# THE NATIONAL TRUST GUIDE
# TO HISTORIC BED & BREAKFASTS,
# INNS, AND SMALL HOTELS

# THE NATIONAL TRUST GUIDE TO HISTORIC

# BED & BREAKFASTS

# INNS AND SMALL HOTELS

## FIFTH EDITION

SUZANNE G. DANE

PRESERVATION PRESS

JOHN WILEY & SONS, INC.
New York • Chichester • Weinheim• Brisbane • Singapore • Toronto

Designed and typeset by Marilyn Appleby, Arnold, Maryland
Cover photo: Inn at Manchester, Manchester Village, VT. Stanley Rosenberg, photographer.
Project Manager, Theresa McDowell

The National Trust for Historic Preservation, chartered by Congress in 1949, is a private, nonprofit organization dedicated to protecting the irreplaceable. It fights to save historic buildings and the neighborhoods and landscapes they anchor. Through education and advocacy, the National Trust is revitalizing communities across the country and challenges citizens to create sensible plans for the future. It has six regional offices, 20 historic sites, and works with thousands of local community groups nationwide. For more information, visit the National Trust's web site at www.nationaltrust.org

This text is printed on acid-free paper. (∞)

This publication is designed to provide accurate and authoritative information in regard to the subject matter covered. It is sold with the understanding that the publisher is not engaged in rendering professional services. If professional advice or other expert assistance is required, the services of a competent professional person should be sought.

*Library of Congress Cataloging in Publication Data:*
Dane, Suzanne G.
   The National Trust guide to historic bed & breakfasts, inns &
      small hotels / Suzanne G. Dane. — 5th ed.
          p.      cm.
     ISBN 0-471-33257-7 (pbk. : alk. paper)
      1. Bed and breakfast accommodations—United States—Guidebooks.
  2. Hotels—United States—Guidebooks.  3. Historic buildings—United
  States—Guidebooks.  4. United States—Guidebooks.  I. National
  Trust for Historic Preservation in the United States.  II. Title.
  TX907.2.D36  1999          96-908
  647.9473'03—dc20

Printed in the United States of America

10  9  8  7  6  5  4  3  2  1

# CONTENTS

| | |
|---|---|
| INTRODUCTION | vii |
| Alabama | 1 |
| Alaska | 3 |
| Arizona | 6 |
| Arkansas | 14 |
| California | 20 |
| Colorado | 71 |
| Connecticut | 86 |
| Delaware | 102 |
| District of Columbia | 108 |
| Florida | 113 |
| Georgia | 134 |
| Hawaii | 148 |
| Idaho | 150 |
| Illinois | 151 |
| Indiana | 157 |
| Iowa | 162 |
| Kansas | 166 |
| Kentucky | 171 |
| Louisiana | 175 |
| Maine | 191 |
| Maryland | 215 |
| Massachusetts | 228 |
| Michigan | 276 |
| Minnesota | 284 |
| Mississippi | 287 |
| Missouri | 297 |
| Montana | 306 |
| Nebraska | 311 |
| Nevada | 312 |
| New Hampshire | 313 |
| New Jersey | 324 |
| New Mexico | 338 |
| New York | 343 |
| North Carolina | 372 |
| Ohio | 392 |
| Oklahoma | 396 |
| Oregon | 398 |
| Pennsylvania | 408 |
| Rhode Island | 442 |
| South Carolina | 452 |
| South Dakota | 464 |
| Tennessee | 465 |
| Texas | 471 |
| Utah | 483 |
| Vermont | 487 |
| Virginia | 510 |
| Washington | 548 |
| West Virginia | 561 |
| Wisconsin | 570 |
| Wyoming | 580 |

# INTRODUCTION

THE NATIONAL TRUST GUIDE TO HISTORIC BED & BREAKFASTS, INNS, AND SMALL HOTELS lists more than 650 historic lodgings across the United States. The diversity of buildings represents the range of American architecture and complexity of our history. There are mansions aplenty and a castle or two, while the lives of everyday people are reflected in their simple, yet elegantly constructed homes. But these are also recycled buildings—historic structures too valuable to discard, yet no longer able to serve their original function: banks, warehouses, schools, gatehouses, kitchen dependencies, and even a jail! Religious freedom is expressed in dwellings that once housed parsons, monks, bishops, and religious orders.

In this guide you will find a gingerbreaded house and a manor on the prairie. You can stay in lighthouses, on ranches in the wide open West, on farms on both coasts and in many places in between, on islands, in major cities, or secluded countryside. Lodgings are found in buildings constructed to house lumberjacks, miners, and lock keepers. Of course, many of today's historic lodgings have always been just that, but they might be resorts at the shore or resorts in the mountains. Perhaps hotels in big cities or small. Some inns have been serving travelers since colonial times and were then known as ordinaries. Whatever style of architecture or period of history you fancy, it can be found in this guide, which provides options for overnight stays that span the country and the centuries.

## ABOUT THE PROPERTIES

To qualify for listing in this guidebook, an inn must be 50 or more years old and must retain its architectural integrity. Homes and inns that have undergone dramatic remodeling that obliterated original structures or historic additions have been excluded.

Descriptions of the inns, compiled from materials supplied by the innkeepers, include information about each building's architecture, construction, and craftsmanship. They describe the importance of the structure to the community, historic events that occurred there, or maybe a note about the not-so-famous people who were once residents. These bits of information set the historic inns apart from their more anonymous modern counterparts; they are the fragments of the past that catch a traveler's imagination.

## ABOUT THE GUIDE

The listing that follows each description summarizes room rates and amenities. It also tells you when the establishment is open for business, how many guest rooms are available, whether or not there are private baths, and if the room rate includes meals. The notation "MAP," which stands for Modified American Plan, means that both breakfast and dinner are included in the rate. **Room rates**, unless otherwise stated, are for double occupancy and are exclusive of taxes. The listing also notes those establishments that offer discounted rates to National Trust members and National Trust Visa cardholders.

**Credit cards** have been abbreviated as follows: AmEx, American Express; MC, Master Card; CB, Carte Blanche; DC, Diners Club. Other credit cards are spelled out.

Some bed and breakfasts cannot accommodate very young **children**. Such restrictions, including an age limit for children, are noted.

Many establishments prohibit cigarette and cigar **smoking** anywhere indoors. "No smoking" will indicate this restriction, even if outside smoking is allowed; "limited" means that smoking is permissible only in certain rooms.

The **On-site activities** section highlights things to do or see *on the premises*. This category most often includes recreational activities but also may list interesting collections, libraries, or just plain peace and quiet, if that's what an establishment specializes in.

**Nearby attractions**, listed under town or city names (rather than the names of specific establishments), include historic sites and other points of interest around which you may want to plan your trip. Places for sightseeing, shopping, and outdoor recreation within an hour's driving time all are listed in this category. Frequently, the attractions are within walking distance of the inn.

Some bed and breakfasts in high-tourism areas have minimum-stay requirements on weekends or in peak seasons. If you are headed to a known tourist region at peak season, be sure to ask about possible restrictions.

The owners and managers of these historic bed and breakfasts, inns, and small hotels have proven their dedication to enriching the present and future by preserving the best of the past. With this guide to historic accommodations you too can take part in the adventure and history offered by these one-of-a-kind establishments.

# ALABAMA

## ANNISTON

**Nearby attractions:** Mt. Cheaha, Anniston Museum of Natural History, Talladega Super Speedway, historic district walking tours, antique hunting

## THE VICTORIA, A COUNTRY INN AND RESTAURANT
1604 Quintard Avenue
P.O. Box 2213
Anniston, Alabama 36202
**Phone:** 205/236-0503 or 800/260-8781
**Fax:** 205/236-1138
**Website:** www.thevictoria.com
**E-mail:** victoria@victoria.com
**Proprietors:** Betty and Earlon McWorter
**Innkeepers:** Beth and Fain Casey

Built in 1888 by John M. McKleroy, a Civil War veteran and attorney, the Victoria is listed in the National Register of Historic Places. A shining example of the Queen Anne style, it is notable for a three-story turret, a mixture of wavy, square, and incised shingles, stained- and etched-glass windows, and colonnaded verandas. The interior boasts oak detailing rich in ornamentation. The inn consists of the original home, which accommodates a full-service restaurant and three suites, plus a recently constructed annex that wraps around a brick courtyard and swimming pool. Each guest room is decorated with brass, wicker, pine, or mahogany furnishings. The Victoria sits grandly on a hill surrounded by trees and well-groomed flower beds.

**Open:** year round **Accommodations:** 60 guest rooms with private baths; 4 are suites **Meals:** continental breakfast included; restaurant on premises **Wheelchair access:** some guest rooms, dining room **Rates:** $79 to $219 **Payment:** AmEx, Visa, MC, CB, DC, Discover, personal and traveler's checks **Restrictions:** no pets **On-site activities:** swimming pool, gazebos, Wren's Nest art gallery

# EUFAULA

**Nearby attractions:** historic district walking and driving tours, house museums, Lake Eufaula water activities, National Wildlife Refuge, golfing, hiking, biking and nature trails

## KENDALL MANOR INN

534 W. Broad Street
Eufaula, Alabama 36027
**Phone:** 334/687-8847
**Fax:** 334/616-0678
**Website:** www.bbonline.com/al/kendallmanor/
**E-mail:** kmanorinn@aol.com
**Proprietors:** Tim and Barbara Lubsen

Situated on a hillside two blocks from the center of historic Eufaula, this 1872 Italianate house is easily recognized by its surrounding, colonnaded porches and a center tower, or belvedere, from which guests can view miles of surrounding landscape. Ruby etched-glass panels set in tall entrance doors, 16-foot ceilings surrounded by elaborate moldings, 13-foot windows topped by gold-leaf cornices, and an array of authentic period furnishings mark the inn as elegant. Reproduction queen- and king-sized beds, private baths, and cozy sitting areas make it comfortable. Ghost stories and a graffiti-filled staircase ascending to the tower room keep it fun-filled. In 1905, the builder's grandson wrote, "I, Joe Kendall, came up here to keep from going to church with my mother." Today's guests are invited to leave behind their own epigraphs. Ideal for private getaways as well as corporate retreats and wedding parties, Kendall Manor Inn has been featured in *Southern Living, Travel & Leisure,* and *Conde Nast Traveler.*

**Open:** year round **Accommodations:** 6 guest rooms with private baths **Meals:** full breakfast included; complimentary refreshments; restaurant on premises **Rates:** $89 to $119; 10% discount offered to National Trust members and National Trust Visa cardholders **Payment:** AmEx, Visa, MC, Discover, personal and traveler's checks **Restrictions:** children over 14 welcome; no smoking; no pets **On-site activities:** croquet, rocking chairs, walk to fitness center

# ALASKA

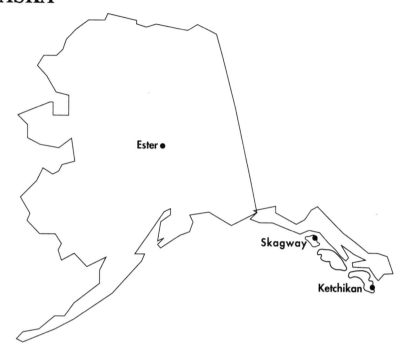

## ESTER

**Nearby attractions:** Riverboat Discovery, University of Alaska Museum, Alaskaland, gold dredge no. 8

### ESTER GOLD CAMP
3660 Main Street
P.O. Box 109
Ester, Alaska 99725
**Phone:** 907/479-2500
**Summer fax:** 907/474-1780
**Winter fax:** 907/456-6997
**Website:** www.alaskabest.com/ester
**E-mail:** intrasea@polarnet.com
**Proprietor:** Brenda Winther

At the turn of the century, the discovery of gold on Ester, Cripple, and Eva creeks drew prospectors. The town of Ester sprang up to meet their needs, boasting numerous hotels, saloons, and shops. Eventually, the pick and pan gave way to partnerships with steam hoists. Those gave way to the hydraulic cannon and gold dredge. The Fairbanks Exploration Company opened Ester Gold Camp to support a large-scale dredge operation in 1936. A bunkhouse and dining hall, homes, offices, and shops were built. The days of the dredge are gone, but Ester Gold Camp still provides overnight accommodations and delicious buffet dinners in the bunkhouse. The camp's 11 buildings have been listed in the National Register and are open to visitors. The blacksmith shop now sells gifts and souvenirs.

**Open:** May to September **Accommodations:** 20 guest rooms with sinks; every 2 rooms share a shower and toilet **Meals:** continental breakfast included; restaurant on premises **Rates:** $50 to $80 **Payment:** Visa, MC, Discover, personal and traveler's checks **Restrictions:** no smoking; no pets **On-site activities:** Malemute Saloon with nightly entertainment, Northern Lights Photosymphony, gift shop

# KETCHIKAN

**Nearby attractions:** historic Creek Street, Southeast Alaska Visitors Center, totem parks, rain forest, museums, salmon hatchery, restaurants and nightclubs, fjords, harbor cruises, fishing for salmon and freshwater trout

## GILMORE HOTEL
326 Front Street
Ketchikan, Alaska 99901
**Phone:** 907/225-9423
**Proprietors:** Terry Wanzer and Kay Sims

Built in 1927 of solid concrete, the Gilmore Hotel sits in the center of downtown, affording guests a delightful view of Alaska's busiest waterfront. Here, commercial fishing boats, luxury cruise liners, freighters, and seaplanes come and go regularly. The hotel, listed in the National Register of Historic Places, provides modern conveniences such as private baths, color television, telephones, and room service. Along with friendly Alaskan hospitality, the Gilmore Hotel offers fishing-vacation packages, freezer space for fish caught by guests, and a courtesy van. The Gilmore Hotel is the home of Annabelle's Famous Keg and Chowder House, which is decorated in a style reminiscent of Ketchikan's earlier days, and a Baskin-Robbins ice cream parlor is located just off the lobby. Ketchikan, Alaska's fourth-largest city, offers a remarkable blend of modern and frontier ways of life and offers a variety of activities within walking distance.

**Open:** year round **Accommodations:** 40 guest rooms (38 have private baths) **Meals:** restaurant on premises **Rates:** $65 to $110; 10% discount to National Trust members and National Trust Visa cardholders **Payment:** AmEx, Visa, MC, DC, Discover, traveler's checks **Restrictions:** Smoking limited; pets permitted with some limitations

# SKAGWAY

**Nearby attractions:** Klondike Gold Rush National Historical Park, hiking and walking trails, fishing, city and area tours by van, train, plane, or helicopter

## GOLDEN NORTH HOTEL AND GOLDBAR PUB
P.O. Box 343
Third and Broadway
Skagway, AK 99840
**Phone:** 907/983-2451 or 888-222-1898
**Fax:** 907/983-2755
**Proprietors:** Dennis and Nancy Corrington

The Alaskan gold rush brought thousands of prospectors to Skagway, including the men of the Klondike Trading Company, whose two-story commercial building was constructed in 1898 on the corner of Third Avenue and State Street. Ten years later, a team of horses helped move the structure a block away to its present location. A third story and the hotel's distinctive golden dome were soon added to this local landmark, the oldest operating hotel in the state. It is also the home of Skagway Brewing Co., established in 1897. Guest rooms feature ocean and glacier views, and each is furnished with period antiques and photos of the gold rush family for whom the room is named. Located in Skagway's historic district, the Golden North Hotel is an excellent jumping off point for exploring the area, and the staff is available to help visitors plan excursions and day trips to the many nearby historic and scenic attractions. The hotel is located in the Klondike Gold Rush National Historical Park, which is listed in the National Register of Historic Places.

**Open:** March to October **Accommodations:** 31 guest rooms (27 have private baths); 1 is a suite **Meals:** Restaurant and brew-pub on premises **Wheelchair access:** Public areas and restaurant only **Rates:** $80 to $100; 10% discount offered to National Trust members and National Trust Visa cardholders **Payment:** AmEx, Visa, MC, Discover, traveler's checks **Restrictions:** Smoking allowed in bar or outdoors only; no pets **On-site activities:** Skagway Tour Company based in hotel; travel desk can assist with sightseeing plans

# ARIZONA

## BISBEE

**Nearby attractions:** Bisbee Mining and Historical Museum, Queen Mine, Lavender Pit Copper Mine, mine tours, Tombstone, art galleries, specialty and Western jewelry shops, antiques hunting, Mexico

## THE BISBEE INN

P.O. Box 1855
45 OK Street
Bisbee, Arizona 85603
**Phone:** 520/432-5131 or 888/432-5131
**Fax:** 520/432-5343
**E-mail:** BisbeeInn@aol.com

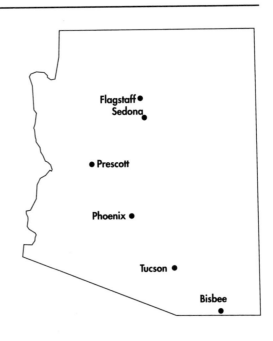

Bisbee's boom days began in the 1880s with the Copper Queen Lode mining rush and, at its peak at the turn of the century, the town was a major business center. In 1917, the Bisbee Inn—originally called the Hotel La More—was built as a miner's hotel, servicing an industry that drew billions of dollars worth of gold, silver, copper, and other minerals from local mines. Rates were just $2 a day for what was then billed as the most modern hotel in town. After its illustrious start, the structure found several other uses including rooming house, Peace Corps training facility, and home to a Pentecostal group. Located in Bisbee's historic district on Chihuahua Hill, the restored brick hotel overlooks Brewery Gulch and treats guests to comfortable surroundings in an old-fashioned setting. Old maps and photos on the walls document Bisbee's and the inn's early years. Guest rooms contain many original and period furnishings, and a full country breakfast is served each morning.

**Open:** Year round **Accommodations:** 24 guest rooms with private baths; 5 are suites **Meals:** Full breakfast included; restaurants nearby **Wheelchair access:** limited **Rates:** $45 to $140; 10% discount offered to National Trust members and National Trust Visa cardholders **Payment:** AmEx, Visa, MC, DC, Discover, traveler's checks **Restrictions:** smoking allowed outside only **On-site activities:** lounge, television

# FLAGSTAFF

**Nearby attractions:** Grand Canyon, Hopi and Navajo Indian reservations, Indian ruins, Meteor Crater, Oak Creek Canyon, San Francisco Peaks, Coconino National Forest, hiking, mountain biking, bird-watching, cross-country skiing, Museum of Northern Arizona, Lowell Observatory, Northern Arizona University, Flagstaff Arboretum, Native American art galleries, antiques hunting

## BIRCH TREE INN BED AND BREAKFAST
824 W. Birch Avenue
Flagstaff, Arizona 86001
**Phone:** 520/774-1042 or 888/774-1042
**Fax:** 520/774-8462
**E-mail:** birch@flagstaff.az.us
**Proprietors:** Rodger and Donna Pettinger; Sandy and Ed Znetko

Located just a short walk from downtown Flagstaff, the Birch Tree Inn began in 1915 as a two-story farmhouse modeled on the Prairie style of architecture: most notable in its low-pitched, hipped roof and wraparound porch, both of which sport widely overhanging eaves. For more than 40 years, beginning in 1928, Flagstaff Mayor Joseph Waldhaus lived here, and it remained a private residence until 1989. The inn's conversion from a fraternity house to a beautifully renovated bed and breakfast inn earned it a 1990 Flagstaff Historic Preservation Award. The owners' artistic and family backgrounds characterize the individually decorated guest rooms, which feature antique furnishings and family heirlooms. The refreshing smell of pine in the air blends well with the Shaker pine furnishings found in Carol's Room, while the Southwest Room's decor takes its cue from the local landscape. Breakfast is served on silver and china in the dining room, and in the late afternoon guests enjoy tea and snacks in the formal living room.

**Open:** Year round **Accommodations:** 5 guest rooms (3 have private baths) **Meals:** full breakfast included; complimentary refreshments; restaurants nearby **Rates:** $69 to $109; 10% discount offered to National Trust members and National Trust Visa cardholders **Payment:** AmEx, Visa, MC, Discover, traveler's checks **Restrictions:** children over 10 welcome; no smoking; no pets **On-site activities:** outdoor spa, pool table, and game room

## THE INN AT 410 BED AND BREAKFAST
410 North Leroux Street
Flagstaff, Arizona 86001
**Phone:** 520/774-0088 or 800/774-2008
**Website:** www.bbonline.com/az/at410/
**Proprietors:** Howard and Sally Krueger

This 1907 Craftsman house was first the residence of a wealthy banker, businessman, and cattle rancher. Now, fully renovated and elegantly decorated, the Inn at 410 offers nine guest rooms filled with a blend of antique and contemporary furnishings in a variety of styles. Rooms include the Southwest, with its Santa Fe decor; Sunflower Fields, abundant with country sunflowers; and Dakota, with Old West furnishings in a cowboy decor. Seven rooms offer fireplaces, two have whirlpool tubs. Stained glass, lace curtains, and local antiques fill the remainder of the inn, where fresh home-baked cookies are offered each afternoon. Located just blocks from downtown Flagstaff, the inn is a perfect base from which to visit the natural splendors of northern Arizona.

**Open:** year round **Accommodations:** 9 guest rooms with private baths; 4 are suites **Meals:** full breakfast included; complimentary refreshments; restaurants nearby **Wheelchair access:** 1 guest room **Rates:** $125 to $175 **Payment:** Visa, MC, personal and traveler's checks **Restrictions:** no smoking; no pets **On-site activities:** books, board games

# PHOENIX

**Nearby attractions:** Arizona Science Center, Deer Valley Rock Art Center, Desert Botanical Garden, Arizona State University, Biltmore Fashion Park, theaters, convention center, Capitol Complex, golfing, tennis, horseback riding, fishing

## MARICOPA MANOR BED AND BREAKFAST INN

15 West Pasadena Avenue
Phoenix, Arizona 85013-2001
**Phone:** 602/274-6302 or 800/292-6403
**Fax:** 602/266-3904
**Website:** www.maricopamanor.com
**E-mail:** mmanor@getnet.com
**Proprietors:** Mary Ellen and Paul Kelley

Maricopa Manor was built in 1928 as a summer home by Byron J. and Neomi Showers, who were early settlers in the Arizona Territory. It was designed in a Spanish Revival style. Guests are invited to share in the use of the spacious gathering room with outside deck, the formal living, dining, and music rooms, the patio, and the gazebo spa. Guest suites are luxuriously furnished in various motifs from the blue-and-white Library Suite, with canopied king bed, to the Victorian Suite, outfitted in satin, lace, antiques, and king bed. The guest house, built on the property in the 1940s, contains two suites—one nostalgic and one modern. All suites have color television and telephones. The one-acre estate sits amid lush gardens, palm and citrus trees, fountains, courtyards, and patios.

**Open:** year round **Accommodations:** 6 guest suites with private baths **Meals:** continental-plus breakfast included; restaurants nearby **Wheelchair access:** 1 room **Rates:** $89 to $229; 10% discount to National Trust members and National Trust Visa cardholders **Payment:** AmEx, Visa, MC, Discover, personal and traveler's checks **Restrictions:** smoking limited; no pets **On-site activities:** swimming pool, spa

---

# PRESCOTT

**Nearby attractions:** Prescott National Forest, Sharlot Hall Museum, Prescott Downs Racetrack, hiking, fishing, horseback riding, rock climbing, antiques hunting, Western shopping

## HOTEL VENDOME

230 S. Cortez Street
Prescott, AZ 86303
**Phone:** 520/776-0900 or 888/468-3583

**Fax:** 520/771-0395
**Website:** www.vendomehotel.com
**Proprietors:** Rama and Amrish Patel

Built in 1917 as lodging for families of recovering tuberculosis patients, the Hotel Vendome has retained its Old West charm and, according to some, the ghost of a former owner. Cowboy actor Tom Mix was a long-time guest and today visitors will enjoy both modern conveniences and an old-fashioned atmosphere. The two-story brick hotel, with its double veranda, offers spacious guest rooms furnished with antiques and claw-foot tubs. Guests can relax in the lobby with a beverage ordered at the handsome, hand-carved cherrywood bar or inquire about having lunch served on the long upstairs porch. Hotel Vendome, a Clarion Carriage House and National Register property, is convenient to Prescott's historic district, county courthouse, and the famed Whiskey Row. The proprietors will gladly help guests plan local sightseeing and can pack a picnic lunch to take along on outings.

**Open:** year round **Accommodations:** 20 guest rooms with private baths; 4 are suites **Meals:** continental-plus breakfast included; wine and beer bar on premises; restaurants nearby **Wheelchair access:** limited **Rates:** $79 to $179; 10% discount offered to National Trust members and National Trust Visa cardholders Sunday through Thursday, except public holidays **Payment:** AmEx, Visa, MC, CB, DC, Discover, traveler's check, personal check (in-state only with check guarantee card) **Restrictions:** smoking limited; no pets **On-site activities:** board games, cards

### MOUNT VERNON INN
204 N. Mt. Vernon Avenue
Prescott, Arizona 86301
**Phone:** 520/778-0886
**Fax:** 520/778-7305
**Website:** prescottlink.com/mtvrnon/
index.htm
**E-mail:** mtvrnon@primenet.com
**Proprietors:** Michele and Jerry Neumann

Located in Prescott's historic district—the largest Victorian neighborhood in the state—the Mount Vernon Inn is a striking Queen Anne house, with its candle-snuffer turret, variety of gables, and Greek Revival porch. Built in 1900, it was home to John H. Robinson, a high-ranking local official whose scandalous murder near the fairgrounds was the talk of the town in 1926. A riveting account of his mysterious demise and the trial that followed can be read in the inn's sitting room after a day spent exploring nearby Courthouse Square, the area's breathtaking natural scenery, or any number of other local attractions. Guests are invited to relax on the wraparound front porch or settle into one of the individually appointed guest rooms: Avalon, Arcana, Arcadia, and Aerie. Each is appointed with period furniture and Victorian motifs, including ceiling fans. The grounds also contain three guest cottages. This National Register property received an Arizona Heritage Preservation Award in 1997.

**Open:** year round **Accommodations:** 4 guest rooms with private baths; 3 cottage suites with private baths **Meals:** full breakfast included; complimentary refreshments; restaurants nearby **Wheelchair access:** Yes **Rates:** $95 to $125; 10% discount offered to National Trust members and National Trust Visa cardholders Sunday-Thursday, November through March **Payment:** Visa, MC, Discover **Restrictions:** no smoking; no pets **On-site activities:** porch sitting, reading, videos

---

# SEDONA

**Nearby attractions:** Hopi mesas, Tlaquepaque, national forests, shops and galleries, horseback riding, golfing, tennis, fishing

### BED AND BREAKFAST AT SADDLE ROCK RANCH
255 Rock Ridge Drive
Sedona, Arizona 86336
**Phone:** 520/282-7640
**Fax:** 520/282-6829
**Website:** saddlerockranch.com
**E-mail:** saddlerock@sedona.net
**Proprietors:** Fran and Dan Bruno

Saddle Rock Ranch is a country estate nestled on three acres of hillside overlooking the town of Sedona. It is surrounded on all sides by breathtaking red rock vistas. The 1926 homestead has native rock and adobe walls, massive-beamed ceilings, and wood and flagstone floors. The spacious parlor, exclusively for guest use, has an 1850s pump organ, fireplace, and Native American artifacts. In the sunny breakfast room works by renowned local artists adorn the rock walls. Each guest room is decorated in romantic themes, enhanced by wood-burning rock fireplaces. Guests are welcome in the courtyard garden to enjoy its deck, lounges, swimming pool, spa, and magnificent views. A guest refrigerator, freezer, and microwave are available. Saddle Rock Ranch is a City of Sedona Historic Landmark.

**Open:** year round **Accommodations:** 3 guest rooms with private baths; 1 is a suite **Meals:** full breakfast included; complimentary refreshments; restaurants nearby **Rates:** $130 to $150 **Payment:** personal and traveler's checks **Restrictions:** children over 14 welcome; no smoking; no pets **On-site activities:** swimming, hiking, Jeep tours

## TUCSON

**Nearby attractions:** University of Arizona, Arizona Sonora Desert Museum, Tucson Convention Center, planetarium, observatories, zoo, state and local parks, golfing, tennis, jogging and hiking trails

### CASA ALEGRE BED AND BREAKFAST INN

316 East Speedway
Tucson, Arizona 85705
**Phone:** 520/628-1800
**Fax:** 520/792-1880
**Proprietor:** Phyllis Florek

Located in the West University Historic District, this distinguished Craftsman bungalow was built in 1915 for Tucson pharmacist Arthur McNeal. The house features built-in mahogany and leaded-glass cabinetry and hardwood floors. Three guest rooms, each with private bath, are uniquely furnished to reflect Tucson's history: the Saguaro Room, named for the indigenous giant cactus, contains natural saguaro ribs; the Hacienda Room features a headboard originally made for a Mexican priest; and the Amethyst Room boasts turn-of-the-century antiques and the house's original claw-foot tub. Two rooms are also available next door in the 1923 Buchanan House. A stuccoed wall encloses the swimming pool and serene patio where guests enjoy a full breakfast. Casa Alegre allows easy access to Tucson's major attractions and business centers.

**Open:** year round **Accommodations:** 5 guest rooms with private baths **Meals:** full breakfast included; complimentary refreshments; restaurants nearby **Rates:** $80 to $125; 10% discount to National Trust members and National Trust Visa cardholders **Payment:** Visa, MC, Discover, personal and traveler's checks **Restrictions:** inquire about children; no smoking; no pets **On-site activities:** swimming pool, hot tub, television room

### EL PRESIDIO BED AND BREAKFAST INN

297 North Main Street
Tucson, Arizona 85701
**Phone:** 520/623-6151 or
800/349-6151
**Fax:** 520/623-3860
**Proprietor:** Patti Toci

Tucson was a frontier village when the Julius Kruttschnitt House was built in 1886. Its location on Main

Street put it in what was then the premier residential area for the young community's important families. Today, the National Register property operates both as an architectural and social museum and as a guest house in the heart of Tucson. The adobe inn is a splendid example of American Territorial style, a compatible blend of Mexican and American Victorian building traditions unique to this city. Guests enjoy spacious accommodations filled with distinctive antiques, original art, and fresh flowers. All guest rooms have kitchenettes and private entrances and each leads to its own courtyard or garden, complete with fountains and lush floral displays. Famous Mexican and gourmet cuisines are within walking distance. This romantic inn has been hailed by *Gourmet, Travel and Leisure*, and *Arizona Highways* magazines.

**Open:** year round **Accommodations:** 3 guest rooms with private baths **Meals:** full breakfast included; complimentary refreshments; restaurants nearby **Rates:** $95 to $115 **Payment:** personal check **Restrictions:** children over 10 welcome; no smoking; no pets **On-site activities:** spacious grounds for bird watching and relaxing

## LA POSADA DEL VALLE
1640 North Campbell Avenue
Tucson, Arizona 85719
**Phone:** 520/795-3840
**Website:** www.bbhast.com-laposadadelvalle
**Proprietors:** Tom and Karin Dennen

This home, designed by renowned Tucson architect Josias T. Joesler, was built in 1929. Constructed of adobe and stucco, La Posada del Valle is a fine example of the Spanish Colonial Revival, or Santa Fe, style of architecture. Each of the five guest accommodations has a private outside entrance and private bath. Room decors range from Victorian in Sophie's Room to Art Deco in Pola's Room. Karin's Cottage, a charming cottage with private entrance from the courtyard and kitchenette, is dressed in an early 1900s African motif. Breakfast is served in the dining room or on the sunporch overlooking the landscaped yard and orange trees. The living room, where afternoon tea is served, is appointed with fine Art Deco furnishings. Located in one of Tucson's finest neighborhoods, La Posada del Valle is central to the city's attractions.

**Open:** year round **Accommodations:** 5 guest rooms with private baths; 1 is a cottage **Meals:** full breakfast included on weekends; continental-plus breakfast included on weekdays; restaurants nearby **Rates:** $90 to $135; 10% discount to National Trust members and National Trust Visa cardholders **Payment:** Visa, MC, personal and traveler's checks **Restrictions:** no smoking; no pets **On-site activities:** patio sitting

# ARKANSAS

## EUREKA SPRINGS

**Nearby attractions:** Eureka Springs Historical Museum, Christ of the Ozarks and Passion Play, Silver Dollar City, Lake Beaver, Inspiration Point artists' colony, country music shows, historic district walking tours, gift shops, antiques hunting, swimming, fishing, boating

### DAIRY HOLLOW HOUSE
515 Spring Street
Eureka Springs, Arkansas 72632
**Phone:** 501/253-7444 or 800/562-8650
**Fax:** 501/253-7223
**Website:** www.dairyhollow.com
**E-mail:**frontdesk@dairyhollow.com
**Proprietors:** Ned Shank and Crescent Dragonwagon

Dairy Hollow House relieves visitors of their jangled nerves with such pleasures as the smell of hot apple cider, or a quilt-covered, canopied bed and a stack of wood by an antique fireplace, or a jug of tulips and books to read in a sunny nook or on a rocker-filled porch. Guest rooms are in either the 1888 farmhouse or the 1940s main house just up the gravel road. In the farmhouse the Tulip Room has a whirlpool tub for two and potbellied stove; the Rose Room and Iris Room feature antiques and fireplaces. Suites in the main house are individually decorated, but all have fireplaces. Breakfast is brought to bedroom doors. The inn features an acclaimed restaurant serving what the innkeepers call "Nouveau 'Zarks" cuisine. Dairy Hollow House has been praised by the *New York Times*, *USA Today*, *Christian Science Monitor*, *Glamour*, and *Chocolatier*, and is a three-time winner of Uncle Ben's Inn of Distinction award.

**Open:** February 1 through December 31 **Accommodations:** 6 guest rooms with private baths; 2 are suites **Rates:** $125 to $175 **Payment:** AmEx, Visa, MC, CB, DC, Discover, personal and traveler's checks **Restrictions:** children welcome in suites; no smoking; no pets **On-site activities:** outdoor hot tub in the woods, porch rocking, bird-watching, reading

# CRESCENT HOTEL
75 Prospect Avenue
Eureka Springs, Arkansas 72632
**Phone:** 501/253-9766 or 800/643-4972
**Fax:** 501/253-5296
**Website:** www.crescent-hotel.com

Perched above the Victorian village of Eureka Springs, the Crescent Hotel was built in 1886 by Governor Powell Clayton, opening on an invitation-only basis. At the time, thousands of tourists arrived each year, eager to sample the healing waters of the local springs. Today, visitors come to the Crescent for its comfortable surroundings and impressive view of the Ozarks. And just as guests of yore did, they can still meet a horse-drawn surrey at the front door for a ride through town. The hotel, a massive four-story structure of rough-faced stonework, has retained its old-fashioned character, from the Victorian-style Crystal Dining Room to the massive grand fireplace in the lobby, while in a newer addition, the New Moon Health Spa is a modern-day take on the health services for which the area was once renowned. The National Register-listed property is located in the Eureka Springs Historic District.

**Open:** year round **Accommodations:** 68 guest rooms with private baths; 8 are suites **Meals:** restaurant on premises **Wheelchair access:** yes **Rates:** $59 to $145; 10% discount to National Trust members or National Trust Visa cardholders **Payment:** AmEx, Visa, MC, Discover, traveler's and personal checks **Restrictions:** smoking limited **On-site activities:** gardens, walking paths, fitness center, health spa, pool, shuffleboard

## ELMWOOD HOUSE
110 Spring Street
Eureka Springs, Arkansas 72632
**Phone:** 501/253-5486
**Fax:** 501/253-7613
**Website:** www.eureka-usa.com/
elmwood
**Proprietors:** Lavenya and Willis
Schenck

Devastating nineteenth-century fires in this old resort town prompted the brick construction of the Elmwood House, the city's first such structure. Completed in 1886 as a lodging facility, the three-story house has a distinctive double-decker porch that wraps around three sides, offering views of the historic district and Elmwood's own garden, pond, and waterfall. The restored house has two spacious, Victorian-style guest suites that also feature modern amenities, including double whirlpool tubs, refrigerators, and air conditioning. Guests are invited to browse through Eggcetera, a gift shop located on the first floor. Here the Elmwood's owners—also egg artists—offer a variety of Faberge-, Ukrainian-, Austrian-and Czechoslovakian-style decorated eggs. The Elmwood House, listed in the National Register of Historic Places, is adjacent to a trolley stop, where guests can begin their sightseeing excursions of the town that once drew thousands to its springs for medicinal cures.

**Open:** year round **Accommodations:** 2 suites with private baths **Meals:** complimentary refreshments; meal coupons to nearby restaurants included in rate **Rates:** $95; 10% discount offered to National Trust members and National Trust Visa cardholders **Payment:** Visa, MC, Discover, traveler's checks and personal check **Restrictions:** children over 12 welcome; no smoking; no pets
**On-site activities:** Eggcetera gift shop

## SINGLETON HOUSE
11 Singleton
Eureka Springs, Arkansas 72632
**Phone:** 501/253-9111 or 800/833-3394
**Proprietor:** Barbara Gavron

This 1890s two-story, bay-front Queen Anne Victorian is located on a ridge above historic Sweet Springs, one of more than 60 springs in the area. Built by a local barber, the house contains many original pieces of furniture, including a barber's cabinet. The present owner, trained as an interior designer, has furnished the light and airy guest rooms with an eclectic collection of treasures and antiques. Full breakfast is served on the balcony overlooking a garden and goldfish pond. Guests can ride an old-fashioned trolley to town or take a one-block stroll down a wooded footpath to shops and cafes. For a very private retreat, ask about the Gardener's Cottage—a 100-year-old cabin filled with country antiques, yet offering the most modern amenities, including a whirlpool tub for two. The innkeeper, who is beginning her fourteenth season, offers a hands-on apprentice-ship program for aspiring bed-and-breakfast owners.

**Open:** year round  **Accommodations:** 5 guest rooms with private baths; separately located guest cottage **Meals:** full breakfast included (optional breakfast served at cottage); complimentary refreshments; restaurants nearby **Rates:** $69 to $105; cottage $95 to $125; 10% discount to National Trust members and National Trust Visa cardholders on midweek stays of two or more nights **Payment:** AmEx, Visa, MC, Discover, personal and traveler's checks **Restrictions:** well-behaved children welcome; no smoking; no pets **On-site activities:** nature trail, porches with swings and rockers, bird-watching, small library

# LITTLE ROCK
**Nearby attractions:** Robinson Center Music Hall, War Memorial Stadium, State House Convention Center, museums, shopping, riverboat rides, hiking, golfing

## THE EMPRESS OF LITTLE ROCK
2120 Louisiana
Little Rock, Arkansas 72206
**Phone:** 501/374-7966
**Fax:** 501/375-4537
**Website:** www.TheEmpress.com
**E-mail:** hostess@theEmpress.com
**Proprietors:** Robert Blair and Sharon Welch-Blair

Described in the National Register of Historic Places as the finest example of ornate Victorian architecture in the state, the aptly named Empress of Little Rock, was the largest and perhaps most opulent house when it was built in 1888 for saloon keeper James H. Hornibrook. A flamboyant display of gables, octagonally shaped rooms, a three-and-a-half-story corner tower, a stained-glass skylight, and exterior trims in Greek, Mexican, and Gothic designs, Hornibrook Mansion became the Arkansas Women's College in 1897. A century later the house earned third place in the National Trust for Historic Preservation's 1997 Great American Home Awards for bed-and-breakfast restoration. The decor of each elegant guest room is inspired by the colorful character in Arkansas history for whom it is named. A full breakfast with silver service is served on the veranda or in the formal dining room. The inn is listed in the National Register of Historic Places.

**Open:** year round **Accommodations:** 5 guest rooms with private baths; 2 are mini-suites **Meals:** full breakfast included; complimentary refreshments; restaurants nearby **Rates:** $100 to $140 **Payment:** AmEx, Visa, MC, traveler's checks and personal check **Restrictions:** children over 10 welcome; no smoking; no pets

## HOTZE HOUSE
1619 Louisiana Street
Little Rock, Arkansas 72206
**Phone:** 501/376-6563
**Fax:** 501/374-5393
**Proprietors:** Suzanne and Steven Gates

Hotze House was built by prominent businessman Peter Hotze in 1900 as a gift to his three children. When built, the elegant Neoclassical mansion was considered to be the finest and most expensive house in Arkansas. Recently restored, the house now offers elegant overnight accommodations. Each room is individually appointed with an attractive and comfortable mixture of antique and traditional furnishings and offers a private bath, telephone, television, individual climate control, and a king- or queen-size bed. Guests may have breakfast in the formal dining room or in the sunny conservatory. Located in the Governor's Mansion District, Hotze House is a downtown landmark and is listed in the National Register of Historic Places.

**Open:** year round **Accommodations:** 5 guest rooms with private baths; 4 have fireplaces **Meals:** full breakfast included; complimentary refreshments; restaurants nearby **Rates:** $90; 10% discount to National Trust members and National Trust Visa cardholders **Payment:** AmEx, Visa, MC, DC, Discover, personal and traveler's checks **Restrictions:** children over 5 welcome; no smoking; no pets

# CALIFORNIA

- Eureka
- Ferndale
- Westport
- Fort Bragg
- Mendocino
- Ukiah
- Healdsburg
- Calistoga
- St. Helena
- Auburn
- Santa Rosa
- Napa
- Sonoma
- Sacramento
- Hope Valley
- Ione
- San Francisco
- Murphys
- Half Moon Bay
- Groveland
- Santa Cruz
- Pacific Grove
- Carmel
- Death Valley
- San Luis Obispo
- Santa Barbara
- Ojai
- South Pasadena
- Santa Monica
- Palm Springs
- Seal Beach
- La Jolla
- San Diego

## AUBURN

**Nearby attractions:** Old Town
Auburn, Gold Country, antiques
hunting, hiking, horseback riding,
snow skiing, hot-air ballooning, hunting, lakes and rivers for fishing, boating,
water skiing, wind surfing, and swimming

## POWER'S MANSION INN
164 Cleveland Avenue
Auburn, California 95603
**Mailing address:**
P.O. Box 602076
Sacramento, California 95860-2076
**Phone:** 530/885-1166
**Fax:** 530/885-1386
**Website:** www.vsr.net/~powerinn
**E-mail:** powerinn@westsierra.net
**Proprietors:** Arno and Jean Lejnieks

Covering a full city block in downtown Auburn, this Queen Anne Victorian house was the turn-of-the-century home of Harold and Mary Power and their six children. The Powers built their home in 1900 with the fortune they had made in gold mining, and spared no expense in making it an elegant showplace. Harold Power was a state assemblyman, and in 1900 he served as a delegate to the Republican National Convention. The Powers often entertained prominent guests in their home, including Senator (later Governor) Hiram Johnson and young mining engineer Herbert Hoover. As the Power's Mansion Inn, the house's 13 rooms are lavishly decorated with Victorian antiques, including an ornate piano in the parlor. Four-poster and brass beds are complemented by satin and lace comforters and curtains. The inn is located less than a block from Main Street.

**Open:** year round **Accommodations:** 13 guest rooms with private baths; 2 are suites **Meals:** full breakfast included; catering for meetings and weddings available; restaurants nearby **Rates:** $79 to $149; 10% discount to National Trust members and National Trust Visa cardholders **Payment:** AmEx, Visa, MC, personal and traveler's checks **Restrictions:** smoking limited; no pets **On-site activities:** patio and garden

# CALISTOGA

**Nearby attractions:** Napa Valley wineries, golfing, tennis, bicycling, spas, hot-air ballooning and glider rides, fishing, water skiing

## SCARLETT'S COUNTRY INN

3918 Silverado Trail
Calistoga, California 94515
**Phone:** 707/942-6669
**Fax:** 707/942-6669
**Website:** members.aol.com/scarletts
**E-mail:** scarletts@aol.com
**Proprietor:** Scarlett Dwyer

This 1900 two-story farmhouse was built on the former site of a Wappo campground, to which these Native Americans migrated when winter cold and snow made hunting poor in the nearby mountains. Their obsidian arrowheads can still be found in the ground around the inn. The farmhouse is set among green lawns and tall pines overlooking nearby vineyards. Guest rooms have private entrances, queen-size beds, air conditioning, mini-refrigerators, microwaves, televisions, and private baths with toiletries. Guests will also find bathrobes in the closets and fresh flowers on the tables. Each room offers a special touch: French doors, a wood-burning stove, a wet bar, a claw-foot tub, or Indian artifacts. Breakfast is served on the deck, under the apple trees, next to the swimming pool, or in guest rooms.

**Open:** year round **Accommodations:** 3 guest rooms with private baths; 2 are suites **Meals:** full breakfast included; complimentary refreshments; restaurants nearby **Rates:** $115 to $175 (children welcome at no charge); 10% discount to National Trust members and National Trust Visa cardholders **Payment:** personal check **Restrictions:** no smoking; no pets **On-site activities:** swimming, sunbathing, hiking, bicycling

# CARMEL

**Nearby attractions:** Old Carmel Mission, Point Lobos State Reserve, 17-Mile Drive, Pebble Beach Golf Course, tennis, fine dining, boutiques, art galleries, beachcombing, Big Sur

## HAPPY LANDING

Monte Verde between Fifth and Sixth Streets
P.O. Box 2619
Carmel, California 93921
**Phone:** 408/624-7917
**Website:** www.virtualcities.com/ons/ca/c/cac8501.htm
**Proprietor:** Dick Stewart **Manager:** Robert Ballard

Built in 1925 as a family retreat, the Happy Landing is a quaint inn offering antique-filled rooms with cathedral ceilings. Its cottage style, featuring small-paned windows, a balcony, and a round tower, gives it a Hansel-and-Gretel-like appearance. Three separate buildings surround a lush central garden with a gazebo, pond, and flagstone paths. Guest rooms are enhanced by fireplaces or stained-glass windows. Many personal touches, including breakfast served in guests' rooms, make the Happy Landing a quiet and romantic place to stay near town and beach.

**Open:** year round **Accommodations:** 7 guest rooms with private baths; 2 are suites **Meals:** continental-plus breakfast included; restaurants nearby **Rates:** $90 to $165 **Payment:** Visa, MC, personal check **Restrictions:** children over 12 welcome; no smoking; no pets

# DEATH VALLEY

**Nearby attractions:** Death Valley National Park, Scotty's Castle, Amargosa Opera House, Stovepipe Wells Village, Borax Museum

## FURNACE CREEK INN
P.O. Box 1
Death Valley, California 92328
**Phone:** 760/786-2345
**Fax:** 760/786-2423
**Website:** www.placestostay.com/DeathValley-FurnaceCreekInn/
**Inn Manager:** Toni Jepson

Originally built in 1927 by the Pacific Borax Company, the Furnace Creek Inn grew in stages until its completion in 1935. The mission-style architecture, red-tiled roof, and use of indigenous stone and adobe bricks created on the site by Shoshone Indians are a tribute to California's rich history. Possibly the most uniquely situated hotel in the United States, Furnace Creek Inn is surrounded by magnificent mountains, inspiring canyons, and the desert panoramas of Death Valley National Park. The extraordinary palm gardens amid meandering natural springs produce a true oasis in the heart of the desert landscape. Some of the guest rooms feature whirlpool tubs or balconies; most offer garden and desert views. A recent renovation has drawn upon the classic style of the 1930s to augment the historical aspects of this four-diamond resort. Furnace Creek Inn is a member of the National Trust's Historic Hotels of America.

**Open:** year round **Accommodations:** 66 guest rooms with private baths; 2 are suites **Meals:** restaurant on premises **Wheelchair access:** yes **Rates:** $215 to $325; 10% discount to National Trust members and National Trust Visa cardholders **Payment:** AmEx, Visa, MC, DC, CB, Discover **Restrictions:** smoking limited; no pets **On-site activities:** massage therapy, spring-fed swimming pool, tennis, golfing, horseback riding, hiking

# EUREKA

**Nearby attractions:** Old Town Eureka, architectural driving tour, Maritime Museum, Clark Museum, Fort Humboldt Logging Museum, Victorian Ferndale, redwood forests, rugged beaches, Humboldt Bay cruises on historic ferry boat, fishing, hiking, golfing, carriage rides, antiques hunting, specialty shops

## ABIGAIL'S "ELEGANT VICTORIAN MANSION" BED AND BREAKFAST INN

1406 C Street
Eureka, California 95501
**Phone:** 707/444-3144
**Fax:** 707/442-5594
**Website:** www.bnbweb.com/abigails.html
or www.bnbcity.com/inns/20016
**Proprietors:** Doug and Lily Vieyra

Replete with ornate vergeboards at the gables, decorative cornice brackets, bay windows, spindlework, and metal roof cresting, this elaborate Victorian house was built in 1888 for Eureka's two-term mayor, William S. Clark. A local newspaper at the time called it "an elegant Victorian mansion." More recently, *Architectural Review* described it as "the best preserved and restored house in Eureka." Listed in the National Register of Historic Places, the mansion offers guests two parlors, a library, and a sitting room, and each morning a multicourse French breakfast is served in the dining room. Guest rooms—some named for past guests such as Lily Langtry and Leland Stanford—provide city, mountain, or bay views as well as elegant period furnishings and all modern comforts. A showcase of authentic high Victorian interiors, the inn provides its guests with a unique living-history experience. The inn has been given three diamonds by AAA.

**Open:** Year round **Accommodations:** 4 guest rooms (2 have private baths); 1 is a suite **Meals:** Full breakfast included; complimentary refreshments; restaurants nearby **Rates:** $85 to $185; guests with a National Trust membership card receive a complimentary horseless-carriage ride ($20 value) **Payment:** Visa, MC **Restrictions:** children over 15 welcome; no smoking; no pets **On-site activities:** croquet, bicycles, silent and classic film shows, classical concerts, Finnish sauna, Swedish massage, game room with Victorian games, mystery weekends, antique automobiles

**BELL COTTAGE (of Carter House Victorians)**
301 L Street
Eureka, California 95501
**Phone:** 707/444-8062 or 800/404-1390
**Fax:** 707/444-8067
**Website:** carterhouse.com
**E-mail:** Carter52@CarterHouse.com
**Proprietors:** Mark and Christi Carter

With a front facade only 20 feet wide, the Bell Cottage gives an unpretentious appearance from the street. But the one-story hip-roofed Victorian cottage is saved from simplicity by tall bay windows and decorative cornice brackets. Built in 1888, the house has recently been renovated to accommodate overnight guests. The interior is decorated in an intriguing blend of new and old: whitewashed walls and original works of art combine with black leather chairs and halogen lighting. Contemporary furniture sits side-by-side with European pine antiques. There are three fireplaces in the house; two are bedside in the guest rooms, the other is in a common area. Bell Cottage provides a fully equipped black marble kitchen for guests' use. Additional amenities include television and VCR, stereo system, and telephones. Bell Cottage is owned and operated by the Carter House Inn across the street, which also operates the adjacent Hotel Carter.

**Open:** year round **Accommodations:** 3 guest rooms with private baths (20 total rooms in three buildings) **Meals:** full breakfast included; complimentary refreshments; restaurant on premises for dinner **Wheelchair access:** guest rooms, bathrooms, dining room **Rates:** $95 to $500 (for full cottage); 10% discount to National Trust members and National Trust Visa cardholders **Payment:** AmEx, Visa, MC, CB, DC, Discover, personal and traveler's checks **Restrictions:** Children over 12 welcome; no smoking; no pets **On-site activities:** reading, conversation, art viewing

# FERNDALE

**Nearby attractions:** historic village, museum, galleries, craft studios, playhouse, hiking trails, redwood forests, ocean, beaches

### GINGERBREAD MANSION INN
400 Berding Street
Ferndale, California 95536
**Phone:** 800/952-4136
**Fax:** 707/786-4381
**Website:** gingerbread-mansion.com
**Proprietor:** Ken Torbert

Well known as one of northern California's most photographed homes, and honored as one of the 10 best inns in California by *San Francisco Focus* magazine, Gingerbread Mansion Inn is an extravaganza of spindlework, bay windows, turrets, and gables trimmed in peach and yellow and surrounded by English gardens. Built as a doctor's residence in 1899, the striking Queen Anne was expanded to twice its original size by the 1920s. It has been used as a hospital, a rest home, an American Legion hall, and an apartment house. Completely restored, the inn pampers guests with luxuriously appointed baths (including his-and-her claw-foot bathtubs), bathrobes, turn-down service, and bedside chocolates. Four guest rooms have fireplaces. Ferndale is California's best preserved Victorian village and has been designated a State Historic Landmark. The inn has been given a four-diamond rating by AAA.

**Open:** year round **Accommodations:** 10 guest rooms with private baths; 4 are suites **Meals:** full breakfast included; complimentary refreshments; restaurants nearby **Rates:** $140 to $350 **Payment:** AmEx, Visa, MC, personal and traveler's checks **Restrictions:** no smoking; no pets **On-site activities:** formal English gardens; four parlors (two with fireplaces) offering games, books, and puzzles

# FORT BRAGG

**Nearby attractions:** Skunk Train, whale-watching, beaches, state parks, hiking, bicycling, tennis, fishing party boats, galleries, theater

## AVALON HOUSE
561 Stewart Street
Fort Bragg, California 95437
**Phone:** 707/964-5555 or 800/964-5556
**Proprietor:** Anne Sorrells

Avalon House was built in 1905 by Horace Weller, a founder of Fort Bragg, as a wedding gift to his son. The redwood building has been restored, preserving the details of its California Craftsman style. Avalon House and its furnishings may be antique, but not at the expense of modern conveniences. In a quiet residential neighborhood three blocks from the ocean, Avalon House offers guest rooms with private baths, fireplaces, whirlpool tubs, down comforters, and ocean views. Rooms also are equipped with individual heat controls, lighted shaving or makeup mirrors, reading lamps, and extra-thick towels. Guest room individuality is expressed through furnishings and the use of stained-glass windows or private decks in some rooms.

**Open:** year round **Accommodations:** 6 guest rooms with private baths **Meals:** full breakfast included; complimentary refreshments; restaurants nearby **Rates:** $70 to $135 **Payment:** AmEx, Visa, MC, Discover, personal and traveler's checks **Restrictions:** no smoking; no pets

# GEYSERVILLE
**Nearby attractions:** golfing, tennis, canoeing, bicycling, wine tasting

## HOPE-BOSWORTH AND HOPE-MERRILL HOUSES
Geyserville Avenue
P.O. Box 42
Geyserville, CA 95441
**Phone:** 707/857-3356 or 800/825-4233
**Fax:** 707/857-4673
**Website:** www.hope-inns.com
**E-mail:** moreinfo@hope-inns.com
**Proprietor:** Cosette Trautman-Scheiber

Facing each other across Geyserville Avenue are the Craftsman-style Hope-Bosworth House (1904) and the Eastlake Stick Style Hope-Merrill House (1876). The Hope-Bosworth House is a pattern-book house ordered from one of the many architectural pattern books of the day. The original oak-grained woodwork is evident throughout the house, from the large pocket doors in the hallway to the upstairs tower bedroom. Polished fir floors and antique light fixtures enhance the period furnishings, completing the comfortable decor. The Hope-Merrill House, built entirely of redwood, is noted for its architectural and historical significance and is listed in the Sonoma County Landmarks Register. Inside, the house is highlighted by original Lincrusta-Walton wainscoting and quarter-sawn oak-grained doors and woodwork. All wallpapers are hand silk-screened in William Morris reproductions by Bruce Bradbury. In recognition of its excellence, the Hope-Merrill House received a first-place award for bed-and-breakfast restoration from the National Trust in its Great American House Awards. Period antiques and whirlpool bathtubs are found in both houses. A glass of wine on the porch or in the parlor brings the day to a quiet end. In the morning, guests rise to the sounds and scents of a home-cooked country breakfast. Guests of both houses are invited to enjoy the relaxing gazebo and heated swimming pool behind the Hope-Merrill House.

**Open:** year round **Accommodations:** 12 guest rooms with private baths; 1 is a suite **Meals:** full breakfast included; complimentary refreshments; restaurants nearby **Rates:** $111 to $179; 10 % discount to National Trust members and National Trust Visa cardholders **Payment:** Amex, Visa, MC, personal and traveler's checks **Restrictions:** not suitable for children; no smoking; no pets **On-site activities:** swimming, croquet

# GROVELAND

**Nearby attractions:** Yosemite National Park, Tuolumne River, horseback riding, hiking, bicycling, mountain climbing, downhill skiing, fishing, white-water rafting, swimming, tennis, golfing

## GROVELAND HOTEL

18767 Main Street
P.O. Box 481
Groveland, California 95321
**Phone:** 209/962-4000 or 800/273-3314
**Fax:** 209/962-6674
**Website:** www.groveland.com
**E-mail:** peggy@groveland.com
**Proprietors:** Peggy A. and Grover C. Mosley
**Location:** 23 miles west of Yosemite National Park

The Groveland Hotel, believed to have been built by Joshua D. Crippen in 1849, is the largest adobe building in Groveland and one of the oldest buildings in Tuolumne County. The adobe structure with two-story wraparound Monterey-style porches served the community first as a trading post, then as a residence until 1865. After that date the building was dedicated exclusively to hotel or boarding house use. Very little alteration has occurred over the years, leaving the hotel with a high degree of architectural integrity. A two-story frame annex that was built next to the hotel in 1914 is considered to be one of the finest examples of the Neoclassical style in Tuolumne County. Today, the Groveland Hotel and Annex offer 17 guest rooms that feature European antiques, down comforters, robes, coffee service, and hair dryers.

**Open:** year round **Accommodations:** 17 guest rooms with private baths; 3 are suites with fireplaces and whirlpool tubs **Meals:** continental-plus breakfast included; complimentary refreshments; restaurant on premises **Rates:** $115 to $195 **Payment:** AmEx, Visa, MC, CB, DC, Discover, personal and traveler's checks **Restrictions:** no smoking; inquire about pets **On-site activities:** murder mystery weekends and seasonal special events; call for free calendar of events

# HALF MOON BAY

**Nearby attractions:** beaches, hiking, tide pooling, fishing, golfing, art galleries, antiques hunting, winery tours, whale-watching, National Trust's Filoli and gardens

## OLD THYME INN

779 Main Street
Half Moon Bay, California 94019
**Phone:** 650/726-1616 or 800/720-4277
**Website:** www.oldthymeinn.com
**E-mail:** innkeeper@oldthymeinn.com
**Proprietors:** Rick and Kathy Ellis

Occupying a prominent position on Main Street, the Old Thyme Inn was built in 1899. Its Queen Anne styling is highlighted by decorative fish-scale shingles on the exterior walls. Guest rooms are all decorated with antiques and offer whirlpool or claw-foot tubs. Some rooms contain fireplaces; one room has a stained-glass window, another a skylight. The guest rooms are named for some of the 80 varieties of herbs grown in the inn's bountiful herb garden. Guests are invited to smell the fragrances and take cuttings home. The Garden Suite has its own private entrance, a four-poster bed, fireplace, and complimentary wine in the refrigerator. Every morning the English-style breakfast includes fresh herbs, as well as homemade scones, egg dishes, and freshly baked breads.

**Open:** year round **Accommodations:** 7 guest rooms with private baths; 1 is a suite **Meals:** full breakfast included; complimentary refreshments; restaurants nearby **Rates:** $105 to $265; 10% discount offered to National Trust members and National Trust Visa cardholders **Payment:** Visa, MC, personal check **Restrictions:** no smoking; no pets **On-site activities:** herb gardens

# HEALDSBURG

**Nearby attractions:** winery tours and tastings, Luther Burbank gardens, historic house tours, antiques hunting, canoeing, golfing, hot-air ballooning, river rafting, swimming, fishing, sailing

## CALDERWOOD INN

25 West Grant Street
Healdsburg, California 95448
**Phone:** 707/431-1110 or 800/600-5444
**Proprietors:** Jennifer and Paul Zawodny

A visitor strolling down West Grant Street will discover Calderwood Inn sitting on a lushly planted acre of land in the heart of Healdsburg's historic district. Surrounded by a filigreed wrought-iron and stone-pillar fence, the property was planted in large part by the famed Luther Burbank at the turn of this century. The house, built in 1902 by the prominent fruit growing and processing John Miller family, is a cross-gabled Victorian exhibiting early Craftsman influences in its overhanging eaves and sturdy porch-roof supports. Large, leaded-glass windows admit plenty of sunlight to the interior, which boasts elegant Victorian ceiling and wallpapers designed by William Morris. Six guest rooms with private baths are furnished in period antiques. Guests are invited to stroll through the estate's gardens.

**Open:** year round **Accommodations:** 6 guest rooms with private baths **Meals:** full breakfast included; complimentary refreshments; restaurants nearby **Rates:** $135 to $185 **Payment:** personal check **Restrictions:** no smoking; no pets **On-site activities:** gardens and ponds, croquet, bicycles, games, books

## CAMELLIA INN

211 North Street
Healdsburg, California 95448
**Phone:** 707/433-8182 or 800/727-8182
**Website:** www.camelliainn.com
**E-mail:** info@camelliainn.com
**Proprietors:** Ray, Del, and Lucy Lewand

More than 50 varieties of camellias bloom on the landscaped grounds of the Camellia Inn and around its terraced swimming pool. The house, built in 1869 by Ransome Powell, is Italianate in design, and its simple facade is made elegant by arched windows and a round-arched doorway and porch. The home was purchased by Dr. J. Walter Seawell in 1892 to serve as his home and offices, and then as the town's first hospital. Heavily carved crown molding, double parlors with twin marble fireplaces, inlaid hardwood floors, and ceiling medallions are

just some of the extant architectural features of the historic home. Guest rooms are decorated individually with antiques, such as a half-testered bed made of tiger maple, which was brought from Scotland. Special amenities may include a gas fireplace or whirlpool bath. Breakfast includes a hearty main dish and freshly baked nut breads.

**Open:** year round **Accommodations:** 9 guest rooms with private baths **Meals:** full breakfast included; complimentary refreshments; restaurants nearby **Wheelchair access:** 1 guest room **Rates:** $75 to $165; 10% discount to National Trust members and National Trust Visa cardholders **Payment:** AmEx, Visa, MC, personal and traveler's checks **Restrictions:** no smoking; no pets **On-site activities:** swimming pool, landscaped gardens

## HEALDSBURG INN ON THE PLAZA
110 Matheson Street
Healdsburg, California 95448
**Phone:** 707/433-6991 or 800/431-8663
**Website:** www.healdsburginn.com
**Proprietor:** Genny Jenkins

Located on the plaza in downtown Healdsburg, the structure known as the Healdsburg Inn first served as the Wells-Fargo Express building, its architecture deemed "modern renaissance" by the *Healdsburg Tribune* in 1901. A grand, paneled staircase leads to the second floor, which once served as the town's center for professional services. The doctors' and dentists' offices and photography studio are now spacious guest rooms. All are furnished with antiques and unique collectibles. Central air and heat, fluffy towels, and rubber duckies are standards. Most rooms have fireplaces and claw-foot tubs. Fine art—for viewing and for sale—is displayed in the reception area and throughout the inn. The first floor also boasts antiques and gift shops. A solarium overlooks the village and provides a comfortable common area.

**Open:** year round **Accommodations:** 10 guest rooms with private baths **Meals:** full breakfast included; complimentary refreshments; restaurants nearby **Rates:** $85 to $240; 10% discount to National Trust members and National Trust Visa cardholders midweek only **Payment:** Visa, MC, personal and traveler's checks **Restrictions:** smoking limited; no pets **On-site activities:** listening to music, games and puzzles, reading, television and VCR, solarium sitting, art gallery, gift shops

## HOPE VALLEY

**Nearby attractions:** Lake Tahoe, historic town of Markleeville, museums, walking tours, downhill skiing (Kirkwood), kayaking, river rafting, canoeing, hot springs

### SORENSEN'S RESORT
14255 Highway 88
Hope Valley, California 96120
**Phone:** 916/694-2203 or 800/423-9949
**Proprietors:** John and Patty Brissenden
**Location:** Sorensen's Resort is located 20 miles south of Lake Tahoe

Set in the striking splendor of the Sierra Nevadas, Sorensen's Resort has been welcoming guests since the 1920s, when cabins were rented for just 25 cents a night. Some of the cabins date back to 1908, others were added to the rustic resort shortly after World War II. In addition to one-bedroom cabins, the resort also offers a replica Norwegian farmhouse that sleeps six, and Sierra House, a two-bedroom split-level cedar cabin with a full kitchen and living room. Breakfast, lunch, and dinner are available daily at the Country Cafe, where complimentary coffee, tea, and cocoa also are offered. A variety of activities are available to fit the season, from skiing to water sports, or hiking the historic Emigrant Trail. With more than 100 lakes and streams and alpine meadows nearby, Sorensen's and the surrounding Hope Valley offer guests endless opportunities for recreation and exploration.

**Open:** year round **Accommodations:** 30 guest rooms (28 have private baths); 2 bed-and-breakfast rooms with shared bath **Meals:** restaurant on premises; restaurants nearby **Wheelchair access:** 1 cabin (summer months only) **Rates:** $80 to $400; 10% discount to National Trust members and National Trust Visa cardholders mid-week and non-holidays only **Payment:** AmEx, Visa, MC, Discover, personal and traveler's checks **Restrictions:** no smoking; pets permitted in some cabins **On-site activities:** cross-country ski center, Horse Feathers Fly Fishing School, hiking, bicycling

---

# IONE

**Nearby attractions:** museums, historic sites, antiques hunting, wineries, art galleries, river, lakes, fishing, swimming, boating

## THE HEIRLOOM
214 Shakeley Lane
P.O. Box 322
Ione, California 95640
**Phone:** 209/274-4468 or 888/628-7896
**Website:** www.theheirloominn.com
**Proprietors:** Melisande Hubbs and Patricia Cross

Nestled among the foothills of the great Sierras lies the small village of Ione and the home of one of the earliest settlers in the valley when it served as a supply center for the rich gold fields nearby. Built in 1863, the two-story brick home adorned by classical columns supporting front and rear porches and balconies is today an inn furnished in family heirlooms and antiques. One of the most remarkable is the square grand piano once owned by gold rush entertainer Lola Montez. Guests are treated to fruit, candy, and flowers in the bedrooms, which are decorated with handmade quilts. Breakfast is served in guest rooms, on private verandas, in the garden, or fireside in the dining room.

**Open:** year round **Accommodations:** 6 guest rooms (4 have private baths) **Meals:** full breakfast included; complimentary refreshments; restaurants nearby **Wheelchair access:** limited **Rates:** $65 to $98 **Payment:** AmEx, Visa, MC, personal and traveler's checks **Restrictions:** children over 8 welcome; no smoking; no pets **On-site activities:** croquet, horseshoe pitching, hammock, glider, piano, games, puzzles, books

# LA JOLLA

**Nearby attractions:** San Diego Zoo, Sea World, Museum of Contemporary Art, Old Town San Diego, Scripps Institution of Oceanography, University of California–San Diego, Cove Beach, ocean, golfing, tennis, swimming, surfing, snorkeling

## BED AND BREAKFAST INN AT LA JOLLA

7753 Draper Avenue
La Jolla, California 92037
**Phone:** 619/456-2066 or 800/582-2466
**Website:** www.innlajolla.com
**Proprietor:** Marilouise Micuda

The Bed and Breakfast Inn at La Jolla offers deluxe accommodations in the building listed as Historical Site 179 on the San Diego Register of Historic Places. The inn is one of architect Irving Gill's finest examples of Cubism. Built in 1913 for George Kautz, the house was home to the John Philip Sousa family during the 1920s. Fireplaces and ocean views are featured in many guest rooms, all of which are decorated in a style that evokes elegant country cottages and contain fresh fruit, sherry, cut flowers, and terrycloth robes for guests. Some rooms also offer refrigerators and hair dryers. Guests are invited to relax in the garden, enjoy the view from the deck, or browse in the library–sitting room. Wine and cheese are served daily. The inn is surrounded by lush gardens originally planned by renowned horticulturist Kate Sessions.

**Open:** year round **Accommodations:** 15 guest rooms with private baths **Meals:** full breakfast included; restaurants nearby **Rates:** $90 to $250; 10% discount offered to National Trust members or National Trust Visa cardholders September through June, midweek only **Payment:** Visa, MC, personal and traveler's checks **Restrictions:** children over 12 welcome; no smoking; no pets

# MENDOCINO

**Nearby attractions:** historic village, shops, art galleries, theater, wineries, redwood forests, four state parks, botanical gardens, horseback riding, canoeing, hiking, bicycling, tennis, golfing, fishing, whale-watching, July music festival

## JOHN DOUGHERTY HOUSE

571 Ukiah Street
P.O. Box 817
Mendocino, California 95460
**Phone:** 707/937-5266 or 800/486-2104
**Website:** www.jdhouse.com
**E-mail:** jdhbmw@mcn.org
**Proprietors:** David and Marion Wells

One of the oldest houses in Mendocino, this historic saltbox home was built in 1867. The main house is furnished with early American antiques and its walls are decorated with stenciling. The guest accommodations range from simple, charming rooms to garden cottages and a unique water tower with an 18-foot-high beamed ceiling, four-poster bed, private bath, sitting room, and wood-burning fireplace. Located in the center of the town's National Register historic district, the inn has some of the best ocean and bay views in the village. John Dougherty House is years removed from twentieth-century bustle but just steps away from great restaurants and shopping.

**Open:** year round **Accommodations:** 6 guest rooms with private baths; 4 are suites **Meals:** continental-plus breakfast included; complimentary refreshments; restaurants nearby **Rates:** $95 to $205; 10% discount offered to National Trust members and National Trust Visa cardholders **Payment:** Visa, MC, personal and traveler's checks **Restrictions:** children over 12 preferred; no smoking; no pets **On-site activities:** ocean viewing, gardens, whale-watching, television, relaxing on verandas

**WHITEGATE INN**
499 Howard Street
P.O. Box 150
Mendocino, California 95460
**Phone:** 707/937-4892 or 800/531-7282
**Fax:** 707/937-1131
**Website:** www.whitegateinn.com
**E-mail:** staff@whitegateinn.com
**Proprietors:** Carol and George Bechtloff

Built in 1883 and described by a local journalist as "one of the most elegant and best appointed residences in town," the Whitegate Inn stands today much as it did then. The first floor is still graced with large double parlors separated by 10-foot-high pocket doors, and the original crystal chandeliers hang as they have for more than a century. The front parlor fireplace still provides warmth. Guest rooms are charming with fireplaces, brass and iron beds, Victorian antiques, and glimpses of the Pacific Ocean. Full breakfasts feature homemade muffins and cinnamon raisin rounds, and delicious entrees such as caramel-apple French toast or eggs Florentine. After a day exploring Mendocino's shops and sites, guests are greeted by the innkeepers with light hors d'oeuvres and a glass of wine.

**Open:** year round **Accommodations:** 7 guest rooms with private baths **Meals:** full breakfast included; complimentary refreshments; restaurants nearby **Rates:** $119 to $239; 10% discount to National Trust members and National Trust Visa cardholders **Payment:** AmEx, Visa, MC, Discover, personal and traveler's checks **Restrictions:** no smoking; no pets **On-site activities:** relaxing, reading

# MURPHYS

**Nearby attractions:** historic Main Street (with shops, galleries, and museum), Calaveras Big Trees State Park, Columbia State Park, winery tours, skiing, river rafting, golfing, seasonal festivals, antiques hunting, museums, art galleries

## DUNBAR HOUSE, 1880

271 Jones Street
Murphys, California 95247
**Phone:** 209/728-2897 or 800/692-6006
**Fax:** 209/728-1451
**Website:** www.dunbarhouse.com
**E-mail:** inkeep@dunbarhouse.com
**Proprietors:** Barbara and Bob Costa

An Italianate home built in 1880 by Willis Dunbar for his bride, Ellen Roberts, this charming bed and breakfast has won acclaim from such publications as *Victorian Homes, Sunset, Gourmet,* and the *Los Angeles Times.* Located in the historic Gold Country of California, Dunbar House offers fine accommodations accented with antiques, lace, claw-foot tubs, and wood-burning stoves. Service is attentive; the innkeepers will make dinner reservations, turn down beds, and leave chocolates at the bedside. Guest rooms come equipped with a refrigerator stocked with ice and a complimentary bottle of local wine. Each room contains a television, VCR, and a classic video library hidden discreetly in an armoire. Reading lights, makeup mirrors, and hair dryers also are provided. Home-baked goods are part of the full breakfast served by the dining room fire, in the garden, or in guest rooms.

**Open:** year round **Accommodations:** 4 guest rooms with private baths; 1 is a suite **Meals:** full breakfast included; complimentary refreshments; restaurants nearby **Rates:** $125 to $225; 10% discount offered to National Trust members and National Trust Visa cardholders midweek only, excluding holidays **Payment:** Visa, MC, personal and traveler's checks **Restrictions:** children over 10 welcome; no smoking; no pets **On-site activities:** reading, gardens, classic videos, music

# NAPA

**Nearby attractions:** winery tours and tastings, Napa Valley Wine Train, hot-air ballooning, glider rides, mud baths, opera house, tennis, golfing, hiking, bicycling, horseback riding

### BEAZLEY HOUSE
1910 First Street
Napa, California 94559
**Phone:** 707/257-1649
or 800/559-1649
**Fax:** 707/257-1518
**Website:**
www.beazleyhouse.com
**E-mail:**
innkeeper@beazleyhouse.com
**Proprietors:** Carol and Jim Beazley

Beazley House opened in 1981 as Napa's first bed and breakfast, and is the only inn in Napa still owned and operated by its founders. Built in 1902, the house was designed by Napa architect Luther Turton for Dr. Adolf Kahn, a local surgeon and politician. The chocolate brown Shingle Style mansion with white trim remains in nearly original condition today. Large, individually decorated guest rooms are appointed with antiques, queen-size beds, and private baths. Guest rooms are also found in the reconstructed carriage house behind the mansion, nestled among gardens and trees. In it, five charming rooms with private spas, baths, and fireplaces are available. A full breakfast buffet and afternoon tea are served. Sitting on half an acre of lawns and gardens, Beazley House is a short stroll from old Napa's shops and restaurants.

**Open:** year round **Accommodations:** 11 guest rooms with private baths; 4 are suites **Meals:** full breakfast included; complimentary refreshments; restaurants nearby **Wheelchair access:** 1 room **Rates:** $115 to $250; 10% discount to National Trust members and National Trust Visa cardholders **Payment:** AmEx, Visa, MC, personal and traveler's checks **Restrictions:** no smoking; no pets (resident cats) **On-site activities:** wine tastings, gardens

## BELLE EPOQUE BED AND BREAKFAST INN
1386 Calistoga Avenue
Napa, California 94559
**Phone:** 707/257-2161
**Fax:** 707/226-6314
**Website:** www.labelleepoque.com
**Proprietor:** Georgia Jump

In 1893, Herman Schwarz, the successful owner of the largest hardware firm in Napa County, commissioned the house at Calistoga and Seminary streets as a wedding gift for his daughter Minnie. This city landmark, designed by respected Bay Area architect Luther Turton, is an extravagant example of Queen Anne styling. Decorative flat and molded carvings can be seen in the gables and bays, and original stained-glass windows remain in the transoms and semicircular windows. Several historic church windows, which predate the house, have been artfully added to the front of the building. The finely crafted and decorated interiors are graced by an exceptional collection of Victorian antiques. Tucked away in the basement is a wine cellar and tasting room. For further investigation, guests can take a short walk to the Napa Valley Wine Train.

**Open:** year round **Accommodations:** 6 guest rooms with private baths, 2 have fireplaces **Meals:** full breakfast included; complimentary wine and appetizers; restaurants nearby **Rates:** $149 to $209; 10% discount to National Trust members and National Trust Visa cardholders midweek only **Payment:** AmEx, Visa, MC, Discover, personal and traveler's checks **Restrictions:** no smoking; no pets **On-site activities:** wine tasting, board games, television and VCR, square grand piano

## CHURCHILL MANOR BED AND BREAKFAST
485 Brown Street
Napa, California 94559
**Phone:** 707/253-7733
**Proprietors:** Joanna Guidotti and Brian Jensen

Built in 1889 for local banker Edward Churchill, the 10,000-square-foot mansion was a showcase for visitors sailing from San Francisco. An expansive veranda supported by 20 fluted Ionic and Doric columns surround the three-story Second Empire mansion. Following Churchill's death in 1903, his daughter Dorothy resided here until 1956, opening the home to boarders and weddings. The first floor boasts a mosaic marble-floored solarium and four spacious parlors separated by massive redwood pocket doors. Each parlor features a fireplace with an ornate mantel and 17 layers of ceiling moldings. American and European antiques fill the luxurious guest rooms. Pedestal sinks, claw-foot tubs, brass fixtures, and hand-painted and gold-laced tiles adorn the private baths. Evenings at Churchill Manor begin with a Napa Valley varietal wine and cheese reception.

**Open:** year round **Accommodations:** 10 guest rooms with private baths; 4 are suites **Meals:** full breakfast included; complimentary wine and cheese and freshly baked cookies; restaurants nearby **Rates:** $95 to $195; 10% discount to National Trust members and National Trust Visa cardholders midweek only **Payment:** AmEx, Visa, MC, Discover, personal and traveler's checks **Restrictions:** children over 12 welcome; no smoking; no pets; two-night minimum with Saturday night booking **On-site activities:** croquet, tandem bicycling, grand piano, library, puzzles, games, television and VCR

## OLD WORLD INN
1301 Jefferson Street
Napa, California 94559
**Phone:** 707/257-0112 or 800/966-6624
**Fax:** 707/257-0118
**Website:** www.napavalley.com/napavalley/lodging/inns/oldworld/
**Proprietor:** Sam VanHoeve

The Old World Inn was built in 1906 by local contractor E. W. Doughty as his private town residence. The home is an eclectic combination of architectural styles detailed with wood shingles, wide shady porches, clinker brick, and leaded and beveled glass. Inside are painted Victorian and other antique furnishings. Each of the eight guest rooms has been decorated with coordinating linens and fabrics, and each has a private bathroom, most with claw-foot tubs. Bright, fresh Scandinavian colors inspired by the works of Swedish artist Carl Larsson dominate the bedrooms as well as the parlor. The latter, with its fireplace and soft classical music, provides a soothing retreat. Complimentary wines, cheeses, appetizers, and desserts are offered daily.

**Open:** year round **Accommodations:** 8 guest rooms with private baths **Meals:** continental-plus breakfast included; complimentary refreshments; restaurants nearby **Rates:** $125 to $275 **Payment:** AmEx, Visa, MC, Discover, personal and traveler's checks **Restrictions:** no smoking; no pets **On-site activities:** outdoor spa, puzzles

---

# OJAI

**Nearby attractions:** Ojai Center for the Arts, Ojai Valley Historical Society and Museum, Lake Casitas recreation area, golfing, tennis, antiques hunting, ongoing festivals

## THEODORE WOOLSEY HOUSE
1484 E. Ojai Avenue
Ojai, California 93023
**Phone:** 805/646-9779
**Fax:** 805/646-4414
**Website:** www.theodorewoolseyhouse.com
**Proprietors:** Ana and Papi Cross

Tucked away on seven oak-shaded acres is the Theodore Woolsey House. A rose-lined drive leads to the two-story stone and clapboard New England-style farmhouse with its 70-foot-long veranda. The house was built in 1887 for Theodore S. Woolsey, professor of international law and dean of Yale University, who moved to the temperate Ojai Valley with his wife in hopes of improving her health. Today, the restored spacious house welcomes guests to experience for themselves the charm of Ojai and the house's relaxing, old-fashioned ambiance. The inn is furnished with a variety of old-time touches, from the 1950s Wurlitzer jukebox in the dining room to antique claw-foot tubs and wood-burning stoves in some of the guest rooms. Whether sitting in the garden room, the screened-in patio breakfast room, or on the sundeck—each overlooking the pool and gardens—guests are treated to the valley's picturesque mountain views.

**Open:** year round **Accommodations:** 6 guest rooms with private baths **Meals:** continental breakfast included; complimentary refreshments; restaurants nearby **Rates:** $85 to $150 **Payment:** personal check **Restrictions:** no smoking; no pets **On-site activities:** sand volleyball court, swimming pool, hot tub, croquet lawn, horseshoe pits, gardens

## PACIFIC GROVE

**Nearby attractions:** historic Pacific Grove, Cannery Row, Monterey Bay Aquarium, Monterey Maritime Museum, Pebble Beach Golf Course, 17-Mile Drive, Carmel-by-the-Sea, Carmel Mission, Big Sur, Point Lobos State Park, tennis, boating, fishing, kayaking, sailing, scuba diving, hiking, biking, butterfly-watching, beaches, gift shops, galleries

### GATEHOUSE INN
225 Central Avenue
Pacific Grove, California 93950
**Phone:** 831/649-8436 or 800/753-1881
**Fax:** 831/648-8044
**Website:** www.sueandlewinns.com
**Proprietors:** Susan Kuslis and Lewis Shaefer

State Senator Benjamin J. Langford built this Italianate house in 1884 as a summer retreat for his family. The inn takes its name from Langford's act of civil disobedience—chopping down the wagon gate that kept the devil out of town, but made getting home a nuisance for Langford. Reminders of the senator's era are seen in the home's Bradbury and Bradbury mosaic wallpapers, tin ceilings, and original moldings. Five guest rooms have ocean views; five, their own entrances. The Captain's room, Steinbeck room, and Cannery Row room all evoke local tradition and influences, while the Italian room, with its rococo flourishes, and the Turkish room, with its exotic flair, offer accommodations a world away. Some rooms contain wood-burning stoves, claw-foot tubs, or fireplaces. The inn faces Monterey Bay and a marine reserve, giving guests a front row seat from which to watch seals, sea lions, and sea otters at play.

**Open:** year round **Accommodations:** 9 guest rooms with private baths **Meals:** full breakfast included; complimentary refreshments; restaurants nearby **Wheelchair access:** 1 guest room and common areas **Rates:** $110 to $165; 10% discount to National Trust members and National Trust Visa cardholders **Payment:** AmEx, Visa, MC, Discover, personal check **Restrictions:** children over 8 welcome; no smoking; no pets **On-site activities:** games, books, bicycles

### GRAND VIEW INN
557 Ocean View Boulevard
Pacific Grove, California 93950
**Phone:** 831/372-4341
**Proprietors:** Susan and Ed Flatley

After half a century as a Methodist summer camp, the town of Pacific Grove was becoming established as a year-round community by 1910, the same year that Dr.

Julia Platt, a noted marine biologist, built her four-story home at the edge of Monterey Bay overlooking Lover's Point. Pacific Grove's first woman mayor, she was instrumental in preserving the Lover's Point beach and park for future generations. Her home has been completely restored by the Flatley family and opened as the Grand View Inn. Along with unsurpassed views of the bay from each room, guests enjoy the elegance of marble-tiled private baths, patterned hardwood floors, antique furnishings, and inviting grounds. The parlor is appointed with oak columns, a marble fireplace, and comfortable seating areas affording wraparound ocean views. A full breakfast and afternoon tea are served overlooking the Pacific Grove coastline.

**Open:** year round **Accommodations:** 10 guest rooms with private baths **Meals:** full breakfast included; complimentary refreshments; restaurants nearby **Wheelchair access:** 1 room **Rates:** $155 to $275 **Payment:** Visa, MC, personal and traveler's checks **Restrictions:** children over 12 welcome; no smoking; no pets **On-site activities:** oceanfront walks, touring, relaxing, gardens, viewing ocean

### MARTINE INN
255 Ocean View Boulevard
Pacific Grove, California 93950-0232
**Mailing address:** P.O. Box 232
**Phone:** 831/373-3388
or 800/852-5588
**Fax:** 831/373-3896
**Website:**
www.martineinn.com
**Proprietor:** Don Martine

This elegant inn, perched high on the cliffs overlooking the rocky coastline of Monterey Bay, dates from 1899, when it was built as a Victorian house. Later, Laura and James Parke of Parke Davis Pharmaceuticals transformed it into a Mediterranean-style house with a stuccoed exterior. Fond of exotic woods, Parke installed gates of Siamese teak, a Spanish cedar staircase, and inlaid oak and mahogany floors. Guest rooms, many with working fireplaces, are furnished with museum-quality American antique bedroom suites. Guests receive fruit in a Victorian silver basket, a fresh rose, and chocolate mints on pillows at evening turn-down. Breakfast is served on antique silver, crystal, and lace in the dining room, which provides views of the bay. In 1993 Martine Inn was selected by *Bon Appétit* as one of eight best bed and breakfasts in historic homes.

**Open:** year round **Accommodations:** 19 guest rooms with private baths; 2 are suites **Meals:** full breakfast included; complimentary refreshments; restaurants nearby **Wheelchair access:** guest rooms, bathrooms, dining facilities **Rates:** $150 to $300 **Payment:** Amex, Visa, MC, personal and traveler's checks **Restrictions:** smoking limited; no pets **On-site activities:** billiards, spa, vintage car collection

## OLD ST. ANGELA INN
321 Central Avenue
Pacific Grove, California 93950
**Phone:** 831/372-3246 or 800/748-6306
**Fax:** 831/372-8560
**Website:** www.sueandlewinns.com
**E-mail:** lew@redshift.com
**Proprietors:** Susan Kuslis and Lewis Shaefer

This charming home, built in 1910 for Roberta and Anne Littlehale, is a happy blend of Cape Cod (one and a half stories, steeply pitched roof) and Craftsman (wide, overhanging eaves and broad, shed dormer) styles. For a token payment of ten dollars in 1928, the house became a rectory for the first St. Angela's Catholic Church and later a convent for the Dominican Sisters. Restored to its original appearance in 1960, the house was expanded and turned into a bed-and-breakfast inn in 1983. Overlooking Monterey Bay, the inn offers guests a warm, relaxing atmosphere with its pine furniture and antiques and bright cut flowers. In the afternoon guests can mingle by the living room fireplace and enjoy wine and cheese and tea service. A full buffet breakfast is served in the redwood and glass

solarium with a view of the garden. The comfortable guest rooms—some with ocean views—are havens of serenity, free of television and telephones. Located only 100 yards from the water, St. Angela's Inn is convenient to Monterey's many fine restaurants, shops, and world-class golf courses.

**Open:** year round **Accommodations:** 8 guest rooms with private baths **Meals:** full breakfast included; complimentary refreshments; restaurants nearby **Wheelchair access:** limited **Rates:** $110 to $150; 10% discount to National Trust members and National Trust Visa cardholders **Payment:** Visa, MC, Discover, personal check **Restrictions:** children over 5 welcome; no smoking; some pets acceptable—limited to certain rooms **On-site activities:** games, books, spa/hot tub

## SEVEN GABLES INN
555 Ocean View Boulevard
Pacific Grove, California 93950
**Phone:** 408/372-4341
**Proprietors:** Susan, Ed, and John Flatley

Built in 1886, the Seven Gables Inn is one of a parade of large, showy Victorian homes found throughout Pacific Grove, a coastal town that began as a Methodist summer retreat in the 1850s. Bought in 1906 by Henry and Lucie Chase, this house was christened "The House of Seven Gables" to honor the Chase's Salem, Massachusetts, origins. The inn is perched on a rocky promontory overlooking Monterey Bay, a location that affords each guest room views of the Pacific coastline and encircling mountains. Ornate stained-glass windows and delicate plaster ceiling medallions are backdrops to the fine European antiques found throughout the inn. The Flatley family has owned this home for 25 years and attends to guests' needs with meticulous care and attention, resulting in a Mobil four-star rating and the honor of being named one of 1994's top 12 inns in the nation by *Country Inns* magazine.

**Open:** year round **Accommodations:** 14 guest rooms with private baths **Meals:** full breakfast included; complimentary afternoon tea; restaurants nearby **Wheelchair access:** 2 rooms accessible with assistance **Rates:** $155 to $350 **Payment:** Visa, MC, personal and traveler's checks **Restrictions:** children over 12 welcome; no smoking; no pets **On-site activities:** relaxing, porch sitting, gardens, viewing ocean

## PALM SPRINGS

**Nearby attractions:** Desert Museum, historic village green, theaters, tennis, golfing, horseback riding, hiking, cross-country skiing, art galleries, shopping, botanical gardens, Aerial Tramway, Cahuilla Reservation

### ORCHID TREE INN
261 South Belardo Road
Palm Springs, California 92262
**Phone:** 760/325-2791 or 800/733-3435
**Fax:** 760/325-3855
**Website:** www.orchidtree.com
**Proprietors:** Robert and Karen Weithorn

Representing five decades of Palm Springs architecture (1910s to 1950s), the Orchid Tree offers accommodations ranging from intimate studios and suites to garden cottages, cabins, and bungalows. In the sheltered area between the famed Palm Springs village and the soaring San Jacinto Mountains, the inn's various—Mediterranean to Modernist—buildings nestle amid flowering gardens, fruit trees, towering palms, and three large swimming pools. Many accommodations offer private balconies, porches, patios, or gardens. Most rooms offer full kitchens, and all have color cable television. A desert garden retreat, the Orchid Tree offers the appeal of the 1920s and 1930s combined with custom-made lodgepole pine funiture and contemporary comfort and convenience.

**Open:** year round **Accommodations:** 40 guest rooms with private baths; 15 are suites **Meals:** continental-plus breakfast included November 1 through May 31; restaurants nearby **Rates:** seasonally variable from $65 to $295; 10% discount offered to National Trust members and National Trust Visa cardholders excluding holidays and high season **Payment:** AmEx, Visa, MC, Discover, travelers check **Restrictions:** inquire about children; smoking limited; no pets **On-site activities:** 3 swimming pools, 2 spas, shuffleboard, library, board games, seminars, retreats, tennis at neighboring private club

### THE WILLOWS—HISTORIC PALM SPRINGS INN
412 West Tahquitz
Palm Springs, California 92262
**Phone:** 760/320-0771
**Fax:** 760/320-0780
**Website:** www.thewillowspalmsprings.com
**E-mail:** innkeeper@thewillowspalmsprings.com

A Mediterranean-style villa and oasis set in Old Palm Springs Village, the Willows was built in 1927, soon becoming the winter estate of famed New York attorney

Samuel Untermeyer. Since then visitors have reveled in the inn's tranquil setting before the looming San Jacinto Mountains. Among the inn's distinctive features are a mountain waterfall that flows into a pool beside the dining room, the veranda's frescoed ceilings, and an enchanted hillside garden. The luxurious guest rooms offer modern amenities as well as antique furnishings, private garden patios, and mountain or garden views. Einstein's Garden Room, with its stylish Art Deco mahogany furniture and French doors opening to the waterfall, hosted Albert Einstein on many occasions, and honeymooners Clark Gable and Carole Lombard stayed in the Library, which boasts a dark cherry hand-carved fireplace and coffered ceiling. The Willows, recipient of AAA's four diamonds and Mobil's four stars, is just a short walk from fine dining, historic sites, and the city's renowned fashion boutiques and antiques shops.

**Open:** September 1 to July 1 **Accommodations:** 8 guest rooms with private baths **Meals:** full breakfast included; complimentary refreshments; restaurants nearby **Rates:** $250 to $500; 10% discount to National Trust members and National Trust Visa cardholders **Payment:** AmEx, Visa, MC, CB, DC, Discover, traveler's and personal checks **Restrictions:** children over 16 welcome; no smoking; no pets **On-site activities:** pool/whirlpool, garden, hiking

## SACRAMENTO

**Nearby attractions:** state capitol, historic Old Sacramento, Crocker Art Museum and Sculpture Garden, Sutter's Fort, Downtown Plaza, Sacramento Community Center, Music Circus, American River Bike Trail, day trips to Napa wine country, San Francisco, Sierra foothills' Gold Country of Lake Tahoe, tennis, jogging, fishing, swimming

### INN AT PARKSIDE
2116 Sixth Street
Sacramento, California 95818
**Phone:** 916/658-1818 or 800/995-7275
**Fax:** 916/658-1809
**Website:** www.innatparkside.com
**E-mail:** gmcgreal@wired2.net
**Proprietor:** Georgia McGreal

A grand mansion, built in 1936 as the official U.S. residence for the North American Ambassador to Nationalist China, the Inn at Parkside overlooks Southside Park in the heart of Sacramento. Its Italian Renaissance styling is emphasized by a low-pitched, hipped roof of ceramic tiles and arched ground floor windows and entryway. Sumptuously decorated, the inn's public rooms feature lofty, hand-painted ceilings, crystal chandeliers, and gleaming hardwood floors and woodwork. Guest rooms, decorated with a mix of elegance and whimsy, have views of Southside Park or the lush foliage of the inn's landscaped grounds. Guests are invited to enjoy the library, deck, or a selection of hundreds of vintage records on the antique phonograph in the ballroom, complete with spring-loaded, maple dance floor. A guest kitchenette is open 24 hours a day. A spa room is equipped with a whirlpool tub for two, wall-to-wall mirror, stained-glass ceiling, and original artwork.

**Open:** year round **Accommodations:** 7 guest rooms with private baths; 1 is a suite **Meals:** full breakfast included; restaurants nearby **Rates:** $79 to $200 **Payment:** AmEx, Visa, MC, Discover, personal and traveler's checks **Restrictions:** no smoking **On-site activities:** parlor games, spa, library, ballroom dancing

## ST. HELENA

**Nearby attractions:** Napa Valley wineries, Robert Louis Stevenson Museum, Petrified Forest, Napa Valley Wine Train, river, lake, hot-air ballooning, bicycling, hiking, tennis, golfing, antiques hunting, shopping

### CINNAMON BEAR BED AND BREAKFAST
1407 Kearney Street
St. Helena, California 94574
**Phone:** 707/963-4653 or (toll free) 888/963-4600
**Fax:** 707/963-0251
**Proprietor:** Cathye Ranieri

A classic Craftsman bungalow with a full-width front porch and gabled dormer, this house was built in 1904 as a wedding gift to Susan Smith from her groom, Walter Metzner, who would later serve as mayor of St. Helena for 20 years. The house is beautifully preserved with gleaming hardwood floors, original light fixtures, and elegant period furnishings. The main floor offers a sitting room with

fireplace, two formal dining rooms with original redwood wainscoting, and a large private suite. Two more guest rooms are upstairs; all are done in antiques with quilts and a collection of antique teddy bears. The innkeepers are professional chefs who love to share their knowledge of food and wine. In the evening guests are invited to relax in front of the living room fireplace or enjoy puzzles, games, and books in the parlor. A hearty country breakfast is served in the dining room or on the porch.

**Open:** year round **Accommodations:** 3 guest rooms with private baths; 1 is a suite **Meals:** full breakfast included; complimentary refreshments; restaurants nearby **Rates:** $115 to $190; 10% discount to National Trust members or National Trust Visa cardholders with stay of more than 1 night **Payment:** AmEx, Visa, MC, traveler's and personal checks **Restrictions:** children over 10 welcome; no smoking; no pets **On-site activities:** bicycles, wine tours, picnics

# SAN DIEGO

**Nearby attractions:** San Diego Zoo, Balboa Park, Sea World, beaches, fishing, diving, tennis, golfing, museums, historic sightseeing

### HERITAGE PARK BED AND BREAKFAST INN
2470 Heritage Park Row
San Diego, California 92110
**Phone:** 619/299-6832 or 800/995-2470
**Fax:** 619/299-9465
**E-mail:**
innkeeper@HeritageParkInn.com
**Proprietors:** Charles and Nancy Helsper

In the heart of the city's historic Old Town is the eight-acre Heritage Park Victorian Village where seven historic homes have been relocated to save them from destruction. The Heritage Park Bed and Breakfast Inn comprises two of these buildings: the 1889 Christian house, a Queen Anne characterized by a variety of chimney and shingle styles, a two-story turret, and an encircling veranda, and the 1887 Italianate Bushyhead house located immediately next door (the two houses were originally next-door neighbors on Cedar Street). The interior of the Christian house boasts three carved-wood fireplaces faced with imported tiles. Many windows are filled with stained glass. A carved balustrade and staircase lead to the second floor. Both floors display curved, ornate, and lacquered redwood molding and trim. Floral wallpapers reproduced from turn-of-the-century designs, antique brass beds, and claw-foot tubs are trademarks of the inn, which has received awards for its full candlelight breakfasts and national recognition in *Country Inns* magazine

**Open:** year round **Accommodations:** 12 guest rooms with private baths **Meals:** full breakfast included; complimentary afternoon tea; restaurants nearby **Rates:** $90 to $225; 10% discount to National Trust members and National Trust Visa cardholders **Payment:** AmEx, Visa, MC, Discover, personal and traveler's checks **Restrictions:** no smoking; no pets **On-site activities:** classic film shows, puzzles, bicycles, croquet

## SAN FRANCISCO

**Nearby attractions:** San Francisco Bay region, Golden Gate Bridge, Fisherman's Wharf, Embarcadero, North Beach, Mission Dolores, historic districts, Japan Center, financial district, Chinatown, dining, theaters, shopping, opera, symphony, ballet, zoo, cable cars, museums, Golden Gate Park, bicycling, jogging paths, tennis, golfing

### GOLDEN GATE HOTEL
775 Bush Street
San Francisco, California 94108
**Phone:** 415/392-3702 or 800/835-1118
**Fax:** 415/392-6202
**Website:** www.goldengatehotel.com
**Proprietors:** John and Renate Kenaston

The Golden Gate Hotel is a bed-and-breakfast hotel located in the Lower Nob Hill Historic District. Built in 1913, the four-story hotel has a double-bay facade, providing many guest rooms with bay-window views and letting in plenty of light and air. The rear of the building faces an open, tree-filled garden. An antique birdcage elevator is a favorite attraction of hotel guests. Furnished with antiques, art, and imagination, the hotel maintains the mood of turn-of-the-century San Francisco, especially in its antique claw-foot tubs. The multilingual hosts of this small, family-owned-and-operated inn take pride in offering individual attention: They brighten each guest room with fresh flowers, provide concierge services, and arrange sightseeing tours. The inn is centrally located in the city with a cable car stop on the corner.

**Open:** year round **Accommodations:** 23 guest rooms (14 have private baths); 1 is a suite **Meals:** continental breakfast included; complimentary afternoon tea; restaurants nearby **Rates:** $65 to $109; 10% discount offered to National Trust members and National Trust Visa cardholders November through April **Payment:** AmEx, Visa, MC, CB, DC, personal and traveler's checks **Restrictions:** smoking limited; with notice, arrangements can be made for pets **On-site activities:** relaxation, classical music in the parlor, conversation

## SHERMAN HOUSE

2160 Green Street
San Francisco, California 94123
**Phone:** 415/563-3600 or 800/424-5777
**Fax:** 415/563-1882
**Website:** www.theshermanhouse.com
**E-mail:** TSHREZ@MHOTELGROUP.com
**Proprietors:** Manou and Vesta Mobedshahi

In 1876, Leander Sherman, an influential patron of the arts, created this elegant Second Empire home, which flourished for decades at the center of San Francisco's musical and artistic life. The focus of the house was a soaring, three-story music recital hall. In 1981 the structure's restoration and conversion into a world-class hotel took 11 months of meticulous work, with an average of 60 craftspeople on the job daily. Sherman House is now filled with antiques and international furnishings. Each unique guest room is designed in either a French Second Empire, Biedermeier, or English Jacobean motif. Canopied feather beds are draped in rich tapestry fabrics. Modern amenities include wet bars, wall safes, and whirlpool baths in the black granite bathrooms. A city and county landmark, Sherman House is a member of Historic Hotels of America.

**Open:** year round **Accommodations:** 14 guest rooms with private baths; 6 are suites **Meals:** restaurant on premises serving breakfast, afternoon tea, and dinner; 24-hour room service; restaurants nearby **Wheelchair access:** 1 suite **Rates:** $310 to $775; 10% discount offered to National Trust members and National Trust Visa cardholders **Payment:** AmEx, Visa, MC, DC, personal and traveler's checks **Restrictions:** no smoking; no pets **On-site activities:** reading and board games in the gallery, relaxing in the garden

## STANYAN PARK HOTEL
750 Stanyan Street
San Francisco, California 94117
**Phone:** 415/751-1000
**Fax:** 415/668-5454
**Website:** www.stanyanpark.com
**E-mail:** info@stanyanpark.com

The Stanyan Park Hotel is significant as the oldest extant hotel on the border of Golden Gate Park. It was built for Henry P. Heagerty, who had run a saloon and small boarding house on the site since 1883. As competition soared, resulting in a dozen hotels serving the park by 1904, Heagerty responded by having an elegant and fashionable structure created by the architectural firm of Martens and Coffey. They gave him the best and costliest ($28,000) of their many buildings in the neighborhood in the Stanyan Park Hotel, an asymmetrical, classically ornamented building with Beaux Arts influences. The hotel is completely restored after many decades of ownership changes and offers today's guests 36 romantic rooms and suites in a variety of period decors. Each of the six suites has a full kitchen, dining room, and living room. The hotel is located next to Golden Gate Park with its world class museums, Japanese Tea Garden, gardens, tennis courts, and jogging and biking trails. Located in a quieter part of this beautiful city, the Stanyan Park is on convenient bus and trolley lines.

**Open:** year round **Accommodations:** 36 guest rooms with private baths; 6 are suites **Meals:** continental-plus breakfast included; complimentary tea service; restaurants nearby **Rates:** $115 to $300 **Payment:** AmEx, Visa, MC, Discover, CB, DC, traveler's check **Restrictions:** no smoking; no pets

## VICTORIAN INN ON THE PARK

301 Lyon Street
San Francisco, California 94117
**Phone:** 415/931-1830 or 800/435-1967
**Fax:** 415/931-1830
**Website:** www.citysearch.com/sfo/victorianinn
**E-mail:** vicinn@aol.com
**Proprietors:** Lisa and William Benau and Shirley and Paul Weber

The Victorian Inn on the Park, also known as the Clunie House, was built in 1897 in the Queen Anne style. Overlooking Golden Gate Park, the house sports decorative gable vergeboards and finials and an octagonal, covered, third-story porch. Each guest room is uniquely designed to reflect Victorian San Francisco and provides comfort with fluffy comforters, down pillows, and private bathrooms. A newspaper and a breakfast of seasonal fruit, cheese, juice, croissants, and freshly brewed coffee greet guests each morning in the oak-paneled dining room. The innkeepers are always available to help guests plan local tours, make dining reservations, or obtain anything from a chauffeured limousine to theater tickets.

**Open:** year round **Accommodations:** 12 guest rooms with private baths; 2 are suites **Meals:** continental-plus breakfast included; complimentary refreshments; restaurants nearby **Rates:** $109 to $169; 10% discount to National Trust members and National Trust Visa cardholders **Payment:** AmEx, Visa, MC, CB, DC, Discover, personal and traveler's checks **Restrictions:** no pets; smoking limited

# SAN LUIS OBISPO

**Nearby attractions:** Hearst Castle, Mission San Luis Obispo, winery tours, walking and house tours, Pismo Beach, Morro Bay, Cambria, mountains, natural hot springs, horseback riding, hiking, picnicking, shopping, golfing, tennis, bicycling, antiques hunting

## GARDEN STREET INN

1212 Garden Street
San Luis Obispo, California 93401
**Phone:** 805/545-9802
**Proprietors:** Dan and Kathy Smith

Behind a wrought-iron fence, one block from an eighteenth-century mission, is this graceful 1887 Italianate building, home of the Garden Street Inn. Its guest rooms are appointed with antiques, fireplaces, whirlpool tubs, armoires, and rich wall coverings and fabrics. Historical, cultural, and personal memorabilia provide each room with its theme, such as Emerald Isle (shamrocks and Lilies of the

Valley), Amadeus (eighteenth-century elegance), Edelweiss (Victorian Austria), and The Lovers (a print of Picasso's famed picture and a private deck). A full breakfast is served in the McCaffrey morning room with original stained-glass windows. Spacious outside decks and the well-stocked Goldtree library are open to guests.

**Open:** year round **Accommodations:** 13 guest rooms with private baths; 4 are suites **Meals:** full breakfast included; complimentary refreshments; restaurants nearby **Wheelchair access:** 1 room **Rates:** $98 to $160; 10% discount to National Trust members and National Trust Visa cardholders (requires two-night stay on weekends) **Payment:** AmEx, Visa, MC, personal and traveler's checks **Restrictions:** not suitable for young children; no smoking **On-site activities:** reading, relaxing, touring historic house

## SANTA BARBARA

**Nearby attractions:** historic sites, mission, beach, ocean swimming, sailing, fishing, hiking, biking, riding, windsurfing, tennis, golfing, botanical gardens, wine-country tours, museums, theaters, shopping

### EL ENCANTO
1900 Lasuen Road
Santa Barbara, California 93103
**Phone:** 805/687-5000
**Fax:** 805/687-3903
**General Manager:** Thom Narozonick

El Encanto—"The Enchanted"—fittingly describes this restored landmark hotel, only 90 minutes from Los Angeles. It is situated amid 10 acres of lush tropical gardens overlooking the Pacific Ocean. Fortunate travelers have been drawn to this site since 1915. Located near historic Mission Santa Barbara, Queen of the Missions (circa 1725), this romantic hideaway offers Craftsman-style cottages and Spanish Colonial Revival villas, two styles for which Santa Barbara is famous. Scores of Hollywood stars have stayed here; Hedy Lamarr moved in. Rooms are individually decorated and offer ocean, city, or garden views. Many rooms have wood-burning fireplaces, hardwood floors, porches, and private or semiprivate patios or balconies. The El Encanto Dining Room, offering breakfast, lunch, and dinner is considered the most beautiful dining room in Santa Barbara by *Gourmet* magazine. The El Encanto is a member of Historic Hotels of America.

**Open:** year round **Accommodations:** 83 cottages and garden villas **Meals:** restaurant on premises **Wheelchair access:** yes **Rates:** $165 to $900; 10% discount to National Trust members and National Trust Visa cardholders **Payment:** AmEx, Visa, MC **Restrictions:** smoking limited; no pets **On-site activities:** swimming pool, tennis court, library, lounge, tour and golf arrangements

## HOTEL SANTA BARBARA

533 State Street
Santa Barbara, California 93101
**Phone:** 805/957-9300 or 888/259-7700
**Fax:** 805/962-2412
**Website:** www.hotelswest.com
**E-mail:** HotelSB@aol.com

Located on Santa Barbara's famed State Street, the Hotel Santa Barbara is within walking distance of many of the city's attractions, such as Stearns Wharf and the beach, museums, theaters, and charming restaurants and shops tucked into Old World-style lanes. Built in 1926, the Mediterranean-style hotel with its graceful arches and wrought-iron balconies was popular with Hollywood's Golden Age stars, including Clark Gable and Carole Lombard; Leo Carrillo, the Cisco Kid's television sidekick, was another frequent visitor who would enter the lobby on horseback. Today the hotel, which underwent a recent multimillion dollar renovation, once more welcomes guests to its handsome accommodations and gracious coastal location. Rates include a continental breakfast, and guests have use of the hotel library and also receive athletic club and pool privileges. Conference and meeting rooms are available.

**Open:** year round **Accommodations:** 75 guest rooms with private baths; 10 are mini-suites **Meals:** continental breakfast included; complimentary refreshments; restaurants nearby **Wheelchair access:** yes **Rates:** $89 to $209; 10% discount to National Trust members and National Trust Visa cardholders **Payment:** AmEx, Visa, MC, DC, Discover, personal and traveler's checks **Restrictions:** smoking limited; no pets **On-site activities:** guest library, athletic club and pool privileges

## MARY MAY INN
111 West Valerio Street
Santa Barbara, California 93101
**Phone and Fax:** 805/569-3398
**Website:** www.silcon.com/~ricky/mary.htm
**Proprietor:** Kathleen M. Pohring

Situated in a residential neighborhood 16 blocks from the beach, the Mary May Inn comprises two historic properties dating from the late nineteenth century. One of them, a Queen Anne structure, was built for the French ambassador to the United States. Both have been fully restored, including interior hand-carved woodwork throughout. Each of the Mary May rooms features a distinctive ambience as the inn is a showcase for extraordinary furnishings. Guest rooms may contain canopied beds, wood-burning fireplaces, claw-foot or whirlpool tubs, or a private entrance. All have private baths. The innkeeper provides a full breakfast and late afternoon tea. Mary May Inn has been awarded three diamonds by AAA.

**Open:** year round **Accommodations:** 12 guest rooms with private baths; 2 are suites **Meals:** full breakfast included; complimentary refreshments and freshly baked cookies; restaurants nearby **Rates:** $100 to $180; 10% discount to National Trust members and National Trust Visa cardholders **Payment:** AmEx, Visa, MC, personal and traveler's checks **Restrictions:** no smoking; some pets allowed **On-site activities:** croquet

## OLD YACHT CLUB INN
431 Corona Del Mar Drive
Santa Barbara, California 93103
**Phone:** 805/962-1277 or 800/676-1676 (reservations)
**Fax:** 805/962-3989
**Proprietors:** Nancy Donaldson and Sandy Hunt

Built as a private home in 1912, this Craftsman house was used during the 1920s as temporary headquarters for the Santa Barbara Yacht Club. The house was restored in 1980 and opened as the city's first bed and breakfast. The Old Yacht Club Inn is furnished with classic European and Early American antiques. Oriental rugs cover the hardwood floors. Four sunny guest rooms are available upstairs and the Captain's Corner downstairs offers a private "aft" deck. The adjacent Hitchcock House features seven additional guest rooms. All rooms have private baths and telephones, fresh flowers, and a decanter of sherry. Guests may relax in front of the fireplace, on the covered front porch, or on the back deck. Gourmet breakfasts are prepared daily by Chef Nancy, who also offers five-course Saturday-night meals, which *Bon Appetit* has said "rival the finest the city has to offer."

**Open:** year round **Accommodations:** 11 guest rooms with private baths **Meals:**full breakfast included; complimentary refreshments; dinner available on Saturdays; restaurants nearby **Rates:** $100 to $185; 10% discount to National Trust members and National Trust Visa cardholders midweek only **Payment:** AmEx, Visa, MC, Discover, personal and traveler's checks **Restrictions:** no smoking; no pets **On-site activities:** bicycles and beach equipment provided

## PARSONAGE BED AND BREAKFAST INN
1600 Olive Street
Santa Barbara, California 93101
**Phone:** 805/962-9336 or 800/775-0352
**Fax:** 805/962-2285
**Website:** www.parsonage.com
**Proprietor:** Kelly Ebert

Built in 1892 as a parsonage for the Trinity Episcopal Church, one of Santa Barbara's most notable Queen Anne Victorians is now a bed-and-breakfast inn. The Parsonage has been furnished with antiques and reproductions to create an atmosphere of comfort and grace. Each guest room has its individual character: the Versailles Room, for example, faithfully reproduces the decor of Louis XIV with period furnishings and distinctive wallpaper; the Honeymoon Suite features a king-size canopy bed and an old-fashioned solarium. A full breakfast is served in the dining room by the fireplace or on the sundeck with its cozy gazebo. The living room with fireplace and garden with arbor are comfortable places to unwind. The Parsonage is located in a quiet residential neighborhood between downtown Santa Barbara and the foothills.

**Open:** year round **Accommodations:** 6 guest rooms with private baths; 1 is a suite **Meals:** full breakfast included; restaurants nearby **Rates:** $125 to $275; 10% discount offered to National Trust members and National Trust Visa cardholders **Payment:** AmEx, Visa, MC, personal and traveler's checks **Restrictions:** smoking limited; no pets

## SIMPSON HOUSE INN

1221 East Arrellaga
Santa Barbara, California 93101
**Phone:** 805/963-7067 or 800/676-1280
**Fax:** 805/564-4811
**Website:** simpsonhouseinn.com
**E-mail:** SimpsonHouse@Compuserve.com
**Proprietors:** Glyn and Linda Davies  **Manager:** Dixie Budke

Scotsman Robert Simpson built this Eastlake-style home in 1874 to remind himself of his native land. Today, the Simpson House Inn is considered one of the most distinguished Victorian homes of southern California and is a Santa Barbara Landmark. Sandstone walls and tall hedges screen the house from the street. Guests pass through wrought-iron gates and landscaped grounds into the house. Here the spacious sitting room adjoins the formal dining room, and French doors open onto garden verandas with teak floors and white wicker furniture. Guest rooms are elegantly appointed with antiques, English lace, oriental rugs, goose-down comforters, and fresh flowers. Four suites in the restored barn and three cottages in the gardens offer understated elegance, privacy, and fireplaces. Simpson House is surrounded by an acre of English gardens, mature oaks, magnolias, fountains, and arbors. Simpson House is North America's only AAA five-diamond bed & breakfast.

**Open:** year round **Accommodations:** 14 guest rooms with private baths; 4 are suites; 3 are cottages **Meals:** full breakfast included; complimentary refreshments; restaurants nearby **Wheelchair access:** 1 barn suite **Rates:** $160 to $365 **Payment:** AmEx, Visa, MC, Discover, personal and traveler's checks **Restrictions:** children over 12 welcome; no smoking; no pets **On-site activities:** English croquet, bicycles, beach chairs and towels available, acre of gardens for sitting and strolling

## UPHAM VICTORIAN HOTEL AND GARDEN COTTAGES

1404 De La Vina Street
Santa Barbara, California 93101
**Phone:** 805/962-0058 or 800/727-0876
**Fax:** 805/963-2825
**Proprietor:** Jan Martin Winn

In 1871, Boston banker Amasa Lincoln sailed to Santa Barbara and built one of the city's first boarding houses to accommodate guests attracted to the area by reports of health-giving hot springs. Lincoln had the building designed in the Italianate style, complete with a wraparound porch and cupola to remind him of his New England origins. Situated on an acre of gardens in the heart of downtown, the Upham is now the oldest continuously operating hostelry in southern California. Antiques and period furnishings highlight the guest rooms, which are located in the main building, five garden cottages, and a carriage house. A breakfast buffet, daily newspaper, and many guest services are provided by the helpful and friendly staff. Louie's Restaurant, adjoining the lobby, offers innovative California cuisine for lunch and dinner, featuring fresh seafood and pasta.

**Open:** year round **Accommodations:** 50 guest rooms with private baths; 4 are suites **Meals:** continental-plus breakfast included; complimentary wine and cheese; restaurant on premises **Wheelchair access:** dining room only **Rates:** $130 to $370 **Payment:** AmEx, Visa, MC, CB, DC, Discover, travelers check **Restrictions:** no pets **On-site activities:** relaxing in the garden

---

## SANTA CRUZ

**Nearby attractions:** beaches; boardwalk and amusement park; swimming; surfing; sailing; seal-watching; tennis; golfing; shopping; wineries; villages of Aptos, Soquel, and Capitola

## APPLE LANE INN

6265 Soquel Drive
Aptos, California 95003
**Phone:** 831/475-6868 or 800/649-8988
**Website:** www.applelaneinn.com
**E-mail:** ali@cruzio.com
**Proprietors:** Doug and Diana Groom
**Location:** 10 miles south of Santa Cruz

Apple Lane Inn is a Victorian farmhouse with wraparound porch, patterned wood shingles, and decorative vergeboards. The house and barn were built in the 1870s on three acres, which included apple orchards. Today, the inn still enjoys its quiet country setting amid trim lawns and flowering gardens. Guest accommodations are handsomely furnished in the Victorian tradition. One elaborate room features redwood wainscoting, a pressed-tin ceiling, and a eighteenth-century Spanish four-poster bed. Others offer antique pine or walnut furnishings, lace canopies, claw-foot tubs, or antique quilts. A full country breakfast is served, always centering on a hearty main course. The brick patio and gazebo offer both afternoon sun and cooling shade under wisteria and roses.

**Open:** year round **Accommodations:** 5 rooms with private baths; 2 are suites **Meals:** full breakfast included **Rates:** $95 to $175; 10% discount offered to National Trust members or National Trust Visa cardholders **Payment:** Visa, MC, Discover, personal check **Restrictions:** children welcome Sunday through Thursday; no smoking **On-site activities:** barn and farm animals, pitching horseshoes, croquet, historic library

## CHATEAU VICTORIAN

118 First Street
Santa Cruz, California 95060
**Phone:** 831/458-9458 or 831/429-6696
**Website:** www.travelguides.com/bb/chateauvictorian
**Proprietor:** Alice June

This Queen Anne–style structure was built around the turn of the century as a single-family residence. In the 1950s the house was converted to apartments, but 30 years later it was restored to its original appearance and opened as a comfortable inn. Fireplaces adorn all of the guest rooms, and each room offers a touch of individuality. Bay Side Room has a marble fireplace and a claw-foot tub with overhead shower. Garden Room, on the main level, contains an original bay window and a canopy bed. Patio Room has a private entrance and an old-fashioned armoire. Two guest rooms are in the cottage on the other side of the brick patio. Guests may choose to enjoy breakfast in the lounge, on the secluded deck, or on the terrace.

**Open:** year round **Accommodations:** 7 rooms with private baths **Meals:** continental-plus breakfast included; complimentary refreshments; restaurants nearby **Rates:** $110 to $140 **Payment:** Visa, MC, personal and traveler's checks **Restrictions:** cannot accommodate children or pets; no smoking **On-site activities:** restful relaxation

## SANTA MONICA

**Nearby attractions:** Palisades Park, Santa Monica Pier, Third Street Promenade, beach, ocean activities, Beverly Hills, Rodeo Drive, Century City

### THE GEORGIAN HOTEL
1415 Ocean Avenue
Santa Monica, California 90401
**Phone:** 310/395-9945
**Fax:** 310/451-3374
**Website:** www.georgianhotel.com
**General Manager:** Paul Hortobagyis

Built in the popular Art Deco style in 1933, this Santa Monica landmark was an immediate attraction for a myriad of silver screen stars as a retreat from the hot summers in the nearby Hollywood Hills. Intentionally created without a large ballroom and the inherent commotion of related social functions, the hotel was designed strictly for comfortable oceanfront lodging, offering refreshing, unfettered enjoyment of soothing afternoon breezes and spectacular Pacific sunsets. Streamlined Art Deco architectural details accent the building's exterior and intimate lobby; spacious guest rooms and casual elegant suites have been restored to reflect the style of The Georgian's debut. Turn-down service, shoe shines, and morning newspapers are complimentary. The Georgian Hotel is a member of Historic Hotels of America.

**Open:** year round **Accommodations:** 84 guest rooms with private baths; 28 are suites **Meals:** restaurant on premises; restaurants nearby on "Restaurant Row" **Wheelchair access:** yes **Rates:** $165 to $315; 10% discount to National Trust members and National Trust Visa cardholders **Payment:** AmEx, Visa, MC, Discover **Restrictions:** smoking limited; pets require a nonrefundable fee

# SANTA ROSA

**Nearby attractions:** Railroad Square, antiques hunting, Sonoma wineries, redwood forests, Pacific coast, San Francisco, museums, Luther Burbank Center for the Arts, art galleries, golfing, hot-air ballooning

## HOTEL LA ROSE

308 Wilson Street
Santa Rosa, California 95401
**Phone:** 707/579-3200 or 800/527-6738
**Fax:** 707/579-3200
**Website:** www.hotellarose.com
**Proprietors:** Debbie, Claus, and Evan Neumann

First settled in the 1850s, Santa Rosa became a center of commerce and transportation when the railroad came to town in 1870. Hotel La Rose was built in 1907—during Santa Rosa's period of continued economic growth—of locally quarried stone. After an extensive renovation in 1984 that garnered top honors from the Sonoma County Historical Society, Hotel La Rose reopened with 29 guest rooms in the original building. Twenty new guest rooms in the adjacent carriage house each have a private balcony or patio overlooking the garden courtyard. Original wainscoting has been preserved in the corridors and the hotel's grand staircase was taken from the San Francisco Cable Car Barn. Josef's Restaurant, in the hotel, serves continental cuisine. Hotel La Rose is a member of Historic Hotels of America.

**Open:** year round **Accommodations:** 49 guest rooms with private baths **Meals:** continental breakfast included; restaurant on premises; restaurants nearby **Wheelchair access:** yes **Rates:** $74 to $184; 10% discount to National Trust members and National Trust Visa cardholders **Payment:** AmEx, Visa, MC, travelers check **Restrictions:** smoking limited; no pets **On-site activities:** specialty packages (hot-air ballooning, golfing, romance)

# SEAL BEACH

**Nearby attractions:** Disneyland, the *Queen Mary*, beach, golfing, tennis, sailing, surfing, theater, antiques hunting, Catalina Island, Hollywood

## SEAL BEACH INN AND GARDENS
212 Fifth Street
Seal Beach, California 90740
**Phone:** 562/493-2416
**Fax:** 562/799-0483
**Proprietor:** Marjorie Bettenhausen

Built in 1918 and 1923, Seal Beach Inn and Gardens has served as a seaside resort since its inception, making it the area's oldest continuously operating business. Architectural details—filigreed iron fences and newel posts, a brick courtyard, curved window arches, window boxes, tile murals, and iron fountains—reflect the area's early European and Mediterranean influences. The inn also features picturesque gardens, an elegant dining room with a fireplace and brass chandeliers, and bedrooms containing original hardwood floors and light fixtures, and many period furnishings. The innkeepers proudly cater special occasions, and will serve lunches, teas, and dinners by request. Picnic baskets are also available. The inn has been designated a historic landmark by the Seal Beach Historical Society. In 1995, the Seal Beach Inn was chosen as one of the top 12 inns of the year by *Country Inns* magazine.

**Open:** year round **Accommodations:** 23 guest rooms with private baths; 14 are suites **Meals:** full breakfast included; gourmet picnics on request; wine and cheese social in evening; restaurants nearby **Rates:** $125 to $225; 10% discount to National Trust members **Payment:** AmEx, Visa, MC, DC, travelers check, personal check for advance reservations only **Restrictions:** children discouraged; no smoking; no pets **On-site activities:** swimming pool, library, board games

# SONOMA

**Nearby attractions:** National Register historic district, Jack London State Park, St. Franci de Solano Mission, wineries, art galleries, historic home tours, golfing, horseback riding, hiking, hot-air ballooning

## SONOMA HOTEL
110 West Spain Street
Sonoma, California 95476
**Phone:** 707/996-2996 or 800/468-6016
**Fax:** 707/996-7014
**Proprietors:** John and Dorene Musilli

Located on Sonoma's tree-lined plaza (a National Register historic district), this vintage hotel has offered accommodations and dining to the discriminating guest since the 1920s. It was first built in 1879 as a two-story adobe structure that housed a grocery shop and entertainment hall across a dirt road from the Sonoma State Depot. In 1922 the building was sold to Samual Sebastiani, who added a third floor and six dormers, and admitted guests to the rechristened Plaza Hotel. In today's Sonoma Hotel, each antique-filled guest room evokes California's early history, while the emphasis on comfort is decidedly European. From the wine offered on arrival to the morning's fresh-baked pastries, guests sample the wine country's hospitality. This romantic inn is a short walk to wineries, historic landmarks, art galleries, and unique shops.

**Open:** year round **Accommodations:** 17 guest rooms (5 have private baths); 1 is a suite **Meals:** continental breakfast included; complimentary refreshments; full bar and restaurant on premises **Rates:** $75 to $125; 10% discount offered to National Trust members and National Trust Visa cardholders November 1 through May 30 **Payment:** AmEx, Visa, MC, personal and traveler's checks

# SOUTH PASADENA

**Nearby attractions:** Norton Simon Museum of Art, Huntington Library, Rose Bowl, Old Town Pasadena, Angeles National Forest, annual Tournament of Roses parade, downtown Los Angeles

## THE ARTISTS' INN

1038 Magnolia Street
South Pasadena, California 91030
**Phone:** 626/799-5668 or 888/799-5668
**Fax:** 626/799-3678
**E-mail:** artistsinn@aol.com
**Proprietor:** Janet Marangi
**Innkeeper:** Leah Roberts

C. R. Johnson's 1895 Victorian farmhouse has retained its historic charm with its artful transformation to a bed-and-breakfast inn. The restored house, furnished with original art, antiques, rich fabrics, and fresh flowers offers guests both an enchanting atmosphere and a lesson in art history. Guest rooms derive their names from the artist or art period that inspired the room's decor: the Van Gogh takes its cue from the artist's painting of his own bedroom; the Fauve uses the color schemes found in the works of Matisse and Dufy; the Impressionist features the soft colors found on Monet's and Renoir's palettes; the Italian Suite recalls Renaissance Italy; and the Eighteenth Century English room includes the works of Gainsborough, Reynolds, and Constable. Guests enjoy breakfast served on the front porch overlooking the garden, or in the dining room, or their own room. A complimentary English tea is served in the afternoon.

**Open:** year round **Accommodations:** 9 guest rooms with private baths; 3 are suites **Meals:** choice of full breakfast or complimentary-plus breakfast included; complimentary refreshments; restaurants nearby **Rates:** $110 to $165; 10% discount to National Trust members and National Trust Visa cardholders **Payment:** AmEx, Visa, MC, Discover, personal and traveler's checks **Restrictions:** no smoking; no pets **On-site activities:** croquet, puzzles, reading on front porch

## UKIAH

**Nearby attractions:** Mendocino coast, redwood forests, museums, water sports

### VICHY HOT SPRINGS RESORT AND INN

2605 Vichy Springs Road
Ukiah, California 95482
**Phone:** 707/462-9515
**Fax:** 707/462-9516
**Website:** www.vichysprings.com
**E-mail:** vichy@pacific.net
**Proprietors:** Gilbert and Marjorie Ashoff
**Location:** 2 hours north of San Francisco via US Highway 101

The only warm and naturally carbonated mineral baths in North America, Ukiah's springs were first used thousands of years ago by Native Americans. The Vichy, a state historic landmark, opened in 1854 and is one of California's oldest continuously operating resorts. It has been renovated to combine its natural and historic charm with modern comfort. Seventeen guest rooms are in redwood buildings dating from the 1860s; three cottages with fully equipped kitchens date from 1854 and are the oldest structures in Mendocino County. A few feet from the individually decorated rooms are 10 natural tubs built in 1860 and used by such guests as Mark Twain, Jack London, Teddy Roosevelt and his daughter Alice, Ulysses S. Grant, and pugilists John L. Sullivan and Jim Corbett.

**Open:** year round **Accommodations:** 17 guest rooms with private baths; 3 cottages **Meals:** full breakfast included; restaurants nearby **Wheelchair access:** 1 cottage fully ADA **Rates:** $99 to $189; 10% discount to National Trust members and National Trust Visa cardholders **Payment:** AmEx, Visa, MC, CB, DC, Discover, personal and traveler's checks **Restrictions:** smoking outside only; no pets **On-site activities:** Swedish massage and herbal facials, communal hot pool, Olympic-size pool, carbonated 90-degree mineral baths, mountain biking, hiking and picnicking on 700-acre ranch

# WESTPORT

**Nearby attractions:** ocean beaches, art galleries, antiques hunting, Skunk Train, Mendocino, deep-sea fishing from Noyo Harbor, wilderness, redwoods, tide pools

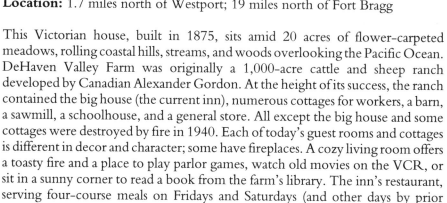

**DEHAVEN VALLEY FARM**
39247 North Highway One
Westport, California 95488
**Phone:** 707/961-1660
**Fax:** 707/961-1677
**Website:** www.dehaven-valley-farm.com
**E-mail:** dehaven@dehaven-valley-farm.com
**Proprietor:** Christa Stapp
**Location:** 1.7 miles north of Westport; 19 miles north of Fort Bragg

This Victorian house, built in 1875, sits amid 20 acres of flower-carpeted meadows, rolling coastal hills, streams, and woods overlooking the Pacific Ocean. DeHaven Valley Farm was originally a 1,000-acre cattle and sheep ranch developed by Canadian Alexander Gordon. At the height of its success, the ranch contained the big house (the current inn), numerous cottages for workers, a barn, a sawmill, a schoolhouse, and a general store. All except the big house and some cottages were destroyed by fire in 1940. Each of today's guest rooms and cottages is different in decor and character; some have fireplaces. A cozy living room offers a toasty fire and a place to play parlor games, watch old movies on the VCR, or sit in a sunny corner to read a book from the farm's library. The inn's restaurant, serving four-course meals on Fridays and Saturdays (and other days by prior arrangement), has been recognized by *Forbes* magazine and given three stars by Mobil.

**Open:** year round **Accommodations:** 8 guest rooms (6 have private baths); 2 are suites **Meals:** full breakfast included; restaurant on premises serves dinner Fridays, Saturdays, and by prior arrangement **Rates:** $85 to $140 **Payment:** AmEx, Visa, MC, Discover, personal and traveler's checks **Restrictions:** children welcome in cottages only; no smoking; no pets **On-site activities:** parlor games, VCR and videos, beach, hot tub, farm animals, 20 acres for walks and picnics

## HOWARD CREEK RANCH

40501 North Highway One
P.O. Box 121
Westport, California 95488
**Phone:** 707/964-6725
**Fax:** 707/964-1603
**Website:** www.HOWARDCREEKRANCH.com
**Proprietors:** Charles (Sunny) and Sally Grigg
**Location:** 3 miles north of Westport, 180 miles north of San Francisco

Once part of a huge sheep and cattle ranch first settled in 1867, Howard Creek Ranch occupies a 40-acre valley on the Mendocino coast. Designated a Mendocino County historic site, the 1871 farmhouse sits on an expanse of green lawns and award-winning flower gardens. A 75-foot-long swinging footbridge spans Howard Creek as the waterway flows past barns and outbuildings to the beach 200 yards away. The ranch buildings are constructed of virgin redwood from the ranch's forest. The inn is furnished with antiques, collectibles, and memorabilia; the original fireplace still warms the parlor. A hot tub and sauna are set into the mountainside, forming a unique health spa with privacy and dramatic views. The magnificent area affords sweeping views of the ocean, sandy beaches, and rolling mountains.

**Open:** year round **Accommodations:** 10 guest rooms (8 have private baths); 3 are cabins **Meals:** breakfast included; barbecue grills available for beach picnics; some rooms with microwaves and refrigerators; restaurants nearby **Rates:** $75 to $160; 10% discount offered off-season **Payment:** AmEx, Visa, MC, personal and traveler's checks **Restrictions:** children by prior arrangement; smoking limited; arrangements can be made for pets **On-site activities:** horseback riding, games, books, musical instruments, beachcombing, watching birds and whales, tide pools, heated pool, hot tub, massages

# COLORADO

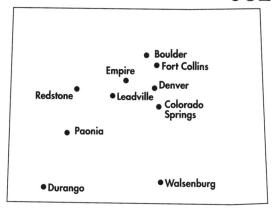

## BOULDER

**Nearby attractions**: University of Colorado, Pearl Street pedestrian mall, Shakespeare festival, Chautauqua festival

### BRIAR ROSE BED AND BREAKFAST
2151 Arapahoe Avenue
Boulder, Colorado 80302
**Phone:** 303/442-3007
**Fax:** 303/786-8440
**Website:** www.globalmall.com/brose/
**E-mail:** brbbx@aol.com
**Proprietors:** Bob and Margaret Weisenbach

In 1904, the McConnel family built a brick bungalow on this site. Over the next 77 years they expanded and improved their home until it was purchased in 1981 and converted to a bed and breakfast.

The house is charmingly styled much like an English country cottage with arched windows, stone lintels and sills, and a shake roof. Period antiques, original art, and fresh flowers fill the nine guest rooms, giving each a distinctive character. All rooms have private baths, telephones, fine linens, and feather comforters on queen-size beds. The

Honeymoon and Anniversary rooms have wood-burning fireplaces. Carefully groomed gardens offer a private retreat for guests, as well as the perfect site for small meetings and receptions. The innkeepers provide a generous breakfast and afternoon tea, featuring the inn's own shortbread cookies.

**Open**: year round **Accommodations**: 9 guest rooms with private baths; 1 is a suite **Meals**: continental-plus breakfast included; complimentary refreshments; restaurants nearby **Rates**: $84 to $159; 10% discount offered to National Trust members and National Trust Visa cardholders **Payment**: check **Restrictions**: no smoking; no pets **On-site activities:** garden strolling, conversation

## COLORADO SPRINGS

**Nearby attractions:** Pikes Peak, Garden of the Gods, Cheyenne Cañon, U.S. Olympic Training Center, U.S. Air Force Academy, Old Colorado City, Manitou Springs, historic district, shopping, hiking, bicycling, fishing, ice skating, horseback riding

### HOLDEN HOUSE—1902 BED AND BREAKFAST INN
1102 West Pikes Peak Avenue
Colorado Springs, Colorado 80904
**Phone:** 719/471-3980
**Fax:** 719/471-4740
**Website:** www.bbonline.com/co/holden/
**E-mail:** HoldenHouse@worldnet.att.net
**Proprietors:** Sallie and Welling Clark

This 1902 turreted Colonial Revival Victorian house, 1906 carriage house, and adjacent 1898 Victorian house were built by Isabel Holden, widow of prosperous Colorado Springs businessman Daniel M. Holden. The five guest suites are named for mining towns in which the Holdens owned interests: the Aspen, Cripple Creek, Silverton, Goldfield, and Independence. All boast private baths, period furnishings, queen beds, fireplaces, private sitting areas, and "tubs for two." The three houses are filled with family treasures, antiques, heirloom quilts, and personal touches. A full gourmet breakfast is served in the formal dining room, and complimentary refreshments are provided. The inn's common areas include the living room with a tiled fireplace, the parlor with television, the veranda with wicker furniture and mountain views, and a back garden with a gazebo.

**Accommodations:** 5 guest suites with private baths **Meals:** full breakfast included; complimentary refreshments; restaurants nearby **Wheelchair access:** 1 suite **Rates:** $115 to $125 **Payment:** AmEx, Visa, MC, CB, DC, Discover, traveler's check, personal check (advance only) **Restrictions:** not suitable for children; no smoking; no pets (resident cats)

## ROOM AT THE INN BED AND BREAKFAST

618 North Nevada Avenue
Colorado Springs, Colorado 80903
**Phone:** 719/442-1896 or 800/579-4621
**Fax:** 719/442-6802
**Website:** www.roomattheinn.com
**E-mail:** roomatinn@pcisys.net
**Proprietors:** Chick and Jan McCormick

A wealthy mine investor and his wife built this Queen Anne home in 1896. They incorporated many elements typical of the style including fish-scale siding, a wraparound porch, and a three-story turret. Inside, original hand-painted murals, Italian tiled fireplaces, and pocket doors remain. Today, as an inn, the house offers five guest rooms with private baths, queen-size beds, period antiques, and oriental rugs. Several rooms have whirlpool tubs and turret sitting areas, while the others have gas fireplaces. The adjacent cottage offers two guest accommodations; one is fully wheelchair accessible, the other has a kitchenette. Designer linens, cotton robes, and evening turn-down service are provided in all rooms. Guests may relax in the hot tub on the sundeck or play games and read in the third-floor upper parlor.

**Open:** year round **Accommodations:** 7 guest rooms with private baths; 2 are suites **Meals:** full breakfast included; complimentary refreshments; restaurants nearby **Wheelchair access:** 1 guest room **Rates:** $89 to $140 **Payment:** AmEx, Visa, MC, CB, DC, Discover, personal and traveler's checks **Restrictions:** children over 12 welcome; no smoking; no pets **On-site activities:** hot tub, library, board games, bicycles

## DENVER

**Nearby attractions:** Denver Museum of Natural History, Colorado History Museum, Denver Art Museum, Molly Brown House Museum, State Capitol, U.S. Mint, Coors Field, Denver Performing Arts Complex, Historic Lower Downtown District (LoDo), Denver Zoo, swimming, golfing, tennis, fishing, and Rocky Mountains for skiing, hiking, and bicycling

## CAPITOL HILL MANSION

1207 Pennsylvania Street
Denver, Colorado 80203
**Phone:** 303/839-5221 or 800/839-9329
**Fax:** 303/839-9046
**Website:** www.capitolhillmansion.com
**Proprietor:** Bill and Wendy Pearson and the King family

Located in the Pennsylvania Street Historic District—an architecturally rich area of grand old houses where some of Denver's most prominent and powerful figures resided—is the Capitol Hill Mansion. Built in 1891 for Jeffrey and Mary Keating, who made their fortune in real estate, insurance, and lumber, the house boasts exceptional Richardsonian Romanesque architecture. It is constructed of local ruby sandstone from the Dakotah Hogback formation and features turrets, towers, balconies, and a semi-wraparound porch. In 1923, the Keating House became the Buena Vista Hotel, and over the next 70 years it saw various owners and uses until its conversion to a luxurious bed-and-breakfast inn. Carefully restored, the inn boasts a high level of craftsmanship from its stained- and beveled-glass windows to the golden oak paneling. The richly appointed guest rooms are individually decorated and offer views of the Rocky Mountains, state capitol, or the historic neighborhood. Capitol Hill Mansion is in the National Register of Historic Places.

**Open:** year round **Accommodations:** 8 guest rooms with private baths; 3 are suites **Meals:** full breakfast included in rate; complimentary refreshments; restaurants nearby **Wheelchair access:** limited **Rates:** $85 to $175 (seasonal); corporate rates available **Payment:** AmEx, Visa, MC, Discover, traveler's check and personal check with credit card **Restrictions:** young children restricted to Bluebell Suite; no smoking; no pets **On-site activities:** games, puzzles, books

## CASTLE MARNE – A LUXURY URBAN INN
1572 Race Street
Denver, Colorado 80206
**Phone:** 303/331-0621 or 800/92MARNE (reservations)
**Fax:** 303/331-0623
**Website:** www.castlemarne.com
**E-mail:** themarne@ix.netcom.com
**Proprietors:** The Peiker family

A grand example of Richardsonian Romanesque architecture, Castle Marne is the work of prominent Denver architect William Lange, who also designed the nearby home of the Titanic's Unsinkable Molly Brown. The mansion, built in 1889, has had among its owners Wilber Raymond, an early Denver silver baron and real estate developer, and John Mason, founder and first curator of Denver's Museum of Natural History. Aside from its striking exterior, the house boasts an impressive circular stained glass "Peacock Window," as well as ornate fireplaces and Victorian decor. Individually appointed guest rooms are furnished with antiques and family heirlooms; some have private balconies, mountain views, and claw-foot tubs. A full breakfast is served in the castle's original cherry-paneled formal dining room, and guests can gather in the parlor for afternoon tea. Located in the Wyman Historic District, Castle Marne is convenient to downtown Denver, and fine dining options are within walking distance of the inn.

**Open:** year round **Accommodations:** 9 guest rooms with private baths; 2 are suites **Meals:** full breakfast included; complimentary refreshments; Victorian luncheons and candlelight dinners available; restaurants nearby **Rates:** $70 to $220; 10% discount to National Trust members and National Trust Visa cardholders **Payment:** AmEx, Visa, MC, CB, DC, Discover, personal and traveler's checks **Restrictions:** children over 10 welcome; no smoking; no pets **On-site activities:** pool table, darts, player piano, games, Victorian garden

## THE OXFORD HOTEL
1600 Seventeenth Street
Denver, Colorado 80202
**Phone:** 303/628-5400
**Fax:** 303/628-5413
**General Manager:** Jane Hugo

Built at the crest of the silver bonanza, The Oxford's classic exterior belied an extravagant interior, as curious opening-day guests discovered on October 3, 1891. There were dining rooms, a barber shop, library, pharmacy, telegraph office, stables, and a saloon. Oak furnishings, marble and carpeted floors, sterling silver chandeliers, and glistening stained glass were features of the sumptuous decor. Expanded in 1912, the hotel was transformed into an Art Deco showcase by architect Charles Jaka in the 1930s. Restored and reopened in 1983, the hotel now displays its original architectural detailing and fine English, French, and American antique furnishings. The Oxford offers turn-down service, complimentary morning newspaper and coffee, afternoon sherry, and shoe shine. Located in the downtown historic district, central to businesses, shopping, entertainment, and Coors Field, the hotel provides valet parking and 24-hour downtown limousine service. This National Register-listed property is a member of the National Trust's Historic Hotels of America.

**Open:** year round **Accommodations:** 81 guest rooms with private baths **Meals:** restaurants on premises; 24-hour room service; restaurants nearby **Wheelchair access:** yes **Rates:** $139 to $315; 10% discount to National Trust members and National Trust Visa cardholders **Payment:** AmEx, Visa, MC, DC, Discover **Restrictions:** no pets **On-site activities:** health club, spa, salon

---

# DURANGO

**Nearby attractions:** Durango–Silverton Narrow Gauge Railroad, Mesa Verde National Park, historic districts, downhill and cross-country skiing, hiking, mountain biking, rafting, kayaking, fishing, rodeo, shopping, galleries, fine dining

## LELAND HOUSE BED AND BREAKFAST
721 E. Second Avenue
Durango, Colorado 81301
**Phone:** 970/385-1920 or 800/664-1920
**Fax:** 970/385-1967
**Website:** www.rochesterhotel.com
**E-mail:** leland@frontier.net
**Proprietors:** Kirk and Diane Komick

Much of the flavor of Old West and gold rush days remains not only on the historic streets of Durango, but also on the walls of the Leland House. Here old photos documenting the town's lively history and framed articles and biographies of its colorful citizens adorn the hallways, inviting visitors to become better acquainted with Durango's past. P. W. Pittman built the two-story Craftsman-style apartment house in 1927, which the family managed until 1947. Today the restored house offers guests six three-room suites with kitchens and four one-bedroom studios with kitchenettes, each named for important figures in Durango's history. The Leland House is under the same management as the Rochester Hotel (see following entry), located across the street, where a breakfast buffet is served each morning.

**Open:** year round **Accommodations:** 10 guest rooms with private baths; 6 are suites **Meals:** full breakfast included; restaurant on premises **Rates:** $95 to $145; 10% discount offered to National Trust members and National Trust Visa cardholders **Payment:** AmEx, Visa, MC, CB, DC, Discover, personal and traveler's checks **Restrictions:** no smoking


## ROCHESTER HOTEL
721 East Second Avenue
Durango, Colorado 81301
**Phone:** 970/385-1920 or 800/664-1920
**Fax:** 970/385-1967
**Website:** www.rochesterhotel.com
**E-mail:** leland@frontier.net
**Proprietors:** Diane and Kirk Komick

This two-story brick structure, built in 1891, was originally known as the Peeples Hotel. Mary Francis Finn, who owned and operated the hotel from 1905 to 1920, renamed it the Rochester. By the 1950s it had sunk into disrepair and continued

to decay until purchased in 1993 by Diane Komick and her son Kirk. Together they completed an extensive restoration, converting the derelict building into a spacious hotel furnished in a "cowboy-Victoriana" style. Original interior features that have been restored include the woodwork, staircase, hardware, doors, windows, and skylight in the upstairs ceiling. The Rochester Hotel offers 15 high-ceilinged rooms, each decorated in an Old West motif inspired by the many movies filmed in and around Durango. Among the rooms available are those named *Viva Zapata*, *Ticket to Tomahawk*, and *How the West Was Won*. The hotel has been featured in *Condé Nast Traveler* and *USA Today*, among many others.

**Open:** year round **Accommodations:** 15 guest rooms with private baths; 2 are suites **Meals:** full breakfast included; complimentary refreshments; restaurant on premises; restaurants nearby **Wheelchair access:** yes **Rates:** $125 to $195; 10% discount to National Trust members and National Trust Visa cardholders **Payment:** AmEx, Visa, MC, Discover, personal and traveler's checks **Restrictions:** no smoking; no pets **On-site activities:** courtyard garden

---

## ELDORA

**Nearby attractions:** Eldora Mountain Resort, downhill and cross-country skiing, ski school, Nederland, Indian Peaks Wilderness Area, Rocky Mountain National Park, hiking, bicycling, fishing, camping, horseback riding, antiques hunting, crafts shops, gambling towns of Central City and Black Hawk

### GOLDMINER HOTEL
601 Klondyke Avenue
Eldora, Colorado 80466
Mailing address:
Box 478
Nederland, Colorado 80466
**Phone:** 800/422-4629
**Fax:** 303/258-3850
**Proprietor:** Scott Bruntjen

The Goldminer Hotel is an 1897 two-story, hipped-roof, long-and-frame structure in the heart of the Eldora National Historic District. The building itself is listed in the National Register of Historic Places and is a Boulder County Landmark. Guest rooms are decorated with period pieces to bring back the rustic and exciting gold-mining days of the area. Some rooms have fireplaces and a hot tub is available to all guests. Adjacent to Eldora Mountain Resort, the hotel offers free daily shuttle transportation to the resort, as well as nightly transportation to the close-by gambling towns of Central City and Black Hawk. The hotel also operates unique horseback, Jeep, cross-country ski, and snowcat tours of the area.

**Open:** year round **Accommodations:** 5 guest rooms (3 have private baths); 1 is a suite **Meals:** full breakfast included; restaurants nearby **Rates:** $69 to $179; 10% discount to National Trust members and National Trust Visa cardholders **Payment:** Visa, MC, traveler's check **Restrictions:** no smoking **On-site activities:** hot tub, hiking

## EMPIRE

**Nearby attractions:** Georgetown-Silver Plume Historic District, ski resorts, horseback riding, fishing, hiking, biking, gambling, factory outlets

### THE PECK HOUSE
83 Sunny Avenue
P.O. Box 428
Empire, Colorado 80438
**Phone:** 303/569-9870
**Fax:** 303/569-2743
**Website:** www.peckhouse.com
**Proprietors:** Gary and Sally St. Clair

Established in 1862, the Peck House, Colorado's oldest continuously operating hotel, has maintained not only its Victorian charm, but also the enticing views of the Empire Valley from its full-length verandah. James Peck, a successful Chicago merchant who also prospered as a gold miner, built the house and later welcomed other prospectors and investors seeking their fortunes. The Peck House's guest registry includes the names of P. T. Barnum, Ulysses S. Grant, and General William Sherman, as the hotel was then the scene of the town's more genteel activities. Decorated with antiques, oak, walnut, and maple furnishings, and photographs from the town's early days, the hotel offers guests comfortable accommodations in a secluded setting at the foot of Berthoud Pass. Guests can also take in the impressive valley views from the hotel dining room, with its original etched-glass gaslight lampshades and exhibit of colored lithographs depicting local mining operations. Peck House is listed in the National Register of Historic Places.

**Open:** year round **Accommodations:** 11 guest rooms (9 have private baths); 1 is a suite **Meals:** continental breakfast included; restaurant on premises **Rates:** $70 to $100 **Payment:** AmEx, Visa, MC, CB, DC, Discover, personal and traveler's checks **Restrictions:** no pets **On-site activities:** whirlpool

# FORT COLLINS

**Nearby attractions:** Rocky Mountain National Park, Fort Collins Museum, historic Old Town Fort Collins, Colorado State University, hiking, golfing, fishing, skiing

## THE EDWARDS HOUSE BED AND BREAKFAST

402 W. Mountain Avenue
Fort Collins, Colorado 80521
**Phone:** 970/493-9191 or 800/281-9190
**Fax:** 970/484-0706
**Website:** www.edwardshouse.com
**E-mail:** edshouse@edwardshouse.com
**Proprietor:** Greg Belcher

Renowned local architect Montezuma Fuller built the Edwards house in 1904 for Alfred Augustus Edwards, who was a leader in developing northern Colorado's first irrigation projects. This four-square-style house, featuring neoclassical designs in its Palladian windows and large, columned front porch and gazebo, remained in the Edwards family until 1981. Today the restored building offers guests gracious accommodations with both an old-fashioned atmosphere and modern amenities. Guests can relax on the covered front porch, the back deck, or in the formal parlor and the library. Comprehensive concierge services are available, and the innkeeper can assist guests in arranging white-water rafting, llama packing trips, day hikes, and other adventures. Located in a quiet residential area, the Edwards House is within walking distance of City Park and Old Town, and is a good base from which to explore Ft. Collins' historic neighborhoods and the abundant scenic areas nearby.

**Open:** year round **Accommodations:** 8 guest rooms (7 have private baths); 4 are suites **Meals:** full breakfast included; complimentary refreshments; restaurants nearby **Rates:** $85 to $145 **Payment:** AmEx, Visa, MC, Discover, personal and traveler's checks **Restrictions:** children over 10 are welcome; no smoking; no pets **On-site activities:** sauna, basketball, front and back porches for relaxing, cable TV and VCRs in each guest room, video library

# LEADVILLE

**Nearby attractions:** National Mining Hall of Fame, Colorado and Southern Scenic Railroad, Heritage Museum, Tabor Opera House, Leadville Music Festival, Mts. Elbert and Massive, historic Ski Cooper, carriage rides, golfing, hiking, white-water rafting, fishing, hunting, bicycling, snowmobiling, downhill and cross-country skiing, antiques hunting, gold panning, swimming, tennis

## DELAWARE HOTEL
700 Harrison Avenue
Leadville, Colorado 80461
**Phone:** 719/486-1418 or 800/748-2004
**Fax:** 719/486-2214
**Proprietors:** Susan and Scott Brackett

Leadville's gold- and silver-mining days brought desperados such as Billy the Kid, Doc Holiday, and Butch Cassidy to the Delaware Hotel. Built in 1886 by three brothers named Callaway from Delaware, and often referred to as the "crown jewel of Leadville," the hotel is notable for its Italianate and Second Empire elements. A recent renovation has resulted in a Victorian-style lobby that contains period antiques, crystal chandeliers, brass fixtures, and oak paneling. Thirty-six guest rooms and suites are appointed with brass and iron bed frames, heirloom quilts, lace curtains, and period antiques. Each room has a private bath and color cable television. In the hotel's restaurant, Callaway's, the breakfast and lunch menu offers local and traditional dishes, while the dinner menu offers continental cuisine.

**Open:** year round **Accommodations:** 36 guest rooms with private baths; 4 are suites **Meals:** full breakfast included; restaurant on premises; restaurants nearby **Rates:** $70 to $115; 10% discount to National Trust members and National Trust Visa cardholders **Payment:** AmEx, Visa, MC, DC, Discover, personal and traveler's checks **Restrictions:** no smoking in restaurant; no pets **On-site activities:** hot tub; library, gift shop

## ICE PALACE INN BED AND BREAKFAST
813 Spruce Street
Leadville, Colorado 80461
**Phone:** 719/486-8272 or 800/754-2840
**Fax:** 719/486-0345
**Website:** http://colorado-b~b.com/icepalace
**E-mail:** ipalace@sni.net
**Proprietors:** Giles and Kami Kolakowski

In the winter of 1896 the citizens of Leadville erected a lumber frame around which they built a palace of ice carved from a nearby lake. The Leadville Ice Palace was the largest ice structure ever built. March that year was unexpectedly warm and the ice palace quickly melted away, leaving a wooden skeleton. An architect named Dimmick used the Ice Palace's wood to build five houses on Spruce Street, including this one, constructed in 1900 as a wedding gift to John Harvey and his wife. Today, the Harvey's home is the Ice Palace Inn, where romantic guest rooms—each with a private bath—are decorated with antiques and quilts. Photos of the Ice Palace are found throughout the house, including guest rooms, which are named after the rooms at the original Ice Palace: Grand Ballroom, Crystal Carnival, Skating Rink, King's Tower, Lady Leadville, and Gaming Room. This house was featured in Leadville's 1994 Victorian Homes Tour and the 1997 Victorian B&B Tour.

**Open:** year round **Accommodations:** 6 guest rooms with private baths; 1 is a suite **Meals:** full breakfast included; complimentary refreshments; restaurants nearby **Rates:** $79 to $119; 10% discount to National Trust members and National Trust Visa cardholders **Payment:** AmEx, Visa, MC Discover, personal and traveler's checks **Restrictions:** no smoking; no pets **On-site activities:** games, croquet, television and VCR, stereo system, garden hot tub

# PAONIA

**Nearby attractions:** Black Canyon National Monument, Grand Mesa and West Elk Loop Scenic Byways, West Elk and Ragged Wilderness areas, river rafting, fishing, bicycling, downhill skiing at Powderhorn, cross-country skiing, ice fishing, orchards and vineyards, art galleries, antiques hunting

## BROSS HOTEL
312 Onarga Street
P.O. Box 85
Paonia, Colorado 81428
**Phone:** 970/527-6776
**Fax:** 970/527-7737
**E-mail:** Bross@fgn.net
**Proprietor:** Julie Andrew
**Innkeeper:** Nina McDugald

When Deputy Sheriff W. T. Bross opened this hotel in 1906, the local newspaper deemed it "the only really first-class hotel in the county." Bross financed the project by mining clay in what is now the basement and firing bricks on site. What bricks he didn't use in constructing the hotel, he sold to local builders. Just one block from Paonia's main street, the hotel flourished for nearly 70 years. In 1994, owner Julie Andrew purchased the hotel and assembled a group of imaginative artisans, skilled carpenters, and other craftspeople to renovate this historic property. Original wood floors and trim were restored, brick interiors exposed, and sunny dormer windows added. Ten guest rooms with private baths boast expansive views. Some open into family-sized suites. The inn is appointed throughout with antiques and handmade quilts. Generous breakfasts and afternoon teas are served daily in the cozy dining room or on the shady porch.

**Open:** year round **Accommodations:** 10 guest rooms with private baths; 4 rooms combine to create 2 suites **Meals:** full breakfast included; complimentary refreshments; special event catering available; restaurants nearby **Rates:** $70 to $80; 10% discount to National Trust members and National Trust Visa cardholders **Payment:** Visa, MC, personal and traveler's checks **Restrictions:** no smoking; no pets **On-site activities:** garden, hot tub, library, game room

# REDSTONE

**Nearby attractions:** West Elk Loop Scenic and Historic Byway, world's largest hot springs pool in Glenwood Springs, horseback riding, river rafting, hiking, cross-country skiing

## CLEVEHOLM MANOR, THE HISTORIC REDSTONE CASTLE
0058 Redstone Boulevard
Redstone, Colorado 81623
**Phone:** 970/963-3463 or 800/643-4837
**Fax:** 970/963-3463
**Proprietor:** Cyd Lange
**Location:** 18 miles south of Carbondale on Highway 133

Cleveholm Manor was built in 1900 as a retreat for industrialist John Cleveland Osgood and his family. With 42 rooms and 27,000 square feet of living area, the castle cost $2.5 million to build. Osgood employed the finest artisans from Austria and Italy to carve stone from nearby red sandstone cliffs for the exterior and to install marble fireplaces throughout the house. Louis Tiffany brasswork, from chandeliers to sconces, was used exclusively. Guests may reserve the entire castle or just one room, but all guests have full use of its library, music room, game room, armory, board room, sun parlor, and grand room with its huge fireplace. The professionally appointed kitchen is available along with the mahogany- and velvet-walled dining room with gold-leaf ceiling.

**Open:** year round **Accommodations:** 15 guest rooms (8 have private baths); 3 are suites **Meals:** continental-plus breakfast included; complimentary refreshments; restaurant on premises serves on weekends; restaurants nearby **Rates:** $105 to $295; 10% discount to National Trust members and National Trust Visa cardholders **Payment:** AmEx, Visa, MC, personal and traveler's checks **Restrictions:** no smoking **On-site activities:** hiking, fishing, cross-country skiing, sledding, snowshoeing, lawn games, game room, billiards

## REDSTONE INN
82 Redstone Boulevard
Redstone, Colorado 81623
**Phone:** 970/963-2526
**Fax:** 970/963-2527
**General Manager:** Deborah Strom

Focal point of this turn-of-the-century model community, the Redstone Inn opened in 1902 as housing for bachelor miners employed by millionaire coal baron John Cleveland Osgood. It was converted into a hotel in 1925. Restored in 1989, the inn showcases the American Arts and Crafts movement, including more than 60 pieces of authentic Gustav Stickley furniture, stunning hand-crafted wrought-iron light fixtures, and locally quarried and hand-cut stone detailing. Overlooking Osgood's company cottages—now a haven for artisans, sculptors, and antiques dealers—the inn's Seth Thomas tower clock has kept time for the villagers for more than 90 years. The Redstone Inn, with its 35 guest rooms on 22 acres is a full-service, four-season resort. Surrounded by National forest, it is a National Historic Landmark and member of the National Trust's Historic Hotels of America.

**Open:** year round **Accommodations:** 35 guest rooms with private baths **Meals:** 2 restaurants on premises **Rates:** $65 to $195; 10% discount to National Trust members and National Trust Visa cardholders **Payment:** AmEx, Visa, MC, Discover **Restrictions:** no smoking; well-behaved pets accepted with extra fee **On-site activities:** fitness center, swimming pool, hot tub, horseback riding, mountain bike rentals, tennis, fishing, winter sleigh rides, cross-country skiing, snowcat powder tours

# WALSENBURG

**Nearby attractions:** Scenic Highway of Legends, towns of Stonewall, Weston, Segundo, and Trinidad, museums, golfing, Lathrop State Park for hiking, bicycling, boating, fishing, wind surfing and water skiing, shopping

## LA PLAZA DE LOS LEONES
118 West Sixth Street
Walsenburg, Colorado 81089
**Phone:** 719/738-5700
**Fax:** 719/738-6220
**Proprietor:** Marti Henderson

The structure that is now La Plaza de los Leones (from the town's earlier name, which means "village of the lions") was built in 1907 by Paul Frohlich. It was then known as the Oxford Hotel. In 1939, local businessman L. H. Kirkpatrick purchased the building and spared no expense in remodeling and refurbishing it to earn the reputation as one of the finest hotels in the Rockies. It was during Kirkpatrick's renovation that the glass block facade and Art Deco style that is still evident throughout the hotel was added. After suffering years of neglect, the building was purchased in 1996 by Marti Henderson who did much of the painting and refurbishing herself. Today's elegant small hotel offers 15 guest rooms, all with private toilet facilities (most have tubs with showers; some have tubs only). Each room is decorated in a different theme from Southwestern to Victorian to Wild West. Many of the furnishings and decorative pieces are Marti's family pieces. La Plaza also offers conference facilities and gladly caters parties, receptions, and weddings.

**Open:** Year round **Accommodations:** 15 guest rooms with private baths; 2 are suites **Meals:** continental-plus breakfast included; restaurant on premises; restaurants nearby **Rates:** $50 to $75; 10% discount for National Trust members and National Trust Visa cardholders **Payment:** Visa, MC, personal and traveler's checks **Restrictions:** no smoking; no pets **On-site activities:** gift shop

# CONNECTICUT

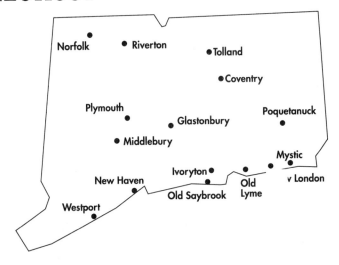

## COVENTRY

**Nearby attractions:** University of Connecticut, Nathan Hale Homestead, homes of Mark Twain and Harriet Beecher Stowe, Caprilands Herb Farm, Strong House Museum, antiques hunting, golfing, hiking, bicycling

**MAPLE HILL FARM BED AND BREAKFAST**
365 Goose Lane
Coventry, Connecticut 06238-1215
**Phone:** 860/742-0635 or 800/742-0635
**Fax:** 860/742-4435
**Website:** www.obs-us.com\chesler\maplehillfarmbnb-ct\
**E-mail:** 73554.172@compuserve.com
**Proprietors:** Tony Felice and Marybeth Gorke-Felice

Nathaniel Woodward built this Cape-style farmhouse in 1731 using stone, oak, and chestnut. The house stands today at the center of Maple Hill Farm as a bed and breakfast inn, the first in Coventry. The four large guest rooms are furnished with antiques. Breakfast by candlelight is accompanied by classical music. The meal is ordered from a small menu offering fresh eggs from the farm's own chickens and homemade granola. The library has a woodstove for winter comfort, and there are fireplaces in the keeping room and parlor. A screened porch, picnic areas, and swimming pool are available in the summer. Guests particularly enjoy the hot tub in the plant-filled solarium. Visitors are encouraged to walk the property, visit the horses and goats, or just relax in a hammock. Hearth cooking demonstrations are available by arrangement.

**Open:** year round **Accommodations:** 4 guest rooms (1 has a private bath; 3 share 2 other baths) **Meals:** full breakfast included; restaurants nearby **Rates:** $65 to $85 **Payment:** Visa, MC, personal and traveler's checks **Restrictions:** children over 4 welcome; no smoking; small dogs accepted **On-site activities:** bicycling, swimming, hot tub, hiking, picnic areas

# GLASTONBURY

**Nearby attractions:** Hartford's historic and cultural sites, including the Harriet Beecher Stowe House, Mark Twain House, Wadsworth Atheneum, Webb-Deane-Stevens Museum; Bushnell Park, state capitol

## BUTTERNUT FARM
1654 Main Street
Glastonbury, Connecticut 06033
**Phone:** 860/633-7197
**Fax:** 860/659-1758
**Proprietor:** Don Reid

Jonathan Hale's classic Georgian house, with its clapboard exterior and large central chimney, was built in two stages starting in 1720. Carefully restored to its original condition, the house showcases a variety of colonial craftsmanship, from paneled fireplaces to fine cornice detailing; the restoration exposed the original wide brick fireplaces and removed layers of paint from paneling in many of the rooms. Also on view is an excellent collection of eighteenth-century Connecticut antiques, such as a cherry highboy, gateleg tables, bannister-back chairs, and a collection of English Delft. Guest rooms are furnished in traditional colonial style, and a full breakfast, including homemade jams, is served in the original kitchen or dining room. The inn is surrounded by herb and flower gardens, and the landscaped grounds are also home to the innkeeper's herd of dairy goats, flocks of chickens, doves, ducks, and geese, not to mention a llama.

**Open:** year round **Accommodations:** 5 guest rooms with private baths; 1 is a suite; 1 is an apartment **Meals:** full breakfast included; restaurants nearby **Rates:** $75 to $95 **Payment:** AmEx, personal check **Restrictions:** no smoking; no pets

# IVORYTON

**Nearby attractions:** Goodspeed Opera House, Ivoryton Playhouse, Connecticut River Musuem, Essex Steam Train, Mystic Seaport and Aquarium, Gillette Castle State Park, sailing, antiques hunting

## COPPER BEECH INN
46 Main Street
Ivoryton, Connecticut 06442
**Phone:** 860/767-0330 or 888/809-2056
**Website:** www.copperbeechinn.com
**Proprietors:** Sally and Eldon Senner

The handsome Copper Beech Inn, once the private home of an ivory importer, stands behind a magnificent copper beech tree, one of the oldest and largest of its type in Connecticut. Lovely turn-of-the-century gardens and native woodlands complete the inn's setting in this quiet village. The house was built in the 1880s as an elegant Victorian country cottage, complete with carriage barn, root cellar, and terraced gardens. It was rescued from disrepair and vacancy in the 1970s, refurbished, and opened as the Copper Beech Inn. Guest rooms in the main house are decorated with country and antique furnishings; the old-fashioned baths are intact. Guest rooms in the renovated carriage house have traditional country furnishings, some with four-poster or canopy beds; all have whirlpool baths and French doors leading to decks. French country-style dining is available in the restaurant.

**Open:** year round, except first week of January **Accommodations:** 13 guest rooms with private baths **Meals:** continental-plus breakfast included; complimentary refreshments; restaurant on premises serving dinner Tuesday through Sunday (Wednesday through Sunday in January, February, and March) **Wheelchair access:** some guest rooms, dining room **Rates:** $105 to $175 **Payment:** AmEx, Visa, MC, CB, DC, personal and traveler's checks **Restrictions:** children over 10 welcome; smoking limited; no pets **Activities:** country gardens, gallery of antique Chinese porcelain

# MIDDLEBURY

**Nearby attractions:** state parks, museums, theaters, concerts, historic sites, antiques hunting, Quassy Amusement Park, water sports, hiking, fishing, golfing, tennis, skiing

## TUCKER HILL INN
96 Tucker Hill Road
Middlebury, Connecticut 06762
**Phone:** 203/758-8334
**Website:** www.bedandbreakfastusa.com
**Proprietors:** Susan and Richard Cebelenski
**Location:** 1/2 hour east of Danbury

Tucker Hill Inn is a typical New England–style Colonial Revival home—large and spacious inside and out, and lightly shaded by ancient oaks and maples. Located one mile from the village green in Middlebury, Tucker Hill opened for business in 1923 as a tearoom, becoming a busy trolley stop on the line from Waterbury. Over time the tearoom evolved into an inn with a restaurant and catering facilities; hundreds of brides have descended the home's center-hall staircase. Today's inn is also host to weary travelers who want to relax and unwind. Guests stay in bright, sunny rooms and are invited to share the downstairs living room. A full breakfast is served either in the formal dining room or on the patio.

**Open:** year round **Accommodations:** 4 guest rooms, 2 with private baths **Meals:** full breakfast included; restaurants nearby **Rates:** $70 to $130; 10% discount to National Trust members and National Trust Visa cardholders **Payment:** AmEx, Visa, MC, personal and traveler's checks **Restrictions:** no smoking; no pets **On–site activities:** library, videotapes, compact discs

# MYSTIC

**Nearby attractions:** Mystic Seaport Museum, Mystic Marinelife Aquarium, Old Mistick Village, Groton Submarine Base, U.S. Coast Guard Academy, tennis, golfing, sailing, deep-sea fishing, antiques hunting, classical music concerts, wildlife sanctuaries, historic houses, shopping

## PALMER INN
25 Church Street
Noank, Connecticut 06340
**Phone:** 860/572-9000
**Website:** visitmystic.com/palmerinn/
**Proprietor:** Patricia Ann White
**Location:** 2 miles south of Mystic

One block from Long Island Sound and two miles from Mystic Seaport, shipyard craftsmen built a grand seaside mansion for shipbuilder Robert Palmer in 1906. The house, described by the architects as a "Classic Colonial Suburban Villa," features a hip roof with dormers, a balustrade, dentil cornices, pilasters, Palladian windows, and a huge portico with two-story Ionic columns. Today, as the Palmer Inn, these architectural details remain, while inside the elegant inn 13-foot ceilings, a mahogany staircase and beams, brass fixtures, intricate woodwork, stained-glass windows, and original wall coverings have been restored. Guest rooms, filled with family heirlooms and antiques, also offer modern luxuries such as hair dryers, makeup mirrors, toiletries, and designer sheets. Balconies offer views of Long Island Sound, and fireplaces warm cold winter evenings.

**Open:** year round **Accommodations:** 6 rooms with private baths **Meals:** continental-plus breakfast included; restaurants nearby   **Rates:** $125 to $225; 10% discount to National Trust members and National Trust Visa cardholders Sunday through Thursday, excluding holidays **Payment:** AmEx, Visa, MC, personal and traveler's checks **Restrictions:** children over 14 welcome; no smoking; no pets **On-site activities:** sailing lessons, tennis, art school in June

## PEQUOT HOTEL BED AND BREAKFAST
Burnett's Corners
711 Cow Hill Road
Mystic, Connecticut 06355
**Phone:** 860/572-0390
**Fax:** 860/536-3380
**Website:** visitmystic.com/pequothotel
**E-mail:** PEQUOTHTL@aol.com
**Proprietors:** Nancy and Jim Mitchell

The Pequot Hotel is an authentically restored 1840 stagecoach stop. The stately Greek Revival landmark is located in the center of the Burnett's Corners historic district, surrounded by many other historic buildings. Inside, original hardware, moldings, and fireplaces enhance the building's historic character. Two guest rooms with 12-foot-high coved ceilings have Rumford fireplaces. A two-room suite offers accommodations for up to four people. Guests will find a rare book collection in the library and wicker furniture on the screened porch. Two parlors are also open to guests. The hotel is surrounded by more than 20 acres of trailed woods, open fields, ponds, spacious lawns, and gardens. The Pequot was included in the National Trust Engagement Calendar for 1998.

**Open:** year round **Accommodations:** 3 guest rooms with private baths; 1 is a suite **Meals:** full breakfast included; complimentary refreshments; restaurants nearby **Rates:** $95 to $155; 10% discount to National Trust members **Payment:** Visa, MC, personal and traveler's checks **Restrictions:** well-supervised children over 8 welcome; no smoking; no pets **On-site activities:** horseshoe pitching, badminton, 22 acres of woods, fields, pond, and stream


## RED BROOK INN
2750 Gold Star Highway, Route 184
P.O. Box 237
Mystic, Connecticut 06372
**Phone:** 860/572-0349 or 800/290-5619
**E-mail:** rkeyes1667@aol.com
**Proprietor:** Ruth Keyes

Red Brook Inn offers guest lodgings in two handsome historic buildings: the Haley Tavern (1740) and the Crary Homestead (1770). The Crary house was built on this site; the Haley Tavern (a National Register property) was moved here by owner Ruth Keyes to prevent its destruction by a proposed highway. For her outstanding preservation efforts, Keyes received an award in 1986 from the U.S. Department of Transportation and President Reagan's Advisory Council on Historic Preservation. Guest rooms in both buildings are appointed with period antiques and original early lighting fixtures. Extensive collections of early American glass, pewter, and lighting devices are on display in the downstairs common rooms. Fireplaces abound throughout the inn. The Red Brook Inn has been featured in *National Geographic Traveler*.

**Open:** year round **Accommodations:** 11 guest rooms with private baths **Meals:** full breakfast included; restaurants nearby **Rates:** $105 to $189; 10% discount to National Trust members and National Trust Visa cardholders **Payment:** Visa, MC, traveler's check **Restrictions:** no smoking; no pets **On-site activities:** picnic area, terrace, woodlands walking

---

## NEW HAVEN

**Nearby attractions:** Yale University, Yale Art Museum, Yale Center for British Art, Peabody Museum, Shubert Theater, Yale Repertory Theater, boutiques, dining

### THREE CHIMNEYS INN AT YALE

1201 Chapel Street
New Haven, Connecticut 06511
**Phone:** 203/789-1201 or 800/443-1554
**Fax:** 203/776-7363
**Website:** www.threechimneysinn.com
**E-mail:** chimneysnh@aol.com
**Proprietor:** Ron Peterson

Three Chimneys Inn is an elegant 1871 two-story, clapboard mansion conveniently located in a vibrant lodging and dining area, one block from the Yale campus. The grand staircase and two parlors with their four period fireplaces showcase the finely detailed oak millwork that was prevalent in the 1870s. The front verandah, with turned-spindle porch supports, overlooks a manicured formal garden of boxwood hedges and perennials. Ten distinctive guest rooms with private baths, three with fireplaces, reflect the Georgian and Federal periods of furniture design with four-poster and canopied beds, rich color palettes, and oriental rugs. Modern amenities include a hair dryer, clock radio, full-size desk, color television, and telephone with data port for PC connection in each room. Small, intimate business meetings are often held in the library; two larger conference rooms accommodate 14 or 24 persons. Complete meeting packages including meals and equipment are available.

**Open:** year round **Accommodations:** 10 guest rooms with private baths; 1 is a suite **Meals:** full breakfast included; complimentary refreshments; restaurants nearby

**Rates:** $160; 10% discount to National Trust members and National Trust Visa cardholders **Payment:** AmEx, Visa, MC, Discover, traveler's check **Restrictions:** children over 6 welcome; no smoking; no pets

# NEW LONDON

**Nearby attractions:** Garde Arts Center, Foxwoods Casino, U.S. Naval Submarine Base, Mystic Seaport Museum and Marinelife Aquarium, Gillette's Castle, Eugene O'Neill Theater Center, U.S. Coast Guard Academy, marinas, beaches, sailing, sport fishing, outlet shops

## LIGHTHOUSE INN
6 Guthrie Place
New London, Connecticut 06320
**Phone:** 203/443-8411
**Fax:** 203/437-7027
**General Manager:** Paul Cullen

In 1902 steel magnate Charles S. Guthrie built his country home overlooking Long Island Sound and called it Meadow Court after the wildflowers that surrounded it. The formal grounds were designed by landscape architect Frederick Law Olmsted, who also designed Central Park. The Mediterranean-style mansion formed a half circle so that every room had a view of either the gardens or the water. Meadow Court became a focal point for society events and a retreat for film stars, including Bette Davis and Joan Crawford. Operated as an inn since 1927, the mansion and adjacent carriage house contain 50 guest rooms dressed in old and new furnishings, some of them original to the Guthrie family. Canopied beds and wing chairs blend easily with color television sets, whirlpool tubs, and bedside telephones. Two restaurants serve three meals daily. Lighthouse Inn, a member of Historic Hotels of America, provides a private beach for its guests just a block away.

**Open:** year round **Accommodations:** 50 guest rooms with private baths **Meals:** 2 restaurants on premises **Rates:** $95 to $255; 10% discount to National Trust members and National Trust Visa cardholders **Payment:** AmEx, Visa, MC, DC, traveler's check **Restrictions:** no pets **On-site activities:** four acres of landscaped grounds, private beach, sailing, sport fishing, business services

## NORFOLK

**Nearby attractions:** skiing, water sports, horseback riding, Norfolk Music Festival, summer theater, antiques hunting, crafts shops, vineyards

### GREENWOODS GATE BED AND BREAKFAST INN

105 Greenwoods Road East
P.O. Box 491
Norfolk, Connecticut 06058
**Phone:** 860/542-5439
**Website:** greenwoodsgate.com
**Proprietor:** George E. Schumaker

Greenwoods Gate exemplifies the tradition of Federal, or Adam, architecture in the northern states with its clapboard exterior, 12-over-12 double-hung windows, and paneled front door flanked by sidelights. Furnished throughout with an eclectic blend of fine antiques and collectibles, the handsome 1797 home is located less than a half-mile east of Norfolk's village green. Brass and iron beds, canopies suspended from walls, oriental rugs, and coordinating fabrics come together in four elegantly designed guest suites filled with such amenities as freshly cut flowers, monogrammed bathrobes, and crisp, ironed linens. All rooms retain original wide-board cherry floors. Afternoon tea is served in the library. Original fireplaces grace the grand parlor and breakfast room. This luxurious inn has been praised by *Ladies Home Journal, Victoria, Country Inns Bed and Breakfast, Innsider* and *Country Accents* magazines.

**Open:** year round **Accommodations:** 4 guest suites with private baths **Meals:** full breakfast included; complimentary refreshments; restaurants nearby **Rates:** $175 to $245; 10% discount to National Trust members and National Trust Visa cardholders **Payment:** personal and traveler's checks **Restrictions:** children over 12 welcome; no smoking; no pets

### MANOR HOUSE

69 Maple Avenue
P.O. Box 447
Norfolk, Connecticut 06058
**Phone:** 860/542-5690
**Website:** www.manorhouse-norfolk.com
**Proprietors:** Hank and Diane Tremblay

The original cherry paneling of the Manor House's foyer and grand staircase typifies the architectural elegance of this home. The Tudor-style house was built in 1898 for Charles Spofford, designer of London's underground system. As a housewarming present, Louis Comfort Tiffany installed 20 stained-glass win-

dows. The baronial living room has a six-foot-wide raised hearth, and several of the bedrooms have fireplaces with ornate mantels. Guest rooms are furnished with four-poster, brass, sleigh, spindle, or lace-canopied beds, all covered with plush down comforters. The hearty breakfast menu changes daily but always includes honey harvested from the Manor House's own hives. A grand piano is available for entertainment and a library offers solitude.

**Open:** year round **Accommodations:** 9 guest rooms with private baths **Meals:** full breakfast included; complimentary refreshments; restaurants nearby **Rates:** $135 to $225; 10% discount offered to National Trust members and National Trust Visa cardholders (some restrictions may apply) **Payment:** AmEx, Visa, MC, personal and traveler's checks **Restrictions:** children over 12 welcome; smoking limited; no pets **On-site activities:** croquet, hiking, bicycling, cross-country skiing

## OLD LYME

**Nearby attractions:** Florence Griswold Museum, Lyme Art Academy, Connecticut River Museum, Mystic Seaport and Aquarium, Gillette Castle, Goodspeed Opera House, Essex Steam Train and Boat Ride, Mystic Seaport, boating, bicycling, swimming, hiking, antiques hunting

### OLD LYME INN
85 Lyme Street
Old Lyme, Connecticut 06371
**Phone:** 860/434-2600 or 800/434-5352
**E-mail:** olinn@aol.com
**Proprietor:** Diana Atwood-Johnson

The Champlain family built this house in the 1850s and worked its 300-acre farm until the turnpike came through town in the 1950s. The rambling farmhouse with its broad front porch was converted to an inn, which later fell into extreme

disrepair following a fire. In 1976 the innkeeper purchased and restored the building, reopening it as the Old Lyme Inn. The inn, listed in the National Register of Historic Places, has a front hall adorned by hand-painted murals and stencils like those that were popular in the 19th century. Elsewhere in the inn are examples of the Old Lyme School of impressionist painting that flourished at the turn of the century. Guest rooms contain Empire and Victorian furnishings, and some rooms have canopied or four-poster beds. Awarded three stars by the *New York Times*, the inn's restaurant continues to be recognized in publications nationwide for its creativity and quality.

**Open:** year round **Accommodations:** 13 guest rooms with private baths; 8 are suites **Meals:** continental-plus breakfast included; restaurant on premises **Wheelchair access:** 4 guest rooms and restaurant **Rates:** $99 to $150; 10% discount offered to National Trust members and National Trust Visa cardholders **Payment:** AmEx, Visa, MC, CB, DC, Discover, personal and traveler's checks **On-site activities:** fine dining, relaxing, listening to classical guitar in the Grill Room

## OLD SAYBROOK

**Nearby attractions:** General William Hart House, Saybrook Point cruises, antique shops, art galleries, factory outlets, Mystic Seaport, Essex Steam Train and Riverboat

### DEACON TIMOTHY PRATT BED AND BREAKFAST

325 Main Street
Old Saybrook, Connecticut 06475
**Phone:** 860/395-1229
**Fax:** 860/395-4748
**Website:** virtualcities.com/ct/pratthouse.htm *or* oldsaybrookct.com/pratt
**Proprietor:** Shelley Nobile

Timothy Pratt built a small portion of this traditional two-story house around 1746, but it was his son, Timothy Pratt, Jr., who constructed the rest of the house in 1771. Since then the five-bay, central chimney house, named for the son who became a deacon in the Congregational Church, has remained a local landmark in the historic seafaring town of Old Saybrook. The restored house welcomes guests to a warm and comfortable atmosphere with romantic accommodations that feature a four-poster bed, working fireplaces, and large private bath in each room. Guests are welcome to relax in the candlelit parlor or in the library, where items of historical note that were found during the house's restoration are on display. The Deacon Timothy Pratt House is within walking distance of shops, restaurants, and museums, and the inn provides guests with beach passes.

**Open:** year round **Accommodations:** 3 guest rooms with private baths; 1 is a suite **Meals:** full breakfast included; complimentary refreshments; restaurants nearby **Rates:** $110 to $150 ($15 less without full breakfast) **Payment:** AmEx, Visa, MC, personal and traveler's checks **Restrictions:** no smoking; no pets **On-site activities:** yard with hammock, swing, gardens; books and games; massage therapy

## PLYMOUTH

**Nearby attractions:** American Clock and Watch Museum, New England Carousel Museum, antiques hunting, vineyards, nature preserves, skiing; historic Litchfield, Hartford 30 minutes away

### SHELTON HOUSE BED AND BREAKFAST
663 Main Street (Route 6)
Plymouth, Connecticut 06782
**Phone and Fax:** 860/283-4616
**E-mail:** SheltonHBB@aol.com
**Proprietors:** Pat and Bill Doherty

Ebenezer Plumb built this impressive Greek Revival house with its distinctive entry pilasters and upper-story frieze in 1825, but it is named for its most well-known owner, A. C. Shelton, a prosperous carriagemaker during the mid-nineteenth century. Now a bed-and-breakfast inn, Shelton House enjoys a parklike setting with its perennial flower gardens and pineapple fountain. The inn's interior boasts ten-foot ceilings, original woodwork, wainscoting, and wideboard chestnut floors as well as period furnishings and antiques, including an ornate hall bench once owned by silent film star Marie Dressler. Four guest rooms offer queen, double, or twin beds and private or semi-private baths. Guests can relax by the fireplace in the spacious parlor and enjoy afternoon tea; each morning a full breakfast is served in the dining room or, on summer days, out on the patio.

Located in the Litchfield Hills, the inn is convenient to many New England villages, and historic Litchfield is just 10 miles away.

**Open:** year round **Accommodations:** 4 guest rooms (2 have private baths) **Meals:** full breakfast included; afternoon tea; restaurants nearby **Rates:** $65 to $95; 10% discount to National Trust members **Payment:** personal and traveler's checks **Restrictions:** not suitable for children; no smoking; no pets **On-site activities:** formal guest parlor with television, reading materials; perennial garden and fountain

## POQUETANUCK

**Nearby attractions:** Mystic Seaport and Aquarium, U.S. Coast Guard Academy, Submarine Force Library and Museum, Gillette Castle, casinos, beaches, wineries, golfing, tennis

### CAPTAIN GRANT'S, 1754
109 Route 2A
Poquetanuck, Connecticut 06365
**Phone:** 860/887-7589 or 800/982-1772
**Fax:** 860/892-9151
**Website:** www.captaingrants.com
**Proprietors:** Ted and Carol Matsumoto

Not only did Captain Grant's home—built in 1754 for his wife, Mercy—house three generations of the Grant family, it also housed soldiers garrisoned in town during the American Revolution. In 1880 the house was divided in half by two feuding sisters; their radical remodeling efforts have been undone by its present owners, who have restored the house's original appearance and outstanding architecture, including a seven-foot-wide staircase and massive oak and chestnut beams. Today the house offers four bedrooms with private baths. Guests are invited to relax in the library or on the two-story deck overlooking the inn's shaded grounds. On request, the innkeepers will give a tour of the abandoned cemetery behind the house, which includes the graves of American Revolution soldiers. Guests will also enjoy taking in the local history of Poquetanuck, which was a stop on the Underground Railroad and is honeycombed with tunnels used by slaves.

**Open:** year round **Accommodations:** 4 guest rooms with private baths **Meals:** full breakfast included; complimentary evening wine; restaurants nearby **Rates:** $80 to $125; 10% discount to National Trust members and National Trust Visa cardholders **Payment:** AmEx, Visa, MC, Discover **Restrictions:** Children over 6 welcome; no smoking; no pets

# RIVERTON

**Nearby attractions:** historic house tours, Hitchcock Chair Company and Museum, Lake Compounce Festival Park, sleigh and carriage rides, state parks and forests, picnicking, fishing, hiking, hunting, cross-country and downhill skiing, camping, golfing, tennis, river tubing, canoeing, horseback riding, swimming, boating, bicycling

## OLD RIVERTON INN

436 East River Road
Riverton, Connecticut 06065
**Phone:** 860/379-8678
**Fax:** 860/379-1006
**Website:** www.newenglandinns.com/inns/riverton/index.html
**E-mail:** mark.telford@snet.net
**Proprietors:** Mark and Pauline Telford

This three-story Federal-style building was opened for business in 1796 by Jesse Ives and was known on the post route between Hartford and Albany as Ives Tavern or Ives Hotel. In the two intervening centuries, the inn has seen various architectural changes, but the National Register property remains true to its origins in style and hospitality. With white shutters gleaming against blue clapboards, the rechristened Old Riverton Inn offers quaint and cozy accommodations, some with canopy beds or fireplaces. All rooms have private baths and color cable television. For relaxing and dining, the inn offers the Hobby Horse Bar, Colonial Dining Room, and Grindstone Terrace.

**Open:** year round **Accommodations:** 12 guest rooms with private baths; 1 is a suite **Meals:** full breakfast included; restaurant on premises **Wheelchair access:** dining facilities **Rates:** $80 to $175; 10% discount offered to National Trust members and National Trust Visa cardholders off-peak only
**Payment:** AmEx, Visa, MC, CB, DC, Discover, traveler's check **Restrictions**: pets accepted with prior approval; smoking limited

## TOLLAND

**Nearby attractions:** Nathan Hale, Mark Twain, and Harriet Beecher Stowe house museums, Old Sturbridge Village, antiques hunting, winery, golfing, bicycling, bird watching, ice skating

### OLD BABCOCK TAVERN
484 Mile Hill Road (Route 31)
Tolland, Connecticut 06084
**Phone:** 860/875-1239
**Fax:** 860/870-9544
**E-mail:** babcockbb@juno.com
**Proprietors:** Barbara and Stuart Danforth

Listed in the National Register of Historic Places as the Sgt. John Cady House, the Old Babcock Tavern was built in 1720 by the sergeant in a typical New England center-chimney plan. That granite chimney services three fireplaces and two bake ovens—all original to the house, all in working order today. The owners have painstakingly restored this house since purchasing it in 1967, opening it as a bed-and-breakfast inn in 1984. Three charming guest rooms reflect the building's origins with Early American antiques and original wide-board floors. A hearty old-fashioned breakfast is served each morning and afternoons may find guests relaxing in the tap room with its polished paneled walls and reconstructed historic bar. A keeping room and parlor are also available. All common rooms have fireplaces as does one of the bedrooms. The innkeepers offer a restoration slide presentation in the evenings for interested guests.

**Open:** year round **Accommodations:** 3 guest rooms with private baths; 1 is a suite **Meals:** full breakfast included; complimentary refreshments; restaurants nearby **Rates:** $70 to $85 **Payment:** cash or check only **Restrictions:** children over 12 welcome; no smoking; no pets **On-site activities:** wine tastings, herb garden, horseshoe pitching, croquet

# WESTPORT

**Nearby attractions:** Westport County Playhouse, historic waterfront district, Westport beaches, art galleries, antiques hunting, health club and indoor pool, shopping, dining

## INN AT NATIONAL HALL

2 Post Road West
Westport, Connecticut 06880
**Phone:** 860/221-1351 or 800/NAT-HALL
**Website:** www.integra.fr/relaischateaux/nationalhall
**Proprietor:** Keith Halford

Built in 1873 as Westport's First National Bank, this distinctive Italianate structure housed the town's meeting place—National Hall—on its third floor. Fashioned after Europe's elite manor houses, the inn displays a delightful mix of whimsy, privacy, and history. A recent rehabilitation produced elegant rooms with state-of-the-art amenities. Selected chambers feature loft bedrooms with soaring two-story ceilings, enhanced by expansive windows and sweeping river views. Guests should keep an eye out for fanciful trompe l'oeil paintings throughout the hotel. Embracing the understated elegance of the inn is its renowned Restaurant at National Hall, serving American regional and continental cuisine. Listed in the National Register of Historic Places, the Inn at National Hall is the cornerstone of Westport's restored historic waterfront district. A member of Relais & Chateaux, the inn has also garnered five diamonds from AAA.

**Open:** year round **Accommodations:** 15 guest rooms with private baths; 7 are suites **Meals:** continental breakfast included; complimentary refreshments; restaurant on premises; restaurants nearby **Wheelchair access:** restaurant **Rates:** $225 to $575; 10% discount offered to National Trust members and National Trust Visa cardholders **Payment:** AmEx, Visa, MC, DC, personal and traveler's checks **Restrictions:** no smoking; no pets **On-site activities:** billiards room, complimentary video library, cable television, complimentary use of local health facility

# DELAWARE

Montchanin ●
● Wilmington
New Castle
● Delaware City
Milford ●
Lewes ●

## DELAWARE CITY

**Nearby attractions:** Fort Delaware, Fort Dupont, Fort Mott, Delaware City Historic District, boating, fishing, golf-ing

## OLDE CANAL INN
Clinton and Harbor Streets
P.O. Box 250
Delaware City, Delaware 19706
Phone: 302/832-5100
Fax: 302/834-7442
Proprietors: Frank S. Luxl and Wendy Grose

The Old Canal Inn has restored and refurbished guest rooms that will charm visitors and a lively past that will intrigue history buffs. The inn was built in 1826 as the Delaware Hotel during construction of the Chesapeake & Delaware Canal. It was a meeting place for government officials and Union officers during the Civil War, and most of the inn's guest rooms have views of Fort Delaware on Pea Patch Island, where 30,000 Confederate soldiers were held prisoner. The inn also prospered during Prohibition, when its riverfront location made suspicious late-night deliveries convenient. Military and government officials once more frequented the inn in large numbers during World War II, when prisoners from General Rommel's African corps were imprisoned on nearby Dupont Island. In addition to waterfront and river views, some guest rooms offer fireplaces and whirlpool tubs, and the Penthouse Suite, with its cathedral ceilings, includes four bedrooms, a kitchen, and private bath. A fine-dining restaurant and riverfront tavern and deck offer guests on-site dining options.

**Open:** year round **Accommodations:** 11 guest rooms with private baths; 4 are suites; 1 is a penthouse suite **Meals:** continental breakfast included; restaurant and tavern on premises **Wheelchair access:** limited to restaurant and tavern **Rates:** $50 to $250; 10% discount to National Trust members and National Trust Visa cardholders **Payment:** Visa, MC, traveler's check; personal check for deposit only **Restrictions:** children over 10 welcome; smoking permitted in tavern and dining room only; no pets **On-site activities:** special event weekends (mysteries, Civil War dramas)

## LEWES

**Nearby attractions:** Zwaanendael Museum, maritime museum, historic town with three centuries of architecture, ocean and bay beaches, watching whales and dolphins, sailing, harbor and Delaware Bay tours, Cape Henlopen State Park, Prime Hook Wildlife Refuge, charter boat fishing

### WILD SWAN INN
525 Kings Highway
Lewes, Delaware 19958
**Phone:** 302/645-8550
**Fax:** 302/645-8550
**E-mail:** wildswan@udel.edu
**Proprietors:** Hope and Michael Tyler

Built just after the turn of the century, this classic example of a Queen Anne home is resplendent with ornate and delicate spindlework, wraparound porches, carved vergeboards, and fancy finials. Its pink-and-white exterior is accented by its surrounding flowering trees and shrubs. Guest rooms are decorated and furnished with an eclectic Victorian flair. All rooms are air conditioned and have private baths. The parlor, with its lavish wallpaper, antique furnishings, and player piano, provides a comfortable place to unwind. In summer months, the patio and pool offer a change of pace. A formal breakfast is served in the spacious dining room

lighted by one of the inn's many antique brass chandeliers. The Wild Swan, which was featured in the National Trust's 1998 Appointment Calendar, is walking distance from downtown Lewes.

**Open:** year round **Accommodations:** 3 guest rooms with private baths **Meals:** full breakfast included; complimentary refreshments; restaurants nearby **Rates:** $85 to $150; 10% discount to National Trust members and National Trust Visa cardholders during off season, excluding holidays **Payment:** personal and traveler's checks **Restrictions:** not suitable for children; no smoking; no pets **On-site activities:** swimming pool, bicycles, music on antique player piano and Edison phonograph, porch sitting

# MILFORD

**Nearby attractions:** Mispillion River; River Walk; Delaware Bay and Atlantic Ocean beaches; Bombay Hook National Wildlife Preserve; Dickerson Plantation; golfing; swimming; tennis; fishing; boating; antiques hunting; historic towns of Lewes, Rehoboth Beach, Odessa, Milton, and Milford

## CAUSEY MANSION BED AND BREAKFAST
2 Causey Avenue
Milford, Delaware 19963
**Phone:** 302/422-0979
**Proprietors:** Kenneth and Frances Novak

In 1763, Levin Crapper built this mansion in the Georgian style on 1000 acres of land, which he farmed with the help of many slaves. Today, one of the original slave quarters remains on the property. After ownership by Governor Daniel Rogers, the house was purchased by Governor Peter F. Causey in 1849. He enlarged the house by adding a third floor, changing the style from Georgian to the popular Greek Revival. Recently renovated, the Causey Mansion now offers accommodations that reflect the house's Early American heritage yet are comfortably modernized with private baths and air conditioning. Sitting on three acres in the heart of Milford, Causey Mansion is convenient to all the area's sites and activities.

**Open:** year round **Accommodations:** 5 guest rooms with private baths; 1 is a suite **Meals:** full breakfast included; complimentary refreshments; restaurants nearby **Wheelchair access:** 1 room **Rate:** $85 **Payment:** Visa, MC, personal and traveler's checks **Restrictions:** no smoking; no pets **On-site activities:** formal boxwood gardens

## THE TOWERS BED AND BREAKFAST
101 Northwest Front Street
Milford, Delaware 19963
**Phone:** 302/422-3814 or 800/366-3814
**Website:** www.mispillion.com
**Proprietor:** Dan Bond

Built in 1783, The Towers is one of the oldest buildings in Milford. Built in a typical Delawarean colonial style, the wooden structure was vastly remodeled in 1891, resulting in an engaging mix of Queen Anne and Steamboat Gothic styles. Craftsmen from the local shipyards enlarged the house, added whimsical embellishments, and created a stunning interior of stained glass and carved woodwork, including a sycamore coffered ceiling in the music room and an elaborate staircase crafted from walnut and mahogany. The carefully restored house sports an exterior paint scheme of six colors. It has been featured in the 1992 book, *America's Painted Ladies*. Inside, the furnishings are primarily French Victorian. Guests often gather in the music room with its fireplace, 1899 grand piano, and working Victrola. In warm weather, guests are invited to enjoy the walled garden, swimming pool, or gazebo porch.

**Open:** Friday and Saturday nights only year round **Accommodations:** 6 guest rooms (4 have private baths); 2 are suites **Meals:** full breakfast included; restaurants nearby **Rates:** $95 to $125; 10% discount to National Trust members and National Trust Visa cardholders **Payment:** Visa, MC, personal and traveler's checks **Restrictions:** children over 13 welcome; no smoking; no pets **On-site activities:** swimming pool, bicycles

---

# MONTCHANIN
**Nearby attractions:** Winterthur, Longwood Gardens, Brandywine River Museum, Hagley Museum and Library, Delaware Art Museum, Delaware Museum of Natural History

## THE INN AT MONTCHANIN VILLAGE
Route 100 and Kirk Road
Montchanin, Delaware 19710
**Phone:** 302/888-2133 or 800/COW-BIRD (800/269-2473)
**Fax:** 302/888-0389
**Website:** www.montchanin.com
**Proprietors:** Dan and Missy Lickle

Montchanin Village is a collection of 11 buildings constructed between 1799 and 1910, all of which have been restored and renovated to provide 26 elegant guest suites with private marble baths, fireplaces, individual garden and terrace settings, and amenities with the sophisticated traveler in mind. Each one- and two-bedroom suite has a different floor plan; some are two stories, and one is three stories high. The village was once the home of workers on the nearby DuPont estate, Winterthur, and accommodations and meeting rooms are in former residences, a barn, and a blacksmith shop. According to the National Register of Historic Places, Montchanin "remains today much as it did at the turn of the century. There are few other hamlets that have survived with so few intrusions in their environment and structural characteristics." The inn is a member of Historic Hotels of America.

**Open:** year round **Accommodations:** 26 guest suites with private baths **Meals:** full breakfast included; complimentary refreshments; award-winning Krazy Kat's restaurant on premises **Rates:** $150 to $350; 10% discount to National Trust members **Payment:** AmEx, Visa, MC, DC, personal and traveler's checks **Restrictions:** no smoking; no pets

---

## NEW CASTLE

**Nearby attractions:** historic New Castle, Longwood Gardens, Winterthur, Brandywine River Museum, historic walking tour of eighteenth- and nineteenth-century buildings, tennis, golfing, biking, shopping, dining, Philadelphia

### ARMITAGE INN
2 The Strand
New Castle, Delaware 19720
**Phone:** 302/328-6618
**Fax:** 302/324-1163
**E-mail:** armitageinn@earthlink.net
**Proprietors:** Stephen and Rina Marks

Built in 1732, the Armitage Inn is situated on the bank of the Delaware River only a few feet from the spot where William Penn first set foot in the New World. The inn is named after Ann Armitage, who married an early owner of the house, Zachariah Van Leuvenigh. One of the rooms on the first floor is believed to have been built in the 1600s, being incorporated into the main house when built. Within this room is an original brick walk-in cooking fireplace. Guest rooms are individually decorated with attention to historic details. All furnishings, beds, linens, and towels have been carefully selected to pamper and comfort guests. Rooms feature king- and queen-size beds, private baths (some with whirlpool tubs), and central air conditioning. Guests are invited to enjoy the dining room, parlor, library, screened porch, and walled garden.

**Open:** year round **Accommodations:** 5 guest rooms with private baths **Meals:** breakfast buffet included; restaurants nearby **Rates:** $105 to $150 **Payment:** AmEx, Visa, MC, Discover, personal check **Restrictions:** children over 12 welcome; no smoking; no pets

# WILMINGTON

**Nearby attractions:** Winterthur, Longwood Gardens, Brandywine River Museum, Olde New Castle, Hagley Museum; Philadelphia, Pennsylvania

### DARLEY MANOR INN BED AND BREAKFAST
3701 Philadelphia Pike
Wilmington, Delaware 19703
**Phone:** 302/792-2127 or 800/824-4703
**Fax:** 302/798-6143
**Website:** www.dca.net/darley
**E-mail:** darley@claymontde.org
**Proprietors:** Ray and Judith Hester

Built in 1790 with four rooms plus attic, Darley Manor was expanded in 1810 and again in 1842. The house is named in honor of its most famous resident, Felix Darley, a popular book illustrator in the mid-nineteenth century. Darley's work was found in books by many notable authors, including Dickens, Poe, Longfellow, and Tennyson. Charles Dickens was guest here during his American tour in 1867. Darley lived in this home from 1859 until 1888. Today's guest rooms are decorated with colonial- and Victorian-style furnishings. All rooms are air conditioned and have refrigerators, coffeepots, pants pressers, and private baths with robes, hair dryers, and individual toiletries. Common rooms, dotted with fine antiques, include two parlors, meeting room, reading room, dining room, and foyer, where some of Darley's prints are on display.

**Open:** year round **Accommodations:** 6 guest rooms with private baths; 4 are suites **Meals:** full breakfast included; complimentary refreshments; 24-hour hospitality table; restaurants nearby **Rates:** $99 to $149 **Payment:** AmEx, Visa, MC, personal and traveler's checks **Restrictions:** children over 10 welcome; no smoking; no pets **On-site activities:** porch rockers, garden swing

# DISTRICT OF COLUMBIA

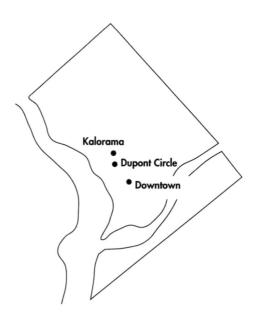

## DOWNTOWN

### HENLEY PARK HOTEL
926 Massachusetts Avenue, N.W.
Washington, D.C. 20001
**Phone:** 202/638-5200 or 800/222-8474
**Fax:** 202/634-6740
**E-mail:** henleypark@aol.com
**General Manager:** Joseph Giannino

Making its debut in 1918 as the upscale Tudor Hall apartments, home to members of Congress and the Senate, this meticulously restored building was converted to a hotel in 1982. The lobby retains its original stained-glass windows and Mercer tile floor; traditional archways and moldings, carved walls, and leaded-glass windows are featured throughout. The facade of the building displays 118 gargoyles including two depicting the faces of the architect and his wife. Four others above the restaurant atrium were rescued from New York's Commodore Hotel when it was razed. Guest rooms are furnished with Queen Anne or

Chippendale reproductions; some rooms feature four-poster beds. Small to midsize business meetings are easily accommodated in the Eton Room. The Henley Park, a member of Historic Hotels of America, is less than one block from the Convention Center and offers off-street parking.

**Open:** year round **Accommodations:** 96 guest rooms with private baths; 17 are suites **Meals:** continental breakfast included; restaurant on premises **Rates:** $125 to $295 **Payment:** AmEx, Visa, MC, DC, Discover, traveler's check, personal check with identification **Restrictions:** children under 16 free with parents; no pets **On-site activities:** fitness center, traditional tea daily, live jazz entertainment nightly, dancing on weekends

## MORRISON-CLARK INN

1015 L Street, N.W.
Washington, D.C. 20001
**Phone:** 202/898-1200 or 800/332-7898
**Fax:** 202/289-8576
**General Manager:** Josette Shelton

The Morrison-Clark Inn, built in 1864 is the only inn in Washington, D.C., to be listed in the National Register of Historic Places. It was originally two detached Victorian mansions built for David Morrison and Reuben Clark. A later owner added a Chinese Chippendale porch covered by a Shanghai mansard roof to the house at 1015 L Street. In 1923 one home became the Soldiers, Sailors, Marines, and Airmen's Club, offering lodging to servicemen for 75 cents per night. In 1930, the two homes were combined and the military club expanded. The late 1980s restoration of the houses created an elegant small hotel that today is a charter member of Historic Hotels of America. Original interior ornaments include 12-foot-high mahogany-framed mirrors and elaborately carved marble fireplaces.

Public and guest rooms are decorated with Victorian, neoclassical, and country furnishings. The inn's highly regarded restaurant has been featured in *Gourmet* and *Conde Nast Traveler.*

**Open:** year round **Accommodations:** 54 guest rooms with private baths; 13 are suites **Meals:** continental breakfast included; restaurant on premises **Rates:** $145 to $260; 10% discount off regular room rates to National Trust members **Payment:** AmEx, Visa, MC, DC, Discover, En Route, personal and traveler's checks **Restrictions:** smoking limited; no pets **Activities:** fine dining, fitness center, conversation, relaxing in courtyard

## THE SWISS INN
1204 Massachusetts Avenue, N.W.
Washington, D.C. 20005
**Phone:** 202/371-1816 or 800/955-7947
**Fax:** 202/371-1138
**Website:** www.theswissinn.com
**E-mail:** SwissInnDC@aol.com

This handsome four-story brownstone, built in 1904, is the smallest hotel in downtown Washington, offering guests comfortable accommodations convenient to the capital's many attractions. A colorful flower garden marks the entrance to the inn, whose west wall features a mural celebrating the life and achievements of abolitionist Frederick Douglass. Outfitted with high ceilings and bay windows, this inn was formerly an efficiency apartment building before it was converted to a hotel in 1982. Each guest room comes with individual climate controls, television, and a fully equipped kitchenette. The Swiss Inn is located in downtown Washington, within walking distance of the White House, The Mall with the Smithsonian museums and national monuments, Embassy Row, Chinatown, the Washington Convention Center, theater district, Union Station, and the subway's Metro Center.

**Open:** year round **Accommodations:** 8 guest rooms with private bath **Meals:** all rooms have kitchenettes **Rates:** $58 to $78; 10% discount to National Trust members and National Trust Visa cardholders **Payment:** AmEx, Visa, MC, Discover, traveler's check **Restrictions:** smoking limited

# DUPONT CIRCLE

## THE DUPONT AT THE CIRCLE
1604 Nineteenth Street, N.W.
Washington, D.C. 20009
**Phone:** 202/332-5251
**Fax:** 202/332-3244
**Website:** www.dupontatthecircle.com
**Proprietors:** Alan and Anexora Skvirsky

In the very heart of one of Washington's most exciting neighborhoods, The Dupont at the Circle is steps away from the Dupont Circle shopping district, dozens of restaurants, museums, galleries, nightclubs, and the clean and efficient Metro subway system. In a restored 1885 brick rowhouse, the inn combines original features such as gas lamps and ornate moldings with tasteful antiques and modern comforts. Each of the guest rooms has a full private bath with pedestal sink and claw-foot or whirlpool tub, a brass or antique Victorian bed fitted with fine linens, and an antique writing desk. Some rooms feature hand-crafted stained-glass windows or decorative fireplaces. Guests can mingle in the living room, parlor with television and VCR, or during nice weather, on the front patio for people watching in this bustling in-town community. District of Columbia residents for more than 25 years, the innkeepers are fully versed in all the city has to offer and welcome the opportunity to assist their guests.

**Open:** year round **Accommodations:** 7 guest rooms with private baths; 1 is a suite **Meals:** continental breakfast included; restaurants nearby **Rates:** $130 to $190; 10% discount to National Trust members and National Trust Visa cardholders **Payment:** AmEx, Visa, MC, personal and traveler's checks **Restrictions:** children over 14 welcome; no smoking; no pets **On-site activities:** patio, access to health club facilities

# KALORAMA

### TAFT BRIDGE INN
2007 Wyoming Avenue, N.W.
Washington, D.C. 20009
**Phone:** 202/387-2007
**Fax:** 202/387-5019
**Website:** www.quikpage.com/T/TaftBridge
**Proprietor:** Yoshie Haga Rozali

Taft Bridge Inn is a turn-of-the-century Georgian-style Colonial Revival mansion in the heart of the exclusive Kalorama district, which includes the former homes of presidents Taft, Eisenhower, Wilson, and Johnson. The inn's location in this intimate neighborhood makes it an easy walk to Dupont Circle, Adams-Morgan, and the Metro subway. The inn contains eleven bedrooms, six fireplaces, a handsome paneled drawing room, porticoed porch, and garden area. Each guest room is individually decorated, with reproduction and antique pieces. A complimentary full breakfast is served daily. Laundry service, on-premises parking, housekeeping service, and small meeting spaces are available. Taft Bridge Inn offers companies and individuals attractive long-term rates in a unique historic bed-and-breakfast setting with the conveniences of home and office.

**Open:** year round **Accommodations:** 11 guest rooms (4 have private baths) **Meals:** full breakfast included; complimentary refreshments; restaurants nearby **Rates:** $49 to $98 **Payment:** Visa, MC, personal and traveler's checks **Restrictions:** not suitable for children; no smoking; no pets

# FLORIDA

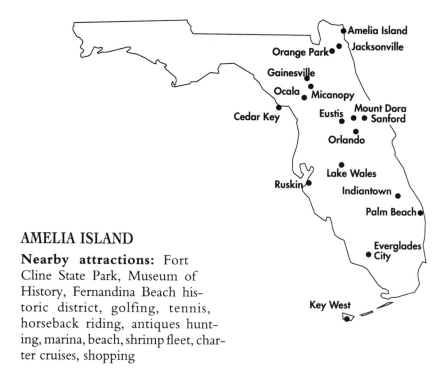

## AMELIA ISLAND

**Nearby attractions:** Fort
Cline State Park, Museum of
History, Fernandina Beach historic district, golfing, tennis,
horseback riding, antiques hunting, marina, beach, shrimp fleet, charter cruises, shopping

## BAILEY HOUSE

28 South Seventh Street
P.O. Box 805
Fernandina Beach, Florida 32034
**Phone:** 800/251-5390
**Fax:** 904/321-0103
**Website:** www.bailey-house.com
**Proprietors:** Tom and Jenny Bishop
**Location:** on Amelia Island, 35 miles northeast of Jacksonville

Bailey House was designed by architect George W. Bailey of Knoxville,
Tennesee, in 1895. With its turrets, gables, bays, stained-glass windows, and fish-
scale shingles, the house took three years to build at the then-extravagant cost of
$10,000. The National Register home, an outstanding example of the Queen
Anne style, is in the heart of Fernandina Beach's historic district. Bailey House
guests enjoy ornately carved antique furniture. There are also brass beds, a pump
organ, fringed lamps, claw-foot bathtubs, and marble-topped dressers and tables.
Four guestrooms were added in 1997; all are furnished with antiques. The most

spectacular of 10 fireplaces, located in the reception hall, bears the inscription on its mantel: "Hearth Hall, Welcome All."

**Open:** year round **Accommodations:** 9 guest rooms with private baths **Meals:** full breakfast included; restaurants nearby **Rates:** $95 to $140 **Payment:** AmEx, Visa, MC, personal and traveler's checks **Restrictions:** children over 8 welcome; no smoking; no pets **On-site activities:** bicycles, porch swings and rocking chairs, croquet

### 1735 HOUSE
584 South Fletcher Avenue
Fernandina Beach, Florida 32034
**Phone:** 904/261-4148 or 800/872-8531
**Fax:** 904/261-9200
**Website:** //ameliaislandlodging.com
**Proprietor:** William L. Auld
**Location:** on Amelia island, 35 miles northeast of Jacksonville

The 1735 House (named for the year Georgia Governor James Oglethorpe claimed the island for England) is a unique country inn situated on one of Amelia Island's beaches. Built in the 1930s, the New England-style clapboard inn offers its guests the relaxation of a beach vacation along with the proximity to golf, tennis, swimming, fishing, and boating activities as well as the charms of historic downtown Fernandina Beach. Each suite accommodates up to four guests and has a private bath and kitchenette. The inn, with Georgia heart-pine paneling, is furnished in wicker and rattan and such nautical antiques as sea chests, maps, and barometers. A continental breakfast is delivered to each suite along with the day's newspaper.

**Open:** year round **Accommodations:** 5 guest suites with private baths **Meals:** continental breakfast included; restaurants nearby **Rates:** $131 to $181 **Payment:** AmEx, Visa, MC, Discover, personal and traveler's checks **Restrictions:** no smoking; no pets **On-site activities:** located on beach

# CEDAR KEY

**Nearby attractions:** wildlife preserve, nature walks, boat tours, walking tours, swimming in freshwater springs, fresh and saltwater fishing, bird-watching

## ISLAND HOTEL

Second and B Streets
P.O. Box 460
Cedar Key, Florida 32625
**Phone:** 352/543-5111 or 800/432-4640
**Fax:** 352/543-6949
**Website:** islandhotel-cedarkey.com
**E-mail:** ishotel@islandhotel-cedarkey.com
**Proprietors:** Dawn and Tony Cousins

Survivor of hurricanes, floods, economic depression, and arson, the 1859 Island Hotel has truly stood the test of time and travail. One reason is its solid construction of 10-inch-thick tabby walls (a composite of oyster shells, sand, lime, and salt water) and 12-inch-thick oak beams. Recently restored by today's innkeepers and listed in the National Register of Historic Places, the hotel is a charming throwback to early life in Cedar Key. The two-story structure began life as a general store and was converted to a hotel in 1915. Its rooms are comfortably furnished in an old Florida style that includes feather beds, claw-foot tubs, mosquito netting and ceiling fans, although the structure is centrally heated and air conditioned. But modern intrusions like telephones and television have been omitted. The hotel's restaurant continues a long tradition of serving gourmet island seafood, and the lounge bar, decorated with murals painted in 1948, has been refinished with genuine cedar from the key. Island Hotel is a favored location for weddings, private functions, and conferences.

**Open:** year round **Accommodations:** 13 guest rooms with private baths **Meals:** full breakfast included; restaurant on premises **Wheelchair access:** dining room **Rates:** $75 to $120; 10% discount to National Trust members and National Trust Visa cardholders **Payment:** Visa, MC, Discover, traveler's check **Restrictions:** not suitable for children; smoking limited **On-site activities:** reading, conversing, dining, balcony sitting

# EUSTIS

**Nearby attractions:** Disney World, Universal Studios, Ocala National Forest, Lakeridge Winery, horseback riding, water sports, Wekiva River, antiques hunting

## DREAMSPINNER, HISTORIC MOSES TAYLOR HOME

117 Diedrich Street
Eustis, Florida 32726
**Phone:** 352/589-8082 or 888/479-1229
**Fax:** 352/589-8860
**E-mail:** dreamspinner@cde.com
**Proprietor:** Jeano Broome
**Location:** 35 miles northwest of Orlando

Moses Taylor, Eustis' first town clerk, built this cross-gabled Victorian house with wraparound porch and decorative vergeboard in 1881. Surrounded by gardens and shaded by oaks, the National Register house retains an old-fashioned atmosphere while the grounds offer restful benches, ponds, antique roses, camellias, and azaleas. Guest rooms are furnished with antiques and English fabrics, and each room is accented with cut flowers and a bowl of fresh fruit. The Dreamspinner provides guests with a number of extra touches, including a coffee tray with newspaper delivered each morning and nightly turn-down service with chocolates. An English tea is served in the afternoon, and in the evening guests can gather for wine and cheese. In addition to on-site activities and a closet full of games, the inn can arrange for trolley and boat tours, golf and tennis outings, and the use of bicycles for exploring the area.

**Open:** Year round **Accommodations:** 5 guest rooms (4 with private baths); 1 is a suite **Meals:** full breakfast included; complimentary refreshments; restaurants nearby **Rates:** $105 to $150; 10% discount to National Trust members and National Trust Visa cardholders **Payment:** personal and traveler's checks **Restrictions:** children over 12 welcome **On-site activities:** new and antique books, croquet, games, bicycles, guided canoe trips, mystery weekends

# EVERGLADES CITY

**Nearby attractions:** Everglades, airboat and swampbuggy rides, boating and fishing excursions, Museum of the Everglades

## ON THE BANKS OF THE EVERGLADES...A BED AND BREAKFAST INN
201 West Broadway
Everglades City, Florida 34139
**Phone:** 941/695-3151 or 888/431-1977
**Fax:** 941/695-3335
**Website:** www.banksoftheeverglades.com
**E-mail:** patty@banksoftheeverglades.com
**Proprietors:** Patty Flick Richards and Bob Flick

Industrialist Barron Collier founded the Bank of the Everglades in 1923, having this imposing Greek Revival structure built in 1926 to house it. The first bank in Collier County, it was in use until the 1960s. Located in the heart of the town's historic district, the bank's solid construction has kept it intact through five hurricanes. Its 7,000 square feet today house an inviting bed-and-breakfast inn, owned and operated by a father-and-daughter team. Clever room names evoke the building's history. Small Shareholders and Small Business Loans rooms are singles; Loan Department, Trust Room, Checking Department, and Stocks and Bonds rooms are doubles. Rooms that accommodate up to four "investors" as this inn's guests are known, are the Board Room, Savings Department, Foreclosure Department, Mutual Funds Department, and the President's Suite, all with private baths, most with full kitchens. A full breakfast is served each morning in the original vault. Bicycles and fishing poles are available for investors' use and the innkeepers will gladly arrange fishing excursions.

**Open:** year round **Accommodations:** 11 guest rooms (5 with private baths); 6 are suites **Meals:** full breakfast included; complimentary refreshments; restaurants nearby **Rates:** $50 to $150; 10% discount to National Trust members and National Trust Visa cardholders **Payment:** AmEx, Visa, MC, Discover, personal and traveler's checks **Restrictions:** all good children welcome; no smoking; some pets accepted with prior notice **On-site activities:** games, bicycles, fishing poles

# GAINESVILLE

**Nearby attractions:** Hippodrome State Theater, cultural arts center, natural springs, canoeing, antiques hunting

## MAGNOLIA PLANTATION BED AND BREAKFAST INN

309 S.E. Seventh Street
Gainesville, Florida 32601
**Phone:** 352/375-6653 or 800/201-2379
**Fax:** 352/338-0303
**Website:** www.magnoliabnb.com
**Proprietors:** Joe and Cindy Montalto

Magnolia Plantation derives its name from the many magnolias that surround the inn, formerly known as the Baird Mansion. The innkeepers and many of their family members have carefully restored this 1885 Italianate house and its gardens, resulting in awards from the city of Gainesville for historic preservation and beautification. The interior of the house boasts an eight-foot-wide central hallway with a mahogany staircase. The parlor and adjoining library, with two of the ten fireplaces at the inn, are favorite gathering spots for guests. Bedrooms feature white iron, sleigh, four-poster, or canopied queen-size beds. Nearly all rooms have gas-log fireplaces and ceiling fans. Each room also contains a music center and a selection of romantic tapes. A full breakfast, evening wine, and stocked guest refrigerator are complimentary.

**Open:** year round **Accommodations:** 5 guest rooms with private baths **Meals:** full breakfast included; complimentary refreshments; candlelight dinners offered; restaurants nearby **Rates:** $85 to $125; 10% discount to National Trust members and National Trust Visa cardholders **Payment:** AmEx, Visa, MC, personal and traveler's checks **Restrictions:** children over 6 welcome; no smoking; no pets **On-site activities:** candlelight dinners, carriage rides, massage therapist on call

# INDIANTOWN

**Nearby attractions:** Barley Barber Swamp, airboat and swampbuggy rides, Owens Citrus Grove, Cracker House museum, Lake Okeechobee fishing, horseback riding

## SEMINOLE COUNTRY INN
15885 S.W. Warfield Boulevard
Indiantown, Florida 34956
**Phone:** 561/597-3777
**Fax:** 561/597-4691
**Website:** www.bbonline.com/fl/seminole/
**Proprietor:** Jonnie Williams

This little one-street town is only 30 miles northwest of Palm Beach, but it is as quiet and rural as that city is sprawling and glamorous. Indiantown is in the heart of citrus and cattle country and the Seminole Country Inn (named for the Indians who settled the area early in the nineteenth century) is in the middle of town. It was built in 1926 by S. Davies Warfield, who planned to make Indiantown the southern headquarters of his Seaboard Airline Railroad. The lobby retains the pecky cypress ceiling and hardwood floors specified in Warfield's original plans and the original fireplace, winding staircase, solid brass wall fixtures, and bronze chandeliers are the same as on opening day when Warfield's niece, Wallis Warfield, later the Duchess of Windsor, attended. History and fate intervened and Warfield's planned model city never came to complete fruition, but his inn remains, today offering guests 25 comfortable rooms that capture the essence of old Florida.

**Open:** year round **Accommodations:** 25 guest rooms with private baths; 3 are suites **Meals:** continental breakfast included; "oldest continually operated restaurant in the state" on premises **Rates:** $65 to $95; 10% discount to National Trust members and National Trust Visa cardholders **Payment:** AmEx, Visa, MC, Discover, personal and traveler's checks **Restrictions:** smoking limited **On-site activities:** butterfly garden, swimming pool, porch rocking

# JACKSONVILLE

**Nearby attractions:** Jacksonville Landing, historic districts, Cummer Art Museum and Gardens, Jacksonville Science Museum, antiques hunting, parks, tennis, swimming, beaches, Okefenokee Swamp, Gator Bowl, jazz festival

## HOUSE ON CHERRY STREET
1844 Cherry Street
Jacksonville, Florida 32205
**Phone:** 904/384-1999
**Fax:** 904/384-5013
**E-mail:** Houseoncherry@compuserve.com
**Proprietor:** Carol Anderson

This Colonial Revival home on the St. John's River was built in 1912. During World War II the Navy leased the residence, converting it into four apartments for military personnel. In 1975, the original floor plan was reestablished and, in 1989, the house's owner received a preservation award from the Jacksonville Historic Landmarks Commission. Today, the bed and breakfast is decorated with antiques, oriental rugs, tall case clocks, a large decoy collection, pewter, and collectibles. Bedrooms have sitting areas, and the canopied beds are covered with woven coverlets. Guests receive complimentary wine and hors d'oeuvres in the evening. A large screened porch looks out on landscaped grounds and the river beyond. The house is located in the historic Riverside section of Jacksonville. Within walking distance of three city parks, the inn can provide complimentary bicycles, kayaks, or canoes with notice.

**Open:** year round **Accommodations:** 4 guest suites with private baths **Meals:** continental-plus breakfast included; restaurants nearby **Rates:** $75 to $105 **Payment:** AmEx, Visa, MC, personal and traveler's checks **Restrictions:** children over 10 welcome; no smoking; no pets **On-site activities:** croquet, fishing

## PLANTATION MANOR INN
1630 Copeland Street
Jacksonville, Florida 32204
**Phone:** 904/384-4630
**Fax:** 904/387-0960
**Website:** www.bbonline.com/fl/plantation/
**Proprietors:** Kathy and Jerry Ray

Plantation Manor was built in 1905 on a high corner lot in the historic Riverside area of Jacksonville, only two blocks from the St. John's River. First owned by a real estate mogul and then a bank president, this elegant Neoclassical house is

distinguished by a full-height entry porch and first-floor wraparound porch supported by rows of massive Doric columns. Inside, crystal and brass chandeliers glow above antique furnishings and oriental carpets. Guest rooms feature either fireplaces or sitting areas, as well as telephones and cable television. Guests are invited to enjoy the lap pool, spa, and garden. Plantation Manor Inn also hosts small business meetings, weddings, and receptions, and features a romantic honeymoon suite.

**Open:** year round **Accommodations:** 9 guest rooms with private baths; 3 are suites **Meals:** continental or full breakfast included; complimentary refreshments; restaurants nearby **Rates:** $125 to $160; 10% discount offered to National Trust members or National Trust Visa cardholders **Payment:** AmEx, Visa, MC, DC, personal and traveler's checks **Restrictions:** children over 12 welcome; no smoking; no pets **On-site activities:** lap pool, spa

## KEY WEST

**Nearby attractions:** Ernest Hemingway Home and Museum, Audubon House and Gardens, Duval Street, theater, beaches, fishing, snorkeling, scuba diving, tennis

## HERON HOUSE
512 Simonton Street
Key West, Florida 33040
**Phone:** 305/294-9227 or 800/294-1644
**Fax:** 305/294-5692
**E-mail:** heronkyw@aol.com

Three old Key West houses combine to create the casually elegant Heron House, just one block from world-famous Duval Street. The house that dates to 1856 is one of the few remaining examples of Classical Revival architecture in Key West. The other two date to around 1900. There are porches, decks, and balconies galore helping private rooms merge with lush gardens in the central courtyard, where a swimming pool is surrounded by towering palms and the inn's trademark: sweet-scented orchids. With attention to artistic detail, the interior and exterior spaces blend and flow together, featuring rooms with walls of teak, oak, or cedar, granite baths with tile floors, and stained-glass transoms above French doors. Original, commissioned watercolors of the Keys, created by local artisans enrich each room in the inn. A low-profile, responsive staff helps create an atmosphere of luxury without pretense.

**Open:** year round **Accommodations:** 21 guest rooms with private baths; 13 are suites plus 2 apartments **Meals:** continental-plus breakfast included; complimentary refreshments; restaurants nearby **Rates:** $119 to $329 (seasonal); 10% discount to National Trust members and National Trust Visa cardholders **Payment:** AmEx, Visa, MC, CB, DC traveler's check **Restrictions:** children over 16 welcome; no smoking; no pets **On-site activities:** heated swimming pool, second-story sundeck, orchid gardens

## ISLAND CITY HOUSE HOTEL
411 William Street
Key West, Florida 33040
**Phone:** 305/294-5702 or 800/634-8230
**Fax:** 305/294-1289
**Proprietors:** Stanley and Janet Corneal

Island City House Hotel comprises three unique guest houses that share private tropical gardens laced with red brick pathways. The Island City House, built as a private home in the 1880s, was enlarged and opened as a hotel in 1912 for the arrival of the railroad in Key West. The Cigar House is a recently built cypress house modeled after the cigar factory that once stood on the site. The Arch House, ca. 1880, the only remaining carriage house on the island, is a two-story, gingerbread-encrusted building. All three buildings offer parlor suites individually furnished with antiques or in contemporary or casual island decors. Hardwood floors, ceiling fans, color television, telephones, and private baths are standard. Most rooms offer balconies or porches.

**Open:** year round **Accommodations:** 24 guest suites with private baths **Meals:** continental-plus breakfast included; restaurants nearby **Rates:** $95 to $155; 10% discount to National Trust members and National Trust Visa cardholders **Payment:** AmEx, Visa, MC, CB, DC, Discover, traveler's check, personal check for advance deposit only **Restrictions:** no pets **On-site activities:** swimming pool, sundecks, gardens

## WATSON HOUSE

525 Simonton Street
Key West, Florida 33040
**Phone:** 305/294-6712 or 800/621-9405
**Fax:** 305/294-7501
**Website:** www.keywestvacations.com
**Proprietors:** Joe Beres and Ed Czaplicki

The front double-decker veranda was one of the first areas that was restored in the 1980s to bring the Watson House back to its original Bahamian style. Built in 1860 by William and Susan Watson, the house was later sold and remodeled as a southern colonial mansion. After completing their restoration and expansion in 1987, the innkeepers received an award for preservation excellence from the Historical Florida Keys Preservation Board. Guest quarters blend tropical decor with Victorian romanticism using wooden paddle fans, wicker and rattan furnishings, floral patterns, and hardwood floors. A four-room apartment in the poolside cabana includes vaulted ceilings and a full kitchen. Guests relax in the swimming pool, heated spa, sundecks, and tropical gardens.

**Open:** year round **Accommodations:** 3 guest suites with private baths **Meals:** continental-plus breakfast included; restaurants nearby **Rates:** $105 to $390; 10% discount to National Trust members and National Trust Visa cardholders **Payment:** AmEx, Visa, MC, traveler's check **Restrictions:** not suitable for children; smoking limited; no pets **On-site activities:** heated swimming pool, spa, sunbathing

## WHISPERS BED AND BREAKFAST INN

409 William Street
Key West, Florida 33040
**Phone:** 305/294-5969
or 800/856-SHHH (800/856-7444)
**Fax:** 305/294-3899
**Website:** www.whispersbb.com
**Proprietor:** John Marburg

This house, listed in the National Register of Historic Places, was built by Gideon Lowe, the youngest son of one of Key West's earliest Bahamian settlers. Located on a sleepy, shaded street within view of the Gulf harbor, the structure is surrounded by a 30-block historic district of distinctive nineteenth-century buildings. The oldest section of the house (ca. 1845) retains numerous significant architectural details. A later section, dating to 1866, reflects a typical Greek Revival floor plan, with Victorian embellishments. The house exhibits Bahamian influences in its scuttles, porches, shuttered windows, and numerous doors—all features well suited to the tropics. Guests can relax on cool porches, in the lush garden, or in rooms quietly cooled by ceiling fans. Whispers has appeared in many publications, including *National Geographic Traveler* and *Colonial Homes*.

**Open:** year round **Accommodations:** 7 guest rooms (5 have private baths) **Meals:** full breakfast included; restaurants nearby **Rates:** $85 to $175; 10% discount offered to National Trust members and National Trust Visa cardholders **Payment:** AmEx, Visa, MC, Discover, personal and traveler's checks **Restrictions:** smoking limited

---

## LAKE WALES

**Nearby attractions:** Bok Tower Gardens, Cypress Gardens, Frank Lloyd Wright building at Florida Southern College, Black Hills Passion Play, tennis, golfing, beaches, central Florida attractions

### CHALET SUZANNE COUNTRY INN AND RESTAURANT

U.S. Highway 27 and County Road 17A
3800 Chalet Suzanne Drive
Lake Wales, Florida 33853-7060
**Phone:** 813/676-6011 or 800/433-6011
**Fax:** 813/676-1814
**Website:** www.chaletsuzanne.com
**E-mail:** info@chaletsuzanne.com
**Proprietors:** Carl and Vita Hinshaw
**Location:** 4 miles north of Lake Wales

A winding road leads travelers to Chalet Suzanne's pastel-tinted cottages. Surrounded by cobblestone walkways and courtyards with fountains, the cottages are attached at odd angles and topped with a storybook assortment of steeples, gables, belfries, and cupolas. Built in various stages throughout the 1920s, 1930s,

and 1940s, the cottages display a decor that is a little bit gingerbread, a little bit baroque, a touch medieval, and a touch Viking. Each guest room is uniquely proportioned and furnished; and fruits, candies, fresh flowers, complimentary sherry, and fine toiletries are standard. Chalet Suzanne is famous for its sprawling restaurant and delicious soups, which have been canned on the premises for more than 30 years. The inn has Mobil four-star and AAA three-diamond ratings and has been listed by *Women's Day* as one of the 10 most romantic spots for a honeymoon in Florida. Chalet Suzanne was voted one of the Top 10 Country Inns for 1991–1992 by Uncle Ben's.

**Open:** year round **Accommodations:** 30 guest rooms with private baths; 4 are suites **Meals:** full breakfast included; restaurants on premises **Wheelchair access:** 2 guest rooms **Rates:** $159 to $219 **Payment:** AmEx, Visa, MC, CB, DC, Discover, personal and traveler's checks **Restrictions:** additional charge for pets **On-site activities:** swimming, lawn games, fishing in private lake, jogging, rowboat, private airstrip, cannery, gift shop, antiques shop, ceramic studio

# MICANOPY

**Nearby attractions:** Payne's Prairie State Park, University of Florida, Hippodrome Theater, Cross Creek, Marjorie Kinnan Rawlings Home, freshwater springs, antiques hunting, canoeing, horseback riding

## HERLONG MANSION

402 N.E. Cholokka Boulevard
P.O. Box 667
Micanopy, Florida 32667
**Phone:** 800/HERLONG (800/437-5664)
**Fax:** 352/466-3322
**Website:** www.afn.org/~herlong/
**Proprietor:** H. C. (Sonny) Howard, Jr.

The Herlong Mansion was originally a two-story Victorian house built in 1845. In 1910 it was encased in brick in a Colonial Revival design. Four two-story, carved-wood, Corinthian columns support the double porch that spans the front facade. Inside, the mansion boasts leaded-glass windows, 10 fireplaces, mahogany inlaid oak floors, 12-foot-high ceilings, walnut and tiger oak paneling, and floor-to-ceiling windows in the dining room. Each guest room offers different amenities, such as fireplaces, claw-foot tubs, private porches, antique brass beds, or leaded-glass windows. All provide private baths. A full breakfast features homemade pastries. Set back from the street, the mansion is surrounded by gardens and old oak and pecan trees.

**Open:** year round **Accommodations:** 12 guest rooms with private baths; 4 are suites **Meals:** full breakfast included; complimentary refreshments; catered meals available; restaurants nearby **Rates:** $65 to $170; 10% discount to National Trust members and National Trust Visa cardholders **Payment:** Visa, MC, personal and traveler's checks **Restrictions:** no smoking; no pets **On-site activities:** complimentary bicycles

## MOUNT DORA

**Nearby attractions:** Lake Dora, national forest, water sports, golfing, fishing, antiques hunting, historic Mount Dora, seasonal festivals, Disney World, Sea World, Universal Studios

### LAKESIDE INN
100 North Alexander Street
Mount Dora, Florida 32757
**Phone:** 352/383-4101
**Fax:** 352/735-2642
**Website:** www.lakeside-inn.com
**General Manager:** Karin Bernard

Follow a quiet lane lined with lampposts to the gentle shoreline of Lake Dora, home of the Lakeside Inn. Originally opened in 1883 as a 10-room hotel, the inn was expanded over the years, ultimately reaching its current proportions in the early 1930s with honored guest Calvin Coolidge on hand to dedicate the Gables and Terrace wings. Listed in the National Register of Historic Places, this charming refuge features guest rooms and public spaces warmly appointed in the English country style. The current proprietors continue to refine the inn to reflect the traditions and hospitality of the 1920s and 1930s. Guest rooms and suites are comfortably furnished and provide terrycloth bathrobes. Guests can indulge in a number of activities at the inn, from swimming to tennis or shopping at the nearby Mount Dora boutiques and antiques shops. The Lakeside Inn, a member of Historic Hotels of America, is convenient to all of central Florida's attractions.

**Open:** year round **Accommodations:** 88 guest rooms with private baths **Meals:** continental breakfast included; restaurants on premises; room service **Wheelchair access:** yes **Rates:** $90 to $205; 10% discount to National Trust members and National Trust Visa cardholders **Payment:** AmEx, Visa, MC, DC, CB, Discover **Restrictions:** smoking limited **On-site activities:** swimming pool, tennis courts, boat rentals, croquet

# OCALA

**Nearby attractions:** Ocala historic district, horse farms, Silver Springs Park and glass-bottom boat rides, Appleton Art Museum, antiques hunting, shopping, golfing, jai alai, hiking, bicycling, tennis, canoeing, and natural springs swimming

## SEVEN SISTERS INN
820 S.E. Fort King Street
Ocala, Florida 34471
**Phone:** 904/867-1170
or 800/250-3496
**Fax:** 352/867-5266
**E-mail:** sistersinn@aol.com
**Proprietors:** Bonnie
Morehardt and Ken Oden

Located in the heart of the city's historic district, this grand Queen Anne house was built in 1888 for a family named Scott. Later owners were the Childs; their six daughters and the Scott family are the namesakes of the Seven Sisters' guest rooms. Laura Ashley prints, Battenburg lace, country quilts, gingham checks, antiques, and canopy or wrought-iron beds adorn these rooms. Full gourmet breakfasts are served in the French Monet room, and may include such treats as baked eggs with caviar or French toast stuffed with three cheeses. The Club Room offers diverting games, and the wraparound porch provides solitude. In 1986, after undergoing extensive work, the house was voted "Best Restoration Project" by the Florida Trust for Historic Preservation. The Seven Sisters Inn, has been voted one of the best twelve inns in America by *Country Inns Bed and Breakfast* magazine and has been featured in many others, including *Southern Living, Glamour,* and *Conde Nast Traveler.*

**Open:** year round **Accommodations:** 9 guest rooms with private baths; 6 are suites **Meals:** full breakfast included; complimentary refreshments; candlelight dinners available; restaurants nearby **Rates:** $125 to $185; 10% discount to National Trust members and National Trust Visa cardholders Sunday through Thursday, excluding holidays **Payment:** AmEx, Visa, MC, Discover, CB, DC, personal and traveler's checks **Restrictions:** children over 12 welcome; no smoking; no pets **On-site activities:** bicycles, massage therapy, books, games, television with VCR

# ORANGE PARK

**Nearby attractions:** St. John's River, historic St. Augustine, Jacksonville, museums, theater, dog track, golfing, swimming, boating, tennis

## THE CLUB CONTINENTAL

2143 Astor Street
Orange Park, FL 32073
**Phone:** 904/264-6070 or 800/877-6070
**Fax:** 904/264-4044
**Website:** www.bbonline.com
**Proprietors:** Caleb Massee and Karrie Stevens
**Location:** 25 miles south of Jacksonville

For more than 70 years the Club Continental property has been preserved by the descendants of Caleb Johnson, founder of the Palmolive Soap company. The 1923 Mediterranean-style mansion, originally known as Mira Rio, offers bed-and-breakfast accommodations individually decorated with an Old World ambience. Guest rooms overlook the river or the immaculate formal gardens and courtyard. At the center of the club is the dining room, open to overnight guests and club members, where French and American cuisine is served. The lush grounds surrounding the house, shaded by moss-draped Live Oaks and dotted with palms and magnolias, include swimming pools, tennis courts, and a riverside walk. A marina is available for guests arriving by boat (with advance reservations), and across from the club is the Riverhouse Pub, a pre-Civil War cottage that has been restored and now offers refreshments and entertainment.

**Open:** year round **Accommodations:** 7 guest rooms with private baths; 1 is a suite; 1 is an apartment **Meals:** continental breakfast included; restaurant on premises; restaurants nearby **Rates:** $65 to $160 **Payment:** AmEx, Visa, MC, DC, Discover, traveler's check **Restrictions:** No pets **On-site activities:** 3 swimming pools, 7 tennis courts, Riverhouse Pub

# ORLANDO

**Nearby attractions:** Disney World, Sea World, Universal Studios, Church Street Station, Kennedy Space Center, river cruises, boating, golfing, fishing, tennis

## COURTYARD AT LAKE LUCERNE

211 North Lucerne Circle, East
Orlando, Florida 32801
**Phone:** 407/648-5188 or 800/444-5289
**Fax:** 407/246-1368
**Website:** www.travelbase.com/destinations/Orlando/LakeLucerne
**Proprietors:** Sam and Eleanor Meiner, Charles Meiner, Paula Bowers

Overlooking the lake and encircling a lush garden, this inn is a cluster of four historic buildings. The Norment-Parry Inn, built in 1883, is Orlando's oldest home. Each of the guest rooms in this clapboard Victorian has been decorated by a different designer; the results range from flowered and airy to opulent and dramatic. The Wellborn is one of Orlando's finest examples of Art Deco design, with its pink stucco, corner and porthole windows, and wrought-iron screen doors. Elegant and streamlined guest suites bring back the 1930s in every detail from colors to furnishings. At the I.W. Phillips House, guests enjoy luxurious rooms furnished in authentic Belle Epoque style. Ceiling fans and a Tiffany window enhance the atmosphere of this late nineteenth-century antebellum-style house complete with broad two-story verandas. The adjoining Dr. Phillips House, dating to 1893, provides an additional six elegantly appointed guest rooms, each with a marble bathroom and double whirlpool tub.

**Open:** year round **Accommodations:**
**Meals:** continental-plus breakfast included; restaurant on premises; restaurants nearby
**Rates:** $95 to $225 **Payment:** AmEx, Visa, MC, DC, traveler's check **On-site activities:** tropical garden with fountain, walking, jogging

## MEADOW MARSH BED & BREAKFAST

940 Tildenville School Road (SR 545)
Winter Garden, Florida 34787
**Phone:** 407/656-2064 or 888/656-2064
**Fax:** 407/654-0656
**Website:** bbonline.com
**Proprietors:** John and Cavelle Pawlack
**Location:** 15 miles west of downtown Orlando

Luther F. Tilden, an early founder of Florida's citrus industry, built this house in 1877. Noted Orlando architect F. H. Trimble designed the massive renovation in 1900 that transformed the original "cracker-style" house into the Neoclassical mansion it is today. Meadow Marsh is nestled on 12 lush acres where visitors can stroll the spacious lawn among azaleas, palms, and live oaks while on the lookout for a variety of wildlife, including owls, eagles, otters, or even a fox. The cozy guest rooms come with antique furnishings and a quaint country atmosphere; the suites also feature two-person whirlpool tubs. A three-course breakfast is served each morning, and special prearranged guest packages with a romantic touch are available, from candy and flowers to a country picnic or private candlelight dinner for two. Meadow March is close to central Florida's premier attractions.

**Open:** year round **Accommodations:** 5 guest rooms with private baths; 3 are suites **Meals:** full breakfast included; complimentary refreshments, restaurant on premises; restaurants nearby **Wheelchair access:** limited **Rates:** $95 to $199 **Payment:** Visa, MC, traveler's check **Restrictions:** children over 12 welcome; no smoking; no pets **On-site activities:** croquet, games and cards, sitting room for reading, swings, badminton, adjacent to biking path

---

## PALM BEACH

**Nearby attractions:** Worth Avenue, Atlantic Ocean beaches, museums, tennis, golfing, swimming, fishing, sailing, boating, horseback riding, polo, jai alai, greyhound racing, ballet, opera, theater, antiques hunting, art galleries, boutiques, planetarium, botanical gardens, sculpture gardens, sightseeing cruises, scuba diving, snorkeling

## PALM BEACH HISTORIC INN

365 South County Road
Palm Beach, Florida 33480
**Phone:** 561/832-4009
**Fax:** 561/832-6255
**Website:** www.palmbeachhistoricinn.com
**E-mail:** palmbeachhistoricinn.worldnet.att.net
**Proprietor:** Chris Lohman

This 1923 Palm Beach landmark building was designed by the architectural firm of Harvey and Clarke, which also designed the town hall. The stucco building with Mission-style parapet and red-tile roof, on a prominent corner lot, is most notable for its arcade of round arches with Tuscan columns that extends around its two street sides. Charming, intimate accommodations are individually appointed with coordinating paints, papers, and fabrics. Each room offers a private bath, refrigerator, color cable television, and telephone. A continental-plus breakfast is delivered to guest rooms, along with the morning newspaper. This historic inn is one block from the beach and two from the shops of world-famous Worth Avenue.

**Open:** year round **Accommodations:** 13 guest rooms with private baths; 4 are suites **Meals:** continental-plus breakfast included; complimentary refreshments; restaurants nearby **Rates:** $75 summer to $225 winter **Payment:** AmEx, Visa, MC, CB, DC, Discover, traveler's check **Restrictions:** smoking limited; no pets

# RUSKIN

**Nearby attractions:** railroad museum, historic house tours, Portavant Indian mound, Little Manatee River, canoeing, manatee watching, bayfront beach

### RUSKIN HOUSE BED AND BREAKFAST
120 Dickman Drive, S.W.
Ruskin, Florida 33570-4611
**Phone:** 813/645-3842
**Website:**
ruskinhouse@compuserve.com
**Proprietor:** Arthur M. Miller

A. P. Dickman was a cofounder in 1906 of this planned Christian Socialist community that was based on the principles of the British thinker John Ruskin. Dickman's house was built in 1911 incorporating the Queen Anne style—asymmetry, varied roof lines, a tower—with Colonial Revival elements, most notably a columned, double-tiered gallery. The house is built entirely of heart pine. The interior boasts a massive dogleg staircase, hardwood floors, high ceilings, and original wall coverings. Every room is furnished with period antiques and oriental rugs; rocking chairs grace the verandas. Both verandas look over a view of the Ruskin Inlet, which winds past the natural waterfront. The second-story veranda is screened and offers a double hammock. Breakfast is served in the dining room on Haviland china. The three-acre property affords quiet walks, tropical glades, and small flowering gardens. In season, guests are welcome to pick fruit from the pink grapefruit, navel orange, tangerine, meyer lemon, and key lime trees on the property.

**Open:** year round **Accommodations:** 3 guest rooms (2 have private baths); 1 is a suite **Meals:** continental breakfast included; restaurants nearby **Rates:** $55 to $75; 10% discount to National Trust members and National Trust Visa cardholders **Payment:** AmEx, Visa, MC, personal and traveler's checks **Restrictions:** children over 6 welcome; no smoking; no pets **On-site activities:** salt-water fishing from front yard, hammock, porch sitting

## ST. AUGUSTINE

**Nearby attractions:** Castillo de San Marcos, Lightner Museum, Ripley's Believe It or Not Museum, alligator farm, beaches, boating, swimming, Intra-coastal Waterway

### ST. FRANCIS INN
279 St. George Street
St. Augustine, Florida 32084
**Phone:** 904/824-6068 or 800/824-6062
**Fax:** 904/810-5525
**Website:** www.st.francisinn.com
**Proprietor:** Joseph P. Finnegan

Built in 1791 by Gaspar Garcia, the St. Francis Inn is a Spanish Colonial structure encircling a private courtyard; balconies adorn the second floor. The first two stories are original; the third, fronted by a mansard roof, was added in 1888. The building is constructed of coquina, a local building material made of compressed sea shells and corals. Because the inn was built at the intersection of two streets that are not perpendicular, it is a trapezoidal building—there are no square or rectangular rooms in the inn! The St. Francis is situated in the center of the National Register historic district of St. Augustine, the oldest city on the North American continent. The courtyard garden contains banana trees, bougainvillea, jasmine, and other tropical flowers and shrubs. Attractive, comfortable accommodations range from single rooms to three-room suites. Some rooms have working fireplaces, kitchenettes, or two-person whirlpool tubs; all are centrally air conditioned.

**Open:** year round **Accommodations:** 11 guest rooms with private baths; 2 are suites **Meals:** full breakfast included; complimentary refreshments; restaurants nearby **Rates:** $85 to $179; 10% discount to National Trust members and National Trust Visa cardholders **Payment:** AmEx, Visa, MC, Discover, DC, personal and traveler's checks **Restrictions:** children over 10 welcome; no smoking; no pets **On-site activities:** swimming pool, bicycles

# SANFORD

**Nearby attractions:** historic Sanford, Centennial Park, St. John's River, Wekiva River, Blue Spring State Park, Central Florida Zoo, Lake Monroe, Mt. Dora, Ocala National Forest, Cape Canaveral Wildlife Refuge, Walt Disney World, Sea World, Universal Studios

## HIGGINS HOUSE VICTORIAN BED AND BREAKFAST

420 South Oak Avenue
Sanford, Florida 32771
**Phone:** 407/324-9238 or 800/584-0014
**Fax:** 407/324-5060
**Website:** www.castlegate.net/higginshouse.com
**Proprietors:** Walter and Roberta Padgett

Higgins House was built in 1894 by James Cochran Higgins, Sanford's railroad superintendent. He chose to build in the Queen Anne style with cross gables, patterned wood shingles, bay windows, turned-post and spindle work, and a second-story round window. The Padgetts purchased the house, in a state of disrepair, in 1990 and performed most of the restoration and landscaping that has resulted in today's bed-and-breakfast inn. Three guest rooms with private baths are in the main house: The Queen Anne Room overlooks the garden, the Wicker Room has a bay window, and the Victorian Country Room has an antique brass bed and stenciled wood floor. Guests are invited to relax in the parlor, the pub, the front porch, the upstairs veranda, or in the hot tub. The adjacent Cochrans Cottage offers a two-bedroom, two-bath suite with full kitchen, living room, and porch. Also on premises is a gift and antiques shop.

**Open:** year round **Accommodations:** 4 guest rooms with private baths; 1 is a suite **Meals:** continental-plus breakfast included; complimentary refreshments; restaurants nearby **Rates:** $80 to $150; 10% discount to National Trust members and National Trust Visa cardholders **Payment:** AmEx, Visa, MC, Discover, personal and traveler's checks **Restrictions:** children welcome in cottage; no smoking; no pets **On-site activities:** hot tub, gardens, porch, bird watching, hiking, canoeing

# GEORGIA

## AMERICUS

**Nearby attractions:** Plains/
Jimmy Carter National Historic Site, restored high school visitor's center, state
welcome center at Plains, Habitat for Humanity headquarters, Americus National
Register historic district, original Tog Shop Catalog outlet, Andersonville
National Historic Site, Civil War Village of Andersonville, National POW
Museum, Rural Georgia Telephone Museum, Providence Canyon, Westville
1850s village, shopping in award-winning Main Street town, golfing, tennis

## WINDSOR HOTEL
125 West Lamar Street
Americus, Georgia 31709
**Phone:** 912/924-1555 or 800/678-8946
**General Manager:** Frank Santoro
**Sales and Marketing Director:** Barbara Taylor
**Location:** 100 miles southwest of Atlanta; 9 miles east of Plains;
11 miles southwest of Andersonville

The 1892 Windsor Hotel is Georgia's Victorian secret—a fairytale castle of
towers, balconies, arches, round-topped windows, and a three-story atrium
lobby. Restored in 1991 at a cost of nearly $6 million, the Windsor received a
preservation award from the National Trust for Historic Preservation and has
been featured in *Southern Living* among other publications. Located in the city's
National Register historic district, the hotel offers round-tower suites, period-
style bed chambers, breezy verandas with wicker rockers, a lively pub, and a grand
dining room. The top of the round tower is the Bridal Chamber with a half-

canopy king bed and sitting area. On the third floor are the Carter Presidential and Jessica Tandy suites, appointed as are all the rooms, with ceiling fans, carved oak beds, and period-style furnishings. The ambience is reminiscent of the Old South, but with all the modern conveniences: air conditioning, cable television, private baths, and room service. A complimentary full breakfast is touted as having the creamiest grits in Georgia. The Windsor Hotel is a member of Historic Hotels of America.

**Open:** year round **Accommodations:** 53 guest rooms with private baths; 4 are suites **Meals:** full breakfast included; restaurant on premises; murder-mystery and madrigal dinners; restaurants nearby **Rates:** $83 to $189; 10% discount to National Trust members and National Trust Visa cardholders **Payment:** AmEx, Visa, MC, Discover, personal and traveler's checks **Restrictions:** no pets **On-site activities:** Floyd's Pub, The Blue Note Lounge (weekend blues club), boutique shopping, tour planning, specialty packages including weddings (rent the whole hotel for ceremony, guest rooms, dinners, and reception)

---

# ATHENS

**Nearby attractions:** Cobbham Historic District, historic downtown, University of Georgia, parks, Georgia Museum of Art, State Botanical Gardens

## MAGNOLIA TERRACE GUEST HOUSE
277 Hill Street
Athens, Georgia 30601
**Phone:** 706/548-3860 or 800/891-1912
**Fax:** 706/369-3439
**Website:** www.ATHENS/GA.com/magnoliaterrace/
**Proprietor:** Shelia Rabun

This spacious Colonial Revival house, built in 1912, is located in the heart of downtown near the University of Georgia. Distinctive architectural features such as Corinthian columns, beveled-glass entrance, and original fireplace mantels showcase the area's talented craftsmen. Comfortably furnished with antiques, each of the seven unique guest rooms offers a large private bath with period claw-foot tub and modern shower or whirlpool. Beautifully appointed public areas are equally suited to intimate conversation and festive functions. Parking is available on premises, a porch is offered for smokers, and children and pets are welcome. Magnolia Terrace is less than a mile from the city's vibrant downtown with shops and restaurants.

**Open:** year round  **Accommodations:** 7 guest rooms with private baths **Meals:** continental-plus breakfast included; complimentary refreshments; restaurants nearby **Wheelchair access:** yes **Rates:** $90 to $150; 10% discount to National Trust members and National Trust Visa cardholders  **Payment:** AmEx, Visa, MC, personal and traveler's checks **Restrictions:** smoking limited **On-site activities:** library with many National Trust publications, porch sitting

## ATLANTA

**Nearby attractions:** Swan House, governor's mansion, state capitol, Margaret Mitchell house, Museum of Science and Technology, Ansley Park, Inman Park, Buckhead, Woodruff Arts Center, Underground Atlanta, World of Coke, Zoo Atlanta, High Museum, World Congress Center, Piedmont Park, Stone Mountain, botanical gardens, symphony, shopping at Lenox Square and Phipps Plaza

### SHELLMONT BED AND BREAKFAST LODGE
821 Piedmont Avenue, N.E.
Atlanta, Georgia 30308
**Phone:** 404/872-9290
**Fax:** 404/872-5379
**Website:** www.INBOOK.com/shell.html
**Proprietors:** Ed and Debbie McCord

A Colonial Revival house designed by renowned architect W. T. Downing in 1891, the Shellmont was owned by a single family until 1982, when it was acquired by the McCords. A thorough restoration has returned to the house original paint colors, period wallpapers, and fancy painted finishes. Stained, leaded, and beveled glass abound. The house is particularly noted for its hand-carved woodwork (both inside and out) depicting seashells, ribbons, garlands, flowers, fruits, and mythical creatures. Rare stenciling in geometric patterns graces the Turkish Corner—a room filled with oriental furnishings and memorabilia. This commendable restoration has gained a National Register listing and city landmark status for the Shellmont. Guests enjoy complimentary beverages, chocolates, and breakfast. Furnishings—beds, armoires, chairs—are Victorian.

Wicker-laden verandas overlook manicured lawns and gardens, including a Victorian fish pond.

**Open:** year round **Accommodations:** 5 guest rooms with private baths; separate carriage house **Meals:** full breakfast included; complimentary beverages; restaurants nearby **Rates:** $89 to $160 **Payment:** AmEx, Visa, MC, DC, personal and traveler's checks **Restrictions:** children over 12 welcome; no smoking; no pets **On-site activities:** games, three verandas with rockers

## CLARKESVILLE

**Nearby attractions:** Chattahoochee National Forest, Tallulah Falls, Helen, Appalachian Trail, Dahlonega, lakes, hiking, white-water rafting, boating, mountain biking, horseback riding, tennis, golfing, gold panning, antiques hunting

### BURNS-SUTTON INN
855 Washington Street
Clarkesville, Georgia 30523
**Phone:** 706/754-5565
**Fax:** 706/754-9698
**Website:** www.georgiamagazine.com/burns-sutton
**Proprietor:** Jaime G. Huffman

Built in 1901 by master carpenters Rush and Cornelius Church for Dr. and Mrs. J. K. Burns, this spacious three-story inn is located in Clarkesville's historic district. Listed in the National Register of Historic Places, the inn showcases

Victorian style in both architectural design and room furnishings. Fine craftsmanship is evident in the wraparound porches, seven brick chimneys and fireplaces, paneled pocket doors, stained-glass windows and doors, and heart pine floors, ceilings, and woodwork. Guest rooms, enhanced by 12-foot ceilings, feature period furnishings; gas fireplaces and canopied beds are in some rooms. A complete breakfast is served daily; the inn's restaurant serves dinner Tuesday through Saturday and Sunday brunch. The inn is situated on an acre of green lawn and country gardens amid towering magnolias, oaks, and hemlocks. The property, recipient of three diamonds from AAA, is within walking distance of Clarkesville's town square with shopping and dining.

**Open:** year round **Accommodations:** 7 guest rooms (5 have private baths); 2 are suites **Meals:** full breakfast included; complimentary refreshments; restaurant on premises; restaurants nearby **Rates:** $65 to $125 **Payment:** Visa, MC, personal and traveler's checks **Restrictions:** children over 12 welcome; no smoking; no pets **On-site activities:** English-style gardens, patio, porch sitting, arrangements made for local golfing, horseback riding, whitewater rafting, fishing, canoeing, kayaking, and bicycling

## MACON

**Nearby attractions:** historic district walking tours, museum houses, antiques hunting, Grand Opera House

### 1842 INN
353 College Street
Macon, Georgia 31201
**Phone:** 912/741-1842 or 800/336-1842
**Fax:** 912/741-1842
**Website:** the1842inn@worldnet.att.net
**Proprietors:** Phillip Jenkins and Richard Meils

Listed in the National Register of Historic Places, the 1842 Inn is a classic example of southern Greek Revival architecture, with its full-colonnaded facade that continues around the sides of the house. Public and guest rooms are in this antebellum mansion and an adjoining Victorian house that share a courtyard and garden. The 21 guest rooms, parlors, and library are tastefully designed with fine English antiques, oriental carpets, tapestries, and paintings. Some bedrooms feature canopied beds, working fireplaces, and whirlpool tubs. An array of services include concierge, nightly turn-down, and complimentary in-room breakfast. Guests are offered access to an exclusive private dining and health club. Equally suited to corporate retreats and romantic getaways, the 1842 Inn is a member of Historic Hotels of America and rates four diamonds from AAA and four stars from Mobil.

**Open:** year round **Accommodations:** 21 guest rooms with private baths **Meals:** continental-plus breakfast included; full breakfast optional; complimentary refreshments; complimentary access to private dining club; restaurants nearby **Wheelchair access:** yes **Rates:** $125 to $185; 10% discount to National Trust members and National Trust Visa cardholders **Payment:** AmEx, Visa, MC, personal check **Restrictions:** children over 12 welcome; smoking limited; no pets **On-site activities:** gift shop, courtyard and garden, whirlpool tubs; VIP guest memberships to local country club

---

# ST. SIMONS ISLAND

**Nearby attractions:** historic St. Simons and Sea Island, golfing, tennis, shopping

## LITTLE ST. SIMONS ISLAND
P.O. Box 1078
St. Simons, Georgia 31522
**Phone:** 912/638-7472
**Fax:** 912/634-1811
**Website:** www.pactel.com.au/lssi
**E-mail:** lssi@mindspring.com
**Proprietor:** Debbie McIntyre

Little St. Simons Island is a secluded, unspoiled, 10,000–acre barrier island along the Georgia coast. Purchased for its lumber in the early 1900s by the owner of the Eagle Pencil Company, Little St. Simons Island proved better suited to a hunting and bird–watching retreat. Still privately owned by the same family, the island now accommodates guests in four separate buildings. Built in 1917, the Hunting Lodge remains the heart of the resort, serving as its dining and social centers; it also offers two guest rooms filled with rustic furniture and family memorabilia. In the lobby is a massive fireplace and vintage bar. The other houses provide a variety of guest lodgings with fireplaces, porches, and decks in natural woodland settings. *Forbes, House Beautiful, Gourmet,* and *Atlanta Magazine* have praised Little St. Simons Island. With never more than 24 visitors sharing the island, it becomes a guest's private retreat.

**Open:** year round **Accommodations:** 15 guest rooms with private baths; 1 is a suite **Meals:** all meals and refreshments provided on premises **Wheelchair access:** 1 room **Rates:** $225 to $540; 10% discount to National Trust members and National Trust Visa cardholders June through September **Payment:** Visa, MC, personal and traveler's checks **Restrictions:** children over 6 welcome October through May, children of all ages welcome June through September; no smoking; no pets **On-site activities:** expertly guided fly-fishing and angling excursions, bird-watching, horseback riding, hiking, bicycling, canoeing, boating, shelling, swimming, sunbathing, interpretive natural history tours, private boat docking

## SAUTEE

**Nearby attractions:** state parks, arts and community center with museum and gallery, historic district

## STOVALL HOUSE
1526 Highway 225 North
Sautee, Georgia 30571
**Phone:** 706/878-3355
**Website:** www.georgiamagazine.com/sh
**Proprietor:** Hamilton Schwartz
**Location:** 5 miles southeast of Helen

Constructed in 1837, the Stovall House was originally a one-story farmhouse with two rooms, each with a fireplace, on either side of a central passage known as a dogtrot hallway. The doors and mantels are made of black walnut taken from the property. William I. Stovall bought the house in 1893, making numerous changes that included the addition of three dormers to create a second floor and a wing to house the dining room and kitchen. Restored as an inn by the current owner in 1983, the Stovall House has been recognized by the Georgia Trust for Historic Preservation and by the Georgia Mountain Regional Planning Commission. Wall stenciling, handmade curtains, family antiques, and a serene mountain setting combine to put guests at their ease. The house, situated on a knoll surrounded by 26 acres of farmland, provides views of the valley and mountains in all directions.

**Open:** year round **Accommodations:** 5 guest rooms with private baths **Meals:** continental breakfast included; restaurant on premises serves dinner **Wheelchair access:** limited **Rates:** $75 to $80; 10% discount offered to National Trust members and National Trust Visa cardholders **Payment:** Visa, MC, personal and traveler's checks **Restrictions:** smoking limited **On-site activities:** walking, bird-watching, boccie

# SAVANNAH

**Nearby attractions:** historic district, River Street, City Market, museums, galleries, beach, riverfront, Fort Pulaski, Savannah Wildlife Refuge, tennis, golfing, deep-sea fishing, antiques hunting

## ELIZA THOMPSON HOUSE
5 West Jones Street
Savannah, Georgia 31401
**Phone:** 912/236-3620 or 800/348-3978
**Fax:** 912/238-1920
**Website:** www.bbonline.com
**E-mail:** Elizath@aol.com

Eliza Thompson, a striking red-haired widow, had this Federal mansion built in 1847. Its styling and architectural details, inside and out, reflect the gentility that pervaded Savannah in the mid-nineteenth century. The facade is distinguished by decorative eaves brackets and filigreed wrought-iron porch and balcony railings. The Eliza Thompson House couples its love for the past (evident in gleaming heart pine floors and antique and reproduction furnishings) with modern comforts and conveniences such as private baths, telephones, and color televisions in the historic house and the courtyard addition (originally the carriage house). Guests will enjoy the fragrant landscaped courtyard with fountain and water sculptures, where afternoon refreshments are often served. The parlor provides a refined setting for evening sherry. The inn, located in the city's National Register historic district, has received three diamonds from AAA and three stars from Mobil.

**Open:** year round **Accommodations:** 23 guest rooms with private baths **Meals:** full breakfast included; complimentary refreshments; restaurants nearby **Rates:** $89 to $189 **Payment:** AmEx, Visa, MC, personal and traveler's checks **Restrictions:** children over 12 welcome; no smoking; no pets

## FOLEY HOUSE INN
14 West Hull Street
Savannah, Georgia 31401
**Phone:** 912/232-6622 or 800/647-3708
**Website:** www.bbonline.com/forward/ga/savannah/foely/index.html
**Proprietors:** Mark A. Moore and Inge Svensson Moore

Two Savannah townhouses combine to create the Foley House Inn in the historic district of the city. Built in 1863 and 1896, the houses have been meticulously restored by master artisans. Each guest room is a seamless blend of traditional furnishings and contemporary pleasures. Antique furniture, silver, rugs, and engravings selected from around the world enhance rooms equipped with working fireplaces, whirlpool baths, and color televisions able to play the many selections in the inn's film library. Breakfast is served in the privacy of guest rooms, in the sunny courtyard, or in the newly expanded lounge. Wine, evening cordials, and tea are served daily in the parlor. Evening turn-down, shoeshine, and concierge services are standard at Foley House, which has been rated as one of the 10 most romantic inns by *Vacations* magazine.

**Open:** year round **Accommodations:** 19 guest rooms with private baths **Meals:** continental-plus breakfast included; complimentary refreshments; restaurants nearby **Rates:** $135 to $250; 10% discount to National Trust members and National Trust Visa cardholders **Payment:** AmEx, Visa, MC, personal and traveler's checks **Restrictions:** smoking limited; no pets **On-site activities:** golf or tennis by arrangement

### LION'S HEAD INN

120 East Gaston Street
Savannah, Georgia 31401
**Phone:** 912/232-4580 or 800/355-5466
**Fax:** 912/232-7422
**Website:** the-lions-headinn.com
**E-mail:** lionshead@syscnn.com
**Proprietor:** Christy Dell'Orco

This three-story 9,000-square-foot townhouse, built in 1883 for the William Wade family, is traditionally styled with dentils at roof and porch cornices and gently arched windows. A wraparound porch is supported by filigreed wrought-iron columns and railings. The fine materials used in the house's construction have been preserved: hand-carved marble mantels, detailed wood and plaster moldings, hardwood floors, a Waterford crystal chandelier in the dining room, and a French bronze chandelier in the parlor. Guest rooms are furnished with nineteenth-century American Federal antiques, king- and queen-size four-poster beds, fireplaces, cable television, and telephones. Guests are welcome in the parlor, library, dining room, and courtyard. The innkeeper serves a traditional English tea, plus wine and cheese each afternoon in the parlor or on the veranda. The elegant Lion's Head Inn has been featured in *Country Inns.*

**Open:** year round **Accommodations:** 6 guest rooms with private baths; 2 are suites **Meals:** continental-plus breakfast included; complimentary refreshments; restaurants nearby **Wheelchair access:** 1 room **Rates:** $105 to $160; 10% discount to National Trust members and National Trust Visa cardholders **Payment:** AmEx, Visa, MC, personal and traveler's checks **Restrictions:** no smoking; no pets **On-site activities:** house tours

## MAGNOLIA PLACE INN

503 Whitaker Street
Savannah, Georgia 31401
**Phone:** 912/236-7674 or 800/238-7674
**Fax:** 912/236-1145
**Website:** www.MagnoliaPlaceInn.com
**E-mail:** B.B.Magnolia@MCI2000.com
**Proprietors:** Rob and Jane Sales; Kathy Medlock

In the heart of Savannah's historic district stands this imposing Second Empire house, the birthplace of Pulitzer Prize-winning poet Conrad Aiken. It was built in 1878 for a descendent of Thomas Weyward, a signer of the Declaration of Independence. Magnolia Place features a mansard roof and two-story verandas overlooking fashionable Forsyth Park. The foyer has an elaborate parquet floor, marquetry below the wainscoting, and an open staircase illuminated by a skylight 30 feet above. Each guest room is individually furnished with English antiques, period prints, and Chinese porcelains. All rooms contain queen or king four-poster beds, fireplaces, private baths, and a television with VCR and a wide selection of videos. Breakfast is served in the parlor, on a silver tray delivered to guest rooms, on one of the many porches, or in the courtyard. Cordials and pralines placed bedside during evening turn-down service are standard at Magnolia Place. The innkeepers are happy to help guests with sightseeing arrangements and dinner or symphony reservations.

**Open:** year round **Accommodations:** 15 guest rooms with private baths **Meals:** continental-plus breakfast included; complimentary refreshments; restaurants nearby **Rates:** $135 to $240 **Payment:** AmEx, Visa, MC, Discover, DC, personal and traveler's checks **Restrictions:** no smoking; no pets **On-site activities:** relaxing on porches and courtyard, honeymoon packages

## THE MANOR HOUSE

201 West Liberty Street
Savannah, Georgia 31401
**Phone:** 912/233-9597 or 800/462-3595
**Website:** www.bbonline.com/ga/savannah/manorhouse/index.html
**Proprietor:** Richard F. Carlson

Built for the Lester Byrd family in the 1830s, this private home was used to house federal officers during Sherman's "march to the sea." Tucked away in the residential section of Savannah's famous historic district, The Manor House is the city's oldest building south of Liberty Street. The inn is furnished with fine English and American antiques and oriental rugs. Architectural integrity has been preserved as evidenced by the warmly polished heart-pine floors, floor-to-ceiling windows, and handsome double parlors with two fireplaces. Each guest accommodation in this intimate, all-suites inn features a master bedroom with private bath and separate sitting room with gas fireplace. Some suites contain double whirlpool tubs. Fresh flowers, bath salts, down-filled pillows, and nightly turn-down service with brandy and chocolates are just a few of the comforts found in the inn. Breakfast is served in suites, on the veranda, or in the main parlor. The Manor House is within easy walking distance of Bull Street and the riverfront.

**Open:** year round **Accommodations:** 5 guest suites with private baths **Meals:** continental breakfast included; honor bar; restaurants nearby **Rates:** $185 to $225; 10% discount to National Trust members and National Trust Visa cardholders **Payment:** AmEx, Visa, MC, personal check **Restrictions:** children over 12 welcome; no smoking; no pets **On-site activities:** televisions with VCRs

## RIVER STREET INN

115 East River Street
Savannah, Georgia 31401
**Phone:** 912/234-6400 or 800/678-8946
**Fax:** 912/234-1478
**Proprietor:** Jack Busser

The River Street Inn was built in 1817 on the banks of the Savannah River for the storing, sampling, grading, and exporting of raw cotton. The structure quickly grew too small to meet the needs of the booming cotton industry, but being hemmed in by the bluff to the south and the Savannah River to the north, the only direction for expansion was up. Three floors were added to the building in 1853, but access was needed to each level in order to move the cotton bales in and out. As a result, a series of alleys and walkways were created on the bluff and bridges were built to provide street access to every floor. Known as "Factor's Walk" after the factors who graded the cotton, the alleys are one of the River

Street Inn's most unique features. Today, the inn welcomes guests to 44 authentically appointed guest rooms, many with French balconies and floor-length windows overlooking the river. Complimentary breakfast, an afternoon wine reception, evening turn-down service, and use of a nearby athletic club are standard amenities at the River Street Inn, a member of Historic Hotels of America.

**Open:** year round **Accommodations:** 44 guest rooms with private baths **Meals:** continental breakfast included; complimentary refreshments; three restaurants on premises; restaurants nearby **Rates:** $89 to $179; 10% discount to National Trust members and National Trust Visa cardholders **Payment:** AmEx, Visa, MC, Discover **On-site activities:** concierge service for arranging tours and reservations, complimentary passes to athletic club

---

# SENOIA

**Nearby attractions:** Warm Springs, Callaway Gardens and Butterfly Center, driving tour of 113 places listed in the National Register, museums, tennis, golfing, antiques hunting, crafts shops, day trips to Atlanta

## THE VERANDA
252 Seavy Street
Box 177
Senoia, Georgia 30276-0177
**Phone:** 770/599-3905
**Fax:** 770/599-0806
**Proprietors:** Jan and Bobby Boal
**Location:** 30 miles south of Atlanta airport

The Veranda, formerly known as the Hollberg Hotel, is a 1906 neoclassical building constructed of heart of pine, its wraparound porch supported by grand

columns. The restored property is listed in the National Register of Historic Places. Among the hotel's many distinguished guests have been statesman William Jennings Bryan and *Gone With the Wind* author Margaret Mitchell, who interviewed Civil War veterans during their annual conventions here. The bookcases in the parlor once graced President McKinley's Ohio law offices. All nine guest rooms contain special touches, such as handmade quilts and antique armoires. Guests enjoy hearty complimentary breakfasts; delicious dinners are served by reservation. A collection of old and new kaleidoscopes, a 1930 Wurlitzer player piano, and an early twentieth-century pump organ provide entertainment. The picturesque town of Senoia was the setting for the films *Fried Green Tomatoes* and *The War.*

**Open:** year round **Accommodations:** 9 guest rooms with private baths **Meals:** full breakfast included; five-course candlelit dinner on premises by reservation; restaurants nearby **Wheelchair access:** 2 guest rooms and public rooms **Rates:** $99 to $150 **Payment:** AmEx, Visa, MC, personal and traveler's checks **Restrictions:** children must be supervised by parents **On-site activities:** bird-watching, nature walks, player piano and pump organ, gift shop, kaleidoscope collection

## THOMASVILLE

**Nearby attractions:** plantation and house tours, historic district, Paradise Park, Rose Test Gardens, Birdsong Nature Center, Gulf coast, golfing, crafts shops, antiques hunting, greyhound racing

### EVANS HOUSE BED AND BREAKFAST
725 South Hansell Street
Thomasville, Georgia 31792
**Phone:** 912/226-1343 or 800/344-4717
**Fax:** 912/226-0653
**Proprietors:** John and Lee Puskar

Located in the Parkfront Historic District, directly across from 27-acre Paradise Park, this late Victorian house is in a transitional style, combining the asymmetry of the Victorian era with the simpler formality of the emerging Neoclassical style. Robert R. Evans built the house for his family in 1898. The second story was added a few years later, then, after suffering the effects of a fire in 1908, the house was again remodeled. Four individually decorated guest rooms are now available,

each with cozy seating area, private bath, and ceiling fan. The bedrooms, entrance hall, library, dining room, and parlor are furnished with antiques and contemporary pieces. Guests are served a full breakfast. Turn-down service and complimentary bicycles are available. Evans House is ideal for corporate retreats, offering all necessary amenities and corporate rates.

**Open:** year round **Accommodations:** 4 guest rooms with private baths; 2 are suites **Meals:** full breakfast included; complimentary refreshments; restaurants nearby **Rates:** $75 to $125 **Payment:** personal and traveler's checks **Restrictions:** children over 12 welcome; no smoking; small pets acceptable, please inquire **On-site activities:** bicycling

# HAWAII

Poipu, Kauai

Lahaina, Maui

## POIPU BEACH, KAUAI

**Nearby attractions**: Spouting Horn, Waimea Canyon, Na Pali Coast, Fern Grotto, Old Koloa Town, beach, water sports, free tennis and pool at neighboring club, golfing, sightseeing tours by helicopter and boat

## POIPU BED AND BREAKFAST INN

2720 Hoonani Road
Poipu Beach, Kauai, Hawaii 96756-9635
**Phone:** 808/742-1146 or 800/552-0095 or 800/22POIPU (800/227-6478)
**Fax:** 808/742-6843
**Website:** www.poipu.net
**E-mail:** Poipu@aloha.net
**Proprietor:** Dotti Cichon
**Location:** 13 miles south of Lihue Airport

This simple, yet elegant wooden house was built in 1933 for a former Kauai County mayor and was moved to its present site in 1969. Its unique all-fir interior and beautiful hand-hewn arch in the living room qualify it as an excellent example of Hawaiian plantation-style architecture. The sympathetically added lanais (porches) and 1987 restoration have won awards, including the Hawaii Visitors

Bureau's prestigious Kahili Award and a Great American Home Award from the National Trust. Furnished with white wicker, pine antiques, tropical prints, and an authentic carousel horse in each room, Poipu Bed and Breakfast Inn offers pampering amenities such as robes, beach towels, fine

toiletries, cool tropical drinks, free videos, concierge services, and an exotic garden where guests can often pick their breakfast fruit fresh from the trees. Guest rooms provide beautiful ocean or garden views.

**Open:** year round **Accommodations:** 11 rooms with private baths; 2 are suites **Meals:** continental-plus breakfast included; complimentary refreshments; restaurants nearby **Wheelchair access:** 1 suite, gathering room, and breakfast area **Rates:** $120 to $255; weekly discounts; 10% discount offered to National Trust members or National Trust Visa cardholders **Payment:** AmEx, Visa, MC, CB, DC, Discover, personal and traveler's checks **Restrictions:** no smoking; no pets; guests are expected to observe local custom of removing shoes before entering **On-site activities:** afternoon tea on lanai, free popcorn and videos on in-room VCR, library, croquet, Trivial Pursuit and Scrabble in the evening

## LAHAINA, MAUI

**Nearby attractions:** Old Lahaina Town historical walks, dining, luaus, antiques hunting, shopping, art galleries, fine dining, sailing, snorkeling, whale watching

### LAHAINA INN
127 Lahainaluna Road
Lahaina, Maui, Hawaii 96761-1502
**Phone:** 808/661-0577 or 800/669-3444
**Fax:** 808/667-9480
**Website:** www.LahainaInn.com
**E-mail:** INNTOWN@aloha.net
**Proprietor:** Rick Ralston  **Manager:** Paul Gomez

The building now known as the Lahaina Inn was built by Tomezo Masuda in 1938 for his Maui Trading Company, a general merchandise store. It was a popular gathering place for servicemen stationed on Maui during World War II. Sold in 1949, the building subsequently changed hands several times and suffered subdivision and a disastrous fire in the 1960s. Rick Ralston bought the neglected building in 1986 and began transforming it into a small luxury inn that has been called "One of the Best Country Inns" by *Glamour.* Twelve individually appointed guest rooms present vignettes of historic Hawaii through rich fabrics and wall coverings, antique leaded-glass lamps, lace curtains, oriental carpets, and antique furnishings. The property is also home to David Paul's Lahaina Grill, voted "Best Maui Restaurant" by the readers of *Honolulu* magazine for the past four years.

**Open:** year round **Accommodations:** 12 guest rooms with private baths; 3 are suites **Meals:** continental breakfast included; restaurant on premises; restaurants nearby **Rates:** $99 to $169; 10% discount to National Trust members and National Trust Visa cardholders **Payment:** AmEx, Visa, MC, Discover, personal and traveler's checks **Restrictions:** children over 15 welcome; no smoking; no pets **On-site activities:** fine dining, antiques shopping, whale-watching from porches

# IDAHO

## STANLEY

**Nearby attractions:** Centennial State Park, Sawtooth National Recreation Area, Salmon River, Sun Valley, hiking, camping, fishing, mountain lakes with endangered salmon, fish hatchery, ghost towns, white-water rafting and canoeing, mountain biking, shopping

● Stanley

## IDAHO ROCKY MOUNTAIN RANCH
H.C. 64, Box 9934
Stanley, Idaho 83278
**Phone:** 208/774-3544
**Fax:** 208/774-3477
**E-mail:** idrocky@cyberhighway.net
**Proprietor:** Rozalys Smith

In 1930, carpenters handcrafted the lodge and surrounding cabins of the Idaho Rocky Mountain Ranch from native lodgepole pines. At that time it was an invitation-only guest ranch. Now open to the public, cozy lodge rooms and authentic duplex log cabins are handsomely decorated with log furniture fashioned by early craftsmen. Massive rock fireplaces warm the public rooms in the lodge as well as each log cabin. All accommodations provide private baths. The ranch is nestled in the heart of the Sawtooth National Recreation Area, surrounded by the Sawtooth and White Cloud mountain ranges of central Idaho. Encircling the ranch are hundreds of miles of trails through meadows and up mountains to trout-filled lakes. Full breakfasts and dinners can be provided. The dining room specializes in country cuisine featuring fresh Idaho trout, lamb, steaks, and vegetarian entrees.

**Open:** June through September and Thanksgiving through March **Accommodations:** 21 guest rooms with private baths; 17 are in log cabins **Meals:** full breakfast and dinner included on modified American Plan (MAP); picnic baskets available; restaurants nearby **Rates:** $85 to $240 MAP **Payment:** Visa, MC, Discover, personal and traveler's check **Restrictions:** no smoking; no pets **On-site activities:** horseback riding, natural hot springs swimming pool, hiking, walking, fishing, wildlife watching, rock climbing, horseshoes, volleyball, mountain biking

# ILLINOIS

Lake Forest ●

Evanston ●

●Pekin

● Springville

● Carlinville

●Jerseyville

Waterloo
●

## CARLINVILLE

**Nearby attractions:** Historic Macoupin Courthouse, Macoupin County Historical Society, nation's largest collection of Sears' mail-order catalog homes, Beaver Dam State Park, Blackburn College, Route 66, Springfield area Lincoln sites, state capitol, Frank Lloyd Wright home, archeological sites at Cahokia Mounds and Kampsville, riverboat casinos, golfing, antiques hunting

## VICTORIA TYME INN BED AND BREAKFAST
511 East First South Street
Carlinville, Illinois 62626
**Phone:** 217/854-8689
**Fax:** 217/854-5122
**E-mail:** victyme@accunet.net
**Proprietors:** Jodie and Jeff Padgett

The main part of this Italianate house was constructed in 1878 by William Burgdorff, a prominent Carlinville citizen. Decorated with antiques and period furnishings, the drawing room, sitting room, and library feature high ceilings, fireplaces, and carved woodwork. Upstairs are the guest rooms with high ceilings, large windows, antiques, private baths, and queen-size beds. The Burgdorff Bedchamber also includes a huge claw-foot tub. At the rear of the house is a two-story ell that had been built earlier as a separate house. This 1868 home was the birthplace of author Mary Hunter Austin, who was also a pioneering naturalist, feminist, and activist for Native American rights. Secluded from the other guest rooms, the Mary Austin Suite features a queen-size bed, whirlpool tub for two, and a separate sitting room with a daybed. A full breakfast is served in the dining room, highlighted by a pressed-tin ceiling and built-in china cabinet, or, in good weather, on the porch overlooking the formal garden.

**Open:** year round **Accommodations:** 4 guest rooms with private baths; 1 is a suite **Meals:** full breakfast included; complimentary refreshments; restaurants nearby **Rates:** $67.50 to $130; 10% discount to National Trust members and National Trust Visa cardholders **Payment:** Visa, MC, Discover, personal and traveler's checks **Restrictions:** children over 12 welcome; no smoking; no pets **On-site activities:** board games, croquet, television with VCR and video library

## EVANSTON

**Nearby attractions:** cultural and educational activities at Northwestern University, Chicago sightseeing, lakefront parks

### THE HOMESTEAD
1625 Hinman Avenue
Evanston, Illinois 60201
**Phone:** 708/475-3300
**Proprietor:** David Reynolds

Evanston architect Philip Danielson designed and built The Homestead in 1927 as a colonial-style residence and hotel. The Depression and subsequent war years necessitated that he and his wife, Ruby, a noted interior decorator, run the hotel themselves. Under their 30-year direction, The Homestead reigned as one of Evanston's premier residences and hotels. Mrs. Herbert Hoover and Sinclair Lewis were among its guests. Lewis included reflections of his Homestead experiences in *Work of Art*, published two years after his visit. The Homestead lies close to Lake Michigan, Northwestern University, and downtown Evanston, and borders Evanston's historic lakeshore district. Its hotel rooms and furnished monthly apartments afford a quiet retreat in a busy metropolitan area.

**Open:** year round **Accommodations:** 35 guest rooms, 55 apartments, all with private baths **Meals:** continental breakfast included; restaurant on premises for dinner; restaurants nearby **Rates:** $85 to $95 **Payment:** personal and traveler's checks **Restrictions:** smoking limited; no pets

# JERSEYVILLE

**Nearby attractions:** Center for American Archaeology, Mississippi River, St. Louis, MO, Springfield, IL, antiques hunting, golfing, tennis

## THE HOMERIDGE BED AND BREAKFAST
1470 North State Street
Jerseyville, Illinois 62052
**Phone:** 618/498-3442
**Proprietors:** Sue and Howard Landon
**Location:** 1 mile north of Jerseyville; 45 minutes from St. Louis airport

The Homeridge is a 14-room Italianate structure with deep eaves, decorative brackets, and a third-story, square cupola. It was built in 1867 by Cornelius B. Fisher. Senator Theodore S. Chapman purchased the home in 1891 and it remained in the Chapman family until 1960. Today, as a bed and breakfast, The Homeridge retains its original woodwork, 12-foot-high ceilings, pocket doors, crown molding, and elegant, hand-carved, curved stairway. The inn offers a choice of king-size, twin, or antique double beds. Each room, with its expansive view of the countryside, has a private bath. Favorite places to relax include the pillared front porch and private swimming pool.

**Open:** year round **Accommodations:** 4 guest rooms with private baths **Meals:** full breakfast included; complimentary refreshments; restaurants nearby **Rates:** $75; 10% discount to National Trust members and National Trust Visa cardholders **Payment:** AmEx, Visa, MC, personal and traveler's checks **Restrictions:** children over 14 welcome; no smoking; no pets **On-site activities:** swimming pool, 20 acres for hiking, walking, jogging, and cross-country skiing

# LAKE FOREST

**Nearby attractions:** Lake Forest Beach, Six Flags Great America, Arlington International Racecourse, botanical gardens, historic estates, Lake Michigan activities

## DEER PATH INN

255 East Illinois Road
Lake Forest, Illinois 60045
**Phone:** 847/234-2280 or 800/678-8946
**Fax:** 847/234-3352
**General Manager:** Michael Lama

Historic Lake Forest lies on the shore of Lake Michigan, just 30 miles north of Chicago. Near the town's Historic Market Square shopping district, Deer Path Inn made its debut in 1929 and grew popular as a retreat for Chicago's elite and visiting guests. Designed by Chicago architect William C. Jones, the half-timbered and stucco Tudor building was modeled after the mid-fifteenth-century Manor House in Chiddingstone, England. Authentic details, including stone fireplaces, leaded-glass windows, beamed ceilings, and an extensive collection of English antiques and artifacts evoke both the charm of Renaissance England and the comfort of country manor houses. Accordingly, each of the inn's guest rooms is named for a property of the British National Trust. The Deer Path Inn is listed in the National Register of Historic Places and is a member of Historic Hotels of America.

**Open:** year round **Accommodations:** 54 guest rooms; 27 are suites **Meals:** breakfast buffet included; restaurant and pub on premises **Rates:** $145 to $300; 10% discount to National Trust members and National Trust Visa cardholders **Payment:** AmEx, Visa, MC, Discover **On-site activities:** health club privileges

---

# PEKIN

**Nearby attractions:** Illinois River, Dirksen Congressional Center, University of Illinois Medical School, Par-a-dice Riverboat Gambling, golfing, fishing

## HERGET HOUSE BED AND BREAKFAST

420 Washington Street
Pekin, Illinois 61554
**Phone:** 309/353-4025
**Proprietor:** Richard T. Walsh

Listed in the National Register of Historic Places, this Neoclassical home was built in 1912, in an era known in England as Edwardian. Accordingly, the house is furnished in an elegant English country style. Bedrooms—named for King Edward himself and some of his contemporaries—feature antiques, four-poster or sleigh beds, fine linens, down comforters and pillows, and writing desks. Guests are invited to have breakfast on the sunporch, take tea in the music room, relax in the living room, or browse through an eclectic selection of books. Herget House, with its four grand columns supporting a large triangular pediment, commands its setting on an acre of grounds. Off-street parking is available.

**Open:** year round **Accommodations:** 5 guest rooms (4 have private baths); 1 is a suite **Meals:** full breakfast included; restaurants nearby **Rates:** $85 to $125; 10% discount to National Trust members **Payment:** personal check **Restrictions:** no smoking; no pets (resident dog and rabbit) **On-site activities:** reading

---

## SPRINGFIELD

**Nearby attractions:** State Capitol, State House, State Museum, State Library, Frank Lloyd Wright-designed Dana Thomas House, Lincoln home and law offices, Old State Capitol, Governor's Mansion

### INN AT 835
835 South Second Street
Springfield, Illinois 62704
**Phone:** 217/523-4466 or 888/217-4835
**Fax:** 217/523-4468
**Website:** www.innat835.com
**Proprietors:** Court and Karen Conn

Listed in the National Register of Historic Places, the Inn at 835 is Springfield's oldest apartment house. Miss Bell Miller, a turn-of-the-century businesswoman, had it built in 1909 by George Helmle. The classically styled, three-story building is accentuated by a fanlighted entryway, dentiled cornice, and balustraded balconies. Constructed during the Arts and Crafts Movement, the interior is graced with exquisite oak detailing and massive fireplaces. All accommodations in the completely renovated building have private baths with plush towels, hand-milled French soaps, soft linens, cable television, and private telephones. Buffet breakfasts are accompanied by the morning newspaper. The inn can accommodate parties, receptions, or business meetings for up to 150 people, fulfilling catering, audio-visual, and entertainment needs.

**Open:** year round **Accommodations:** 7 guest rooms with private baths **Meals:** full breakfast included; complimentary refreshments; restaurants nearby **Wheelchair access:** yes **Rates:** $92.50 to $145; 10% discount to National Trust members and National Trust Visa cardholders **Payment:** AmEx, Visa, MC, CB, DC, Discover, personal and traveler's checks **Restrictions:** children over 12 welcome; no smoking; no pets **On-site activities:** relaxing by sitting room fireplace, veranda sitting

---

## WATERLOO

**Nearby attractions:** historic district, St. Louis, Mississippi River, Cahokia Mounds World Heritage Site, Waterloo Winery, Illinois Caverns, Fort de Chartres site, Prairie du Rocher Historic Village, seasonal festivals

**SENATOR RICKERT RESIDENCE
BED AND BREAKFAST**
216 East Third Street
Waterloo, Illinois 62298
**Phone:** 618/939-8242
**E-mail:** eweil@dpc.net
**Proprietors:** Ed and
Kathi Weilbacher

Located in Waterloo's historic district, this bed and breakfast was constructed in 1866 as a one-story brick house. Senator Joseph Rickert enlarged the house in 1897 to its present size. Fascinated with the French Second Empire style of architecture, he added a mansard roof, tower, widow's walk, and gingerbread detailing. The house is currently undergoing restoration and offers one guest suite. The spacious bedroom boasts antiques once owned by the senator's wife's family. Through pocket doors, the bedroom opens to a bright sitting room featuring a three-piece parlor set. The large bath includes a footed tub with oak rail. The country kitchen, formal dining room, and brick patio are available for enjoying full breakfasts that feature house specialties such as spinach and sausage strata.

**Open:** year round **Accommodations:** 1 guest suite with private bath **Meals:** full breakfast included; restaurants nearby **Rate:** $75; 10% discount offered to National Trust members and National Trust Visa cardholders **Payment:** Visa, MC, Discover, personal and traveler's checks **Restrictions:** no smoking; no pets

# INDIANA

## COLUMBUS

**Nearby attractions:** historical and contemporary architecture tours, outlet shops, golfing, hiking, walking and bicycling trails

### COLUMBUS INN BED AND BREAKFAST
445 Fifth Street
Columbus, Indiana 47201
**Phone:** 812/378-4289
**Fax:** 812/378-4289

The Columbus Inn was built in 1895 as the Columbus City Hall, the hub of this scenic small town for many years. The building housed public offices, a town library, a market house, and an auditorium for everything from dances to basketball and poultry shows. After standing empty for several years, this National Register building has been transformed into the Columbus Inn, the only historic lodging in downtown Columbus. Guest rooms are furnished with reproduction furnishings and are decorated with bright, bold wall coverings and paint schemes. Public rooms include the elegant lobby, lounges, and a library. In the heart of downtown, the Columbus Inn has meeting rooms fully equipped for business functions, and has been awarded four diamonds by AAA.

**Open:** year round  **Accommodations:** 34 guest rooms with private baths; 5 are suites **Meals:** full breakfast included; complimentary refreshments; lunch and dinner for groups by reservation; restaurants nearby **Wheelchair access:** yes **Rates:** $105 to $250; 10% discount to National Trust members and National Trust Visa cardholders **Payment:** AmEx, Visa, MC, CB, DC, Discover, personal and traveler's checks **Restrictions:** smoking limited; no pets **On-site activities:** library

## GOSHEN

**Nearby attractions:** Notre Dame University, Goshen College, Shipshewana auction and flea market, Elkhart County fairgrounds, Mennonite Relief Sale, factory outlets, golfing, fishing, boating, hiking, bicycling

### PRAIRIE MANOR BED AND BREAKFAST

66398 U.S. 33 South
Goshen, Indiana 46526
**Phone:** 219/642-4761 or 800/791-3952
**Fax:** 219/642-4762
**Website:** www.prairiemanor.com
**Proprietors:** Jean and Hesston Lauver
**Location:** 5 miles southeast of Goshen

Prairie Manor's four comfortable guest accommodations are housed in this spacious country manor-style home built in 1925 by a Wall Street banker. It was designed by the renowned New York architect Julius Gregory, widely regarded as a transitional architect. During his 42-year career, he designed the "Ideal House" for *House and Garden* and the "Pacesetter House" for *House Beautiful*, as well as numerous churches. At Prairie Manor the living room replicates the builder's favorite painting at the Metropolitan Museum of Art—an English baronial hall featuring a fireplace big enough to walk into. Guests also enjoy a wood-paneled library with inviting window seats and fireplace. Interesting architectural details abound throughout the estate, including arched doorways, wainscoting, and a hidden compartment for the family silver. Breakfast is served in the dining room or sunroom. Prairie Manor is situated on 12 acres of lawns, shade trees, flowers, meadowland, and woods.

**Open:** year round **Accommodations:** 4 guest rooms with private baths **Meals:** full breakfast included; complimentary refreshments; restaurants nearby **Rates:** $70 to $100 **Payment:** Visa, MC, personal and traveler's checks **Restrictions:** no smoking; pets may stay in horse barn **On-site activities:** library, swimming pool, hiking and jogging trail

# INDIANAPOLIS

**Nearby attractions:** Monument Circle, RCA Dome, Indianapolis Zoo, Indiana State Museum, Eiteljorg Museum, theaters, dining

## RENAISSANCE TOWER HISTORIC INN
230 East Ninth Street
Indianapolis, Indiana 46204
**Phone:** 317/261-1652 or 800/676-7786
**Fax:** 317/262-8648

Constructed in 1922 by the E. G. Spink Company, this six-story structure was one of the earliest high-rise apartment buildings in Indianapolis. Edgar G. Spink, founder of this company, was a leader in the development of multifamily housing in this city. Originally named The Spink and later renamed The Jefferson, the building was redeveloped in the mid-1980s by Borns Management Corporation and is now the Renaissance Tower Historic Inn. Located in the heart of the prestigious Historic St. Joseph District, the inn features 80 fully furnished studio suites. Complete kitchens with full-size appliances and all necessary tableware, utensils, and cookware are standard. Each graciously appointed bedroom features a cherry four-poster bed and spacious living rooms are decorated in reproduction Queen Anne cherry furnishings. The inn provides free local calls and voice mail, fully equipped laundry facilities, complimentary parking, and cable television.

**Open:** year round **Accommodations:** 80 guest suites with private baths **Meals:** fully equipped kitchens in each suite; restaurants nearby **Rates:** $75 to $250; 10% discount to National Trust members and National Trust Visa cardholders; weekly and monthly rates available **Payment:** AmEx, Visa, MC **Restrictions:** smoking limited; no pets

---

# MADISON

**Nearby attractions:** historic district, house tours, Ohio River walk, Clifty Falls State Park, antiques hunting

## SCHUSSLER HOUSE BED AND BREAKFAST
514 Jefferson Street
Madison, Indiana 47250
**Phone:** 812/273-2068 or 800/392-1931
**Website:** the-mid-west-web.com/schussler.htm
**Proprietors:** Judy and Bill Gilbert

In 1849 physician Charles Schussler had this combination home and office built in a blend of the popular Federal and Greek Revival architectural styles. Three spacious, elegantly appointed guest rooms feature antique and reproduction furniture, coordinating fabrics and wall coverings, reading areas, and private baths. Guests may also relax in the front parlor with soft music and an abundance of reading materials. A full breakfast is served in the sun-filled dining room and may feature such treats as apple flan or caramel-glazed French toast. Additional amenities include afternoon refreshments and evening turn-down service. The Ohio River is within walking distance of Schussler House.

**Open:** year round **Accommodations:** 3 guest rooms with private baths **Meals:** full breakfast included; complimentary refreshments; restaurants nearby **Rates:** $89 to $139; 10% discount to National Trust members and National Trust Visa cardholders **Payment:** Visa, MC, personal and traveler's checks **Restrictions:** children over 12 welcome; no smoking; no pets

# ROCKVILLE

**Nearby attractions:** downtown Rockville and historic district, Turkey Run State Park, Shades State Park, Billie Creek Village, Raccoon Lake, museums, Parke County Covered Bridge Capital, 32 covered bridges throughout county, Bridgeton, Mansfield, crafts shops, tennis, canoeing

## SUITS US BED AND BREAKFAST
514 North College
Rockville, Indiana 47872
**Phone:** 317/569-5660 or 888-4-SUITS-US
**Proprietors:** Marty and Bev Rose

Built in 1883 by the Beadle family, this white clapboard house later became the property of Isaac and Juliet Strauss. Both Strausses were editors with the *Rockville Tribune* and Juliet was later a writer for *Ladies Home Journal*. Her pen name became "The Country Contributor" and it was during this time that their house guests included Woodrow Wilson, Senator John Kern, Annie Oakley, and James Whitcomb Riley. With tall windows and decorative eave brackets from the Italianate era and a two-story entry portico supported by two massive columns from the Neoclassical, this house handsomely blends architectural styles. Three charming guest rooms feature antique furnishings; a family suite has bedroom, bath, kitchen, and living area. It will sleep up to six people and has a private entrance. Guests are invited to enjoy the inn's formal living room, the library, exercise equipment, and spacious front porch.

**Open:** year round **Accommodations:** 4 guest rooms with private baths; 1 is a suite **Meals:** full breakfast included; complimentary refreshments; restaurants nearby **Rates:** $55 to $125 **Payment:** personal and traveler's checks **Restrictions:** no smoking; no pets **On-site activities:** exercise porch, video library, front-porch sitting

# RUSHVILLE

**Nearby attractions:** six covered bridges and the Moscow Covered Bridge Festival; Metamora with 180 crafts shops; Knightstown and Centerville for antiques hunting (more than 400 shops); golfing, dining

## GREYSTONE INN BED AND BREAKFAST

525 North Main Street
Rushville, Indiana 46173
**Phone:** 765/932-5922 or 888/276-0022
**Fax:** 765/932-2192
**Website:** www.thegreystoneinn.com
**Proprietors:** Ranny and Denise Grady

The Greystone Inn was lumber baron Jasper Case's mansion that he built in 1918. After his death, it was purchased by the Wyatt-Moore families and served as a mortuary for more than 40 years. The innkeepers bought the property in 1996, converting it into a hospitable inn offering spiritual as well as physical refreshment. The 25-room Indiana stone mansion shows a strong Prairie influence in design: low-pitched, hipped roof, gables and dormers; widely overhanging eaves; and one-story porches that emphasize the house's horizontal lines. Inside there are eight Rookwood Pottery-tiled fireplaces and six guest rooms, each named for a flower and individually decorated with antiques. One of the suites has two fireplaces and bath with whirlpool tub. Public areas include the music room, fellowship room, and a recreation and fitness room. A full breakfast is served.

**Open:** year round **Accommodations:** 6 guest rooms (3 have private baths); 2 are suites **Meals:** full breakfast included; complimentary refreshments; restaurants nearby **Rates:** $84 to $132.25; 10% discount to National Trust members and National Trust Visa cardholders **Payment:** Visa, MC, personal and traveler's checks **Restrictions:** children over 14 welcome; no smoking; no pets **On-site activities:** recreation and fitness room, snooker

# IOWA

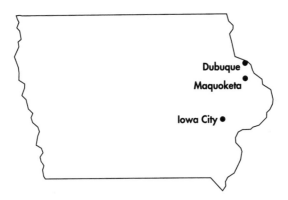

## DUBUQUE

**Nearby attractions:** five historic districts, Mississippi River paddlewheel cruises, Cable Car Square, Woodward Riverboat Museum, National Rivers Hall of Fame, gambling, dog track, parks, walking trails, golfing, downhill and cross-country skiing

### THE RICHARDS HOUSE
1492 Locust Street
Dubuque, Iowa 52001
**Phone:** 319/557-1492
**Website:** www.the-richards-house.com
**Proprietor:** David C. Stuart

Constructed in 1883 by manufacturer and financier B. B. Richards, this four-story Stick Style house with Eastlake effects is one of the finest and most original homes in Dubuque. Occupied by the same family until 1989, The Richards House features nearly ninety stained-glass windows, eight ornate fireplaces, seven types of woodwork, ten patterns of embossed wallcoverings, original chandeliers, hand-painted tiles, and elaborate built-in cupboards. Guest rooms are furnished with period antiques. Most have concealed television sets and telephones, and working fireplaces. Bathrooms feature original fixtures. Queen-size beds and air conditioning are standard. Guests are served a full breakfast by the fireplace in the dining room, surrounded by pocket doors with stained-glass inserts, a bay window, and ornate fretwork. A music room with grand piano is open to guests at this National Register–listed inn.

**Open:** year round **Accommodations:** 6 guest rooms (4 have private baths); 1 is a suite **Meals:** full breakfast included; complimentary refreshments; restaurants nearby **Rates:** $40 to $95; 10% discount to National Trust members and National Trust Visa cardholders **Payment:** AmEx, Visa, MC, CB, DC, Discover, personal and traveler's checks **Restrictions:** smoking limited

---

## IOWA CITY

**Nearby attractions:** University of Iowa, Kinnick Stadium, MacBride Museum, University of Iowa Art Museum, Amana Colonies Amish community of Kalona, city park, Herbert Hoover birthplace and library

### HAVERKAMPS LINN STREET HOMESTAY BED AND BREAKFAST
619 North Linn Street
Iowa City, Iowa 52245
**Phone:** 319/337-4363
**Fax:** 319/354-7057
**Proprietors:** Clarence and Dorothy Haverkamp

John Koza emigrated from Czechoslovakia in 1868 when he was 19. His future wife, Barbara, had emigrated in 1857 at the age of 4. After they were married, they built this handsome house on North Linn Street in 1907. The house's design owes much to the Prairie style, evident in its hipped roof with widely overhanging eaves and massive square porch supports. Original floor plans and building contracts and old photographs indicate that little has been changed inside or out during the house's nearly 90 years and six family changes. Today's bed and breakfast

welcomes children and, in fact, offers a crib for small visitors. Wake-up coffee is offered along with a full breakfast. Off-street parking is available.

**Open:** year round **Accommodations:** 3 guest rooms share a bath **Meals:** full breakfast included; restaurants nearby **Rates:** $30 to $45; 10% discount to National Trust members and National Trust Visa cardholders **Payment:** personal and traveler's checks **Restrictions:** no smoking; no pets **On-site activities:** television, reading, card games

## 2 BELLA VISTA PLACE BED AND BREAKFAST

2 Bella Vista Place
Iowa City, Iowa 52245
**Phone:** 319/338-4129
**Proprietor:** Daissy P. Owen

Bella Vista Place, aptly named for its beautiful view of the Iowa River and Hancher Auditorium on Iowa City's historic north side, is conveniently located in a quiet neighborhood of stately homes within walking distance of downtown and the University of Iowa. This 1920 house with Prairie School styling offers two guest suites with private baths and two rooms with a shared bath. Each room is distinctively decorated; one has a canopied bed. All accommodations have a view of the Iowa River. The innkeeper has traveled extensively in Europe and Latin America and filled her home with international artifacts. Guests may gather in the comfortable living room with a complimentary glass of wine or soft drink upon arrival. A hearty breakfast is served in the dining room or on the deck overlooking the water. The innkeeper is fluent in Spanish and speaks some French.

**Open:** year round **Accommodations:** 4 guest rooms (2 have private baths); 2 are suites **Meals:** full breakfast included; complimentary refreshments; restaurants nearby **Rates:** $55 to $95 **Payment:** personal check **Restrictions:** no smoking; no pets

# MAQUOKETA

**Nearby attractions:** Maquoketa State Caves Park, Lime Kilns, art galleries, Banowetz Antiques

## SQUIERS MANOR BED AND BREAKFAST

418 West Pleasant
Maquoketa, Iowa 52060
**Phone:** 319/652-6961 or 319/652-2359
**Proprietors:** Kathy and Virl Banowetz

Squiers Manor, built in 1882, was the first house in Maquoketa to have running water and electric power. It was home to members of the Squiers family for more than 60 years. The Queen Anne brick mansion is notable for its massive brick chimneys, corbeling, and rectangular bays. The original cast-iron fence surrounds the property. Through the front door, with its stained-glass window, guests will note walnut, cherry, butternut, and pine woodwork as well as original light fixtures, louvered shutters, and fireplace mantels. The innkeepers, who also run an antiques business known as Banowetz Antiques, have filled the inn with outstanding American Victorian furnishings, including a seven-foot-high brass bed and a mahogany bed carved with birds and flowers that is original to the house. Guest rooms also feature all modern comforts, including whirlpool baths and color television.

**Open:** year round **Accommodations:** 8 guest rooms with private baths; 3 are suites **Meals:** full breakfast and candlelight evening dessert included; complimentary refreshments; restaurants nearby **Rates:** $75 to $195; 10% discount to National Trust members and National Trust Visa cardholders midweek only, no holidays **Payment:** AmEx, Visa, MC, personal check **Restrictions:** smoking limited; no pets **On-site activities:** Victorian garden, grape arbor, front porch swing

# KANSAS

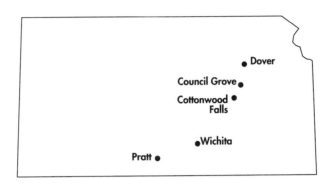

## COTTONWOOD FALLS

**Nearby attractions:** historic sites, proposed Tall Grass Prairie National Park, antiques hunting, crafts shops, bicycling

### 1874 STONEHOUSE ON MULBERRY HILL
R.R. 1, Box 67A
Cottonwood Falls, Kansas 66845
**Phone:** 316/273-8481
**Website:** www.Kansas-stonehouse.com
**E-mail:** SHMH1874@aol.com
**Proprietor:** Diane Ware

Mulberry Hill contains 60 acres of river valley woods, a half-mile of old stone fencing, a stretch of Cottonwood River for wading and fishing, an old stone barn and corral ruins, an abandoned railway right-of-way, and the 1874 farmhouse,

built of locally quarried stone. On the first floor is the fireplace room for reading and conversation and where breakfast is served, and the parlor where guests can enjoy music and television. Three upstairs guest rooms have private baths. The Rose Room has a sleigh bed; the Blue Room overlooks the quarry pond; and the Yellow Room has a vista of the flint hills. With its rural setting and historic buildings, the 1874 Stonehouse appeals to naturalists, hikers, hunters, fishermen, and historians alike.

**Open:** year round **Accommodations:** 3 guest rooms with private baths **Meals:** full breakfast included; complimentary refreshments; restaurants nearby **Rate:** $80 to $90; 10% discount to National Trust members and National Trust Visa cardholders **Payment:** AmEx, Visa, MC, personal and traveler's checks **Restrictions:** children over 12 welcome; no smoking; pets welcome in kennel facilities on property **On-site activities:** hiking, bird-watching, fishing, hunting

---

## COUNCIL GROVE
**Nearby attractions:** Old Santa Fe Trail, "Old West" historic sites, lakes, boating, fishing, water skiing, golfing, shopping

**COTTAGE HOUSE HOTEL**
25 North Neosho
Council Grove, Kansas 66846
**Phone:** 316/767-6828 or 800/727-7903
**Proprietor:** Connie Essington

This unusually styled brick hotel began as a three-room cottage in 1867, but was encapsulated in an 1871 two-story brick building. Then in 1879 the building gained a 5,000-square-foot addition that encompassed a two-story turret with stained-glass windows to the east, a bank of bay windows on the northeast side, a corbelled brick parapet, and gazebo-style porches. Many of the interior's

Victorian features have been restored, including pressed-tin ceilings in the hallways. Selected antique furnishings and lace curtains are featured throughout the building. Each guest room, from Aunt Minnie's Room to the Anniversary Suite, is individually decorated and contains a special accent, such as a stained-glass window, claw-foot tub, or brass bed. Private baths and all modern amenities complete each room.

**Open:** year round **Accommodations:** 26 guest rooms with private baths; 2 are suites **Meals:** continental-plus breakfast included; famous Hays House restaurant nearby **Wheelchair access:** limited **Rates:** $60 to $130; 10% discount offered to National Trust members and National Trust Visa cardholders **Payment:** AmEx, Visa, MC, CB, DC, Discover, personal and traveler's checks **Restrictions:** smoking limited; pets accepted at manager's discretion with an $8 charge **On-site activities:** porch sitting, whirlpool and sauna room

# DOVER

**Nearby attractions:** state capitol, Washburn University, Kansas Museum of History, Kansas Expocentre, Menninger Institute, Topeka Zoo, Topeka Performing Arts Center, Lake Shawnee, Heartland Park Race Track, golfing, shopping

## HISTORIC SAGE INN

13553 S.W. K-4 Highway
P.O. Box 13
Dover, Kansas 66420
**Phone:** 785/256-6566 or 888/256-6566
**Proprietors:** Bob and Janice Dunwell

Mark Sage was a stonemason from England. He worked on the east wing of the state capitol in nearby Topeka and, with his brother Alfred, built the structure now known as the Historic Sage Inn between 1865 and 1878. Constructed along the Mission Creek ford of the Southwest Trail, the building served as a hotel, stagecoach stop, and livery, and possible station along the Underground Railroad. Listed in the National Register of Historic Places, it is a two-story limestone building of dressed and rough stones. In 1982, the inn's 18-inch stone walls were tuckpointed, wood trim repainted in its original colors, pine floors refinished, cedar shingles on roof restored, and all mechanical systems were modernized, resulting in today's modern inn in a historic setting. Three charming guest rooms are available; two with king-size beds and one with a queen. Meals, under the direction of the inn's executive chef, a graduate of the Scottsdale Culinary

Institute, are served in the dining room. Menus can be adapted to meet any special dietary needs.

**Open:** year round **Accommodations:** 3 guest rooms with private baths **Meals:** full breakfast included; complimentary refreshments; picnic lunches and dinners available; restaurants nearby **Rates:** $65 to $75 **Payment:** personal and traveler's checks **Restrictions:** no smoking **On-site activities:** bird watching on the banks of Mission Creek, bicycling, Southwest Trail Trading Post with Southwest Native American arts and crafts

---

## PRATT

**Nearby attractions:** Pratt County Historical Museum, Kansas Wildlife and Parks Museum and Ponds, Cheyenne Bottoms/Quivira National Wildlife Refuge, antiques hunting, auction houses, Santa Fe Trail

### PRATT GUEST HOUSE BED AND BREAKFAST INN
105 North Iuka Street
P.O. Box 326
Pratt, Kansas 67124
**Phone:** 316/672-1200
**Proprietor:** Marguerite Flanagan

A classic example of Colonial Revival architecture, Pratt Guest House was built in 1910 by Samuel P. "Geb" Gebhart, founder of the *Pratt Union* newspaper, and one-time mayor and councilman. Gebhart resided in this home until his death in 1935. Now listed in the National Register of Historic Places and the Register of Historic Kansas Places, the house recently was rehabilitated; an elegant oak staircase with hand-carved newel posts, leaded-glass windows and doors, and quarter-sawn oak cabinetry have been beautifully restored. Period antiques and family heirlooms complete the decor. A large third-floor suite has a king-size bed; all other guest rooms have queen-size beds. Whirlpool tubs are available in some bathrooms. Guests are welcome to relax in the parlor or gardens. Breakfast is served in the dining room.

**Open:** year round **Accommodations:** 5 guest rooms with private baths **Meals:** full breakfast included; complimentary refreshments; restaurants nearby **Rates:** $65 to $89 **Payment:** Visa, MC, personal and traveler's checks **Restrictions:** inquire about children; no smoking; no pets **On-site activities:** backyard bird-watching, reading, porch rockers

## WICHITA

**Nearby attractions:** Old Town Wichita, Arkansas River, boathouse, tennis, Indian Center, Botanical Gardens, Cow Town, museums, convention center

### CASTLE INN RIVERSIDE
1155 North River Boulevard
Wichita, Kansas 67203
**Phone:** 316/263-9300 or 800/580-1131
**Website:** www.castleinnriverside.com
**E-mail:** 1castle@GTE.net
**Proprietors:** Dr. and Mrs. Terry Lowry

This castle of Richardsonian Romanesque architecture was built in 1888 by cattle baron Colonel Burton Campbell, who modeled it after a castle in Scotland. The rough-faced stonework mansion, with round-arched porches and porte cochere, is notable for its five-story castellated tower. Completely restored and listed in the National Register of Historic Places, the house boasts original stained-glass windows, intricately carved woodwork in oak, mahogany, cherry, and walnut, and nine European fireplace mantels. Public areas include the foyer, parlor, library, coffee bar, solaruim, and dining and billiard rooms. Guest rooms—most with working fireplaces—are furnished with antiques and reproduction pieces. Beds, dressed in luxurious linens, are brass and cast iron. Guests are served a full, seasonally changing breakfast, afternoon hors d'oeuvres and aperitifs, and evening desserts, coffee, and cordials.

**Open:** year round **Accommodations:** 14 guest rooms with private baths; 2 are suites **Meals:** full breakfast included; complimentary refreshments; restaurants nearby **Wheelchair access:** 1 room **Rates:** $125 to $275; 10% discount to National Trust members and National Trust Visa cardholders midweek only **Payment:** AmEx, Visa, MC, Discover, personal and traveler's checks **Restrictions:** children over 12 welcome; no smoking; no pets **On-site activities:** exercise and meeting facilities, croquet, board games, book and videotape libraries, two acres of grounds with gardens and strolling paths

# KENTUCKY

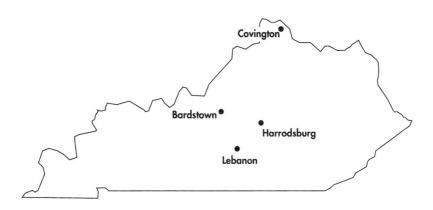

## BARDSTOWN

**Nearby attractions:** Lincoln's birthplace, Federal Hill, Stephen Foster outdoor drama, Civil War battlefield, My Old Kentucky Home State Park, My Old Kentucky Dinner Train, Kentucky bourbon distilleries

### JAILER'S INN
111 West Stephen Foster Avenue
Bardstown, Kentucky 40004
**Phone:** 502/348-5551 or 800/948-5551
**Website:** www.jailersinn.com
**E-mail:** CPaul@jailersinn.com
**Proprietor:** Fran McCoy

Built as a jail in 1819, the building originally housed prisoners upstairs while the jailer lived below. In 1874 prisoners were moved to a new jail built behind the old one, which remained the jailer's residence. Both facilities were used until 1987, at which time the complex was the oldest operating jail in the state of Kentucky. Listed in the National Register of Historic Places, the 1819 building has been completely rehabilitated to offer six individually decorated guest rooms filled with antiques, original rugs, and heirlooms. Accommodations range from the Victorian Room and the Garden Room to the former women's cell, which is adorned in prison black and white and features two of the original bunk beds and a more modern waterbed. Another room contains a double whirlpool bathtub. Guests are treated to refreshments and a hearty continental-plus breakfast.

**Open:** March to January **Accommodations:** 6 guest rooms with private baths **Meals:** continental-plus breakfast included; complimentary refreshments; restaurants nearby **Wheelchair access:** limited **Rates:** $65 to $105 **Payment:** AmEx, Visa, MC, Discover, personal and traveler's checks **Restrictions:** smoking limited; no pets **On-site activities:** touring old jails, playing cards, board games, tandem bicycle

---

## COVINGTON

**Nearby attractions:** Riverfront Stadium, Kings Island, horse racing at Turfway River Downs, boating, opera, ballet, symphony, walk to downtown Cincinnati

### AMOS SHINKLE TOWNHOUSE BED AND BREAKFAST
215 Garrard Street
Covington, Kentucky 41011
**Phone:** 606/431-2118 or 800/972-7012
**Website:** www.bbonline.com/ky/shinkle
**Proprietors:** Bernie Moorman and Don Nash
**Location:** less than 1 mile south of downtown Cincinnati, Ohio

A fine example of upper-class lifestyle in antebellum northern Kentucky, this 1854 brick house was built for entrepreneur Amos Shinkle, one of the area's leading business figures in the mid-nineteenth century. The restored home, winner of several preservation awards, features an Italianate facade with a cast-iron filigreed porch. Superior local craftsmanship is evident in the plaster chandelier medallions—preserved intact—and interior cornices, elaborate crown moldings, and Italianate mantels. Guest rooms have four-poster or Victorian-style beds and period furnishings. Behind the house is the Carriage House, where original horse stalls have been redesigned as delightful sleeping accommodations for children.

**Open:** year round **Accommodations:** 7 guest rooms with private baths; 1 is a suite **Meals:** full breakfast included; restaurants nearby **Wheelchair access:** 2 guest rooms and baths **Rates:** $79 to $140; 10% discount to National Trust members and National Trust Visa cardholders **Payment:** AmEx, Visa, MC, CB, DC, Discover, personal and traveler's checks **Restrictions:** no pets

# HARRODSBURG

**Nearby attractions:** Ft. Harrod State Park, Constitution Square Park, Kentucky Horse Park, Bright Leaf Golf Resort, fishing, boating

## SHAKER VILLAGE OF PLEASANT HILL

3500 Lexington Road
Harrodsburg, Kentucky 40330
**Phone:** 606/734-5411 or 800/734-5611
**Website:** www.shakervillageky.org
**Proprietor:** James C. Thomas
**Location:** 7 miles east of Harrodsburg

Shaker Village of Pleasant Hill preserves 33 original nineteenth-century buildings (built between 1809 and 1844) that have been accurately restored to provide visitors with an insight into the Shaker way of life. To make a stay at Shaker Village even more interesting, visitors are invited to lodge in one of 80 guest rooms scattered throughout 15 of these buildings. Guest rooms are furnished with reproduction Shaker furniture and handwoven rugs and curtains. Despite their nineteenth-century decor, all rooms are air conditioned and have private baths. Pleasant Hill, a National Historic Landmark, provides a relaxing, yet educational look at one of America's most successful communal religious societies.

**Open:** year round **Accommodations:** 80 guest rooms with private baths; 7 are suites **Meals:** restaurant on premises **Wheelchair access:** Trustee's Office dining room **Rates:** $60 to $80 **Payment**: Visa, MC, personal check **Restrictions**: no pets **On-site activities:** touring historic village, hiking, riverboat excursions, nature programs, shopping for handmade crafts and reproductions

# LEBANON

**Nearby attractions:** Maker's Mark Bourbon Distillery tours, Perryville Battlefield, Lebanon National Cemetery, My Old Kentucky Home State Park, historic Bardstown, Lincoln Birthplace National Landmark, Gethsemani Trappist Monastery, Green River Reservoir State Park, Shaker Village of Pleasant Hill, boating, fishing, swimming, bicycling

## MYRTLEDENE BED AND BREAKFAST

370 North Spalding Avenue
Lebanon, Kentucky 40033
**Phone:** 502/692-2223 or 800/391-1721
**Website:** www.bbonline.com/ky/myrtledene//
**Proprietor:** James Spragens

For more than 150 years, travelers coming into Lebanon from the north along Spalding Avenue have faced Myrtledene at the bend of the road. The imposing Greek Revival home was built for Benedict and Elizabeth McElroy Spalding in 1833—the year before Marion County was carved out of Washington, with Lebanon as its county seat. In 1862, General John Hunt Morgan used Myrtledene as headquarters during his raids on Lebanon and when he returned in 1863 intending to destroy the town, it was at Myrtledene that the flag of truce was flown. The house has been designated a Kentucky Landmark by the Kentucky Heritage Committee. Today, guests are offered gracious accommodations in one of four bedrooms and are invited to relax in the family room, garden, or in the Victorian swing in the front yard. On cold days, a fire is always set in the living room. A full breakfast is served daily. The innkeepers will gladly help visitors with plans to see the area's many attractions.

**Open:** year round **Accommodations:** 4 guest rooms (2 have private baths) **Meals:** full breakfast included; restaurants nearby **Rates:** $65 to $75; 10% discount to National Trust members and National Trust Visa cardholders **Payment:** Visa, MC, personal and traveler's checks **Restrictions:** smoking limited; no pets **On-site activities:** library of old and rare books, television with VCR

# LOUISIANA

## BREAUX BRIDGE

**Nearby attractions:** Bayou Teche Tourist Information Center, Cajun and Zydeco dance halls, swamp tours, antiques and specialty shopping, fishing, golfing, bird watching

### MAISON DES AMIS
140 East Bridge Street
Breaux Bridge, Louisiana 70517
**Phone:** 318/332-5273
**Fax:** 318/332-2227
**Proprietors:** Cynthia and Dickie Breaux

Located in historic downtown Breaux Bridge, "Crawfish Capital of the World," Maison des Amis has as its origin an 1810 two-room bousillage (adobe mud and moss) structure that was encapsulated by the main structure around 1880. The original two rooms are now guest baths and a bedroom. The entire house, which was in a state of severe disrepair when the innkeepers purchased it in 1994 and began restoration, is one story with a Queen Anne-influenced polygonal bay and Eastlake galleries. The clapboard structure is unusual for this part of Louisiana and

has been called Caribbean-Creole in design. Now listed in the National Register of Historic Places, the inn was the recipient of a National Preservation Award in 1997. Four high-ceilinged guest rooms are professionally decorated with period antiques, fine linens, original art, and two cozy robes in the armoire. The innkeepers also own the Cafe des Amis down the street, where bed and breakfast guests are invited to enjoy a complimentary full breakfast.

**Open:** year round **Accommodations:** 4 guest rooms with private baths; 2 can be joined as a suite **Meals:** full breakfast included (off premises) except Mondays when a continental breakfast is served at the inn; complimentary refreshments; restaurants nearby **Rates:** $75 to $90; 10% discount to National Trust members and National Trust Visa cardholders **Payment:** AmEx, Visa, MC, Discover, personal and traveler's checks **Restrictions:** no smoking; no pets **On-site activities:** gazebo overlooking the bayou, landscaped grounds, games, books

---

## CHENEYVILLE
**Nearby attractions:** Kent Plantation, antiques hunting, gaming

### LOYD HALL PLANTATION BED AND BREAKFAST
292 Loyd Bridge Road
Cheneyville, Louisiana 71325
**Phone:** 318/776-5641 or 800/240-8135
**Fax:** 318/776-5886
**E-mail:** loydhall@linknet.net
**Proprietors:** Dr. and Mrs. Frank Fitzgerald and Melinda F. Anderson
**Location:** 16 miles south of Alexandria

Situated on the banks of Bayou Boeuf, Loyd Hall Plantation's colorful past is marked by countless tales of survival throughout its 175-year history. The house had once been in such disrepair it wasn't even listed on legal deeds, although the 640-acre plantation has been in continuous operation since 1800. Today it provides guests with a hands-on look at Louisiana agriculture, with crops of corn, cotton, soybeans, and cattle. Now exquisitely restored, Loyd Hall features ornate plaster ceilings, suspended staircases, and rare antiques. Overnight guests are offered accommodations in five smaller houses scattered around the property, including the restored nineteenth-century Commissary or Carriage House with exposed brick walls and floors and a wood-burning fireplace. The houses offer views of pastures and farmland or the swimming pool with patio and pavilion. The plantation house is open daily for tours and takes reservations for lunches, private receptions, candlelight dinners, poolside parties, and seminars.

**Open:** year round (except Thanksgiving, Christmas, and New Year's days) **Accommodations:** 6 guest suites with private baths and kitchens **Meals:** continental-plus breakfast provided; complimentary refreshments; restaurants nearby **Wheelchair access:** limited **Rates:** $85 to $155 **Payment:** AmEx, Visa, MC, personal and traveler's checks **Restrictions:** no smoking; no pets **On-site activities:** swimming, bicycling, fishing, walking, observing farm and animals

# NAPOLEONVILLE

**Nearby attractions:** plantation tours, swamp tours, Cajun Research Center, Baton Rouge

## MADEWOOD PLANTATION HOUSE
4250 Highway 308
Napoleonville, Louisiana 70390
**Phone:** 504/369-7151 or 800/375-7151
**Website:** www.madewood.com
**E-mail:** madewoodpl@aol.com
**Proprietor:** Keith Marshall
**Location:** 30 miles south of Baton Rouge

Madewood, a National Historic Landmark, is a 21-room Greek Revival mansion designed by noted Irish architect Henry Howard. Built in 1846 for Colonel Thomas Pugh, the house was originally part of a large sugar plantation on Bayou Lafourche. Its name derives from the fact that it is constructed of wood from trees on the property. A century later, its grand design of six massive Ionic columns, central portico, and triangular pediment had fallen into disrepair when it was purchased for $70,000 in 1964 and restoration was begun. Accommodations in the again gleaming white mansion feature canopied or half-tester beds in rooms furnished with antiques and fresh flowers. Dinner by candlelight and turn-down service are supplied. Rooms are also available in two smaller buildings on the property: Charlet House, a restored 1820 Greek Revival cottage with a fireplace, or the small, rustic four-room cabin with canopied bed and pot-bellied stove.

**Open:** year round **Accommodations:** 8 guest rooms with private baths: 3 are suites **Meals:** full breakfast and dinner included; complimentary wine-and-cheese reception **Rate:** $215 **Payment:** AmEx, Visa, MC, Discover, personal and traveler's checks **Restrictions:** children over 8 welcome; no smoking; no pets **On-site activities:** relaxing, house tours

---

## NEW IBERIA

**Nearby attractions:** National Trust's The Shadows-on-the-Teche, Lake Peigneur, Tabasco factory, Jungle Gardens on Avery Island, Rip Van Winkle Gardens, Konriko Rice Mill, airboat tours of Atchafalaya Swamp

### COOK'S COTTAGE AT RIP VAN WINKLE GARDENS ON JEFFERSON ISLAND

5505 Rip Van Winkle Road
New Iberia, Louisiana 70560
**Phone:** 318/365-3332 or 800/375-3332
**Fax:** 318/365-3354
**Website:** www.ripvanwinkle.com
**E-mail:** rvw@1stnet.com
**Executive Director:** Shereen Minvielle

The quaint Cook's Cottage was built in 1925 to serve as a home for the cook who prepared meals for employees of the Diamond Crystal Salt Company, which mined the salt dome below Jefferson Island. This salt dome is the geological feature that gives the site its "island" formation, being at a higher elevation than the surrounding area. The island is named for the nineteenth-century actor Joseph Jefferson, who built his 22-room mansion here in 1870. The surrounding gardens—a 25-acre semitropical paradise—are named for the famous character he portrayed in more than 3,000 performances in theaters around the world. Guests on Jefferson Island can enjoy the gardens, greenhouse and nursery, mansion, and gift shop, then sleep over in the Cook's Cottage with its luxurious amenities, including complimentary liqueurs, aromatherapy kit, and whirlpool tub.

**Open:** year round **Accommodations:** 1 private cottage **Meals:** continental breakfast included; complimentary refreshments; restaurant on premises; restaurants nearby **Rates:** $175; 10% discount to National Trust members and National Trust Visa cardholders **Payment:** AmEx, Visa, MC, Discover, personal and traveler's checks **Restrictions:** well-behaved children welcome; no smoking; no pets **On-site activities:** complimentary tours of Joseph Jefferson House, 25 acres of blooming gardens; discounts for boat excursions on Lake Peigneur

## INN AT LE ROSIER

314 East Main Street
New Iberia, Louisiana 70560
**Phone:** 318/367-5306 or 888/804-ROSE (7673)
**Fax:** 318/365-1216
**Website:** www.leRosier.com
**Proprietors:** Mary Beth and Hallman Woods

Located in the New Iberia historic district, le Rosier was once a family home, built around 1870 directly across from the famed Shadows-on-the-Teche. The white-frame cottage with shuttered windows and full-length front porch is now a charming country inn and world-class restaurant. Six guest rooms are furnished with antiques and elegant appointments. Each room has its own stocked refrigerator, bath, telephone, and television. Le Rosier restaurant, under the direction of Chef Hallman Woods III, named one of the Best New Chefs in America by *Food and Wine* magazine, presents an original genre of cooking—New Acadian. In the spring and summer, the rose bushes at le Rosier fill the air with their intoxicating fragrance, adding to the romantic atmosphere that pervades the inn. Le Rosier has received accolades from *Southern Living* and *Country Inns*.

**Open:** year round **Accommodations:** 6 guest rooms with private baths **Meals:** full breakfast included; restaurant on premises; restaurants nearby **Rates:** $95 to $115 **Payment:** AmEx, Visa, MC **Restrictions:** children over 12 welcome; no smoking; no pets

---

# NEW ORLEANS

**Nearby attractions:** Audubon Park and Zoological Gardens, French Quarter, St. Louis Cathedral, Tulane University, Woldenberg Park, Riverwalk Mall, central business district, Superdome, U.S. Mint, Cajun food and dancing, Natchez paddlewheeler on Mississippi River, streetcar rides, antiques hunting, tennis, swimming, nature trips through swamps

## BENACHI HOUSE, ONE OF THE COTTON BROKERS' HOUSES

2257 Bayou Road
New Orleans, Louisiana 70119
**Phone:** 504/525-7040 or 800/308-7040
**Fax:** 504/525-9760
**Website:** www.nolabb.com
**E-mail:** cotton@nolabb.com
**Proprietors:** James G. Derbes and Cecilia J. Rau

This Greek Revival house was constructed in 1858 for Nicolas M. Benachi,

cotton broker, Consul of Greece, and a founder of the city's Greek Orthodox church. The home is located in the Esplanade Ridge National Register historic district; eighteenth- and nineteenth-century artifacts have been found in the inn's yard. An award-winning restoration by the innkeepers is evident in 14-foot ceilings with banded cornices and medallions, carved black marble mantels, Rococo Revival chandeliers, Greek key doorways, and heart-of-pine floors. The entire house is furnished with nineteenth-century American antiques. Guests are welcome in the parlor, library, and dining room, and are invited to stroll the tree-shaded grounds with gazebo and fountain. The inn has been featured in such publications as *American Home* and the *Times-Picayune* and two feature films have been filmed here.

**Open:** year round **Accommodations:** 4 guest rooms (3 with private baths); 1 is a suite **Meals:** full breakfast included; complimentary refreshments; restaurants nearby **Rates:** $105 to $125; 10% discount to National Trust members and National Trust Visa cardholders **Payment:** AmEx, Visa, MC, Discover, personal and traveler's checks **Restrictions:** no smoking; no pets

## COLUMNS HOTEL
3811 Saint Charles Avenue
New Orleans, Louisiana 70115
**Phone:** 504/899-9308 or 800/445-9308
**Fax:** 504/899-8170
**Proprietors:** Claire and Jacques Creppél

Designed by architect Thomas Sully and built by wealthy tobacco merchant Simon Hernsheim in 1883, the Columns is the only remaining example of a large group of Italianate houses Sully designed between 1883 and 1885. The surviving interior features are considered to be among the grandest known in any late nineteenth-century Louisiana residence. One of the most dramatic is a mahogany stairwell that rises to meet an extraordinary square-domed skylight made of stained glass in a stylized sunburst motif. The house is listed in the National Register and was the location for Louis Malle's film, *Pretty Baby*, which won an award at Cannes. Guest rooms, furnished with antiques, each feature some small delight—a unique fireplace, an armoire, or a claw-foot bathtub. The Columns serves New Orleans–style food, which combines the best of Creole, Cajun, and European cuisines, and also offers Sunday brunch.

**Open:** year round **Accommodations:** 20 guest rooms with private baths; 3 are suites **Meals:** continental breakfast included; complimentary refreshments; restaurants and lounge on premises; catered parties available **Wheelchair access: yes Rates:** $90 to $200; 10% discount offered to National Trust members and National Trust Visa cardholders **Payment:** AmEx, Visa, MC, personal and traveler's check **On-site activities:** jazz nights, international nights

## DUSTY MANSION
2231 General Pershing Street
New Orleans, Louisiana 70115
**Phone:** 504/895-4576
**Fax:** 504/891-0049
**Proprietor:** Cynthia Riggs

This homey, casual inn is on a quiet residential street on the edge of the Garden District in the historic Bouligny Plantation District. The turn-of-the-century, two-story frame house sports a wide front porch where guests often relax on the wicker swing. Inside, the house is trimmed in original hardwood floors and cypress woodwork and doors. Guest rooms are air conditioned, have ceiling fans and televisions, and are furnished with antiques and reproduction pieces. Queen-size beds may be brass, canopied, sleigh, or white enameled iron. Guests are invited to linger over breakfast in the dining room, play pool in the game room, or relax on the sundeck or shaded patio. Just six blocks from the St. Charles Avenue streetcar, Dusty Mansion offers off-street parking.

**Open:** year round **Accommodations:** 4 guest rooms (2 have private baths) **Meals:** continental-plus breakfast included; champagne brunch on Sundays; complimentary refreshments; restaurants nearby **Rates:** $50 to $80; 10% discount to National Trust members and National Trust Visa cardholders **Payment:** personal and traveler's checks **Restrictions:** no smoking; no pets **On-site activities:** gazebo with hot tub, pool table, table tennis

## ESPLANADE VILLA
2216 Esplanade Avenue
New Orleans, Louisiana 70119
**Phone:** 504/525-7040 or 800/308-7040
**Fax:** 504/525-9760
**E-mail:** cotton@nolabb.com
**Proprietor:** James G. Derbes

When it was constructed in 1880, this Italianate house—notable for its profusion of arched windows and doorways—reflected the prosperity of Esplanade Avenue, the grand promenade of Creole New Orleans. Its two-family occupancy was a local tradition in building, often connecting successive generations of the same family. On the first floor were double foyers, double parlors, and a dining room and kitchen on both sides. Upstairs, each family enjoyed four bedrooms and one bath. Purchased in a state of severe disrepair, the house has been recently restored by the innkeepers, and now proudly shows off its ceiling medallions, cornice moldings, and pocket doors. Five two-room guest suites are furnished with an outstanding collection of American antiques from the last quarter of the nineteenth century. All suites contain a private Victorian bath that includes a footed, cast-iron tub with shower and a pedestal sink. Each room also contains its original mantel and fireplace, and modern conveniences are included: telephone, cable television, central heating and air conditioning, and ceiling fans.

**Open:** year round **Accommodations:** 5 guest suites with private baths **Meals:** full breakfast included, served at Nicolas M. Benachi House; complimentary refreshments; restaurants nearby **Rates:** $125 to $135 **Payment:** AmEx, Visa, MC, Discover, personal and traveler's checks **Restrictions:** no smoking; no pets **On-site activities:** landscaped patio and garden

## FRENCH QUARTER LANAUX HOUSE
Esplanade Avenue at Chartres Street
Box 52257
New Orleans, Louisiana 70152-2257
**Phone:** 504/488-4640 or 800/729-4640
**Fax:** 504/488-4639
**Proprietors:** Ruth Bodenheimer and Hazell Boyce

Charles Andrew Johnson built this Italianate town house in 1879. Although he died unmarried in 1896, he willed his 11,000-square-foot mansion to Marie Andry Lanaux, the daughter of his business partner, and object of his affections. The Lanaux family owned this home for generations. Ms. Bodenheimer has meticulously restored the house. The original ceiling medallions and moldings are in nearly perfect condition. The seven fireplaces wear their original mantels. A

number of furnishings owned by Johnson remain in the house today. A private entrance leads to each guest suite, which includes a private sitting room, queen bed, bathroom, and country kitchenette. A self-served continental breakfast is provided for guests to enjoy at their leisure.

**Open:** year round **Accommodations:** 4 guest suites with private baths **Meals:** continental breakfast included; restaurants nearby **Rates:** $142 to $252; 10% discount to National Trust members **Payment:** personal and traveler's checks **Restrictions:** no smoking; no pets **On-site activities:** historic house tour

## HOTEL MAISON DE VILLE AND THE AUDUBON COTTAGES
727 Rue Toulouse
New Orleans, Louisiana 70130
**Phone:** 504/561-5858 or 800/678-8946
**Fax:** 504/528-9939
**Website:** www.maisondeville.com/
**General Manager:** Jean-Luc Maumus

The main structure of the Maison de Ville, whose name in French means town house, was just that—a two-story dwelling rebuilt circa 1800 after a fire destroyed most of the French Quarter. Today, the house contains the hotel's reception room, parlor, concierge, and nine guest rooms. Across the courtyard with its cast-iron fountain and bricks original to the location, four former slave quarters, constructed some 50 years earlier, have been renovated as luxurious guest accommodations. The adjacent carriage house is now a two-story suite. On nearby Dauphine Street are seven cottages named for John James Audubon who, in 1821, produced a portion of his *Birds of America* series while residing there. All

guest rooms are furnished with antiques, four-poster beds, and period paintings. The hotel and its Bistro have been praised by *Conde Nast Traveler, Gourmet, Bon Appetit,* and *Wine Spectator.* This is a Historic Hotel of America.

**Open:** year round **Accommodations:** 23 guest rooms with private baths; 7 are suites **Meals:** continental breakfast included; complimentary refreshments; restaurants nearby **Rates:** $185 to $325; 10% discount to National Trust members and National Trust Visa cardholders **Payment:** AmEx, Visa, MC, DC, Discover, traveler's check **Restrictions:** children over 12 welcome; no smoking; no pets **On-site activities:** swimming pool

## LAFITTE GUEST HOUSE
1003 Bourbon Street
New Orleans, Louisiana 70116
**Phone:** 800/331-7971 or 504/581-2678
**Fax:** 504/581-2677
**Website:** www.lafitteguesthouse.com
**Innkeeper:** Andy Crocchiola

According to *Dixie Magazine*, Lafitte Guest House is "as New Orleans as streetcars, jazz musicians, and voodoo queens." Located in the heart of the French Quarter, the Lafitte offers easy access to the district's antiques shops, museums, world-famous restaurants, Bourbon Street nightclubs, and rows of colorful Creole and Spanish cottages. The inn, built in 1849 by P. J. Gelieses, is a four-story, New Orleans–style French Colonial, complete with lacy wrought-iron balconies. Each guest room is individually decorated with antiques and reproduction furnishings. A continental breakfast is served on the balconies or in the intimate courtyard. The tranquil and gracious atmosphere has been hailed by *Glamour, McCall's, Antique Monthly*, and *Country Living.*

**Open:** year round **Accommodations:** 14 guest rooms with private baths; 2 are suites **Meals:** continental breakfast included; complimentary refreshments; restaurants nearby **Rates:** $99 to $179 **Payment:** AmEx, Visa, MC, Discover, DC, traveler's check **Restrictions:** no pets

## MCKENDRICK-BREAUX HOUSE
1474 Magazine Street
New Orleans, Louisiana 70130
**Phone:** 504/586-1700 or 888/570-1700
**Fax:** 504/522-7138
**Website:** www.mckendrick-breaux.com
**E-mail:** mckenbro@cmq.com
**Proprietor:** Eddie Breaux

In 1865, Scotsman Daniel McKendrick, a well-to-do plumber, built a three-story, masonry home on land originally part of the Sarpy Plantation. Now part of the historic Lower Garden District, this is one of the most comprehensive nineteenth-century Greek Revival neighborhoods remaining in the country. Today, McKendrick's gracious home is connected at the rear of the property by a courtyard and patio to a two-story frame house built in 1857. Both have been meticulously restored by the innkeeper to highlight their original plasterwork, woodwork, and flooring. Seven guest rooms, comfortably furnished with antiques, family collectibles, and fresh flowers, have private baths. Some rooms open onto the courtyard. Breakfast is served in the double parlors and the library offers information related to local culture and destinations. World-class antiques shops, the convention center, and the historic French Quarter are only minutes away from the inn, which has received numerous preservation and hospitality awards.

**Open:** year round **Accommodations:** 7 guest rooms with private baths **Meals:** continental-plus breakfast included; restaurants nearby **Rates:** $95 to $150; 10% discount to National Trust members and National Trust Visa cardholders **Payment:** AmEx, Visa, MC, personal check **Restrictions:** no smoking; no pets

## PRYTANIA PARK HOTEL
1525 Prytania Street
New Orleans, Louisiana 70130
**Phone:** 504/524-0427 or 800/682-1984
**Fax:** 504/522-2977
**Website:** www.prytaniaparkhotel.com
**Proprietor:** Edward Halpern

Located in the historic Garden District, the Prytania Park Hotel is only a half block from St. Charles Avenue, where the world's oldest continuously operating streetcar provides 24-hour access to the French Quarter. The original portion of this hotel is in a beautifully restored 1856 Greek Revival townhouse, complete with high ceilings, shiny heart-pine floors, exposed brick walls, and old English

furniture. Wrought-iron second-floor balconies lend the building an authentic New Orleans air. Many of the hotel's guest rooms are located in the recently constructed addition and are furnished with microwave ovens and refrigerators. All rooms have air conditioning, ceiling fans, cable television, and voice mail. The courtyard provides a comfortable setting for a New Orleans continental breakfast. AAA gives Prytania Park three diamonds.

**Open:** year round **Accommodations:** 62 guest rooms with private baths; 6 are suites **Meals:** continental breakfast included; restaurants nearby **Rates:** $59 to $229; 10% discount offered to National Trust members and National Trust Visa cardholders **Payment:** AmEx, Visa, MC, CB, DC, traveler's check; personal check in advance only **Restrictions:** no pets

## RATHBONE INN

1227 Esplanade Avenue
New Orleans, Louisiana 70116
**Phone:** 504/947-2100 or 800/947-2101
**Fax:** 504/947-7454
**Website:** www.rathboneinn.com
**E-mail:** rathbonein@aol.com
**Proprietor:** Ray Peacock

The Rathbone Inn was built in 1850 as a single-family residence. The Greek Revival building is adorned with a two-story front porch supported by Ionic columns on the first floor and Corinthian on the second. The wrought-iron front fence with filigreed gate is one of the finest in New Orleans. The house was restored in 1985 so that most rooms sport their original high ceilings and interesting architectural details. Accommodations range from small rooms with a king- or queen-size bed to large two- and three-room suites. All guest rooms have private baths and kitchenettes. The Rathbone Inn is located less than two blocks from the French Quarter.

**Open:** year round **Accommodations:** 9 guest rooms with private baths and kitchenettes **Meals:** continental breakfast included; restaurants nearby **Rates:** $90 to $145; 10% discount to National Trust members and National Trust Visa cardholders **Payment:** AmEx, Visa, MC, CB, DC, Discover, traveler's check **Restrictions:** no pets **On-site activities:** patio with hot tub

## SULLY MANSION
2631 Prytania Street
New Orleans, Louisiana 70130
**Phone:** 504/891-0457
**Fax:** 504/899-7237
**Proprietor:** Maralee Prigmore

Sully Mansion, designed by renowned architect Thomas Sully in 1890, is the most intact of the few remaining "Sullys" in New Orleans. Original stained-glass windows, ornate ceiling medallions, heart-of-pine floors, a grand stairway, 10-foot-high cypress doors, and 12-foot-high coved ceilings are just a few of the features of this rare Queen Anne–style home. A tasteful blend of antiques and today's comfortable furnishings creates an intimate atmosphere. Sully Mansion is located in the heart of New Orleans's historic Garden District. Nearby, the historic St. Charles streetcar takes visitors to all the city's attractions.

**Open:** year round **Accommodations:** 5 guest rooms with private baths; 2 suites **Meals:** continental breakfast included; restaurants nearby **Rates:** $125 to $225 **Payment:** Visa, MC, personal and traveler's checks **Restrictions:** not suitable for children

# RAMSAY/COVINGTON
**Nearby attractions:** St. Joseph's Abbey Benedictine monastery and liberal arts college, Dom Gregory DeWitt painted frescoes, antiques hunting on Lee Lane and in town

## MILL BANK FARMS
75654 River Road
Ramsay/Covington, Louisiana 70435
**Phone:** 504/892-1606 or 800/935-5485 (PIN 56)
**Proprietor:** "Miss Katie" Planche Friedrichs
**Location:** 4 miles outside Covington, 35 minutes north of New Orleans

Mill Bank Farms bed and breakfast was originally built in 1832 as the office of a lumber company and mill. The mill operated until 1915 when it was purchased by M. P. Planche, Sr., for farming. Guests have the use of the large living room and dining room with open fireplaces. Each of the bedrooms are enhanced by antique furnishings and private baths. Wake-up calls are made with coffee or tea served in bed. Then a full plantation breakfast is served indoors or on the front porch overlooking the pecan orchard and grazing horses. Mill Bank (a working farm) sits back off River Road, one of the oldest and most scenic roads in the state, in the middle of 70 acres on the bluffs of the Bogue Falaya River, a registered Lousisana scenic river.

**Open:** year round **Accommodations:** 2 guest rooms with private baths **Meals:** full plantation or continental breakfast included; complimentary refreshments; restaurants nearby **Rates:** $100 with continental to $125 with full breakfast; 10% discount to National Trust members and National Trust Visa cardholders **Payment:** AmEx, Visa, MC, Discover, personal check **Restrictions:** no smoking; no pets **On-site activities:** fishing, bicycling, river swimming, hiking

---

## ST. FRANCISVILLE
**Nearby attractions:** golfing, historic sightseeing, plantations

### BUTLER GREENWOOD PLANTATION
8345 U.S. Highway 61
St. Francisville, Louisiana 70775
**Phone:** 504/635-6312
**Website:** ww.butlergreenwood.com
**Proprietor:** Anne Butler
**Location:** 2 1/2 miles north of St. Francisville

This plantation was established in 1796; the main house was built around 1810. Guest accommodations are in six dependencies located on the extensive grounds filled with moss-draped live oaks and antebellum gardens of mature azaleas and camellias. The Old Kitchen, built in 1796, features exposed beams and bricks made on the plantation by its slaves. The nineteenth-century Cook's Cottage has a working fireplace, claw-foot tub, and porch swing. The Gazebo is notable for its three nine-foot-tall antique stained-glass church windows. The Pond House sleeps six and has a shaded gingerbread-trimmed porch overlooking the pond. The Treehouse is at the edge of a steep wooded ravine. It has a three-level deck, a king-size cypress four-poster bed, and a fireplace. The shingled, three-story Dovecote has two bedrooms, a whirlpool tub, fireplace, and deck. All accommodations have kitchens and private baths.

**Open:** year round **Accommodations:** 6 guest cottages with private baths and kitchens **Meals:** continental-plus breakfast included; restaurants nearby **Wheelchair access:** limited **Rates:** $100 to $110 **Payment:** AmEx, Visa, MC, personal and traveler's checks **Restrictions:** no smoking in main plantation house **On-site activities:** gardens, swimming pool, pond with ducks and geese, guided nature walks and bird-watching, historic home tour

## COTTAGE PLANTATION
10528 Cottage Lane
St. Francisville, Louisiana 70775
**Phone:** 504/635-3674
**Proprietors:** Harvey and
Mary T. Brown
**Location:** 5 miles north of
St. Francisville

Cottage Plantation, built between 1795 and 1850, is one of the few complete antebellum plantations remaining in the South. The mansion—an English cottage with broad galleries and a steeply pitched roof with dormers—and its outbuildings stand as tributes to the skill and imagination of the designers and artisans of the early nineteenth century. In its time the cottage entertained such eminences as Andrew Jackson, who stopped on his way to Natchez as a guest of the original owner, shortly after the Battle of New Orleans. Today, the house and guest rooms are furnished with antiques, many original to the home. Located on nearly 400 rolling acres with moss-draped oaks and old gardens, this National Register property conveys the charm and hospitality of the Old South.

**Open:** year round **Accommodations:** 6 guest rooms with private baths **Meals:** full breakfast included; restaurant on premises **Rate:** $85 to $95 **Payment:** Visa, MC, personal and traveler's checks **Restrictions:** children over 12 welcome; smoking limited; no pets **On-site activities:** horseshoes, croquet, swimming pool, antiques shop

---

# ST. MARTINVILLE

**Nearby attractions:** Bayou Teche, National Register historic district, St. Martin Square, St. Martin Catholic Church, Presbytère, Petit Paris Museum

## OLD CASTILLO BED AND BREAKFAST

220 Evangeline Boulevard
P.O. Box 172
St. Martinville, Louisiana 70582
**Phone:** 318/394-4010 or 800/621-3017
**Fax:** 318/394-7983
**Proprietor:** Peggy Hulin

Pierre Vasseur built this stately Greek Revival structure in 1829 as a combination inn and residence. Later, under the management of Mrs. Edmond Castillo, widow of a well-known steamboat captain, the hotel became renowned as a center of superb hospitality, gala balls, and fine operas. Between 1899 and 1986 the building was owned by the Sisters of Mercy, who operated it as a high school for girls. Today, the building has been restored to its original use, now housing five antiques-filled guest rooms and La Place d'Evangeline restaurant featuring Acadian cuisine. The building's careful restoration has earned it a listing in the National Register of Historic Places.

**Open:** year round **Accommodations:** 5 guest rooms with private baths; 3 are suites **Meals:** full breakfast included; restaurants nearby **Wheelchair access:** limited **Rates:** $50 to $80; 10% discount to National Trust members and National Trust Visa cardholders **Payment:** AmEx, Visa, MC, traveler's check **Restrictions:** well-behaved children are welcome; smoking limited; no pets **On-site activities:** relaxing on balcony or along bayou

# MAINE

## BAR HARBOR

**Nearby attractions:** Acadia National Park, Cadillac Mountain, museums, art galleries, water activities and sports, bicycling, hiking, golfing, nature tours, whale watching, summer concert series

## GRAYCOTE INN

40 Holland Avenue
Bar Harbor, Maine 04609
**Phone:** 207/288-3044
**Fax:** 207/288-2719
**Website:** www.graycoteinn.com
**E-mail:** graycote@acadia.net
**Proprietors:** Roger and Pat Samuel

A "cote" is a small cottage, thus the name of this inn means "small gray cottage." While the 1881 inn is a substantial house by today's standards, it was a small cottage in comparison with the very large ones being built in Bar Harbor at the end of

the nineteenth century by families with names like Morgan, Vanderbilt, Astor, and Pulitzer. Today, the rambling gray clapboard inn sits on nearly an acre of land in the village of Bar Harbor. Twelve elegantly appointed guest rooms are furnished with Victorian antiques, canopied beds, lace, and wicker. All rooms are spacious with king- or queen-size beds and private baths; some rooms offer a fireplace, private sunporch, or balcony. A full breakfast is served on the sunny breakfast porch; early risers will find a coffee and tea tray ready. The innkeepers are happy to help guests plan their visits to this quaint seaside resort and all the sites and activities it offers. For those who enjoy quiet times, the inn offers games, a grand piano, and a library.

**Open:** year round **Accommodations:** 12 guest rooms with private baths; 2 are suites **Meals:** full breakfast included; complimentary refreshments; restaurants nearby **Rates:** $65 to $155 (seasonal) **Payment:** AmEx, Visa, MC, Discover, traveler's check **Restrictions:** children over 10 welcome; no smoking; no pets **On-site activities:** wicker-filled front porch, hammocks, croquet, garden

## INN AT BAY LEDGE
1385 Sand Point Road
Bar Harbor, Maine 04609
**Phone:** 207/288-4204
**Fax:** 207/288-5573
**Website:** maineguide.com/barharbor/bayledge
**E-mail:** bayledge@downeastnet.com
**Proprietors:** Jack and Jeani Ochtera

Eagles fly by at eye level at this inn, perched on an 80-foot cliff overlooking Frenchman's Bay. On two acres of pine forest, only two miles from the entrance to Acadia National Park, the Inn at Bay Ledge provides 79 steps from the top of the cliff to the stone beach below, which is part of the historic areas known as The Ovens and Cathedral Rock. Begun in 1901, and enlarged throughout the decades, the inn possesses an upscale country ambiance. All guest rooms are decorated with antiques and offer king or queen canopied or antique four-poster beds covered with designer linens, down quilts, and feather beds. Breakfast is served before a roaring fire or on the deck, from which seals and dolphins can be seen eating their breakfasts on the rocks and in the waters below. Guests are invited to enjoy a dip in the pool, a sauna, a steam shower, or a book in the hammock overlooking the water. The Inn at Bay Ledge offers its guests the finest blend of luxury and rustic living.

**Open:** May to October **Accommodations:** 10 guest rooms with private baths **Meals:** full breakfast included; complimentary refreshments and high tea; restaurants nearby **Rates:** $135 to $275; 10% discount to National Trust members and National Trust Visa cardholders May 1-20 only **Payment:** Visa, MC, personal and traveler's checks **Restrictions:** children over 16 welcome; no smoking; no pets **On-site activities:** in-ground pool, sauna, steam room, private beach, library

## MIRA MONTE INN

69 Mount Desert Street
Bar Harbor, Maine 04609
**Phone:** 207/288-4263 or 800/553-5109
**Fax:** 207/288-3115
**Website:** maineinns.com
**E-mail:** mburns@acadia.net
**Proprietor:** Marian Burns

This elegant summer retreat was built in 1864 and was named Mira Monte ("behold the mountains") in 1892 by its wealthy Philadelphia owners. The rambling clapboard building is graced by porches, balconies, and bay windows, as well as several fireplaces. The wraparound porch, paved terraces, gardens, and sweeping lawns are a testament to style and beauty. Guests may relax in the living room or library and are encouraged to use the piano for their enjoyment. Each guest room is furnished in the Victorian style and offers a special feature: a balcony or porch, a bay window, an alcove, or a fireplace. Fresh flowers, freshly baked breads, and a friendly staff are relaxing additions.

**Open:** early May to late October **Accommodations:** 15 guest rooms with private baths **Meals:** full breakfast included; complimentary refreshments; restaurants nearby **Wheelchair access:** yes **Rates:** $125 to $180; 10% discount offered to National Trust members and National Trust Visa cardholders **Payment:** AmEx, Visa, MC, Discover, personal and traveler's checks **Restrictions:** smoking limited; no pets **On-site activities:** badminton, croquet, library, piano, chess and board games

## BATH

**Nearby attractions:** historic Bath, Kennebec River, Maritime Museum, Chocolate Church Cultural Center, Bowdoin College, antiques hunting, art gallery, outlet shopping, beaches, state parks

### GALEN C. MOSES HOUSE
1009 Washington Street
Bath, Maine 04530
**Phone:** 207/442-8771 or 888/442-8771
**Fax:** 207/443-6861
**Website:** www.galenmoses.com
**E-mail:** galenmoses@clinic.net
**Proprietors:** James M. Haught and Larry E. Kieft

Built in 1874 for Galen Clapp Moses, this Italianate house stands out in its National Register historic district thanks not only to its outstanding architecture but also to its current paint scheme of plum, pink, and teal. The interior of the house is just as commanding: fireplaces with elaborately carved and mirrored overmantels, built-in bookcases, leather upholstered seats, paneled walls, bay windows, plaster friezes. Guest rooms are individually appointed and dressed with antiques ranging from Victorian to vintage 1950s. Porches and elegant gardens are also open to guests. Surprises are found throughout the house, from the full theater located on the third floor that was once used to entertain officers from the nearby naval air station during World War II to the reputed friendly ghosts who often make their presence felt. AAA recommends the inn with three diamonds.

**Open:** year round **Accommodations:** 4 guest rooms with private baths **Meals:** full breakfast included; complimentary refreshments; restaurants nearby **Rates:** $69 to $99; 10% discount to National Trust members and National Trust Visa cardholders weekdays only **Payment:** Visa, MC, personal and traveler's checks **Restrictions:** no smoking; no pets **On-site activities:** porch sitting, garden strolling, reading

# BELFAST

**Nearby attractions:** walking tours of historic Belfast, Penobscot Marine Museum, four state parks, swimming, golfing, tennis, train excursions, sailing, fishing, windjammer cruises, ferry boat rides, art galleries, shopping, antiques hunting, summer theater

## JEWELED TURRET INN

40 Pearl Street
Belfast, Maine 04915
**Phone:** 207/338-2304 or 800/696-2304
**Website:** www.bbonline.com/me/jeweled turret/
**Proprietors:** Carl and Cathy Heffentrager

Built in 1898 for prominent attorney James S. Harriman and his wife Nell, the Jeweled Turret Inn derives its name from the grand stairway, which is housed in a round turret with stained- and leaded-glass panels and jewel-like embellishments. The exterior of this Queen Anne structure features many gables, three turrets, and rubble-stone verandas. Inside, unique oak, maple, fir, and pine woodwork has been restored. An unusual room is the den with its dark pine-beamed ceiling and wainscoting framed in rattan. Here, one of the house's four ornate fireplaces is constructed of rocks and semiprecious stones from every state in the Union at the time the house was built. Guest rooms are inviting and romantic with four-poster and scrolled-iron beds, beautiful linens, and antique furnishings. Breakfast is served in the oak-paneled dining room and features fresh fruits, scones, and a house specialty such as German pancakes or sourdough gingerbread waffles. The inn has been given three diamonds by AAA.

**Open:** year round **Accommodations:** 7 guest rooms with private baths **Meals:** full breakfast included in rate; complimentary refreshments; restaurants nearby **Rates:** $75 to $100; 10% discount to National Trust members and National Trust Visa cardholders **Payment:** Visa, MC, personal and traveler's checks **Restrictions:** children over 12 welcome; no smoking; no pets **On-site activities:** veranda sitting, gardens

## THE WHITE HOUSE AT NO. 19 CHURCH STREET

19 Church Street
Belfast, Maine 04915
**Phone:** 207/338-1901 or 888/290-1901
**Fax:** 207/338-5161
**Website:** www.mainebb.com
**E-mail:** whitehouse@mainebb.com
**Proprietors:** Dianne Porter, Robert Hansen, and Terry Prescott

For more than 150 years, the White House has been an impossible sight to ignore for visitors entering this seaside community from the South. The man who built it, James Patterson White, and the man who designed it, Calvin Ryder, conspired to make the house one of the most dramatic in Maine. Its unique design places The White House among the top Greek Revival homes in Maine. With its graceful symmetry and templelike facade crowned by an octagonal cupola, The White House is one of the most photographed homes on Maine's coast. The interior is as exquisite with ornate plaster ceiling medallions, marble fireplaces, and intricate moldings. Finely appointed guest rooms are furnished with antiques and reproductions, king or queen beds, and plush linens. A triangle of landscaped grounds and gardens surrounds the home. The largest copper beech tree in Maine spreads its branches to shade the terrace, a favorite place for guests to enjoy the view of the gardens and the English tea that is served each afternoon.

**Open:** year round **Accommodations:** 6 guest rooms with private baths; 2 are suites **Meals:** full breakfast included; complimentary refreshments and afternoon tea; restaurants nearby **Rates:** $75 to $125; 10% discount to National Trust members and National Trust Visa cardholders **Payment:** Visa, MC, Discover, personal and traveler's checks **Restrictions:** children over 10 welcome; no smoking; no pets **On-site activities:** baby grand piano, board games, reading and video libraries, croquet, landscaped gardens with gazebo and terrace

# BOOTHBAY HARBOR

**Nearby attractions:** lighthouses, boating, fishing, sightseeing, tennis, golfing, theaters, museums, specialty shops, restaurants, antiques hunting

## HARBOUR TOWNE INN ON THE WATERFRONT

71 Townsend Avenue
Boothbay Harbor, Maine 04538
**Phone:** 207/633-4300 or 800/722-4240
**Fax:** 207/633-4300
**Website:** www.acadia.net/harbourtowneinn
**E-Mail:** mainco@gwi.net
**Proprietors:** The Thomases

This rambling Queen Anne inn sits among colorful gardens and giant shade trees on the shore of beautiful Boothbay Harbor. Built just before the turn of the century, this fully refurbished structure offers scenic views of the quaint village and harbor that, together, are known as the "Boating Capital of New England." Waterfront accommodations in the inn have outside decks, good for catching fresh breezes. A modern, spacious penthouse accommodates six people and affords a panoramic view not only of the harbor but also of outlying islands and the ocean. A deluxe continental breakfast is served in the sunroom. In cold weather, the parlor fireplace is kept burning. With charming accommodations and special off-season packages, the inn's proprietors and guests have deemed it "The Finest B&B on the Waterfront."

**Open:** mostly year round **Accommodations:** 6 guest rooms with private baths; 1 is a penthouse suite **Meals:** continental-plus breakfast included; restaurants nearby **Rates:** $69 to $249 (seasonal); 10% discount off rack rate to National Trust members and National Trust Visa cardholders **Payment:** AmEx, Visa, MC, Discover, traveler's check, personal check with credit card and driver's license **Restrictions:** well-behaved children welcome; no smoking; no pets

# BRIDGTON

**Nearby attractions:** Shaker Village, restored nineteenth-century village of Willowbrook, antiques and crafts shops, Jones Gallery of glass and ceramics

## THE NOBLE HOUSE

37 Highland Road
P.O. Box 180
Bridgton, Maine 04009
**Phone and Fax:** 207/647-3733
**Proprietors:** Dick and Jane Starets
**Location:** 38 miles west of Portland, 1/2 mile from Bridgton

In the heart of the Lakes Region of Maine in the quaint town of Bridgton, this 1903 Queen Anne home overlooks peaceful Highland Lake. Built for State Senator Winfred Staples, the house is most notable for a second-story balcony topped by an unusual round arch tucked under a steep gable and for its wraparound porches. Inside, the inn is understated yet elegant. A front parlor contains the library, a grand piano, a pump organ, and a fireplace. The lounge in the rear of the house provides a comfortable setting for meeting other guests over complimentary refreshments or for watching television and videotapes. Some guest rooms have private porches; others provide whirlpool tubs. A full breakfast is served on the porch, by the fireside, or family-style in the dining room.

**Open:** year round **Accommodations:** 7 guest rooms (5 have private baths); 3 are suites **Meals:** full breakfast included; restaurants nearby **Rates:** $78 to $125 **Payment:** AmEx, Visa, MC, personal and traveler's checks **Restrictions:** no infants on weekends in season; no smoking; no pets **On-site activities:** swimming, canoeing, fishing, croquet, lakeside hammock

# BROOKSVILLE

**Nearby attractions:** nature trails, hiking, beach, fishing, boating, museums, antiques and arts-and-crafts shops, seasonal concerts and fairs

## OAKLAND HOUSE'S SHORE OAKS SEASIDE INN

R.R. 1, Box 400
Herrick Road
Brooksville, Maine 04617
**Phone:** 207/359-8521 or 800/359-RELAX
**Website:** www.acadia.net/oaklandhse
**Proprietors:** Jim and Sally Littlefield
**Location:** 50 miles south of Bangor

Twenty-five miles from the nearest traffic light, in a rural setting off paved roads, Oakland House's 200-year-old property extends along a half-mile of oceanfront and is complete with dock, rowboats, moorings, firewood, salt- and freshwater beaches, and hiking trails and dirt roads that lead to magnificent overlooks. Shore Oaks Seaside Inn is nestled among Oakland House's extensive property. The inn was built by the Spencer family in 1907 on a rocky point of land overlooking Eggemoggin Reach. It is a classic Maine coast cottage that, having been renovated in 1995, contains original Craftsman and Victorian antiques, a living room with fireplace, library, dining room, piazza, and bayfront gazebo. Ten individually decorated guest rooms (two with fireplaces) are on three floors. Intended as a place to relax and unwind, Shore Oaks purposefully has neither televisions nor telephones.

Open: year round **Accommodations:** 10 guest rooms (7 have private baths) **Meals:** full breakfast included in summer, continental breakfast included remainder of the year; dinners can be included in summer; complimentary refreshments; restaurant on premises at Oakland House **Rates:** $75 to $115 low season (B&B); $146 to $190 high season (MAP); packages and specials available that may include lobster dinners, schooner trips, cruises, or discounted rates **Payment:** personal check **Restrictions:** children over 14 welcome; no smoking; no pets **On-site activities:** hiking, boating, swimming, lawn games

# CAMDEN

**Nearby attractions:** Camden Harbor, Camden Opera House, Camden Hills State Park, shopping, museums, boating, cruises, lake swimming, windjammers, lighthouses, island day trips, golfing, tennis, hiking, horseback riding, downhill and cross-country skiing and all winter sports

## BLACKBERRY INN
82 Elm Street
Camden, Maine 04843
**Phone:** 207/236-6060 or 800/388-6000
**Website:** www.bbonline.com/me/blackberryinn
**E-mail:** blkberry@midcoast.com
**Proprietors:** Cynthia and James Ostrowski

A stay at Blackberry Inn is made special by its spacious guest rooms decorated in Victorian style with brass beds, curved love seats, and antique dressers, and extra touches such as blackberry candies and large fluffy towels. Each morning brings a gourmet breakfast with entrees like brie souffle and cheese blintzes with blackberry sauce. Two new deluxe rooms contain king-size beds, whirlpool tubs, and wood-burning fireplaces. Guests also enjoy the 1849 Victorian home for its airy parlors (one furnished with Bar Harbor wicker), polished parquet floors, original tin ceilings, working fireplaces, and ornate plaster moldings. The inn has been fitted with sprinklers for the safety of its guests and has been described as "just delightful" by the *Miami Herald*. This is a unique home, the only one from Maine featured in *Daughters of Painted Ladies: America's Resplendent Victorians*.

**Open:** year round **Accommodations:** 10 guest rooms with private baths  **Meals:** full breakfast included; dinner available by special arrangement; restaurants nearby **Wheelchair access:** 3 guest rooms, dining room, parlors **Rates:** $85 to $155 (seasonal) **Payment:** Visa, MC, personal and traveler's checks  **Restrictions:** no smoking; no pets (resident dog)

# EASTPORT

**Nearby attractions:** Campobello Island and the Roosevelt summer cottage, whale-watching, Reversing Falls, hiking, fishing trips, tennis, beachcombing, museums, historic district walking tours, art galleries

## TODD HOUSE
1 Capen Avenue
Todd's Head
Eastport, Maine 04631
**Phone:** 207/853-2328
**Proprietor:** Ruth M. McInnis

Built in 1775, Todd House is a classic New England Cape Cod house with a massive center chimney and a unique "good morning" staircase that rises toward the chimney, then divides left and right to lead toward two opposing bedroom doors. (When occupants of each room awake in the morning and open their doors, they are facing each other, hence the nickname.) One of these bedrooms has a working fireplace. In 1801, Eastern Lodge No. 7 of the Masonic Order was chartered here; a cornerstone marks the event. During the Civil War, the Todd House served as barracks for soldiers. The house, currently owned by a historian and listed in the National Register, has many volumes of local history in its library. Breakfast is served in the common room before a fireplace and bake oven in surroundings reminiscent of the Revolutionary era. The yard affords a view of Passamaquoddy Bay and its islands.

**Open:** year round **Accommodations:** 6 guest rooms (2 have private baths); 2 are suites **Meals:** continental-plus breakfast included; two rooms have kitchenettes; complimentary refreshments; restaurants nearby **Wheelchair access:** some guest rooms, common rooms **Rates:** $45 to $80 **Payment:** personal and traveler's checks **Restrictions:** no smoking **On-site activities:** deck and barbecue with water view, library of local history

## WESTON HOUSE
26 Boynton Street
Eastport, Maine 04631
**Phone:** 207/853-2907 or 800/853-2907
**Fax:** 207/853-0981
**Proprietors:** Jett and John Peterson

Jonathan Weston built this Federal house in 1810 on a hill overlooking Passamaquoddy Bay. John James Audubon stayed here while awaiting passage to Labrador in 1833. At today's inn, listed in the National Register of Historic Places,

afternoon sherry and tea are offered to guests in surroundings elegantly furnished with collections of antiques and oriental rugs. Some of the large and comfortable guest rooms overlook the bay while others afford views of the expansive lawn and garden. Sumptuous breakfasts are served in the dining room amid family treasures, to the relaxing strains of classical music.

**Open:** year round **Accommodations:** 5 guest rooms with shared baths **Meals:** full breakfast included; complimentary refreshments; dinners and picnic lunches by reservation; restaurants nearby **Rates:** $60 to $75; 10% discount offered to National Trust members **Payment:** personal and traveler's checks **Restrictions:** smoking limited; no pets **On-site activities:** croquet, badminton, porch sitting to view the bay, gardens

---

## FREEPORT

**Nearby attractions:** Maine Maritime Museum, famous Freeport factory outlets, including L. L. Bean; Bowdoin and Bates colleges; boat cruises; fishing; beaches; four state parks with nature trails; Marine Museum; golfing; bicycling; hiking; cross-country skiing

### BAGLEY HOUSE BED AND BREAKFAST
1290 Royalsborough Road
Durham, Maine 04222
**Phone:** 207/865-6566 or 800/765-1772
**Fax:** 207/353-5878
**Website:** members.aol.com/bedandbrk/bagley
**E-mail:** bglyhse@aol.com
**Proprietors:** Suzanne O'Connor and Susan Backhouse
**Location:** 6 miles north of Freeport on Route 136 in Durham; exit 20 of I-95

Tranquility and history prevail in this National Register-listed home, the oldest in Durham. Only 10 minutes from downtown Freeport, the Bagley House offers a rural retreat from the bustle of traffic and shoppers. Opened in 1772 as a public house by Captain O. Israel Bagley, it also served as the first house of worship and first school in town, then known as Royalsborough. Today, the Bagley House contains five guest rooms, each furnished with antiques and custom-crafted pieces. Most have queen-size beds and one offers a wood-burning fireplace. The adjacent Bliss Barn offers three rooms with gas fireplaces and king or queen beds. Downstairs is a spacious common room suitable for small conferences, receptions, or showers. In the main house, the kitchen boasts a huge brick fireplace and beehive oven. This is where guests gather for a full country breakfast. Cold drinks and chocolate-chip cookies are always available. The inn is located on six acres of fields and woods.

**Open:** year round **Accommodations:** 8 guest rooms with private baths **Meals:** full breakfast included; complimentary refreshments; restaurants nearby **Rates:** $85 to $140 **Payment:** AmEx, Visa, MC, Discover, personal and traveler's checks **Restrictions:** no smoking; no pets (resident dog and cat) **On-site activities:** games, books, hiking, bird-watching, studying wildflowers, berry picking, cross-country skiing, quilting weekends

---

## FRYEBURG

**Nearby attractions:** White Mountain National Forest, hiking, golfing, fishing, canoeing, skiing, summer concert series, theater, Fryeburg Fair, outlet shopping, antiques hunting

### ADMIRAL PEARY HOUSE BED AND BREAKFAST

9 Elm Street
Fryeburg, Maine 04037
**Phone:** 207/935-3365 or 800/237-8080
**Fax:** 207/935-3365
**Website:** www.mountwashingtonvalley.com/admiralpearyhouse
**E-mail:** adpeary@nxi.com
**Proprietors:** Ed and Nancy Greenberg

The Admiral Peary House is a sprawling white home surrounded by acres of manicured lawns and award-winning perennial gardens. Admiral Robert Edwin Peary lived here with his mother after graduating from Bowdoin College in 1877. They were the first occupants of the house, and Peary often wrote about its beauty in his journal. The house's three gables are gambreled and flared, much like the early Dutch tradition and it was known for a time as the "house of three gables." Today it is carefully preserved, offering guests a well-stocked library and formal living room, as well as a wicker-furnished screened porch with adjoining red cedar deck overlooking the lawn and eight acres of forest. Antiques are found throughout the inn. Each of the five guest rooms has been tastefully decorated to complement the period of the house while offering twentieth-century comforts. Spacious grounds provide hours of entertainment including tennis, and a guest living room with billiards is in what was once an attached barn.

**Open:** year round **Accommodations:** 6 guest rooms with private baths **Meals:** full breakfast included; complimentary refreshments; restaurants nearby **Rates:** $70 to $128 **Payment:** AmEx, Visa, MC, personal and traveler's checks **Restrictions:** children over 10 welcome; no smoking; no pets **On-site activities:** piano, library, billiards, clay tennis court, outdoor spa, bicycles, snowshoe trail, lawn games

---

## GREENVILLE

**Nearby attractions:** Steamboat Katahdin lake cruises, Moosehead Lake for water activities, skiing on Squaw Mountain, golfing, tennis, sightseeing plane rides, snowmobile trails

### GREENVILLE INN
P.O. Box 1194
Norris Street
Greenville, Maine 04441-1194
**Phone:** 207/695-2206 or 888-695-6000
**Website:** www.greenvilleinn.com
**E-mail:** glinn@moosehead.net
**Proprietors:** Elfi, Susie, and Michael Schnetzer

In 1895 William Shaw, a wealthy lumber baron, fell in love with the dramatic vista of Moosehead Lake and Squaw Mountain from this site and so had his elegant

mansion built here. Ships' carpenters worked 10 years to complete the carved embellishments and paneling of cherry, mahogany, and oak found throughout the inn. A spruce tree painted on a leaded-glass window graces the stairway landing. Embossed Lincrusta and gaslights adorn the walls. Fireplaces are ornamented with carved mantels, mosaics, and English tiles. Individually appointed guest rooms and cottages are furnished with attention to detail and comfort. Guests begin a memorable evening with cocktails on the veranda, or by fireside in the drawing room. Dining rooms with lake and mountain views provide a romantic setting for an elegant dinner. Innovative menus feature fresh Maine seafood, roast duckling, rack of lamb, steaks, and other local specialties. The homemade desserts and pastries are famous.

**Open:** year round **Accommodations:** 6 guest rooms (1 is a suite) and 5 cottages with private baths **Meals:** continental-plus breakfast included; restaurants on premises **Wheelchair access:** limited **Rates:** $95 to $195; 10% discount to National Trust members and National Trust Visa cardholders **Payment:** Visa, MC, Discover, personal and traveler's checks **Restrictions:** children over 7 welcome; no smoking; no pets

---

# KENNEBUNK

**Nearby attractions:** museums, theaters, galleries, beaches, hiking bicycling, canoeing, nature preserves, wildlife refuges, antiques hunting, boutique and outlet shopping, golfing, tennis, sailing, whale watching, deep sea fishing, skiing, skating, sledding

### THE KENNEBUNK INN
45 Main Street
Kennebunk, Maine 04043
**Phone:** 207/985-3351
**Fax:** 207/985-8865
**Proprietors:** John and Kristen Martin

Two hundred years old, The Kennebunk Inn stands in the center of downtown Kennebunk on Main Street. Having been established so long ago, it is not surprising that the inn is the oldest operating business on Main Street. The white clapboard building sports handsome touches in the form of cornice dentils, upper and lower front porches, pediments, and dormers. A classic inn, it offers 28 newly appointed guest rooms, each with a distinctive personality set by antique claw-foot porcelain bathtubs, four-poster beds, hardwood floors or, perhaps, cozy quilts. All rooms include private baths. Televisions and room phones are also available for those who must stay in touch. Guests are invited to enjoy the sitting rooms where shelves of books, and games await. The Kennebunk Inn Restaurant serves an ever-changing, provocative menu seven nights a week.

**Open:** year round **Accommodations:** 28 guest rooms with private baths; 4 are suites **Meals:** continental breakfast included; restaurant on premises; restaurants nearby **Wheelchair access:** yes **Rates:** $80 to $160 **Payment:** AmEx, Visa, MC, Discover, personal and traveler's checks **Restrictions:** smoking limited

# KENNEBUNKPORT

**Nearby attractions:** Dock Square shops, walking tours, tennis, golfing, boating, deep-sea fishing, watching birds and whales, bicycling, hiking, beaches, museums, outlet shops, theaters, concerts, art galleries, antiques hunting

### 1802 HOUSE BED AND BREAKFAST INN
15 Locke Street
P.O. Box 646A
Kennebunkport, Maine 04046
**Phone:** 207/967-5632 or 800/932-5632
**Fax:** 207/967-0780
**Website:** www.1802inn.com
**Fax:** inquiry@1802inn.com
**Proprietors:** Ron and Carol Perry

Like the great sailing ships that are dragged down the Kennebunk River to be launched into the Atlantic Ocean, this house was pulled by oxen from nearby Waterboro where it was built in 1802 to its present location on Locke Street. At that time it was a one-story structure. Several years later, a second story was added, resulting in the inn as it is seen today. Each of the inn's six guest rooms (one is a three-room suite) is furnished with antiques, original art, and four-poster beds and features either a fireplace or whirlpool tub; some have both. Amenities abound in each room, including bathrobes and slippers, make-up and shaving mirrors, hair dryers, CD player, television and VCR, candles, and wine glasses with a corkscrew. The fireplace in the guest parlor is a focal point for those guests who like to mingle. Breakfast is served in the guest dining room, originally a barn. Behind the inn is the fifteenth fairway of the Cape Arundel Golf Club. The innkeepers are happy to make arrangements for golf tee times, complimentary use of the local health club, special occasion stays, or special dietary needs.

**Open:** year round **Accommodations:** 6 guest rooms with private baths; 1 is a suite **Meals:** full breakfast included; complimentary refreshments; restaurants nearby **Rates:** $129 to $329 **Payment:** AmEx, Visa, MC, Discover, personal and traveler's checks **Restrictions:** children over 12 welcome; no smoking; no pets **On-site activities:** bird watching, gardens

## INN ON SOUTH STREET
5 South Street
Kennebunkport, Maine 04046
**Phone:** 207/967-5151 or 800/963-5151
**Fax:** 207/967-4385
**Website:** www.innonsouthst.com
**E-mail:** innkeeper@innonsouthst.com
**Proprietor:** Eva M. Downs

Built between 1806 and 1823 by sea captain Ivory Goodwin, this three-story Greek Revival home was one of many built with profits earned when clipper ships made the long voyage to the East and returned with tea, silk, and porcelain and, indeed, the inn today retains a decor reminiscent of Kennebunkport's link with the early China trade. Fully restored and listed in the National Register of Historic Places, the inn boasts a handsome "good morning" staircase, original pine-plank floors, and an old-fashioned herb garden. Spacious guest rooms feature antiques and traditional furnishings. Comfort is ensured with down comforters, piles of pillows, thick towels, fine soaps, telephones, and interesting reading materials. A full breakfast is served in the second-floor country kitchen with views of the river and ocean. Guests are invited to stroll through the formal herb garden or lounge in the secret garden. Located in a quiet corner of the historic village, the inn is within easy walking distance of shops, restaurants, and beaches.

**Open:** year round **Accommodations:** 4 guest rooms with private baths; 1 is a three-room suite **Meals:** full breakfast included; complimentary refreshments; restaurants nearby **Rates:** $105 to $225 **Payment:** Visa, MC, personal and traveler's check **Restrictions:** no smoking; no pets

## KENNEBUNKPORT INN
One Dock Square
P.O. Box 111
Kennebunkport, Maine 04046
**Phone:** 207/967-2621 or 800/248-2621
**Fax:** 207/967-3705
**Website:** kennebunkportinn.com
**Proprietors:** Rick and Martha Griffin

The Kennebunkport Inn began in 1890 as a private residence for wealthy tea and coffee merchant Burleigh S. Thompson. The Colonial Revival mansion boasted 400 feet of river frontage and was furnished without regard to expense. Today, guest rooms in the mansion and in the attached 1930s River House are individually decorated with period antiques. All accommodations include private baths and color television. The inn's dining room is renowned for its fresh native seafood and regional cuisine. The turn-of-the-century pub includes a piano bar. The inn boasts a swimming pool, deck, and white sand beach. Just steps from the inn are numerous shops and galleries.

**Open:** year round **Accommodations:** 34 guest rooms with private baths **Meals:** continental breakfast include in winter months; restaurant on premises serves breakfast and dinner; restaurants nearby **Wheelchair access:** yes **Rates:** $89.50 to $265 (seasonal) **Payment:** AmEx, Visa, MC, traveler's check **Restrictions:** smoking limited; no pets **On-site activities:** swimming pool, piano bar and lounge

## MAINE STAY INN
34 Maine Street
P.O. Box 500A-NT
Kennebunkport, Maine 04046-1800
**Phone:** 207/967-2117 or 800/950-2117
**Fax:** 207/967-8757
**Website:** www.mainestayinn.com
**E-mail:** innkeeper@mainestayinn.com
**Proprietors:** Carol and Lindsay Copeland

Built as a home in 1860 in a square-block, Italianate style with a contoured, low-hipped roof, the Maine Stay Inn underwent numerous alterations around the turn of the century. The house's fine craftsmanship is still evident in a suspended flying staircase, sunburst-crystal glass windows, ornately carved mantels and moldings, a spacious wicker-bedecked wraparound porch, and a cupola that was once used to spot rum-runners offshore and now offers lovely views of the town. The delightful guest rooms, some with fireplaces, offer comfort and solitude. Both the house and surrounding district are listed in the National Register of Historic Places. The innkeepers join with Maine Stay guests each afternoon for tea and conversation, sharing the latest happenings in the "Port."

**Open:** year round **Accommodations:** 6 guest rooms with private baths; 2 are suites **Meals:** full breakfast included; complimentary afternoon refreshments; restaurants nearby **Rates:** $95 to $225 **Payment:** AmEx, Visa, MC, personal and traveler's checks **Restrictions:** no smoking; no pets **On-site activities:** lawn games, porch for reading and relaxing

## TIDES INN BY-THE-SEA

R.R. 2, 737 Goose Rocks Beach
Kennebunkport, Maine 04046
**Phone:** 207/967-3757
**Fax:** 207/967-5183
**Website:** www.tidesinnbythesea.com
**E-mail:** innkeeper@mainestayinn.com
**Proprietor:** Marie B. Henriksen
**Location:** On a 3-mile sandy beach, 6 miles from center of Kennebunkport

Exceptionally clean, homey New England lodging is what guests encounter at the Tides Inn, a three-story Victorian clapboard-and-shingle hotel, designed by John Calvin Stevens and built in 1899. In its infancy, the inn was called the New Belvidere, and hosted such luminaries as Theodore Roosevelt and Sir Arthur Conan Doyle, whose signatures are in the guest register. The lobby boasts its original beachstone fireplace and an antique cabinet displaying items found in the hotel walls during its most recent renovation: snuff boxes, love letters, photographs, a large hat pin, and black hosiery! The front rooms, dining rooms, and open porches afford sunny, unobstructed views of the Atlantic Ocean. Guests enjoy a cozy pub, terrific Maine cooking, and a relaxed atmosphere.

**Open:** mid-May to mid-October **Accommodations:** 22 guest rooms (19 have private baths); 2 are suites **Meals:** restaurants on premises; restaurants nearby **Rates:** $105 to $250 **Payment:** AmEx, Visa, MC, personal and traveler's check **Restrictions:** smoking limited; no pets **On-site activities:** three miles of sandy beach for jogging, swimming, collecting shells, and building sand castles

# KINGFIELD

**Nearby attractions:** Sugarloaf Ski and Golf Resort, Lakewood Theater, Stanley School Museum, Phillips Historical Society, restored narrow gauge railroad, Kennebec and Dead rivers, hiking, bicycling, whitewater rafting, fishing

## THE HERBERT – A COUNTRY INN

Main Street
P.O. Box 67
Kingfield, Maine 04947
**Phone:** 207/265-2000 or 800/THE-HERB
**Website:** www.byme.com/theherbert
**E-mail:** herbert@somtel.com
**Proprietor:** Bud Dick

Judge and member of the Maine House of Representatives Herbert Wing had this striking Beaux Arts hotel built in 1918, using only the finest materials: fumed oak paneling in the lobby; white oak and terrazzo floors with Italian marble; and solid brass light fixtures (the hotel was one of the first buildings in town to be completely electrified from the start). Following abandonment and bankruptcy, the Herbert was rescued in the early 1980s by Bud Dick who sent it through a $1 million restoration. Original features survive throughout, including those brass light fixtures and electrical outlet covers, all sparkling like new once again. New are the roof, private baths for each of the 33 guest rooms, and heating, sprinkling, and fire alarm systems. Many guest rooms feature brass beds and most have whirlpool tubs. The hotel's dining room (rated with four stars by the *Boston Globe*) features upscale New England cuisine, accompanied by a choice of 115 wines. Ensuring a stress-free environment is the absence of telephones and televisions from guest rooms.

**Open:** year round **Accommodations:** 33 guest rooms with private baths; 6 are suites **Meals:** continental-plus breakfast included; restaurant on premises; restaurants nearby **Rates:** $59 to $199 (seasonal); 10% discount to National Trust members and National Trust Visa cardholders **Payment:** AmEx, Visa, MC, Discover, CB, DC, personal and traveler's checks **Restrictions:** smoking limited **On-site activities:** hot tub and sauna

# OAKLAND

Nearby attractions: Belgrade Lakes Chain, swimming, boating, water skiing, fishing, ice skating, cross-country skiing, snowmobiling, ice fishing

## PRESSEY HOUSE
85 Summer Street
Oakland, Maine 04963
**Phone:** 207/465-3500
**E-mail:** presshse@mint.net
**Proprietors:** Terry and JoAnne Badger

Pressey House is a fine example of an architectural rarity: an octagon house. Built in the 1850s by H. T. Pressey, this local landmark (one of 14 known octagonal structures in the state of Maine) incorporates elements of the Greek Revival style in its simple ornamentation. Located in the quaint village of Oakland on Messalonskee Lake, Pressey House has an attached ell and barn in the typical New England rural style. The house boasts 22 rooms and five original fireplaces in 8,000 square feet of living space. The rambling structure also includes five guest suites, many with excellent lake views. Listed in the National Register of Historic Places, Pressey House is decorated with traditional and Victorian furnishings.

**Open:** year round **Accommodations:** 5 guest suites with private baths **Meals:** full breakfast included; complimentary refreshments; restaurants nearby **Rates:** $75 to $100; 10% discount to National Trust members and National Trust Visa cardholders **Payment:** personal and traveler's checks **On-site activities:** lake beach, swimming, fishing, boating, gardens

# PORTLAND

**Nearby attractions:** historic district walking tours, fine art museum, symphony, theater, beaches, Casco Bay, Calendar Islands, harbor cruises, whale-watching, ice skating, cross-country skiing, outlet shops, international ferry to Nova Scotia

## POMEGRANATE INN
49 Neal Street
Portland, Maine 04102
**Phone:** 207/772-1006 or 800/356-0408
**Fax:** 207/773-4426
**Proprietor:** Isabel Smiles

In 1884, E. Russell Barbour built a Victorian house on this corner lot. In 1919 the house was sold to Frank E. Milliken, who remodeled it to its current Colonial Revival style, which features a two-story bow window, and a classical portico. Today, the house is the Pomegranate Inn, an imaginative small inn dressed in eclecticism and offering personalized service. The walls of each bedroom have been painted by artist Heidi Gerquest in unique floral abstractions and geometric patterns that blend seamlessly with the elegant furnishings, which include four-poster beds and gas fireplaces in some rooms. All rooms are appointed with antiques, fine linens, telephone, television, air conditioning, and private bath. The inn's individuality extends to breakfast, with entrees such as currant pancakes. French doors lead from the dining room out to the gardens. Pomegranate Inn has been featured in *Travel and Leisure*.

**Open:** year round **Accommodations:** 8 guest rooms with private baths; 1 is a suite **Meals:** full breakfast included; restaurants nearby **Wheelchair access:** 1 room **Rates:** $95 to $165; 10% discount to National Trust members and National Trust Visa cardholders **Payment:** AmEx, Visa, MC, DC, Discover, personal and traveler's checks **Restrictions:** children over 16 welcome; no smoking; inquire about pets

## WEST END INN
146 Pine Street
Portland, Maine 04102
**Phone:** 207/772-1377 or 800/338-1377
**Fax:** 207/828-0984
**Proprietor:** John Leonard

Situated in Portland's historic Western Promenade, the West End Inn provides a convenient location and thoughtful hospitality in a restored 1871 city landmark building. Originally owned by Freedom Nash, "Portland's Stove Maker," the house is in the handsome Second Empire style. The innkeeper bought it in 1994

and put it through a complete renovation, introducing a blend of antiques, contemporary pieces, and
unique accessories from around the
world. Six tastefully decorated rooms
feature rice-carved canopy beds
(queen- and king-size) dressed in designer linens, including comfy flannel
sheets in winter. A room on the first
floor has a private deck; another features a whirlpool tub. All rooms are
air conditioned and offer cable televi-

sion. His and her bathrobes are provided in each room for added convenience and
comfort. Breakfast is cooked to order and served in the formal dining room by
the fireplace.

**Open:** year round **Accommodations:** 6 guest rooms with private baths **Meals:** full
breakfast included; restaurants nearby **Rates:** $89 to $169; 10% discount to National Trust
members and National Trust Visa cardholders **Payment:** AmEx, Visa, MC, CB, DC,
personal and traveler's checks **Restrictions:** no smoking; no pets

---

# WALPOLE

**Nearby attractions:** Fort William Henry, lighthouses, Audubon Center,
museums, beaches, fresh and saltwater fishing, boating, hiking, bicycling, golfing,
tennis, seal watching

## BRANNON–BUNKER INN
349 State Road 129
Walpole, Maine 04573
**Phone:** 207/563-5941 or 800/563-9225
**E-mail:** brbnkinn@lincoln.midcoast.com
**Proprietors:** Jeanne and Joe Hovance
**Location:** 4 miles south of Damariscotta

In the 1920s the owners of this Cape-style house, which had been built one
hundred years earlier, turned the barn behind the house into a dance hall known
as La Hacienda. In the 1950s the owners converted the old barn and adjacent
carriage house to comfortably furnished sleeping rooms and opened the inn, then
known as the Homeport. It was the area's first bed and breakfast. Today, eight
sleeping rooms are furnished in colonial, Victorian, and Empire themes. Stenciled
walls and floors, quaint wallpapers, homemade quilts, dried flowers, and country
crafts meld with each room's antique furnishings. Antiques also fill the breakfast

nook and public room with fieldstone fireplace. The upstairs sitting area showcases the innkeeper's World War I memorabilia.

**Open:** April to December **Accommodations:** 8 guest rooms (6 have private baths) 1 is a suite **Meals:** continental-plus breakfast; restaurants nearby **Wheelchair access:** 3 rooms **Rates:** $55 to $110; 10% discount to National Trust members and National Trust Visa cardholders **Payment:** AmEx, Visa, MC, personal check **Restrictions:** no smoking; no pets **On-site activities:** badminton, board games, television, reading, stream and pond

## WISCASSET

**Nearby attractions:** Reid State Park beaches, Wiscasset, Pemaquid Point scenic area, Boothbay Harbor, sailing, tour boats, deep sea fishing, shopping, Maritime Museum, Center for the Arts, Montsweag Flea Market, Musical Wonder House

### SQUIRE TARBOX INN
Box 1181
Westport Island
Wiscasset, Maine 04578
**Phone and Fax:** 207/882-7693
**Website:** www.innbook.com/squiretarbox
**E-mail:** squiretarbox@ime
**Proprietors:** Karen and Bill Mitman
**Location:** 10 miles south of Wiscasset

Squire Samuel Tarbox built the main portion of this New England farmhouse in 1825, although an earlier section dates to 1763. The original floors, carvings, beams, molding, and fireplaces have been carefully preserved, resulting in an inn that offers the charm of antiquity and the personal comforts of today. A major attraction of this inn is its herd of dairy goats, which provides milk for the inn's famous chèvre cheeses. Equally well known is the inn's dining room, offering five-course dinners made from the freshest ingredients. After dinner, guests are invited to enjoy games in the old barn, or a stroll down wooded paths, or the comfort of a warm fire and a good book. In a pastoral setting, the Squire Tarbox Inn provides a place to escape tourist crowds, yet is close to many of Maine's famous attractions.

**Open:** mid May to late October **Accommodations:** 11 guest rooms with private baths **Meals:** full breakfast and dinner included **Rates:** $145 to $225 **Payment:** AmEx, Visa, MC, Discover, personal and traveler's checks **Restrictions:** children over 12 welcome; smoking limited; no pets **On-site activities:** farm animals, rowboat, game room, walking the grounds

# MARYLAND

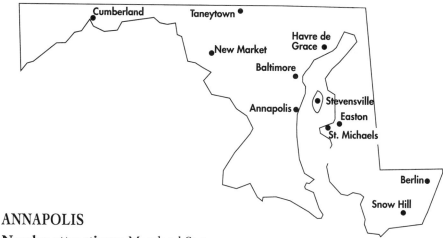

## ANNAPOLIS

**Nearby attractions:** Maryland State
Capitol, William Paca House, walking tours
of historic district, City Dock, Chesapeake Bay, boating, U.S. Naval
Adacemy, antiques hunting, shopping, dining

## HISTORIC INNS OF ANNAPOLIS

16 Church Circle
Annapolis, Maryland 21401
**Phone:** 410/263-2641 or 800/678-8946
**Fax:** 410/268-3813
**General Manager:** Homan Cull

Three restored buildings in the heart of the historic district comprise this
establishment: Two of the inns face the State Capitol on State Circle. The oldest,
the Governor Calvert House, was built in 1727 as a two-story brick building with
attached shed, smokehouse, and frame outbuilding. The Robert Johnson House
was built in 1765. On Church Circle, the Maryland Inn was constructed as a home
in 1776 and was described as "an elegant brick house...in a dry and healthy part
of the city." All guest rooms have been handsomely restored and individually
furnished with period antiques and reproductions. Historic Inns of Annapolis also
offers a renowned restaurant, the Treaty of Paris, and live musical shows at the
King of France, an eighteenth-century tavern that features top name jazz and big
band performers. Banquet and meeting facilities are available. Each of the Historic
Inns is located just steps from the State House, U.S. Naval Academy, and
downtown Old Annapolis. The group of inns is a member of Historic Hotels of
America.

**Open:** year round **Accommodations:** 128 guest rooms with private baths; 12 are suites **Meals:** complimentary refreshments; restaurant on premises; restaurants nearby **Wheelchair access:** yes **Rates:** $125 to $300; 10% discount to National Trust members and National Trust Visa cardholders **Payment:** AmEx, Visa, MC, DC, personal and traveler's checks **Restrictions:** smoking limited; no pets **On-site activities:** nightclub

## WILLIAM PAGE INN

8 Martin Street
Annapolis, Maryland 21401
**Phone:** 410/626-1506 or 800/364-4160, ext. 8
**Fax:** 410/263-4841
**Website:** www.wmpageinn.com
**E-mail:** WmPageInn@aol.com
**Proprietor:** Robert L. Zuchelli

Built in 1908, this four-square, cedar shake Shingle house was, for more than 50 years, the Democratic Club in the Historic District. In 1987 it was handsomely renovated into the William Page Inn. The first floor entry contains an open stairway flanked by crystal chandeliers. The common room offers an inviting gathering area with its wood-burning fireplace and wet bar. Five distinctively appointed guest rooms range from the first-floor Fern Room with queen-size Victorian bed and direct access to the wraparound porch to the Marilyn Suite, a spacious third-floor accommodation with skylight, dormer window seats, sitting area, and whirlpool tub. A full breakfast is accompanied by a selection of local and national newspapers. The innkeepers are eager to assist guests with local attractions, dining reservations, and recommendations. The elegant William Page Inn has been featured in *Country Inns, Bed and Breakfast,* and *National Geographic Traveler* magazines, among others and holds three diamonds from AAA.

**Open:** year round **Accommodations:** 5 guest rooms (3 have private baths); 1 is a suite **Meals:** full breakfast included; restaurants nearby **Rates:** $105 to $200; 10% discount to National Trust members and National Trust Visa cardholders **Payment:** Visa, MC, personal and traveler's checks **Restrictions:** children over 12 welcome; no smoking; no pets

# BALTIMORE

**Nearby attractions:** National Aquarium, Inner Harbor, Oriole Park at Camden Yard, Maryland Science Center, Johns Hopkins University, historic Fell's Point, Little Italy, Pimlico Race Course (home of the Preakness), Baltimore Zoo, Babe Ruth Baseball Museum, H. L. Mencken House, Edgar Allan Poe House, Baltimore Symphony, Mechanic Theatre, historic neighborhoods, antiques hunting, tennis, bicycling, boating, swimming

## ADMIRAL FELL
888 South Broadway
Baltimore, Maryland 21231
**Phone:** 410/522-7377 or 800/292-INNS (4667)
**Fax:**410/522-0707
**Website:** www.admiralfell.com
**Proprietors:** Nancy Caudill

In the historic Fell's Point section of Baltimore is the mischievously named Admiral Fell Inn, seven adjoining buildings of Victorian design dating from 1850 to 1910. Originally a boardinghouse for sailors, later a YMCA, and then a vinegar bottling plant, this delightful facility was completely renovated in 1985, then expanded and renovated in 1995. The public areas include an antique-filled lobby and library, an English-style pub for light fare, and a full-service restaurant specializing in fresh seafood dishes. The 80 individually decorated guest rooms, many with four-poster beds, are named after figures in Maryland history. Ultimate convenience is provided by modern bathrooms (some with whirlpool tubs) containing color cable television sets and telephones. In addition to free continental breakfasts and daily newspapers, the inn provides complimentary transportation to the Inner Harbor, downtown, and Johns Hopkins Medical Institutions. The Admiral Fell Inn is a charter member of Historic Hotels of America.

**Open:** year round **Accommodations:** 80 guest rooms with private baths; 4 are suites **Meals:** continental breakfast included; restaurants on premises; restaurants nearby **Wheelchair access:** guest rooms, bathrooms, dining rooms **Rates:** $195 to $355; 10% discount to National Trust members and National Trust Visa cardholders **Payment:** AmEx, Visa, MC, Discover, personal and traveler's checks **Restrictions:** no smoking; call for guidelines for pets **On-site activities:** pub and restaurant, courtyard for relaxing, books and games

## BETSY'S BED AND BREAKFAST

1428 Park Avenue
Baltimore, Maryland 21217
**Phone:** 410/383-1274 or 800/899-7533
**Fax:** 410/728-8957
**Website:** www.bandbworldwide.org
**E-mail:** amandasRS@aol.com
**Proprietor:** Betsy Grater

Betsy's Bed and Breakfast is in an 1870 four-story townhouse with center staircase that rises to a skylight. The interior features six carved marble fireplace mantels and 12-foot ceilings with medallions. A hallway is inlaid with strips of oak and walnut. The walls are decorated with handsome brass rubbings and family heirloom quilts and coverlets. Spacious guest rooms with marble mantelpieces contain queen- or king-size beds. The living room, in the back of the house, opens through French doors onto a garden, deck, and hot tub. Bolton Hill is a historic neighborhood, primarily residential, with tree-lined streets and brick sidewalks. Once it was home to F. Scott Fitzgerald and Gertrude Stein. Betsy's is within walking distance of Baltimore's cultural center and just seven minutes' driving time to the inner harbor and Harbor Place or a quick ride on the light rail to Camden Yard.

**Open:** year round **Accommodations:** 4 guest rooms with private baths **Meals:** continental breakfast included; restaurants nearby **Rates:** $65 to $85; 10% discount offered to National Trust members **Payment:** AmEx, Visa, MC, Discover, personal and traveler's checks **Restrictions:** no smoking; no pets **On-site activities:** hot tub in season

## MR. MOLE BED AND BREAKFAST

1601 Bolton Street
Baltimore, Maryland 21217
**Phone:** 410/728-1179
**Fax:** 410/728-3379
**Proprietors:** Collin Clarke and Paul Bragaw

Mr. Mole Bed and Breakfast is located in historic Bolton Hill, a neighborhood of quiet, tree-lined streets and spacious brick row houses. The neighborhood was built by wealthy merchants of mid-nineteenth-century Baltimore. This house, built in 1870, is decorated in a comfortable English style with many eighteenth- and nineteenth-century antiques. On the first floor, the living, breakfast, and drawing rooms are made elegant by 14-foot-high ceilings, bay windows, and marble fireplaces. Each guest room is individually decorated to create a distinctive mood like that in the Explorer Suite, a soothing blue-and-white room appointed with prints and artifacts collected from around the world. The Garden Suite, with its third-floor sunroom and sitting area, is bright in floral prints. Garage parking (with an automatic garage door opener) is available. Mr. Mole Bed and Breakfast has a Mobil four-star rating.

**Open:** year round **Accommodations:** 5 guest rooms with private baths; 2 are suites **Meals:** continental breakfast included; restaurants nearby **Rates:** $105 to $165 **Payment:** AmEx, Visa, MC, DC, Discover, personal and traveler's checks **Restrictions:** children over 10 welcome; no smoking; no pets

---

# BERLIN

**Nearby attractions:** Assateague Island National Seashore, Ocean City, antiques hunting, museums, horseback riding, golfing, tennis, fishing, crabbing, boating, swimming, beachcombing

## MERRY SHERWOOD PLANTATION

8909 Worcester Highway
Berlin, Maryland 21811
**Phone:** 410/641-2112 or 800/660-0358
**Fax:** 410/641-9528
**Website:** www.atbeach.com
**Proprietor:** Kirk Burbage
**Location:** 6 miles west of Ocean City, Maryland

On 18 acres of Maryland's scenic Eastern Shore, Merry Sherwood is an Italianate plantation home built in 1859. Outside, the stately structure is heavily orna-

mented with decorative cresting along the roofs of the main three-story house, the two-story wing, the wraparound arcaded porch, and the central tower. Inside, marble fireplaces, hardwood floors, fine antiques, and period light fixtures are complemented by deep, rich wall paints and Victorian-style papers. Each large guest room has been decorated with differently styled Victorian antiques. Bathrooms are luxurious with marble tile floors, marble showers, antique fixtures, and period wallcoverings. Guests are invited into the ballroom, parlor, dining room, library, and sunporch. Landscaped grounds include rare varieties of trees and shrubs. The plantation is listed in the National Register of Historic Places.

**Open:** year round **Accommodations:** 8 guest rooms (5 have private baths); 1 is a suite **Meals:** full breakfast included; complimentary refreshments; restaurants nearby **Rates:** $150 to $175; 10% discount to National Trust members and National Trust Visa cardholders **Payment:** Visa, MC, personal and traveler's checks **Restrictions:** no smoking; no pets **On-site activities:** lawn games, swings, bird-watching

## CUMBERLAND

**Nearby attractions:** historic districts, History House Museum, Western Maryland Station and Museum, Western Maryland Scenic Railroad, C&O Canal towpath, Cumberland Theater, Rocky Gap and New Germany state parks, Frostburg State University, Savage River and Greenridge recreation areas, bicycling, Frank Lloyd Wright's Fallingwater

### INN AT WALNUT BOTTOM
120 Greene Street
Cumberland, Maryland 21502
**Phone:** 301/777-0003 or 800/286-9718
**Fax:** 301/777-8288
**Website:** www.iwbinfo.com
**E-mail:** iwb@hereintown.net
**Proprietor:** Grant M. Irvin

The Inn at Walnut Bottom comprises the 1820 Federal-style Cowden House, the adjoining 1890 Dent House, the Oxford House Restaurant, and from May through October, the Haystack Mountain Art Workshops. All guest rooms are uniquely decorated with antique and period reproduction furniture. All rooms have television and private telephones. The inn is air conditioned and bathrooms are modern. Two parlors and a gift shop are available to overnight guests. In addition to the art workshops hosted by the inn from spring to fall, the inn offers a variety of packages based on such activities as canoeing the Potomac River, bicycling along the C&O Canal, and Mountain Club golfing. The restaurant serves traditional country-inn fare.

**Open:** year round **Accommodations:** 12 guest rooms (8 have private baths); 2 are suites **Meals:** full breakfast included; complimentary refreshments; restaurant on premises; restaurants nearby **Wheelchair access:** 2 rooms **Rates:** $79 to $130; 10% discount to National Trust members and National Trust Visa cardholders Sunday through Thursday **Payment:** AmEx, Visa, MC, Discover, traveler's check **Restrictions:** no smoking; no pets **On-site activities:** parlor games, library, in-room cable television

# EASTON

**Nearby attractions:** historic district walking tours, specialty and antiques shops, art galleries, museums, golfing, bicycling, tennis, boating, sailing, historic Oxford and St. Michaels

## BISHOP'S HOUSE BED AND BREAKFAST
214 Goldsborough Street
P.O. Box 2217
Easton, Maryland 21601
**Phone:** 410/820-7290 or 800/223-7290
**Website:** www.traveldata.com/inns/data/bishop.html
**E-mail:** bishopshouse@skipjack:bluecrab.org
**Proprietors:** Diane M. Laird-Ippolito and John Ippolito

Conveniently located in Easton's historic district, this house was built in 1880 for Philip Francis Thomas, Maryland's governor from 1848 to 1851. After his death in 1892, the house and property were sold to the Episcopal Church, serving as the Bishop's residence for the next 60 years. The three-story clapboard house evokes the Gothic Revival style in its steeply pitched gables and dormers. The innkeepers' restoration has returned the 14-foot ceilings, plaster moldings and medallions, and working fireplaces to their former beauty. The six guest rooms have individually controlled air conditioning and feature Victorian carved and sleigh beds. Three rooms have fireplaces and two bathrooms feature whirlpool tubs. The entire home, including the spacious foyer and two drawing rooms with fireplaces, is furnished with classic Victorian antiques. The wraparound porch is ideal for socializing or relaxing with a cold drink in warm weather. The inn provides a full breakfast, off-street parking, and cycling tour maps.

**Open:** year round **Accommodations:** 6 guest rooms (5 have private baths) **Meals:** full breakfast included; restaurants nearby **Rates:** $85 to $120 **Payment:** personal and traveler's checks **Restrictions:** children over 12 welcome; no smoking; no pets

## FREDERICK

**Nearby attractions:** historic district, carriage rides, Civil War battlefields and tours, antiques hunting, golfing, tennis, bicycling, swimming

### SPRING BANK, A BED AND BREAKFAST INN

7945 Worman's Mill Road
Frederick, Maryland 21701
**Phone:** 301/694-0440 or 800/400-INNS
**Fax:** 301/694-5926 (call first)
**Website:** www.bbonline.com/md/springbank/
**E-mail:** springbnk@aol.com
**Proprietor:** Ray Compton

Gothic Revival meets Italianate in this high-style Maryland farmhouse built in 1880 by George Houck. Lancet-arched windows set in steeply pitched gables combine with tall, thin first- and second-floor windows and a rooftop belvedere to present a handsome brick dwelling unique to this part of rural Frederick County. Inside, all original materials remain, including brass hardware with flowers and bird motifs, paneled louvered shutters, and heart-pine floors. Guests enter the foyer on a diamond-patterned floor of slate and marble. Five guest rooms are offered. There are fireplaces in three of them. Some rooms have bay-windowed sitting areas; some have claw-foot tubs in the baths. Antiques—furniture, oriental rugs, books, and decorative arts—fill the spacious inn. Guests are invited to relax in the parlor or on any of the three long porches. The inn is listed in the National Register of Historic Places and is a designated Frederick County Landmark Home.

**Open:** year round **Accommodations:** 5 guest rooms (1 has a private bath) **Meals:** continental-plus breakfast included; restaurants nearby **Rates:** $80 to $95; 10% discount to National Trust members and National Trust Visa cardholders mid-week only, excluding holidays **Payment:** AmEx, Visa, MC, Discover, personal and traveler's checks **Restrictions:** children over 11 welcome; no smoking; no pets **On-site activities:** half-mile walking path around perimeter of property

# HAVRE DE GRACE

**Nearby attractions:** Concord Point Lighthouse, boat rentals, decoy museum, swimming, antiques hunting, walking tour of historic district, state park

## SPENCER SILVER MANSION
200 South Union Avenue
Havre de Grace, Maryland 21078
**Phone:** 410/939-1097 or 800/780-1485
**E-mail:** SpencerSilver@erols.com
**Proprietor:** Carol Nemeth

Located in the heart of Havre de Grace's National Register historic district, the Spencer Silver Mansion is just two blocks from the water. The inn is a stone mansion in the Queen Anne style, its design embellished by a two-story bay window, a tower, four gables, a dormer, and a variety of window shapes and placements. The house was constructed in 1896 for John Spencer, a merchant and foundry owner. Later the house was purchased by Charles Silver, a local canner. Restored to reflect late Victorian styles, the house features intricate oak woodwork, impressive fireplace mantels, 10-foot-high quarter-sawn oak doors, and parquet floors with fancy inlaid borders. Guest rooms are decorated with Victorian antiques. A reading nook invites guests to curl up with a good book and relax. The recently restored carriage house (ca. 1919) has become a luxurious suite for four with whirlpool bath.

**Open:** year round **Accommodations:** 4 guest rooms (2 have private baths); 1 is a carriage house **Meals:** full breakfast included; restaurants nearby **Rates:** $70 to $140; 10% discount offered to National Trust members **Payment:** personal check **Restrictions:** smoking limited; no pets **On-site activities:** croquet, badminton

## NEW MARKET

**Nearby attractions:** historic New Market; antiques hunting, historic Frederick; Cunningham Falls National Park; Washington, D.C.; Gettysburg, Pa.; Baltimore; Harpers Ferry

### STRAWBERRY INN
17 West Main Street
New Market, Maryland 21774
**Phone:** 301/865-3318
**Website:** www.newmarketmd.com/straw.htm
**Proprietors:** Jane and Ed Rossig

This 1837 wood-siding farmhouse shows a Gothic influence in its steeply pitched center gable with arched window. Across the symmetrical facade are slightly arched windows. The house is located in the heart of New Market, founded in 1793, and now a National Register historic district. New Market is also known as the antiques capital of Maryland, thus all rooms at the Strawberry Inn are furnished with antiques, including the five guest rooms with private baths. The first-floor guest room is wheelchair accessible and has a private porch. A large grape arbor covers the cafe-style back porch, where breakfast is served on warm mornings, allowing guests to appreciate the landscaped yard. Afternoon tea is served in the Victorian gazebo.

**Open:** year round **Accommodations:** 5 guest rooms with private baths **Meals:** full breakfast included; complimentary refreshments; restaurants nearby **Wheelchair access:** 1 room **Rates:** $95 to $125; 10% discount to National Trust members and National Trust Visa cardholders **Payment:** personal check, cash **Restrictions:** children over 7 welcome; no smoking; no pets **On-site activities:** garden, gazebo

---

## ST. MICHAELS

**Nearby attractions:** Chesapeake Bay Maritime Museum, St. Mary's Square Museum, St. Michael's historic district, antiques hunting, golfing, tennis, hunting, boating, bicycling, fishing, crabbing

### PARSONAGE INN
210 North Talbot Street
St. Michaels, Maryland 21663
**Phone:** 410/745-5519 or 800/394-5519
**Website:** www.virtualcities.com
**Proprietors:** Anthony and Jodie Deyesu

Henry Clay Dodson, a prominent businessman and politician, built this house as his private residence in 1883, using bricks from his St. Michaels brickyard. This Victorian house, with its steeple-topped entry tower flanked by paneled chimneys and its porches adorned with gingerbread, is one of the major architectural gems in the town's historic district. Dodson's daughter donated this building to the Union Methodist Church in 1924, and it served as the parsonage until 1985, when it was purchased by the current owners and meticulously restored. The Parsonage Inn is furnished in late Victorian garb, right down to its lighting fixtures, yet modern amenities assure guest comfort. Guest rooms are decorated with English country-style fabrics, bed linens, and wallpapers. Three guest rooms have working fireplaces, as does the parlor.

**Open:** year round **Accommodations:** 7 guest rooms with private baths; 1 is a suite **Meals:** full breakfast included; catering available for lunch and business meetings; restaurants nearby **Wheelchair access:** 1 guest room and bath **Rates:** $110 to $160; 10% discount offered to National Trust members weeknights **Payment:** Visa, MC, personal and traveler's checks **Restrictions:** no smoking; no pets **On-site activities:** bicycles, patio and charcoal grill, library

---

## SNOW HILL

**Nearby attractions:** historic Snow Hill (founded 1642), Pocomoke River, canoeing, ocean beaches, museums, Chincotegue and Assateague National Wildlife Refuge, parks, Crisfield, Chesapeake Bay, bicycling, swimming

### RIVER HOUSE INN
201 East Market Street
Snow Hill, Maryland 21863
**Phone:** 410/632-2722
**Fax:** 410/632-2866
**Website:** www.riverhouseinn.com
**E-mail:** innkeeper@riverhouseinn.com
**Proprietor:** Larry Knudsen

River House Inn comprises three historic buildings situated on more than two acres of lawn that lead to the Pocomoke River. The Little House is an 1835 Tidewater cottage with wide floorboards and a picket fence. The River Cottage was built in 1890 as a carriage barn and now offers private accommodations with a porch overlooking the river. The Main House is a stunning 1860 Gothic Revival home. It was built by a Mr. Smith, and shortly thereafter sold to a Mr. Payne. In 1877 it was purchased by George Washington Purnell, an attorney. The house stayed in Purnell's family, being owned by his youngest daughter, Frances Thebaud, until 1975. Today, the inn combines modern amenities with the charm

of fireplaces in spacious rooms and old-fashioned porches. All guest rooms have private baths. Guests may tie up their boats along the inn's waterfront at no charge.

**Open:** year round **Accommodations:** 8 guest rooms with private baths; 2 are suites **Meals:** full breakfast included; complimentary refreshments; dinner available by arrangement; restaurants nearby **Wheelchair access:** River Cottage **Rates:** $100 to $175; 10% discount to National Trust members and National Trust Visa cardholders **Payment:** AmEx, Visa, MC, personal and traveler's checks **Restrictions:** no smoking; no pets **On-site activities:** fishing, river tours, bicycling, canoe rentals

## STEVENSVILLE

**Nearby attractions:** Thompson Creek, Horsehead Wildlife Nature Preserve, Chesapeake Bay, sailing, boating, bicycling, Queenstown Factory Outlet shopping

### KENT MANOR INN
500 Kent Manor Drive
Stevensville, Maryland 21666
**Phone:** 410/643-5757 or 800/678-8946
**Fax:** 410/643-8315
**Website:** www.kentmanor.com
**Proprietor:** Dave Meloy

The Kent Manor Inn was, and still is, a masterpiece of design and craftsmanship. The inn features three stories with walk-out porches and working fireplaces. The original wing of the house was built circa 1820. The center portion of the home was added by Alexander Thompson in 1865. The property changed hands several times and has been known as "The Brightworth Inn" and "Kent Hall." The inn was purchased in 1987 for complete restoration and expansion, and now includes 24 individually decorated guest rooms, featuring Victorian furnishings. Kent Manor Inn is situated on a 226-acre plantation with one and a half miles of waterfront on the Chesapeake Bay. Water activities are easily available for guests at this Historic Hotel of America.

**Open:** year round **Accommodations:** 24 guest rooms with private baths; 2 are suites **Meals:** restaurant on premises **Wheelchair access:** yes **Rates:** $130 to $220; 10% discount to National Trust members and National Trust Visa cardholders **Payment:** AmEx, Visa, MC, DC, CB, Discover **On-site activities:** walking trails, lawn games, complimentary paddle boats and bicycles, 8 boat slips on Thompson Creek

---

# TANEYTOWN

**Nearby attractions:** Carroll County Farm Museum, Homestead Museum, antiques hunting, golfing, bicycling, hiking; Gettysburg, Pennsylvania

## ANTRIM 1844
30 Trevanion Road
Taneytown, Maryland 21787
**Phone:** 410/756-6812 or 800/858-1844
**Fax:** 410/756-2744
**Proprietors:** Richard and Dorothy Mollett

An antebellum plantation in the rolling Catoctin Mountains in central Maryland, Antrim 1844 seeks to meet every need of its guests. Elegantly restored and refurbished, the house offers nine guest rooms with antiques, fireplaces, canopied beds, and either marble baths or double whirlpool tubs. Five additional suites are located in the plantation's outbuildings: the Ice House, the Barn (with two rooms), and the Cottage. Each of these special rooms has its own fireplace and is furnished with a queen- or king-size bed. Antrim 1844 is noted for its superb cuisine, prepared with the freshest seasonal ingredients. An early continental breakfast is served daily, followed by a formal breakfast. A five-course dinner is available. The Greek Revival brick mansion is surrounded by 23 acres of countryside. Listed in the National Register and lauded by numerous publications, including *Conde Nast Traveler*, *Country Inns*, *Colonial Homes*, and *Victoria*, the inn is a welcome respite from urban life. It is equally suited to lavish weddings and corporate retreats.

**Open:** year round **Accommodations:** 15 guest rooms with private baths; 5 are suites **Meals:** continental-plus and full breakfasts included; restaurant on premises; catered functions on premises **Rates:** $150 to $300 **Payment:** AmEx, Visa, MC, Discover, DC, personal and traveler's checks **Restrictions:** children over 14 welcome; smoking limited; no pets **On-site activities:** swimming pool, croquet, tennis, putting green, cigar smoking

# MASSACHUSETTS

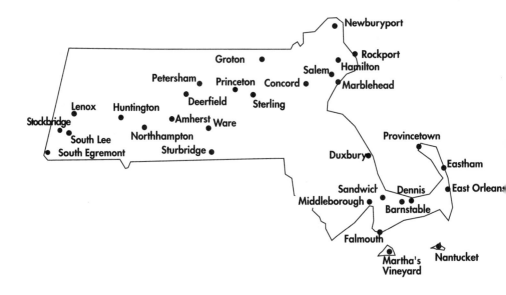

Newburyport

Rockport
Salem Hamilton
Groton
Petersham
Princeton Concord
Marblehead
Deerfield
Lenox Huntington Sterling
Stockbridge ●Amherst Ware
South Lee Northhampton Provincetown
South Egremont Sturbridge Duxbury
Eastham
Sandwich Dennis East Orleans
Middleborough Barnstable
Falmouth
Martha's Nantucket
Vineyard

## AMHERST

**Nearby attractions:** Emily Dickinson Homestead, historic Deerfield, Old Sturbridge Village, Hancock Shaker Village, Yankee Candle Co., galleries, museums, theaters, shopping, five-college area: Amherst College, University of Massachusetts, Hampshire College, Smith College, Mount Holyoke College

Millikan

**ALLEN HOUSE VICTORIAN INN**
599 Main Street
Amherst, Massachusetts
01002
**Phone:** 413/253-5000
**Website:**
www.allenhouse.com
**Proprietors:** Alan and
Ann Zieminski

Allen House was built in the Stick Style—steeply pitched gables contain decorative trusses and patterned stickwork accentuates the clapboard walls. On three scenic acres, just across the road from Emily Dickinson's home, Allen House was built in 1886 by Lysander H. Allen, a local wire goods manufacturer. A detailed restoration has earned a Historic Preservation Award from the Amherst Historical Commission. Guest accommodations are spacious and comfortable with private baths, telephones, and air conditioning. Eastlake-style furnishings are enhanced by reproduction wallcoverings from the Aestheic period of Victorian design. The innkeepers provide a full breakfast, afternoon tea, free pickup service from the nearby train and bus stations, and a complimentary collection of selected poems by Emily Dickinson. The inn has been featured in *Boston* magazine.

**Open:** year round **Accommodations:** 7 guest rooms with private baths **Meals:** full breakfast included; complimentary refreshments; restaurants nearby **Rates:** $45 to $135; 10% discount to National Trust members and National Trust Visa cardholders **Payment:** Visa, MC, CB, DC, Discover, personal and traveler's checks **Restrictions:** children over 10 welcome; no smoking; no pets **On-site activities:** chamber music concerts, baby grand piano, flower gardens, cross-country skiing

---

# BARNSTABLE (CAPE COD)

**Nearby attractions:** Barnstable Harbor for fishing and whale watching, Sturgis Library, historic courthouse, Old King's Highway, Sandy Neck beach, Sandwich Glass Museum and Heritage Plantation, antiques hunting, gift shops, arts-and-crafts galleries, museums, auctions, tennis, golfing, biking, island ferries

## ASHLEY MANOR
3660 Old King's Highway (Route 6A)
P.O. Box 856
Barnstable, Massachusetts 02630
**Phone:** 508/362-8044 or 888/535-2246
**Fax:** 508/362-9927
**Website:** www.capecod.net/ashleymn
**E-mail:** ashleymn@capecod.net
**Proprietor:** Donald Bain
**Location:** 1/2 mile east of Barnstable Village

Intimate and romantic, Ashley Manor occupies a two-acre estate in the heart of one of Cape Cod's historic districts. Built in 1699, the inn has seen many additions. Evidence of its age and history is in the wide-board flooring (made of wood usually reserved for the king during colonial times), huge open-hearth fireplaces, and a secret passageway connecting the upstairs and downstairs suites; the passageway is thought to have been a hiding place for Tories during the Revolutionary War. Elegant public rooms and spacious guest rooms are furnished

with antiques, oriental rugs, and graceful country furniture. All but one guest room contain working fireplaces; three suites feature whirlpool tubs. A full gourmet breakfast is served fireside in the formal dining room or on the charming brick terrace. The beach, village, and harbor are within walking distance.

**Open:** year round **Accommodations:** 6 guest rooms with private baths; 4 are suites **Meals:** full breakfast included; complimentary refreshments; restaurants nearby **Rates:** $130 to $180 **Payment:** Visa, MC, Discover, personal and traveler's checks **Restrictions:** children over 14 welcome; smoking limited; no pets **On-site activities:** tennis, croquet, bicycles, board games

---

## CONCORD

**Nearby attractions:** Walden Pond; Old North Bridge; wildlife sanctuary; canoeing; picnicking; walking; homes of Emerson, Alcott, and Hawthorne

### COLONEL ROGER BROWN HOUSE
1694 Main Street
Concord, Massachusetts 01742
**Phone:** 978/369-9119 or 800/292-1369
**Fax:** 978/369-1305
**Proprietor:** William Sullivan
**Innkeeper:** Laurie Berlied

Roger Brown was framing his house on April 19, 1775, when news arrived that the British army was advancing on Concord. He responded to the call to arms becoming a corporal in the Framingham Minutemen. He returned 10 days later to finish building this center-chimney clapboard Georgian house and later went on to become a Colonel in the Massachusetts Militia. Today, his house is restored to show off its original woodwork, raised paneling and hand-hewn beams. Guests are invited to relax before the fireplace in the living room or help themselves to refreshments in the guest kitchen. Six bedrooms are available, each with private bath, individual climate control, color television, and direct-dial telephones. Guests enjoy complimentary use of the fitness center in an adjacent mill. Listed in the National Register of Historic Places, the inn opened on April 19, 1987; its first guest book entry was made by Roger Brown, the builder's descendant.

**Open:** year round **Accommodations:** 6 guest rooms with private baths; 1 is a suite **Meals:** continental-plus breakfast included; complimentary refreshments; restaurants nearby **Rates:** $80 to $120; 10% discount to National Trust members and National Trust Visa cardholders with stays of three or more nights **Payment:** AmEx, Visa, MC, CB, personal and traveler's checks **Restrictions:** no smoking; no pets **On-site activities:** fitness center with swimming, sauna, massage, aerobics classes, treadmill, rowing machines and weight systems

## HAWTHORNE INN
462 Lexington Road
Concord, Massachusetts 01742
**Phone:** 978/369-5610
**Fax:** 978/287-4949
**Website:** www.concordmass.com
**Proprietor:** Marilyn Mudry

Located in Concord's historic district, the Hawthorne Inn was built in 1870 on the famed Battle Road once traveled by revolutionists. The site has an impressive literary pedigree: at various times the land was owned by Ralph Waldo Emerson, Louisa May Alcott, and Nathaniel Hawthorne. The inn itself sits across the road from Hawthorne's house, Wayside; the Alcott's Orchard House; and Grapevine Cottage, where the Concord grape was developed. The Hawthorne Inn's rooms are appointed with antique furnishings, handmade quilts, and oriental and rag rugs on the hardwood floors. Original art, displayed throughout the inn, includes antique Japanese ukiyoe prints and sculptures by the innkeeper. Guest rooms feature canopy beds, fresh flowers or fruit, and a selection of poetry books. When the weather turns cold, the common room's fireplace is kept burning.

**Open:** year round **Accommodations:** 7 guest rooms with private baths **Meals:** continental-plus breakfast included; complimentary refreshments; restaurants nearby **Rates:** $150 to $215 **Payment:** AmEx, Visa, MC, Discover, personal and traveler's checks **Restrictions:** no smoking; no pets (resident dogs and cats) **On-site activities:** playground for children, gardens and paths, lily pool, many works of art, poetry books

# DEERFIELD

**Nearby attractions:** Historic Deerfield, Yankee Candle Co., Hancock Shaker Village, country fairs, auctions, antiques hunting, five-college area: Amherst College, University of Massachusetts, Hampshire College, Smith College, Mount Holyoke College

## DEERFIELD'S YELLOW GABLED HOUSE

111 North Main Street
Deerfield-South, Massachusetts 01373
**Phone:** 413/665-4922
**Proprietor:** Edna J. Stahelek
**Location:** 1/2 mile from South Deerfield Center; 4 miles from Historic Deerfield

When early colonists settled in this area in 1660, they encountered hostility from the native population of Pocumtuck, Mohawk, and Iroquois Indians. Among the most famous of these conflicts were the 1675 Bloody Brook Massacre and the Deerfield Massacre of 1704. The Yellow Gabled House is located at the site of the former. The house was built circa 1810—more than a century after that sad time. It is a picturesque frame house, distinguished by three gables across its front. Decorated with traditional furnishing and period antiques set on gleaming hardwood floors, the house is imbued with a cozy character. The warm, elegant living and dining rooms are for guests' use. Three comfortable, carefully decorated bedrooms are offered and a full breakfast is served in the dining room overlooking the garden.

**Open:** year round **Accommodations:** 3 guest rooms (1 has a private bath); 1 is a suite **Meals:** full breakfast included; restaurants nearby, including the four-star Sienna **Rates:** $75 to $140; 10% discount to National Trust members and National Trust Visa cardholders **Payment:** personal check **Restrictions:** not suitable for children; no smoking; no pets **On-site activities:** croquet, gardens

# DENNIS (CAPE COD)

**Nearby attractions:** beach, swimming, theater, antiques hunting, crafts shops, museums, sightseeing, golfing, tennis, bicycling

## ISAIAH HALL BED AND BREAKFAST INN
152 Whig Street
P.O. Box 1007
Dennis, Massachusetts 02638
**Phone:** 508/385-9928 or 800/736-0160
**Website:** www.capecod.com/isaiahhall/
**E-mail:** isaiah@capecod.net
**Proprietor:** Marie Brophy

Tucked away on a quiet historic street, this 1857 Greek Revival farmhouse was the home of Isaiah B. Hall, a builder and cooper. A short distance behind the house, his brother Henry cultivated the first cranberry bogs in America. The house has been kept as an inn since 1948, with cheerful guest rooms in both the main house and carriage house featuring iron and brass beds and homemade quilts. All guest rooms enjoy private baths and air conditioning. Guests enjoy relaxing on porch rockers, in front of a Victorian parlor stove surrounded by antiques and oriental rugs, or in the converted carriage house, decorated in white wicker and knotty pine. Centrally located on the Cape, the inn is within walking distance of the beach or village.

**Open:** April through mid-October **Accommodations:** 10 guest rooms with private baths; 1 is a suite **Meals:** continental-plus breakfast included; complimentary refreshments; restaurants nearby **Wheelchair access:** limited **Rates:** $59 to $112 **Payment:** AmEx, Visa, MC, personal and traveler's checks **Restrictions:** children over 7 welcome; smoking limited; no pets **On-site activities:** board games, badminton, croquet, library, television

# DUXBURY

**Nearby attractions:** Bradford House, John Alden House, Myles Standish Monument, King Caesar House, Powder Point Bridge, beaches, sailing, tennis, golfing, cross-country skiing, gift and antiques shops

## WINSOR HOUSE INN
390 Washington Street
Duxbury, Massachusetts 02332
**Phone:** 781/934-0991
**Fax:** 781/934-5955
**Proprietor:** David M. O'Connell

Originally a private residence, the Winsor House Inn was built in 1803 by Nathaniel Winsor—patriarch, merchant, and sea captain—for his daughter Nancy, and her husband, John Howland. The house stayed in the Winsor family for generations and was inherited by Daniel Winsor in 1915. With his wife Marie, they converted the house to an inn in 1932 and it was a popular gathering spot in the town until they retired in 1962. It then fell into disrepair, passing through numerous ownerships, until the innkeepers purchased and restored it in 1976. Today, the inn is cozy and inviting with original hardwood floors, hand-hewn beams, exposed brick, gleaming woodwork, and cheery fireplaces. Sunlit bedrooms with canopy beds and fireplaces make guests feel welcome. A full breakfast is complimentary and the inn also has a restaurant and pub offering lunch and dinner. Winsor House Inn offers a 36-foot cutter-rigged Cape Dory sailboat for charter.

**Open:** year round **Accommodations:** 4 guest rooms with private baths; 2 are suites **Meals:** full breakfast included; restaurant on premises; restaurants nearby **Rates:** $130 to $210 **Payment:** AmEx, Visa, MC, Discover, personal and traveler's checks **Restrictions:** smoking limited to pub; no pets

# EASTHAM (CAPE COD)

**Nearby attractions:** Cape Cod National Seashore, bicycle trail, Audubon Wildlife Sanctuary, Nauset Lighthouse, hiking, swimming, windsurfing, museums, historic homes, antiques hunting, art galleries

## OVER LOOK INN, CAPE COD
3085 County Road (Route 6)
Eastham, Massachusetts 02642
**Phone:** 508/255-1886
**Fax:** 508/240-0345
**Website:** www.overlookinn.com
**E-mail:** stay@overlookinn.com
**Proprietors:** Aitchison family

This Victorian house, built in 1869 by Captain Barnabus Chipman as a wedding gift to his wife Sarah, sits on a hill across from the saltpond and marshes of Coast Guard Beach and the first visitors center of the Cape Cod National Seashore. Carefully restored, the Over Look is furnished in comfortable antiques and period reproductions of the Victorian era, including queen-size brass beds, cozy wicker, down comforters, and lace. A Scottish breakfast is served in the Edward Hopper Dining Room. Afternoon tea is served in the Sarah Chipman Parlor. Guests will also enjoy the Winston Churchill Library and the Ernest Hemingway Billiard Room. The inn has played host to such notables as Henry Beston, the author and naturalist, and the mayor and mayoress of Eastham, England.

**Open:** year round **Accommodations:** 10 guest rooms with private baths **Meals:** full breakfast included; complimentary afternoon tea; restaurants nearby **Rates:** $95 to $165; 10% discount to National Trust members and National Trust Visa cardholders **Payment:** AmEx, Visa, MC, CB, DC, Discover, personal and traveler's checks **Restrictions:** smoking limited; no pets **On-site activities:** billiards, library, porches

# EAST ORLEANS

**Nearby attractions:** Nauset Beach swimming and sunbathing, bicycle trails, fishing, sailing, boating, whale watching, golfing, horseback riding, antiques hunting, shopping

## NAUSET HOUSE INN
143 Beach Road
P.O. Box 774
East Orleans, Massachusetts 02643
**Phone:** 508/255-2195
**Website:** www.virtualcapecod.com/market/nausethouse/
**Proprietors:** Diane and Al Johnson and Cindy and John Vessella

At the Nauset House Inn, sea and shore, orchard and field create a refreshing, tranquil setting. Built in 1810 in the Cape Cod style, the Nauset House Inn has undergone numerous changes over the years, including the addition of dormers and a turn-of-the century conservatory filled with flowering plants and wicker furniture. The brown clapboard inn with a cherry red front door also offers a large common room with fireplace and 14 cozy guest rooms. An old-fashioned country breakfast is served. A warm and intimate atmosphere permeates the inn, and the hosts are happy to share their love for the Cape with their guests. Nauset House, only a half mile to the beach, has been recommended by *Country Living, Travel and Leisure*, and *Glamour*.

**Open:** April through October **Accommodations:** 14 guest rooms (8 have private baths) **Meals:** full breakfast included; complimentary refreshments; restaurants nearby **Rates:** $75 to $135 **Payment:** Visa, MC, personal and traveler's checks **Restrictions:** children over 12 welcome; no smoking; no pets **On-site activities:** relaxing in conservatory, in front of fireplaces, on brick patio, or under 100-year-old apple trees

## SHIP'S KNEES INN
186 Beach Road
P.O. Box 756
East Orleans, Massachusetts 02643
**Phone:** 508/255-1312
**Fax:** 508/240-1351
**Website:** www.capecodtravel.com/shipskneesinn
**Proprietors:** Donna Anderson and Peter Butcher

Built more than 170 years ago, with a section added in 1970, this rehabilitated sea captain's home offers an intimate setting just a short walk from the sand dunes of beautiful Nauset Beach. Inside the lantern–lighted doorways are 19 guest rooms, each distinctively decorated in a nautical style and furnished with such antiques as hand-painted trunks, braided rugs, four-poster beds, and authentic ship's knees (the wooden braces used in shipbuilding). Some rooms have an ocean view, and the master suite has a working fireplace. The inn has a swimming pool and tennis court. Three miles away overlooking Town Cove, the proprietors also offer accommodations in three quaint buildings: a turn-of-the-century Cape Cod–shuttered house with three guest rooms (with private baths) and an efficiency apartment, and two cedar-shingled cottages (a one-bedroom unit and a two-bedroom unit) that predate World War II. This cluster of buildings is nestled on a small hillside leading to the water's edge.

**Open:** year round **Accommodations:** 19 guest rooms (8 have private baths) **Meals:** continental breakfast included; restaurants nearby **Rates:** $45 to $100; 10% discount offered to National Trust members and National Trust Visa cardholders **Payment:** Visa, MC, personal and traveler's checks **Restrictions:** no smoking, no pets **On-site activities:** swimming pool, tennis

# FALMOUTH (CAPE COD)

**Nearby Attractions:** Shining Sea Bikeway, Woods Hole Oceanographic Institute, Plymouth, ferry to Martha's Vineyard and Nantucket, historic district, museums, shopping, beach, swimming, boating, golfing, fishing, tennis

### CAPTAIN TOM LAWRENCE HOUSE, BED AND BREAKFAST

75 Locust Street
Falmouth, Massachusetts 02540
**Phone:** 508/540-1445 or 800/266-8139
**Fax:** 508/457-1790
**Website:** www.sunsol.com/captaintom/
**Proprietor:** Barbara Sabo-Feller
**Location:** southwestern corner of Cape Cod, 68 miles south of Boston

Tom Lawrence first sailed on a Nantucket whaler in 1838. As he met with success, he built a fine residence on Locust Street, sparing no expense. His Italianate home, built in 1861, is today an intimate bed-and-breakfast inn. With its circular staircase, hardwood floors, and high ceilings, the house remains much as it was when Captain Lawrence lived here although it is fully air conditioned today. Guests may play the Steinway piano or read by a cozy fire in the sitting room, with its antique furnishings and old paintings. Six corner guest rooms are available, all with private baths, designer linens, and color television, and some with canopy beds. The complimentary full breakfast includes specialties like Belgian waffles with strawberry sauce and whipped cream. The innkeeper speaks German.

**Open:** year round **Accommodations:** 6 guest rooms with private baths **Meals:** full breakfast included; restaurants nearby **Rates:** $95 to $165; 10% discount to National Trust members and National Trust Visa cardholders **Payment:** Visa, MC, personal and traveler's checks **Restrictions:** children over 12 welcome; no smoking; no pets **On-site activities:** relaxing, playing piano, bicycling

## GRAFTON INN
261 Grand Avenue, South
Falmouth Heights, Massachusetts 02540
**Phone:** 508/540-8688 or 800/642-4069
**Fax:** 508/540-1861
**Website:** www.sunsol.com/graftoninn/
**Proprietors:** Elizabeth and Rudy Cvitan

Grafton Inn, an oceanfront bed and breakfast, was built in 1880 when the area known as Falmouth Heights was being developed as a popular summer resort. The house was enlarged in 1905, taking on its current Queen Anne style, complete with turret. All interior walls are constructed of tongue-and-groove white pine to allow for the expansion and contraction that is common in seaside climates. Today's inn provides 10 guest rooms attractively decorated with period furnishings, antiques, and original art. Soft colors, thoughtful amenities such as French-milled soaps, color cable television, air conditioning, hair dryers, home-made chocolates, and fresh flowers from the inn's English-style garden provide an atmosphere of leisure and indulgence. Large windows throughout the inn offer beautiful ocean views. Guests can stare dreamily out to sea while breakfast is served at private tables in the enclosed porch. AAA gives the Grafton Inn three stars.

**Open:** mid-February to mid-November **Accommodations:** 10 guest rooms with private baths **Meals:** full breakfast included; complimentary refreshments; restaurants nearby **Rates:** $105 to $179 **Payment:** AmEx, Visa, MC, traveler's checks **Restrictions:** not suitable for children; no smoking; no pets **On-site activities:** enclosed garden with tables and umbrellas, board games on porch, 30 steps to ocean beach, sand chairs and towels, swimming, reading, fishing

## MOSTLY HALL BED AND BREAKFAST INN
27 Main Street
Falmouth, Massachusetts 02540
**Phone:** 508/548-3786 or 800/682-0565
**Fax:** 508/457-1572
**Website:** www.sunsol.com/mostlyhall/
**E-mail:** mostlyhl@cape.com
**Proprietors:** Caroline and Jim Lloyd
**Location:** southwestern corner of Cape Cod

In 1849 Albert Nye built this striking home for his New Orleans bride. The house, Falmouth's first summer residence, features a wide porch completely surrounding the house, a front-to-back central hallway, and 13-foot-high ceilings. Its name derives, legend has it, from a young child who, upon entering, exclaimed, "Why, it's mostly hall!" Majestically set back from the road, Mostly Hall provides comfortable seclusion in more than an acre of gardens, yet is close to shops, beaches, and island ferries. The spacious corner guest rooms are furnished with antiques and canopied, queen-size beds. All rooms are air conditioned and have comfortable reading areas with large windows, ensuring plenty of light and fresh air. Breakfast is served either fireside in the dining room or on the porch overlooking the gazebo; the menu is highlighted by recipes that have been featured in *Bon Appetit*, the *Boston Globe*, and in the cookbook *Mostly Hall Breakfast at 9.*

**Open:** February 15 through December 31 **Accommodations:** 6 guest rooms with private baths **Meals:** full breakfast included; complimentary refreshments; restaurants nearby **Rates:** $95 to $135; 10% discount to National Trust members and National Trust Visa cardholders **Payment:** AmEx, Visa, MC, Discover, traveler's check **Restrictions:** not suitable for children; no smoking; no pets **On-site activities:** piano, library, veranda, widow's walk and garden gazebo for relaxing and reading, bicycles to use on the Shining Sea Bikeway to Woods Hole

## VILLAGE GREEN INN
40 Main Street
Falmouth, Massachusetts 02540
**Phone:** 508/548-5621or 800/237-1119
**Fax:** 508/457-5051
**Website:** villagegreeninn.com
**E-mail:** vgi40@aol.com
**Proprietors:** Diane and Don Crosby

Built in 1804 in the Federal style, Village Green Inn stands today as it has since being remodeled in 1875 and 1894, making it Victorian in appearance with a wraparound porch, decorative shingles, bay windows, and a turretlike dormer. Today, the house contains tastefully appointed guest rooms decorated in soft colors. Each room has a private bath and uniquely designed fireplace. Two large porches furnished in white wicker and hanging pots of red geraniums overlook

the flower gardens and lawns that surround the inn and adjacent carriage house. A formal parlor is well stocked with a varied choice of books, magazines, and games. Breakfast may include such specialties as apple-plum crumble or tangy ambrosia.

**Open:** year round **Accommodations:** 5 guest rooms with private baths; 1 is a suite **Meals:** full breakfast included; complimentary refreshments; restaurants nearby **Rates:** $85 to $160 **Payment:** AmEx, Visa, MC, personal and traveler's checks **Restrictions:** children over 12 welcome; no smoking; no pets

## WILDFLOWER INN

167 Palmer Avenue
Falmouth, Massachusetts 02536
**Phone:** 508/548-9524 or 800/294-5459
**Fax:** 508/548-9524
**Website:** www.bbonline.com/ma/wildflower
**E-mail:** WLDFLR167@aol.com
**Proprietor:** Donna Stone

Although the innkeepers originally thought this two-story frame house had been built in 1910 (based on a deed from that year), in early 1997, they heard from a woman whose father had been born in this house in 1898. She gave the Stones photos of the house from that time, which they have put on display in the inn. As the Wildflower Inn, the house retains its original floors and woodwork, all completely restored to their original beauty. Guests enter the house through a wraparound porch lined with rockers. Inside is a fireplaced gathering room, then a wide staircase leading up to guest rooms. Each room is named for a wildflower and distinctively decorated. All have private baths, some with whirlpool tubs. Colorful cozy quilts add to the decor. A separate suite with private entrance and porch has a full kitchen, living room, and romantic loft bedroom. The inn, surrounded by award-winning flower gardens, has been featured on a PBS country inn cooking television program.

**Open:** year round **Accommodations:** 6 guest rooms with private baths; 1 is a suite **Meals:** full breakfast included; complimentary refreshments; restaurants nearby **Rates:** $85 to $195; 10% discount to National Trust members and National Trust Visa cardholders **Payment:** AmEx, Visa, MC, traveler's checks **Restrictions:** children over 12 welcome; no smoking; no pets **On-site activities:** bicycling, porch rocking, flower gardens

# GROTON

**Nearby attractions:** Northeast's largest collection of Indian artifacts and antiques, Fruitlands Shaker Village, Mt. Wachusett and Nashoba Valley skiing, canoeing, golfing, hiking, fishing, bicycling, horseback riding, Boston

## STAGECOACH INN AND TAVERN

128 Main Street
Groton, Massachusetts 01450
**Phone:** 978/448-5614
**Fax:** 978/448-0016
**Proprietor:** George Pergantis

Serving travelers since 1780, this inn has hosted such luminaries as Henry Wadsworth Longfellow, Julia Ward Howe, and presidents Grant, Cleveland, Roosevelt, and Taft. In the town center on a gentle slope shaded by large elm trees, the Stagecoach Inn is a harmonious blend of three historic structures. The first part was built circa 1723 by Samuel Parker and enlarged in 1761 by Samuel Dana. The wainscoting in the lobby dates from this period as does the hand-printed French wallpaper in one of the upstairs guest rooms. A second building (circa 1714) was joined to the back of the Dana house in the 1790s. A third building was added onto the north side in 1840. This structure is thought to have been the Richardson Tavern, built as early as 1678 as a dwelling. The inn's famous "rocking porch" was added during the 1840 renovation. Today's 17 guest rooms, many with canopied beds, all feature private baths. There are four dining rooms, a lounge, and a function hall. The decor is in keeping with the buildings' historic origins.

**Open:** year round **Accommodations:** 17 guest rooms with private baths; 2 are suites **Meals:** full breakfast included; restaurant, lounge, and function hall on premises **Wheelchair access:** limited (1 guest room) **Rates:** $85 to $120; 10% discount to National Trust members and National Trust Visa cardholders, and to seniors, retired veterans, and military personnel **Payment:** AmEx, Visa, MC, DC, personal and traveler's checks **Restrictions:** no smoking; no pets **On-site activities:** swimming pool

# HAMILTON

**Nearby attractions:** world-class horse e~
ing, Cape Ann and Crane's beaches, hik~
cross-country skiing, whale-watching, Pa

## MILES RIVER COUNTRY INN

823 Bay Road
Hamilton, Massachusetts 01936
**Phone:** 978/468-7206
**Fax:** 978/468-3999
**Website:** milesriver.com
**E-mail:** milesriver@mediaone.net
**Proprietor:** Gretel T. Clark

244   HISTORIC BED & BREAKFAST

HUNTINGTON
**Nearby attracti**
Westfield Riv
series

CARM
8 M

Set among Boston's fabled North Shore estates, this New England farmhouse was built in the late eighteenth century. In 1919 the president of Harvard gave the house to his daughter and son-in-law as a wedding gift, moving it to its present site from his estate a half mile away. A ballroom and glassed-in porch were added at that time. Today the 24-room house with 12 fireplaces (four in guest rooms) is filled with the family's antique furniture. The grounds—more than 30 acres— are landscaped in the grand estate style of the early 1900s with sweeping lawns, a grass allée (passage between two rows of trees), ponds, streams, and a giant arborvitae "secret garden" to explore. The estate contains a flock of chickens that provide fresh eggs, gardens that produce fresh fruit, and an apiary that offers honey for country breakfasts. The Miles River flows through the property. Surrounding meadows and woodlands invite countless varieties of ducks, geese, birds, and other wildlife.

**Open:** year round **Accommodations:** 8 guest rooms (3 have private baths) **Meals**: full breakfast included; complimentary refreshments and afternoon tea; restaurants nearby **Rates:** $90 to $165; 10% discount to National Trust members and National Trust Visa cardholders **Payment:** personal check **Restrictions:** no smoking **On-site activities:** walking, hiking, jogging, bird-watching, croquet, badminton, cross-country skiing, ice skating

**ns:** Five-College area, Jacob's Pillow, Tanglewood, ski resorts, Wild Water Canoe Club, summer theaters, festivals, concert

## LWOOD
Montgomery Road
Huntington, Massachusetts 01050
**Phone:** 413/667-5786 or 877/227-6593
**Proprietor:** Katheryn Corrigan

The house now called Carmelwood was built in 1860 by Horace Taylor as a wedding gift for his daughter. It had four rooms: the present kitchen, den, and two bedrooms upstairs. In 1885 the front rooms, foyer, central fireplace, two bedrooms, bath, and porches were added and an oval stained-glass window was placed at the landing of the staircase. The steeply pitched roof with its unusual barrel dormer windows gives the house a style all its own. The house takes its name from Claire and Richard Carmel who owned the house beginning in the 1930s. Claire, an art teacher, painted a series of wall murals in the dining room that depict New England scenes. These works of art are currently being restored after years of hiding behind wallpaper. Four guest rooms are furnished with antiques, heirlooms quilts, and original art. Country breakfasts feature fresh, organically grown produce. The innkeeper is an avid gardener and runs a garden shop on the premises.

**Open:** year round **Accommodations:** 4 guest rooms with 2 shared baths **Meals:** full breakfast included (vegetarian menus available); restaurants nearby **Rates:** $70 to $90; 10% discount to National Trust members and National Trust Visa cardholders **Payment:** Visa, MC, Discover, personal and traveler's checks **Restrictions:** children over 12 welcome; no smoking; no pets (resident long-haired cat) **On-site activities:** piano, board games, library, croquet, volleyball, hiking and cross-country skiing trails, fishing, canoeing, bicycling, 2 par-3 golf holes

# LENOX

**Nearby attractions:** Tanglewood, Jacob's Pillow, Berkshire Theater Festival, Shakespeare and Company, Wharton and Melville houses, National Trust's Chesterwood, Hancock Shaker Village, Norman Rockwell Museum, Williams College, Clark Art Institute, Bashbish Falls, Appalachian Trail, Mount Greylock, Berkshires, downhill and cross-country skiing, tennis, golfing, swimming, horseback riding, fishing, hiking

## AMADEUS HOUSE

15 Cliffwood Street
Lenox, Massachusetts 01240
**Phone:** 413/637-4770 or 800/205-4770
**Fax:** 413/637-4484
**Website:** www.amadeushouse.com
**E-mail:** info@amadeushouse.com
**Proprietors:** Martha Gottron and John Felton

Amadeus House is named in honor of its proximity to Tanglewood, summer home of the Boston Symphony Orchestra. The elegant yet comfortable Adam-style house originated in 1820 but was enlarged, gaining its wraparound porch with unusual decorative detailing in 1903. Guest rooms, named for the innkeepers' favorite composers, range from the cozy (Schubert and Sibelius) to the spacious (Bach, Brahms, and Mozart). Bernstein and Copland are rooms in between. The Beethoven Suite, on the third floor, is a two-bedroom apartment with fully equipped kitchen, bathroom, and living room. The inn is furnished with antiques and wicker. Soothing colors and classical music complete the relaxing atmosphere. Afternoon refreshments are served on the wraparound porch with its rockers or before a crackling fire in the living room (where guests are encouraged to pick up a baton and conduct a symphony, if the mood strikes). Each morning begins with a nourishing breakfast featuring a special entree.

**Open:** year round **Accommodations:** 8 guest rooms (6 have private baths); 1 is a suite **Meals:** full breakfast included; complimentary refreshments; restaurants nearby **Rates:** $65 to $195 **Payment:** AmEx, Visa, MC, Discover, personal and traveler's checks **Restrictions:** children over 10 welcome; no smoking; no pets **On-site activities:** porch rocking, listening to music

## BIRCHWOOD INN
7 Hubbard Street
P.O. Box 2020
Lenox, Massachusetts 01240
**Phone:** 413/637-2600 or 800/524-1646
**Website:** www.bbonline.com/ma/birchwood
**E-mail:** detoner@bcn.net
**Proprietors:** Joan, Dick, and Dan Toner

The Birchwood Inn, located at the top of a hill overlooking the historic village of Lenox, is the town's only inn listed in the National Register of Historic Places. The inn's tradition of hospitality dates to 1767 when the first town meeting was held in this building, replete with dormers and chimneys. Guests enjoy the large library and common rooms with fireplaces, antiques, and colonial-era decor. A spacious, covered porch and gardens enclosed by authentic New England stone fences offer outdoor places to relax. A multicourse, country breakfast is served daily, complemented by homemade breads and muffins. The inn is adjacent to Kennedy Park, a popular place for hiking, bicycling, and cross-country skiing.

**Open:** year round **Accommodations:** 12 guest rooms (10 have private baths); 2 are suites **Meals:** full breakfast included; restaurants nearby **Rates:** $60 to $199 **Payment:** AmEx, Visa, MC, CB, DC, Discover, personal and traveler's checks **Restrictions:** children over 12 welcome; no smoking; no pets **On-site activities:** library, videotapes, croquet, therapeutic massage

## GARDEN GABLES INN
141 Main Street
Lenox, Massachusetts 01240
**Phone:** 413/637-0193
**Fax:** 413/637-4554
**E-mail:** gardeninn@aol.com
**Proprietors:** Mario and Lynn Mekinda

Built as a private residence in 1780, Garden Gables Inn was converted into a country inn in the late 1940s. The green-shuttered, white clapboard rambling house is notable for its unusual combination of gambrel and steeply pitched gables. Sitting on five acres of landscaped and natural grounds, the inn offers 18 different cozy, air-conditioned guest rooms, wallpapered in soft floral patterns. All rooms have private baths and telephones. Some have whirlpool tubs, fireplaces, or private porches. All are decorated with American country furniture. The living rooms and dining room feature English antiques and nineteenth-century Dutch watercolors. A full buffet breakfast is served daily. In summer, guests are invited to swim in the 72-foot outdoor swimming pool, the largest in the Berkshires. Garden Gables is close to all the area's seasonal attractions.

**Open:** year round **Accommodations:** 18 guest rooms with private baths; 6 are suites **Meals:** full breakfast included; complimentary refreshments; restaurants nearby **Rates:** $95 to $225 **Payment:** AmEx, Visa, MC, Discover, personal and traveler's checks **Restrictions:** children over 12 welcome; smoking limited; no pets **On-site activities:** 72-foot swimming pool, built in 1911

## VILLAGE INN
16 Church Street
P.O. Box 1810
Lenox, Massachusetts 01240
**Phone:** 413/637-0020 or 800/253-0917
**Fax:** 413/637-9756
**Website:** www.villageinn-lenox.com
**E-mail:** villinn@vgernet.net
**Proprietors:** Clifford Rudisill and Ray Wilson

In 1771 the Whitlock family built a large residence and two nearby barns on their property. In 1775 they connected the barns to the main house by building an adjoining dining room. Then the barns were adapted to provide guest accommodations. That was the beginning of the Village Inn, which has operated continuously ever since. Except for two bay windows added in the Victorian era, the building has retained its eighteenth-century architectural styling. In recent years the interior has been renovated and decorated with antiques, oriental

carpets, and period wallpapers. Some guest rooms have working fireplaces and four-poster canopied beds. To promote its pre-Revolutionary heritage, the inn serves authentic English high tea in the afternoon and British beers and ales in the cellar pub.

**Open:** year round **Accommodations:** 32 guest rooms with private baths; 1 is a suite **Meals:** continental breakfast included November through June; restaurant on premises serves breakfast, English tea, and dinner **Wheelchair access:** guest rooms, bathrooms, dining facilities **Rates:** $50 to $225 (seasonal); 10% discount to National Trust members and National Trust Visa cardholders midweek only **Payment:** AmEx, Visa, MC, CB, DC, personal and traveler's checks **Restrictions:** children over 6 welcome; smoking limited; no pets **On-site activities:** tavern; television room; common room with games, piano, and reading; weekend packages

## WALKER HOUSE
64 Walker Street
Lenox, Massachusetts 01240
**Phone:** 413/637-1271 or 800/235-3098
**Fax:** 413/637-2387
**Website:** www.walkerhouse.com
**E-mail:** Phoudek@vgernet.net
**Proprietors:** Richard and Peggy Houdek

Built in 1804 in historic Lenox Village, Walker House is one of the town's last remaining examples of Federal architecture. Among its residents have been two judges and a state senator. Guest rooms in the restored building, situated on three acres of woods and gardens, bear the names of composers—Mozart, Chopin, Beethoven, and others—and are decorated with art and antiques that recall the lives and times of their namesakes. Some rooms have warming fireplaces. The parlor contains a grand piano, lots of books, and a fireplace with hearth. Guests can relax on the open and screened porches in warm weather. A video theater shows classic films, operas, plays, and notable events nightly on a seven-foot screen. Breakfast and afternoon tea are served in the dining room.

**Open:** year round **Accommodations:** 8 guest rooms with private baths **Meals:** continental-plus breakfast included; complimentary refreshments; restaurants nearby **Wheelchair access:** 1 guest room **Rates:** $80 to $200; 10% discount offered to National Trust members and National Trust Visa cardholders from November 1 to April 30, excluding holidays **Payment:** personal check **Restrictions:** children over 12 welcome; no smoking; pets accepted with prior approval **On-site activities:** croquet, tennis, library

# LYNN

**Nearby attractions:** Lynn Historical Society, Mary Baker Eddy home, beach, walking and jogging paths, Salem, Marblehead

### DIAMOND DISTRICT BREAKFAST INN
142 Ocean Street
Lynn, Massachusetts 01902-2007
**Phone:** 781/599-5122 or 800/666-3076
**Fax:** 781/599-4470
**Website:** www.bbhost.com/diamonddistrict
**E-mail:** diamonddistrict@msn.com
**Proprietors:** Sandra and Jerry Caron

This 17-room architect-designed clapboard mansion was built in 1911 by a Lynn shoe manufacturer. Its Colonial Revival design is defined by its hipped roof,

pedimented dormers, modillions, quoins, and Palladian-style window above the front door. The 44-page architect specifications permitted only the best of materials, evident, for example, in the Mexican mahogany used in the living room. This room features a large fireplace and French doors leading to a veranda that overlooks the gardens and ocean. A winding staircase ascends three floors. Like the remainder of the house, guest rooms are furnished with antiques and oriental rugs. Two suites have working fireplaces, whirlpool tubs, and decks. A piece of note is the 1895 rosewood Knabe concert grand piano.

**Open:** year round **Accommodations:** 11 guest rooms (7 have private baths); 2 are suites **Meals:** full breakfast included; complimentary refreshments; restaurants nearby **Rates:** $90 to $225 **Payment:** AmEx, Visa, MC, CB, DC, Discover, personal and traveler's checks **Restrictions:** not suitable for young children; no smoking; inquire about pets **On-site activities:** ocean watching

## MARBLEHEAD

**Nearby attractions:** Audubon bird sanctuary, historic homes and sites, Abbott Hall Spirit of '76 painting, museums, antiques hunting, art galleries, swimming, sailing, tennis, windsurfing, harbor cruises, whale watching, seasonal festivals, Boston, Salem

### HARBOR LIGHT INN
58 Washington Street
Marblehead, Massachusetts 01945
**Phone:** 781/631-2186
**Fax:** 781/631-2216
**Website:** www.harborlightinn.com
**Proprietors:** Peter and Suzanne Conway

Located in this sailing capital's National Register historic district, the Harbor Light Inn was first constructed in 1712. An 1820 remodeling transformed the building into a Federal mansion. Completely renovated in 1986, it is today an elegant, modern inn that preserves its rich past. The feeling of a previous era is conveyed by the brass chandeliers, finely tooled eighteenth-century mahogany furniture, bedside fireplaces, local period art, and authentic oriental rugs— treasures frequently brought home from exotic ports. Many guest rooms offer fireplaces, and some have whirlpool tubs. The inn has a conference room and easily accommodates business meetings. A swimming pool offers exercise and a rooftop walk provides a clear view of the famous Marblehead Light.

THE HARBOR LIGHT INN, MARBLEHEAD, MASSACHUSETTS

**Open**: year round **Accommodations**: 21 guest rooms with private baths **Meals**: continental breakfast included; restaurants nearby **Rates**: $125 to $245; 10% discount offered to National Trust members and National Trust Visa cardholders **Payment**: AmEx, Visa, MC, personal and traveler's checks **Restrictions**: children over 6 welcome; smoking limited; no pets

## HARBORSIDE HOUSE

23 Gregory Street
Marblehead, Massachusetts 01945
**Phone:** 781/631–1032
**Website:** www.shore.net/~swliving
**E-mail:** swliving@shore.net
**Proprietor:** Susan Livingston
**Location:** 1/2 hour to Boston/Logan Airport

This handsome 1850 home, built by a ship's carpenter, overlooks the picturesque harbor in the historic district of Marblehead. Guests enjoy water views from the wood-paneled and beamed living room with fireplace, the period dining room, the sunny breakfast porch, and the third-story deck. Antique furnishings and reproduction wallpapers enhance the charm of this comfortable, quiet home. One large guest room with twin beds overlooks the harbor. Another, a romantic room with a double bed and an antique mirrored dressing table, looks out on flower gardens and the deck. A generous breakfast features homemade breads and muffins. Guests are just a short stroll from historic sites, quaint shops, and fine restaurants.

**Open:** year round **Accommodations:** 2 guest rooms share a bath **Meals:** continental-plus breakfast included; afternoon tea available; restaurants nearby **Rates:** $70 to $90; 10% discount to National Trust members and National Trust Visa cardholders **Payment:** personal and traveler's checks **Restrictions:** children over 10 welcome; smoking limited; no pets **On-site activities:** television, sundeck, secluded garden, quiet relaxation

## SPRAY CLIFF

25 Spray Avenue
Marblehead, Massachusetts 01945
**Phone:** 781/631-6789 or 800/626-1530
**Fax:** 781/639-4563
**Website:** www.marblehead chamber.org/spraycliff
**E-mail:** spraycliff@aol.com
**Proprietors:** Roger and Sally Plauche

The sea is the most enticing amenity offered at Spray Cliff. It is viewed through picture windows from nearly every room in this 1910 Tudor-style mansion. Built as a summer home, Spray Cliff offers seven spacious bedrooms, elegantly appointed with antiques, wicker, and fresh-cut flowers. In addition to the panoramic vistas, each room contains a sitting area, refreshments, reading materials, and toiletries. Living and dining areas for guests are cozy and relaxed. But it is the brick terrace, nestled in lush flower gardens, that is most memorable with its sights and sounds of the ocean. Three guest rooms and the hospitality room offer working fireplaces.

**Open:** year round **Accommodations:** 7 guest rooms with private baths **Meals:** continental-plus breakfast included; restaurants nearby **Rates:** $150 to $210; 10% discount offered to National Trust members and National Trust Visa cardholders **Payment:** AmEx, Visa, MC, personal and traveler's checks **Restrictions:** not suitable for children, no smoking

## MARTHA'S VINEYARD (CAPE COD)

**Nearby attractions:** villages of Edgartown, Oak Bluffs, and Vineyard Haven; beaches; bicycle rentals; tour buses; fishing; sailing; movie house; health club; tennis; golfing; summer theater; shopping; antiques hunting; island ferries; yacht club

### CAPTAIN DEXTER HOUSE

92 Main Street
P.O. Box 2457
Vineyard Haven, Massachusetts 02568
**Phone:** 508/693-6564
**Fax:** 508/693-8448
**Proprietor:** Roberta Pieczenik

This country colonial home was built in 1843 as the home of sea captain Rodolphus Dexter. Its original wide floorboards, graceful molding, Rumford fireplaces, and hand-stenciled walls have been meticulously restored, and the house is now furnished with eighteenth-century antiques, early American oil paintings, and oriental rugs. Each guest room is unique in style and distinctive in decor. Several rooms have working fireplaces and four-poster beds with white lace canopies. All rooms are air conditioned. In-room amenities include color-coordinated linens and comforters, period reproduction wallpapers, velvet wing chairs, fresh-cut flowers, and complimentary sherry. The home-baked continental breakfast is served in the formal dining room or in the garden. The inn is located in the heart of town on a street of fine historic homes, only a short stroll to the beach, shops, and restaurants.

**Open:** April to December **Accommodations:** 8 guest rooms with private baths; 1 is a suite **Meals:** continental-plus breakfast included; restaurants nearby **Rates:** $95 to $225; 10% discount to National Trust members and National Trust Visa cardholders **Payment:** AmEx, Visa, MC, DC, personal and traveler's checks **Restrictions:** no smoking; no pets **On-site activities:** garden lounge chairs

### CAPTAIN DEXTER HOUSE OF EDGARTOWN
35 Pease's Point Way
P.O. Box 2798
Edgartown, Massachusetts 02539
**Phone:** 508/627-7289
**Fax:** 508/627-3328
**Proprietor:** Roberta Pieczenik

Built in 1840 by a seafaring merchant, this country colonial inn on the island of Martha's Vineyard is traditionally New England—from its white clapboard siding and black shutters to its original double width floorboards. The home is located on a quiet residential street, just a short stroll to the harbor, shops, and restaurants. Guest rooms retain their colonial character with canopied beds, period antiques, and working fireplaces, yet offer all of today's conveniences, including air-conditioning. The cutting garden provides fresh flowers for the inn, while the landscaped garden is a haven for relaxation. Guests start their days with a home-baked continental breakfast served in the elegant dining room or flower-filled garden. Afternoon brings a complimentary aperitif or lemonade.

**Open:** May through October **Accommodations:** 11 guest rooms with private baths **Meals:** continental-plus breakfast included; complimentary refreshments; restaurants nearby **Rates:** $95 to $225; 10% discount offered to National Trust members and National Trust Visa cardholders **Payment:** AmEx, Visa, MC, DC, personal and traveler's checks **Restrictions:** smoking limited; no pets **On-site activities:** sunbathing, garden lounge chairs

## EDGARTOWN INN
56 North Water Street
Edgartown, Massachusetts 02539
**Phone:** 508/627-4794
**Fax:** 508/627-9420
**Website:** www.vineyard.net/biz/edgartowninn
**Proprietors:** Liliane and Earle Radford

Whaling captain Thomas Worth built this Federal home in 1798. His son, William Jenkins Worth, later became a hero of the Mexican War and the namesake of Fort Worth, Texas. The house was first used for lodging in 1820. During its long career, the house has been host to many notable guests, including Daniel Webster, Nathaniel Hawthorne, Senator Charles Sumner, and later, Senator John F. Kennedy. The inside of Captain Worth's house is much unchanged, except for the addition of spotless tiled baths and a paneled dining room at the rear of the building. Here are served full country breakfasts, featuring homemade breads and muffins. Beyond the patio is the Garden House with two spacious rooms with private balconies. Many period antiques are found throughout the property.

**Open:** April to November **Accommodations:** 20 guest rooms (16 have private baths) **Meals:** full and continental breakfast served; restaurants nearby **Rates:** $80 to $190 **Payment:** personal and traveler's checks **Restrictions:** children over 6 welcome; no pets **On-site activities:** television, sunbathing, porch sitting

## LOTHROP MERRY HOUSE
P.O. Box 1939
Vineyard Haven, Massachusetts 02568
**Phone:** 508/693-1646
**Website:** tiac.net/users/lothmer
**E-mail:** lothmer@tiac.net
**Proprietors:** John and Mary Clarke

The Lothrop Merry House is an eighteenth-century guest house overlooking Vineyard Haven harbor and the ocean beyond. Built in the late 1790s, the house retains its original latch-lock doors, wide pine floors, and wainscoting. Most guest rooms offer a harbor view; some have their own fireplaces. All are charmingly furnished with antiques. The lawn slopes gently down to the inn's private beach. Continental breakfasts, featuring homemade breads, are served outside on the sunny, flower-bordered terrace in warm weather. For those who enjoy sailing, the inn owns and operates a 54-foot Alden ketch, which can be chartered for daily, evening, or overnight cruises among the many coves and harbors of the Vineyard and the Elizabeth Islands. In addition, the inn offers free use of a canoe and sunfish.

**Open:** year round **Accommodations:** 7 guest rooms (4 have private baths) **Meals:** continental breakfast included; restaurants nearby **Wheelchair access:** 1 guest room **Rates:** $68 to $215 **Payment:** Visa, MC, traveler's check **Restrictions:** no pets **On-site activities:** private beach, swimming, canoeing, sunfish sailing

## MARTHA'S PLACE B&B

114 Main Street
Vineyard Haven, Massachusetts 02568
**Phone:** 508/693-0253
**Website:** www.marthasplace.com
**Proprietors:** Richard Alcott and Martin Hicks

Built in 1840 by Nathaniel Mayhew, a descendant of the founder of Martha's Vineyard, Martha's Place is an outstanding example of Greek Revival architecture. Located in the historic district overlooking the harbor, the inn has been elegantly restored to show off its gleaming hardwood floors with oriental carpets, crystal chandeliers, eight working fireplaces, and antique furnishings. There is a harbor-view front porch with antique white wicker furniture, a brick back courtyard for sunning, and a private brick side courtyard. The grounds are landscaped with pink rose and boxwood hedges, azaleas, heather, and a weeping pink cherry tree. Guest rooms are luxuriously appointed with such amenities as Egyptian cotton linens, terrycloth robes, and Crabtree & Evelyn toiletries. Most rooms have fireplaces and some have whirlpool tubs. Consider Martha's Empire room with antique brass half-tester bed draped in blue velvet. The inn is one block from the ferry dock, village shops, and restaurants.

**Open:** year round **Accommodations:** 6 guest rooms with private baths **Meals:** continental-plus breakfast included; complimentary refreshments; restaurants nearby **Rates:** $100 to $295 (seasonal); 10% discount to National Trust members and National Trust Visa cardholders during off season **Payment:** Visa, MC **Restrictions:** quiet children welcome; no smoking; no pets **On-site activities:** complimentary use of bicycles, tennis racquets, beach towels and chairs, coolers; sailboat for charter

# MIDDLEBOROUGH

**Nearby attractions:** historic district walking tours, Town Hall, antiques hunting, Tom Thumb Museum, Middleborough Historical Museum, Plymouth, Cranberry Harvest Festival, Boston

## ZACHARIAH EDDY HOUSE BED AND BREAKFAST

51 South Main Street
Middleborough, Massachusetts 02346
**Phone:** 508/946-0016
**Fax:** 508/946-2603
**Website:** www.bbhost.com/zacheddyhouse
**E-mail:** zacheddy@aol.com
**Proprietor:** Cheryl Leonard

The house's namesake and original owner was a noted nineteenth-century attorney. Son of one of Middleborough's founding fathers and descended from Pilgrims, Zachariah Eddy was an associate of Daniel Webster and friend of John Quincy Adams. A large Greek Revival house, it was built on granite block in 1831 and renovated with Colonial Revival details in the late 1800s. The interior of the inn is enhanced by patterned parquet floors, a hand-carved floor-to-ceiling oak fireplace with European tiled hearth, and the unusual "chapel bath" with a magnificent oriel stained-glass window. Three guest rooms are furnished with a blend of antiques, reproductions, and collectibles. Each room is equipped with cable television, paddle ceiling fans, and/or air-conditioning. Hearty, creative breakfasts are a staple at the Zachariah Eddy House. Guests may be served bread pudding with amaretto sauce, breakfast pizza, or the seasonal house specialty, lobster omelet. The inn is located in the heart of the town's South Main Street historic district.

**Open:** year round **Accommodations:** 3 guest rooms; 1 has a private bath **Meals:** full breakfast included; restaurants nearby **Rates:** $75 to $125; 10% discount to National Trust members and National Trust Visa cardholders **Payment:** AmEx, Visa, MC, Discover, traveler's check **Restrictions:** inquire about young children; no smoking; no pets

## NANTUCKET (CAPE COD)

**Nearby attractions:** Steamship Wharf, swimming, beaches, boating, wind surfing, tennis, golfing, bicycling, historic sites, museums, shopping, antiques hunting, theaters, nature walks

### COBBLESTONE INN

5 Ash Street
Nantucket, Massachusetts 02554
**Phone:** 508/228-1987
**Proprietors:** Robin Hammer-Yankow and Keith Yankow

Built in 1725 as a simple, two-story dwelling by Tristram Coffin, a member of one of Nantucket's founding families, this house was later expanded to a six-bedroom guest house offering charm and privacy (no two guest rooms have adjoining walls). The weathered-shingle building managed to survive the great fire of 1846 and now proudly displays its plaque from the Nantucket Historical Association. Retained are such original features as four fireplaces, wide floorboards, and curved corner support posts from a ship's frame. Guest rooms are spacious and contain period furnishings including some canopy beds. A suite with harbor view is also available. A sunporch, fenced yard, brick patio, and garden are delightful places to relax. Guests like to gather around the living-room fireplace in cold weather. A guest pantry is always open for snacks and beverages.

**Open:** year round **Accommodations:** 5 guest rooms with private baths; 1 is a suite **Meals:** continental-plus breakfast included; complimentary refreshments; restaurants nearby **Rates:** $75 to $250 (seasonal); 10% discount to National Trust members and National Trust Visa cardholders **Payment:** Visa, MC, personal and traveler's checks **Restrictions:** no smoking; no pets **On-site activities:** books about Nantucket, games, croquet, television–VCR and film library

### THE PINEAPPLE INN

10 Hussey Street
Nantucket, Massachusetts 02554
**Phone:** 508/228-9992
**Fax:** 508/325-6051
**Website:** www.nantucket.net/lodging/pineappleinn
**E-mail:** pineappl@nantucket.net
**Proprietors:** Caroline and Bob Taylor

Named for the colonial symbol of gracious hospitality, the Pineapple Inn lives up to that standard with elegant furnishings, thoughtful amenities, and conscientious service. The full restored inn began in 1838 as home to whaling ship captain Uriah Russell. A stately Georgian manse, the inn is appointed throughout with fine reproduction furniture, authentic nineteenth-century antiques, original works of art, and oriental carpets. In the guest rooms are handmade four-poster canopy beds, designer linens, goose-down comforters, and white marble baths. Each room also features a king or queen bed, air conditioning, cable television, and a telephone with voice mail and computer access. The innkeepers, former restaurateurs, offer delectable continental-plus breakfasts daily, served in the formal dining room or on the bricked garden patio with fountain. Located on a quiet side street in the historic district, the inn offers both convenience and peacefulness.

**Open:** May to October **Accommodations:** 12 guest rooms with private baths **Meals:** continental-plus breakfast included; complimentary refreshments; restaurants nearby **Rates:** $175 to $250; 10% discount to National Trust members and National Trust Visa cardholders off-peak only **Payment:** AmEx, Visa, MC, personal and traveler's checks **Restrictions:** children over 8 welcome; no smoking; no pets **On-site activities:** library, television

## 1739 HOUSE
43 Centre Street
P.O. Box 997
Nantucket, Massachusetts 02554
**Phone:** 508/228-0120 or 800/672-0908
**Proprietor:** Robert (Bob) Martin

In the early eighteenth century Solomon Gardner gave this parcel of Centre Street land to his daughter Sarah and her husband, David Joy. They built their clapboard, Georgian-style home here in 1739, and it stands just as elegantly today. Its five fireplaces and center chimney still provide warmth and comfort, and the wide floorboards have been carefully preserved. The 1739 House is furnished with antiques, oriental rugs, and canopy beds. Guests are invited to enjoy two living rooms, the garden patio, and a rose garden. Located in the heart of Nantucket's historic district, the house is a short walk to shops, restaurants, museums, wharves, and beaches.

**Open:** May 20 to October 20 **Accommodations:** 6 guest rooms (3 have private baths); 2 are suites **Meals:** continental breakfast included; restaurants nearby **Rates:** $89 to $132 **Payment:** personal and traveler's checks **Restrictions:** no pets **On-site activities:** television-VCR and movie library, patio parties

## WOODBOX INN
29 Fair Street
Nantucket, Massachusetts 02554
**Phone:** 508/228-0587
**Website:** www.woodboxinn.com
**Proprietor:** Dexter Tutein

The Woodbox is Nantucket's oldest inn. Built in 1709 by a whaling captain named Bunker, it was joined to its neighboring 1711 house in the early 1900s to create a guest establishment. The low-beamed, pine-paneled dining room serves breakfast (some say the best on the island) and gourmet dinners by the light of tall candles in brass candlesticks. Furnishings throughout the Woodbox feature fine American antiques from the colonial period. Six of the nine guest rooms are suites with fireplaces, and some contain canopy beds. Less than two blocks from Main Street, the Woodbox Inn is located in a quiet part of town, promising peaceful nights.

**Open:** June through mid-October **Accommodations:** 9 guest rooms with private baths; 6 are suites with fireplaces **Meals:** restaurant on premises serving breakfast and gourmet dinners **Wheelchair access:** limited **Rates:** $150 to $250; 10% discount to National Trust members and National Trust Visa cardholders midweek, off season only **Payment:** personal and traveler's checks **Restrictions:** no pets

## NEWBURYPORT

**Nearby attractions:** Custom House Maritime Museum, Plum Island National Wildlife Refuge, Cushing House; Maudslay State Park for cross-country skiing, hiking, picnicking, and bird-watching; concerts and plays, Firehouse Center for Performing and Visual Arts, antiques hunting, speciality shops, golfing, swimming, tennis, fishing, boating, Lowell's Boat Shop, Sturbridge Village, Hancock Shaker Village, New Hampshire's White Mountains

## CLARK CURRIER INN
45 Green Street
Newburyport, Massachusetts 01950
**Phone:** 508/465-8363 or 800/360-6582
**Proprietors:** Mary, Bob, and Melissa Nolan

The Clark Currier Inn is a classic Federal home built in 1803 by Thomas March Clark, a prominent citizen, entrepreneur, and shipbuilder. Lovely architectural details such as a wide center hall, decorative dentil moldings, window seats, Indian shutters, and an elegant "good morning" staircase, lend grace to the dwelling. The name of the inn honors memories of its builder and a longtime owner, and each guest room bears the name of a former owner or resident. All rooms are furnished with antiques and have private baths and air conditioning. There is a sunny garden room, comfortable parlor, library, and garden for guests to enjoy. The inn is located just one block from an award-winning restored historic downtown and three blocks from the waterfront.

**Open:** year round **Accommodations:** 8 guest rooms with private baths **Meals:** buffet breakfast included; complimentary afternoon tea; restaurants nearby **Wheelchair access:** 3 guest rooms, common areas **Rates:** $85 to $155; 10% discount offered to National Trust members and National Trust Visa cardholders **Payment:** AmEx, Visa, MC, personal and traveler's checks **Restrictions:** children over 12 welcome; smoking limited; no pets **On-site activities:** reading

## WINDSOR HOUSE
38 Federal Street
Newburyport, Massachusetts 01950
**Phone:** 978/462-3778 or 888/TRELAWNY
**Fax:** 978/465-3443
**E-mail:** tintagel@greennet.net
**Proprietors:** Judith and John Harris

This three-story Federal-style brick building was constructed in 1786 to serve as both a ship's chandlery and residence. It was Aaron Pardee's wedding gift to Jane Perkins. Each spacious room in today's Windsor House has been refurbished to hold a memory of its original use. The Merchant Suite contains the hand-hewn beamed ceiling that was part of the ships' chandlery. The Bridal Suite was first the bedroom shared by Jane and Aaron Pardee. The Library was Aaron's study; today it houses 500 books on one wall. The inn's newest room, England's Rose, honors the late Diana, Princess of Wales and recalls a typical English cottage bedroom. All guest rooms have private baths. Traditional Cornish and English regional cooking is featured for breakfast and tea. The Windsor House has an ideal location two blocks from the center of Newburyport, within walking distance of the historic harbor, Merrimack River, shops, restaurants, and museums.

**Open:** year round **Accommodations:** 4 guest rooms with private baths **Meals:** full breakfast included; complimentary afternoon tea; restaurants nearby **Rates:** $95 to $135; 10% discount to National Trust members and National Trust Visa cardholders **Payment:** AmEx, Visa, MC, Discover, personal and traveler's checks **Restrictions:** no smoking **On-site activities:** Avalon Travel Associates on site offering specialized tours to ancient sites in Britain

# NORTHAMPTON

**Nearby attractions:** Smith College, theaters, art galleries, specialty shopping, fine dining

## THE HOTEL NORTHAMPTON
36 King Street
Northampton, Massachusetts 01060
**Phone:** 413/584-3100 or 800/678-8946
**Fax:** 413/584-9455
**Website:** www.hotelnorthampton.com
**General Manager:** Mansour Ghalibaf

The rich heritage of the landmark Hotel Northampton, built in 1927, owes much to its first manager, Lewis Wiggins. An avid collector of American antiques, Wiggins sought to achieve museum status for the hotel's public areas and furnishings, to which he added new finds virtually every day. By 1937, he employed a full-time antiquarian-curator with a staff of 15. Some public rooms were outfitted with paneling, timbers, and doors salvaged from early homes; the authentic, colonial-styled Wiggins Tavern, created from an adjacent century-old structure, opened in 1930. Today, Wiggins Tavern is one of Northampton's oldest operating restaurants. The charm, comfort, and gracious elegance of a traditional New England inn is found everywhere in this grand hotel. Guest rooms feature classic furnishings in Chippendale, Federal, and Duncan Phyfe styles. Nestled in the heart of Northampton, the hotel is adjacent to shops, theaters, galleries, and eateries, and is blocks away from prestigious Smith College. The Hotel Northampton is a member of Historic Hotels of America.

**Open:** year round **Accommodations:** 77 guest rooms with private baths **Meals:** continental breakfast included; restaurants on premises; restaurants nearby **Rates:** $90 to $300; 10% discount to National Trust members and National Trust Visa cardholders **Payment:** AmEx, Visa, MC, Discover, traveler's checks **Restrictions:** smoking limited; no pets **On-site activities:** exercise room, business services

# PETERSHAM

**Nearby attractions:** Harvard University forestry division, golfing, hiking, skiing, summer band concerts, museums, Old Sturbridge Village

### WINTERWOOD AT PETERSHAM
19 North Main Street
Petersham, Massachusetts 01366
**Phone:** 978/724-8885
**Proprietors:** Jean and Robert Day

Winterwood is an elegant 16-room country inn just off the common in the historic district of Petersham. The inn was built in 1842 in the Greek Revival style as a private summer home. Recently restored, the house has undergone few changes over the years and is listed in the National Register of Historic Places. Guest rooms are professionally decorated to reflect the grace and history of the house; most rooms have working fireplaces. Guests may enjoy tea or linger over cocktails in front of the living room fireplace or on one of the inn's several porches. Across from a 32-acre wildlife meadow preserve, Winterwood offers views of Mount Wachusett and the countryside.

**Open:** year round **Accommodations:** 6 guest rooms with private baths; 1 is a suite **Meals:** continental breakfast included; restaurant on premises for private parties; restaurants nearby **Rates:** $65 to $125; 10% discount offered to National Trust members and National Trust Visa cardholders **Payment:** AmEx, Visa, MC, Discover, personal and traveler's checks **Restrictions:** no smoking in guest rooms; no pets

---

# PRINCETON

**Nearby attractions:** Old Sturbridge Village, Worcester museums, Worcester Science Center, antiques hunting, hiking, bicycling, berry picking, cross-country and downhill skiing, hawk watching, Wachusett Meadows wildlife preserve

### FERNSIDE BED AND BREAKFAST
162 Mountain Road
Princeton, Massachusetts 01541
**Phone:** 978/464-2741 or 800/545-2741
**Fax:** 978/464-2065
**E-mail:** fernside@msn.com
**Proprietor:** Jocelyn Morrison

Located on the eastern slope of Mount Wachusett in Princeton, this elegant Federal mansion was built in 1838 as a private residence by Captain Benjamin

Harrington. Operated as a tavern and boardinghouse for Harvard professors and students between 1870 and 1889, Fernside was purchased in 1890 by the Girls' Vacation House Association of Boston and served as a summer house for working women for more than 100 years. Recently restored by the innkeepers, the house is furnished with exquisite antiques and period reproductions, including the guest rooms. Here visitors will also enjoy oriental rugs, down comforters, and fully tiled baths. Some guest rooms feature fireplaces and four-poster queen-size beds. Guests are invited to relax in one of the numerous sitting rooms or porches, or read a book before one of the eight fireplaces. Breakfast is made from the freshest ingredients and served in the dining room.

**Open:** year round **Accommodations:** 6 guest rooms with private baths; 2 are suites **Meals:** full breakfast included; complimentary refreshments; restaurants nearby **Rates:** $110 to $175; 10% discount to National Trust members and National Trust Visa cardholders midweek only **Payment:** AmEx, Visa, MC, Discover, personal and traveler's checks **Restrictions:** children over 12 welcome; no smoking; no pets **On-site activities:** piano, books, games, bird watching, hiking, bicycling, croquet, wild berry picking

## ROCKPORT

**Nearby attractions:** Cape Ann, art colony and galleries, ocean beaches, swimming, sailing, park, whale-watching, boating, shopping, antiques hunting, golfing, tennis, trolley tours, schooner trips, June chamber music festival, fine dining

### INN ON COVE HILL

37 Mount Pleasant Street
Rockport, Massachusetts 01966
**Phone:** 978/546-2701 or 888/546-2701
**Website:** www.cape-ann.com/covehill
**Proprietors:** John and Marjorie Pratt

Behind a white picket fence just a block from the harbor is this gracious Federal home built in 1791, many of its decorative and architectural features carefully preserved or restored. On arrival, guests are welcomed into the entrance hall, with its artfully crafted spiral staircase. The living room is an inviting blend of comfortable and antique furnishings. Wide pine floorboards and dentil molding remind visitors of the inn's 200-year heritage. Guest rooms feature canopy beds and period antiques. Carefully selected wallcoverings and fabrics create a cozy yet lavish atmosphere, while personal touches and amenities add comfort.

**Open:** April through October **Accommodations:** 11 guest rooms (9 have private baths) **Meals:** continental breakfast included; restaurants nearby **Rates:** $49 to $113 **Payment:** personal and traveler's checks **Restrictions:** appropriate for children over 16; no smoking; no pets **On-site activities:** reading, relaxation

## RALPH WALDO EMERSON INN

Pigeon Cove
Box 2369
Rockport, Massachusetts 01966
**Phone:** 978/546-6321
**Fax:** 978/546-7043
**E-mail:** emerson@cove.com
**Proprietor:** Gary Wemyss

A large, pillared white hotel, the Ralph Waldo Emerson Inn is named for the nineteenth-century author who wrote from this place that he had "returned from Pigeon cove...where we made acquaintance with the sea." The original building dates to 1840, about a decade before Emerson's visit. The newer section was added in 1912. Today at the Emerson, the fast pace of modern life yields to tranquil days filled with sun and sea, much as it did during its early days. Spacious landscaped lawns and wide, breezy porches promote the peacefulness of the setting. Guest rooms are attractively furnished and offer private baths and telephones. The large dining room provides a view of the ocean. Guests will find much to do in the recreation rooms, heated saltwater pool, and whirlpool and sauna. The inn, awarded three diamonds by AAA, is convenient to Rockport's many activities.

**Open:** April 1 to November 30 **Accommodations:** 36 guest rooms with private baths; 2 are suites **Meals:** restaurant on premises **Rates:** $90 to $145; 10% discount to National Trust members and National Trust Visa cardholders midweek, off season only **Payment:**

Visa, MC, Discover, personal and traveler's checks **Restrictions:** no pets **On-site activities:** heated saltwater swimming pool, hiking trail, whirlpool and sauna, recreation room, movie theater

SEACREST MANOR
99 Marmion Way
Rockport, Massachusetts 01966
**Phone:** 978/546-2211
**Website:** www.rockportusa.com/seacrestmanor/
**Proprietors:** Leighton T. Saville and Dwight B. MacCormack, Jr.

Seacrest Manor is decidedly small, intentionally quiet. Situated on the rugged heights of Cape Ann, surrounded by acres of garden and woodland, it offers a panoramic view of the sea. Built in 1911 as a luxurious Colonial Revival home, it has operated as an inn for more than 40 years, garnering countless accolades from guests and travel critics. Guest rooms are large and sunny, tastefully furnished with antiques and traditional pieces. Turn-down service, evening mints, shoe-shine service, floral bouquets, and morning newspapers are some of the amenities that have earned Seacrest Manor its Mobil three-star rating. A hearty breakfast is served in the dining room overlooking the gardens. The inn's natural setting is furthered by the John Kieran nine-acre nature preserve across the street.

**Open:** April through November **Accommodations:** 8 rooms (6 have private baths) **Meals:** full breakfast included; complimentary afternoon tea; restaurants nearby **Rates:** $98 to $146 **Payment:** personal and traveler's checks **Restrictions:** not recommended for children; no smoking; no pets **On-site activities:** gardens, woods, bird-watching, sundeck, library, bicycles, antiques hunting, relaxation

# SALEM

**Nearby attractions:** Witch Museum, Essex Institute, Peabody Museum, Salem Maritime National Historic Site, House of the Seven Gables, Pickering Wharf, historic homes, harbor cruises, whale-watching, boat rentals, swimming, movie theaters

## AMELIA PAYSON HOUSE

16 Winter Street
Salem, Massachusetts 01970
**Phone:** 978/744-8304
**Website:** www.salemweb.com/biz/ameliapayson/
**E-mail:** bbamelia@aol.com
**Proprietors:** Ada May and Donald C. Roberts

Built in 1845 for Amelia and Edward Payson, 16 Winter Street is one of Salem's finest examples of Greek Revival architecture, its front-gabled facade distinguished by four two-story pilasters. Carefully restored, the elegant inn offers individually decorated guest rooms featuring period antiques, charming wallpapers, and hardwood floors. A generous continental breakfast is served family style, providing guests with an opportunity to learn about historic Salem and its witchcraft mystique from the innkeepers. Guests appreciate the inn's convenient location within the town's historic district.

**Open:** March through December **Accommodations:** 4 guest rooms with private baths; 1 is a suite **Meals:** continental-plus breakfast; restaurants nearby **Rates:** $75 to $125 **Payment:** AmEx, Visa, MC, traveler's check **Restrictions:** children over 12 welcome; no smoking; no pets

## STEPHEN DANIELS HOUSE

1 Daniels Street (corner of Essex)
Salem, Massachusetts 01970
**Phone:** 978/744-5709
**Proprietor:** Catherine B. Gill

The Stephen Daniels House was built in 1667 by a sea captain and remained a family home until it was converted to an inn in 1945. Originally a four-room gambrel-roofed building, the house was greatly enlarged in 1756. Since then there have been no major changes except for the installation of modern plumbing and electricity; all the eighteenth-century architectural details—and some from the seventeenth century—are intact. The house is of such significance that its plans are in the Library of Congress. Of ten working fireplaces, three are in guest rooms. Another is in the dining room and breakfast is served before it. The rooms are large, colorful, and furnished with antiques, including canopy beds. At the inn, listed in the National Register, great care has been taken to ensure that nothing intrudes on the eighteenth-century New England atmosphere.

**Open:** year round **Accommodations:** 6 guest rooms (3 have private baths); 1 is a suite **Meals:** continental breakfast included; complimentary refreshments; restaurants nearby **Rates:** $105 to $120; 10% discount to National Trust members and National Trust Visa cardholders **Payment:** AmEx, personal and traveler's checks **On-site activities:** checkers, board games, private English garden, conversing

## SANDWICH (CAPE COD)

**Nearby attractions:** Sandwich Glass Museum, Heritage Plantation, Thornton Burgess Museum, Hoxie House, Yesteryear's Doll Museum, Cape Cod Bay Beach, antiques hunting, whale-watching, golfing, tennis

### DAN'L WEBSTER INN

149 Main Street
Sandwich, Massachusetts 02563
**Phone:** 508/888-3622 or 800/444-3566
**Fax:** 508/888-5156
**Website:** www.danlwebsterinn.com
**E-mail:** dwi@capecod.net
**Proprietors:** Catania family

The history of the Dan'l Webster Inn dates as far back as 1644 when William Newland was given a license to keep an ordinary. Several buildings occupied this site over the next two centuries, always playing host to travelers and locals needing fine company and strong spirits. During the early decades of the nineteenth century, Daniel Webster, noted politician and orator, stayed at the inn frequently. That historic structure was destroyed by fire in 1971, and was rebuilt in 1973. Guest rooms dressed in period decor are offered there today, along with four suites in an 1826 sea captain's house and five rooms in the circa 1850 house that once belonged to the owner of the Sandwich Glass Company. The three buildings constitute today's Dan'l Webster Inn. All rooms are air conditioned and have cable television, telephones, and private baths. Some offer whirlpool tubs and working fireplaces. The gathering room is always open for reading, cards, or just plain relaxing. Three dining rooms serve three meals daily.

**Open:** year round (except Christmas Day) **Accommodations:** 47 guest rooms with private baths; 9 are suites **Meals:** continental breakfast included; complimentary refreshments; restaurants nearby **Wheelchair access:** yes **Rates:** $99 to $270 (seasonal)

**Payment:** AmEx, Visa, MC, CB, DC, Discover, traveler's check **Restrictions:** smoking limited; no pets **On-site activities:** outdoor swimming pool, landscaped grounds with gazebo, local health club privileges

## SUMMER HOUSE
158 Main Street
Sandwich, Massachusetts 02563
**Phone:** 508/888-4991 or 800/241-3609
**E-mail:** sumhouse@capecod.net
**Proprietors:** Phyllis Bury and Eric Suby

Summer House is a beautiful example of Cape Cod Greek Revival architecture set among other equally grand historic homes and public buildings. Built around 1835 by Dr. Jonathan Leonard, Jr., Summer House is located in the heart of the historic district of Sandwich Village, the oldest town on Cape Cod (settled in 1637). Guest rooms are decorated to evoke the spirit of previous centuries. Antiques, hand-stitched quilts, heirloom linens, working fireplaces, painted hardwood floors, and original woodwork and hardware set the mood of a gracious nineteenth-century home. Breakfast is served in the vibrant breakfast room, where Chinese red walls contrast with white window molding and paneling, a black-and-white checkerboard floor, and a black marble fireplace. Afternoon tea is served on the wicker-furnished porch or in the flower garden.

**Open:** year round **Accommodations:** 6 guest rooms with private baths **Meals:** full breakfast included; complimentary afternoon tea; restaurants nearby **Rates:** $80 to $105; 10% discount offered to National Trust members and National Trust Visa cardholders **Payment:** AmEx, Visa, MC, Discover, personal and traveler's checks **Restrictions:** children over 6 welcome; no smoking; no pets **On-site activities:** flower gardens and lawns, library

## SOUTH EGREMONT

**Nearby attractions:** Tanglewood, Norman Rockwell Museum, Appalachian Trail, golfing, skiing, hiking

## THE EGREMONT INN

10 Old Sheffield Road
South Egremont, Massachusetts 01258
**Phone:** 413/528-2111 or 800/859-1780
**Fax:** 413/528-3284
**Proprietors:** Karen and Steven Waller

Located by a gentle stream in the historic village of Egremont, this inn was built in 1780 by Frances Haere, a Revolutionary War veteran. It has served travelers since its inception being known alternately as Haere's Tavern, Mt. Everett House, and finally the Egremont Inn. Today's inn offers 19 antiques-filled guest rooms, three spacious sitting rooms made cozy in winter by wood-burning fireplaces, and wicker rocker-filled wraparound porches that span the first and second floors. The elegant dining room and informal tavern feature classic American cuisine. Acoustic Jazz and popular vocals are performed by outstanding local musicians. Both the inn and the village of South Egremont are listed in the National Register of Historic Places. In the heart of the southern Berkshires, the Egremont is a perfect home base from which to explore the area's many attractions.

**Open:** year round **Accommodations:** 19 guest rooms with private baths; 1 is a suite **Meals:** continental (weekdays) or full (weekends) breakfast included; restaurants on premises **Wheelchair access:** limited **Rates:** $85 to $170; 10% discount to National Trust members and National Trust Visa cardholders, off-peak only **Payment:** AmEx, Visa, MC, Discover, personal and traveler's checks **Restrictions:** smoking limited; no pets **On-site activities:** in-ground pool, 2 tennis courts, books, chess, television

# STERLING

**Nearby attractions:** Wachusett Mountain skiing, Worcester Art Museum, Sterling Millworks, historic Lexington and Concord

## STERLING INN
240 Worcester Road
Route 12
Sterling, Massachusetts 01564
**Phone:** 978/422-6592 or 800/370-0239
**Proprietors:** Mark and Patricia Roy
**Location:** 15 miles north of Worcester

The Sterling Inn has served central Massachusetts since 1890. The current building was designed in 1907 by G. Henri Desmond, a Boston architect. The inn is an excellent example of the Craftsman style of architecture that swept the country at the turn of the century, and its half-timbering and flower-filled window boxes give it a Swiss chalet feel. The dining rooms and tap room, where working fireplaces generate warmth on chilly evenings, have always been popular with both travelers and local patrons. For generations local families have considered the inn a second home where they entertain at holidays, hold intimate wedding receptions, or simply sit together on the front porch. The second floor has six comfortable guest rooms decorated in a homespun, country style.

**Open:** year round **Accommodations:** 6 guest rooms with private baths **Meals:** continental-plus breakfast included (full breakfast on Sunday); complimentary refreshments; restaurant on premises **Wheelchair access:** dining rooms and public bathrooms **Rates:** $60 to $69; 10% discount offered to National Trust members and National Trust Visa cardholders **Payment:** AmEx, Visa, MC, personal and traveler's checks **Restrictions:** children over 8 welcome; no pets

## STOCKBRIDGE–SOUTH LEE

**Nearby attractions:** Tanglewood Music Festival; Jacob's Pillow Dance Festival; Berkshire Festival Theater; skiing; fall foliage tours; Norman Rockwell Museum; National Trust's Chesterwood, Wharton, and Melville houses; Hancock Shaker Village; Mission House; Naumkeag

### INN AT STOCKBRIDGE
30 East Street (Route 7 North)
P.O. Box 618
Stockbridge, Massachusetts 01262
**Phone:** 413/298-3337 or 888/466-7865
**Fax:** 413/298-3406
**Website:** www.stockbridgeinn.com
**E-mail:** innkeeper@stockbridgeinn.com
**Proprietors:** Alice and Len Schiller

In 1906, Boston attorney Philip Blagdon built an elegant vacation home in Stockbridge. He had it designed in the Colonial Revival style, complete with Georgian detailing and classical columns. The house, now the Inn at Stockbridge, remains structurally unchanged; its interior still boasts finely detailed molding throughout the first floor and on the staircase. The inn, on 12 secluded acres, offers an atmosphere of warmth and friendliness attested to by numerous publications, including *Country Inns*, *New York Magazine,* and the *Boston Globe*. Individually decorated guest rooms are traditional and cozy. A full breakfast is served on a grand mahogany table set with china, silver, crystal, linen, and lighted candles. Guests also gather for wine and cheese each afternoon, often after a dip in the pool.

**Open:** year round **Accommodations:** 12 guest rooms with private baths; 4 are suites **Meals:** full breakfast included; complimentary refreshments; restaurants nearby **Rates:** $125 to $270; 10% discount offered to National Trust members and National Trust Visa cardholders off-peak only **Payment:** AmEx, Visa, MC, personal and traveler's checks **Restrictions:** children over 12 welcome; no smoking; no pets **On-site activities:** swimming, exploring 12 acres, extensive library

## RED LION INN
Main Street
Stockbridge, Massachusetts 01262
**Phone:** 412/298-5545
**Fax:** 413/298-5130
**Website:** www.redlioninn.com
**Proprietors:** Fitzpatrick family

Established as a stagecoach stop in 1773 by Silas Pepoon and rebuilt in 1897 following a devastating fire, the Red Lion is one of the few remaining American inns in continuous use since the eighteenth century. Immortalized in Norman Rockwell's painting *Main Street, Stockbridge,* the inn epitomizes New England hospitality. It is filled with a fine collection of Staffordshire china, colonial pewter, and eighteenth-century furnishings, many of which have belonged to the inn for more than a century. Every guest room is uniquely decorated in keeping with the inn's history. Contemporary New England cuisine is served in the main dining room, cozy tavern, or the Lion's Den Pub. Host to five presidents as well as Nathaniel Hawthorne, William Cullen Bryant, and Henry Wadsworth Longfellow, the Red Lion Inn is central to Stockbridge's and the Berkshires' historic and cultural attractions.

**Open:** year round **Accommodations:** 111 guest rooms (93 have private baths); 19 are suites **Meals:** restaurants on premises **Rates:** $95 to $370; 10% discount to National Trust members and National Trust Visa cardholders **Payment:** AmEx, Visa, MC, CB, DC, Discover, personal and traveler's checks **Restrictions:** no pets **On-site activities:** massage therapist, outdoor swimming pool, exercise room, pub with nightly entertainment

# STURBRIDGE

**Nearby attractions:** Old Sturbridge Village, museums, galleries, tennis, golfing, hiking trails, antiques hunting, shopping

## EBENEZER CRAFTS INN
66 Fiske Hill Road
Sturbridge, Massachusetts 01566
**Phone:** 800/PUBLICK (782-5425)
**Fax:** 508/347-5073
**Website:** www.publickhouse.com
**Proprietors:** Publick House Historic Inn

This classic New England Federal farmhouse was built in 1786 by David Fiske. The house is owned and operated today by the nearby Publick House, first opened in 1771 by Colonel Ebenezer Crafts. Except for the addition of modern conveniences, Fiske's house is as it was when built. Large, airy guest rooms are individually furnished with colonial antiques and period reproductions. Each has its own bath. All offer sweeping views of unspoiled rolling hills. On arrival, guests are given a tour of the historic house. Before retiring at night, beds are turned down, terrycloth robes are laid out, and chocolates are left on bedside tables. A fresh bakery breakfast and afternoon tea are offered daily. The entire inn may be reserved for special occasions.

**Open:** year round **Accommodations:** 8 guest rooms with private baths; 2 are suites **Meals:** continental breakfast included; complimentary refreshments; restaurants nearby **Rates:** $74 to $155; 10% discount to National Trust members and National Trust Visa cardholders **Payment:** AmEx, Visa, MC, CB, DC, personal and traveler's checks **Restrictions:** smoking limited; no pets **On-site activities:** swimming pool, hiking, lawn games, specialty packages

# WARE

**Nearby attractions:** Springfield Quadrangle Museums, Old Sturbridge Village, Basketball Hall of Fame, Higgins Armory Museum, Riverside Park, Quabbin Reservoir Wilderness, Five-College Area, boating, swimming, tennis, cross-country and downhill skiing, ice skating

## WILDWOOD INN BED AND BREAKFAST

121 Church Street
Ware, Massachusetts 01082
**Phone:** 413/967-7798 or 800/860-8098
**Proprietors:** Fraidell Frenster, Richard Watson

Midway between Boston and the Berkshires, the town of Ware is an ideal location from which to explore central Massachusetts. In Ware, on a quiet street lined with Victorian-era houses, the Wildwood Inn is a large Queen Anne structure surrounded by two acres of lawns, gardens, and woods. Brothers named Southworth built the house in 1880 using all the classic elements of that style, including a turret, wraparound porch, bay windows, and fishscale shingles. Polished wood floors, a welcoming fireplace, and comfy furnishings make visitors feel welcome. Nine sunny guest rooms are furnished with American primitive antiques, except for the aptly named Victorian room, which features mahogany, lace, and oriental rugs. Each of the other rooms is named for the handmade quilt or afghan across the bed. Views are of maple and fir trees, the inn's mini-orchard, or perennial gardens. Ample "no lunch" breakfast is served each day, family style.

**Open:** year round **Accommodations:** 9 guest rooms (7 have private baths); 2 are suites **Meals:** full breakfast included; complimentary refreshments; restaurants nearby **Rates:** $50 to $90 **Payment:** AmEx, Visa, MC, Discover, DC, personal and traveler's checks **Restrictions:** children over 6 welcome; no smoking; no pets **On-site activities:** lawn games, hammock, porch sitting, 10 cultivated gardens, stone barbeque

# MICHIGAN

## BIG BAY

**Nearby attractions:** maritime museum, harbor cruises, walking tours, antiques hunting, hiking, waterfall tours, fishing, rock climbing, canoeing, downhill and cross-country skiing, art and music festivals

### BIG BAY POINT LIGHTHOUSE BED AND BREAKFAST
3 Lighthouse Road
Big Bay, Michigan 49808
**Phone and Fax**: 906/345-9957
**Website**: www.lighthousebandb.com
**Proprietors**: Linda and Jeff Gamble
**Location**: 30 miles north of Marquette

Beginning in 1896, the Big Bay Point Lighthouse guided mariners on Lake Superior from its vantage point high atop a cliff jutting into the water. Although automated signals replaced the original lamp in 1941, the 1500-pound Third Order Fresnel Lens, the second largest ever used on the Great Lakes, is still intact and available for inspection by guests. In 1986 the two-story brick building and its adjoining 60-foot-high square tower were adapted to a bed-and-breakfast facility. The 18-room inn has seven guest rooms and a common living room with fireplace, a dining room, a library, and a sauna located in the tower. A visit to the lantern, 125 feet above the lake surface, reveals vistas of Lake Superior, the Huron Mountains, fields of wildflowers, dense forests, and the drama of offshore lightning bolts and the Aurora Borealis in the night sky.

**Open:** year round **Accommodations:** 7 guest rooms (5 have private baths); 2 are suites **Meals:** full breakfast included; restaurants nearby **Rates:** $85 to $175; 10% discount to National Trust members **Payment:** traveler's check **Restrictions:** not suitable for children; no smoking; no pets **On-site activities:** sauna, nature trail, 1/2 mile of lakefront, cross-country skiing

# COLDWATER

**Nearby attractions:** Tibbits Opera House, Shipshewana Amish Country, Allen (antiques capital of Michigan), Colon Magic Festival, Michigan International Speedway, Kalamazoo, winery, museums, Pokagon State Park, golfing, boating, fishing, ice fishing, swimming, cross-country skiing, hiking, Binder Park Zoo

### CHICAGO PIKE INN
215 East Chicago Street
Coldwater, Michigan 49036
**Phone:** 517/279-8744
**Fax:** 517/278-8597
**Proprietors:** Harold, Jane, and Rebecca Schultz

Built for Morris G. Clarke, a wealthy Coldwater merchant, this 1903 mansion exhibits elegant neoclassical styling in its full-height porch supported by massive columns with Ionic capitals. After more than 50 years as a rooming house, it was sold in 1988 and transformed into the luxurious bed and breakfast of today. A careful restoration preserved the sweeping cherry staircase, stained-glass windows, parquet and marble floors, and gas and electric chandeliers. Richly designed wallpapers and fabrics from Schumacher and Waverly are accentuated by oriental rugs and Victorian-era antiques. Guest rooms, recalling former house occupants with names like Miss Sophia's Suite, the Hired Girls' Suite, and the Grandchildrens'

Room, all assure comfort, with individual climate controls and comfortable chairs and reading lamps. Chicago Pike Inn has been featured in an *Innsider* cover story.

**Open:** year round **Accommodations:** 8 guest rooms with private baths; 1 is a suite **Meals:** full breakfast included; complimentary refreshments; restaurants nearby **Rates:** $90 to $180 **Payment:** AmEx, Visa, MC, personal check **Restrictions:** children over 12 welcome; smoking limited; no pets **On-site activities:** bicycling, reading, relaxing in gazebo, gift shop

## HOLLAND

**Nearby attractions:** Windmill Island, DeWitt Cultural Center, Manufacturers' Marketplace, Lake Michigan beaches, bicycle paths, cross-country skiing, boating, golfing, tennis, tulips in May

### BONNIE'S PARSONAGE 1908
6 East Twenty-fourth Street
Holland, Michigan 49423
**Phone:** 616/396-1316
**Proprietor:** Bonnie McVoy-Verwys

Situated in a quiet residential area, this American Foursquare house (also sometimes called Prairie Box) with hipped roof and dormers was built in 1908 as a parsonage by the Prospect Reformed Church in order to call their first minister.

The interior glows with the warmth of rich oak woodwork. Original leaded-glass windows and pocket doors add to its beauty. Antique furnishings are found in two cozy sitting rooms and the formal dining room, on a summer porch, and in the charming guest rooms. On arrival, guests are greeted with lemonade in the garden patio or hot spiced cider in front of the fireplace in the country kitchen. Conveniently located near the shores of Lakes Michigan and Macatawa and only five minutes from Hope College and the Hedcore business district, the inn accommodates leisure and business travelers. The Parsonage 1908 is AAA approved and has been featured in the *Detroit Free Press*.

**Open:** March 15 to February 15 **Accommodations:** 3 guest rooms (2 have private baths) **Meals:** full breakfast included; complimentary refreshments; restaurants nearby **Rates:** $100 to $110; 10% discount to National Trust members and National Trust Visa cardholders first night only **Payment:** personal and traveler's checks **Restrictions:** not suitable for young children; no smoking; no pets **On-site activities:** patio, garden, croquet, rest and relaxation

---

# LAKESIDE

**Nearby attractions:** Lake Michigan beaches, swimming, state parks, art galleries, summer theater, antiques hunting, winery tours, cross-country skiing

## PEBBLE HOUSE
15093 Lakeshore Road
Lakeside, Michigan 49116
**Phone:** 616/469-1416
**Proprietors:** Jean and Ed Lawrence

The Pebble House, consisting of three guest buildings, a screened summer house, and a tennis court, was built in 1912 as a vacation retreat. Buildings are connected by wooden walkways and pergolas covered with wisteria and grapevines. The main house and fence posts are built of decorative stones that inspired the inn's name. The house decor celebrates the American Arts and Crafts Movement, which flourished between 1900 and 1916 as a rebellion against the excesses of Victorian design. The inn's emphasis on handcraftsmanship and simple, solid construction typifies Arts and Crafts design. Guest rooms are furnished in either Mission or Victorian styles. The glassed-in porch is a welcoming retreat, with rockers surrounding the stone fireplace.

**Open:** year round **Accommodations:** 7 guest rooms with private baths; 4 are suites **Meals:** full breakfast included; complimentary refreshments; restaurants nearby **Wheelchair access:** 1 guest room and bath; dining room with assistance **Rates:** $100 to $140 **Payment:** Visa, MC, personal and traveler's checks **Restrictions:** smoking limited; no pets (resident cats) **On-site ac**tivities: tennis, parlor games, library, screenhouse for hammocks, games, picnicking

---

## LUDINGTON

**Nearby attractions:** Lake Michigan beaches, Ludington State Park, Stearns Park, White Pine Village, Michigan–Wisconsin car ferry

### THE INN AT LUDINGTON
701 East Ludington Avenue
Ludington, Michigan 49431
**Phone:** 616/845-7055 or 800/845-9170
**Website:** www.com.bbonline/mi/ludington
**Proprietor:** Diane Shields

The Inn at Ludington occupies an antique-laden Queen Anne house that was built in 1889 by Dr. F. R. Latimer. The corner tower is the focal point of this

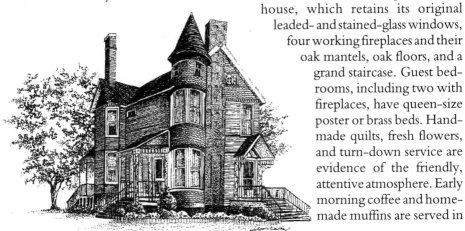

house, which retains its original leaded- and stained-glass windows, four working fireplaces and their oak mantels, oak floors, and a grand staircase. Guest bedrooms, including two with fireplaces, have queen-size poster or brass beds. Handmade quilts, fresh flowers, and turn-down service are evidence of the friendly, attentive atmosphere. Early morning coffee and homemade muffins are served in the parlor, followed by a complete breakfast in the dining room. The inn also offers spring and fall murder-mystery weekends.

**Open:** year round **Accommodations:** 6 guest rooms with private baths; 1 is a suite **Meals:** full breakfast included; complimentary refreshments; restaurants nearby **Wheelchair access:** 1 guest room, dining room, parlor **Rates:** $70 to $90; 10% discount offered to National Trust members and National Trust Visa cardholders **Payment:** AmEx, Visa, MC, personal and traveler's checks **Restrictions:** smoking limited; no pets (resident dog) **On-site activities:** library, relaxing before fire or on patio

# ONEKAMA

**Nearby attractions:** Victorian port city of Manistee, ferry to Wisconsin, antiques hunting, sightseeing

## PORTAGE POINT INN
8513 South Portage Point Road
Onekama, Michigan 49675
**Phone:** 616/889-4222 or 800/878-7248
**Fax:** 616/889-4260
**Website:** www.portagepointinn.com
**E-mail:** mdevoe@portagepointinn.com
**Proprietors:** Mike and Jane Devoe

With an architectural style similar to the Grand Hotel on Mackinac Island, Portage Point Inn is often called the "Baby Grand." It is positioned on a wooded peninsula with miles of sandy Lake Michigan dunes and beaches to the west and the clear, protected waters of Portage Lake to the east. Listed in the National Register of Historic Places, Portage Point Inn consists of 14 buildings on 18 acres with more than 1,000 feet of lake frontage. The sprawling white main hotel with distinctive gambreled gables and grand portico supported by huge fluted columns sits on the shore of Portage Lake. Ten charming cottages of various sizes are tucked in the woods that separate the two lakes. Guest rooms are available in the main hotel, cottages and newer condominiums throughout the property. The lobby and dining room retain the knotty pine paneling installed at the hotel's inception. This is a year-round resort offering limitless activities.

**Open:** year round **Accommodations:** 80 guest accommodations in hotel rooms, cottages, and condominiums (most with private baths) **Meals:** restaurant on premises; many packages include meal plans; catered events **Rates:** $75 to $245; cottages and condos rent by the week only (inquire about rates); 10% discount to National Trust members and National Trust Visa cardholders **Payment:** AmEx, Visa, MC, personal and traveler's checks **Restrictions:** no smoking **On-site activities:** swimming, sunning, fishing, soccer, softball, beaches, bicycling, hiking, boating, snowmobiles, cross-country skiing

## SALINE

**Nearby attractions:** University of Michigan, Greenfield Village, Henry Ford Museum, Ford Heritage Trails, Ann Arbor Antiques Market, Irish Hills, golfing, tennis, theaters

### THE HOMESTEAD BED AND BREAKFAST

9279 Macon Road
Saline, Michigan 48176-9305
**Phone:** 734/429-9625
**Proprietor:** Shirley H. Grossman

Saline is named for the local salt wells where Native Americans once salted their fish for preservation. Their arrowheads and stone axes are still found among the woods and fields of the Homestead's 50-acre organic farm. The country and Victorian antiques throughout the farmhouse have been here for more than 100 years. (The Grossman family purchased the large, two-story brick farmhouse completely furnished more than 36 years ago.) Bedrooms also contain antiques, and each room has a sitting area. Bathrooms are in the hall, so robes and towels are provided in each bedroom. The living room, library, and parlor are open to guests at all times, as is the upright grand piano. Complimentary refreshments are served in the living room each evening. The Homestead is convenient to Saline, Ann Arbor, and Ypsilanti.

**Open:** year round **Accommodations:** 5 guest rooms with shared baths **Meals:** full breakfast included; complimentary refreshments; restaurants nearby **Rates:** $35 to$60 single; $65 to $70 double; 10% discount to National Trust members **Payment:** AmEx, Visa, MC, Discover, personal and traveler's checks **Restrictions:** smoking limited; no pets (resident cats) **On-site activities:** walking, cross-country skiing, reading, piano

## SAUGATUCK

**Nearby attractions:** Holland Tulip Festival, Lake Michigan beaches and charter fishing, Dune State Park for hiking and cross-country skiing, farmers' markets, museums, golfing, shopping

### KEMAH GUEST HOUSE

633 Pleasant Street
Saugatuck, Michigan 49453
**Phone:** 616/857-2919
**Website:** www.bbonline.com/mi/kemah/
**Proprietors:** Phillip and Carolyn Caponigro

Kemah Guest House is a turn-of-the-century mansion evocative of an English cottage with false thatched roof and a porte cochere. The interior sports a combination of Old World charm in its antiques and Bavarian rathskeller, Art Deco grace from a 1920s remodeling, and Southwestern airiness in a solarium designed by a local artist, Carl Hoerman. Six quaint guest rooms combine antique furnishings and hardwood floors with original tile bathrooms for a charming historic atmosphere. Chantilly Corner is accented with lace. The Captain's Quarters features an oak gentleman's suite with six-foot headboard. The Deco Dormer's unique mahogany bedroom suite was featured in a 1926 issue of *Architectural Digest*. Needlepoint Nook is cozy, country Victorian. The study provides a warming fireplace; the parlor contains a baby grand piano. In the rathskeller, a game room offers billiards and television.

**Open:** year round **Accommodations:** 6 guest rooms (4 have private baths) **Meals:** continental-plus breakfast included; complimentary refreshments, restaurants nearby **Rates:** $85 to $140; 10% discount offered to National Trust members and National Trust Visa cardholders **Payment:** AmEx, Visa, MC, Discover, personal and traveler's checks **Restrictions:** not suitable for children; no smoking; no pets **On-site activities:** game room, bird watching, strolling the grounds

## THE KIRBY HOUSE

294 West Center
Douglas, Michigan 49406
**Phone:** 616/857-2904 or 800/521-6473
**Website:** members.aol.com/kirbyinn/bb.html
**E-mail:** kirbyinn@aol.com
**Proprietors:** Ray Riker and James Gowran

First-time visitors to the Saugatuck/Douglas area are usually surprised to discover that the sister towns lie on opposite sides of Campbell Road, one large sand dune away from Lake Michigan. This stylish 1890 Queen Anne house, once owned by Sarah and Frank Kirby, is in the resort community of Douglas. After Frank's death in 1896, Sarah opened it as a rooming house. Later it was turned into a convalescent home and then, in 1932, the house became the Saugatuck/Douglas Hospital, serving the community until 1960. After falling into disrepair during the Sixties and Seventies, the beautiful old house was saved and rehabilitated by the previous owners who opened it as a bed and breakfast in 1984. There are eight handsomely decorated guest rooms, some with canopied beds, three with fireplaces. The first-floor guest room was the hospital's operating room. Two other fireplaces warm public rooms on the first floor. A guest kitchen with microwave is always available and the innkeepers offer a full breakfast daily.

**Open:** year round **Accommodations:** 8 guest rooms (6 have private baths) **Meals:** full breakfast included; guest kitchen; restaurants nearby **Rates:** $100 to $135; 10% discount to National Trust members and National Trust Visa cardholders **Payment:** AmEx, Visa, MC, Discover, personal and traveler's checks **Restrictions:** no smoking; no pets **On-site activities:** heated swimming pool, hot tub, bicycles

# MINNESOTA

## DUNDAS

**Nearby attractions:** Cannon Valley Wilderness for hiking and cross-country skiing, Dundas Dukes baseball, St. Olaf and Carleton colleges, canoeing, antiques hunting, golfing, state parks, Mall of America

### MARTIN OAKS BED AND BREAKFAST

(Historic Archibald–Martin House)
107 First Street
P.O. Box 207
Dundas, Minnesota 55019
507/645-4644
**Proprietors:** Marie and
Frank Gery

Built in 1869 by the treasurer of the thriving Archibald Mills, this Italianate house is now in the National Register of Historic Places. It is one of several large homes built at the same time in the Cannon River community of Dundas, then a thriving mill

town. Guest rooms at Martin Oaks are decorated with antique furnishings. Martin Suite features a spoon-carved high bed and a Baltimore Album quilt. Sarah Etta's Room was stenciled in 1811 and looks out on spring and summer gardens. The tiny Hideaway offers a quiet retreat. An elegant candlelight breakfast is served in the Victorian dining room. Afternoon tea is available on request.

**Open:** year round **Accommodations:** 3 guest rooms with shared baths **Meals:** full breakfast included; complimentary refreshments; restaurants nearby **Rates:** $60 to $85; 10% discount to National Trust members and National Trust Visa cardholders **Payment:** Visa, MC, personal and traveler's checks **Restrictions:** not suitable for children; no smoking; no pets (resident cat)

# RED WING

**Nearby attractions:** Goodhue County Historical Museum, Mississippi River cruises, riverside parks, Sheldon Theater, cable-car tours, picnicking, hiking, downhill skiing, golfing

## ST. JAMES HOTEL
406 Main Street
Red Wing, Minnesota 55066
**Phone:** 612/388-2846 or 800/678-8946
**Fax:** 612/388-5226
**Website:** www.st-james-hotel.com

Nestled between limestone bluffs on the banks of the Mississippi River, Red Wing was the world's largest wheat market in the early 1870s. To celebrate the city's prosperity, local businessmen built the St. James Hotel in 1875. At the turn of the century, the Italianate hotel was purchased by the Lillyblad family, who operated it for 72 years. In the 1970s the hotel was purchased by the Red Wing Shoe Company, which completed a detailed restoration in 1979. Each guest room, named for a nineteenth-century riverboat, is decorated with Victorian antiques and reproductions, including handmade quilts and period wallpapers. Guests receive welcoming champagne, daily newspapers, and turn-down service. The St. James boasts two restaurants, two lounges, nine meeting rooms, a free parking ramp, and a 10-store shopping court. A member of Historic Hotels of America, the St. James holds a AAA four-diamond rating.

**Open:** year round **Accommodations:** 60 guest rooms with private baths (some with whirlpool tubs) **Meals:** restaurants and lounges on premises; restaurants nearby **Wheelchair access:** yes **Rates:** $120 to $170 **Payment:** AmEx, Visa, MC, DC, personal and traveler's checks **Restrictions:** smoking limited; no pets **On-site activities:** shopping arcade

## STILLWATER

**Nearby attractions:** St. Croix River, art galleries, antiques hunting, skiing, hot-air ballooning, trolley tours, golfing, water and jet skiing, paddlewheeler rides

### WILLIAM SAUNTRY MANSION
626 North Fourth Street
Stillwater, Minnesota 55082
**Phone:** 612/430-2653 or 800/828-2653
**Fax:** 612/351-7872
**Website:** www.cotn.com/sauntryinn
**Proprietors:** Elaine and Art Halbardier

Listed in the National Register of Historic Places, this 25-room Queen Anne mansion with Eastlake detailing was built in 1890 by lumber baron William Sauntry. The house reflects Sauntry's penchant for the opulent, with 10 fireplaces, parquet floors, painted canvas ceilings, cherry and oak woodwork, and many stained-glass windows. The house is furnished in the late Victorian style. Each guest room is a tribute to an original family member with colors and decor selected to reflect their personalities. Each room has either a king- or queen-size bed; most rooms have fireplaces, and four have double whirlpool tubs. A four-course breakfast is served in the dining room, and guests are invited to enjoy the parlors, music room, porches, and grounds.

**Open:** year round **Accommodations:** 7 guest rooms with private baths **Meals:** full breakfast included; restaurants nearby **Rates:** $109 to $189 **Payment:** Visa, MC, Discover, personal and traveler's checks **Restrictions:** children over 12 welcome; no smoking; no pets

# MISSISSIPPI

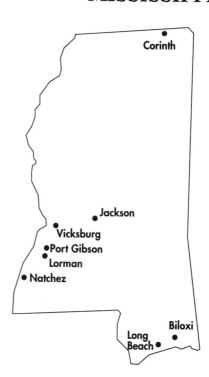

Corinth

Jackson

Vicksburg
Port Gibson
Lorman
Natchez

Biloxi

Long
Beach

## BILOXI

**Nearby attractions:** 12 casinos, Mississippi Beach, Biloxi Lighthouse, historic homes walking and driving tours, Jefferson Davis's home, Mississippi coliseum, art galleries, Marineland, NASA Space Center, antiques hunting, factory outlet mall, charter boating, fishing, sailing, swimming, para-sailing, jet-skiing

## THE OLD SANTINI HOUSE BED AND BREAKFAST INN

964 Beach Boulevard
Biloxi, Mississippi 39539
**Phone:** 228/436-4078 or 800/686-1146
**Fax:** 228/436-4078
**Website:** www.waidsoft.com/santinibnb
**Proprietors:** James and Patricia Dunay

Local historians consider this one-story, wood frame dwelling with hipped tin roof and gabled dormer the earliest example of the "American Cottage" style in Biloxi, having been built circa 1837. Spanning the facade is a gallery with squared, Doric columns. Joseph Santini purchased the home in 1867 and it remained in his family until 1972. Extensive renovation has landed the charming home in the National Register of Historic Places. Guest rooms are decorated to reflect Santini's occupation as an international importer: Oriental, African, and Western rooms. The Honeymoon Cottage is at the rear of the property. A continental breakfast is served in the formal dining room on china and crystal. On cool evenings a fire warms the Louis XIV-decorated living room. Afternoon wine and cheese is served on the garden trellis, where guests enjoy the view and breezes of the Gulf of Mexico.

**Open:** year round **Accommodations:** 4 guest rooms with private baths; 1 is a cottage **Meals:** full breakfast included; complimentary refreshments; restaurants nearby **Rates:** $100 to $160; 10% discount to National Trust members and National Trust Visa cardholders **Payment:** Visa, MC, personal and traveler's checks **Restrictions:** children over 12 welcome; no smoking; no pets **On-site activities:** parlor games, badminton, horseshoes, bicycles

## CORINTH

**Nearby attractions:** walking and driving tours of Civil War sites, including a national cemetery, Battery Robinett, Curlee House, and a Civil War Museum; state parks for boating, bicycling, picnicking; Shiloh National Military Park; Elvis Presley birthplace in Tupelo

### RAVENSWOOD BED AND BREAKFAST
1002 Douglas Street (at Linden)
Corinth, Mississippi 38834-4227
**Phone:** 601/665-0044
**Proprietors:** Timothy Hodges, Ron W. Smith

Ravenswood was built in 1929, in the popular Craftsman style, for Rufus Galyean, a lumberyard owner and contractor. The interior features original woodwork throughout, including hardwood ceiling moldings, floors, and many built-ins. The library, originally a child's room, has unique, hand-cut baseboards and door frames. In the living room, the large gas fireplace is flanked by built-in bookcases and features two original stained-glass windows in Frank Lloyd Wright designs. From the large living room, guests enter a private side porch with swing. Guest rooms are furnished in a mix of antique and contemporary styles. Also upstairs is a sitting room for late-night reading or morning coffee. The inn is located on over an acre of land filled with trees, shrubs, birds, and squirrels. Of note is the crescent-shaped Civil War breastwork mound at the rear of the property. It is a prime example of the tactics employed to protect the railroad, which runs a block behind the house.

**Open:** February through December **Accommodations:** 3 guest rooms with private baths; 1 is a suite **Meals:** continental breakfast included; restaurants nearby **Rates:** $75 to $125; 10% discount to National Trust members and National Trust Visa cardholders **Payment:** Visa, MC, personal and traveler's checks **Restrictions:** no smoking **On-site activities:** Salon at Ravenswood, in an adjacent building on the property, offers hair, nail, skin, and massage services

## SAMUEL D. BRAMLITT HOUSE
1125 Cruise Street
Corinth, Mississippi 38834
**Phone:** 601/286-5370
**Website:** www.tsixroad.com/corinth/bramlitt.html
**E-mail:** thom112@avsia.com
**Proprietors:** Cindy and Kevin Thomas

Sitting atop a hill in Corinth's historic district is this National Register-listed 1892 Queen Anne home built by Samuel D. Bramlitt. It has also been owned by author and playwright Hal Phillips, and hosted such notables as Charlie Rich and Loretta Lynn. The house is virtually wrapped in upper and lower verandas dressed in gingerbread detailing. Visitors enter through the Eastlake-carved door to find a walnut staircase with carved keyhole design winding its way to the second floor. There, guest rooms with fireplaces and private baths are furnished with Victorian antiques, as is the rest of the inn. Public rooms include a formal parlor with antique pump organ, a well-stocked library, and a formal dining room, all with ornately carved fireplaces. Outdoors, guests enjoy the formal gardens, lawn games, and four verandas with ceiling fans, rockers, and swings.

**Open:** year round **Accommodations:** 3 guest rooms with private baths **Meals:** full breakfast included; complimentary refreshments; restaurants nearby **Rates:** $75 to $85; 10% discount to National Trust members and National Trust Visa cardholders **Payment:** AmEx, Visa, MC, personal and traveler's checks **Restrictions:** children over 12 welcome; no smoking; no pets (resident dog) **On-site activities:** lawn and parlor games, porch sitting

---

# JACKSON
**Nearby attractions:** Old Capitol Museum, Mississippi Museum of Art, New Stage Theater, Dizzy Dean Baseball Museum, Jackson Zoological Park, Petrified Forest, Natchez, Vicksburg, golfing, tennis

## FAIRVIEW INN
734 Fairview Street
Jackson, Mississippi 39202-1624
**Phone:** 601/948-3429 or 888/948-1908
**Fax:** 601/948-1203
**Website:** www.fairviewinn.com
**E-mail:** fairview@teclink.net
**Proprietors:** William J. and Carol N. Simmons

This elegant Colonial Revival mansion was built by lumber tycoon Cyrus G. Warren in 1908. In 1930 it was purchased by banker D. C. Simmons, in whose family the house remains today. Designed by the Chicago architectural firm of Spencer and Powers, the house is one of a small number of architecturally designed homes remaining in Jackson. The Simmonses have gathered a rich array of antiques from the surrounding area as well as from their travels in New England and Europe. Eight guest rooms and suites, located in the main building and in the carriage house, are appointed with fine antiques and heirlooms. Hardwood floors gleam throughout the house. Rich tapestries, fine oil paintings, marble mantels, and crystal chandeliers add to the warm opulence of the home. Fairview offers catering services and chef-prepared dinners and is a favorite setting for weddings. The inn has been featured on the cover of *Country Inns*.

**Open:** year round **Accommodations:** 8 guest rooms with private baths; 5 are suites **Meals:** full breakfast included; complimentary refreshments; dinners available with advance notice; restaurants nearby **Wheelchair access:** some rooms **Rates:** $100 to $150; 10% discount to National Trust members and National Trust Visa cardholders **Payment:** AmEx, Visa, MC, Discover, personal and traveler's checks **Restrictions:** no smoking; no pets **On-site activities:** walking and jogging track, library, exercise equipment

## LONG BEACH

**Nearby attractions:** Jefferson Davis home, 14 golf courses, 26 miles of gulf beaches, 12 casinos, historic sites, canoe and kayak rentals

### RED CREEK INN, VINEYARD & RACING STABLE
7416 Red Creek Road
Long Beach, Mississippi 39560
**Phone:** 228/452-3080 or 800/729-9670
**Website:** members@aol.com/KarlMertz
**Proprietor:** Karl Mertz
**Innkeepers:** Karl and "Toni" Mertz

In 1899 a retired Italian sea captain built this house to entice his young bride to move here from her parents' home in New Orleans. He copied that home's raised French Colonial style with its high brick foundation, 64-foot-long front porch, 10 1/2 -foot-high ceilings, six fireplaces, and roof dormers. Six ceiling fans help cool the house, which is also air conditioned. A variety of antiques from different periods help define the Victorian, French, and English rooms. The most elaborate room features an 8 1/2-foot-high headboard and a pink marble-topped dresser and chest of drawers. The inn's 11-plus acres are punctuated by huge magnolias and ancient live oak trees (two of which are registered with the Live Oak Society). An electrified Victorian organ and a wooden tabletop radio with an overseas band provide entertainment.

**Open:** year round **Accommodations:** 5 guest rooms (4 have private baths); 1 is a suite with whirlpool **Meals:** continental-plus breakfast included; restaurants nearby **Rates:** $49 to $134; 10% discount offered to National Trust members and National Trust Visa cardholders **Payment:** personal check **Restrictions:** no smoking; no pets **On-site activities:** porch swings, organ, Victrola, radio, strolling

# LORMAN

**Nearby attractions:** historic homes, antiques hunting; battlefields in Natchez, Vicksburg, and Port Gibson

## ROSSWOOD PLANTATION
Route 552 East
Route 1, Box 6
Lorman, Mississippi 39096
**Phone:** 601/437-4215 or 800/533-5889
**Fax:** 601/437-6888
**Proprietors:** Jean and Walt Hylander
**Location:** 2¹/2 miles east of U.S. 61

Rosswood Plantation, completed in 1857, is a Greek Revival mansion of 14 rooms and 10 fireplaces that Dr. Walter Wade built for his bride Mabella Chamberlain. The journal he kept of their life on a cotton plantation before and during the Civil War makes fascinating reading for overnight guests. The National Register house has 14-foot-high ceilings, a winding staircase, columned galleries, and slave quarters. It is completely restored and furnished with antiques, such as the Jacobean dining table, where breakfast is served. Four-poster beds and fireplaces grace each guest room. Rosswood occupies 100 acres of rolling fields

where deer and other wildlife abound, and Christmas trees stand where cotton once grew.

**Open:** March through December **Accommodations:** 4 guest rooms with private baths **Meals:** full breakfast included; complimentary refreshments; restaurants nearby **Wheelchair access:** bathrooms, dining facilities **Rates:** $115 to $135 **Payment:** Visa, MC, personal and traveler's checks **Restrictions:** no pets **On-site activities:** walking, fishing, movies on videotape, antiques, Civil War history, swimming pool and heated spa

---

## NATCHEZ

**Nearby attractions:** Mississippi River, riverboat gambling, Native American sites, Natchez Trace, historic house tours, golfing, fishing, tennis, antiques hunting

### DUNLEITH
84 Homochitto Street
Natchez, Mississippi 39120
**Phone:** 601/446-8500 or 800/433-2445
**Proprietor:** William F. Heins

Surrounded by 40 acres of pastures and bayous, Dunleith stands as a monument to the southern Greek Revival tradition of architecture. Somtimes called the most-photographed house in America, the white-colonnaded Dunleith has been the backdrop for numerous feature films and has appeared in the Southern Accents book *Historic Houses of the South*. Having undergone extensive restoration since the 1970s, the mansion now offers 11 guest rooms in the main house and the courtyard wing. Each room has a unique decor and contains a fireplace, television, and telephone. The walls in the dining room are covered with rare turn-of-the-century French Zuber wallpaper printed from wood blocks carved in 1855. The mural-like paper reflects the climatic zones of the world: arctic, temperate, and tropical. A southern breakfast is served in the renovated poultry house. Dunleith is a National Historic Landmark.

**Open:** year round except Sundays, Thanksgiving, and Christmas **Accommodations:** 11 guest rooms with private baths **Meals:** full breakfast included; complimentary refreshments; restaurants nearby **Rates:** $95 to $140 **Payment:** Visa, MC, Discover, traveler's check **Restrictions:** not suitable for children; smoking limited; no pets **On-site activities:** daily house tours, strolling through gardens and grounds, gallery sitting

## MONMOUTH PLANTATION

36 Melrose Avenue
P.O. Box 1736
Natchez, Mississippi 39120
**Phone:** 601/442-5852 or 800/828-4531
**Fax:** 601/446-7762
**Website:** www.monmouthplantation.com
**E-mail:** luxury@monmouthplantation.com
**General Manager:** John Lambdin

During the golden age of Natchez, this imposing 1818 Greek Revival mansion was the residence of General John A. Quitman, a Mexican War hero and early governor of Mississippi. The home gradually fell into disrepair after the death of Quitman's last descendants. Beginning in 1977, the plantation house underwent a thorough restoration, including the removal of an artillery shell from the second floor. Surrounded by 26 acres of lawns, pebbled paths, magnolias, and moss-draped oaks, Monmouth is furnished in period antiques, notably an outstanding collection of carved four-poster and canopy beds. Guest rooms are located in the main house, slaves' quarters, cottages, and carriage house. First-rate services and amenities have earned Monmouth a AAA four-diamond rating. A National Historic Landmark and member of Historic Hotels of America, Monmouth Plantation has been rated "one of the top ten most romantic places in the U.S.A." by *Glamour* magazine and *USA Today*.

**Open:** year round **Accommodations:** 28 guest rooms with private baths; 14 are suites **Meals:** full breakfast included; Monday through Sunday a five-course candlelight dinner is offered; restaurants nearby **Rates:** $135 to $365; 10% discount to National Trust members and National Trust Visa cardholders **Payment:** AmEx, Visa, MC, Discover, personal and traveler's checks **Restrictions:** children over 14 welcome; no smoking; no pets **On-site activities:** croquet, fishing, walking paths

## RAVENNASIDE

601 South Union Street
Natchez, Mississippi 39120
**Phone:** 601/442-8015 or 888/442-8015
**Fax:** 601/446-7441
**Website:** www.bbonline.com/ms/ravennaside
**Proprietor:** Sara Coleman

Designed for entertaining, Ravennaside was built in 1899 by Mr. and Mrs. James S. Fleming. Living up to its purpose, the grandly styled Neoclassical house with two-story Ionic columns supporting a large triangular pediment, hosted many famous writers, politicians, foreign dignitaries, and historians. This was also the home of the Fleming's daughter, Mrs. Roane Fleming Byrnes (known affection-ately as "Sweet Auntie"), founder of the Natchez Trace parkway and president of its association from 1935 until her death in 1970. The house retains its numerous unique features, including a one-of-a-kind parquet floor, hand-tinted wallpaper of the Natchez Trace, a bas relief design around the ceiling in the dining room, a copper whaling ship lamp that has always hung in the house, and blue mosaic tiles surrounding the Blue Room's fireplace. Six elegantly furnished guest rooms feature period antiques, including four-poster and tester beds. Ravennaside is listed in the National Register of Historic Places.

**Open:** year round **Accommodations:** 6 guest rooms with private baths **Meals:** full breakfast included; complimentary refreshments; restaurants nearby **Rates:** $85 to $135 **Payment:** Visa, MC, personal and traveler's checks **Restrictions:** no smoking; no pets **On-site activities:** complimentary carriage tour of the historic district; horseshoes, bocci, croquet, billiards, hot tub

---

## PORT GIBSON

**Nearby attractions:** Grand Gulf Military State Park, driving and walking tours of historic town, hiking, bicycling; Civil War battlefields, museums, and forts

### OAK SQUARE PLANTATION
1207 Church Street
Port Gibson, Mississippi 39150
**Phone:** 601/437-4350 or 800/729-0240
**Fax:** 601/437-5768
**E-mail:** kajunmade@aol.com
**Proprietors:** Mr. and Mrs. William D. Lum

Oak Square, named for the massive trees on its grounds, was once the home of a cotton planter. Built in 1850, the house is Greek Revival in design with six 22-foot-tall fluted Corinthian columns supporting the front gallery. Inside, the house's grandeur endures in ornate millwork, a grand staircase, and spacious, high-ceilinged rooms. Fine rare antiques fill the house's public rooms. Guest rooms in the mansion and the guest house are furnished with family heirlooms and have canopied beds. Guests receive a full southern breakfast and a tour of the mansion. National Register–listed Oak Square is the largest antebellum mansion in Port Gibson, the town Ulysses S. Grant said was "too beautiful to burn." Rated with four diamonds by AAA, Oak Square is home to the annual 1800s Spring Festival, a "top 20 event" in the southeast.

**Open:** year round **Accommodations:** 11 guest rooms with private baths **Meals:** full breakfast included; complimentary refreshments; restaurants nearby **Rates:** $95 to $125 **Payment:** AmEx, Visa, MC, Discover, personal check **Restrictions:** not suitable for young children; no smoking; no pets **On-site activities:** house tours, nineteenth-century Spring Festival last weekend of March each year with 200 costumed participants creating a living history weekend

# VICKSBURG

**Nearby attractions:** Vicksburg National Military Park, Center for Southern Culture, Old Court House Museum, historic house tours, casinos, boat rides, golfing

## BALFOUR HOUSE
1002 Crawford Street
P.O. Box 781
Vicksburg, Mississippi 39181
**Phone:** 601/638-7113 or 800/294-7113
**Fax:** 601/638-8484
**E-mail:** shumble@vicksburg.com
**Proprietors:** Bob and Sharon Humble

Balfour House is considered to be one of the finest Greek Revival structures in the state by the Mississippi Department of Archives and History. The house was a center of activity during the Siege of Vicksburg and became the business headquarters for the Union Army after the fall of the city. In 1982, when the house was restored according to the Secretary of the Interior's Standards for Rehabilitation, a cannonball and other Civil War artifacts were discovered hidden in the walls. The restoration, which included work on the three-story elliptical staircase and patterned, inlaid, hardwood floors, received the 1984 Award of Merit from the state historical society. Balfour House, a National Register property and designated Mississippi landmark, offers overnight guests authentically decorated bedrooms, house tours, and a full southern-style breakfast.

**Open:** year round **Accommodations:** 4 guest rooms with private baths **Meals:** full breakfast included; complimentary refreshments; restaurants nearby **Rates:** $85 to $150; 10% discount to National Trust members and National Trust Visa cardholders **Payment:** AmEx, Visa, MC, personal and traveler's checks **Restrictions:** smoking limited **On-site activities:** house tours; fall and spring Pilgrimage; reenactment of 1862 Christmas ball held annually on second Saturday in December

## DUFF GREEN MANSION
1114 First East Street
Vicksburg, Mississippi 39180
**Phone:** 800/992-6037 or 601/636-6968
**Proprietors:** Harry Carter Sharp and Alicia Shrader

Listed in the National Register of Historic Places, the Duff Green Mansion is located in Vicksburg's historic district. The home is noted for the lacy wrought-iron double porches that span its front facade. Built in 1856 by Duff Green, a prosperous merchant, the 12,000-square-foot mansion was the site of many parties in the antebellum days, but was hastily converted to a hospital for both Confederate and Union soldiers during the siege of Vicksburg and the remainder of the war. Recently restored, the mansion offers six elegant guest rooms furnished with antiques and private baths, room service, a swimming pool, and a southern breakfast served in the formal dining room under a grand crystal chandelier.

**Open:** year round **Accommodations:** 6 guest rooms with private baths **Meals:** full breakfast included; complimentary refreshments; dinner available by request; restaurants nearby **Wheelchair access:** yes **Rates:** $85 to $160 **Payment:** AmEx, Visa, MC, personal and traveler's checks **Restrictions:** smoking limited **On-site activities:** swimming pool

# MISSOURI

## CARTHAGE

**Nearby attractions:** Lowell David Foxfire Farm, Powers Museum, George Washington Monument, Harry Truman's birthplace, Precious Moments Chapel

### GRAND AVENUE BED AND BREAKFAST
1615 Grand Avenue
Carthage, Missouri 64836
**Phone:** 417/358-7265 or 888/380-6786
**E-mail:** jeanne1962@aol.com
**Proprietors:** Jeanne and Michael Goolsby

Built in 1893 by S. H. Hauser for $6,000, this spacious Queen Anne has been carefully restored to show off its original stained-glass windows, including the unique circular and semicircular windows that face the street. The original massive polished oak staircase and three oversized pocket doors are still in the house as well as original woodwork, all in prime condition. Spacious guest rooms are named in honor of favorite authors and include selections of the authors' works. Most rooms contain queen- or king-size beds. The E. B. White room can connect to the Mark Twain room to create a suite. A full breakfast is served in the formal dining room with entrees ranging from omelets to fruit-covered blintzes. Grand Avenue Bed and Breakfast is in the heart of this historic town, once able to boast the highest number of millionaires per capita in the country.

**Open:** year round **Accommodations:** 5 guest rooms (4 have private baths) **Meals:** full breakfast included; restaurants nearby **Rates:** $69 to $89; 10% discount to National Trust members and National Trust Visa cardholders **Payment:** Visa, MC, Discover, personal and traveler's checks **Restrictions:** no smoking; no pets **On-site activities:** swimming pool, reading and video libraries

# HANNIBAL

**Nearby attractions:** Mark Twain Historic District, Mark Twain boyhood home, water sports at Mark Twain Lake, Mississippi riverboat cruises, caves, antiques hunting, golfing, tennis

## GARTH WOODSIDE MANSION
R.R. #3, Box 578
Hannibal, Missouri 63401
**Phone:** 573/221-2789
**Website:** www.hanmo.com/garth
**E-mail:** garth@nemonet.com
**Proprietor:** Irv Feinberg

A Second Empire house of grand proportions, the Garth Woodside Mansion stands as a testament to nineteenth-century craftsmanship. The three-story, mansard-roofed manse with center tower, bay windows, and porches has been fully restored by the innkeepers to highlight its many architectural details. The house, on 39 acres of meadows and woodlands, was built for John and Helen Garth who welcomed many prominent people to their elegant home, including their childhood friend Sam Clemens, otherwise known as Mark Twain. Today's fully restored inn is a liveable museum of Victoriana with furnishings original to the home combined with the innkeeper's vast collection of antiques. A spectacular flying staircase vaults three stories without any visible means of support, leading to eight ornately decorated guest rooms with 14-foot stenciled ceilings and marble fireplaces. The inn's authenticity, elegance, and comforts have been lauded by many publications including *Country Inns, Glamour, Conde Nast Traveler, Victoria,* and *Country Living.* The house is listed in the National Register of Historic Places.

**Open:** year round **Accommodations:** 8 guest rooms with private baths **Meals:** full breakfast included; complimentary refreshments; restaurants nearby **Rates:** $77 to $107 **Payment:** Visa, MC, traveler's checks **Restrictions:** children over 12 welcome; no smoking; no pets **On-site activities:** veranda rocking; pond fishing

# KANSAS CITY

**Nearby attractions:** Nelson Atkins Museum of Art, Kemper Museum of Contemporary Art and Design, Country Club Plaza, Royals and Arrowhead Stadium, toy and miniature museum, theater, University of Missouri, carriage rides

## THE DOANLEIGH INN

217 East Thirty-Seventh Street
Kansas City, Missouri 64111
**Phone:** 816/753-2667
**Fax:** 816/531-5185
**Website:** www.doanleigh@aol.com
**Proprietors:** Cynthia Brogdon and Terry Maturo

Overlooking historic Hyde Park, the Doanleigh Inn was originally the Colonial Revival home of the William Marsh family who moved here in 1907. After several changes in ownership and a stint as an apartment house, the Doanleigh was restored in the 1980s. Furnished throughout with American and European antiques, the inn offers five individually appointed guest rooms with thoughtful modern amenities such as speaker telephone, computer data port, cable television, clock radio, and private bath in each accommodation. The house's former master bedroom is now the Hyde Park room and features one of the original baths as well as an original fireplace. A full two-course breakfast, evening wine and hors d'oeuvres and a 24-hour complimentary snack bar are provided. Guests also receive free off-street parking and privileges at a local athletic club. Ideally located between the famed Country Club Plaza and Hallmark Crown Center, the Doanleigh Inn provides a unique setting for private parties, business functions, weddings, and receptions.

**Open:** year round **Accommodations:** 5 guest rooms with private baths **Meals:** full breakfast included; complimentary refreshments; restaurants nearby **Rates:** $95 to $150 **Payment:** AmEx, Visa, MC, Discover, personal and traveler's checks **Restrictions:** children over 12 welcome; no smoking; no pets **On-site activities:** video library, whirlpool tubs

## SOUTHMORELAND ON THE PLAZA – AN URBAN INN
116 East 46th Street
Kansas City, Missouri 64112
**Phone:** 816/531-7979
**Fax:** 816/531-2407
**Proprietors:** Susan Moehl and Penni Johnson

Centuries-old shade trees, native-rock walls, sweeping lawns, and formal gardens create a feeling of country in the city at Southmoreland on the Plaza. The Colonial Revival styling of the 1913 mansion inspires quaint touches such as a white wicker solarium and traditional decor enhanced by antiques. The Plaza locale calls for sophisticated conveniences like in-room telephones, parking, fax service, and airport shuttle for business travelers. Guest rooms are named after notable Kansas Citians, with each room reflecting the era and personality of its namesake. The rooms all boast some special feature, such as a private deck, wood-burning fireplace, or double whirlpool bath. Guests also enjoy membership privileges at a nearby Plaza athletic club. Southmoreland on the Plaza holds a four-star rating from the *Mobil Travel Guide* and is the only inn in the Midwest so honored for the last four years.

**Open:** year round **Accommodations:** 12 guest rooms with private baths **Meals:** full breakfast included; complimentary wine and hors d'oeuvres; restaurants nearby **Wheelchair access:** 1 guest room and bath, dining room, common rooms **Rates:** $115 to $170 **Payment:** AmEx, Visa, MC, personal and traveler's checks **Restrictions:** children over 13 welcome; no smoking; no pets **On-site activities:** conference facilities for up to 18 (A/V equipment available)

# NEW FRANKLIN

**Nearby attractions:** Katy Trail State Park, Old Cooper County Jail and Hanging Barn, start of the Santa Fe Trail, Boone's Lick State Park, Kemper Military Academy and Junior College, Missouri River Festival of the Arts, antiques hunting, hiking, bicycling

**RIVERCENE BED AND BREAKFAST**
127 County Road 463
New Franklin, Missouri 65274
**Phone:** 660/848-2497
or 800/531-0862
**Fax:** 660/848-2142
**Website:** www.katytrail.showmestate.com/Rivercene
**E-mail:** rivercene@showmestate.com
**Proprietors:** Jody and Ron Lenz
**Location:** 4 miles north of Boonville, just over the Missouri River

Rivercene was built in 1869 by riverboat captain Joseph Kinney. After selecting this site directly on the Missouri River, Captain Kinney was warned by the locals that the river would claim his home, and thus it was dubbed Kinney's Folly. But Kinney persevered, building a Second Empire mansion containing nine Italian marble fireplaces, black walnut front doors, and a hand-carved mahogany grand staircase. So spectacular was the house that the state of Missouri duplicated its architectural plan for the present governor's mansion. Restoration has resulted in nine spacious guest rooms filled with period antiques. Nearly all rooms have private baths, one has a whirlpool tub. Guests are served a full breakfast in the dining room or cozy breakfast room.

**Open:** year round **Accommodations:** 9 guest rooms (8 have private baths); 1 is a suite **Meals:** full breakfast included; restaurants nearby **Rates:** $85 to $140 **Payment:** AmEx, Visa, MC, Discover, personal and traveler's checks **Restrictions:** children over 10 welcome; no smoking; no pets **On-site activities:** horseshoe pitching, softball, volleyball, badminton, porch sitting

# ROCHEPORT

**Nearby attractions:** The Katy Trail (a 200-mile-long hiking/biking path), winery, antiques hunting, University of Missouri

## SCHOOL HOUSE BED AND BREAKFAST INN
504 Third Street
Rocheport, Missouri 65279
**Phone:** 573/698-2022
**Proprietors:** Vicki and John Ott

Memories of school days come alive in guest rooms with names like Show 'n Tell, Spelling Bee, Honor Roll, Graduate, Schoolmaster, and Dick & Jane at this former schoolhouse for grades one through twelve. The brick building was constructed in 1914, using brick and lumber salvaged from earlier structures. The original mahogany front doors are intact, the oak steps and polished brass handrails remain, the classroom blackboards now serve as black slate flooring, and large framed prints from the *Dick and Jane Primer* line the walls. Light from the large schoolhouse windows, covered with custom-made plantation shutters, accents the floral wallpapers and brings a glow to the antiques that fill each guest room. The outdoor basketball court is now surrounded by brick patios, flower gardens, and fountains. The School House Inn has been featured in *Midwest Living* and Gail Greco's *The Romance of Country Inns—a Decorating Book for your Home* as well as in a series of Hallmark greeting cards.

**Open:** year round **Accommodations:** 10 guest rooms with private baths; 1 is a suite **Meals:** full breakfast included; complimentary refreshments; restaurants nearby **Rates:** $85 to $155; 10% discount to National Trust members and National Trust Visa cardholders midweek only **Payment:** Visa, MC, personal and traveler's checks **Restrictions:** children over 10 welcome; no smoking; no pets **On-site activities:** library, television room, gift shop with school/teacher memorabilia

---

# STE. GENEVIEVE

**Nearby attractions:** historic French Colonial Ste. Genevieve, Hawn State Park, historic sites of the Mississippi River Valley (Kaskasia, Fort du Chartres, Maeystown)

## MAIN STREET INN
221 North Main Street
P.O. Box 307
Ste. Genevieve, Missouri 63670
**Phone:** 573/883-9199 or 800/918-9199

**Fax:** 573/883-3024
**Website:** www.rivervalleyinns.com
**E-mail:** msinn@ldd.net
**Proprietors:** Ken and Karne Kulberg

Built in 1883, the Second Empire style Main Street Inn has always been a lodging establishment, being known originally as the Meyer Hotel. At today's inn the rooms are spacious, airy, and free of clutter. The ceilings are high, the tall windows dressed with lace curtains, and the floors are refinished original wood. Many of the pieces of furniture were found in the attic and have been carefully restored. Guest rooms are named in recognition of someone significant to the history of Ste. Genevieve, but they are not theme rooms; the innkeepers have simply combined comfortable traditional and antique furniture with vintage linens and new, but old-styled, plumbing. Each bedroom has a fully enclosed private bath with shower; two have very large whirlpools. Substantial breakfasts combine hearty Midwestern ingredients, locally smoked meats, and seasonal fruits creating menus that are special but familiar. Guests are invited to gather in the parlor for wine or soft drinks in the evening.

**Open:** year round **Accommodations:** 8 guest rooms with private baths; 1 is a suite **Meals:** full breakfast included; complimentary refreshments; restaurants nearby **Rates:** $70 to $125; 10% discount to National Trust members and National Trust Visa cardholders **Payment:** AmEx, Visa, MC, Discover, personal and traveler's checks **Restrictions:** children over 12 welcome; no smoking; no pets

## ST. LOUIS

**Nearby attractions:** Gateway Arch, Museum of Westward Expansion, Busch Stadium, Union Station, Anheuser–Busch Brewery, Missouri Botanical Gardens, Laclede's Landing, St. Louis Zoo, art and history museums, Muny Opera, Fox Theater, Science Center, shopping, dining

### LAFAYETTE HOUSE
2156 Lafayette Avenue
St. Louis, Missouri 63104
**Phone:** 314/772-4429 or 800/641-8965
**Fax:** 314/664-2156
**Website:** www.bbonline.com/mo/lafayette/
**Proprietors:** Annalise Millet and Nancy Buhr

Located in a National Register historic district overlooking Lafayette Park, Lafayette House sits in the center of action in St. Louis. The 14-room brick mansion, with Queen Anne and Italianate styling, was built in 1876 by Captain James Eads, who designed the first iron-trussed bridge across the Mississippi River, as a wedding gift for his daughter Margaret. Walnut woodwork, 14-foot ceilings, spacious fireplaced rooms, and a carved walnut staircase are intact and restored. Guest rooms tastefully furnished with antiques include the third-floor suite with kitchen and the single and double rooms on the second floor. In the Lafayette room, guests will find an original speaking tube and brass fixtures. In addition to the living room with fireplace, the inn offers a guest lounge with television and VCR, games, books, and a stocked refrigerator. In good weather, guests are invited to the rear deck with hot tub.

**Open:** year round **Accommodations:** 6 guest rooms (3 have private baths); 1 is a suite **Meals:** full breakfast included; complimentary refreshments; restaurants nearby **Rates:** $50 to $135; 10% discount to National Trust members and National Trust Visa cardholders **Payment:** AmEx, Visa, MC, Discover, CB, DC, personal and traveler's checks **Restrictions**: no smoking; no pets (resident cats)


## LEHMANN HOUSE BED AND BREAKFAST

10 Benton Place
St. Louis, Missouri 63104
**Phone:** 314/231-6724
**Proprietors:** Marie and Michael Davies

This 20-room Richardsonian Romanesque mansion, in historic Lafayette Square, was built in 1893 for Edward S. Rowse, a wealthy financier. But the house's second owners, Frederick and Nora Lehmann, who lived there for 31 years, are best remembered and today's inn bears their name. The current owners are carefully restoring the oak, maple, and cherry woodwork throughout the house. For their lodging, guests may choose from the Sun Room, the Maids' Room, the Map Room, or the President's Room, so named because Lehmann, a lawyer and statesman, is reputed to have entertained William Howard Taft and possibly two other presidents in this home. Breakfast is served in the formal dining room with oak-paneled walls and ceiling. Children are welcome at Lehmann House, and cribs and highchairs are available.

**Open:** year round **Accommodations:** 4 guest rooms (2 have private baths) **Meals:** full breakfast included; complimentary refreshments; restaurants nearby **Rates:** $65 to $90; 10% discount offered to National Trust members and National Trust Visa cardholders **Payment:** AmEx, Visa, MC, DC, Discover, personal and traveler's checks **Restrictions:** no smoking; no pets

# WINTER HOUSE

3522 Arsenal Street
St. Louis, Missouri 63118-2004
**Phone:** 314/664-4399
**E-mail:** kwinter@swbell.net
**Proprietors:** Kendall and Sarah Lee Winter

This 1907 brick house shows Richardsonian Romanesque influences in its round-arched windows and two-story round tower with conical roof. The dining room is in this turret on the first floor. Here breakfast is served on antique Wedgewood china to the soothing piano music of Mozart or Beethoven. Guest rooms feature pressed-tin ceilings and the suite, which accommodates up to four people, contains an original (now decorative) coal-burning fireplace. A balcony enhances these rooms. In the living room guests may enjoy the fireplace and piano. Rooms throughout the house are furnished with antiques and family heirlooms. Winter House is less than a block from Tower Grove Park, a Victorian walking park listed in the National Register of Historic Places, and adjacent to the Missouri Botanical Garden.

**Open:** year round **Accommodations:** 3 guest rooms with private baths; 1 is a suite **Meals:** full breakfast included; complimentary refreshments; restaurants nearby **Rates:** $85 to $125; 10% discount to National Trust members and National Trust Visa cardholders **Payment:** AmEx, Visa, MC, Discover, CB, DC, personal and traveler's checks **Restrictions:** well-behaved children welcome; no smoking; no pets (resident cats and dog) **On-site activities:** piano played by professional musician at breakfast

# MONTANA

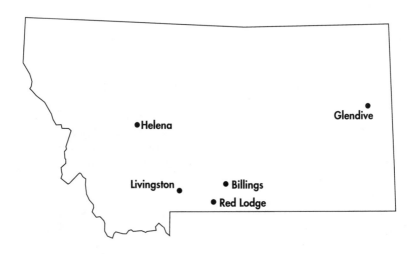

## BILLINGS

**Nearby attractions:** Old Railroad Depot, Boot Hill, Yellowstone Art Center, ZooMontana, Pictograph Caves, Little Bighorn Battlefield, Western Heritage Center, Yellowstone River, museums, theaters, parks, golfing

### THE JOSEPHINE BED AND BREAKFAST
514 North Twenty-Ninth Street
Billings, Montana 59101
**Phone:** 406/248-5898 or 800/552-5898
**Website:** www.thejosephine.com
**E-mail:** josephine@imt.net
**Proprietors:** Douglas and Becky Taylor

"Grandpa" Lehfeldt, a rancher north of Billings, built this clapboard house in 1912 as a town home for his family. Later it became a rooming house, then a boarding school for young women. Today, the restored house sits behind a picket fence, underneath huge shade trees, a quiet oasis in the heart of Montana's largest city. Each of the large rooms is individually decorated with antiques, collectibles, and old photographs. Guests are invited into the dining room, parlor, and library. The wraparound porch, with its swing and quaint seating, offers the ideal place for breakfast or relaxation. Elegant yet comfortable guest rooms offer shared or private baths. The Josephine, named for the Josephine Riverboat that once plied the Yellowstone River, is a refreshing alternative for the business traveler, a perfect romantic getaway destination, or an ideal location for small meetings or gatherings.

**Open:** year round **Accommodations:** 6 guest rooms (4 have private baths); 1 is a suite **Meals:** full breakfast included; complimentary refreshments; restaurants nearby **Rates:** $48 to $88; 10% discount to National Trust members and National Trust Visa cardholders **Payment:** AmEx, Visa, MC, personal and traveler's checks **Restrictions:** children over 8 welcome; no smoking; no pets

---

## GLENDIVE

**Nearby attractions:** Yellowstone River, Dawson Community College, museum, art gallery, downtown historic district, Makoshika State Park, antiques hunting, fishing, hunting, cross-country skiing, hiking, mountain biking

### HOSTETLER HOUSE BED AND BREAKFAST
113 North Douglas Street
Glendive, Montana 59330
**Phone:** 406/365-4505 or 800/965-8456
**Fax:** 406/365-8456
**Proprietors:** Craig and Dea Hostetler

Hostetler House is a classic example of the Prairie School's American Foursquare, a design associated most heavily with Frank Lloyd Wright. Built in 1912, this charming home offers two comfortable guest rooms with shared bath. The guest accommodations are furnished in a casual country decor with handmade quilts on the double beds. Many of the furnishings throughout the house are handmade; others are family heirlooms and treasured collectibles. All combine for a feeling of warmth and hospitality. Guests are invited to enjoy the hot tub and gazebo, the sitting room full of books, the enclosed sun porch, or the deck. A color, cable television with VCR is in the living room. The aromas of freshly ground coffee and home-baked breads and muffins greets guests each morning as they arrive downstairs to enjoy a full breakfast served on Grandma's china in the dining room or on the sun porch. Hostetler House is only one block from the Yellowstone River and two from downtown shopping and restaurants.

**Open:** year round **Accommodations:** 2 guest rooms with shared bath **Meals:** full breakfast included; restaurants nearby **Rates:** $50; business rates and secretarial services available **Payment:** Visa, MC, Discover, personal and traveler's checks **Restrictions:** no smoking; no pets **On-site activities:** hot tub, television with VCR, reading, tandem bicycle

# HELENA

**Nearby attractions:** St. Helena's Cathedral, the original Governor's Mansion, State Capitol, Montana Historical Museum, Holter Museum, Grand Street Theater, fishing on the Missouri River

## APPLETON INN BED AND BREAKFAST

1999 Euclid Avenue
Helena, Montana 59601
**Phone:** 406/449-7492
or 800/956-1999
**Fax:** 406/449-1261
**Website:** www.appletoninn.com
**E-mail:** appleton@ixi.net
**Proprietors:** Tom Woodall and
Cheryl Boid

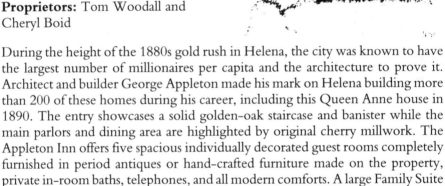

During the height of the 1880s gold rush in Helena, the city was known to have the largest number of millionaires per capita and the architecture to prove it. Architect and builder George Appleton made his mark on Helena building more than 200 of these homes during his career, including this Queen Anne house in 1890. The entry showcases a solid golden-oak staircase and banister while the main parlors and dining area are highlighted by original cherry millwork. The Appleton Inn offers five spacious individually decorated guest rooms completely furnished in period antiques or hand-crafted furniture made on the property, private in-room baths, telephones, and all modern comforts. A large Family Suite is also available. Breakfast is served on original Franciscan Appleware. The inn has been given three diamonds by AAA and three crowns by the American Bed and Breakfast Association.

**Open:** year round **Accommodations:** 5 guest rooms with private baths; 2 are suites **Meals:** full breakfast included in rate; complimentary refreshments and afternoon tea; restaurants nearby **Rates:** $75 to $125 **Payment:** AmEx, Visa, MC, Discover, DC, personal and traveler's checks **Restrictions:** no smoking; pets accepted with prior approval **On-site activities:** perennial gardens, croquet, mountain bikes, hammock, therapeutic massage

## THE SANDERS – HELENA'S BED AND BREAKFAST

328 North Ewing
Helena, Montana 59601
**Phone:** 406/442-3309 or 888/442-3309
**Fax:** 406/443-2361
**Website:** www.sandersbb.com
**E-mail:** thefolks@sandersbb.com
**Proprietors:** Bobbi Uecker and Rock Ringling

Wilbur Sanders, Montana's first U.S. senator, built this three-story Victorian home in 1875. His family, and only one other, owned the house until it was purchased by the innkeepers in 1986. After a thorough restoration, the house was opened as a bed and breakfast, incorporating Sanders' original furnishings in the elegant and comfortable bedrooms and public areas. Each richly detailed guest room has a private bath, telephone, color television, alarm clock, hair dryer, and easy chair, and provides views of the mountains and downtown Helena. Gourmet Montana breakfasts, featuring such specialties as orange souffle and Grand Marnier French toast, are served in the wainscoted dining room. The Sanders has welcomed guests from around the world, most notably Archbishop Desmond Tutu. The inn has been featured in the *Washington Post*, the *New York Times*, and the *Boston Sunday Globe*.

**Open:** year round **Accommodations:** 7 guest rooms with private baths **Meals:** full breakfast included; catering available; restaurants nearby **Rates:** $80 to $110 **Payment:** Visa, MC, Discover, personal and traveler's checks **Restrictions:** no smoking; no pets **On-site activities:** reading, listening to music, porch sitting

# LIVINGSTON

**Nearby attractions:** Yellowstone River, fly fishing, hiking, horseback riding, rafting, bicycling, cross-country and downhill skiing, hunting, golfing, art galleries, museums, theaters, Yellowstone Park

## MURRAY HOTEL
201 West Park Street
Livingston, Montana 59047
**Phone:** 406/222-1350
**Fax:** 406/222-6500
**Website:** murrayhotel.com
**Proprietors:** Dan and Kathleen Kaul

The Murray Hotel has been Livingston's only downtown hotel since it opened in 1905. A four-story brick building touted as "comfortable and fireproof" when built, the Murray is as unique as its Wild West setting. Celebrities, authors, and movie stars have stopped here for years, rubbing elbows with cowpokes, railroaders, and other travelers who provide a hotel's life blood. Restored to its historic place as the premier lodging in Livingston, the Murray still plays a traditional role as a gathering and mixing place for locals and visitors. Guest rooms—accessed by a 1905 hand-cranked Otis elevator—are decorated in turn-of-the-century western charm coupled with all the amenities today's travelers expect. A roof-top hot tub (with spectacular vistas of three mountain ranges), award-winning restaurant, workout room, art gallery, and upscale cigar lounge with live entertainment are on premises. The Murray has been featured in *The New York Times*, *The Oregonian*, and *Minneapolis Star Tribune*. *The Chicago Tribune* calls the Murray "the quintessential old Montana kind of lodging."

**Open:** year round **Accommodations:** 30 guest rooms with private baths; 6 are suites

**Meals:** restaurant on premises serving breakfast, lunch, and dinner; lounge on premises **Rates:** $49 to $150; 10% discount to National Trust members and National Trust Visa cardholders **Payment:** AmEx, Visa, MC, Discover, traveler's checks **On-site activities:** roof-top hot tub, lounge, cafe, art gallery

## RED LODGE

**Nearby attractions:** Yellowstone and Grand Teton National Parks, Red Lodge Mountain Ski Area, scenic Beartooth Highway, Coal Miner's Park, Festival of Nations, Winter Carnival, Home of Champions Rodeo and Parade, Little Big Horn Battlefield, Peaks to Plains Museum, Buffalo Bill Historical Center, golfing, hiking, horseback riding, bicycling, river rafting, fishing, downhill and cross-country skiing, horse-drawn wagon rides

### THE POLLARD
2 North Broadway Avenue
P.O. Box 650
Red Lodge, Montana 59068
**Phone:** 406/446-0001 or 800/POLLARD (765-5273)
**Fax:** 406/446-0002
**Website:** www.pollardhotel.com
**E-mail:** pollard@pollardhotel.com
**Proprietor:** David Knight

The Rocky Fork Coal Company opened the Spofford Hotel on July 4, 1893, the first brick building in the new town site of Red Lodge. Renamed the Pollard in 1902, the hotel was a regular host to Buffalo Bill Cody; William Jennings Bryan and Calamity Jane also signed the guest register. With the 1936 opening of the Beartooth Highway—called the "most beautiful road in America" by Charles Kuralt—the hotel became a popular rest stop for visitors to Yellowstone and Grand Teton National Parks. The hotel reopened in 1994, after a complete restoration. Today's guests will find private baths, fluffy towels and bathrobes, and cable television in their comfortable and inviting rooms. Some guest rooms offer whirlpool tubs and balconies overlooking the Gallery, an interior atrium. Fine dining and Western charm have been combined in the hotel's restaurant, Greenlee's at The Pollard. A full library of Western lore and a health club offering the latest in exercise equipment soothe mind and body. The Pollard is a member of Historic Hotels of America.

**Open:** year round **Accommodations:** 38 guest rooms with private baths; 6 are suites **Meals:** full breakfast included; restaurant on premises; restaurants nearby **Wheelchair access:** some guest rooms, bathrooms, restaurant **Rates:** $95 to $235; 10% discount to National Trust members (subject to availability) **Payment:** AmEx, Visa, MC, Discover, traveler's checks **Restrictions:** no smoking; no pets (arrangements can be made at nearby kennel) **On-site activities:** racquetball courts, fully equipped exercise room, hot tub, saunas

# NEBRASKA

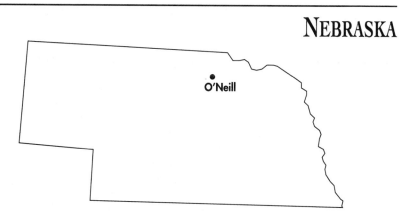

## O'NEILL

**Nearby attractions:** Kincaid Museum, Ashfall Fossil Beds State Park, Ft. Randall Casino, Ft. Randall Dam

### GOLDEN HOTEL
406 East Douglas
O'Neill, Nebraska 68763
**Phone:** 402/336-4436 or 800/658-3148
**Fax:** 402/336-3549
**Proprietor:** David G. Boice

The building of the Golden Hotel in 1913 signified the start of the modern era for the prospering city of O'Neill. Built of brick and steel, the hotel was completely fireproof; the only wood used was in the doors and window frames. On completion, the Golden offered 46 guest rooms with hot and cold water, electricity, and private telephone. Renovated and listed in the National Register of Historic Places, the hotel has been altered only enough to provide private baths for each guest room. The lobby retains its original marble and cast-iron staircase, Art Deco light fixtures, and patterned ceramic tile floor. The two-story annex on the hotel's north side, originally the 1911 Land Office, has been adapted to provide seven small apartments for long-term stays. Golden's Barber Shop, original to the hotel, has been reopened to serve guests. The Golden Hotel proudly provides a pleasant atmosphere at reasonable prices and that most precious of commodities, a good night's sleep.

**Open:** year round **Accommodations:** 34 guest rooms with private baths; 7 are apartments with kitchens **Meals:** continental breakfast included; complimentary refreshments; restaurants nearby **Rates:** $25 to $47; 10% discount to National Trust members and National Trust Visa cardholders **Payment:** AmEx, Visa, MC, Discover, personal and traveler's checks **Restrictions:** smoking limited; small pets accepted **On-site activities:** sauna, gym with exercise equipment

# NEVADA

## EAST ELY

**Nearby attractions:** Nevada Northern Railway Museum and steam train excursions, Great Basin National Park, Cave Lake State Park, garnet hunting, back country trails, ghost towns, golfing, tennis

## STEPTOE VALLEY INN
220 East 11th Street
P.O. Box 151110
East Ely, Nevada 89315-1110
**Phone:** 702/289-8687 (June–September) or 702/435-1196 (October–May)
**Website:** www.nevadaweb.com/steptoe
**Proprietors:** Jane and Norman Lindley

East Ely •

When the Nevada Northern Railway reached the copper mines of Eastern Nevada, promoters laid out a new community called Ely City to attract miners and their families. Steptoe Valley Inn was built in 1907 as the Ely City Grocery and Meat Market and had rooms upstairs for railroad workers. In 1990 the structure was remodeled into Steptoe Valley Inn, with a Victorian cottage decor accentuated by hand-painted accents, decorative wood trim, brass hardware, high embossed ceilings, etched and stained glass, and an old-fashioned rose garden with gazebo. Guest rooms contain white iron, canopy, pine, or wicker beds, lace curtains, and ceiling fans. Each room has a private balcony overlooking mountains, valley, or rose garden. A library, television room, living room, and upstairs veranda are open to guests.

**Open:** June through September **Accommodations:** 5 guest rooms with private baths **Meals:** full breakfast included; complimentary refreshments; restaurants nearby **Rates:** $68 single to $90 triple **Payment:** AmEx, Visa, MC **Restrictions:** supervised, well-behaved children welcome; no smoking; no pets **On-site activities:** croquet, parlor games, television and VCR, chess, library, rose garden and gazebo

# NEW HAMPSHIRE

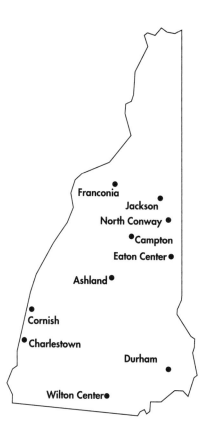

## ASHLAND

**Nearby attractions:** White Mountains, Squam and Winnepesaukee lakes, Plymouth State College, Science Center of New Hampshire, Wellington State Park, Franconia Notch State Park, downhill and cross-country skiing, antiques hunting, swimming, boating, hiking, bicycling, fishing, golfing, tennis, covered bridges

## GLYNN HOUSE VICTORIAN INN
43 Highland Street
P.O. Box 710
Ashland, New Hampshire 03217
**Phone:** 603/968-3775
or 800/637-9599
**Fax:** 603/968-3129
**Website:** www.nettx.com/glynnhouse.html
**E-mail:** glynnhse@lr.net
**Proprietors:** Betsy and Karol Paterman

From its round tower and patterned shingles to its irregular roof line and gingerbreaded wraparound porch, Glynn House is a fine example of Queen Anne architecture. Built in 1897, the house boasts gleaming carved oak woodwork, pocket doors, and fireplace mantels. Elegant period wallpapers are found throughout the house, complemented by Victorian antiques. Each bedroom has its own mood, distinguished by unique interior decor featuring period furnishings, such as lace-draped four-poster beds. Whirlpool tubs are featured in each of the two suites. Fireplaces throughout the house, including one in the Honeymoon Suite, create a cozy ambience. Nestled in the Lakes Region and the White Mountains, Glynn House is in the quaint village of Ashland, central to all the area's attractions.

**Open:** year round **Accommodations:** 8 guest rooms with private baths; 2 are suites **Meals:** full breakfast included; restaurants nearby **Rates:** $95 to $155; 10% discount to National Trust members and National Trust Visa cardholders **Payment:** AmEx, Visa, MC, personal and traveler's checks **Restrictions:** no smoking; no pets **On-site activities:** tennis and swimming

## CAMPTON

**Nearby attractions:** White Mountain National Forest, Squam ("On Golden Pond") Lake, Franconia Notch, Mount Washington, skiing, hiking, rock climbing, canoeing, bicycling, swimming, golfing, tennis, sightseeing

### MOUNTAIN-FARE INN
Mad River Road
Box 553
Campton, New Hampshire 03223
**Phone:** 603/726-4283
**Fax:** 603/726-4285
**E-mail:** mtnfareinn@cyberport.net
**Proprietors:** Susan and Nick Preston

The white clapboards, Gothically styled roof peaks, broad porches, and wide pine floors of this 1830s farmhouse all evoke the agricultural and logging heritage of the area. The house is the oldest place of lodging in the region, hosting first summer then winter travelers as long ago as the late 1800s. Ranging from cozy to spacious, guest accommodations are delightfully decorated with antiques, cottage-style fabrics, quilts, and down comforters. Home-cooked, family-style breakfasts are standard. In spring, summer, and fall, the Mountain-Fare is ideal for family reunions, clubs, and retreats; a charming spot with gardens, fields, and outdoor games. In winter, the innkeepers, avid skiers, enjoy providing lodging for serious skiers, teams, and competitors, with space to store and tune guests' skis.

**Open:** year round **Accommodations:** 10 guest rooms (9 have private baths); 3 are suites **Meals:** full breakfast included; restaurants nearby **Rates:** $75 to $95; 10% discount to National Trust members and National Trust Visa cardholders, off-peak only **Payment:** personal and traveler's checks **Restrictions:** no smoking; inquire about pets **On-site activities:** soccer, volleyball, croquet, billiards

# CHARLESTOWN

**Nearby attractions:** French and Indian War Fort at No. 4, St. Gauden's National Historic Site, covered bridges, Simon Pearce Glass Blowers, Connecticut River Valley, water sports, golfing, hiking, skiing, antiques hunting

### MAPLE HEDGE BED AND BREAKFAST INN
Main Street
Charlestown, New Hampshire 03603
**Phone:** 603/826-5237 or 800/9-MAPLE
**E-mail:** debrine@fmis.net
**Proprietors:** Joan and Dick DeBrine

Maple Hedge has stood beside the Great Road (Route 12) for almost 250 years. Built in 1755 with an addition in 1830, this large colonial home is listed in the National Register of Historic Places. Each of the five bedrooms has been decorated with distinctive antiques and memorabilia to create unique settings: the Victorian Beale Room, the elegant Ellcee's Boudoir, the pine-wainscoted Lt. R.A.D.'s Quarters, the mahogany-furnished Cobalt Room, and the wicker-filled Butterfly Suite. The innkeepers host a predinner social time and provide a full breakfast. This historic home has been updated to include all modern amenities, including central air conditioning and alarm system, smoke detectors, and sprinklers.

**Open:** year round **Accommodations:** 5 guest rooms with private baths; 1 is a 2-bedroom suite **Meals:** full breakfast included; complimentary refreshments; restaurants

nearby **Rates:** $85 to $100; 10% discount to National Trust members and National Trust Visa cardholders excluding September 20 through October 20 and some weekends **Payment:** Visa, MC, personal and traveler's checks **Restrictions:** children over 12 welcome; no smoking; no pets **On-site activities:** horseshoe pitching, croquet, games, books, puzzles

## CORNISH

**Nearby attractions:** Saint-Gaudens National Historic Site, Connecticut River Valley, Dartmouth College, downhill and cross-country skiing, ice skating, bicycling, hiking, fishing, canoeing, antiques hunting, museums, crafts and specialty shops, seasonal theater and concerts

### THE CHASE HOUSE—BED AND BREAKFAST INN
Route 12A
R.R. 2, Box 909
Cornish, New Hampshire 03745
**Phone:** 603/675-5391 or 800/401-9455
**Fax:** 603/675-5010
**Website:** www.chasehouse.com
**Proprietors:** Bill and Barbara Lewis

The Chase House, situated on 160 acres on the New Hampshire bank of the Connecticut River, offers outstanding views of Vermont's Mount Ascutney and the scenic Upper Valley. The original portion of the house was built in 1766. In 1795 it was joined to a Federal-style building. The house's most famous resident was Salmon Portland Chase, born there in 1808. He is remembered as a founder of the Republican Party, namesake of the Chase Manhattan Bank, and as the man on the first $1 bill in 1862 and on the recently retired $10,000 bill. Today, the Chase House is honored as one of 22 National Historic Landmarks in New Hampshire. Furnishings and decor, including canopied beds, antiques, and period pieces, reflect the house's historic and elegant past. A function room, previously the second story of an 1810 house moved from West Topsham, Vermont, accommodates up to 70 people.

**Open:** year round **Accommodations:** 8 guest rooms with private baths; 2 are suites **Meals:** full breakfast included; complimentary refreshments; restaurants nearby **Rates:** $105 to $125 **Payment:** AmEx, Visa, MC, personal check **Restrictions:** children over 12 welcome; no smoking; no pets **On-site activities:** Alpine and Nordic skiing, hiking, canoeing, bicycling

## DURHAM

**Nearby attractions:** University of New Hampshire, Whittemore Center Stadium and Center for the Arts, theaters, art galleries, historic district, walking trails, historic Portsmouth, Strawberry Banke Village living museum, antiques hunting, Isles of Shoals, boating, beaches, outlet shopping in Maine

### THREE CHIMNEYS INN
17 Newmarket Road
Durham, New Hampshire 03824
**Phone:** 603/868-7780 or 888/399-9777
**Fax:** 603/868-2964
**Website:** www.threechimneysinn.com
**E-mail:** chimney3@threechimneysinn.com

The newly restored Three Chimneys Inn overlooks the Oyster River and Old Mill Falls. The earliest part of the house was built by Valentine Hill in 1649. His son, Nathaniel, added to it in 1699 and the attached barn was built in 1795. Guest rooms are in the historic buildings, and are elegantly appointed with Georgian mahogany furnishings, fireplaces, four-poster canopied beds with Edwardian drapes, rich tapestries, oriental rugs, and phones with data ports. Added comforts include full private baths; some with whirlpool or two-person tubs. A full, hearty breakfast, welcome basket on arrival, traditional afternoon tea, and turn-down service are all provided with the inn's compliments. A restaurant, Maples, with its four fireplaces offers fine dining by candlelight. The Tavern with its granite walls, summer kitchen fireplace, and massive beamed ceilings provides a cozy spot for casual fare. The Conservatory is a delightful outdoor place to enjoy casual dining or a beverage in the shade of an old English grape arbor.

**Open:** year round **Accommodations:** 24 guest rooms with private baths; 2 are suites **Meals:** full breakfast included; restaurant and tavern on premises **Rates:** $149 to $189; 10% discount to National Trust members and National Trust Visa cardholders **Payment:** AmEx, Visa, MC, Discover, traveler's checks **Restrictions:** children over 6 welcome; no smoking; no pets **On-site activities:** strolling through formal gardens, bocci, fishing

## EATON CENTER

**Nearby attractions:** White Mountain National Forest, Mount Washington Valley, Crystal Lake, Ossipee Lake, canoeing, boating, ice skating, cross-country and downhill skiing, sleigh rides, snowmobiling, shopping

### INN AT CRYSTAL LAKE

Route 153
P.O. Box 12
Eaton Center, New Hampshire 03832
**Phone:** 603/447-2120 or 800/343-7336
**Fax:** 603/447-3599
**Website:** www.nettx.com/crystallake/index.html
**Proprietors:** Richard and Janice Octeau

In 1884, Nathaniel G. Palmer built a home with spacious rooms and airy balconies around a small home previously built by his father. Making enterprising use of a steep hillside site, Palmer built a Victorian-influenced Greek Revival split-level home—a highly unusual architectural style. By the turn of the century, Palmer was taking in overnight guests who came to enjoy the mountains during the summer, and the establishment became known as Palmer House. After stints as a day camp and a school, the house was converted back to an inn in the 1970s. Now known as the Inn at Crystal Lake, the house has been renovated to include private baths for all guest rooms and to remove 1960s paneling and restore original plaster walls. Victorian lighting and antiques are found throughout. A full country breakfast is served in the sun-filled dining room.

**Open:** year round **Accommodations:** 11 guest rooms with private baths; 2 are suites sleeping up to 7 people **Meals:** full breakfast included; complimentary refreshments; restaurants nearby **Rates:** $70 to $140; 10% discount to National Trust members and National Trust Visa cardholders during off-season **Payment:** AmEx, Visa, MC, DC, Discover, personal and traveler's checks **Restrictions:** smoking limited; no pets **On-site activities:** across the street is Crystal Lake for swimming, fishing, hiking, and cross-country skiing

# FRANCONIA

**Nearby attractions:** White Mountain National Forest, Franconia Notch State Park, Cannon Mountain Aerial Tramway, Appalachian Trail, Lost River and Polar Caves, Mt. Washington Cog Railway, Conway Scenic Railroad, Robert Frost Home, Franconia Village, ski and maple sugar museums, downhill skiing, antiques hunting, golfing

## FRANCONIA INN

1300 Easton Road
Franconia, New Hampshire 03580
**Phone:** 603/823-5542 or 800/473-5299
**Fax:** 603/823-8078
**Website:** www.franconiainn.com
**Proprietors:** Morris Family

The rambling, white Franconia Inn is situated on 107 acres in Easton Valley, affording breathtaking views of the surrounding mountain ranges. Although the site had been settled as early as 1772 and a country inn established here after the Civil War, this inn was not built until 1936, after the previous building was destroyed by fire in 1934. The picturesque Colonial Revival structure contains an oak paneled library and living room with fireplaces, two dining rooms, and East- and West-facing porches. Guest rooms, recently renovated, are simple yet beautifully decorated, all with private baths. A Family Suite—two rooms connected by one common bath—is available. The Inn Suite has a queen bed, living room with fireplace, and a balcony. The Franconia Inn is a year-round resort providing myriad activities and limitless relaxation. Quality service in an informal atmosphere is the hallmark of the inn, which is run by third-generation innkeepers.

**Open:** year round **Accommodations:** 34 guest rooms with private baths; 3 are suites **Meals:** full breakfast included (European and Modified American plans are also available); restaurant on premises **Rates:** $83 to $158; 10% discount to National Trust members and National Trust Visa cardholders **Payment:** AmEx, Visa, MC, traveler's checks **Restrictions:** smoking limited; no pets **On-site activities:** outdoor heated pool, whirlpool, clay tennis courts, mountain bikes, horseback riding, glider rides, lighted ice-skating rink, sleigh rides, cross-country skiing on groomed trails

# JACKSON

**Nearby attractions:** village of Jackson, Mount Washington, four downhill ski areas, North Conway outlet shops, golfing, tennis

**EAGLE MOUNTAIN HOUSE, EST. 1879**
Carter Notch Road
Jackson, New Hampshire 03846
**Phone:** 603/383-9111 or 800/966-5779
**Fax:** 603/383-0854
**Website:** www.eaglemt.com
**E-mail:** reservations@eaglemt.com
**Proprietor:** Paul W. Mayer

Up the hill from the village of Jackson, past the falls of the Wildcat River, stands the Eagle Mountain House, a resort inn built in 1915 to replace the inn that was originally built here in 1879. The vast white structure with black-shuttered windows, cross gables, and dentils has been restored to offer cozy guest rooms and suites, all with private baths, decorated with a country flair. The hotel dining room serves breakfast, brunch, and dinner featuring New England specialties. Lunch and cocktails are available in the Eagle Landing Tavern. Each season at Eagle Mountain House presents an array of activities, from golf, tennis, and swimming in the heated pool to viewing fall foliage and cross-country and downhill skiing. A health club with whirlpool is available year round. Eagle Mountain House is a member of Historic Hotels of America.

**Open:** year round **Accommodations:** 94 guest rooms with private baths; 30 are suites **Meals:** complimentary refreshments; restaurants on premises **Wheelchair access:** yes **Rates:** $69 to $159; 10% discount to National Trust members and National Trust Visa cardholders **Payment:** AmEx, Visa, MC, CB, DC, Discover, personal and traveler's checks **On-site activities:** golfing, tennis, trout fishing, cross-country skiing, swimming pool

## NORTH CONWAY

**Nearby attractions:** downhill and cross-country skiing, ice skating, hiking and walking trails, bicycling, climbing, mountaineering, golfing, fishing, canoeing, white-water rafting, river and lake swimming, tennis, outlet shops, summer theater

## NERELEDGE INN

P.O. Box 547
River Road
North Conway, New Hampshire 03860
**Phone:** 603/356-2831
**Website:** www.nereledgen.com
**E-mail:** nereledge@landmarknet.net
**Proprietors:** Valerie and Dave Halpin

Built in 1787 by Moses Randel, the Cape Cod-style house that became the Nereledge Inn was expanded during the early nineteenth century to its current size—two full stories plus a dormered third. But inside, its colonial post-and-beam construction is still evident, and the original wide-plank pine and oak floors withstand twentieth-century use. The atmosphere at the inn is friendly and informal, and the furnishings are eclectic: Antiques mix with contemporary pieces. Guest rooms reflect warmth and old-fashioned comfort with English eiderdown quilts and rocking chairs. Two relaxing sitting rooms, one with a wood-burning stove, provide games, books, and television. An English-style pub offers darts, backgammon, and cribbage for guests' entertainment.

**Open:** year round **Accommodations:** 11 guest rooms, 6 have private baths **Meals:** full breakfast included; restaurants nearby **Rates:** $59 to $119 **Payment:** AmEx, Visa, MC, personal and traveler's checks **Restrictions:** no smoking; no pets **On-site activities:** front-porch rocking, reading, darts, backgammon, cribbage

## THE 1785 INN

3582 White Mountain Highway
P.O. Box 1785
North Conway, New Hampshire 03860-1785
**Phone:** 603/356-9025 or 800/421-1785
**Fax:** 603/356-6081
**Website:** www.journeysnorth.com/1785
**E-mail:** the1785inn@aol.com
**Proprietors:** Becky and Charlie Mallar

The original section of this house with its commanding views of the Saco River Valley, Mount Washington, Presidential Range, was built in 1785 by Elijah

Dinsmore, veteran of the French and Indian War and American Revolution. That structure today comprises the inn's living and dining rooms. The original chimney with its fireplaces and brick oven forms a beehive structure the size of a small room in the middle of the house. The central chimney floor plan, exposed corner posts, and hand-hewn beams illustrate vividly the construction techniques of the late 1700s. Later additions in the 1800s brought the house to its present size. For overnight guests, the inn has 17 cheerful, individually decorated rooms, two guest living rooms with original working fireplaces, a casual lounge, and more than six acres of beautiful grounds and gardens to explore. The cuisine and wine selection in the dining room here have been heralded by *Wine Spectator* and *Bon Appetit* magazines. AAA gives the 1785 Inn three diamonds.

**Open:** year round **Accommodations:** 17 guest rooms (12 have private baths); 1 is a suite **Meals:** full breakfast included; restaurants and pub on premises; restaurants nearby **Rates:** $49 to $199; 10% discount to National Trust members and National Trust Visa cardholders **Payment:** AmEx, Visa, MC, Discover, DC, CB, personal and traveler's checks **Restrictions:** no smoking; no pets **On-site activities:** four seasons of activities—cross-country skiing, hiking/nature trails, fishing, canoeing, swimming pool, shuffleboard, volleyball

## STONEHURST MANOR

Route 16
P.O. Box 1937
North Conway, New Hampshire 03860
**Phone:** 603/356-3113 or 800/525-9100
**Website:** www.stonehurstmanor.com
**Proprietor:** Peter Rattay
**Location:** 1 mile north of North Conway Village

In 1876, Erastus and Eliza Bigelow, owners of Bigelow Carpet Mills, built a summer home on this piece of pine-forested hillside. Their daughter Helen embarked on a massive remodeling job in 1894 that transformed the simple structure into her vision of a grand English country manor. The two-story clapboard house became a three-story, multigabled, dormered mansion. Rooms were added, existing ones enlarged. A library was created, featuring a massive hand-carved oak mantelpiece imported from England. Windows were replaced with stained and cut glass, and a stone porte cochere was added. This grandeur remains for the pleasure of overnight guests. Wicker abounds in the bedrooms and dining rooms, and seven guest rooms contain fireplaces or porches.

**Open:** year round **Accommodations:** 24 guest rooms (22 have private baths); 2 are suites **Meals:** breakfast and dinner included; restaurant and lounge on premises **Rates:** $48 to $78 per person **Payment:** Visa, MC, traveler's check **Restrictions:** no pets **On-site activities:** hot tub, swimming pool, tennis, guided or unguided walking and hiking tours beginning at the inn, free cross-country skiing on 65 miles of groomed trails

## WILTON CENTER

**Nearby attractions:** three summer theaters (including one for children), antiques hunting, flea markets, arts center, summer chamber-music concerts, hiking, nature center, golfing, canoeing

### STEPPING STONES BED AND BREAKFAST
R.F.D. 1, Box 208
Bennington Battle Trail
Wilton Center, New Hampshire 03086
**Phone:** 603/654-9048 or 888/654-9048
**Fax:** 603/654-6821
**Proprietor:** Ann Carlsmith
**Location:** 5 miles west of Wilton (town); 3/4 mile north of Wilton Center (village)

The house that is Stepping Stones Bed and Breakfast was originally a settler's cabin built in the early nineteenth century. In the late 1800s the original structure was incorporated into a country-style Greek Revival house with gable front and wing. This quaint structure sits along the route taken by the militia from nearby towns as they joined to fight the Revolutionary Battle of Bennington. Visitors will enjoy the artistry of the innkeeper, a garden designer, in the extensively landscaped terraces, paths, and gardens that surround the house. Inside, handwoven throws, pillows, and rugs display her talent as a weaver. Fresh flowers, quilts, down comforters, and an art collection contribute to the comfortable atmosphere. Home-baked breakfast specialties are served in a solar-heated garden room.

**Open:** year round **Accommodations:** 3 guest rooms with private baths **Meals:** full breakfast included; complimentary refreshments; restaurants nearby **Rates:** $40 single to $60 double; 10% discount offered to National Trust members and National Trust Visa cardholders **Payment:** personal and traveler's checks **Restrictions:** no smoking; well-behaved and controlled pets allowed **On-site activities:** gardens, weaving studio, television, library, bird-watching (birdhouses, baths, and feeders)

# NEW JERSEY

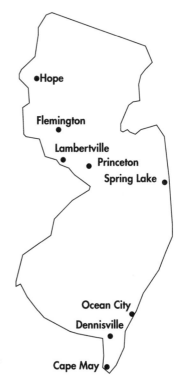

## CAPE MAY

**Nearby attractions:** National Historic Landmark district, Victorian house tours, antiques hunting, horse and buggy rides, trolley and walking tours, bicycling, beach and swimming, Cape May Lighthouse, boating, fishing, bird sanctuary, nature walks, hiking, golfing, tennis, festivals (music, seafood, and kite), theater, shopping

## THE ABBEY

34 Gurney Street at Columbia Avenue
Cape May, New Jersey 08204
**Phone:** 609/884-4506
**Fax:** 609/884-2379
**Website:** www.beachcomber.com
**Proprietors:** Jay and Marianne Schatz

In 1987 the two houses that were in the John B. McCreary family were joined to form The Abbey: a Gothic Revival structure (now the main house), dating to 1869, and a Second Empire cottage, dating to 1873. The main house is dominated by a 60-foot-high tower and accented by ruby-glass arched windows, spacious rooms, and shaded verandas. The cottage boasts an unusual convex man-

sard roof. Both houses are furnished with Victorian antiques, including 12-foot-wide mirrors, ornate glass fixtures, tall walnut beds, and marble-topped dressers. The Abbey is listed in the National Register of Historic Places, and measured drawings of it are recorded in the Library of Congress. Fine accommodations and merriment are The Abbey's trademarks; an evening hat fashion show often takes place with hats from the innkeepers' extensive—and exotic—collection. This establishment has been heralded by many, including the *New York Times* and *Conde Nast Traveler*.

**Open:** April to January **Accommodations:** 14 air-conditioned guest rooms with private baths and mini-refrigerators; 2 are suites **Meals:** full breakfast included; complimentary afternoon tea and refreshments; restaurants nearby **Rates:** $95 to $275 **Payment:** Visa, MC, Discover, traveler's check; personal check for room deposit only **Restrictions:** young adults over 12 welcome; no smoking **On-site activities:** house tours, croquet, rocking and people-watching on veranda

## CARROLL VILLA HOTEL
19 Jackson Street
Cape May, New Jersey 08204
**Phone:** 609/884-9619
**Fax:** 609/884-0264
**Website:** www.beachcomber.com/capemay/bbs/carroll.html
**E-mail:** Madbatter@cyberenet.net
**Proprietors:** Pamela Huber and Mark Kulkowitz

The four-gabled cupola perched atop the fourth floor of this striking Italianate structure makes the Carroll Villa a landmark in Cape May's National Register historic district. The hotel, built in 1882, is named for Thomas Carroll of Maryland, signer of the Declaration of Independence. Just a half-block from the ocean, beaches, and promenade, the Carroll Villa offers 22 Victorian-styled guest rooms furnished with period antiques. Each has a private bath, air conditioning, ceiling fans, and telephone. Sumptuous breakfasts, prepared by the chefs of the Mad Batter Restaurant (which also serves lunch and dinner) are served on the front porch, in the dining room with fireplace, or in the secluded garden terrace. The hotel is equipped to host corporate meetings, weddings, and rehearsal dinners. Carroll Villa has been recommended by the *New York Times* and the *Philadelphia Inquirer*.

**Open:** year round **Accommodations:** 22 guest rooms with private baths **Meals:** full breakfast included; restaurant on premises; restaurants nearby **Rates:** $66 to $165 **Payment:** AmEx, Visa, MC, Discover, DC, personal and traveler's checks **Restrictions:** no smoking; no pets **On-site activities:** stroll to beach

## GINGERBREAD HOUSE
28 Gurney Street
Cape May, New Jersey 08204
**Phone:** 609/884-0211
**Website:** www.gingerbreadinn.com
**Proprietors:** Fred and Joan Echevarria

Built in 1869, the Gingerbread House is one of the original Stockton Row Cottages designed by Stephen Decatur Button and intended as a summer retreat for wealthy families, their servants, and nannies. This charming Victorian house, loaded with gingerbread woodwork, has been skillfully restored, incorporating the innkeeper's craftsmanship as a cabinetmaker: he recreated the double front doors of teak and beveled glass that provide an inviting entrance. His handmade furniture complements the Victorian furnishings, lace curtains, and period wallpapers that decorate the house. Original watercolors by the innkeeper's mother, award-winning photographs, and fresh bouquets from the garden add to the lovely atmosphere. In the heart of the historic district, Gingerbread House is less than a block from the beach.

**Open:** year round **Accommodations:** 6 guest rooms (3 have private baths); 1 is a suite with private porch **Meals:** full breakfast included; complimentary afternoon tea; restaurants nearby **Rates:** $98 to $240 **Payment:** Visa, MC, personal and traveler's checks **Restrictions:** children over 7 welcome; smoking limited; no pets

## LEITH HALL HISTORIC SEASHORE INN
22 Ocean Street
Cape May, New Jersey 08204
**Phone:** 609/884-1934
**Website:** www.capenet.com/capemay/leith
**Proprietors:** Elan and Susan Zingman-Leith

A deep mansard roof, bay windows, a wraparound porch, and ocean views from every room define Leith Hall, an 1885 seaside structure. Inside, Leith Hall has been decorated with rich wall coverings and paint to faithfully reproduce the Victorian era in which it was built. Bedrooms are furnished with Victorian antiques, including walnut or brass beds, handcarved mahogany tables, laces and linens, fringes and tassels.

Each room offers a private bath, and several rooms include refrigerators. Downstairs are a parlor and library for guests' use; stained-glass French doors open onto the chair-lined veranda. Breakfast is served from antique silver, crystal, and Royal Worcester china. An English tea is offered in the afternoon.

**Open:** year round **Accommodations:** 8 guest rooms with private baths; 3 are suites **Meals:** full breakfast included; complimentary refreshments; restaurants nearby **Rates:** $85 to $280 **Payment:** Visa, MC, personal and traveler's checks **Restrictions:** children over 12 welcome; no smoking; no pets **On-site activities:** library, cabinet grand piano, parlor games

## MAINSTAY INN AND COTTAGE

635 Columbia Avenue
Cape May, New Jersey 08204
**Phone:** 609/884-8690
**Website:** www.mainstayinn.com
**Proprietors:** Tom and Sue Carroll

A pair of wealthy gamblers pooled their resources in 1872 to build an exclusive gambling club. They hired an architect to design a grand Italianate villa with 14-foot-high ceilings, ornate plaster moldings, a sweeping veranda, and a cupola to top it off. For the interior, they selected the finest, richly ornamented furnishings: 12-foot-wide mirrors, glittering chandeliers, marble-topped sideboards, and graceful love seats. Yesterday's gambling palace has become today's Mainstay Inn, an elegant Victorian inn in the heart of historic Cape May. All rooms are furnished in antiques, most in a somewhat ornate manner suited to the period. This applies even to rooms in the Cottage, an 1870s summer cottage adjacent to the inn. The Mainstay is listed in the National Register and has been lauded by the *New York Times*, *Town and Country*, *Good Housekeeping*, and *Smithsonian*.

**Open:** year round **Accommodations:** 16 guest rooms with private baths (some with whirlpool tubs and fireplaces); 7 are suites **Meals:** full breakfast included; restaurants nearby **Wheelchair access:** 1 guest suite **Rates:** $95 to $255; discounts available off-season **Payment:** personal and traveler's checks **Restrictions:** children over 12 welcome; no smoking; no pets **On-site activities:** croquet, porch rocking, conversation, tour of historic inn

## MANOR HOUSE
612 Hughes Street
Cape May, New Jersey 08204
**Phone:** 609/884-4710
**Fax:** 609/898-0471
**Website:** www.innbook.com
**Proprietors:** Nancy and Tom McDonald

Nestled in central Cape May, in the stretch of Victorian architecture on Hughes Street, is Manor House, a turn-of-the-century beach cottage with a decidedly Colonial Revival air. Guests enter through a classic chestnut and oak foyer and will find large, airy rooms with cheerful Victorian print wallpapers. Guest rooms vary in size from cozy on the first floor to spacious in the third-floor three-room suite. All provide views and glimpses of gardens, rooftops, or the ocean. Room amenities like hair dryers, iron and ironing board, fluffy robes, and soaps and body lotions are standard. And Manor House hospitality includes complimentary beach chairs, towels and tags, outside hot and cold shower. Breakfasts of fresh-squeezed juices and made-from-scratch entrees are the beginnings of every day at Manor House.

**Open:** February through December **Accommodations:** 10 guest rooms with private baths; 1 is a suite **Meals:** full breakfast included; restaurants nearby **Rates:** $90 to $250 **Payment:** Visa, MC, Discover, personal and traveler's checks **Restrictions:** children over 12 welcome; no smoking; no pets **On-site activities:** porch rocking, reading by fireplace, jigsaw puzzles

## SEVENTH SISTER GUESTHOUSE
10 Jackson Street
Cape May, New Jersey 08204
**Phone:** 609/884-2280
**Fax:** 609/898-9899
**Proprietors:** Bob and Jo-Anne Echevarria-Myers

One of seven identical houses built in 1888, the Seventh Sister was designed by prominent nineteenth-century architect Stephen Decatur Button. Three floors are joined by a central circular staircase. The inn features 80 percent of its original furniture, which was specified by the architect, and a collection of more than 50 wicker pieces. Most of the six individually designed guest rooms have ocean views. A guest living room has the original coal fireplace, and a sunporch faces the ocean. The Seventh Sister, a contributing structure to Cape May's National Historic Landmark district, also earned an individual listing in the National Register of Historic Places on the basis of its own historic merit. The house is decorated to reflect the skills of its owners, an artist and a designer.

**Open:** year round **Accommodations:** 6 guest rooms with shared baths **Meals:** no meals on premises; guest refrigerator available; restaurants nearby **Rates:** $70 to $150; 5% discount offered to National Trust members and National Trust Visa cardholders, excluding holidays **Payment:** Visa, MC, personal and traveler's checks **Restrictions:** children over 7 welcome; smoking limited; no pets **On-site activities:** croquet

## THE SOUTHERN MANSION
720 Washington Street
Cape May, New Jersey 08204
**Phone:** 609/884-7171 or 800/381-3888
**Fax:** 609/898-0492
**Website:** www.southernmansion.com
**Proprietors:** J. Beyer and Mary Bray

An 1863 Italianate mansion designed by renowned architect Samuel Sloan, the Southern Mansion is a masterpiece of craftsmanship. It was built for Philadelphia businessman George Allen and remained in his family until 1946. What followed was 50 years of neglect. In a state of total disrepair in 1994, the house has been impeccably restored to showcase its exquisite mahogany woodwork, intricately carved crown moldings, soaring 15-foot ceilings, giant gilded mirrors, two grand ballrooms, and 5,000 square feet of verandas. Circular or flying, brick or mahogany, there are 10 staircases in the Southern Mansion; the main one climbs six stories from the basement to the cupola. Guest rooms are plush and spacious with private marble and tiled baths. With millions of dollars worth of antiques, the mansion is a virtual Gilded Age showcase. The *New York Times* has said the Southern Mansion is "not to be missed." The National Register-listed inn is equally suited to romantic getaways and corporate retreats.

**Open:** year round **Accommodations:** 23 guest rooms with private baths; 9 are suites **Meals:** restaurant on premises; catering for events; restaurants nearby **Rates:** $125 to $300; 10% discount to National Trust members and National Trust Visa cardholders **Payment:** AmEx, Visa, MC, personal and traveler's checks **Restrictions:** children over 6 welcome; no smoking; no pets **On-site activities:** croquet, bocci, heated indoor pool, hot tub, sauna, gaming room, shuffleboard, horseshoes

## WHITE DOVE COTTAGE
619 Hughes Street
Cape May, New Jersey 08204
**Phone:** 609/884-0613 or 800/321-DOVE
**Proprietors:** Frank and Sue Smith

Built in 1866, this Second Empire–style house boasts a mansard roof faced with original octagonal slate tiles. The three floors were built with spacious rooms and large windows to take advantage of ocean breezes. The inn, furnished with American and European antiques, is decorated with period wallpapers, soft carpeting, paintings, prints, and hand-made quilts. Blending seamlessly with the old are the new: modern private baths, air conditioning, up-to-date systems. Guests enjoy a multicourse breakfast at a banquet table set with lace, fine china, and heirloom crystal. The wicker-furnished front veranda looks out on a quiet, gaslit residential street in the historic district.

**Open:** year round **Accommodations:** 6 guest rooms with private baths; 2 are suites **Meals:** full breakfast included; complimentary afternoon tea; restaurants nearby **Rates:** $100 to $215; 10% discount to National Trust members and National Trust Visa cardholders **Payment:** personal and traveler's checks **Restrictions:** children over 12 welcome; no smoking; no pets **On-site activities:** total relaxation, mystery and romance packages

# DENNISVILLE
**Nearby attractions:** historic Dennisville, Wheaton Village colonial glassworks, New Jersey Wetlands Institute, Leaming's Run Botanical Gardens, Belleplain State Forest, Cape May, Wildwood, Avalon, Stone Harbor, Atlantic City, swimming, bird watching, hiking, bicycling, antiques hunting, theaters

## HENRY LUDLAM INN
1336 Route 47
Dennisville, New Jersey 08214
**Phone:** 609/861-5847
**Proprietors:** Chuck and Pat DeArros
**Location:** 7 miles northwest of Cape May Court House

Located in historic Dennisville, once a colonial shipbuilding center, the Henry Ludlam Inn sits on the bank of a freshwater lake. The home was built for a wealthy landowning and merchant family in the late eighteenth century. The innkeepers have refurbished the house with great care, allowing the stenciled walls, glowing brass fixtures, and rag-rugged staircase to reflect the house's heritage. Each of the five guest rooms has its own character, created by a blend of antique furnishings, personal touches, and modern conveniences. Three of the rooms contain working fireplaces. All have antique double feather beds, piled high with feather pillows and handmade quilts. In warm weather a gourmet breakfast is served on the lakefront porch; in winter it is served fireside in the commons room. The inn, listed in the National Register of Historic Places, is minutes from the varied activities of the New Jersey shore.

**Open:** year round **Accommodations:** 5 guest rooms with private baths **Meals:** full breakfast included; complimentary refreshments; restaurants nearby **Rates:** $85 to $120; 10% discount to National Trust members and National Trust Visa cardholders **Payment:** Visa, MC, traveler's check **Restrictions:** no smoking; no pets (resident cats) **On-site activities:** fishing and canoeing on lake

# FLEMINGTON

**Nearby attractions:** Flemington outlet shops, New Hope and Bucks County, Pa.; antiques hunting; summer theater; Princeton University; hiking; bicycling; Delaware River tubing and rafting

## MAIN STREET MANOR
194 Main Street
Flemington, New Jersey 08822
**Phone:** 908/782-4928
**Fax:** 908/782-4928
**Website:** www.bbianj.com/mainstreet
**Proprietors:** Elinor Hitchner and Dennis Lengle

The house at 194 Main Street was built in 1901 by the locally prominent Schenk family. In 1919, the house was doubled in size and, in 1939, the tower and bay windows in the dining room and the room above were added. The composite has resulted in a restrained Queen Anne styling with asymmetrical massing, projecting bays, varied roof lines, and patterned shingles on the third floor. Entry is through a grand foyer with crystal chandelier and sweeping staircase. Upstairs are five guest rooms named for people important in New Jersey's history: The Lindbergh, dressed in an elegant 1930s style, is the largest with a porch; the Edison is done in a Renaissance Revival style with window seat and claw-foot tub original to the house. All rooms are air-conditioned and have private baths and sitting areas. Guests are invited to breakfast in the dining room with fireplace. Homemade cookies and drinks are always available from the Butler's pantry.

**Open:** year round **Accommodations:** 5 guest rooms with private baths **Meals:** full breakfast included on weekends; continental-plus breakfast included weekdays; complimentary refreshments; restaurants nearby **Rates:** $95 to $135; 10% discount to National Trust members and National Trust Visa cardholders **Payment:** AmEx, Visa, MC, personal check **Restrictions:** children over 12 welcome; no smoking; no pets

# HOPE

**Nearby attractions:** Delaware Water Gap National Recreation Area, Pocono Mountains, skiing, golfing, bicycling, antiques hunting, historic Moravian village tours

### INN AT MILLRACE POND
Box 359
Hope, New Jersey 07844
**Phone:** 908/459-4884or 800/746-6467
**Fax:** 908/459-5276
**Proprietors:** Charles and Cordie Puttkammer

The Inn at Millrace Pond sits on a hillside on 23 acres in historic Hope. The town was founded in 1769 by Moravian pioneers and is now listed in the National Register of Historic Places. The inn comprises three historic buildings: the grist mill, a landmark limestone building constructed in 1770; the miller's house; and the wheelwright's cottage. For 150 years the mill was the heart of Hope's economy. Now it offers colonial-styled overnight accommodations furnished with period reproductions and handcrafted oriental rugs. Original wide-board pumpkin-pine floors gleam throughout the inn. A massive stone wall and exposed beams accent the formal dining room, where award-winning meals are served. From the dining room a staircase descends to the Tavern, which is highlighted by a walk-in fireplace, grain chute, and 180 years of mill memorabilia.

**Open:** year round **Accommodations:** 17 guest rooms with private baths **Meals:** continental breakfast included; restaurant on premises **Wheelchair access:** 2 guest rooms **Rates:** $100 to $160; 10% discount to National Trust members and National Trust Visa cardholders **Payment:** AmEx, Visa, MC, CB, DC, personal and traveler's checks **Restrictions:** smoking limited; no pets **On-site activities:** tennis, hiking

# LAMBERTVILLE

**Nearby attractions:** historic Lambertville, art galleries, antiques hunting, Delaware River, Raritan Canal, horseback riding, mule-drawn barges, carriage rides, symphony, Bucks County Center for the Performing Arts, New Hope, PA

## YORK STREET HOUSE

42 York Street
Lambertville, New Jersey 08530
**Phone:** 609/397-3007 or 888/398-3199
**Fax:** 609/397-9677
**Website:** www.virtualcities.com/ons/nj/t/njt3601.htm
**Proprietors:** Beth A. Wetterskog and Nancy J. Ferguson

For her twenty-fifth wedding anniversary in 1909, Mrs. George W. Massey of Lambertville received this elegant 13-room Colonial Revival house on three-quarters of an acre. Mr. Massey was one of the early industrialists who had settled his family in this historic river village just after the turn of the century. In 1911, the home was featured as *House & Garden* magazine's Home of the Year, with all the modern conveniences including a central vacuum that still stands in the cellar. The heart of today's bed-and-breakfast inn is a three-story staircase leading to six gracious guest rooms, some with queen-size canopy beds. The public rooms are warmed by Mercer Tile fireplaces, the original Waterford crystal chandelier, and a baby grand piano. Breakfast is served in the oak-trimmed dining room with its built-in leaded-glass china and large oak servers, overlooking the lawn and sitting porch.

**Open:** year round **Accommodations:** 6 guest rooms (3 have private baths) **Meals:** full breakfast included; complimentary refreshments; restaurants nearby **Rates:** $85 to $165; 10% discount to National Trust members and National Trust Visa cardholders **Payment:** AmEx, Visa, MC, Discover, personal check **Restrictions:** not suitable for children; no smoking; no pets **On-site activities:** porch rocking, flower garden, hot tub

# OCEAN CITY

**Nearby attractions:** Ocean City boardwalk with shops, amusement arcades, and bicycling; historic walking tours; Leaming Run Gardens; Cape May

## NORTHWOOD INN
401 Wesley Avenue
Ocean City, New Jersey 08226
**Phone:** 609/399-6071
**Website:**
www.northwoodinn.com
**E-mail:**
nwoodin@bellatlantic.net
**Proprietors:** Marj and John
Loeper

The Northwood Inn, a capacious
Queen Anne was built circa 1894
and is a key building in the Ocean
City Historic District, being one of the first 200 houses built on the island. With
the main living space located on the second floor, this style of home is also called
Upper Cottage. It is a style of architecture unique to the Jersey Shore area. A
1901 remodeling removed the Victorian brackets and vergeboards, a six-room
addition was built on, and the structure was turned into a rooming house. Today,
the Northwood is one of the oldest ongoing rooming establishments in Ocean
City. Purchased as a gutted shell in 1989, the house was completely restored by
the innkeepers. The sweeping staircase and hardwood floors throughout show
the skill applied to the inn's finishing touches. Guest rooms are air conditioned,
have private baths, and are distinctively decorated.

**Open:** February 1 to January 2 **Accommodations:** 7 guest rooms with private baths;
2 are suites **Meals:** full breakfast included on weekends; continental-plus breakfast
included weekdays; restaurants nearby **Rates:** $100 to $165; 10% discount to National
Trust members and National Trust Visa cardholders **Payment:** AmEx, Visa, MC,
personal and traveler's checks **Restrictions:** children over 9 welcome; no smoking; no
pets **On-site activities:** rooftop hot tub, pool table, board games, reading and video
libraries, complimentary bicycles and beach tags

# PRINCETON

**Nearby attractions:** Princeton University, McCarter Theater, governor's mansion, antiques hunting in Bucks County, Pa.

## PEACOCK INN
20 Bayard Lane
Princeton, New Jersey 08540
**Phone:** 609/924-1707
**Fax:** 609/924-0788
**Proprietor:** Candy Lindsay

The gambrel-roofed building that houses the Peacock Inn was built in 1775 on the campus of Princeton University. It was moved to its present location, one block from the campus, 100 years later. Originally the home of John Deare, the Peacock Inn has been a Princeton landmark and gathering place since opening its doors to the public in 1912 and has hosted many illustrious guests, such as Bertrand Russell, Albert Einstein, and F. Scott Fitzgerald. Guest rooms are decorated with individually chosen antiques in a number of styles, including French, Early American, and English. Each room is decorated with a cheerful mixture of prints, plants, and authentic country crafts. Guests are served a continental-plus breakfast and the inn's elegant restaurant, Le Plumet Royal, serves fresh, seasonal French cuisine for dinner and lunch.

**Open:** year round **Accommodations:** 15 guest rooms **Meals:** continental-plus breakfast included; restaurant on premises; restaurants nearby **Rates:** $115 to $150; 10% discount to National Trust members and National Trust Visa cardholders **Payment:** AmEx, Visa, MC, personal and traveler's checks **Restrictions:** smoking limited

# SPRING LAKE

**Nearby attractions:** ocean beach, tennis, golfing, antiques hunting, state park, horseback riding, surf and deep-sea fishing, thoroughbred racing

## NORMANDY INN

21 Tuttle Avenue
Spring Lake, New Jersey 07762
**Phone:** 732/449-7172 or 800/449-1888
**Fax:** 732/449-1070
**Website:** www.normandyinn.com
**E-mail:** normandy@bellatlantic.net
**Proprietors:** Mike and Jeri Robertson

This National Register house stands as a prime example of a Victorian seaside inn. Built as a summer home in 1888, the Normandy is an Italianate villa (square towers and tall, round-arched windows) with Queen Anne modifications (wraparound porches and lacey brackets). Formerly known as the Audenried House, the original structure was moved to its present location—only five houses from the beach—in the early 1900s and became known as one of the Johnson cottages. The Johnson family began the Normandy's heritage of innkeeping nearly 90 years ago. The prized furnishings of all common rooms and each guest room are original American Victorian antiques that are accented with reproduction wallpaper. A full country breakfast is served, after which guests often explore this picturesque oceanfront village on bicycles provided by the inn.

**Open:** year round **Accommodations:** 17 guest rooms with private baths; 2 are suites **Meals:** full breakfast included; complimentary refreshments; restaurants nearby **Rates:** $98 to $199 **Payment:** AmEx, Visa, MC, DC, Discover, personal and traveler's checks **Restrictions:** smoking limited; no pets **On-site activities:** bicycles, beach chairs, and towels provided free of charge

# NEW MEXICO

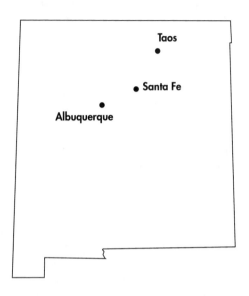

## ALBUQUERQUE

**Nearby attractions:** Indian Pueblo Cultural Center, Albuquerque Museum, Museum of Natural History, Petroglyph Park, Coronado Monument, Old Town, Sandia Peak Tramway, aquarium, botanical gardens, hiking, skiing, bicycling, hot air balloons, horseback riding

### HACIENDA ANTIGUA BED AND BREAKFAST

6708 Tierra Drive, N.W.
Albuquerque, New Mexico 87107
**Phone:** 505/345-5399 or 800/201-2986
**Fax:** 505/345-3855
**Website:** www.haciendantigua.com/bnb/
**E-mail:** antigua@swcp.com
**Proprietors:** Ann Dunlap and Melinda Moffitt

The hacienda has been standing since the 1790s, in part because of the 30-inch thick terrones (mud brick) walls. Don Pablo Yrisarri, an emissary of King Charles III of Spain, ensured his family's protection with these bricks and the massive carved gates that guard the inner courtyard of this classic Southwestern hacienda. At one time, there were as many as 28 rooms that housed a variety of activities (tool making, blacksmithing, grain storage, and even a chapel) in addition to the family's living quarters. In the late nineteenth century, the hacienda served as a stagecoach stop between Mexico City and Santa Fe. Today, it continues to offer comfort and shelter to travelers with five traditionally styled guest rooms, each offering a special attraction such as a kiva fireplace, claw-foot tub, or private patio. Mobil gives Hacienda Antigua three stars and it has been featured on The Learning Channel program "Great Country Inns."

**Open:** year round **Accommodations:** 5 guest rooms with private baths; 1 is a suite **Meals:** full breakfast included; restaurants nearby **Rates:** $95 to $150; 10% discount to National Trust members and National Trust Visa cardholders **Payment:** AmEx, Visa, MC, Discover, personal and traveler's checks **Restrictions:** no smoking; no pets **On-site activities:** swimming pool in summer, outdoor spa all year

---

## SANTA FE

**Nearby attractions:** Indian pueblos, museums, art galleries, shopping, mountains, desert, skiing

### DON GASPAR COMPOUND

623 Don Gaspar
Santa Fe, New Mexico 87501
**Phone:** 505/986-8664 or
888/986-8664
**Fax:** 505/986-0696
**Website:** www.dongaspar.com
**E-mail:** dongaspar@sfol.com
**Proprietors:** David and Shirley
Alford

Built in 1912 in Santa Fe's Don Gaspar historic district, the compound is a classic example of Mission and Territorial architecture. Six private suites enjoy a secluded adobe-walled garden courtyard with fountain and heirloom flowers. The Main House, in the Mission style, is rented to one party at a time. It has two wood-burning fireplaces, three bedrooms, two baths, and a fully equipped kitchen. There are two casitas overlooking the fountain, both with saltillo-tiled floors, gas-burning fireplaces, and fully equipped kitchens. One has a whirlpool tub for two. The Southwest Suite has a wood-burning fireplace and Mexican-tiled bath. The Aspen Suite with king-size bed has a kitchenette. The western-style Colorado Room opens onto a patio through French doors. The compound is a short walk from Santa Fe's famed Plaza.

**Open:** year round **Accommodations:** 6 guest rooms with private baths; 5 are suites **Meals:** continental-plus breakfast included; restaurants nearby **Rates:** $95 to $245 May through October; $85 to $195 November through April; 10% discount to National Trust members and National Trust Visa cardholders during low season only **Payment:** AmEx, Visa, MC, personal and traveler's checks **Restrictions:** no smoking; no pets **On-site activities:** gardens with fountain

## LA TIENDA INN
445-447 West San Francisco Street
Santa Fe, New Mexico 87501
**Phone:** 505/989-8259 or 800/889-7611
**Website:** www.latiendabb.com
**Proprietors:** Leighton and Barbara Watson

Sixty years ago the common room of the inn was a small, neighborhood market (*tienda*). It had been built of adobe by Adolfo Montoya next door to his classic Territorial-style house (circa 1900) to serve a growing community. Today, the buildings are combined to form La Tienda Inn. Seven guest rooms have been designed and furnished with careful attention to comfort. Antiques, artifacts, and hand-built furniture showcase Santa Fe's Spanish and Native American history. The three rooms in the Territorial House feature original moldings and details. Four rooms are nestled in the Old Store adobe wing, three with fireplaces. Each room, with private entrance and bath, overlooks the garden or tree-canopied courtyard. Just four blocks from the Plaza, the inn is quiet and secluded, yet convenient. Its year-long renovation earned an award from the City of Santa Fe.

**Open:** year round **Accommodations:** 7 guest rooms with private baths; 2 rooms can be combined as a suite **Meals:** continental-plus breakfast included; complimentary refreshments; restaurants nearby **Wheelchair access:** yes **Rates:** $100 to $160; 10% discount to National Trust members and National Trust Visa cardholders **Payment:** Visa, MC, personal and traveler's checks **Restrictions:** no smoking; no pets

## PRESTON HOUSE
106 Faithway Street
Santa Fe, New Mexico 87501
**Phone:** 505/982-3465 or 888/877-7622
**Fax:** 505/988-2397
**Website:** www.prestonhouse.com/santafe
**E-mail:** alexinn@aol.com
**Proprietor:** Carolyn Lee

In a land of adobe, the Preston House is distinctive as the only Queen Anne structure in the city of Santa Fe (in fact, there is only one other Queen Anne building in the state!). Built in 1886 by George Cuyler Preston, an easterner who made a name in the territory as a land speculator, the house is made with fired bricks under a coat of stucco. Shingles on the second and third floors and roof are of pressed metal. The house has been operated as a bed and breakfast since 1981, when nationally known artist Signe Bergman purchased it and, using her artistic and design talents, successfully combined the comforts of the present with the elegance of the turn of the century. Guest rooms are dressed in period furnishings; most have private baths and some have fireplaces. Listed in the National Register of Historic Places, Preston House has been the subject of many articles in newspapers across the country and has been featured on The Discovery Channel program "Great Country Inns."

**Open:** year round **Accommodations:** 8 guest rooms (6 have private baths); 1 is a suite **Meals:** continental-plus breakfast included; complimentary refreshments; restaurants nearby **Wheelchair access:** limited **Rates:** $70 to $160; 10% discount to National Trust members and National Trust Visa cardholders **Payment:** Visa, MC, personal and traveler's checks **Restrictions:** children over 10 welcome; no smoking **On-site activities:** gardens and patio

## PUEBLO BONITO BED AND BREAKFAST INN

138 West Manhattan
Santa Fe, New Mexico 87501
**Phone:** 505/984-8001 or 800/461-4599
**Fax:** 505/984-3155
**E-mail:** pueblo@roadrunner.com
**Proprietors:** Herb and Amy Behm

Once a circuit judge's estate with stables and servants quarters, Pueblo Bonito still boasts quiet courtyards, narrow brick paths, wrought-iron gates, adobe archways to the street, and a shady garden. Built in 1872, the estate, with its foot-thick adobe walls was later a boarding house for artists. Three signed paintings still remain in the upstairs hallway, compliments of a resident who could not pay his rent. Today, 18 cozy guest rooms in the main house and casitas around the grounds are furnished with works from local artists and artisans and feature handcrafted wooden furniture, antiques, viga ceilings, nichos, kiva fireplaces, and wooden, flagstone, or brick floors. Each room has a private entrance and bath, cable television, and telephone. Reinforcing the area's proud multicultural heritage, each casita is named after an area Indian tribe. A create-your-own breakfast buffet is offered each morning and visitors can return home after a full day of sightseeing to tea, wine, or the house specialty, a Pueblo Margarita.

**Open:** year round **Accommodations:** 18 guest rooms with private baths; 7 are suites **Meals:** continental-plus breakfast included; complimentary refreshments; restaurants nearby **Wheelchair access:** yes **Rates:** $80 to $150 **Payment:** Visa, MC, personal and traveler's checks **Restrictions:** no smoking; no pets **On-site activities:** hot tub, sun deck, outside dining, reading

---

# TAOS

**Nearby attractions:** Rio Grande, Sangre de Cristo mountains, downhill and cross-country skiing, rafting, fishing, horseback riding, world-famous art galleries and studios

## LA POSADA DE TAOS

309 Juanita
P.O. Box 1118
Taos, New Mexico 87571
**Phone:** 505/758-8164 or 800/645-4803
**Fax:** 505/751-3294
**Website:** www.taosnet.com/laposada/
**E-mail:** laposada@newmex.com
**Proprietor:** Bill Swan and Nancy Brooks-Swan

Bert Phillips, a founder of the Taos art colony, built this adobe house in 1907 in the Pueblo Revival style with flat roofs, parapets, canales or rainwater gutters for drainage, and thick walls for insulation. His family lived here for 50 years and then, in 1982, it was turned into the town's first bed and breakfast. La Posada is surrounded by adobe walls and "coyote" fencing made of small, whole aspen tree trunks. Guest rooms are individually decorated with country antiques, handmade quilts, local arts, and hand-crafted furniture. An adobe kiva fireplace, private entrance, whirlpool tub, or private patio distinguishes each guest accommodation. Generous breakfasts in the sun-filled dining room are famous at the inn, which has been featured in *Country Inns, Bed and Breakfast,* and *Bon Appétit.*

**Open:** year round **Accommodations:** 6 guest rooms with private baths **Meals:** full breakfast included; restaurants nearby **Wheelchair access:** limited **Rates:** $85 to $135; 10% discount to National Trust members and National Trust Visa cardholders excluding holidays **Payment:** personal and traveler's checks **Restrictions:** children over 12 welcome; no smoking; no pets

# NEW YORK

## BERLIN

**Nearby attractions:** Tanglewood, Shaker Village, Williamstown, museums, National Trust's Chesterwood, state parks, swimming, hiking, cross-country and downhill skiing

**SEDGWICK INN**
Route 22
Berlin, New York 12022
**Phone:** 518/658-2334 or 800/845-4886
**Fax:** 518/658-3998
**Website:** www.regionnet/colberk/sedgwickinn.html
**E-mail:** sedgwickin@aol.com
**Proprietor:** Edith Evans

Located on the New York side of the Berkshire Mountains, the Sedgwick Inn sits on 12 acres in the scenic Taconic Valley. The original deed to the property, dated 1791 and signed by Stephen Van Rensselaer, hangs in library of the house, which was built in that same year. The elegant Federal-style house is filled with antiques and has a large parlor with fireplace and a well-stocked library. In summer, the wraparound porch with wicker furniture provides a cool place to relax. For many years the building was known as the Ranch Tavern. Now, as the Sedgwick Inn, it offers distinctive period accommodations and a choice of dining areas—the original tavern room or the airy dining porches overlooking the garden. The inn's restaurant has an outstanding reputation in the area. Behind the mansion, a converted carriage house has been turned into a gift shop, and an unusual one-room, tin-lined building dating from 1834 now serves as an antiques shop.

**Open:** year round **Accommodations:** 5 guest rooms with private baths; 1 is a suite **Meals:** full breakfast included; restaurant on premises **Wheelchair access:** restaurant **Rates:** $65 to $145 (seasonal); 10% discount offered to National Trust members and

National Trust Visa cardholders **Payment:** AmEx, Visa, MC, DC, Discover, personal and traveler's checks **Restrictions:** children over 12 welcome; smoking limited; no pets (a motel annex accepts children of all ages and pets) **On-site activities:** gift and antiques shops

## BUSHNELL BASIN

**Nearby attractions:** Finger Lakes, Strong Museum, George Eastman House, International Museum of Photography, Letchworth Park, Niagara Falls

### OLIVER LOUD'S INN
Mailing address:
1474 Marsh Road
Pittsford, New York 14534
**Phone:** 716/248-5200 or 716/248-5000—restaurant only
**Fax:** 716/248-9970
**Website:** www.frontiernet.net/~rchi
**Proprietor:** Vivienne Tellier
**Location:** 12 miles southeast of Rochester in Bushnell Basin; 4 miles from New York State Thruway exit 45

Oliver Loud built this simple Federal-style tavern around 1812 in the hamlet of Egypt on a busy stagecoach route to Syracuse. In 1825 the opening of the Erie

Canal a few miles away cost the tavern much of its trade. By the 1980s the building was abandoned and slated for demolition. Fortunately, it was rescued by Vivienne Tellier. Moved in 1985 to its present location on the canal, it was reopened as an inn after a painstaking restoration in which wood moldings and wallpapers were reproduced from remnants. Today, high-quality reproduction furniture and artifacts grace the building's interior. Faux-grained doors follow Loud's "recipe for making any wood look like mahogany," spelled out in his almanac. Guest rooms are elegantly appointed in period furnishings, yet contain modern amenities. The innkeeper speaks French and Spanish.

**Open:** year round **Accommodations:** 8 guest rooms with private baths **Meals:** continental breakfast included; complimentary refreshments; restaurant on premises **Wheelchair access:** yes **Rates:** $135 to $155; corporate rates available; 10% discount offered to National Trust members and National Trust Visa cardholders **Payment:** AmEx, Visa, MC, DC, CB, personal and traveler's checks **Restrictions:** children over 12 welcome; smoking limited; no pets (kennels nearby) **On-site activities:** Erie Canal towpath, walking, jogging, cross-country skiing, croquet, restaurant

## CANANDAIGUA

**Nearby attractions:** Finger Lakes wineries, Bristol Mountain ski resort, Sonnenberg Gardens and Mansion, Granger Homestead and Carriage Museum, Finger Lakes Performing Arts Center, Cumming Nature Center, Canandaigua Lake, boating, fishing, swimming, golfing, hiking, tennis, downhill and cross-country skiing

### ACORN INN
4508 Route 64 South, Bristol Center
Canandaigua, New York 14424
**Phone:** 716/229-2834
**Fax:** 716/229-5064
**Website:** www.acorninnbb.com
**Proprietors:** Joan and Louis Clark
**Location:** 8 miles west of Canandaigua, 30 miles south of Rochester

This brown-shingled Federal stagecoach inn was built by Ephraim Wilder in 1795. Today it is a gracious bed and breakfast. The large, book-lined gathering room with Rumford fireplace and adjacent dining room are decorated in Williamsburg colors and furnished with early nineteenth-century English and American antiques and reproductions. The inn has four large, air-conditioned, soundproofed guest rooms, each with a draped canopy bed, comfortable sitting area, excellent reading lamps, and large, private bath. The Hotchkiss Room on the first floor has a private terrace, fireplace, and whirlpool bath. The inn's former ballroom (with spring dance floor) is now the Bristol Room and has a fireplace and window seat large enough for two. Beds are turned down nightly and chocolates are placed on each room's refreshment table. A guest closet contains complimentary beverages, snacks, ice, and wine buckets. The gardens have brick walks, two frog ponds, and a whirlpool spa on brick terrace. Acorn Inn is rated by AAA with four diamonds.

**Open:** year round **Accommodations:** 4 guest rooms with private baths **Meals:** full breakfast included; complimentary refreshments **Rates:** $105 to $185; 10% discount to National Trust members and National Trust Visa cardholders; 50% discount on second night, Monday through Thursday, November through April with continental breakfast, subject to availability **Payment:** AmEx, Visa, MC, Discover, personal and traveler's checks **Restrictions:** children over 12 welcome; no smoking; no pets **On-site activities:** extensive libraries, gardens, whirlpool spa

## CANDOR

**Nearby attractions:** Cornell University, Ithaca College, Watkins Glen, wineries, state parks, Mark Twain country, Tioga Train Ride

### EDGE OF THYME
6 Main Street
P.O. Box 48
Candor, New York 13743
**Phone:** 607/659-5155 or 800/722-7365 (outside New York state)
**Fax:** 607/659-5155
**Website:** www.clarityconnect.com/webpages2/edgeofthyme
**Proprietors:** Frank and Eva Mae Musgrave

At the turn of the century, Rosa Murphy, the private secretary of John D. Rockefeller, met Dr. Amos Canfield in New York City. They married and decided to spend their summers in Candor, New York. Their Georgian home

was built in the center of the village, and Rosa's elegant style of entertaining became widely known. The well-maintained formal home retains its marble fireplaces, parquet floors, porch with leaded-glass windows, sweeping stairway, gardens, pergola, and gracious atmosphere. The decor is in keeping with the Canfield's era, as are the recipes used for the full breakfasts. The Edge of Thyme is located in the center of the Finger Lakes region, a short drive to Cornell University and Ithaca College.

**Open:** year round **Accommodations:** 4 guest rooms (2 have private baths); 1 is a suite **Meals:** full breakfast included; complimentary refreshments; high tea by appointment; restaurants nearby **Rates:** $75 to $125; 10% discount offered to National Trust members **Payment:** AmEx, Visa, MC, personal and traveler's checks **Restrictions:** no smoking; no pets (kennels nearby) **On-site activities:** parlor games, croquet, gift shop

# CHESTERTOWN

**Nearby attractions:** Glen Falls, Chapman Historical Museum, Forts Ticonderoga and William Henry, Adirondack Museum, Lakes Champlain and George, Gore Mountain, skiing, mountain biking, snowmobiling, golfing, tennis, hiking, outlet shopping, antiques hunting

### FRIENDS LAKE INN
963 Friends Lake Road
Chestertown, New York 12817
**Phone:** 518/494-4751
**Fax:** 518/494-4616
**Website:** www.friendslake.com
**E-mail:** friends@netheaven.com
**Proprietor:** Sharon Taylor

Friends Lake Inn had its humble origins in the southern Adirondack tanning industry. Known as Murphy's Friends Lake Inn, it was built in 1862 as a boarding house for men working in the local tanneries. (The bark of the region's prevalent hemlock tree was a main component in the hide tanning process.) During Prohibition, the inn became one of a popular Adirondack summer retreat. But business slackened for the next several decades and the inn closed in 1969, sitting vacant until the mid-1980s when it was rescued by the innkeepers. A massive renovation project restored the dining room's painted tin ceiling, maple floor, and wood-burning fireplaces. Private baths were built for guest rooms and newer accommodations were added. Today's inn offers 16 charming guest rooms decorated with turn-of-the-century style in mind. The dining room serves imaginative New-American cuisine and its wine collection received *Wine*

*Spectator's* 1997 Grand Award. An on-site Nordic ski center offers 32 kilometers of groomed trails.

**Open:** year round **Accommodations:** 16 guest rooms with private baths; 10 are suites **Meals:** full breakfast included; restaurant and bar/lounge on premises; restaurants nearby **Rates:** $135 to $285; 10% discount to National Trust members and National Trust Visa cardholders midweek only, excluding holidays; MAP rates available **Payment:** AmEx, Visa, MC, personal and traveler's checks **Restrictions:** not suitable for children; smoking limited; no pets (resident pets) **On-site activities:** cross-country skiing, outdoor hot tub, hiking, Friends Lake across street with swimming and canoeing

---

## CLARENCE

**Nearby attractions:** Niagara Falls, Amherst Old Colony Museum, Lancaster Opera House, Buffalo, antiques hunting, Town Park, tennis, golfing, swimming, skiing, Fort Niagara, Genesee County Village, winery tours

### ASA RANSOM HOUSE
10529 Main Street (Route 5)
Clarence, New York 14031
**Phone:** 716/759-2315 or 800/844-1735
**Fax:** 716/759-2791
**Website:** www.asaransom.com
**Proprietors:** Robert Lenz, Judy Lenz
**Location:** 16 miles northeast of Buffalo

In 1799 the Holland Land Company offered a lot to anyone who would build and operate a tavern on it. Asa Ransom was first to accept this offer, building a combination tavern and log cabin home. He also built a sawmill (1801) and a gristmill (1803), the ruins of which are at the rear of the property. Another building, incorporating the original tavern, was constructed in 1853. Today, it offers guest accommodations plus a library, gift shop, and tap room. Guest rooms are furnished with antiques and period reproductions. Some rooms have fireplaces, some have canopied beds, all have private baths. Guests are invited to work puzzles, play board games, read, or listen to old radio program tapes in the antiques-appointed library. The inn offers two fine restaurants featuring fresh New York farmland fare.

**Open:** February 1 to December 31 **Accommodations:** 9 guest rooms with private baths; 2 are suites **Meals:** full breakfast included; complimentary refreshments; restaurants on premises **Wheelchair access:** yes **Rates:** $95 to $145; 10% discount to National Trust members and National Trust Visa cardholders Monday through Thursday **Payment:** Visa, MC, Discover, personal and traveler's checks **Restrictions:** no smoking; no pets **On-site activities:** library, chess, board games, more than 200 old-time radio program tapes, gift shop

## COOPERSTOWN

**Nearby attractions:** National Baseball Hall of Fame, Farmers' Museum/ Fenimore House, Glimmerglass Opera, art galleries, Lake Otsego, Glimmerglass State Park, golfing, boating, fishing, swimming, hiking, bicycling, antiques hunting, museums

### ÄNGELHOLM BED AND BREAKFAST

14 Elm Street
Cooperstown, New York 13326
**Phone:** 607/547-2483
**Fax:** 607/547-2309
**E-mail:** angelholm@telnet.net
**Proprietors:** Fred and Janet
Reynolds

Ängelholm is a Federal-style home
built in 1805 on historic Phinney's Farm, now in the heart of Cooperstown. Phinney's Farm was the site of the first baseball game, invented by Abner Doubleday. Today, Ängelholm's backyard and Doubleday Field have common boundaries. Charming air-conditioned guest rooms are decorated individually: the Doubleday room with white iron bed has a view of historic Doubleday Field and Stadium; the Elihu Phinney and Roby Mae rooms each boast original board-and-batten walls; the Glimmerglass room is early American in style; Ann's Cabbage Rose room is Victorian. A living room and library are offered to guests, along with the veranda overlooking the formal flower gardens. Guests are provided with off-street parking.

**Open:** year round **Accommodations:** 5 guest rooms with private baths **Meals:** full breakfast included; complimentary refreshments; restaurants nearby **Rates:** $95 to $110 (seasonal) **Payment:** Visa, MC, personal check **Restrictions:** children over 6 welcome; no smoking; no pets

### COOPER INN

Chestnut Street
P.O. Box 311
Cooperstown, New York 13326
**Phone:** 607/547-2567 or 800/348-6222
**Fax:** 607/547-1271
**Website:** www.cooperinn.com
**Proprietor:** Steven Walker

The Cooper Inn is a classic Federal brick structure, built in 1812 as the private residence of publisher Henry Phinney, whose father started the first newspaper west of the Hudson River in New York state, the *Cooperstown-Otsego Herald*. The local landmark house at the corner of Main and Chestnut in the Village of Cooperstown was originally known as Willowbrook for the willow-lined stream running through its property. The inn's guest rooms and suites are traditionally styled and offer private bath, telephone, cable television, and air conditioning. The Cooper Inn is affiliated with the Otesaga Resort Hotel in Cooperstown; all inn guests are invited to use the facilities of the historic resort, including the Leatherstocking Golf Course and the dining room for a complimentary continental breakfast.

**Open:** year round **Accommodations:** 15 guest rooms with private baths; 5 are suites **Meals:** continental breakfast included; affiliation with the Otesaga Hotel permits meal specials; restaurants nearby **Rates:** $150 to $230 **Payment:** AmEx, Visa, MC, personal and traveler's checks **Restrictions:** no smoking; no pets **On-site activities:** library, reading rooms, games, television, grounds with stream and willows

## INN AT COOPERSTOWN

16 Chestnut Street–
NT
Cooperstown,
New York 13326
**Phone:**
607/547-5756
**Fax:** 607/547-8779
**Website:**
cooperstown.net/
theinn
**E-mail:**
theinn@telenet.net
**Proprietor:** Michael
Jerome

The Inn at Cooperstown, built in 1874 as an annex to the Hotel Fenimore, was designed by Henry J. Hardenbergh, architect of the Dakota Apartments and the Plaza Hotel in New York City. Originally known as the Fenimore Cottages, the inn is an excellent example of Second Empire style. The impressive three-story structure has a sweeping veranda, bracketed cornices, and large dormered windows gracing the mansard roof. The innkeeper's restoration of the building earned him the New York State Certificate of Achievement for Historic Preservation in 1986 and the tourism award from the Preservation League of New York in 1992. The 18 guest rooms are comfortably furnished with period reproductions. The sitting rooms, furnished with antiques, are inviting places to watch television or enjoy a book by a warming fire. Or guests may choose to rock idly on the porch.

**Open:** year round **Accommodations:** 18 guest rooms with private baths **Meals:** continental breakfast included; restaurants nearby **Wheelchair access:** 1 room **Rates:** $85 to $125 **Payment:** AmEx, Visa, MC, Discover, DC, personal and traveler's checks **Restrictions:** smoking limited; no pets **On-site activities:** reading, porch rocking, television

# DEERFIELD

**Nearby attractions:** Utica Club Brewery, Fort Stanwix Museum, Children's Museum, Stanley Performing Arts Center, Utica Zoo, minor league baseball, Erie Canal and locks, downhill and cross-country skiing, golfing, fishing, antiques hunting, Oneida Indian Nation Casino

### PRATT SMITH HOUSE BED AND BREAKFAST
10497 Cosby Manor Road
Deerfield, New York 13502
**Phone:** 315/732-8483
**Proprietors:** Anne and Alan Frederick

In 1815, Pratt Smith, a son of New England farmers, bought land in what is now the town of Deerfield and built a house of brick and wood, using the abundant local maple trees. This historic Federal house still stands and had been tastefully updated for comfort and convenience while retaining its original character, from the wide-plank maple floors to the perfectly preserved curved bannister on the center hall staircase. Two guest rooms are available, each with private bath and large windows overlooking the Mohawk Valley and the city of Utica. A full breakfast is served daily. Guests may want to enjoy the large shaded lawn, surrounded by cool fragrant evergreens, or take a stroll down the bridle path through part of the 22 wooded acres that remain from the original farmland. In winter, explore it on cross-country skis. Next door to the house is the Eagles' Club, a nine-hole public golf course.

**Open:** year round **Accommodations:** 2 guest rooms with private baths **Meals:** full breakfast included; fresh fruit in rooms; restaurants nearby **Rates:** $55 to $60; 10% discount to National Trust members and National Trust Visa cardholders **Payment:** personal and traveler's checks **Restrictions:** children over 12 welcome, call about younger children; no smoking; no pets **On-site activities:** cross-country skiing, walking trail

## DOVER PLAINS

**Nearby attractions:** Hyde Park, Roosevelt, and Vanderbilt estates; Culinary Institute of America; Hudson riverboat tours; Mary Flagler Cary Arboretum; wineries; Tanglewood; antiques hunting; canoeing; horseback riding; golfing

## OLD DROVERS INN

Old Route 22
Dover Plains, New York 12522
**Phone:** 914/832-9311
**Fax:** 914/832-9311
**Website:** www.olddroversinn.com
**E-mail:** old_Drovers_Inn@juno.com
**Proprietors:** Alice Pitcher and Kemper Peacock

Nestled in the Berkshire foothills, the Old Drovers Inn is a traditional colonial inn that has survived almost 250 years of continuous service. Guests enter the original Tap Room, with its crackling fire, heavy wood-smoked beams, and stone walls, that greeted cattle drovers in 1750. These New England "cowboys" purchased herds of cattle and swine and drove them down the post roads to New York City markets. The drovers disappeared in the mid-nineteenth century, but their stopping place remains. Today's guests may choose from four antique-furnished bedrooms: the largest has a unique barrel-shaped ceiling; three have working fireplaces; all have private baths. The inn is famed for its blend of traditional and innovative fare at breakfast, lunch, and dinner. As only the third owners of Old Drovers, the proprietors continue the inn's heritage of hospitality and comfort.

**Open:** year round **Accommodations:** 4 guest rooms with private baths **Meals:** continental breakfast included weekdays; full breakfast and dinner included weekends; restaurant on premises **Wheelchair access:** dining room and bathrooms **Rates:** $150 to $395; 10% discount offered to National Trust members and National Trust Visa cardholders on Mondays and Thursdays **Payment:** Visa, MC, CB, DC, personal and traveler's checks **Restrictions:** pets allowed with a $20 per night charge **On-site activities:** biking, croquet, badminton, cross-country skiing

---

## EAST AURORA

**Nearby attractions:** Frank Lloyd Wright's Darwin D. Martin house, Kleinhan's Music Hall, Chautauqua Institution

### ROYCROFT INN
40 South Grove Street
East Aurora, New York 14052
**Phone:** 716/652-5552
**Fax:** 716/655-5345
**Website:** www.someplacesdifferent.com
**E-mail:** info@roycroftinn.com
**Proprietor:** Martha Augat
**Location:** 15 miles southeast of Buffalo

In 1895, Elbert Hubbard founded the Roycroft community to celebrate and promote hand-crafted, guildlike workmanship based on the Arts and Crafts movement begun in England. His community turned into a 14-building campus dedicated to printing and publishing, metalworking, mission-style furniture making, and the manufacturing of leather goods and other Roycroft-labeled objects. At the social center of the campus was the Roycroft Inn. After suffering financial failure, the campus closed in 1983. Saved by the Wendt Foundation of Buffalo and a grass-roots organization of preservationists, the Roycroft Inn is fully restored. Because of its National Landmark status, the inn retains historically accurate elements, including wooden blinds, wicker and Stickley furniture, wooden doors carved with individual room names, Roycroft lamps and wall sconces, and wallpaper in the artistic style of the influential William Morris. Each suite comprises a sitting room, dressing/reading room, bathroom, and bedroom. The inn also features three dining rooms, a lounge with fireplace, and courtyard garden.

**Open:** year round **Accommodations:** 22 guest suites with private baths **Meals:** continental breakfast included; restaurant on premises; restaurants nearby **Wheelchair access:** yes **Rates:** $120 to $250; 10% discount to National Trust members and National Trust Visa cardholders **Payment:** AmEx, Visa, MC, Discover, DC, personal and traveler's checks **Restrictions:** no smoking; no pets

# GARRISON

**Nearby attractions:** West Point, Boscobel restoration, Hudson River, Franklin Roosevelt home, Vanderbilt mansion

## BIRD AND BOTTLE INN

Old Albany Post Road
Route 9
Garrison, New York 10524
**Phone:** 914/424-3000 or 914/424-4035
**Fax:** 914/424-3283
**Website:** www.birdbottle.com
**E-mail:** birdbottle@aol.com
**Proprietor:** Ira Boyar and Jane Goldberg
**Location:** 8 miles north of Peekskill, 8 miles south of Fishkill and Route 84

Since opening in 1761, Warren's Tavern—now the Bird and Bottle Inn—has been closely identified with the history of the Hudson River Valley. It was a stagecoach stop on the New York–Albany Post Road (a National Historic Landmark) and quartered defense troops during the Revolutionary War. The Bird and Bottle Inn is a three-story, wood-frame structure, decorated in authentic American colonial style. Low-timbered ceilings and long, narrow hallways look today as they did when the building was constructed more than 200 years ago. Well known since 1940 for its extraordinary cuisine, the inn recently reopened for overnight accommodations. Wood-burning fireplaces warm the guest rooms, each of which is meticulously furnished with period furniture and a four-poster or canopied bed.

**Open:** year round **Accommodations:** 4 guest rooms with private baths **Meals:** full breakfast and dinner included; restaurant on premises **Wheelchair access:** guest rooms, bathrooms, dining facilities **Rates:** $210 to $240; 10% discount offered to National Trust members and National Trust Visa cardholders **Payment:** AmEx, Visa, MC, DC **Restrictions:** no pets

# GENEVA

**Nearby attractions:** Finger Lakes wineries, Watkins Glen, Corning Glass Center, Sonnenberg Gardens

## BELHURST CASTLE
Route 14 South
Geneva, New York 14456
**Phone:** 315/781-0201
**Proprietor:** Duane R. Reeder

Belhurst Castle was constructed over a four-year period beginning in 1885. The turreted, red medina-stone structure was built mostly of materials imported from Europe in a style known as Richardsonian Romanesque, which emphasizes round-topped arches over windows. In the century since the structure was completed, Belhurst Castle has been at various times a home, speakeasy, casino, and restaurant. Today the 100-year-old mansion contains 11 romantic bedrooms; two guest houses offering unique accommodations are also located on the grounds. The castle features atmospheric dining in the library, parlor, center room, conservatory, or on the veranda overlooking Seneca Lake. Belhurst Castle is rated with four diamonds by AAA.

**Open:** year round **Accommodations:** 13 guest rooms with private baths; 2 are suites **Meals:** restaurant on premises **Rates:** $75 to $315 **Payment:** Visa, MC **Restrictions:** no pets **On-site activities:** fishing and sailing 100 yards from castle

---

# HAGUE

**Nearby attractions:** Lake George, boating, town beach, swimming, lake cruises, water skiing, fly fishing, golfing, tennis, Saratoga Springs, horse racing, Saratoga Performing Arts Center

## LOCUST INN
Route 9N
P.O. Box 569
Hague, New York 12836
**Phone:** 518/543-6035
**Website:** www.locustinn.com
**Proprietor:** James Coates

Built in 1865, this frame Victorian house with tall windows and decorative front porch was rennovated in 1992, opening as a bed and breakfast. Furnished in period antiques from the early 1900s, the inn features an extensive collection of regional art. Five guest suites have private baths, sitting areas, and views of northern Lake George and the surrounding Adirondack Mountains. Guests are served a home-cooked country breakfast each morning. In season, Saturday nights feature a casual gathering for a barbecue or lobster bake dinner. Next door to the inn is Hague Brook, a salmon and smelt spawning ground well known as a fly-fisherman's paradise. The inn is also adjacent to the town beach and a boat ramp.

**Open:** year round **Accommodations:** 5 guest suites with private baths **Meals:** continental-plus breakfast included; restaurants nearby **Rates:** $105 to $125 **Payment:** Visa, MC, Discover, personal and traveler's checks **Restrictions:** smoking limited

---

# HAMMONDSPORT

**Nearby attractions:** historic village walking tours, Finger Lakes winery tours, Watkins Glen, Corning Glass Museum, Glenn Curtiss Museum of Aviation, Keuka Lake, boat dock and launch, swimming, fishing, bicycling, picnicking

### BLUSHING ROSÉ BED AND BREAKFAST
11 William Street
Hammondsport, New York 14840
**Phone:** 607/569-3402 or 800/982-8818
**Fax:** 607/569-2504
**Website:** blushingroseinn.com
**E-mail:** blusrose@ptd.net
**Proprietors:** Ellen and Bucky Laufersweiler

An Italianate home with Greek Revival detailing, the Blushing Rosé Bed and Breakfast was built in 1843 as the Keeler homestead. It offers quiet, romantic accommodations in the middle of the state's famed wine country at the southern end of the Finger Lakes region. There are four guest rooms, each furnished with nineteenth-century antiques, handmade quilts, and a private bath. Ruffles, lace, wall stenciling, eyelet, and rattan are just some of the details that adorn the individually decorated rooms. Breakfasts include such treats as lemon poppy-seed waffles and strawberry bread, along with cinnamon coffee and fresh seasonal fruit. Guests have access to a telephone, refrigerator, picnic baskets, and a guest parlor with television and soft music.

**Open:** May 1 to December 31 **Accommodations:** 4 guest rooms with private baths; 2 are mini-suites **Meals:** full breakfast included; complimentary refreshments; restaurants nearby **Rates:** $85 to $95 **Payment:** Visa, MC, personal and traveler's checks **Restrictions:** children over 12 welcome; no smoking; no pets **On-site activities:** flower garden with small pond, games, reading

# HIGH FALLS

**Nearby attractions:** Catskill Mountains, Hudson River cruises, winery tours, scenic drives, Mohonk Preserve, New Paltz, Woodstock, Culinary Institute of America, Delaware and Hudson Canal Museum, Delaware and Ulster Rail Ride, state parks, hiking, swimming, skiing, F.D.R.'s Hyde Park, Vanderbilt and Roosevelt estates

### CAPTAIN SCHOONMAKER'S BED AND BREAKFAST
913 Route 213
High Falls, New York 12440
**Phone:** 914/687-7946
**Fax:** 914/687-4250
**Proprietors:** Bill and Judy Klock

The inn's namesake was a Hudson Valley Revolutionary War hero who built this stone cottage in 1760 and lived here with his 13 sons before they were summoned to serve in the regiment protecting New York's then-capital, Kingston. Original fireplaces, beams, and flooring in this early Dutch Colonial home have all been preserved and restored to their original beauty. Early American country antiques add to the house's warmth and hospitality. The post-and-beam barn, once part of the working farm, has been renovated to house guests. The 1810 structure, situated along a creek and waterfall, provides private porches overlooking woodlands. Canopy beds and puffy feather beds are part of the early American decor. A six-course breakfast features home-baked breads and sweet cakes.

**Open:** year round **Accommodations:** 4 guest rooms share 2 baths **Meals:** six-course breakfast included; complimentary refreshments; restaurants nearby **Rate:** $85; 10% discount offered to National Trust members and National Trust Visa cardholders **Payment:** personal check **Restrictions:** not suitable for children under 12 on weekends; no pets **On-site activities:** trout fishing in stocked stream, library

## LOCKTENDER COTTAGE AT DEPUY CANAL RESTAURANT

Route 213
P.O. Box 96
High Falls, New York 12440
**Phone:** 914/687-7700
**Fax:** 914/687-7073
**E-mail:** johnnovi@aol.com
**Proprietor:** John N. Novi

The locktender along the stretch of the old Delaware and Hudson Canal in High Falls once lived in this charming 1860 Victorian cottage. Set neatly behind a picket fence, it offers a choice of three bedrooms, each with a private bath, air conditioning, and individually controlled heat in winter. One bedroom has a fireplace. There is also a cozy Chef's Quarters, complete with kitchenette and whirlpool tub. Across the street is the world-renowned, four-star Depuy Canal House Restaurant where Chef John Novi imaginatively combines food from around the world with fresh local produce to create menus for which he has been acclaimed "The Father of American Nouvelle Cuisine" by *Time* magazine. The restaurant is housed in a 1797 tavern. A collection of original paintings, authentic folk art, antiques, maps, and newspaper clippings adorn the many intimate dining rooms, four with their original fireplaces. Guests are invited to view the preparation of their meals from a balcony overlooking the kitchen. Lectures, music, art shows, and other happenings take place in the stone cellar Cabaret Gallery.

**Open:** year round **Accommodations:** 3 guest rooms with private baths; 1 is a suite **Meals:** continental breakfast included, served in suite; $10 voucher at Depuy Canal House Restaurant **Rates:** $85 to $110; 10% discount to National Trust members and National Trust Visa cardholders **Payment:** AmEx, Visa, MC, Discover, DC, personal check **Restrictions:** no pets

# ITHACA

**Nearby attractions:** Salmon Creek and Falls, Finger Lakes region, Cornell University, Ithaca College, wineries, state parks, Lake Cayuga, swimming, fishing, boating, picnicking, bicycling

## FEDERAL HOUSE BED AND BREAKFAST

P.O. Box 4914
Ithaca, New York 14852
**Phone:** 607/533-7362 or 800/533-7362
**Fax:** 607/533-7899
**Website:** wordpro.com/FedH/FH.htm
**E-mail:** innkeeper@clarityconnect.com
**Proprietor:** Diane Carroll

Constructed circa 1815 by Abijah Miller, the Federal House features spacious rooms furnished with antiques, original woodwork, and handcarved mantels that are reputedly the work of Brigham Young, who served as apprentice carpenter in the area. It was at the Federal House that William Seward, secretary of state under Abraham Lincoln, courted his wife Frances, Squire Miller's niece. At today's inn, four individually appointed guest rooms, each with private bath and air conditioning, offer such amenities as a gas fireplace, canopy bed, handpainted furniture, or private staircase. A formal breakfast is served in the elegant dining room where early coffee and tea is always available. Guests are invited to sit on the porch or in the gazebo surrounded by gardens and share homemade afternoon refreshments while listening to the tranquil sounds of nearby Salmon Creek Falls.

**Open:** year round **Accommodations:** 4 guest rooms with private baths; 1 is a suite **Meals:** full breakfast included; complimentary refreshments and stocked guest refrigerator; restaurants nearby **Rates:** $65 to $160; 10% discount to National Trust members and National Trust Visa cardholders **Payment:** AmEx, Visa, MC, Discover, personal and traveler's checks **Restrictions:** children over 14 welcome; no smoking; no pets **On-site activities:** gardens with gazebo and swing, bicycles

# KEENE

**Nearby attractions:** Lake Placid, Olympic Village, downhill and cross-country skiing, mountain climbing, luging, bobsledding, hiking, mountain biking, canoeing, kayaking, swimming, tennis, golfing, shopping, dining, world-class competitions in ice skating, ski jumping, canoeing, rowing

## THE BARK EATER INN

Alstead Mill Road
Keene, New York 12942
**Phone:** 518/576-2221 or 800/232-1607
**Fax:** 518/576-2071
**Website:** www.tvenet.com/barkeater
**E-mail:** barkeater@tvenet.com
**Proprietor:** Joe Pete Wilson

This old farmhouse also served as a stagecoach stopover in the early nineteenth century. Today, as the Bark Eater Inn (the name derives from the Iroquois phrase "ratirontak," a derisive term for their enemies the Algonquin, who shared the region) is a haven for those seeking simple but gracious accommodations, memorable dining, and easy access to the out-of-doors. Fireplaces grace the downstairs public rooms. Antiques adorn every room, including the seven guest rooms upstairs. The renovated Carriage House provides charming rooms with private baths. A hand-hewn log cottage in a quiet woodland setting on a hill above the inn is ideal for families or groups. The inn provides a hearty country breakfast; dinner is available. The inn has a riding stable with horses to suit riders from novice to expert. In winter guests enjoy cross-country skiing on the property's groomed trails.

**Open:** year round **Accommodations:** 15 guest rooms (9 with private baths); 2 are suites **Meals:** full breakfast included; complimentary refreshments; restaurant on premises; restaurants nearby **Rates:** $65 to $136; 10% discount to National Trust members and National Trust Visa cardholders; riding and skiing packages and MAP rates available **Payment:** AmEx, Visa, MC, Discover, personal and traveler's checks **Restrictions:** no smoking; no pets **On-site activities:** cross-country skiing on groomed trails, horseback riding with instruction, polo matches, hiking

# KINGSTON

**Nearby attractions:** Hudson River cruises, lighthouses, Urban Cultural Park, Trolley Museum of New York, Firemen's Museum, Old Dutch Church and Museum, Maritime Museum, Senate House and Museum, historic Stockade area of New York's first capital, art galleries, theaters, antiques hunting, specialty shops

## RONDOUT BED AND BREAKFAST

88 West Chester Street
Kingston, New York 12401
**Phone:** 914/331-2369
**Fax:** 914/331-9049
**Website:** www.pojonews.com/rondout
**E-mail:** calcave@ibm.net
**Proprietors:** Adele and Ralph Calcavecchio

It is said that J. Graham Rose, the wealthy industrialist who built this Colonial Revival home in 1906, had piles of dirt dumped at the building site at $1 per truckload in order to make his home the highest in Kingston. Then he had built this 4000-square-foot, 12-room house with lofty ceilings, numerous windows (some with leaded and beveled glass), and chestnut paneling. Nearly all of the house's original architectural details remain intact, including brass wall sconces, having been converted from gas to electricity. Both the living and dining rooms contain pianos, and the entire house is filled with antiques and paintings, prints, and ceramics by local artists. The glassed-in porch sports rattan and wicker furniture that belonged to Adele Calcavecchio's grandmother. Hearty breakfasts feature Belgian waffles and homemade maple syrup.

**Open:** year round **Accommodations:** 4 guest rooms (2 have private baths) **Meals:** full breakfast included; complimentary refreshments; restaurants nearby **Rates:** $65 to $100; 10% discount offered to National Trust members and National Trust Visa cardholders **Payment:** AmEx, Visa, MC, personal check **Restrictions:** no smoking; no pets **On-site activities:** croquet, boccie, bicycles, player piano, television, reading

# LAKE PLACID

**Nearby attractions:** U.S. Olympic Training Center, John Brown's grave and homestead, Adirondack Park, Lake Center for the Arts, Whiteface Mountain Ski Center, golfing, tennis, canoeing

## STAGECOACH INN
370 Old Military Road
Lake Placid, New York 12946
**Phone:** 518/523-9474
**Proprietor:** Peter Moreau

The Stagecoach Inn has been serving travelers—many in stagecoaches—since 1833. The two-story clapboard building with gabled dormers is distinguished outside by its balustraded porch and balcony and inside by its unique yellow birch staircase. Nine guest rooms are individually furnished with brass or white iron beds, handmade quilts, wicker pieces, and antiques. Memorable breakfasts may feature cheese souffles, French toast, or homemade breads. The inn was host to the CBS Sports broadcast team during the 1980 Winter Olympics and has been praised by *Gourmet* and *Vogue.*

**Open:** year round **Accommodations:** 9 guest rooms (5 have private baths); 2 are suites **Meals:** full breakfast included; restaurants nearby **Rates:** $60 to $190; 10% discount to National Trust members and National Trust Visa cardholders **Payment:** Visa, MC **Restrictions:** no pets

---

# LEW BEACH

**Nearby attractions:** Beaverkill Valley, Catskill Mountains, downhill skiing, fly-fishing museum, Wulff Fishing School, boating, horseback riding

## BEAVERKILL VALLEY INN
Beaverkill Road
Box 136
Lew Beach, New York 12753
**Phone:** 914/439-4844
**Fax:** 914/439-3884
**Website:** wwwbeaverkillvalley.com
**Proprietor:** Laurance Rockefeller

Since 1893 this inn in the Beaverkill Valley has hosted sportsmen and nature enthusiasts. First opened as the Bonnie View Inn, it was in a state of decline when purchased in 1981 by Larry Rockefeller, an environmental lawyer, who restored the white clapboard, red-shingled building and set about claiming surrounding acreage for conservation and protection. Now listed in the National Register of Historic Places, the inn contains 20 guest rooms individually outfitted with brass-and-iron beds, quilts, oak furniture, and Laura Ashley wallpapers. The inn also contains game rooms, a Victorian bar, a sundeck, and a dining room featuring seasonal foods and home-baked breads and pastries. An old barn has been renovated to include a 60-foot heated indoor swimming pool and a self-serve ice cream parlor. Sixty acres of pristine wilderness surround the inn.

**Open:** year round **Accommodations:** 20 guest rooms (15 have private baths) **Meals:** breakfast, lunch, and dinner included on Full American Plan (FAP) **Rates:** $160 to $195 single FAP; $260 to $330 double FAP **Payment:** AmEx, Visa, MC, personal and traveler's checks **Restrictions:** no smoking; no pets **On-site activities:** fly fishing, cross-country skiing, indoor swimming pool, tennis, ice cream parlor

---

## RHINEBECK

**Nearby attractions:** FDR library and home, Old Rhinebeck Aerodrome, state historic sites of Clermont and Olana, mansion tours, Culinary Institute of America, golfing, tennis, skiing

### DELAMATER HOUSE
44 Montgomery Street (Route 9)
Rhinebeck, New York 12572
**Phone:** 914/876-7080
**Fax:** 914/876-7062
**Website:**
www.bekmanarm@aol.com
**Proprietors:** Doris Masten
and Chuck LaForge

Delamater House is one of the architectural jewels of the Hudson Valley. Built in 1844, it was designed by noted architect Alexander Jackson Davis for Henry Delamater, founder of the First National Bank of Rhinebeck. Davis designed many state capitol buildings as well as mansions, the most famous of which is the National Trust's Lyndhurst in Tarrytown. Delamater House has been excellently preserved (it is listed in the National Register of Historic Places) and is one of few early examples of an American Gothic residence still in existence. It is elaborately decorated with fancy vergeboards, pointed-arched windows, and diamond-paned sashes. Accommodations at Delamater House are reminiscent of those at a country manor. A living room, enclosed porch, and pantry also are available for guests.

**Open:** year round **Accommodations:** 7 guest rooms with private baths **Meals:** continental breakfast included; complimentary refreshments; restaurants nearby **Wheelchair access:** limited **Rates:** $85 to $99; 10% discount offered to National Trust members and National Trust Visa cardholders **Payment:** AmEx, Visa, MC, personal and traveler's checks **Restrictions:** children over 12 welcome; no pets **On-site activities:** spacious lawns for strolling, lounging, and croquet

# SARATOGA SPRINGS

**Nearby attractions:** National Museum of Dance, National Museum of Racing, Saratoga Raceway, Saratoga Performing Arts Center, New York City Ballet in July, New York City Opera in June, state park, Lake George, mineral baths, antiques hunting, Saratoga National Battlefield, tennis, golfing, swimming, downhill and cross-country skiing, outlet shops

## ADELPHI HOTEL
365 Broadway
Saratoga Springs, New York 12866
**Phone:** 518/587-4688 or 800/860-4086
**Fax:** 518/587-0851
**Website:** www.adelphihotel.com
**Proprietors:** Gregg Siefker, Sheila Parkert

The Adelphi was built in 1877 when Saratoga reigned as a world-class spa. Its exuberant Italianate style is embellished by three-story wooden columns topped with decorative fretwork and tracery. The interior is elaborate Victoriana, with fringed draperies, stenciled ceiling, wall coverings, and antique furnishings giving an original interpretation to a historical period. The spacious guest rooms feature lofty ceilings and windows and ornate woodwork. All are decorated with rich window treatments and wallpapers to accent antique rugs and furniture. All rooms have also been updated with private baths, air conditioning, direct-dial telephones, and cable television. A piazza runs the length of the building on the second floor. Outfitted with flower boxes and rocking chairs, it overlooks Broadway and all its activity. Numerous periodicals have extolled the Adelphi's virtues, including the *New York Times*, *Details*, *Victorian Homes*, *Vogue*, and *Forbes*.

**Open:** mid-May through October **Accommodations:** 39 guest rooms with private baths; 18 are suites **Meals:** continental breakfast included; restaurant on premises serves dinner in July and August only; restaurants nearby **Rates:** $95 to $330 **Payment:** AmEx, Visa, MC, personal and traveler's checks **Restrictions:** no pets **On-site activities:** outdoor swimming pool

## WESTCHESTER HOUSE
102 Lincoln Avenue
P.O. Box 944
Saratoga Springs, New York 12866
**Phone:** 518/587-7613 or 800/581-7613
**Website:** www.westchester-bb.saratoga.ny.us
**Proprietors:** Bob and Stephanie Melvin

This 1885 Queen Anne Victorian was built by master carpenter Almeron King as his family home. Examples of King's skill and imagination abound. A main staircase and two elaborate hand-carved fireplace mantels reflect a strong Eastlake influence. The whimsical roofline includes a cupola and balcony. Decorative exterior shingles, a wraparound porch, and a seven-color paint scheme tie the whole together. The proprietors have combined antique furnishings with contemporary art and collectibles and up-to-date comforts. Guest rooms contain luxury linens, queen- and king-size beds, ceiling fans, air conditioning, and chocolates. Guests may enjoy the library, baby grand piano, and gardens. The dining room, where breakfast is served on crystal and china, is brightened by large arched windows. The innkeepers have earned several local and state awards for their extensive restoration work on the house.

**Open:** February through December **Accommodations:** 7 guest rooms with private baths **Meals:** continental-plus breakfast included; complimentary refreshments; restaurants nearby **Rates:** $85 to $165; $195 to $275 in racing season; 10% discount to National Trust members and National Trust Visa cardholders, restrictions may apply **Payment:** AmEx, Visa, MC, personal and traveler's checks **Restrictions:** well-behaved children welcome; smoking limited; no pets (resident dog) **On-site activities:** library, games, piano, gardens, walking distance to all Saratoga attractions

## SPENCERTOWN

**Nearby attractions:** Tanglewood, Jacob's Pillow, McHayden Theater, Spencertown Academy, historic sites, antiques hunting, Hancock Shaker and Mount Lebanon Shaker Villages, hiking, skiing, bicycling, fishing

### SPENCERTOWN COUNTRY HOUSE, A BED AND BREAKFAST
1909 County Route 9
P.O. Box 279
Spencertown, New York 12165
**Phone:** 518/392-5292 or 888/727-9980
**Fax:** 518/392-7453
**Website:** spencertowncntryhouse.com
**E-mail:** info@spencertowncntryhouse.com
**Proprietor:** Heather Spitzer

The Spencertown Country House rests like an architecturally eclectic jewel on the five landscaped acres that remain from its once-large farm. Built in 1803 in a traditional center-hall Federal style, it was expanded in 1877 and twice more again at the turn of the century. The result is a rambling, gabled building that has seen years of previous service as farmhouse and a lodge. Today it is a warm and welcoming bed and breakfast offering five guest rooms decorated with period furniture, each with a private bath. A popular place for guests to relax is the formal parlor with piano. Guests may also gather around the cozy fireplace, play games, or watch television in the second parlor. Breakfast is served in the dining room, which opens onto a large porch, where guests may enjoy morning coffee or an afternoon tea. The inn is conveniently located near all the area's scenic, cultural, and sporting attractions.

**Open:** February 1 to December 31 **Accommodations:** 5 guest rooms with private baths **Meals:** full breakfast included; complimentary refreshments; restaurants nearby **Rates:** $60 to $138; 10% discount to National Trust members and National Trust Visa cardholders excluding July, August, and October **Payment:** AmEx, Visa, MC, personal and traveler's checks **Restrictions:** children over 12 welcome; no smoking; no pets

# STONE RIDGE

**Nearby attractions:** Catskill Mountains, lakes, Woodstock art colony, Kingston, Hyde Park, hiking, bicycling, cross-country skiing, ice skating, fishing, tennis, golfing, Hudson River cruises, bird-watching, wine region, antiques hunting, crafts shops

## INN AT STONE RIDGE – HASBROUCK HOUSE
Route 209
Stone Ridge, New York 12484
**Phone:** 914/687-0736
**Fax:** 914/687-0112
**Proprietors:** Dan and Suzanne Hauspurg

This eighteenth-century Dutch colonial mansion, with a full-facade double-decker porch, is set on 40 acres of lawns, gardens, and woods with a lake. The guest parlor area includes a full-size antique billiard table, a sitting room with library, and a television room. Guest rooms are furnished in colonial and Victorian antiques. Located on the first floor of the mansion, Milliways Restaurant features regional cuisine and specials representing America's different heritages. A craft and gift shop, located in the original carriage house of the estate, features the works of local artisans. Hasbrouck House, only 95 miles from midtown Manhattan, is listed in the National Register of Historic Places.

**Open:** year round **Accommodations:** 11 guest rooms (2 have private baths); 1 is a suite **Meals:** full breakfast included; restaurant on premises; restaurants nearby **Rates:** $60 to $145; 10% discount to National Trust members and National Trust Visa cardholders **Payment:** AmEx, Visa, MC, Discover, personal and traveler's checks **On-site activities:** gardens, hiking, swimming, billiards

# THENDARA

**Nearby attractions:** Adirondack Museum, Fulton Chain of Lakes, arts center, Old Forge, Blue Mountain Museum, Enchanted Forest, Water Safari, golfing, horseback riding, hiking, downhill and cross-country skiing

## MOOSE RIVER HOUSE BED AND BREAKFAST
12 Birch Street
Thendara, New York 13472
**Phone:** 315/369-3104
**E-mail:** mrheb@telenet.net
**Proprietors:** Kate and Bill Labbate

Built in 1884 as a small hotel, Moose River House was then accessible only by boat. The double-decked *Fawn*, a tiny sidewheeler, steamed upstream from

Minnehaha, where the only wooden train rails ended. Four delightful guest rooms overlook the river, which offers miles of canoeing and fishing. Guests are also welcome in the fireplaced living room for conversation, reading, games, or television. A full breakfast is served in the dining room or on the outside deck, both of which overlook Moose River. A canoe trip originates at the inn that goes through the eight lakes of the Fulton Chain as well as Raquette, Forked, Long, and Saranac lakes.

**Open:** year round **Accommodations:** 4 guest rooms (2 have private baths) **Meals:** full breakfast included; restaurants nearby **Rates:** $70 to $95 **Payment:** Visa, MC, personal and traveler's checks **Restrictions:** children over 12 welcome; no smoking; no pets **On-site activities:** gardens, hiking, canoeing, mountain biking

---

## TRUMANSBURG

**Nearby attractions:** Cayuga and Seneca Lakes, Ithaca, Watkins Glen, Taughannock Falls State Park, wineries, golfing

### THE ARCHWAY BED AND BREAKFAST

7020 Searsburg Road
Trumansburg, New York 14886
**Phone:** 607/387-6175 or
800/387-6175
**Website:**
www.fingerlakes.net/archway
**E-mail:**
archway@lightlink.com
**Proprietors:** Meredith
Pollard and Joe Prevost

The archway at this charming country bed and breakfast is the vine-covered trellis set in the house's surrounding white picket fence. The 1861 house is a classic Greek Revival but possesses an unusual spiral staircase (one of two in the county) said to have been designed by a boat builder. The innkeepers offer double, queen, king, or twin accommodations in rooms that please the mind and heart. Bedding is line dried when weather permits. Shared and private baths are available. A full breakfast provides healthy choices for hearty appetites. Guests may enjoy their meals by the cozy fireplace or in the sunroom overlooking the Trumansburg Public Golf Course. A hammock on the porch and one in the trees are just two of the tranquil spots at this bed and breakfast. Guests are invited to wander through the inn's ever-expanding old-fashioned gardens.

**Open:** year round **Accommodations:** 3 guest rooms (1 has a private bath) **Meals:** full breakfast included; complimentary refreshments; restaurants nearby **Rates:** $65 to $85; 10% discount to National Trust members and National Trust Visa cardholders **Payment:** AmEx, Visa, MC, Discover, personal and traveler's checks **Restrictions:** all children are loved and welcome; no smoking; no pets **On-site activities:** books, music, piano, television

## UPPER SARANAC LAKE

**Nearby attractions:** Upper Saranac Lake with boating, fishing, swimming, ice skating, and ice fishing; cross-country skiing

### THE WAWBEEK ON UPPER SARANAC LAKE
Panther Mountain Road
Upper Saranac Lake, New York 12986
**Phone:** 518/359-2656 or 800/953-2656
**Fax:** 518/359-2475
**Website:** www.wawbeek.com
**E-mail:** wawbeek@capital.net
**Proprietors:** Nancy and Norman Howard

The Wawbeek is a turn-of-the-century Great Camp resort set on 40 acres extending from dense woods to a glade of giant hemlocks, from a wildflower field to lawns and a lovely beach and bay, from a bike and cross-country ski trail to a nature trail that meanders along the shoreline. Two of the original Great Camp buildings, designed by William Coulter (the acknowledged father of Adirondack camp architecture) in 1898, are the Mountain House with its knotty pine paneling and great room with massive stone fireplace and the Wawbeek Restaurant with diamond-paned windows, beamed ceiling, and huge fireplace. Fully appointed yet rustic in charm, accommodations are in the Mountain House and in log cabins and cottages that dot the property. With something for everyone each season of the year, the Wawbeek is ideal for weddings, conferences, and reunions. *Travel & Leisure* calls it "one of the best new American destinations."

**Open:** year round **Accommodations:** 20 guest rooms with private baths; 12 are suites or cabins **Meals:** full breakfast included in summer and fall; continental-plus breakfast included winter and spring; restaurant and lounge on premises **Rates:** $130 to $400 **Payment:** AmEx, Visa, MC, personal and traveler's checks **Restrictions:** no pets **On-site activities:** sand beach, boats, canoes, docks, fishing, bicycles, tennis courts, walking trails, snowshoeing, cross-country skiing, ice fishing

# WARRENSBURG

**Nearby attractions:** Lake George, Gore Mountain, hot air balloon festival, boating, swimming, downhill skiing, golfing, tennis, lake cruise ships, antiques hunting, outlet shops, public beaches, water skiing, Fort Ticonderoga, Fort William Henry

## WHITE HOUSE LODGE

53 Main Street
Warrensburg, New York 12885
**Phone:** 518/623-3640
**Proprietors:** Jim and Ruth Gibson

Warrensburg, in the heart of the Adirondacks, is home to the White House Lodge. An 1847 white clapboard house with dark red shutters and an inviting wraparound porch, the White House is picturesque in its setting under shady maple trees set back from the main street in this historic downtown. Comfortably furnished with antiques and oriental rugs, the inn offers guests three bedrooms with Victorian-styled furnishings, ceilings and window fans, and an air-conditioned television lounge, all on the second floor, providing privacy. A continental breakfast is served in the lounge. With its convenient location, White House Lodge is an easy stroll to restaurants and shops.

**Open:** year round **Accommodations:** 3 guest rooms share 2 baths **Meals:** continental breakfast included; restaurants nearby **Rate:** $85 **Payment:** Visa, MC **Restrictions:** children over 7 welcome; smoking limited; no pets

# WESTHAMPTON BEACH

**Nearby attractions:** Quogue Wildlife Refuge, Montauk Point, ocean and beach, golfing, fishing, shopping

## 1880 SEAFIELD HOUSE
2 Seafield Lane
P.O. Box 648
Westhampton Beach, New York 11978
**Phone:** 516/288-1559 or 800/346-3290
**Fax:** 516/288-7696
**Website:** www.1880-house.com
**Proprietor:** Elsie Pardee Collins

Seafield House is a rural retreat just 90 minutes from Manhattan but 100 years from the present in style, decor, and atmosphere. The estate, including a swimming pool and tennis court, is only a short, brisk walk to the ocean beach. The home is filled with family heirlooms, antiques, and personal touches, especially in the guest suites, with their flower arrangements, fruit and candies, and English toiletries. The eclectic furnishings harmonize to create a casual, country-inn feeling. When the weather turns cool, the parlor fire and 1907 potbelly stove continually blaze to keep Seafield House warm and comforting. Guests are treated to a full breakfast, and all leave Seafield House carrying one of Mrs. Collins's complimentary home-baked goodies.

**Open:** year round **Accommodations:** 3 guest suites with private baths **Meals:** full breakfast included; complimentary refreshments; restaurants nearby **Rates:** $100 to $200; 10% discount to National Trust members **Payment:** AmEx, Visa, MC, personal and traveler's checks **Restrictions:** children over 5 welcome; no smoking; no pets **On-site activities:** swimming pool, tennis

# NORTH CAROLINA

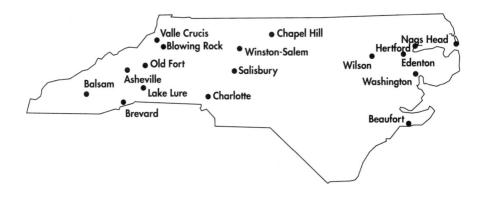

## ASHEVILLE

**Nearby attractions:** Biltmore Estate, Thomas Wolfe home, Carl Sandburg home, Great Smoky Mountains National Park, Blue Ridge Parkway, arts and science center, crafts shops, tennis, golfing, hiking, white-water rafting, horseback riding

### CEDAR CREST VICTORIAN INN
674 Biltmore Avenue
Asheville, North Carolina 28803
**Phone:** 828/252-1389
**Fax:** 828/252-5522
**Website:** www.cedarcrestvictorianinn.com
**Proprietors:** Jack and Barbara McEwan

Perched on a hill just north of Biltmore Village, this opulent Queen Anne mansion is prominently situated on its four-acre site. Built in 1891 for Confederate veteran and businessman William E. Breese, Cedar Crest is known for its captain's walk, turrets, and expansive verandas. Ornate woodwork, said to be that of the same artisans employed by Vanderbilt at his nearby Biltmore estate, is featured prominently inside, perhaps most ornately in the parlor's carved oak corner mantel and crown molding. Spacious bedrooms are furnished with period antiques and may have canopied or brass beds, Victorian laces, fireplaces, or clawfoot tubs. The Guest Cottage, just above the garden, is a 1915 bungalow ideal for families and those seeking additional privacy. Cedar Crest is listed in the National Register of Historic Places.

**Open:** year round **Accommodations:** 11 guest rooms with private baths; 3 are suites **Meals:** full breakfast included; complimentary refreshments; restaurants nearby **Rates:** $130 to $220; winter discounts; 10% discount offered to National Trust members and National Trust Visa cardholders **Payment:** AmEx, Visa, MC, DC, Discover, personal and traveler's checks **Restrictions:** children over 10 welcome; no smoking; no pets **On-site activities::** croquet, badminton, gardens, music room

## INN ON MONTFORD
296 Montford Avenue
Asheville, North Carolina 28801
**Phone:** 828/254-9569 or 800/254-9569
**Fax:** 828/254-9518
**Website:** innonmontford.com
**Proprietor:** Alexa Royden

The Inn on Montford sits behind a boxwood-lined walkway, under enormous shade trees, on a street traveled by Scott and Zelda Fitzgerald and memorialized by Thomas Wolfe. Architect Richard Sharp Smith, supervising architect of nearby Biltmore house, designed this house in an English cottage style with its two front gables, eaves flared, and an expansive wraparound porch. Today, the inn is furnished with English and American antiques, fine paintings, oriental rugs, and porcelains. Guest rooms feature canopied beds and fireplaces. Three bathrooms have whirlpool tubs and one has an old-fashioned claw-foot tub. All are stocked with scented soaps and plush towels. The innkeeper serves a full breakfast that features daily specialties and an afternoon tea.

**Open:** year round **Accommodations:** 4 guest rooms with private baths **Meals:** full breakfast included; complimentary refreshments; restaurants nearby **Rates:** $135 to $180 **Payment:** AmEx, Visa, MC, Discover, personal and traveler's checks **Restrictions:** no smoking; no pets (resident dogs) **On-site activities:** porch sitting

## OLD REYNOLDS MANSION
100 Reynolds Heights
Asheville, North Carolina 28804
**Phone:** 828/254-0496
**Proprietors:** Helen and Fred Faber

One of the few brick houses in Asheville that predates the Civil War, the Old Reynolds Mansion maintains its solitary perch on Reynolds Mountain surrounded by acres of trees. This large home was built in 1855 by Daniel and Susan Reynolds. Their son Nathaniel renovated it, adding a third story with a mansard roof, a kitchen, and two verandas, and transformed the house to a Second Empire style. Restored by the innkeepers, the Old Reynolds Mansion is listed in the National Register of Historic Places. All guest rooms are adorned with antiques, and most have private baths and fireplaces. Guests can enjoy breakfasts and sunsets on the verandas, stroll through the pines surrounding the house, or tour historic Asheville.

**Open:** year round, weekends only January and February **Accommodations:** 10 guest rooms (8 have private baths); 1 is a cottage suite **Meals:** continental-plus breakfast included; complimentary refreshments; restaurants nearby **Rates:** $60 to $130 **Payment:** personal and traveler's checks **Restrictions:** children over 12 welcome; no pets; no smoking **On-site activities:** swimming pool, porch sitting, walking

## RICHMOND HILL INN
87 Richmond Hill Drive
Asheville, North Carolina 28806
**Phone:** 828/252-7313 or 800/545-9238
**Fax:** 828/252-8726
**Website:** www.richmondhillinn.com
**Proprietors:** Dr. Albert J. and Margaret Michel

An impressive Queen Anne Victorian, this mansion was built in 1889 as the private residence of Richmond Pearson, a former congressman and ambassador. Designed by James. G. Hill, supervising architect for the U.S. Treasury buildings, the home was one of the most elegant and innovative residential structures of its era, with running water, its own communication system, and a pulley-operated elevator for luggage. The Richmond Hill Inn, as the house is known today, boasts a grand entrance hall paneled in rich native oak and 10 fireplaces with neoclassical mantels. The cottages and garden rooms at Richmond Hill reflect the Victorian style of the mansion. The house, listed in the National Register of Historic Places, the cottages, and the garden complex offer guests individually decorated, antique-filled bedrooms with such extras as turn-down service, fresh flowers, and down pillows.

**Open:** year round **Accommodations:** 12 rooms with private baths in the mansion, 1 is a suite; 15 rooms with private baths in garden complex, 1 is a suite; 9 rooms with private baths in the cottages, 1 is a suite **Meals:** full breakfast included; complimentary refreshments; 2 restaurants on premises **Wheelchair access:** limited **Rates:** $135 to $375 **Payment:** AmEx, Visa, MC, personal and traveler's checks **Restrictions:** no smoking; no pets **On-site activities::** croquet, rare book collection

## WRIGHT INN AND CARRIAGE
235 Pearson Drive
Asheville, North Carolina 28801
**Phone;** 828/251-0789 or 800/552-5724
**Fax:** 828/251-0929
**Website:** www.wrightinn.com
**Proprietors:** Carol and Art Wenczel

Asheville's historic Montford District contains the grand homes of turn-of-the-century industrialists and real estate developers. The fully restored Wright Inn is one of the finest examples of Queen Anne architecture found in the district and in all of western North Carolina. Built in 1899 for Osella B. and Leva Wright, the house, heavily ornamented with gingerbread trim and known fondly by local residents as "Faded Glory," features original hand-fashioned oak trim inside and numerous gables outside. Each guest room is decorated in early twentieth-century style; two rooms have fireplaces. A Victorian parlor and drawing room, each with a fireplace, provide restful places for afternoon tea. In warm weather, tea is served in the gazebo. The Carriage House contains a living room, dining room, kitchen, three bedrooms, and two baths for group vacationers, especially those with children. The former owners of the Wright Inn received two preservation awards for their work on the historic home.

**Open:** year round **Accommodations:** 9 guest rooms with private baths; 1 carriage-house unit with 3 bedrooms and 2 baths **Meals:** full breakfast included in the inn rates; complimentary refreshments; restaurants nearby **Rates:** $95 to $145; carriage house $215 **Payment:** Visa, MC, Discover, personal and traveler's checks **Restrictions:** children over 12 welcome in the inn **On-site activities:** reading, porch sitting, bicycling (bicycles provided free of charge)

# BALSAM

**Nearby attractions:** Blue Ridge Parkway, Great Smoky Mountain National Park, Smoky Mountain Scenic Railroad, Shining Rock National Wilderness Area, Biltmore Estate, fishing, hiking, white-water rafting

## BALSAM MOUNTAIN INN
Balsam Mountain Inn Road (S.R. 1700)
P.O. Box 40
Balsam, North Carolina 28707
**Phone:** 828/456-9498 or 800/224-9498
**Fax:** 828/456-9298
**Website:** www1.aksi.net/~cmark/balsam.htm
**E-mail:** mteasley@dnet.net
**Proprietor:** Merrily Teasley

Built in 1908, the year the railroad came to Balsam, Balsam Mountain Inn is situated just above the highest depot east of the Rockies. A symmetrical Colonial Revival structure, it is dominated by broad double-decker porches across the main facade, bounded on each end by three-story towers capped with hipped roofs. At an elevation of 3500 feet, Balsam Mountain Inn provides guests with crisp, cool air and a dramatic view of the surrounding mountains. Many original furnishings remain, including pretty iron beds, wicker chairs, oak rockers, and dressers, but modern comforts have been added along with firm mattresses and springs. Delightful areas to relax and make friends include the wicker- and chintz-filled lobby, game room, library, porches, and dining room, where plentiful meals are served.

**Open:** year round **Accommodations:** 50 guest rooms with private baths; 8 are suites **Meals:** full breakfast included; restaurant on premises **Wheelchair access:** some guest rooms, dining room, public bathrooms, lobby, library **Rates:** $90 to $150; 10% discount to National Trust members and National Trust Visa cardholders **Payment:** Visa, MC, personal and traveler's checks **Restrictions:** smoking limited; no pets **On-site activities:** hiking on 26 acres with trails, library, croquet, game room with cards and puzzles

# BEAUFORT

**Nearby attractions:** historic homes tours, antiques hunting, specialty shopping, shelling, North Carolina Maritime Museum, North Carolina Aquarium, scuba diving, deep sea fishing, ferry service to Cape Lookout Lighthouse, Fort Macon State Park, Rachel Carson National Estuary, Shackleford Island with wild ponies

## THE CEDARS INN
305 Front Street
Beaufort, North Carolina 28516
**Phone:** 252/728-7036
**Fax:** 252/728-1685
**Website:** www.cedarsinn.com
**Proprietors:** Sam and Linda Dark

The house built by William Borden has been standing watch over the harbor of this seaport town for more than 200 years. Built in 1768, The Cedars has undergone at least five major renovations in its history, including the one that added its distinctive double-porch Greek Revival facade, but most recently was restored in accordance with the Secretary of the Interior's Standards. The adjacent Belcher Fuller House was built in 1852. Together they compose The Cedars Inn, which contains three suites and two guest rooms in the Borden House, while the Belcher Fuller House has two suites and four guest rooms. All feature the modern comforts of private baths, air conditioning, and cable television. Some have fireplaces and claw-foot tubs. A generous breakfast is served daily. Wide porches and balconies with rockers catch sea breezes and afford sweeping vistas of the harbor and historic town.

**Open:** year round **Accommodations:** 11 guest rooms with private baths; 5 are suites **Meals:** full breakfast included; catered special events available; restaurants nearby **Rates:** $95 to $165; 10% discount to National Trust members and National Trust Visa cardholders midweek only September through April **Payment:** AmEx, Visa, MC, Discover, personal and traveler's checks **Restrictions:** children over 10 welcome; no smoking; no pets **On-site activities:** porch rocking, cooking classes offered during off season

## BLOWING ROCK

Nearby attractions: Blue Ridge Parkway, Grandfather Mountain, Mile High Swinging Bridge, Blowing Rock resort village, Blowing Rock State Company, Appalachian Summer Music Festival, hiking, horseback riding, golfing, bicycling, white-water rafting, canoeing, fly fishing, antiques hunting, specialty shopping, art galleries

### INN AT RAGGED GARDENS

P.O. Box 1927
203 Sunset Drive
Blowing Rock, North Carolina 28605
**Phone:** 828/295-9703
**Website:** ragged-gardens.com
**E-mail:** ragged-gardens.inn@blowingrock.com
**Proprietors:** Lee and Jama Hyett

Surrounded by an acre of formal and "ragged" gardens, this inn is an enchanting hideaway in the heart of the village of Blowing Rock. Built in 1900 as a summer retreat, the stone-and-shingle mansion abounds with architectural craftsmanship. Native stone is used extensively in the walls, porch columns, floors, fireplaces, and even the staircase. Walls are chestnut paneled. Guest rooms are richly appointed with antique or hand-crafted beds, fireplaces, Victorian lace and silk wallpapers, tapestries, goosedown comforters and pillows, and private baths. Some offer a private balcony, whirlpool tub, or sitting area. A bountiful breakfast is served and afternoon refreshments are available in the butler's pantry. From the covered garden veranda off the dining room guests can enjoy the sights and sounds that whisper from the formal rock-walled garden.

**Open:** year round **Accommodations:** 12 guest rooms with private baths; 5 are suites **Meals:** full breakfast included; complimentary refreshments; restaurants nearby **Rates:** $125 to $200; 10% discount to National Trust members and National Trust Visa cardholders **Payment:** Visa, MC, personal and traveler's checks **Restrictions:** children over 12 welcome; no smoking; no pets **On-site activities:** strolling through gardens

# BREVARD

**Nearby attractions:** Pisgah National Forest, Brevard Music Center, Flat Rock Playhouse, Blue Ridge Mountains, Looking Glass Falls, Sliding Rock, Biltmore Estate, Thomas Wolfe home, Carl Sandburg home

## THE RED HOUSE INN
412 Probart Street
Brevard, North Carolina 28712
**Phone:** 828/884-9349
**Proprietor:** Marilyn Ong

For many years before Brevard or Transylvania County were established, the Red House on Probart Street served as a trading post. Built in 1851, it has survived many years of neglect and several attempts to destroy it during the Civil War. As the area grew, the Red House developed first into a railroad station, then the county's first courthouse, Brevard's first post office, a private school, and the predecessor to Brevard College. This local landmark house has been carefully restored and opened as a bed and breakfast. Charmingly furnished in turn-of-the-century antiques, each guest room has a distinctive character. Accommodations range from single to queen beds, and there is a small efficiency cottage with queen bed. Broad double-decker porches span the building's facade, providing ideal locations from which to take in the clear mountain air.

**Open:** year round **Accommodations:** 4 guest rooms with private baths and 1 cottage with bath **Meals:** full breakfast included; complimentary refreshments; restaurants nearby **Rates:** $59 to $89; 10% discount to National Trust members and National Trust Visa cardholders **Payment:** Visa, MC, personal and traveler's checks **Restrictions:** children over 12 welcome; no smoking; no pets **On-site activities:** the inn is at the entrance to Pisgah National Forest

# CHAPEL HILL

**Nearby attractions:** University of North Carolina, historic Hillsborough, Raleigh/Durham, Research Triangle Park, Burlington outlet shops, fishing

### INN AT BINGHAM SCHOOL
P.O. Box 267
Chapel Hill, North Carolina 27514
**Phone:** 919/563-5583 or 800/566-5583
**Fax:** 919/563-9826
**E-mail:** Fdeprez@aol.com
**Proprietors:** François and Christina Deprez
**Location:** 11 miles west of Chapel Hill

Bingham School was a preparatory school that operated from 1845 to 1865. The school is no longer standing, but the headmaster's house, listed in the National Register of Historic Places, has received an award for its meticulous restoration. A combination of Greek Revival and Federal styles, the early nineteenth-century house contains five spacious guest rooms with private baths. Guests will find thick bathrobes, designer soaps, and homemade cookies in their rooms. Two guest rooms offer pencil-post canopy beds, another has a whirlpool tub. Elaborate breakfasts include such entrees as pear-almond waffles or baked German pancakes. Guests are invited to relax on a porch, roam the surrounding woodlands, swing in a hammock, or play a game of croquet. Books, games, and old movies are provided for indoor entertainment.

**Open:** year round **Accommodations:** 5 guest rooms with private baths; 1 is a suite **Meals:** full breakfast included; complimentary wine and cheese; restaurants nearby **Rates:** $75 to $120; 10% discount to National Trust members and National Trust Visa cardholders midweek only **Payment:** AmEx, Visa, MC, Discover, personal and traveler's checks **Restrictions:** no smoking; no pets **On-site activities:** croquet, hammocks, books, games

# CHARLOTTE

**Nearby attractions:** Discovery Place Science Museum, Spirit Square Center for the Arts, North Carolina Blumenthal Performing Arts Center, Carolina Panthers, Charlotte Hornets, Charlotte Knights, Charlotte Motor Speedway

## THE DUNHILL HOTEL
237 North Tryon Street
Charlotte, North Carolina 28202
**Phone:** 704/332-4141 or 800/678-8946
**Fax:** 704/376-4117
**Website:** www.dunhillhotel.com
**General Manager:** John Cunningham

Designed by architect Louis Asbury, Sr., The Dunhill opened in 1929 as the Mayfair Manor apartment hotel. Half the original 100 rooms were rented by permanent tenants. The hotel passed through various owners, operating continuously until 1981. After sitting idle for six years, the hotel was fully restored in 1987. The lobby and guest rooms blend the elegance of eighteenth-century European furnishings with original art, hand-sewn draperies, and four-poster beds, creating an ambience reminiscent of famous hotels of the 1920s and 1930s. The penthouse retains its original marble floor and double balconies offering beautiful views of the city. Guest amenities include stocked refrigerators, complimentary newspaper, turn-down service, and athletic facility privileges. The hotel's Monticello Restaurant prepares light luncheon fare and elegant evening dinners in an intimate atmosphere. The Dunhill is a member of Historic Hotels of America.

**Open:** year round **Accommodations:** 60 guest rooms and suites with private baths **Meals:** restaurant on premises; room service; restaurants nearby **Rates:** $129 to $400 **Payment:** AmEx, Visa, MC **On-site activities:** meeting space for up to 50 guests

# EDENTON

**Nearby attractions:** historic downtown walking tours, waterfront parks, Hope Plantation and Somerset Place museum homes, golfing, swimming, tennis

## THE LORDS PROPRIETORS' INN
300 North Broad Street
Edenton, North Carolina 27932
**Phone:** 919/482-3541 or 800/678-8946
**Fax:** 919/482-2432
**Website:** www.lordspropedenton.com
**Proprietors:** Arch and Jane Edwards

The *New York Times* calls Edenton, founded in 1722 and once the colonial capital of North Carolina, "the South's prettiest town." The quiet tree-lined streets of the extensive historic district are flanked by fine eighteenth and nineteenth-century homes, three of which make up The Lords Proprietors' Inn, established in 1982. The largest of the homes on the one-acre site is a stately brick Victorian with a wraparound porch. Next door is a charming frame house built in 1801, and to the rear are unique lodgings converted from a former tobacco pack house, boasting Edenton's longest porch. Visitors enjoy three spacious parlors with fireplaces, a library, and large, graciously appointed guest rooms. The dining room serves a full breakfast daily and dinner Tuesday through Saturday evenings. The inn is a member of Historic Hotels of America.

**Open:** year round **Accommodations:** 20 guest rooms with private baths **Meals:** full breakfast included Sunday and Monday (B&B rates apply); full breakfast and dinner included Tuesday through Saturday (MAP rates apply) **Wheelchair access:** limited to one guest room and dining room (advance notice requested) **Rates:** $155 to $190 (B&B); $225 to $265 (MAP) **Payment:** personal and traveler's checks **Restrictions:** all children welcome but formal dinner unsuitable for children under 10; smoking limited; no pets **On-site activities:** historic preservation weekend packages in November, February, and March include tour of private historic homes and after-dinner entertainment on Saturday

# HERTFORD

**Nearby attractions:** historic Edenton, Hope Plantation, Somerset Plantation, Newbold–White house, golfing, canoeing

## BEECHTREE INN

Route 1, Box 517 (Pender Road)
Hertford, North Carolina 27944
**Phone:** 252/426-7815
**E-mail:** jhobbs@ecsu.campus.mci.net
**Proprietors:** Ben and Jackie Hobbs

Beechtree Inn consists of the rear wing of the Richard Pratt House, built in 1760 by brick mason Richard Pratt; the Bear Swamp House, ca. 1800, with plaster walls, original woodwork, and fireplace; and the Bennetts Creek House, a ca. 1790 frame house with fireplace and loft bedroom. The three buildings are furnished with period reproduction furniture made by the Hobbses in their on-site shop, where furniture-making classes are offered each month. A full breakfast, served in the dining room of the Pratt House, may include country sausage, corn fritters, or pecan waffles. The inn is in a secluded wooded setting, sharing its grounds with 14 pre–Civil War buildings that have been moved here for protection and restoration.

**Open:** year round **Accommodations:** 3 guest houses with private baths **Meals:** full breakfast included; complimentary refreshments; restaurants nearby **Rates:** $50 to $85; 10% discount to National Trust members and National Trust Visa cardholders **Payment:** personal and traveler's checks **Restrictions:** no smoking **On-site activities:** bicycles, table tennis, furniture-making classes, studying pre–Civil War buildings

---

# LAKE LURE

**Nearby attractions:** Chimney Rock Park, Biltmore Estate, Thomas Wolfe home, hiking, sightseeing, golfing, tennis

## LAKE LURE INN

P.O. Box 10
Lake Lure, North Carolina 28746
**Phone:** 704/625-2525 or 800/678-8946
**Fax:** 704/625-9655
**Website:** www.lakelureinn.com
**General Manager:** Sherry Phelps

Nestled in the beautiful North Carolina mountains, the Lake Lure resort area was begun in 1901, the plan of Dr. Lucius B. Morse. News stories of the time reported,

"He visualized a Great National Mountain Lake Pleasure Resort in a non-duplicatable setting which the world has not yet realized." The inn opened in 1927. This lively Mediterranean-style hostelry has been restored to its original grandeur with 50 attractive guest rooms and suites, many with spectacular views of the lake and surrounding mountains. The hotel has played host to such notables as Presidents Roosevelt and Cleveland, F. Scott Fitzgerald, and Emily Post. During World War II, it served U.S. Air Force officers for "R and R." The cast and crew of the popular movie *Dirty Dancing* were housed at the inn and *The Last of the Mohicans* was filmed in this scenic valley. The inn is a member of Historic Hotels of America.

**Open:** year round **Accommodations:** 50 guest rooms and suites with private baths **Meals:** continental breakfast included; restaurant on premises serves dinner and Sunday buffet **Rates:** $109 to $159 **Payment:** AmEx, Visa, MC **Restrictions:** no pets **On-site activities:** water sports and activities on lake, swimming pool

## NAGS HEAD

**Nearby attractions:** Jockey's Ridge State Park, Wright Brothers Memorial, Cape Hatteras National Seashore, Oregon Inlet Fishing Center, Pea Island Wildlife Refuge, Roanoke Island, North Carolina Aquarium, Fort Raleigh, Elizabethan Gardens, *Queen Elizabeth II*, charter fishing, lighthouses, shipwrecks, bird-watching, beachcombing, sand dunes, wild ponies, golfing, tennis, swimming, sailing, hang gliding, surfing, jet skiing, shopping, art galleries

### FIRST COLONY INN

6720 South Virginia Dare Trail
Nags Head, North Carolina 27959
**Phone:** 252/441-2343 or 800/368-9390
**Fax:** 252/441-9234
**Website:** www.firstcolonyinn.com
**E-mail:** innkeeper@firstcolonyinn.com
**Proprietor:** The Lawrences

Built in 1932 as LeRoy's Seaside Inn, and renamed in 1937, the First Colony Inn is the only remaining beach hotel from Nags Head's early glory days. Slated for demolition in the 1980s, the Shingle-style hotel was saved only by moving it in three pieces nearly four miles down the road. A three-year historic rehabilitation returned the multidormered roof and encircling double veranda to their original appearances, and earned the building a place in the National Register and a preservation award from the Preservation Foundation of North Carolina. A reconfigured interior transformed 60 tiny bedrooms into 26 deluxe rooms plus a breakfast room and elegant library with exposed beams and fireplace. Wet bars

or kitchenettes with dishwashers, remote-controlled television and VCR, individual climate control, heated towel bars, and imported toiletries complement antique-filled rooms. The inn has been rated with four diamonds by AAA.

**Open:** year round **Accommodations:** 26 guest rooms with private baths; 6 are suites **Meals:** full breakfast included; afternoon tea; restaurants nearby **Wheelchair access:** limited **Rates:** $140 to $275 in season; $80 to $160 off season **Payment:** Visa, MC, Discover, personal and traveler's checks **Restrictions:** no smoking; no pets **On-site activities:** boardwalk to beach, pool and ocean swimming, croquet, board games, reading, fishing, hot tub, porch rocking

## OLD FORT

**Nearby attractions:** Blue Ridge Parkway, Chimney Rock, Biltmore House, Mt. Mitchell, Lake Lure, Pisgah National Forest, museums, antiques hunting, crafts shops, golfing, hiking, white-water rafting, horseback riding

### INN AT OLD FORT
106 West Main Street
P.O. Box 1116
Old Fort, North Carolina 28762
**Phone:** 828/668-9384 or 800/471-0637, ext. 1709
**Proprietors:** Debbie and Chuck Aldridge

The Inn at Old Fort was built in 1871 as a summer retreat. Twin, steeply pitched, front gables and pointed-arched windows announce this two-story, frame house's style as Gothic Revival. It is one of the best remaining examples of the style in McDowell County. Located on more than three acres, the house is surrounded by terraced lawns and gardens that were created when the house was built. Furnished with antiques, the house has been extensively renovated and now welcomes overnight guests to its comfortable accommodations. Rooms may be rented individually with private baths or may be combined to create a two-bedroom suite with den and private bath. Guests are invited to relax in the library, parlor, garden, and on the rocker-filled front porch.

**Open:** year round **Accommodations:** 4 guest rooms with private baths; 1 is a suite **Meals:** continental-plus breakfast included; complimentary refreshments; restaurants nearby **Rates:** $50 to $95; 10% discount to National Trust members and National Trust Visa cardholders **Payment:** personal and traveler's checks **Restrictions:** no smoking **On-site activities:** porch rocking, garden walks and sitting areas, croquet, library, parlor games

---

## SALISBURY

**Nearby attractions:** historic districts, Civil War sites, historic railroad museum, state park, swimming, tennis, antiques hunting, High Point furniture market

### ROWAN OAK HOUSE
208 South Fulton Street
Salisbury, North Carolina 28144-4845
**Phone:** 704/633-2086 or 800/786-0437
**Fax:** 704-633-2084
**Website:** www.bbonline.com/nc/rowanoak/
**Proprietors:** Barbara and Les Coombs

Milton S. Brown, a wealthy merchant, built this Queen Anne home for his bride in 1901. Attention to detail is evident in the carved oak door surrounded by stained glass. There are seven tiled fireplaces, each with a uniquely carved mantel; one is bird's-eye maple and another features the ribbon-and-leaf motif found on the front of the house and in the stained-glass Palladian window in the library. Over-sized guest rooms are furnished with antiques, historically patterned wallpaper, down comforters, reading lights, fruit, and fresh flowers. Rowan Oak House, with its octagonal cupola, is located in Salisbury's 14-block historic district, and is close to the Charlotte Motor Speedway and furniture shopping in High Point.

**Open:** year round **Accommodations:** 4 guest rooms with private baths **Meals:** full breakfast included; complimentary refreshments; restaurants nearby **Rates:** $85 to $125; 10% discount offered to National Trust members and National Trust Visa cardholders **Payment:** AmEx, Visa, MC, Discover, personal check **Restrictions:** children over 12 welcome; smoking limited; no pets **On-site activities:** reading, board games, garden strolling, porch sitting

# VALLE CRUCIS

**Nearby attractions:** USS *North Carolina*, golfing, swimming, tennis, boating, historic house tours, fishing, canoeing, downhill skiing, craft fairs, hiking

## MAST FARM INN
Camp Broadstone Road
P.O. Box 704
Valle Crucis, North Carolina 28691
**Phone:** 828/963-5857 or 888/963-5857
**Fax:** 828/963-6404
**Website:** www.mastfarminn.com
**E-mail:** stay@mastfarminn.com
**Innkeepers:** Wanda Hinshaw and Kay Philipp

The Mast Farm has been operated as an inn since the early 1900s by descendants of the Mast family, who built this mountain home in 1885. Placed in the National Register of Historic Places as one of the best examples of a self-contained mountain homestead in North Carolina, the 18-room farmhouse has been restored by the current innkeepers, along with a two-room log cabin, and a variety of outbuildings. Originally a 13-bedroom, 1-bath house, it now has 9 guest rooms, 7 with private baths. Guest accommodations are also available in the Loom House, Blacksmith Shop, and Woodwork Shop. Rooms are furnished with plain, turn-of-the-century antiques and are tastefully decorated with mountain crafts and fresh flowers. Mast Farm Inn has been featured in *Country* magazine, the *New York Times*, and on the PBS television series "Inn Country USA."

**Open:** May through February **Accommodations:** 9 guest rooms and 4 cottages all with private baths; **Meals:** continental-plus breakfast included; restaurant on premises **Wheelchair access:** 1 room **Rates:** $95 to $175 MAP **Payment:** Visa, MC, Discover, personal check **Restrictions:** children over 12 welcome; no smoking; no pets **On-site activities:** fishing, walking, vegetable and flower gardens

# WASHINGTON

**Nearby attractions:** historic district walking tours, North Carolina Estuarium, Beaufort County Arts Council productions, golfing

## ACADIAN HOUSE BED AND BREAKFAST

129 Van Norden Street
Washington, North Carolina 27889
**Phone:** 252/975-3967 or 888/975-3393
**Fax:** 252-975-1148
**Website:** washington-nc.com/acadian
**E-mail:** acadianbb@aol.com
**Proprietors:** Johanna and Leonard Huber

Before there was one on the Potomac River to the North, there was a Washington on the Pamlico River in North Carolina. Quaint and quiet, this smaller version is a haven from hectic life, and just a block from the historic downtown and river is Acadian House. The 1902 hipped roof house is surrounded by an original broad veranda whose roof is supported by a rank of stately columns. Inside is airy with high ceilings and warm with original heart-pine floors. Four comfortable guest rooms are available, as are the downstairs parlor and the upstairs hall library. Here the business traveler will also find a writing table, telephone, and fax and copy machines. The innkeepers, transplants from New Orleans, prepare a breakfast of southern Louisiana delicacies, such as beignets, cafe au lait, and pain perdu. Acadian House is ideal for small workshops, retreats, family reunions, and weddings. Sailing and golfing packages are available.

**Open:** February 1 to December 15 **Accommodations:** 4 guest rooms with private baths; 2 can be combined as a suite **Meals:** full breakfast included; complimentary refreshments; restaurants nearby **Rates:** $60 to $100; 10% discount to National Trust members and National Trust Visa cardholders **Payment:** AmEx, Visa, MC, personal and traveler's checks **Restrictions:** children over 6 welcome; no smoking; no pets **On-site activities:** small library, games, veranda swing, gardens

# WILSON

**Nearby attractions:** antiques hunting, Arts Council, Imagination Station (children's science museum), Tobacco Farm Life Museum, Doctor's Museum, tennis, golfing, swimming

## MISS BETTY'S BED AND BREAKFAST AND EXECUTIVE SUITES
600 West Nash Street
Wilson, North Carolina 27893-3045
**Phone:** 252/243-4447 or 800/258-2058
**Fax:** 252/243-4447
**Proprietors:** Betty and Fred Spitz

Wilson, known as the "antique capital of North Carolina," is a fitting site for Miss Betty's Bed and Breakfast Inn, an 1858 Italianate home listed in the National Register of Historic Places with carved eave brackets and detailed window surrounds. A multicolored paint scheme highlights the house's decorative trim, especially on the porch, which spans the facade. The inn also includes the adjacent Riley House (circa 1900), 1943 house known as Rosebud, and a recently renovated 1911 Queen Anne that contains four executive suites for extended-stay guests. Accommodations at Miss Betty's range from twin-bed rooms to suites with king-size beds. Each room provides a cable television and private telephone with data port. Located in Wilson's downtown historic district, Miss Betty's offers 14 Victorian-styled guest rooms and four spacious parlors. Seven covered porches provide ample space to relax and enjoy the mature trees, shrubs, and rose gardens on the landscaped grounds.

**Open:** year round **Accommodations:** 14 guest rooms with private baths; 7 are suites **Meals:** full breakfast included; restaurants nearby **Wheelchair access:** limited **Rates:**

$60 to $80 **Payment:** AmEx, Visa, MC, CB, DC, Discover, personal and traveler's checks **Restrictions:** no smoking; no pets **On-site activities:** VCR available with classic film library, reading, board games, American Victorian antiques for sale

# WINSTON-SALEM

**Nearby attractions:** Old Salem National Register historic district, Museum of Early Southern Decorative Arts, Revolutionary War military park, Reynolda Village, Tanglewood Park, tennis, swimming, hiking, golfing

## AUGUSTUS T. ZEVELY INN
803 South Main Street
Old Salem
Winston-Salem, North Carolina 27101
**Phone:** 336/748-9299 or 800/928-9299
**Fax:** 336/721-2211
**Proprietor:** Linda Anderson

Augustus Theophilus Zevely purchased this house in 1845, a year after its construction. The symmetrical brick house is a contributing structure in the National Register village known as Old Salem, founded by the Moravian religious sect in 1766. Zevely began using his house as an inn in 1848; that use continued until around 1900. After nearly a century as a tenement and apartment house, Zevely's house received a museum-quality restoration in 1993. It is the only lodging in the historic district. The Zevely Inn is furnished today with Old Salem licensee's furniture, fixtures, accessories, textiles, and floor coverings. Each individually decorated guest room has a private bath, television, radio-alarm clock, and built-in hairdryer. Some rooms have fireplaces, whirlpool tubs, steam baths, refrigerators, and microwaves. The parlor and dining room each contain a corner fireplace, a characteristic of Moravian architecture. A two-story porch at the rear of the building is comfortable even on cool days, due to its radiant-heated floors.

**Open:** year round **Accommodations:** 12 guest rooms with private baths; 1 is a suite **Meals:** full breakfast included on weekends; continental-plus breakfast included week-days; complimentary refreshments; restaurants nearby **Wheelchair access:** yes **Rates:** $80 to $205; 10% discount to National Trust members and National Trust Visa cardholders **Payment:** AmEx, Visa, MC, personal and traveler's checks **Restrictions:** children over 10 welcome; smoking limited; call about pets **On-site activities:** period gardens

## COLONEL LUDLOW INN

434 Summit at West Fifth Street
Winston-Salem, North Carolina 27101
**Phone:** 336/777-1887 or 800/301-1887
**Fax:** 336/777-0518
**Website:** www.bbinn.com
**E-mail:** innkeeper@bbinn.com
**Proprietor:** Ken Land

The Colonel Ludlow Inn comprises two neighboring Victorian homes: the 1887 Queen Anne–styled Jacob Lott Ludlow House and the 1895 Benjamin Joseph Sheppard House. Located in the West End historic district, both homes are listed in the National Register of Historic Places. Guest rooms are furnished with Victorian antiques accented by works of art, books, fresh flowers, and plants. Nearly all rooms have king-size beds and whirlpool tubs, and all feature a stereo system with a wide selection of tapes, television and VCR, telephone, coffeemaker, iron, hair dryer, microwave, and mini-refrigerator. Some rooms have working fireplaces. Bathrobes have been thoughtfully provided by the innkeeper, as are a full breakfast, a morning newspaper, and in-room movies. Guests can walk to restaurants, shops, and parks.

**Open:** year round **Accommodations:** 9 guest rooms with private baths; 3 are suites **Meals:** full breakfast included; restaurants nearby **Rates:** $89 to $219 **Payment:** AmEx, Visa, MC, Discover, personal and traveler's checks **Restrictions:** children over 12 welcome; no pets **On-site activities:** exercise room, recreation room with bar and pool table, golf practice cage

# OHIO

Poland •

Worthington •

Cincinnati
• Williamsburg

## CINCINNATI

**Nearby attractions:** King's Island, downtown Cincinnati, picturesque Mariemont village for strolling and shopping, pond, parks, convention center

## BEST WESTERN
## MARIEMONT INN
6880 Wooster Pike
Cincinnati, Ohio 45227
**Phone:** 513/271-2100 or 800/528-1234
**Fax:** 513/271-1057
**General Manager:** Bonnie Malone

The Cincinnati suburb of Mariemont was designed and constructed in the 1920s as a planned community modeled after English country villages. It was envisioned as a rural alternative to nearby Cincinnati. Now a Cincinnati suburb listed in the National Register of Historic Places, Mariemont is still a quaint village of English Tudor-style commercial buildings and quiet, tree-lined residential neighborhoods. At the Tudor-style Mariemont Inn, guest rooms contain four-poster or canopy beds and Queen Anne chairs, along with antiques and portraits of British

royalty. Massive beams stretch across the ceilings, and polished dark wood accents each room. Modern amenities include television and hair dryers. Hearty meals and grog are served up in the National Exemplar restaurant and Southerby's Pub.

**Open:** year round **Accommodations:** 60 guest rooms with private baths; 2 are suites **Meals:** restaurant and pub on premises **Rates:** $69 to $79; 10% discount offered to National Trust members and National Trust Visa cardholders **Payment:** AmEx, Visa, MC, Discover, CB, DC, personal and traveler's checks **Restrictions:** no pets

# POLAND

**Nearby attractions:** historic Poland Village, boyhood home of President William McKinley; Village Woods with hiking, jogging, and cross-country skiing trails; Mill Creek Park with golfing, tennis, walking trails, and gardens; Butler Institute of American Art; Amish country; antiques hunting

### INN AT THE GREEN
500 South Main Street
Poland, Ohio 44514
**Phone:** 330/757-4688
**Proprietors:** Ginny and Steve Meloy
**Location:** 7 miles southeast of Youngstown

The Inn at the Green, an 1876 Second Empire home notable for its steeply pitched mansard roof and decorative eave brackets, sits on a slight rise at the southern end of the Poland Village green in a National Register historic district. Its interior architecture is dignified by 12-foot-high ceilings, wood moldings, five fireplaces, interior window shutters, and original poplar floors. Three of the four guest rooms have working fireplaces, and all are furnished with four-poster beds and antiques. The inn's various public rooms are furnished with original American art, antiques, and oriental rugs. The greeting room and parlor contain working fireplaces. A pantry with sink, refrigerator, and microwave is available for guests. An enclosed porch and an English perennial garden with deck and patio offer outdoor relaxation.

**Open:** year round **Accommodations:** 4 guest rooms with private baths **Meals:** continental breakfast included; complimentary refreshments; restaurants nearby **Rates:** $55 to $60; 10% discount offered to National Trust members and National Trust Visa cardholders **Payment:** Visa, MC, personal and travelers checks **Restrictions:** no pets **On-site activities:** library, piano, classical music on compact disc, audiotape library with players in rooms, room televisions, video collection, lawn games, garden

# WILLIAMSBURG

**Nearby attractions:** East Fork State Park, Rocky Fork State Park, Riverbend Amphitheater, Cincinnati Nature Center, downtown Cincinnati, boating, fishing, swimming, horseback riding, hunting

## LEWIS McKEVER FARMHOUSE BED AND BREAKFAST

4475 McKeever Pike
Williamsburg, Ohio 45176
**Phone:** 513/724-7044
**Proprietors:** John and Carol Sandberg
**Location:** 30 miles east of Cincinnati

This elegant example of rural Italianate architecture was built in 1841 by Lewis McKever, a prominent businessman, farmer, and horse breeder. The two-story farmhouse was part of the Underground Railroad during the Civil War and was forced to host some of Morgan's raiders when they passed through Williamsburg. Listed in the National Register of Historic Places, the bed and breakfast is located on 10 acres of rolling fields and woods. Three spacious guest rooms have private baths and queen beds, air conditioning, and ceiling fans. The library has an inviting fireplace and a second-floor porch is a comfortable alternative to the spacious dining room for breakfast.

**Open:** year round **Accommodations:** 3 guest rooms with private baths **Meals:** continental-plus breakfast included; complimentary refreshments; restaurants nearby **Rates:** $65 to $75 **Payment:** Visa, MC, personal and traveler's checks **Restrictions:** inquire about children; no smoking; no pets **On-site activities:** walking paths, country tranquility

# WORTHINGTON

**Nearby attractions:** Ohio State University, Ohio State Fair, Columbus Museum of Art, Center of Science and Industry, Worthington Historical Society, Columbus Zoo, Olentangy Indian Caverns, skiing, hiking, jogging, shopping, swimming, Wexnee Center, Tuttle Mall

## WORTHINGTON INN
649 High Street
Worthington, Ohio 43085
**Phone:** 614/885-2600
**Fax:** 614/885-1283
**Website:** worthingtoninn.com
**E-mail:** worthinn@midohio.net
**Proprietors:** Steve and Susan Hanson

The Worthington Inn was built as a residence in 1831 by Rensselaer W. Cowles. After Cowles's death, the house was enlarged by the new owner and became a stagecoach stop on the toll road, and later a hotel. Originally a Federal structure, it was altered numerous times, and after a fire in 1901, the third floor and mansard roof were added. This National Register property has recently been renovated and provides guest rooms handsomely appointed with vintage furnishings and antiques, personally collected by the owners in a five-state search. Reproductions of rich textiles and period wallpapers complete the turn-of-the-century effect. A full-service restaurant specializes in regional American cuisine. The Worthington Inn has been featured in *Country Inns* magazine and has received Mobil's four-star award.

**Open:** year round **Accommodations:** 26 guest rooms with private baths; 5 are suites **Meals:** full breakfast included; complimentary refreshments; restaurant on premises; restaurants nearby **Wheelchair access:** yes **Rates:** $150 to $260 **Payment:** AmEx, Visa, MC, DC, Discover, personal and traveler's checks **Restrictions:** smoking limited; no pets

# OKLAHOMA

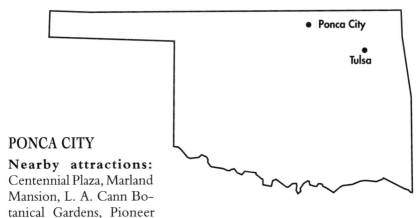

## PONCA CITY

**Nearby attractions:**
Centennial Plaza, Marland
Mansion, L. A. Cann Bo-
tanical Gardens, Pioneer
Woman State Memorial, five museums, Poncan Theater, Tallgrass Prairie
Preserve, Standing Bear Memorial, two lakes

## ROSE STONE INN

120 South Third Street
Ponca City, Oklahoma 74601
**Phone:** 580/765-5699 or 800/763-9922
**Fax:** 580/762-0240
**Proprietor:** David Zimmerman

Savings and loans in oil-boom towns were a risk and novel idea in 1918, when
E. W. Marland, founder of Conoco, and other powerful businessmen decided to
start a bank where oil workers could save money for a home down payment, then
get a loan for a 20-year mortgage. Ponca City Building and Loan was one of the
first savings and loans west of the Mississippi. It was headquartered in this
International-style, rosestone granite-clad building. Inside, it was handsome with
Missouri brown marble and walnut paneling, all beautifully preserved. Now, the
history-making structure houses a small luxury hotel with guest rooms in former
vaults and boardrooms. Bedrooms have individual climate controls and themes
that pay tribute to the area's cattle ranches, oil fields and barons, and pioneers.
Business guests will appreciate dataport telephones, full-size desks, and fax and
copier services. All visitors enjoy the exercise room, video library, and evening
snack.

**Open:** year round **Accommodations:** 25 guest rooms with private baths **Meals:**
continental-plus breakfast included; restaurants nearby **Wheelchair access:** yes **Rates:**
$49 to $79; 10% discount to National Trust members and National Trust Visa cardholders
**Payment:** AmEx, Visa, MC, CB, DC, Discover, personal and traveler's checks
**Restrictions:** no smoking **On-site activities:** health club privileges, VCRs and video
library

# TULSA

**Nearby attractions:** Philbrook Art Museum, Utica Square Shopping Center, antiques hunting on Cherry Street, Gilcrease Museum of American Western Art, River Parks with 12 miles of jogging/biking trails

## MCBIRNEY MANSION

1414 South Galveston
Tulsa, Oklahoma 74127
**Phone:** 918/585-3234
**Fax:** 918/585-9377
**Website:** www.mcbirneymansion.com
**Proprietors:** Kathy Collins and Renita Shofner

This 12,000-square-foot Tudor style mansion, built in 1928 by John Long of Kansas City for Vera and James McBirney is listed in the National Register of Historic Places. The classic design exhibits all the trademarks of this exuberant style: steeply pitched cross gables, tall chimneys capped by chimney pots, diamond-paned casement windows, and decorative half-timbering over stucco. The newly refurbished interior is equally elegant. Sumptuous fabrics and upholstered pieces lend warmth and comfort. Antiques culled from local estate sales and auctions provide character and a long-lived-in look. Guest accommodations each feature a unique touch: a fireplace, a reading nook, or perhaps a porch. All are equipped with private telephone and cable television. A full breakfast is served and early-morning coffee is always ready. Or, for guests who prefer privacy, a continental breakfast can be brought to the bedroom. The inn sits atop a hill on three acres overlooking the Arkansas River.

**Open:** year round **Accommodations:** 7 guest rooms with private baths; 3 are suites **Meals:** full breakfast included; complimentary refreshments; restaurants nearby **Rates:** $129 to $225; 10% discount to National Trust members and National Trust Visa cardholders **Payment:** AmEx, Visa, MC, Discover, personal and traveler's checks **Restrictions:** children over 10 welcome; no smoking; no pets **On-site activities:** house tours, 3 acres with gardens, terraces, and ponds

# OREGON

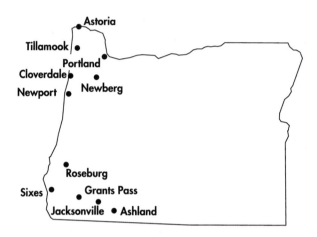

## ASHLAND

**Nearby attractions:** historic district, Oregon Shakespeare Festival, Britt Music Festival, Natural History Museum, Crater Lake National Park, fishing, downhill and cross-country skiing, Rogue and Klamath Rivers, rafting, wineries, historic Jacksonville, golfing, tennis, horseback riding

### IRIS INN
59 Manzanita Street
Ashland, Oregon 97520
**Phone:** 541/488-2286 or 800/460-7650
**Fax:** 541/488-3709
**Website:** www.ccxn.com/ccxn?ccxn;irisinn
**E-mail:** irisinnbb@aol.com
**Proprietors:** Greg and Vicki Capp

A beautiful iris design in the front door's stained-glass window gives this 1905 Victorian frame house its name. Five guest rooms are delicately decorated with antique iron beds, flower-printed fabrics and wallpapers, and antique oak, maple, and wicker furniture. Private bathrooms contain thoughtful touches of hospitality, including terry robes. Elegant and creative breakfasts start the day. A favorite of visitors to Ashland since 1982, the inn is situated in a quiet neighborhood with views of the Rogue Valley and the Grizzly and Siskiyou Mountains. Guests often spend time relaxing on the deck overlooking these sights and the inn's own rose garden.

**Open:** year round **Accommodations:** 5 guest rooms with private baths **Meals:** full breakfast included; complimentary refreshments; restaurants nearby **Rates:** $70 to $110; 10% discount offered to National Trust members and National Trust Visa cardholders **Payment:** Visa, MC, personal and traveler's checks **Restrictions:** children over 7 welcome; no smoking; no pets

---

## CLOVERDALE

**Nearby attractions:** Three Capes Scenic Loop, state parks, nature preserves, whale watching, hiking, beachcombing, fishing, horseback riding

### SANDLAKE COUNTRY INN
8505 Galloway Road
Cloverdale (Sandlake), Oregon 97112
**Phone:** 503/965-6745
**Fax:** 503/965-7425
**Proprietors:** Femke and David Durham
**Location:** 16 miles south of Tillamook

On Christmas morning in 1890, Ezra Chamberlain received an unusual gift—one million board feet of virgin red fir bridge timbers dumped on his beach by a shipwrecked Norwegian schooner. By 1894, his neighbor, William Clent King, had lugged enough of the massive timbers to his homestead to construct a sturdy farmhouse. Now that house is the Sandlake Country Inn offering four whimsical and romantic guest rooms that combine canopied beds, fireplaces, and claw-foot or whirlpool tubs with wicker, Battenberg lace, and floral motifs. One room has a private entrance from the country garden; another a private deck. One suite is in a separate cottage with fully furnished kitchen and a black marble fireplace.

Breakfasts are served in the privacy of guest rooms. Tucked into a bower of roses on more than two acres, the inn is perfect for nature and privacy lovers.

**Open:** year round **Accommodations:** 4 guest rooms with private baths; 2 are suites **Meals:** full breakfast included; complimentary refreshments; restaurants nearby **Rates:** $90 to $135; 10% discount to National Trust members and National Trust Visa cardholders **Payment:** AmEx, Visa, MC, Discover, personal and traveler's checks **Restrictions:** not suitable for children; no smoking; no pets **On-site activities:** strolling, reading, vintage films

---

## GRANTS PASS

**Nearby attractions:** Cascade Mountains, Oregon Caves, Crater Lake, Rogue River, fishing, rafting, hiking, bicycling, skiing, shopping, Ashland Shakespeare, Festival, historic Jacksonville

### WEASKU INN HISTORIC RESORT
5560 Rogue River Highway
Grants Pass, Oregon 97527
**Phone:** 541/471-8000 or 800/4-WEASKU
**Fax:** 541/471-7038
**Website:** www.weasku.com
**General Manager:** Dayle Sedgmore

In November 1927, when the Savage Rapids Dam was built along the Rogue River, it created superb angling along Alfred E. Smith's adjacent 10-acre property. In 1924, Smith opened his rustic log lodge and cabins, which he called Weasku Inn. W. E. "Rainbow" and Peggy Gibson purchased the property in 1927, continuing the tradition of hospitality in the wilderness and bringing along a contingent of friends including Clark Gable, Carole Lombard, Zane Grey, Walt

Disney, and Bing Crosby. Most of the cabins have been dismantled, but the original lodge remains today, completely restored and offering distinctive accommodations with vaulted, beamed ceilings, impressive pine furnishings, and queen-size beds with cozy comforters. Riverfront cabins are also available; these with fireplaces, some with whirlpool tubs. All modern amenities are standard throughout. Guests receive a continental breakfast buffet in the lodge.

**Open:** year round **Accommodations:** 17 guest rooms with private baths; 3 are suites **Meals:** continental breakfast included; complimentary refreshments; restaurants nearby **Rates:** $85 to $295; 10% discount to National Trust members and National Trust Visa cardholders **Payment:** AmEx, Visa, MC, CB, DC, Discover, traveler's check **Restrictions:** not suitable for children; no smoking; no pets **On-site activities:** bank fishing on the Rogue River for salmon or steelhead (Hook a Chinook!), hiking, picnicking, bird-watching, relaxing

## JACKSONVILLE

**Nearby attractions:** historic Jacksonville, museums, Beekman House, Britt Music Festival, Ashland Shakespeare Festival, skiing, hiking, golfing, trolley and carriage rides, antiques hunting

### ORTH HOUSE BED AND BREAKFAST
### "THE TEDDY BEAR INN"
105 West Main Street
Jacksonville, Oregon 97530
**Phone:** 541/899-8665 or 800/700-7301
**Fax:** 541/899-9146
**Website:** www.historicorthhousebnb.com
**Proprietors:** Lee and Marilyn Lewis

Rancher John Orth had this in-town Italianate house built in 1880 of local brick. The huge pocket doors that divide the parlors were brought by mule train from San Francisco. The plans for these doors and the unique, precision-cut stone steps at the front entry are registered with the Library of Congress. The house has been fully restored and offers three guest rooms named for the Orth daughters: Josie, Flora, and Celia. The rooms carry a Victorian motif and feature antiques, brass or carved beds, and teddy bears and toys from the innkeepers' collection of vintage toys. Bathrooms feature claw-foot tubs and all rooms are air conditioned. Guests receive a full breakfast and evening tea and treats. The handsome inn is located one block from downtown and two from the Britt Music Festival Grounds.

**Open:** year round **Accommodations:** 4 guest rooms (3 have private baths); 2 rooms can be combined into a suite **Meals:** full breakfast included; complimentary refreshments;

restaurants nearby **Rates:** $85 to $150; 10% discount to National Trust members and National Trust Visa cardholders **Payment:** Visa, MC, personal and traveler's checks **Restrictions:** children welcome with prior notice; no smoking; no pets **On-site activities:** tandem bicycle, games, books, television in parlor

# NEWBERG

**Nearby attractions:** wineries, hot-air ballooning, bicycling, antiques hunting, Portland

## SPRINGBROOK HAZELNUT FARM

30295 North Highway 99W
Newberg, Oregon 97132
**Phone:** 503/538-4606 or 800/793-8528
**Fax:** 503/537-4004
**Website:** www.nutfarm.com
**E-mail:** ellen@nutfarm.com
**Proprietors:** Chuck and Ellen McClure

Springbrook Hazelnut Farm, with its four matching Craftsman-style buildings dating from 1912, is listed in the National Register of Historic Places. The main residence has a spectacular entry hall extending from the covered front porch to the comfortably furnished back porch. A glassed-in sunporch is filled with plants and wicker furniture. Breakfast is served in the paneled dining room. Four guest rooms provide views of the pond or gardens. The historic carriage house and cottage have master bedrooms, adjoining baths, living rooms, and kitchens. The buildings are nestled among 10 acres of gardens and enormous old trees. The grounds are further enhanced by a pool, tennis court, and pond, complete with canoe and resident blue heron. Beyond the garden is a 60-acre hazelnut orchard, through which guests can walk to the adjoining winery.

**Open:** year round **Accommodations:** 6 guest rooms (4 have private baths); 2 are cottages **Meals:** full breakfast included; restaurants nearby **Rates:** $95 to $175; 10% discount to National Trust members and National Trust Visa cardholders **Payment:** personal and traveler's checks **Restrictions:** inquire about children; no smoking; no pets **On-site activities:** swimming pool, tennis court, pond with canoe, orchard walking, bicycling

# NEWPORT

**Nearby attractions:** Oregon Coast Aquarium, Hatfield Marine Science Center, Yaquina Bay Lighthouse, historic Nye Beach, historic bayfront, shopping, dining

## OAR HOUSE BED AND BREAKFAST

520 S.W. Second Street
Newport, Oregon 97365
**Phone:** 541/265-9571 or 800/252-2358
**Website:** www.newportnet.com/oarhouse
**Proprietor:** Jan LeBrun

Oar House is centrally located in the historic Nye Beach area of Newport and has, since the early 1900s, offered comfort and conviviality to guests. Originally the Bradshaw Boarding House (and once a bordello), Oar House is a cross-gabled Craftsman-style building. Five guest rooms centering on a nautical theme are individually styled—a sleigh bed here, a highboy there, a library, or a sitting room—and provide ocean views. In addition, the house offers a sitting room with fireplace, a living room with television, a guest refrigerator, and a large deck that is sheltered from the wind. A seasonal, healthful breakfast is served family style at the dining room table or at the breakfast bar in the renovated kitchen. Oar House is within walking distance of the beach and bayfront. Panoramic views are available from the house's enclosed cupola with widow's walk.

**Open:** year round **Accommodations:** 5 guest rooms with private baths; 1 is a suite **Meals:** full breakfast included; restaurants nearby **Rates:** $95 to $125 **Payment:** Visa, MC, traveler's check **Restrictions:** not suitable for children; no pets **On-site activities:** cable television with movie channels, reading, deck, cupola for taking in vistas

# PORTLAND

**Nearby attractions:** Oregon Historical Society museum, Performing Arts Center, Riverplace, YMCA, historic conservation district, Oregon Health Science Center, Portland State University, parks, Mt. Hood, Mt. St. Helens, jogging tracks, shopping, convention center, ocean beaches, wineries

## JOHN PALMER HOUSE BED AND BREAKFAST INN

4314 North Mississippi Avenue
Portland, Oregon 97217
**Phone:** 503/284-5893
**Fax:** 503/284-1239
**E-mail:** marysauter@ethergate.com
**Proprietors:** Mary and Richard Sauter

This elaborate Queen Anne residence was erected in 1890 by builder John Palmer. The house delights the eye with its fish-scale shingles, lacy wrought-iron roof cresting, decorative vergeboards, and porches and balconies dripping with gingerbread and spindles. Inside this National Register house, Victorian furnishings provide an elegant and relaxing atmosphere, which is carried through to the bedrooms, decorated with much attention to detail. Walls are covered with 1880-period wallpapers by Christopher Dresser and William Morris. The gas-electric light fixtures, with their ceiling medallions, reflect the colors in the original stained-glass windows. Leisurely breakfasts are served daily. Like the Victorians, guests may "take the waters," meaning today that a relaxing hot tub is in the gazebo.

**Open:** year round **Accommodations:** 2 guest suites with private baths **Meals:** full breakfast included; high tea and dinner available; restaurants nearby **Rates:** $65 to $95; two night minimum stay **Payment:** AmEx, Visa, MC, Discover, personal and traveler's checks **Restrictions:** no smoking; no pets **On-site activities:** reading, piano, hot tub, high teas, seasonal carriage transport to city center and return

# ROSEBURG

**Nearby attractions:** Umpqua River, Crater Lake, museums, fishing, rafting, art galleries, wineries, antiques hunting, Wildlife Safari

## HOKANSON'S GUEST HOUSE

848 S.E. Jackson
Roseburg, Oregon 97470
**Phone:** 541/672-2632
**Fax:** 541/673-5253
**Proprietors:** John and Victoria Hokanson

The land on which this house stands was once owned by Roseburg's founding father, Aaron Rose. The house, built in 1882 in the Gothic Revival style, is Roseburg's only bed and breakfast listed in the National Register of Historic Places. The steep front gable and dormers are fitted with decorative vergeboards and topped with finials. The house has been fully restored by the innkeepers. Two upstairs guest rooms share a common sitting room. Each bedroom has a private bath with claw-foot tub. The Marietta Room contains original vertical-grained fir walls, a king-size and a double bed, and handmade quilts. The Frances Room features period oak furniture, including a queen-size, high-backed bed. The Hokanson's children and Fritz the cat are in residence at the Guest House.

**Open:** year round **Accommodations:** 2 guest rooms with private baths **Meals:** full breakfast included; Victorian high tea served on several holidays; restaurants nearby **Rates:** $75 to $95; 10% discount to National Trust members and National Trust Visa cardholders **Payment:** Visa, MC, personal and traveler's checks **Restrictions:** children over 11 welcome; no smoking; no pets **On-site activities:** piano, porch with swing, pond, garden, parlor games and puzzles

# SIXES

**Nearby attractions:** whale watching and beachcombing at Cape Blanco, the most westerly point in the state of Oregon; fishing and boating on the Sixes and Elk Rivers; windsurfing at nearby Floras Lake; hiking and bicycling the South Oregon Coast area

## SIXES RIVER HOTEL
93316 Sixes River Road
Sixes, Oregon 97476
**Phone:** 541/332-3900 or 800/828-5161
**Fax:** 541/332-9063
**Website:** www.sixeshotel.com
**Proprietors:** Bert and Elizabeth Teitzel

The Sixes River Hotel exemplifies early pioneer architecture based on a Victorian design. The former farmhouse underwent a recent two-year restoration and has been placed in the National Register of Historic Places. Much of the hotel was built of white Port Orford cedar and Douglas fir. The southern portion of the building sits on hand-sawn cedar beams, which were hand-notched to carry the floor joists and wall studs. The floors and ceilings are vertical grain tongue- and-groove Douglas fir cut from the middle section of old-growth timber. The light in the dining room is hand-painted cast aluminum that was installed in the hotel in the early 1940s when power first came to rural Curry County. Four guest rooms are offered with private baths. The *Oregon Coast* recently described this as a "rustically fancy historical hotel."

**Open:** year round **Accommodations:** 4 guest rooms with private baths **Meals:** full breakfast included in rate; restaurant on premises serves guests and special events only; restaurants nearby **Rate:** $85; 10% discount to National Trust members and National Trust Visa cardholders **Payment:** personal check **Restrictions:** no smoking; no pets **On-site activities:** fishing, hiking, bicycling

# TILLAMOOK

**Nearby attractions:** world's largest cheese factory, air museum, beaches, golfing, sand dunes, surfing

## BLUE HAVEN INN
3025 Gienger Road
Tillamook, Oregon 97141
**Phone or Fax:** 503/842-2265
**E-mail:** JAR@oregoncoast.com
**Proprietor:** Joy Still

Located on a two-acre parklike setting, surrounded by tall evergreens, is the Blue Haven Inn, a 1916 two-story, country frame house. Adorned by a broad front porch and decorative vergeboard, the house is painted in soothing shades of blue, highlighted by the white picket fence that fronts the property. After 80 years of service to seven families and a stint as a restaurant catering to officers from the nearby Tillamook Naval Air Station, the charming house was fully renovated by the innkeepers. Guest rooms are furnished with antiques and limited edition collectibles, with all the modern amenities for a comfortable stay. A country breakfast is served on bone china and crystal in the formal dining room with coffered ceiling. An "overflow shop" in the converted garage next door offers antiques, glassware, limited edition plates, dolls, old sewing machines, and claw-foot bathtubs for sale.

**Open:** year round **Accommodations:** 3 guest rooms (1 has a private bath) **Meals:** full breakfast included; restaurants nearby **Rates:** $70 to $85; 10% discount to National Trust members **Payment:** personal and traveler's checks **Restrictions:** not suitable for children; no smoking; no pets **On-site activities:** porch swing, gardens, croquet, library/ game room, antique gramophone

# PENNSYLVANIA

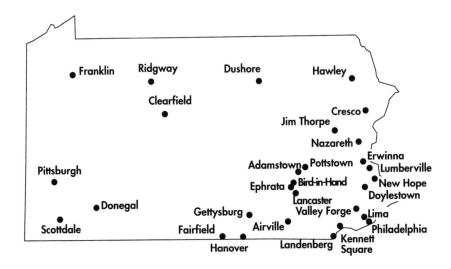

## ADAMSTOWN

**Nearby attractions:** antiques hunting, Pennsylvania Dutch country, Amish farms, Reading outlet shops, hiking and bicycling trails, golfing, tennis, swimming

### ADAMSTOWN INN
62 West Main Street
Adamstown, Pennsylvania 19501
**Phone:** 717/484-0800 or 800/594-4808
**Fax:** 717/484-1384
**Website:** www.adamstown.com
**E-mail:** info@adamstown.com
**Proprietors:** Tom and Wanda Berman

Although this house was built in the early nineteenth century, it was remodeled in 1925, resulting in this handsome two-story, hipped roof house with broad wraparound porch supported by stout columns. Leaded-glass windows and doors were added, as well as elegant chestnut woodwork. The innkeepers renovated the house in 1988, refinishing the woodwork and hardwood floors, adding modern baths, and papering walls in Victorian motifs. Today's guest rooms are decorated with family heirlooms, handmade quilts, lace curtains, and fresh flowers. All rooms have private baths; two feature two-person whirlpool tubs. Each day begins with hot beverages waiting at guest room doors. A continental-plus breakfast that includes muffins, sweet breads, cheeses, or sausage balls, is served downstairs. Adamstown Inn is located in a small town brimming with antiques dealers and is only minutes from Reading and Lancaster.

**Open:** year round **Accommodations:** 4 guest rooms with private baths; 1 is a suite **Meals:** continental-plus breakfast included; complimentary refreshments; restaurants nearby **Rates:** $70 to $125; 10% discount to National Trust members and National Trust Visa cardholders **Payment:** Visa, MC, personal and traveler's checks **Restrictions:** children over 12 welcome; no smoking; no pets (resident dog) **On-site activities:** picnic area, lawn games

# AIRVILLE

**Nearby attractions:** Amish country, horseback riding, fishing, swimming, canoeing, wineries, antiques hunting, golfing, scenic railroad rides, museums, auctions

### SPRING HOUSE
1264 Muddy Creek Forks Road
Airville, Pennsylvania 17302
**Phone:** 717/927-6906
**Proprietor:** Ray Constance Hearne
**Location:** in Muddy Creek Forks, 5 miles south of Brogue and Route 74

Built of local fieldstone in 1798 by Pennsylvania legislator Robert Turner, Spring House was for years the main residence of the village of Muddy Creek Forks, first settled in the 1730s. Now listed in the National Register of Historic Places, the house is situated over and protects an abundant spring, the village's main source of water. The house has massive, 26-inch-thick fieldstone walls that have been restored inside to their original whitewash and stenciling. Spring House offers local wine and Amish-made cheeses to travelers. Sunlit guest rooms, furnished with country antiques and handwoven rugs, are made cozy with feather beds in winter and freshened by fragrant breezes in summer. The porch swing is a relaxing place to take in the beautiful rural setting and scenic Muddy Creek.

**Open:** year round **Accommodations:** 5 guest rooms (3 have private baths) **Meals:** full breakfast included; complimentary refreshments; restaurants nearby **Rates:** $60 to $85; 10% discount offered to National Trust members and National Trust Visa cardholders **Payment:** personal and traveler's checks **Restrictions:** no smoking; pets can be accommodated outside or in nearby kennels (resident dog and cats) **Activities:** bird-watching, herb gardening, porch swing, rockers, games, library, music room

# BIRD-IN-HAND

**Nearby attractions:** Lancaster County, Amish farms, farmers' market, quilt and crafts shops, outlet shops, antiques hunting, golfing, Gettysburg, Hershey

## VILLAGE INN OF BIRD-IN-HAND
2695 Old Philadelphia Pike
P.O. Box 253
Bird-in-Hand, Pennsylvania 17505
**Phone:** 717/293-8369
**Fax:** 717/768-1117
**Website:** www.bird-n-hand.com/villageinn
**E-mail:** lodging@bird-n-hand.com
**Proprietors:** John and Jim Smucker; George
and Pat Desmond

The Old Philadelphia Pike was surveyed and built in 1734, the same year the Village Inn of Bird-in-Hand was built. The inn is a three-story brick building; its facade features an unusual second-story porch with fretwork railings, supported by turned Tuscan columns. A Quaker by the name of William McNabb was the inn's first proprietor. Today, the inn still welcomes guests traveling along the pike. Each guest room has a private bath and deluxe down-filled bedding. Six rooms are suites, three with king-size beds, two with whirlpool baths, one with a working wood stove, and one with a fireplace. The decor is in the Victorian tradition. Breakfast is served on the sunporch. Guests can enjoy free use of indoor and outdoor swimming pools and tennis courts located within walking distance of the inn. A complimentary tour of the surrounding Amish farmlands is offered daily.

**Open:** year round **Accommodations:** 11 guest rooms with private baths; 6 are suites **Meals:** continental breakfast included; complimentary refreshments; restaurants nearby **Rates:** $69 to $149 **Payment:** AmEx, Visa, MC, Discover, personal and traveler's checks **Restrictions:** smoking limited; no pets

# CLEARFIELD
**Nearby attractions:** Clearfield County Historical Museum, antique car museum, historic district walking tours, Elliott and Parker Dam's State Parks, Clearfield County Fair, antiques hunting, regional theater, golfing, boating, hiking, fishing

## CHRISTOPHER KRATZER HOUSE BED AND BREAKFAST
101 East Cherry Street
Clearfield, Pennsylvania 16830
**Phone:** 814/765-5024 or 888/252-2632
**Website:** www.virtualcities.com/pa/kratzerhouse.htm
**Proprietor:** Bruce and Ginny Baggett

Christopher Kratzer, lumberman, architect, politician, and owner of the county's first newspaper, built this striking Greek Revival house in 1840. The oldest house in Clearfield, it is painted a warm yellow with white trim and soft green shutters. The interior reflects the innkeepers' interest in historic preservation as well as their enjoyment of many styles of furniture with a mix of antiques, fine reproductions, and purely contemporary pieces. The eclectic decor also shows their interest in art and music. As a professional artist, Ginny has filled the rooms with a varied collection of objets d'art and colorful silkscreen prints. Bruce's music profession is well represented with musical instruments and more then 30 years of show business memorabilia. Guest rooms with views of river and park are offered. A full country breakfast is served in the dining room; afternoon tea or wine in the fireplaced living room or spacious back porch.

**Open:** year round **Accommodations:** 4 guest rooms (1 has a private bath); 2 rooms connect for a suite **Meals:** full breakfast included; complimentary refreshments; restaurants nearby **Rates:** $45 to $70; 10% discount to National Trust members and National Trust Visa cardholders **Payment:** Visa, MC, Discover, personal and traveler's checks **Restrictions:** smoking limited; no pets **On-site activities:** reading, music, art gallery, attic flea market, porch sitting, television

---

# CRESCO

**Nearby attractions:** Pocono Mountains, state parks, waterfalls, Lake Wallenpaupack, boating, hiking, golfing, swimming, tennis, downhill and cross-country skiing

### LA ANNA GUEST HOUSE
R.R. 2, Box 1051
Cresco, Pennsylvania 18326
**Phone and Fax:** 717/676-4225
**Proprietor:** Kathryn Gilpin Swingle
**Location:** 8 miles north of Cresco in village of LaAnna on Route 191

In 1877, Kay Swingle's grandfather, Civil War veteran and owner of the Gilpin lumber mill, built this Victorian farmhouse of hemlock clapboards. He adorned the house with an elaborately trimmed wraparound porch, which stands intact today. Mrs. Swingle, who grew up in this house and raised her own family here, has maintained the house in much the same fashion as when her grandparents were living, furnishing rooms with their Victorian and Empire furniture, oriental rugs, and Victorian reproduction wallpapers. Two guest rooms look out on a pond, where guests are invited to paddle the inn's canoe. Strolling the grounds, guests will encounter breathtaking views of waterfalls and surrounding mountains.

**Open:** year round **Accommodations:** 4 guest rooms share a bath **Meals:** continental-plus breakfast included; restaurants nearby **Rates:** $30 single to $40 double **Payment:** personal and traveler's checks **Restrictions:** no smoking; no pets **On-site activities:** hiking, fishing, canoeing, cross-country skiing

## DONEGAL

**Nearby attractions:** Frank Lloyd Wright's Fallingwater, Kentuck Knob, Laurel Highlands, Fort Ligonier, Fort Necessity, skiing (Hidden Valley and Seven Springs), hiking, golfing, white-water rafting

### MOUNTAIN VIEW BED AND BREAKFAST INN

Mountain View Road (Exit 9, Pennsylvania Turnpike)
Donegal, Pennsylvania 15628
**Phone:** 724/593-6349 or 800/392-7773
**Fax:** 724/593-6345
**Website:** www.shol.com/mtviewbb
**E-mail:** mtviewbb@westol.com
**Proprietors:** Gerard and Lesley O'Leary

Mountain View, a classically styled farmhouse built in 1853, is located on 10 acres of the Pennsylvania land patent given to John Alexander in 1788 and witnessed by Benjamin Franklin. The property was then defined as "Alexandria." The house's windows still contain original hand-blown glass, and the interior retains original moldings, doors, and a carved walnut center-hall staircase. Guest rooms in the farmhouse as well as in the adjacent converted barn are furnished with eighteenth- and early nineteenth-century American antiques. Mountain View is in a quiet, pastoral setting with a magnificent view of the surrounding Laurel Mountains.

**Open:** year round **Accommodations:** 7 guest rooms with private baths **Meals:** full breakfast included; restaurants nearby **Wheelchair access:** some guest rooms, dining facilities **Rates:** $95 to $185 **Payment:** AmEx, Visa, MC, CB, DC, Discover, personal and traveler's checks **Restrictions:** children over 10 welcome; no smoking; no pets

## DOYLESTOWN

**Nearby attractions:** Mercer Museum, Moravian Tileworks, Delaware River, New Hope, Peddler's Village, antiques hunting, crafts shops, hiking, river tubing, swimming, sailing, bicycling, horseback riding, tennis, golfing, skiing

## INN AT FORDHOOK FARM
105 New Britain Road
Doylestown, Pennsylvania 18901
**Phone:** 215/345-1766
**Fax:** 215/345-1791
**Website:** partyspace.com
**Proprietors:** Jonathan Burpee and Blanche Burpee Dohan

For more than 100 years Fordhook Farm has been the private home of W. Atlee Burpee, founder of the Burpee Seed Company, and his family. Nine major historic buildings constitute Fordhook Farm. Three of these are used for the inn: the main house, which began as a typical mid-eighteenth-century Pennsylvania fieldstone farmhouse; the two-story carriage house, built in 1868 and converted into a private library in 1915 (it features a Gothic-style great room with exposed beams and rafters and chestnut paneling); and the converted Bucks County–style barn. Guest rooms and common areas are filled with family antiques, furnishings, and mementos. There are 60 acres of meadows, woodlands, gardens, and seed-development trial grounds to explore.

**Open:** year round **Accommodations:** 7 guest rooms (5 have private baths); 2 have working fireplaces; 2 are suites **Meals:** full breakfast included; complimentary refreshments; restaurants nearby **Rates:** $100 to $300; 10% discount offered to National Trust members and National Trust Visa cardholders except in October **Payment:** AmEx, Visa, MC, personal and traveler's checks **Restrictions:** children over 12 welcome; no smoking; no pets **On-site activities:** gardens, paths through meadows and woods, badminton, croquet, cross-country skiing, tobogganing

## DUSHORE

**Nearby attractions:** Four State parks (Ricketts Glen, Salt Spring, Mt. Pisgah, and World End), hiking swimming, bicycling, river rafting, skiing, golfing, antiques hunting

## CHERRY MILLS LODGE
Route 87 South
RR 4, Box 1270
Dushore, Pennsylvania 18614
**Phone:** 717/928-8978
**Website:** www.endlessmountains.org
**Proprietors:** Florence and Julio Suarez

Once known as the John Gross Hotel, this building served travelers and itinerant workers during the heyday of the logging industry. During the 1860s, the village

of Cherry Mills had a grist mill, saw mill, school and hotel, general store and post office, and several small homes and farms adjoining the Little Loyalsock stream, along which the inn is situated today. A loving restoration of the hotel has resulted in a master suite with private bath and fireplace plus six cozy guest rooms typical of the nineteenth century. Guests share the living room with stone fireplace, large parlor with wood stove, dining room also with wood stove. Family-style breakfasts are served on the 18-foot oak table. A primitive, storybook cabin with pot-bellied stove is also available. The atmosphere here is entirely casual where activities range from reading books to rambling along trails by bicycle or foot.

**Open:** year round **Accommodations:** 7 guest rooms (2 have private baths); 1 is a suite **Meals:** full breakfast included; complimentary refreshments; restaurants nearby **Rates:** $35 to $75; 10% discount to National Trust members and National Trust Visa cardholders **Payment:** personal check **Restrictions:** children over 12 welcome; smoking limited; no pets **On-site activities:** hillside trail, creekside nature trail, fishing in trout stream, croquet, picnicking, village ruins

---

## EPHRATA

**Nearby attractions:** Ephrata Cloister; Pennsylvania Farm Museum; Pennsylvania Dutch country; historical sites; museums; farmers' market; art studios and galleries; shopping for antiques, collectibles, and fine fashions

### HISTORIC SMITHTON INN
900 West Main Street
Ephrata, Pennsylvania 17522
**Phone:** 717/733-6094
**Proprietors:** Dorothy Graybill and Allan Smith

The people of the religious Ephrata Cloister community built this inn in 1763; it has taken in guests ever since. Big square guest rooms are bright and airy and can be lighted by candles during evening hours. Each room has a working fireplace and a sitting area with comfortable leather-upholstered chairs, reading lamps, and a writing desk. Canopy or four-poster beds are made up with goosedown pillows and handmade Pennsylvania Dutch quilts. All rooms are provided with chamber music, books, and a refrigerator. Night shirts are available for guests to wear, and fresh flowers are in every room. Leisurely evenings can be enjoyed before the fire in the great room or in the adjacent library. Antiques and gleaming hardwood floors unite each room in the inn.

**Open:** year round **Accommodations:** 8 guest rooms with private baths; 1 is a suite **Meals:** full breakfast included; complimentary refreshments; restaurants nearby **Wheelchair access:** 1 room **Rates:** $75 to $175 **Payment:** AmEx, Visa, MC, personal and traveler's checks **Restrictions:** well-mannered, supervised children welcome; no smoking; well-trained, supervised pets allowed **On-site activities:** library, gardens, fountains and fish pond, parlor games

## 1777 HOUSE AT DONECKERS

301 West Main Street
Ephrata, Pennsylvania 17522
**Phone:** 717/738-9515 or 800/377-2217
**Website:** www.doneckers.com
**Proprietor:** H. William Donecker

Named after the year of its construction, the 1777 House at Doneckers is a stately, late-Georgian home built by Jacob Gorgas, a clockmaker in the religious Ephrata Cloister community located in scenic Lancaster County. Later the house was run as a tavern for travelers in Conestoga wagons en route from Philadelphia to Pittsburgh. A careful restoration has retained the structure's original stone masonry, handsome tile flooring, and many other authentic architectural details. Guest rooms (some with fireplaces) are named for brothers and sisters of the cloister, and are decorated with beautiful linens, fine antiques, and hand-cut stenciling. For the comfort of guests, the 1777 House has added queen-size beds and whirlpool baths in many rooms. The adjacent Carriage House offers two suites with lofts.

**Open:** year round **Accommodations:** 12 guest rooms with private baths; 6 are suites **Meals:** continental-plus breakfast included; restaurants nearby **Wheelchair access:** some guest rooms, dining room **Rates:** $75 to $210 **Payment:** AmEx, Visa, MC, CB, DC, Discover, personal and traveler's checks **Restrictions:** no pets

## ERWINNA

**Nearby attractions:** Michner Museum, Pearl Buck house, Mercer Museum, historic New Hope, winery, antiques hunting, historic sites, galleries, parks, canoeing, horseback riding, bicycling, rafting, shopping

### EVERMAY ON-THE-DELAWARE
River Road
Erwinna, Pennsylvania 18920
**Phone:** 610/294-9100 or 877/864-2365
**Fax:** 610/294-8249
**Website:** www.evermay.com
**Proprietors:** William T. and Danielle A. Moffly

Evermay, constructed in the 1700s, then remodeled and enlarged in 1871, is listed in the National Register of Historic Places. Its three stories are covered in clapboard, its facade evenly punctuated by rows of shuttered windows. A broad porch spans the first level. Evermay on-the-Delaware was a popular riverfront resort from 1871 until the 1930s, frequented by prominent families, including the theatrical Barrymores. The inn is located on 25 acres of pastures, woodlands, and gardens. Guest rooms with private baths are furnished with collectibles and antiques from the Victorian era as well as fresh flowers and fruit. Some guest rooms are contained in the restored carriage house. Afternoon tea is served in the parlor or on the patio.

**Open:** year round **Accommodations:** 16 guest rooms with private baths; 1 is a two-bedroom suite **Meals:** continental-plus breakfast included; complimentary refreshments and afternoon tea; restaurant on premises serving dinner **Wheelchair access:** carriage house guest rooms, dining rooms **Rates:** $135 to $235; 10% discount offered to National Trust members and National Trust Visa cardholders **Payment:** Visa, MC, personal and traveler's checks **Restrictions:** children over 12 welcome; smoking limited; no pets **On-site activities:** strolling grounds and gardens, hiking, bicycling, Delaware River swimming and fishing

### GOLDEN PHEASANT INN
763 River Road
Erwinna, Pennsylvania 18920
**Phone:** 610/294-9595 or 800/830-4GPI (4474)
**Fax:** 610/294-9882
**Website:** www.goldenpheasant.com
**Proprietors:** Barbara and Michel Faure

Romantic French country dining and lodging are the fare at the Golden Pheasant Inn, an 1857 Bucks County fieldstone building. Built as a rest stop for bargemen on the Delaware Canal, which is mere yards from the door, the inn is perhaps best known locally for its exceptional cuisine. Chef Michel Faure, a native of Grenoble, France, presents his creative dishes in three dining rooms; one with wood-burning fireplace, beamed ceiling, and exposed stone walls. This room is accented with copper pots and a collection of Quimper pottery from Brittany. Another dining room is in a candlelit greenhouse overlooking the canal. Lodging is available in six antiques-filled rooms featuring queen-size canopied beds and private baths. All offer river and canal views. Listed in the National Register of Historic Places, the inn has been given three diamonds by AAA and three stars by Mobil.

**Open:** year round **Accommodations:** 6 guest rooms with private baths; 1 is a suite **Meals:** continental-plus breakfast included; complimentary refreshments; restaurant on premises serves dinner and Sunday brunch **Wheelchair access:** limited **Rates:** $95 to $165; 10% discount to National Trust members and National Trust Visa cardholders **Payment:** AmEx, Visa, MC, CB, DC, Discover, personal and traveler's checks **Restrictions:** children and pets welcome in cottage suite only; smoking limited **On-site activities:** country garden

---

# FAIRFIELD

**Nearby attractions:** Gettysburg Battlefield, Amish farms, state parks, winery tours, antique hunting, fishing, hiking, golf, skiing

## MAPLEWOOD INN BED AND BREAKFAST
18 East Main Street
Fairfield, Pennsylvania 17320
**Phone and fax:** 717/642-6290
**E-mail:** maplewoodinn@mail.org
**Proprietors:** Marilyn and Robert Henderson

This 1801 log and fieldstone home is the oldest continuously inhabited residence in Fairfield. The Blythe-Cunningham family lived here for more than 125 years. During that time, the original building was enlarged with log and clapboard in 1850 and again in 1900. Today, the Hendersons carefully maintain the historic wide plank flooring, woodwork, hardware, exposed hand-hewn logs and stone masonry that compose this fine home. Guest rooms have queen-size beds, antiques, handmade quilts and pillows, and air conditioning. Two have ornamental fireplaces. Common rooms are cozy with warm fireplaces. A full country breakfast, served on china and crystal, features homemade specialties complemented by homegrown herbs from the inns extensive gardens. Specialty weekend packages are offered.

**Open:** year round **Accommodations:** 4 guest rooms share 2 baths **Meals:** full breakfast included; complimentary refreshments; restaurants nearby **Rates:** $75 to $90; 10% discount to National Trust members and National Trust Visa cardholders **Payment:** Visa, MC, personal check **Restrictions:** children over 12 welcome; no smoking; no pets **On-site activities:** reading, cards, games, television, colonial cutting gardens, specialty weekends

# FRANKLIN

**Nearby attractions:** walking tour of historic district, DeBence Antique Music World, Barrow Civic Theater, Oil Creek–Titusville Railroad, Allegheny River, bicycling, canoeing, fishing, hunting

## QUO VADIS BED AND BREAKFAST

1501 Liberty Street
Franklin, Pennsylvania 16323
**Phone:** 814/432-4208 or 800/360-6598
**Proprietors:** Allan and Janean Hoffman

Quo Vadis, listed individually and as a contributing structure to a historic district in the National Register of Historic Places, is an 1867 Queen Anne house built by lawyer Samuel Plumer. Detailed woodwork and friezes, parquet floors, and terra-cotta tile distinguish the house. Later owned by David Barcroft, the house contains heirloom furniture that has been owned now by his family for four generations. David and Anna Barcroft's daughters, Grace and Maude, made all the quilts, embroidery, and crocheting that are in Quo Vadis today. Also remaining is their hand-painted china. Spacious guest rooms with private baths are offered. The town of Franklin, which celebrated its bicentennial in 1995, is noted for its Victorian architecture, and the historic area has recently been designated as the Oil Region Heritage Park by the state of Pennsylvania.

**Open:** year round **Accommodations:** 6 rooms with private baths **Meals:** full breakfast included; restaurants nearby **Rates:** $60 to $80 **Payment:** AmEx, Visa, MC, personal and traveler's checks **Restrictions:** no smoking; no pets **On-site activities:** piano, Victrola, games, books

# GETTYSBURG

**Nearby attractions:** Gettysburg Battlefield; Lancaster Amish farms; skiing; golfing; antiques hunting; winery tours; Codorus State Park for swimming, boating, fishing, hiking, bicycling, golfing, and horseback riding

**BEECHMONT INN**
315 Broadway,
Route 194
Hanover, Pennsylvania 17331
**Phone:** 717/632-3013 or 800/553-7009
**Proprietors:** William and Susan Day
**Location:** 13 miles east of Gettysburg

Restored to its Federal-period elegance, Beechmont Inn offers traditional hospitality to visitors to historic Hanover and Gettysburg. The 1834 house has changed little except for a pantry and side porch added in 1900. The additions mirror the style of the main section with matching brick and woodwork. Guests at Beechmont can relax in the parlor, the library, or the quiet, formally landscaped courtyard. A winding staircase leads to guest rooms named in honor of the Civil War generals who fought at the Battle of Hanover; the rooms are appointed with period furnishings. Suites with working fireplaces may also feature whirlpool tubs or balconies. Breakfasts feature Beechmont's own granola (which took a prize at the York Fair) and gourmet entrees such as sausage crepes with corn soufflé or herb cheese tart with ambrosia cup.

**Open:** year round **Accommodations:** 7 guest rooms with private baths; 3 are suites **Meals:** full breakfast included; complimentary refreshments; restaurants nearby **Rates:** $80 to $135; 10% discount to National Trust members **Payment:** AmEx, Visa, MC, Discover, personal and traveler's checks **Restrictions:** children over 12 welcome; no smoking; no pets **On-site activities:** honeymoon, anniversary, and golf packages available

## BRAFFERTON INN

44 York Street
Gettysburg, Pennsylvania 17325
**Phone:** 717/337-3423
**Website:** www.bbonline.com/pa/brafferton
**Proprietors:** Jane and Sam Back

In 1786 James Gettys bought 116 acres of farmland from his father. Soon after, he erected this fieldstone house and the village of Gettysburg was born. Today, this National Register stone structure and an adjoining nineteenth-century brick-and-clapboard building house the Brafferton Inn. A National Register home, it has been fully restored to show off its original woodwork, hardwood floors, wall stenciling, and fireplaces. During the Battle of Gettysburg in 1863 a bullet shattered the glass in an upstairs window of the house, lodging in the fireplace mantel, where it remains. Guest rooms, retaining the flavor of colonial times, are comfortably furnished with handmade quilts, pine antiques, samplers, and nineteenth-century wall hangings. Guests often gather in the atrium, garden, or patio. The Brafferton has been featured in *Country Living* and *Early American Life*.

**Open:** year round **Accommodations:** 10 guest rooms with private baths; 2 are suites **Meals:** full breakfast included; complimentary refreshments; restaurants nearby **Rates:** $90 to $125; 10% discount to National Trust members and National Trust Visa

cardholders, Sunday through Thursday **Payment:** AmEx, Visa, MC, Discover, personal and traveler's checks **Restrictions:** children over 8 welcome; smoking limited; no pets **On-site activities:** reading, relaxation

## JAMES GETTYS HOTEL
27 Chambersburg Street
Gettysburg, Pennsylvania 17325
**Phone:** 717/337-1334
**Fax:** 717/334-2103
**Website:** www.jamesgettyshotel.com
**General Manager:** Stephanie McSherry

For nearly 200 years, the building on this site has served as an inn, tavern, or hotel. In 1804, a tavern, the Sign of the Buck, was built here. During the Battle of Gettysburg it was used as a hospital for wounded soldiers. In 1888, the third and fourth floors were added to accommodate the veterans who returned for the twenty-fifth anniversary of the battle. The building continued to serve travelers until the 1930s when it took on the role of apartment building. But it later reverted to its original purpose, becoming a youth hostel until purchased in 1995, being renovated and reborn as the James Gettys Hotel. Eleven tastefully appointed suites each have a sitting area, kitchenette, bedroom, and private bath. Welcome in-room amenities include fresh coffees and teas, fine soaps, evening turn-down service, and continental breakfast. The hotel's management is happy to make area travel and tour arrangements.

**Open:** year round **Accommodations:** 11 guest suites with private baths **Meals:** continental breakfast included; restaurant on site; restaurants nearby **Rates:** $115 to $135; 10% discount to National Trust members and National Trust Visa cardholders **Payment:** AmEx, Visa, MC, Discover, personal and traveler's checks **Restrictions:** no smoking; no pets

## OLD APPLEFORD INN
218 Carlisle Street
Gettysburg, Pennsylvania 17325
**Phone:** 717/337-1711 or 800/275-3373
**Fax:** 717/334-6228
**Website:** www.bbonline.com/pa/appleford
**E-mail:** jwiley@cvn.net
**Proprietors:** John and Jane Wiley

Built in 1867 on what is known as the Historic Pathway to the Battle of Gettysburg, the inn is a three-story, painted brick Italianate house. It was first the home of Robert McCurdy, a captain in the Gettysburg Troop and later county judge. During the period that the home was owned by the John Keith family, it saw such notable visitors as Dwight and Mamie Eisenhower and President Herbert Hoover. As the Old Appleford Inn, the mansion features 10 charming bedrooms, all with private baths, including the Lincoln and Grant rooms with their canopied beds. The library and spacious parlor with baby grand piano and plant-filled sun room provide warm and comfortable places to relax. All are elegantly furnished with antiques. Original hardwood floors are adorned with handmade Persian rugs. Each morning a full breakfast is served in the dining room. The extensively landscaped inn has earned three diamonds from AAA.

**Open:** year round **Accommodations:** 10 guest rooms with private baths **Meals:** full breakfast included; complimentary refreshments; restaurants nearby **Rates:** $85 to $125; 10% discount to National Trust members and National Trust Visa cardholders **Payment:** AmEx, Visa, MC, Discover, personal and traveler's checks **Restrictions:** children over 6 welcome; no smoking; no pets **On-site activities:** library and sun room for reading and games

## HANOVER

**Nearby attractions:** Gettysburg, Battlefield, Amish farms, Hersey Park, Kids's Kingdom, state parks, antiques hunting

### BEECHMONT INN
315 Broadway, Route 194
Hanover, Pennsylvania 17331
**Phone:** 717/632-3013 or 800/553-7009
**Website:** www.virtualcities.com
**Proprietors:** William and Susan Day
**Location:** 13 miles east of Gettysburg

Restored to its Federal-period elegance, Beechmont Inn offers traditional hospitality to visitors to historic Hanover and Gettysburg. The 1834 house has changed little except for a pantry and side porch added in 1900. The additions mirror the style of the main section with matching brick and woodwork. Guests at Beechmont can relax in the parlor, the library, or the quiet, formally landscaped courtyard. A winding staircase leads to guest rooms, appointed with period furnishings, named in honor of the Civil War generals who fought at the Battle of Hanover. Suites with working fireplaces may also feature whirlpool tubs or balconies. Breakfasts feature Beechmont's own granola (which took a prize at the York Fair) and gourmet entrees such as sausage crepes with corn souffle or herb cheese tarts with ambrosia cup. The Beechmont Inn has been awarded a three-diamond rating by AAA.

**Open:** year round **Accommodations:** 7 guest rooms with private baths; 3 are suites **Meals:** full gourmet breakfast included; complimentary refreshments; restaurants nearby **Rates:** $80 to $135; 10% discount offered to National Trust members when paying by cash or check **Payment:** Amex, Visa, MC, Discover, personal and traveler's checks **Restrictions:** children over 12 welcome; no smoking; no pets **On-site activities:** honeymoon/anniversary, weekend and golf packages available

---

# HAWLEY

**Nearby attractions:** Poconos, Lake Wallenpaupack, swimming, boating, golfing, picnicking, blueberry picking, antiques hunting, theater

### ACADEMY STREET BED AND BREAKFAST
528 Academy Street
Hawley, Pennsylvania 18428
**Phone:** 717/226-3430
**Fax:** 717/226-1910
**Proprietor:** Judith Lazan

Academy Street Bed and Breakfast is an outstanding Italianate Victorian built in 1863 by Civil War Captain, Joseph Atkinson, whose family was one of the earliest settlers in the Wayne County-Hawley area. Atkinson was discharged after being badly wounded at Gettysburg and became the first Sheriff of Wayne County. Conveniently located near beautiful recreational Lake Wallenpaupack and all its activities, the inn boasts antique-furnished rooms throughout. All guest rooms are large, bright, and air conditioned. The innkeeper, an avid cook, serves a full gourmet buffet breakfast and afternoon high tea.

**Open:** May to October **Accommodations:** 6 guest rooms (3 have private baths) **Meals:** full breakfast included; complimentary refreshments; restaurants nearby **Rates:** $68 to $85; 10% discount offered to National Trust members and National Trust Visa cardholders **Payment:** Visa, MC **Restrictions:** children over 12 welcome; smoking limited; no pets

## JIM THORPE

**Nearby attractions:** historic district of Victorian architecture, museums, train rides, shopping, skiing, rafting, swimming, fishing, boating

### THE HARRY PACKER MANSION
Packer Hill
Jim Thorpe, Pennsylvania 18229
**Phone:** 717/325-8566
**Website:** www.murdermansion.com
**E-mail:** mystery@murdermansion.com
**Proprietors:** Pat and Bob Handwerk

Constructed in 1874 of local brick, stone, and New England sandstone, the Harry Packer Mansion stands as a monument to an opulent and affluent age. So Gothically imposing is the mansion's facade that it was used as the model for the haunted house at Disney World. The Second Empire mansion is filled with solid walnut woodwork, oak parquet floors, marble mantels, bronze and polished brass chandeliers, English Minton tiles, hand-painted ceilings, oriental rugs, and period antiques. In the dining room, three Tiffany windows depict morning, noon, and evening in seascapes. The front veranda features Minton tile flooring, ornately carved columns of sandstone and a picturesque view of historic Jim Thorpe. Guest rooms are distinctively decorated with period antiques. Murder-mystery weekends are standard at the inn. Victorian balls, high tea, and a Sherlock Holmes chess set complete the setting. AAA has awarded four diamonds to the inn.

**Open:** year round **Accommodations:** 13 guest rooms (11 have private baths); 3 are suite **Meals:** full breakfast included; complimentary refreshments; restaurants nearby **Rates:** $75 to $150 (B&B); $350 to $495 (murder-mystery weekends); 10% discount to National Trust members and National Trust Visa cardholders midweek only **Payment:** Visa, MC **Restrictions:** not suitable for children; no smoking; no pets **On-site activities:** murder-mystery weekends, Victorian balls, high tea, game room

### THE INN AT JIM THORPE
24 Broadway
Jim Thorpe, Pennsylvania 18229
**Phone:** 717/325-2599 or 800/329-2599
**Fax:** 717/325-9145
**Website:** innjt.com
**E-mail:** innjt@ptd.net
**Proprietor:** David Drury

Rebuilt in 1848 after a fire destroyed the wooden structure known as the White Swan, the Inn at Jim Thorpe sits in the center of the Mauch Chunk historic district. It has provided comfort to some of the nineteenth century's most influential and colorful people, including Ulysses S. Grant, William Howard Taft, Thomas Edison, Buffalo Bill, and John D. Rockefeller. With its double wrought-iron balcony, the Italianate building wears a look that hints of New Orleans. Each guest room at the inn is elegantly appointed with furnishings reminiscent of the Victorian age. Lace curtains grace the windows. Ornate headboards adorn the beds. Private baths are complete with pedestal sinks and genuine marble floors. Modern comforts have not been overlooked: air conditioning, remote cable television, and telephones also are in each room. A Victorian dining room and authentic Irish pub are complete with original tin ceilings. The inn holds a three-diamond rating from AAA.

**Open:** year round **Accommodations:** 37 guest rooms with private baths; 5 are suites **Meals:** continental-plus breakfast included; restaurant and pub on premises; restaurants nearby **Rates:** $65 to $250; 10% discount to National Trust members and National Trust Visa cardholders midweek only excluding holidays **Payment:** AmEx, Visa, MC, DC, Discover, personal check in advance **On-site activities:** game room

---

## KENNETT SQUARE

**Nearby attractions:** Longwood Gardens, Brandywine River Museum, Winterthur, Chadds Ford Winery, Hagley Museum, Nemours, Franklin Mint, Rockland Museum, Philadelphia, Pennsylvania Dutch country, Valley Forge Park, antiques hunting, canoeing and tubing on the Brandywine River, bicycling, flea markets and auctions, hiking, outlet shopping

### SCARLETT HOUSE BED AND BREAKFAST
503 West State Street
Kennett Square, Pennsylvania 19348
**Phone:** 610/444-9592 or 800/820-9592
**Fax:** 610/925-0373
**Website:** www.traveldata.com/inns/data/scarlett.html
**E-mail:** janes10575@aol.com
**Proprietors:** Jane and Sam Snyder

The land on which Scarlett House sits was originally deeded to the Scarlett family by William Penn. In 1910, the Scarletts built this massive granite American Foursquare house. Their previous homestead, a farmhouse, was part of the Underground Railroad. This beautiful gray stone house is accentuated by wide bracketed eaves and a broad wraparound porch supported by stone pillars. Four centrally air-conditioned guest rooms each provide scented soaps, bathrobes, extra pillows, and ceiling fans for comfort and are distinctively furnished with antiques. A plentiful breakfast and evening refreshments are served daily. Two Victorian-styled parlors with fireplaces are open to guests. Scarlett House is ideal for small business meetings, corporate retreats, and small weddings.

**Open:** year round **Accommodations:** 4 guest rooms (2 have private baths); 1 is a suite **Meals:** full breakfast included; complimentary refreshments; restaurants nearby **Rates:** $85 to $135; 10% discount to National Trust members and National Trust Visa cardholders **Payment:** AmEx, Visa, MC, Discover, traveler's check **Restrictions:** not suitable for children; no smoking; no pets **On-site activities:** porch sitting, garden with pond

---

# LANCASTER

**Nearby attractions:** Amish country tours, antiques and quilt auctions, villages of Bird-in-Hand and Intercourse, Valley Forge, Gettysburg, Winterthur, Longwood Gardens, Hershey, historic walking tours, museums, outlets shops, golfing

## AUSTRALIAN WALKABOUT INN
837 Village Road
P.O. Box 294
Lancaster, Pennsylvania 17537
**Phone:** 717/464-0707
**Fax:** 717/464-2501
**Website:** www.bbonline.com/pa/walkabout
**Proprietors:** Richard and Margaret Mason

Originally a Mennonite farmhouse, Walkabout Inn was built in 1925 by a local master cabinetmaker. He used solid chestnut for the doors and trim throughout and for the floor-to-ceiling kitchen cabinets. Evidence of his skill is seen in the wood floors, which are laid in decorative patterns. The inn, now owned by an Australian family, is a British-style bed and breakfast located in the heart of Amish country. All guest rooms contain antique furnishings, Pennsylvania Dutch quilts, and hand-painted wall stenciling. Breakfast at the inn is served by candlelight on silver and crystal. Featured are the innkeeper's homemade Australian and British pastries, muffins, and jellies. Guests relax on the wraparound porch, sipping a cup of imported Australian tea while watching the Amish buggies go by and enjoying the grounds, which feature Australian and American wildflower gardens, a mermaid fountain, and exotic fish pond.

**Open:** year round **Accommodations:** 5 guest rooms with private baths; 3 are suites and 1 is a fantasy cottage **Meals:** full breakfast included; restaurants nearby **Rates:** $99 to $299; 10% discount offered to National Trust members and National Trust Visa cardholders **Payment:** AmEx, Visa, MC, personal and traveler's checks **Restrictions:**

children over 12 welcome; no smoking; no pets **On-site activities:** croquet, badminton, sunbathing in garden or park behind inn, outdoor whirlpool in cedar-lined spa house, picnics, barbecues, three-hour car-cassette tours of the Amish countryside

## GARDENS OF EDEN BED AND BREAKFAST
1894 Eden Road
Lancaster, Pennsylvania 17601
**Phone:** 717/393-5179
**Fax:** 717/393-7722
**Website:** www.paduthchinns.com
**Proprietors:** Marilyn and Bill Ebel

This classically styled brick home (circa 1840) was owned in the 1860s by W. C. Beecher, of the nearby Beecher Iron Works. It is to him that the house owes its cast-iron ornamentation: pedimented window hoods with dentils, dogwood flowers, and central floral motif. Situated on 3.5 acres overlooking the Conestoga River with terraced grounds that include wildflowers, perennials, woodland trails, and song birds, the inn offers four country-styled guest rooms. Each contains antiques, family-made quilts, woven coverlets, framed needlework, and floral designs. A private guest cottage (in the restored summer house) has a working fireplace and efficiency kitchen. Bountiful breakfasts, featuring herbs and flowers, are served on the screened porch overlooking the river falls in warm weather. Gardens of Eden has been featured in national publications including *Country Inns* and *Country Decorator*.

**Open:** year round **Accommodations:** 4 guest rooms with private baths; 1 guest cottage **Meals:** full breakfast included; restaurants nearby **Rates:** $95 to $130 **Payment:** Visa, MC, personal and traveler's checks **Restrictions:** children welcome in guest cottage; no smoking; no pets **On-site activities:** wandering grounds with gardens, canoeing and fishing on river

## WITMER'S TAVERN — HISTORIC 1725 INN AND MUSEUM
2014 Old Philadelphia Pike
Lancaster, Pennsylvania 17602
**Phone:** 717/299-5305
**Website:** www.800.padutch.com/1725histwit/index.html
**Proprietors:** Jeanne, Brant, Pamela, Keith, and Melissa Hartung

Witmer's Tavern is the sole survivor of 62 inns that once lined the nation's first turnpike joining Philadelphia and Lancaster. It is the oldest Pennsylvania inn still lodging travelers in the original building. The four-story blue limestone inn with individual room fireplaces, original iron door hinges and latches, nine-over-six bubbly glass windows, and handcrafted woodwork was built in 1725 and underwent several expansions through 1773. Witmer's provisioned thousands of immigrants with Conestoga wagons, rifles, and other supplies and put together the wagon trains heading into the wilderness. It also housed many members of the Continental Congress. Listed in the National Register of Historic Places, Witmer's has been described by historians as "the most completely intact and authentic eighteenth-century inn in south-central Pennsylvania." Today's guests enjoy fresh flowers, antiques, quilts, and fireplaces in every romantic room. A scenic Amish farm is at the rear of the property and a park is across the street.

**Open:** year round **Accommodations:** 7 guest rooms (2 have private baths) **Meals:** continental-plus breakfast included; restaurants nearby **Rates:** $60 to $90 **Payment:** personal and traveler's checks **Restrictions:** no cigars; no pets **On-site activities:** Pandora's Antique Shop, library, tavern, museum collections, therapeutic massage and reflexology, Witmer's Heritage Tours

# LANDENBERG

**Nearby attractions:** Brandywine River Museum, Winterthur, Longwood Gardens, Brandywine Battlefield, Hagley Museum, University of Delaware, Delaware and Lincoln Univerity, Equestrian Center, golfing, antiques hunting, outlet shops

## DAYBREAK FARM BED AND BREAKFAST
476 Chesterville Road (Route 841)
Landenberg, Pennsylvania 19350
**Phone:** 610/255-0282
**Proprietors:** Meg and Bill Ward
**Location:** 15 miles south of Kennett Square

Daybreak Farm Bed and Breakfast, a 1744 Quaker farmhouse, is situated on 20 wooded acres in historic southern Chester County, near the village of Kemblesville. The house flawlessly combines historic details such as deep window sills, five working fireplaces (one walk-in), random-width floors, built-in chimney cupboards, and exposed beams with modern amenities such as central air conditioning and an in-ground swimming pool. Guest rooms feature telephone and computer access for business travelers. The farm's fresh garden vegetables, herbs, and fruit are prepared for a full country breakfast. Guests are invited to relax before the living room fireplace in winter or enjoy the swimming pool and screened porch in warm weather.

**Open:** year round **Accommodations:** 3 guest rooms (2 have private baths); 1 is a suite **Meals:** full breakfast included; complimentary refreshments; restaurants nearby **Rates:** $75 to $95; 10% discount to National Trust members **Payment:** AmEx, Visa, MC, personal and traveler's checks **Restrictions:** children over 12 welcome; no smoking; no pets **On-site activities:** swimming pool, horseshoe pitching, croquet, bass pond (bring your fishing pole), 20 acres for walking and hiking

## LIMA

**Nearby attractions:** Brandywine Valley, Longwood Gardens, Winterthur, Brandywine Museum (Wyeth), Brandywine Battlefield, canoeing, bicycling, Tyler Arboretum, hot-air ballooning, Chadds Fords, antiques hunting

### HAMANASSETT BED AND BREAKFAST
P.O. Box 129
Lima, Pennsylvania 19037
**Phone and Fax:** 610/459-3000
**Website:** www.bbonline.com/pa/hamanassett/
**E-mail:** hamanasset@aol.com
**Proprietor:** Evelene H. Dohan
**Location:** 15 miles southwest of Philadelphia; 15 miles northeast of Wilmington, Del.

Hamanasset, convenient to all Brandywine Valley attractions, was built in 1856 by Dr. Charles D. Meigs. The estate has been in the innkeeper's family since 1870. Built of dark gray fieldstone, the house is distinguished by a cross-grambrel roof and a massive Palladian window, which illuminates the staircase landing. Guest rooms feature canopied beds, private baths, television, fresh flowers and fruit, and comfortable seating arrangements. The living room contains more than 2,000 contemporary and classical books. A full breakfast is served in the formal dining room before the corner fireplace and alcoved floor-to-ceiling French doors that overlook gardens, lawns, and ancient trees. Afternoon tea and refreshments may be enjoyed in the drawing room, in the solarium, or on the loggia in warm weather. Forty-eight acres of gardens, fields, and trails are available for guests to wander through.

**Open:** September to July **Accommodations:** 6 guest rooms with private baths; 1 is a suite **Meals:** full breakfast included; complimentary refreshments; restaurants nearby **Wheelchair access:** first-floor common rooms **Rates:** $90 to $125 **Payment:** personal and traveler's checks **Restrictions:** children over 14 welcome; no smoking; no pets **On-site activities:** trail walking, bird-watching, gardens, television, video & reading libraries

# LUMBERVILLE

**Nearby attractions:** Washington's Crossing, New Hope, Peddler's Village, winery, state parks, antiques hunting, fishing, golfing, tennis, summer theater, barge rides, museums, shopping

## BLACK BASS HOTEL
Route 32, River Road
Lumberville, Pennsylvania 18933
**Phone:** 215/297-5770
**Fax:** 215/297-0262
**Website:** www.blackbasshotel.com
**E-mail:** info@blackbasshotel.com
**Proprietor:** Herbert Ward
**Location:** 8 miles north of New Hope

The Black Bass Hotel was built in the 1740s as a fortified haven for river travelers anxious to steer clear of Native Americans who roamed the forest. It prospered as an inn for early traders. Since that time, the Black Bass has hosted thousands of guests. In 1949, when the current innkeeper took over, the structure underwent a thorough restoration. The guest rooms were filled with eighteenth- and nineteenth-century antiques, creating the mellow atmosphere of an English pub or colonial tavern. Hospitality—the inn's trademark—is readily conveyed in its several dining rooms as well as in the guest rooms, some of which have private balconies viewing the Delaware River. Dining is also available on the screened-in veranda, and the hotel boasts an unusual pewter bar from the famed Maxim's in Paris. The Black Bass is located next to the only footbridge across the Delaware River.

**Open:** year round **Accommodations:** 9 guest rooms (2 have private baths); 2 are suites **Meals:** continental breakfast included; restaurant on premises; restaurants nearby **Wheelchair access:** dining rooms **Rates:** $65 to $175 **Payment:** AmEx, Visa, MC, DC, Discover, personal and traveler's checks **On-site activities:** river boating, fishing, hiking

# NAZARETH

**Nearby attractions:** Jacobsburg Environmental Park, historic Nazareth (oldest Moravian settlement in North America), Moravian Historical Society, Bethlehem, Dorney Park

## CLASSIC VICTORIAN BED AND BREAKFAST
35 North New Street
Nazareth, Pennsylvania 18064
**Phone:** 610/759-8276
**Fax:** 610/434-1889
**Website:** www.insandouts.com
**Proprietors:** Irene and Dan Sokolowski

This 1907 Colonial Revival house was originally occupied by the M. H. Kessler family who manufactured hosiery in Nazareth. During the 1920s, Frank Schmidt, the chief executive officer of the Nazareth National Bank, purchased the property. It is distinguished by bay windows, denticulated eaves, and a sweeping wraparound porch. Inside are beautifully preserved chestnut woodwork and pocket doors, stained-glass windows, and an elevator. Three guest rooms offer period furnishings, oriental carpets, and lace curtains. A candlelight breakfast is served in the formal dining room using Wedgwood china and fine linens. Weather permitting, guests may choose to dine on the front veranda, the second-floor terrace, or under the wisteria-draped arbor. The parlor with carved mantle contains a television. The drawing room provides a place for reading and listening to classical music. The inn has received three diamonds from AAA.

**Open:** year round **Accommodations:** 3 guest rooms with private baths; 1 is a suite **Meals:** full breakfast included; restaurants nearby **Rates:** $85 to $105 **Payment:** AmEx, Visa, MC, personal and traveler's checks **Restrictions:** gardens, hammock, television, reading, listening to music

# NEW HOPE

**Nearby attractions:** New Hope historic district, Delaware River and canal, Bucks County Playhouse, Washington Crossing State Park, Mercer Museum, Fonthill, antiques hunting, arts and crafts shops, tileworks, galleries, scenic Bucks County, bicycling, skiing, ice skating, swimming pool, tennis

## AARON BURR HOUSE

80 West Bridge Street
New Hope, Pennsylvania 18938
**Phone:** 215/862-2520 or 215/862-2343
**Fax:** 215/862-2570
**Website:** www.new-hope-inn.com
**E-mail:** glassmans@erols.com
**Proprietors:** Nadine and Carl Glassman

In the heart of New Hope's historic district, the Aaron Burr House is named for the vice-president who sought a haven in Bucks County after his famous duel with Alexander Hamilton in 1804. Nestled under century-old shade trees, the 1873 inn is a two-story clapboard home, accented by the tall arched windows, single-story bay window, and decorative eave brackets characteristic of the Italianate style. High ceilings and beautifully restored black-walnut floors grace the interior, as does a fireplace that warms the parlor in cold months. Antique-filled guest rooms have four-poster canopy beds and private baths; some have fireplaces. Evening turn-down service includes chocolate mints and homemade almond liqueur at bedside. Guests have 24-hour access to a telephone, fax–copier machine, television, and kitchen.

**Open:** year round **Accommodations:** 6 guest rooms with private baths; 2 are suites with fireplaces **Meals:** continental-plus breakfast included; complimentary refreshments; restaurants nearby **Wheelchair access:** guest rooms, bathrooms, dining facilities **Rates:** $120 to $195; 10% discount offered to National Trust members and National Trust Visa cardholders **Payment:** Visa, MC, personal and traveler's checks **Restrictions:** no smoking; no pets **On-site activities:** croquet, badminton, swimming pool, tennis

## HOLLILEIF BED AND BREAKFAST
677 Durham Road
Wrightstown, Pennsylvania 18940
**Phone:** 215/598-3100
**Website:** www.bbhost.com/hollileif
**E-mail:** hollileif@aol.com
**Proprietors:** Ellen and Richard Butkus
**Location:** 6 miles west of New Hope

The name Hollileif honors the 40-foot holly trees that grace the entrance to this pre-Revolutionary plaster-and-fieldstone farmhouse. Family artwork and antiques collected over many years adorn the establishment. Guest rooms are nostalgically appointed with lace, frills, and fresh flowers. Each room has a comfortable sitting area and two have gas fireplaces. All are centrally air conditioned and have private baths. A full breakfast is served in the intimate paneled-and-beamed breakfast room. Afternoon refreshments are enjoyed before the parlor fireplace or on the arbor-covered patio. Hollileif is in a natural setting of more than five rolling acres marked by trees, flowers, gardens, a stream, and occasional wildlife.

**Open:** year round **Accommodations:** 5 guest rooms with private baths **Meals:** full breakfast included; complimentary refreshments; restaurants nearby **Rates:** $85 to $160; 10% discount to National Trust members and National Trust Visa cardholders, Sunday through Thursday, excluding holidays **Payment:** AmEx, Visa, MC, Discover, personal and traveler's checks **Restrictions:** children over 10 welcome; no smoking; no pets **On-site activities:** badminton, croquet, hammocks, sledding, gardens, bocci

## PINEAPPLE HILL
1324 River Road
New Hope, Pennsylvania 18938
**Phone:** 215/862-1790
**Fax:** 215/862-5273
**Website:** www.pineapplehill.com
**E-mail:** ktriolo@pineapplehill.com
**Proprietors:** Charles "Cookie" and Kathryn Triolo

This 1790 Bucks County manor home rests midway between the center of New Hope and Washington Crossing Park. The restored home with 18-inch-thick walls and original woodwork and floors exemplifies fine early American craftsmanship. Pineapple Hill has five guest rooms and three suites; all feature either a private balcony or fireplace. Each room is individually furnished with locally obtained antiques, collectibles, and original artwork. Suites are accompanied by separate living rooms, one with a fireplace. A full breakfast is served at individual candlelit tables. A common room with fireplace is available for reading, watching videos, or just relaxing. On the grounds, the stone walls of a barn enclose a hand-tiled swimming pool; the rose garden lies where the spring house once stood; and the ruins of the original summer kitchen surround an outdoor sitting area.

**Open:** year round **Accommodations:** 8 guest rooms with private baths; 3 are suites **Meals:** full breakfast included; complimentary refreshments; afternoon tea on weekends; restaurants nearby **Rates:** $75 to $185 **Payment:** AmEx, Visa, MC, traveler's check **Restrictions:** children over 12 welcome; no smoking; no pets **On-site activities:** swimming pool, croquet, bird and butterfly watching

## WEDGWOOD INN
111 West Bridge Street
New Hope, Pennsylvania 18938
**Phone:** 215/862-2570
**Website:** www.new-hope-inn.com
**E-mail:** stay@new-hope-inn.com
**Proprietors:** Nadine Silnutzer and Carl Glassman

Wedgwood Inn offers lodgings in three adjacent historic houses. The 1870 clapboard Victorian is distinguished by a wraparound porch, hipped gables, and a porte cochere. The stone and plaster house next door, built in 1833, boasts 26-inch-thick stone walls. The 1869 Dutch clapboard fits the term "painted lady." Each of the inn's distinctive accommodations offers lofty windows, hardwood floors, and brass ceiling fans. The rooms are furnished with antiques, original art, scented English soaps, plush towels, and handmade quilts and comforters. Guests are served breakfast on the sunporch, in the gazebo, or in the privacy of their rooms. Evening turn-down service includes mints and liqueur at bedside. The inn, once featured on the cover of *National Geographic Traveler*, is just steps from New Hope's National Register historic district.

**Open:** year round **Accommodations:** 10 guest rooms with private baths; 2 are suites with fireplaces **Meals:** continental-plus breakfast included; complimentary refreshments; restaurants nearby **Wheelchair access:** limited **Rates:** $105 to $195; 10% discount to National Trust members and National Trust Visa cardholders **Payment:** Visa, MC, personal and traveler's checks **Restrictions:** no smoking; no pets **On-site activities:** badminton, croquet, porch swings, parlor fireplace, 2 acres of landscaped grounds, Victorian gazebo

## PHILADELPHIA

**Nearby attractions:** Independence National Historic Park, Independence Hall, downtown Philadelphia, Penn's Landing, National Trust's Cliveden, theaters, museums, shopping, Academy of Music and Philadelphia Orchestra

### SHIPPEN WAY INN
418 Bainbridge Street
Philadelphia, Pennsylvania 19147
**Phone:** 215/627-7266 or 800/245-4873
**Fax:** 215/627-7781
**Proprietors:** Raymond Rhule and Ann Foringer

Two eighteenth-century houses—one brick, the other frame (which is unusual in Philadelphia)—constitute Shippen Way Inn. The houses are listed in the National Register and are located in the historic Queens Village district. Nine guest rooms are available ranging from spacious to cozy. One room has a fireplace, some rooms are reached via a spiral staircase, one is a third-floor dormer room, two have private garden entrances. Antiques, Laura Ashley wallpapers, and stenciling (on floors as well as walls) adorn the rooms. A courtyard with rose and herb gardens is shared by the two houses. The courtyard garden is where breakfast is served in warm weather. Afternoon wine and cheese may be enjoyed in the garden or before the living room fireplace.

**Open:** year round **Accommodations:** 9 guest rooms with private baths **Meals:** continental-plus breakfast included; complimentary refreshments; restaurants nearby **Rates:** $90 to $110; 10% discount to National Trust members and National Trust Visa cardholders **Payment:** AmEx, Visa, MC, personal and traveler's checks **Restrictions:** limited space available for children; smoking limited; no pets

## THOMAS BOND HOUSE BED AND BREAKFAST

129 South Second Street
Old City
Philadelphia, Pennsylvania 19106
**Phone:** 215/923-8523 or 800/845-BOND (800/845-2663)
**Fax:** 215/923-8504
**Website:** www.libertynet.org/phila-visitor
**Proprietor:** Rita McGuire

Dr. Thomas Bond, together with Benjamin Franklin and Dr. Benjamin Rush, founded the the first public hospital in the United States in 1751. Bond built this house in 1769 in the Georgian style, the Ionic-modillioned cornice being its most elaborate feature. Additions were made in 1824 and 1840. The "borrowed-light" window on the garret floor, which allows light to get from an outside room to an inside room, is an interesting architectural detail. The house served as a residence until 1810 and then as several kinds of factories and businesses, until restored as a bed and breakfast in 1988. Thomas Bond House offers guest rooms furnished with canopy, four-poster, wrought-iron, or cannonball beds. Chippendale-style and period pine furnishings fill the rooms. Two suites contain fireplaces and whirlpool baths. The parlor, with Rumford fireplace, and dining room are designed in late eighteenth-century style.

**Open:** year round **Accommodations:** 12 guest rooms with private baths; 2 are suites **Meals:** full breakfast included on weekends; continental-plus breakfast included on weekdays; complimentary refreshments; restaurants nearby **Rates:** $95 to $175; 10% discount to National Trust members and National Trust Visa cardholders **Payment:** AmEx, Visa, MC, personal and traveler's checks **Restrictions:** no pets **On-site activities:** access to health club next door, parlor games

## PITTSBURGH

**Nearby attractions:** Three Rivers Stadium, Carnegie Science Center, Pittsburgh Aviary and Children's Museum, Andy Warhol Museum, Mattress Factory Museum, historic house tours, symphony, opera, ballet, galleries, riverboat cruises

### THE PRIORY
614 Pressley Street
Pittsburgh, Pennsylvania 15212
**Phone:** 412/231-3338
**Fax:** 412/231-4838
**Website:** www.sgi.net/thepriory/
**Proprietor:** Mary Ann Graf

Carefully restored and updated, the Priory is a European-style hotel with the appointments of a large establishment and the personality of a small inn. The Priory was once a temporary haven for Benedictine priests traveling through Pittsburgh. Built in 1888, the red brick building, notable for its Romanesque-arched windows and parapeted gables, is adjacent to St. Mary's German Catholic Church, the oldest Catholic church in Pittsburgh. The Priory's maze of rooms and corridors is distinctly Old World. Each guest room is uniquely decorated with Victorian-style furnishings and has a telephone, private bath, hair dryer and cable television. Complimentary evening wine is enjoyed by guests in the sitting room, library, or courtyard. The Priory offers free parking and complimentary morning shuttle service to downtown.

**Open:** year round **Accommodations:** 24 guest rooms with private baths; 3 are suites **Meals:** continental-plus breakfast included; complimentary refreshments; restaurants nearby **Wheelchair access:** limited **Rates:** $100 to $175; 10% discount to National Trust members and National Trust Visa cardholders **Payment:** AmEx, Visa, MC, CB, DC, Discover, personal and traveler's checks **Restrictions:** no pets

## POTTSTOWN

**Nearby attractions:** Valley Forge, Brandywine Valley Museum, Longwood Gardens, Philadelphia, Audubon Wildlife Sanctuary, Chadds Ford, Bryn Mawr College, Villanova University, Valley Forge Music Fair, Amish country, antiques hunting, tennis, golfing, state and local parks

## COVENTRY FORGE INN
3360 Coventryville Road
Pottstown, Pennsylvania 19465
**Phone:** 610/469-6222
**Proprietors:** June and Wallis Callahan
**Location:** 14 miles west of Valley Forge Park

Coventry Forge Inn comprises a guest house, built in 1806, and a restaurant, built in 1717. The guest house, resting among gardens and rolling pastures, offers comfortable and simple accommodations in a quiet rural setting. These spacious rooms, each with a private bath and air conditioning, are decorated in period antiques and reproductions. Breakfast is served on the porch of the restaurant next door. The inn is notable for its fine French cuisine. For more than 30 years, Coventry Forge Inn has offered the freshest, locally obtained ingredients, prepared according to classic French recipes, and served with the care and expertise that continue to gain national recognition, including a four-star rating from the *Mobil Travel Guide*.

**Open:** year round **Accommodations:** 5 guest rooms with private baths **Meals:** continental breakfast included; restaurant on premises **Rates:** $70 to $75 **Payment:** AmEx, Visa, MC, DC **Restrictions:** children over 12 welcome; no pets **On-site activities:** French dining, relaxation

# RIDGWAY

**Nearby attractions:** Allegheny National Forest region, Clairon-Little Toby Creek Rail-Trail, Clarion River canoeing, cross-country skiing, antiques hunting, brewery and wineries, only elk herd east of the Mississippi

## THE TOWERS VICTORIAN INN
330 South Street
Ridgway, Pennsylvania 15853
**Phone:** 814/772-7657
**Website:** www.ncentral.com/~towers
**E-mail:** lauricde@ncentral.com
**Proprietor:** Dale Lauricella

Built in 1865 by the town's first mayor, Jerome Powell, this Italianate house is made remarkable by such features as a wraparound front porch, unusual rounded front gable, and central tower. Around the turn of the century, the house was enhanced with Hyde Murphy woodwork and fireplaces, all meticulously restored today. The Hyde Murphy Company was a premier wood-working firm in Ridgway that provided the interiors of many public buildings, including the U.S.

Supreme Court, the Pentagon, and the Smithsonian Institution. The inn's dining room features cherry paneling and fireplaces, antique stained-glass windows, and a hand-crafted parquet floor. The original Bradley and Hubbard lighting has been completely refurbished, along with all of the 1870s brass door and window hardware. Decorated throughout with antiques, The Towers offers modern amenities for today's travelers: private telephones/modem lines, cable television, wet bars, work desks, and kitchenettes.

**Open:** year round **Accommodations:** 6 guest rooms (4 have private baths); 2 are suites with kitchen facilities **Meals:** full breakfast included; complimentary refreshments; restaurants nearby **Rates:** $65 to $110; 10% discount to National Trust members and National Trust Visa cardholders; specialty weekend packages available, call for rates (wilderness excursion, antiques-lovers, golfers, Victorian romance) **Payment:** Visa, MC, personal and traveler's checks **Restrictions:** children over 12 welcome; no smoking; no pets **On-site activities:** badminton, croquet, horseshoes, board games, massage therapy, bicycles

---

## SCOTTDALE

**Nearby attractions:** Frank Lloyd Wright's Fallingwater, Kentuck Knob, West Overton Museum, Forts Necessity and Ligonier, Bushy Run Battlefield, Compass Inn Museum, Hannastown Museum, Seven Springs and Hidden Valley ski resorts, theater, bicycling, tennis, white-water rafting at Ohiopyle, hiking, nature walks, antiques hunting

### ZEPHYR GLEN BED AND BREAKFAST
205 Dexter Road
Scottdale, Pennsylvania 15683
**Phone:** 724/887-6577
**Proprietors:** Noreen and Gilbert McGurl

Abraham Stauffer, the son of a Mennonite minister, built this Federal brick home in the 1820s. The house is nestled in a glen called Zephyr, which means gentle west wind. Three guest rooms are offered with private baths. All three have stenciled walls and ceiling fans. Anna's Room has two antique beds, hooked rugs, and antique quilts. Elizabeth's Room has two Victorian antique beds—one single, one double. Katrina's Room has a working fireplace, and antique quilts on the 1850 Jenny Lind double bed. Guests are invited for tea and cookies before the fireplace in the parlor or on the front porch, which spans the facade. The yard is filled with trees, wildflowers, and perennial and herb gardens. The innkeepers operate an antiques shop on the property.

**Open:** year round **Accommodations:** 3 guest rooms with private baths **Meals:** full breakfast included; complimentary refreshments; grill and picnic table provided; restaurants nearby **Rates:** $70 to $80 **Payment:** Visa, MC, Discover, personal and traveler's checks **Restrictions:** inquire about children; no smoking; no pets **On-site activities:** musical instruments, porch sitting, garden strolls, antiques shop, board games

# VALLEY FORGE

**Nearby attractions:** Valley Forge National Historical Park, Brandywine Valley Museum, Longwood Gardens, Philadelphia, Audubon Wildlife Sanctuary, Chadds Ford, Bryn Mawr College, Villanova University, King of Prussia Mall, antiques hunting, tennis, golfing

## GREAT VALLEY HOUSE OF VALLEY FORGE

110 Swedesford Road
R.D. 3
Malvern, Pennsylvania 19355
**Phone:** 610/644-6759
**Fax:** 610/644-7019
**Website:** pages.prodigy.com/greatvalleyhouse
**E-mail:** greatvalleyhouse@prodigy.net
**Proprietor:** Pattye Benson
**Location:** 2 miles west of Valley Forge

A Welsh settler began building this fieldstone farmhouse in 1690. It was added to in 1740, and again in 1791. One of the oldest homes in the area, the Great Valley House, is complete with original fireplaces, random-width wood floors, and hand-hewn nails. Also notable are the hand-forged iron hinges used throughout and an old stone sink, said to be one of only two such pre-1700 sinks in the country. The old kitchen contains a walk-in fireplace with its original swing crane and 300-year-old mantel. Each of the three guest rooms are hand stenciled, decorated with antiques, and accented with handmade quilts. A refrigerator, coffeepot, and microwave oven are located in the center hall for guests' convenience. The surrounding three acres contain an old smokehouse, a cold storage keep, and ancient trees as well as a more modern diversion—a large swimming pool. The inn has been featured in the *Washington Post, New York Times,* and *Philadelphia Inquirer,* as well as the television program *"Historic Traveler."*

**Open:** year round **Accommodations:** 3 guest rooms (2 have private baths) **Meals:** full breakfast included; complimentary refreshments; restaurants nearby **Rates:** $75 to $100; 10% discount offered to National Trust members and National Trust Visa cardholders **Payment:** AmEx, Visa, MC, Discover, personal and traveler's checks **Restrictions:** no smoking; no pets **On-site activities:** swimming pool, hiking, walking, fishing

# RHODE ISLAND

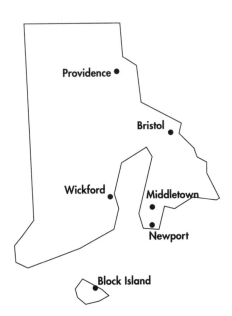

## BLOCK ISLAND

**Nearby attractions:** art galleries, bicycling, swimming, beaches, sailing, bluffs, lighthouses, national landmarks, Nature Conservancy trails, bird-watching, shopping

## HOTEL MANISSES
1 Spring Street
Block Island, Rhode Island 02807
**Phone:** 401/466-2421 or 800/MAN-ISSE
**Fax:** 401/466-3162
**E-mail:** biresorts@aol.com
**Proprietors:** Joan and Justin Abrams

When the Manisses was built in 1870, it was known as one of the best summer hotels in the east. With its mansard roof, clapboard siding, and lookout tower, it was a picturesque beach structure. The current innkeepers purchased this Block Island landmark in 1972 and began restoring it. Now listed in the National Register of Historic Places, the inn has 17 Victorian-style guest rooms featuring turn-of-the-century furniture and some fireplaces, as well as modern conveniences such as private baths (some with whirlpool tubs) and telephones. Brandy and candy are bedside treats. The hotel has a restaurant of note, serving meals in the gar-

den terrace dining room or on the deck in summer. Many of the herbs, vegetables, and flowers used are grown in the hotel's own gardens.

**Open:** year round **Accommodations:** 17 guest rooms with private baths; 4 are suites **Meals:** full breakfast included; complimentary refreshments; restaurant on premises serving dinner **Wheelchair access:** some guest rooms, bathrooms, dining room **Rates:** $90 to $260; 10% discount to National Trust members **Payment:** AmEx, Visa, MC, personal and traveler's checks **Restrictions:** children over 10 welcome; smoking limited; no pets **On-site activities:** lawn games, petting zoo, sailing, bicycling

# BRISTOL

**Nearby attractions:** historic waterfront district, seven museums, Prudence Island and ferry, sailing from Bristol Yacht Club, 15-mile bike path, shopping, dining

## PARKER BORDEN HOUSE
736 Hope Street
Bristol, Rhode Island 02809
**Phone:** 401/253-2084
**Proprietors:** Jean and Bob Tischer

In 1798 sea captain Parker Borden built this stylish Federal house on Hope Street overlooking the piers where his ships sailed into Bristol Harbor. His descendants continued to live here until 1985, when the present owners purchased it. Remarkably, very few changes have been made to the original architectural details. Intricate carving around the front door and the Palladian window above have been painstakingly restored, and the entire front of the house has been painted an eye-catching rich red. The Parker Borden House has 10 fireplaces, including one in each of the guest rooms. The Carter Room overlooks the harbor and has a queen-size bed and private bath. The Bradford Room also overlooks the harbor, and has twin beds, and shares a bath with the intimate Susan B. Anthony Room with double bed that overlooks the garden. All guests may use the adjoining sitting room. Mornings bring full breakfasts in the elegant dining room. The inn is located within walking distance of many of Bristol's attractions.

**Open:** year round **Accommodations:** 3 guest rooms (1 has a private bath); 2 can be joined as a suite **Meals:** full breakfast included; restaurants nearby **Rates:** $70 to $95; 10% discount to National Trust members and National Trust Visa cardholders **Payment:** Visa, MC, personal and traveler's checks **Restrictions:** no smoking; no pets **On-site activities:** relaxing in yard with garden

# MIDDLETOWN

**Nearby attractions:** Newport mansion tours, Cliff Walk, Touro Synagogue, Newport Art Museum, Museum of Yachting, Tennis Hall of Fame, antiques hunting, Brick Market Place shops, Redwood Library, live theater, beaches, sailing, swimming, boating, fishing, golfing, hiking, bicycling, tennis

## THE INN AT SHADOW LAWN

120 Miantonomi Avenue
Middletown, Rhode Island 02842
**Phone:** 401/847-0902 or 800/352-3750
**Fax:** 401/848-6529
**Website:** www.shadowlawn.com
**E-mail:** Randy@shadowlawn.com
**Proprietors:** Selma and Randy Fabricant

The Inn at Shadow Lawn is an 1856 Italianate and Stick Style house designed by Richard Upjohn. Its arcaded front veranda is accented with green-and-white striped awnings, and its white clapboards are set off by green window shutters. Inside, the inn has been elegantly styled, from original French crystal chandeliers and stained-glass windows to tasteful wallcoverings and parquet floors. Each color-coordinated guest room is individually decorated and provides an intimate sitting area, private tiled bath, color cable television, air conditioning, and refrigerator. All bedrooms have working fireplaces and a complimentary bottle of wine. The first floor contains a parlor, a paneled library with unique elephant-skin wallcovering, and a dining room with exquisite stained-glass window and restored, elaborately styled, hand-painted friezes. Weddings, parties, and business meetings can be held in the newly restored ballroom.

**Open:** year round **Accommodations:** 8 guest rooms with private baths **Meals:** full breakfast included; restaurants nearby **Rates:** $65 to $175; 10% discount to National Trust members and National Trust Visa cardholders **Payment:** AmEx, Visa, MC, CB, DC, Discover, traveler's check **Restrictions:** no smoking; no pets **On-site activities:** television, newspapers, magazines, books

# NEWPORT

**Nearby attractions:** mansion tours, Cliff Walk, Touro Synagogue, Newport Art Museum, Tennis Hall of Fame, more than 500 restored colonial homes, antiques hunting, Brick Market Place shops, oldest continuously used library in the country, live theater, beaches, sailing, swimming, boating, fishing, golfing, hiking, bicycling, tennis

## ADMIRAL BENBOW INN

93 Pelham Street
Newport, Rhode Island 02840
**Phone:** 401/848-8000 or 800/343-2863
**Fax:** 401/848-8006
**Website:** www.admiralsinns.com
**E-mail:** 5star@admiralsinns.com
**Proprietors:** Jane and Bruce Berriman

The Admiral Benbow was built in 1855 by a Block Island sea captain, Augustus Littlefield. He designed the house after those he had seen in Italy, incorporating an octagonal, two-story tower and tall, arched windows. The house was built as an inn and, for a few years, operated as a speakeasy. Accordingly, the inn has hosted many famous—and infamous—guests. Today's guest rooms are decorated with brass beds and fine antiques. A collection of eighteenth- and nineteenth-century barometers are on display and for sale in the hall and common room. The inn is a short walk from Bellevue Avenue shops, restaurants, art galleries, and all that Newport has to offer. Listed in the National Register and named after Mrs. Hawkins' inn in *Treasure Island,* the Admiral Benbow has been featured in *Country Inns, Bed and Breakfast,* and *New York* magazines.

**Open:** year round **Accommodations:** 15 guest rooms with private baths; 1 has a private deck with harbor view **Meals:** continental-plus breakfast included; restaurants nearby **Rates:** $65 to $185; 10% discount to National Trust members and National Trust Visa cardholders **Payment:** AmEx, Visa, MC, DC, personal and traveler's checks **Restrictions:** children over 12 welcome; smoking limited; no pets

## ADMIRAL FARRAGUT INN

31 Clarke Street
Newport, Rhode Island 02840
**Phone:** 401/848-8000 or 800/343-2863
**Fax:** 401/848-8006
**Website:** www.admiralsinns.com
**E-mail:** 5star@admiralsinns.com
**Proprietors:** Jane and Bruce Berriman

The original portion of this nearly 300-year-old home was built in 1702 by a man named Stevens. He expanded the two-story, two-room house to its present configuration in 1755. It was left untouched until 25 years ago, thus preserving all original features. Twelve-over-twelve double-hung windows and authentic colonial cove moldings outside give no hint of the modern conveniences inside. The current owners upgraded the interior in 1987 with new wiring and plumbing, salvaged beams, and wrought-iron hardware. Throughout the inn, guests will find a fresh interpretation of colonial themes. Each guest room is different with a combination of handmade and antique furnishings. There are Shaker-style four-poster beds, painted and stenciled armoires, and imported English antiques. Breakfast is served in the keeping room. This National Register property has been featured in *Country Living*.

**Open:** year round **Accommodations:** 9 guest rooms with private baths **Meals:** full breakfast included; restaurants nearby **Rates:** $55 to $175 **Payment:** AmEx, Visa, MC, DC, personal and traveler's checks **Restrictions:** children over 12 welcome; no smoking; no pets

## ADMIRAL FITZROY INN

398 Thames Street
Newport, Rhode Island 02840
**Phone:** 401/848-8000 or 800/343-2863
**Fax:** 401/848-8006
**Website:** www.admiralsinns.com
**E-mail:** 5star@admiralsinns.com
**Proprietors:** Jane and Bruce Berriman

Built in 1854 to designs by architect Dudley Newton, the Admiral Fitzroy is a three-story weathered-shingle structure sitting above an English basement, which houses fashionable shops. The inn's guests rooms are decorated in a distinctive fashion with unique hand-painted details, and furnished with brass or sleigh beds, marble-topped tables, reading lamps, and comfortable sitting areas. Several rooms have fireplaces. A full breakfast is served in the breakfast room. The

Admiral Fitzroy is named for the famous Englishman who commanded the *Beagle* on Charles Darwin's voyage while he was writing the *Origin of Species*. Careful attention to its restoration has earned the Admiral Fitzroy a listing in the National Register of Historic Places.

**Open:** year round **Accommodations:** 17 guest rooms with private baths **Meals:** full breakfast included; restaurants nearby **Wheelchair access:** 1 room **Rates:** $85 to $225 **Payment:** AmEx, Visa, MC, DC, personal and traveler's checks **Restrictions:** smoking limited; no pets

## CASTLE HILL INN AND RESORT

590 Ocean Avenue
Newport, Rhode Island 02840
**Phone:** 401/849-3800 or 888/466-1355
**Fax:** 401/849-3838
**Website:** www.castlehillinn.com

Alexander Agassiz, a renowned scientist and explorer, chose the peninsula known as Castle Hill in 1874 as the site for his summer home and marine laboratory. The home, a Queen Anne mansion became a resort after World War II. The laboratory, in a building similar to the chalets of Agassiz's native Switzerland, became part of the hotel in 1985. Guest rooms are in the restored mansion, private harbor houses, the chalet-style building, and beach cottages. All are sumptuously decorated in individual styles, many offering king-size beds, whirlpool or claw-foot tubs, fireplaces, or semiprivate decks. Spectacular views are everywhere. The inn's dining room is renowned, having won an Award of Excellence from Wine Spectator. The *New York Times* calls Castle Hill, "truly a gem of a hotel."

**Open:** year round **Accommodations:** 38 guest rooms (32 have private baths); 2 are suites **Meals:** continental-plus breakfast included; complimentary refreshments; restaurant and lounge on premises **Rates:** $95 to $325; 10% discount to National Trust members and National Trust Visa cardholders, off-season only **Payment:** AmEx, Visa, MC, Discover, traveler's check **Restrictions:** children over 12 welcome; smoking limited to lounge; no pets **On-site activities:** private white-sand beach, hiking trails

## MELVILLE HOUSE
39 Clarke Street
Newport, Rhode Island 02840
**Phone:** 401/847-0640
**Fax:** 401/847-0956
**Website:** www.melvillehouse.com
**E-mail:** innkeeper@ids.net
**Proprietors:** Vince DeRico and David Horan

A country inn located in bustling Newport, Melville House is a 1750 shingled colonial structure built by Henry Potter, who once quartered officers of the French army here during the Revolutionary War. It was later owned by the Melville family (no relation to Herman) and is listed today in the National Register of Historic Places. Melville House is one of the few inns in Newport dedicated to the colonial style and decorated in the simple tastes of the early colonists. A full breakfast is served in the sunny breakfast room and features the inn's homemade granola, muffins, and home-baked breads. Afternoon tea is served daily and includes homemade biscotti and a hearty soup on cold days. The inn has earned a AAA three-diamond rating and has been featured in *Good Housekeeping* magazine.

**Open:** year round **Accommodations:** 7 guest rooms (5 have private baths); 1 is a winter fireplace suite **Meals:** full breakfast included; complimentary afternoon tea; restaurants nearby **Rates:** $95 to $165; 10% discount to National Trust members and National Trust Visa cardholders **Payment:** AmEx, Visa, MC, Discover, personal and traveler's checks **Restrictions:** children over 12 welcome; no smoking; no pets **On-site activities:** bicycles available

## MILL STREET INN
75 Mill Street
Newport, Rhode Island 02840
**Phone:** 401/849-9500 or 800/392-1316
**Fax:** 401/848-5131
**Website:** millstreetinn.com
**General Manager:** Janie McHenry

The Mill Street Inn began in 1902 as J. D. Johnston's wood-finishing mill and architectural offices. Johnston is known in Newport for designing and building the city hall and numerous other commercial and residential buildings. His original mill on this site was destroyed by fire at the turn of the century. The current building was then constructed of brick, two courses thick, with an interior beam structure that could survive a fire or the fiercest storms off the Atlantic. It stands solidly today, having been renovated to house an all-suites hotel with junior, deluxe, and townhouse accommodations. All rooms offer color cable television, fine toiletries, bathrobes, and mini-bars. In fair weather, the continental-plus breakfast is offered on the rooftop deck. Listed in the National Register of Historic Places, Mill Street Inn is ideally located in Newport's Historic Hill neighborhood.

**Open:** year round **Accommodations:** 23 guest suites with private baths **Meals:** continental-plus breakfast included; catering for groups; restaurants nearby **Rates:** $75 to $350; 10% discount to National Trust members and National Trust Visa cardholders **Payment:** AmEx, Visa, MC, DC, personal and traveler's checks **Restrictions:** no pets

## THE WILLOWS OF NEWPORT, ROMANTIC INN AND GARDEN
8 and 10 Willow Street, Historic Point
Newport, Rhode Island 02840
**Phone:** 401/846-5486
**Website:** www.newportri.com/users/willows
**Proprietor:** Pattie Murphy

The Willows of Newport begins with the 1740 John Rogers House at number 10 Willow Street. Attached to its side is a Greek Revival house, which was built onto the Rogers House in 1840 so that family and friends could vacation in Newport, fast becoming the country's first summer resort. Listed as a National Landmark, the Willows is an inn that caters to the romantic traveler. Five guest rooms are uniquely designed, each with a private bath. Most rooms have canopied brass beds; one has an antique rosewood bedroom suite. Bone china and silver are used for breakfast, which is served to guests in bed by a black-tied host. Evening turn-down service with mints on pillows is standard. Guests are invited to use the wet bar and parlor with fireplace. The inn's award-winning flower gardens also contain a waterfall and heart-shaped fish pond. Private garage parking is provided at this Mobil three-star inn.

**Open:** year round **Accommodations:** 5 guest rooms with private baths **Meals:** continental-plus breakfast in bed included; complimentary refreshments; restaurants nearby **Rates:** $108 to $225 **Payment:** personal and traveler's checks **Restrictions:** not suitable for children; no smoking; no pets **On-site activities:** garden; ask about the new Silk and Chandelier Collection

---

# PROVIDENCE

**Nearby attractions**: historic architecture, Trinity Repertory Theater, Rhode Island School of Design, Brown University, shopping

## OLD COURT BED AND BREAKFAST

144 Benefit Street
Providence, Rhode Island 02903
**Phone:** 401/751-2002 or 401/351-0747
**Fax:** 401/272-4830
**Website:** www.oldcourt.com
**E-mail:** reserve@oldcourt.com
**General Manager:** David Dolbashian

Originally a rectory built in 1863 by Alpheus Morse, Old Court sits next to the historic Rhode Island Courthouse, which currently houses the Rhode Island Historical Preservation Commission. The Italianate inn reflects early Victorian taste in its ornate Italian mantelpieces, plaster moldings, and 12-foot ceilings. Antique furniture, chandeliers, and memorabilia display a range of nineteenth-century styles from the ornate Rococo Revival to the intricate and refined Eastlake. Yet contemporary standards of luxury and comfort are ever present. Breakfast, with espresso or cappuccino, is served in the dining room at the antique claw-foot table. Listed in the National Register of Historic Places, the inn is only a three-minute walk from downtown Providence or the campuses of Brown University and the Rhode Island School of Design.

**Open:** year round **Accommodations:** 11 guest rooms with private baths; 3 are suites **Meals:** full breakfast included; restaurants nearby **Rates:** $125 to $145; 10% discount offered to National Trust members and National Trust Visa cardholders **Payment:** Visa, MC, Discover, personal and traveler's checks

# WICKFORD

**Nearby attractions:** Narragansett Bay, beach, sailing, swimming, boating, kayaking, hiking, tennis, historic Wickford Village, Newport mansion tours, Narragansett, Block Island Ferry

## THE HADDIE PIERCE HOUSE
146 Boston Neck Road
Wickford, Rhode Island 02852
**Phone or Fax:** 401/294-7674
**Website:** www.bestinns.net/usa/ri/hp.html
**E-mail:** haddie@bigplanet.com
**Proprietors:** Darya and John Prassl

In 1906, Haddie and Christopher Pierce built their American Foursquare clapboard home, complete with widow's walk, on a busy street corner in the village of Wickford. The town had been enjoying a newfound reputation as a summer resort thanks to the Seaview Railroad and steamships that sailed into Wickford's harbor. The train and ships have passed into history, but the Haddie Pierce House remains in its excellent location close to all that Wickford offers. The double parlor with its parquet floors, antiques and period furnishings set the tone of Victorian quietude. Guest rooms are light and airy and may have a private or shared bath. A fireplace suite of rooms is also available. A hearty breakfast is served and tea is always available for sipping on the front porch.

**Open:** year round **Accommodations:** 5 guest rooms (1 has a private bath); 1 is a suite **Meals:** full breakfast included; complimentary refreshments; restaurants nearby **Rates:** $85 to $95; 10% discount to National Trust members and National Trust Visa cardholders **Payment**: AmEx, Visa, MC, DC, Discover, personal and traveler's checks **Restrictions:** no smoking; no pets

# SOUTH CAROLINA

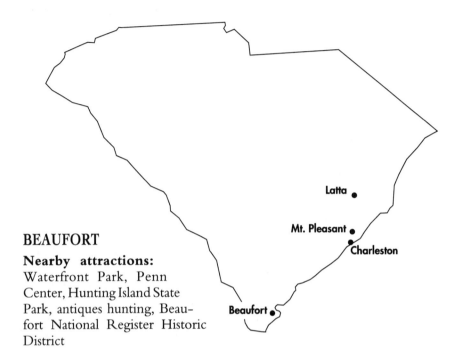

Latta

Mt. Pleasant
Charleston

Beaufort

## BEAUFORT

**Nearby attractions:**
Waterfront Park, Penn
Center, Hunting Island State
Park, antiques hunting, Beau-
fort National Register Historic
District

## TWOSUNS INN BED AND BREAKFAST
1705 Bay Street
Beaufort, South Carolina 29902
**Phone:** 843/522-1122 or 800/532-4244
**Fax:** 843/522-1122
**E-mail:** twosuns@islc.net
**Proprietors:** Carrol and Ron Kay

Designed by Savannah architect Morton Levy, this Neoclassical home, built for
the Keyserling family in 1917, incorporated a host of modern conveniences:
central baseboard vacuum system, a Roman heat distribution system, a brass full-
body shower, an electric call-box system, and an open floor-plan ventilation
system culminating in a classic hipped-roof skylight. Five guest rooms in today's
inn are furnished with antiques and collectibles and decorated with Carrol Kay's
custom window and bed ensembles. The parlor features Carrol's weaving looms,
the living room is cozy with a fireplace, and the veranda rockers invite a lazy
afternoon overlooking Beaufort Bay. Guest bicycles are available for touring
Beaufort's National Landmark historic district.

Open: year round **Accommodations:** 6 guest rooms with private baths **Meals:** full breakfast included; complimentary afternoon "tea and toddy"; restaurants nearby **Wheelchair access:** yes **Rates:** $105 to $135; 10% discount to National Trust members and National Trust Visa cardholders **Payment:** AmEx, Visa, MC, personal and traveler's checks **Restrictions:** children over 12 welcome; no smoking; no pets **On-site activities:** lawn games, bicycles, reading, specialty weekends and B&B workshops available

# CHARLESTON

**Nearby attractions:** Battery, Charleston Harbor, White Point Gardens, Fort Sumter, Gibbes Art Gallery, Charleston Museum, National Trust's Drayton Hall, plantations, waterfront park, beaches, golfing, hiking, swimming, tennis, fishing, concerts, theaters, shopping

## BATTERY CARRIAGE HOUSE INN
20 South Battery
Charleston, South Carolina 29401
**Phone:** 800/775-5575
**Fax:** 843/727-3130
**Proprietors:** Katharine and Drayton Hastie

Built in 1843 and renovated in 1870, this antebellum mansion on the Battery was purchased in 1874 by the innkeeper's great-great grandfather, Andrew Simonds. Guests are invited to stay in the historic carriage house and kitchen of this landmark home in White Point Gardens, the most stately residential district of old Charleston. Elegant rooms overlooking a serene, private garden combine a romantic and historical ambience with many amenities, including private steam baths, whirlpool tubs, terrycloth robes, cable television, afternoon wine, turn-down service, free local phone calls, and ample free parking. Guests are served breakfast and a morning newspaper on silver trays in the privacy of their rooms or under the rose arbor in the garden.

Open: year round **Accommodations:** 11 guest rooms with private baths **Meals:** continental breakfast included; complimentary refreshments; restaurants nearby **Rates:**

$99 to $199 **Payment:** AmEx, Visa, MC, Discover, personal and traveler's checks **Restrictions:** not suitable for young children; smoking limited; no pets **On-site activities:** relax in garden, house tour

## BELVEDERE BED AND BREAKFAST
40 Rutledge Avenue
Charleston, South Carolina 29401
**Phone:** 843/722-0973
**Proprietor:** David S. Spell   **Manager:** Rick Zender

A handsome white house dominated by a two-story circular portico supported by massive columns with Ionic capitals, the Belvedere is an impressive example of the Neoclassical style so popular in 1900, when the house was built. A local physician, who bought the home in 1925, salvaged elegant Adam-style wood-work from nearby Belvedere Plantation (ca. 1800) and had the carved door surrounds and mantels installed in all the rooms and hallways of this house, where they remain today. Belvedere's guest rooms surround a large common sitting area that opens to the spacious round porch overlooking Colonial Lake and the Ashley River beyond. Each bedroom features high ceilings, an ornamental fireplace, antique furnishings with oriental rugs, a private bath, and color television. The house is located in the downtown historic district.

**Open:** year round **Accommodations:** 3 guest rooms with private baths **Meals:** continental-plus breakfast included; complimentary refreshments; restaurants nearby **Rates:** $125 to $150; 10% discount offered to National Trust members **Payment:** personal and traveler's checks **Restrictions:** not suitable for children; no smoking; no pets

## BRASINGTON HOUSE BED AND BREAKFAST
328 East Bay Street
Charleston, South Carolina 29401
**Phone:** 843/722-1274 or 800/722-1274
**Fax:** 843/722-6785
**Proprietors:** Dalton and Judy Brasington

Located in the heart of Charleston's historic district, Brasington House, a 200-year-old antebellum Charleston "single house," was meticulously restored in 1987 by its current owners. The antique furnishings blend with the Greek Revival features, marble mantels, and decorative plaster cornices in the formal living and dining rooms. The raised foundation and wide piazzas running the length of the facade are typical of this Charleston-style house. Four guest rooms appointed in period furnishings include telephones, cable television, and tea, coffee, and hot chocolate-making services. Late each afternoon, the proprietors serve wine and cheese in the living room. Elegant breakfasts are served on fine china, crystal, and silver in the dining room.

**Open:** year round **Accommodations:** 4 guest rooms with private baths; 1 is a suite **Meals:** full breakfast included; complimentary refreshments; restaurants nearby **Rates:** $115 to $154 **Payment:** Visa, MC, personal and traveler's checks **Restrictions:** not suitable for children; no smoking; no pets

## FULTON LANE INN
202 King Street
Charleston, South Carolina 29401
**Phone:** 843/720-2600 or 800/720-2688
**Fax:** 843/720-2940
**Website:** www.charminginns.com
**Proprietor:** Mary Kay Smith

This 1902 brick inn is on a quiet pedestrian lane just off King Street, in the heart of the city's famous historic district. The inn is decorated in a classic blend of contemporary and traditional styling. Many of the spacious guest rooms feature large whirlpool baths and tall, canopied beds draped with hand-strung netting. Other rooms enjoy cathedral ceilings and several offer fireplaces. Each room is furnished with a private stocked refrigerator. Throughout, soaring windows frame vistas of the city's historic skyline, punctuated with the many trademark church spires. Complimentary breakfast is delivered to guest rooms on silver trays. Wine and sherry are offered in the lobby each evening and nightly turn-down service is provided along with chocolates. Fulton Lane Inn has been awarded four diamonds by AAA.

**Open:** year round **Accommodations:** 27 guest rooms with private baths; 5 are suites **Meals:** continental-plus breakfast included; complimentary refreshments; restaurants nearby **Wheelchair access:** 2 rooms **Rates:** $120 to $275; 10% discount to National Trust members and National Trust Visa cardholders **Payment:** Visa, MC, traveler's check **Restrictions:** no smoking; no pets

## GOVERNOR'S HOUSE INN

117 Broad Street
Charleston, South Carolina 29401
**Phone:** 843/720-2070 or 800/720-9812
**Website:** www.governorshouse.com
**Proprietor:** Karen Spell Shaw and Robert Hill Shaw, III

Built in 1760 in the Georgian style for James Laurens by architects Miller and Fullerton, this stately home with full-length double piazzas, is best known for its purchase in 1788 by Edward Rutledge, the youngest signer of the Declaration of Independence. Rutledge later was elected governor of South Carolina. The first floor common rooms are palatial in size, featuring crystal chandeliers and nine fireplaces, and fine family antiques. Guests may select one of 12 elegantly appointed guest rooms with private baths and hardwood floors. The Grand Rooms each have 12-foot ceilings, fireplace, and private veranda. The Roofscape room showcases a colorful view of Charleston. The Kitchen House Suite has a separate living room, private porch, wet bar, and an original 1760 fireplace. Gracious hospitality is extended to guests in the Southern continental breakfast, lowcountry afternoon tea, and evening sherry in the parlor.

**Open:** year round (except 3 days at Christmas) **Accommodations:** 12 guest rooms with private baths; 4 are suites **Meals:** continental-plus breakfast included; afternoon tea and evening sherry; restaurants nearby **Rates:** $165 to $330; 10% discount to National Trust members **Payment:** personal and traveler's checks **Restrictions:** children over 12 welcome; no smoking; no pets **On-site activities:** gardens designed by leading landscaper Robert C. Chestnut

## HAYNE HOUSE
30 King Street
Charleston, South Carolina 29401
**Phone:** 843/577-2633
**Fax:** 843/577-5906
**Proprietors:** Brian and Jan McGreevy

This National Register property is a veritable lesson book in the city's architecture, with the original colonial portion (1755) following the Charleston single-house style and the kitchen house featuring colonial brickwork, the Regency wing dating from the 1820s showing the robustness of interior decoration from the era, and the stair tower, built following the 1886 earthquake, showing Victorian influence. Six guest rooms, all with private baths, are furnished with family antiques and art, much of which has been in the owner's family for generations. Most have original fireplaces. All guests may enjoy the private garden and the piazza with its swing, as well as the drawing room and library. A southern breakfast is served in the formal dining room at the family table.

**Open:** year round **Accommodations:** 6 guest rooms with private baths; 3 are suites **Meals:** full breakfast included; complimentary refreshments; restaurants nearby **Rates:** $95 to $285; 10% discount to National Trust members and National Trust Visa cardholders **Payment:** Visa, MC, personal and traveler's checks **Restrictions:** no smoking; no pets **On-site activities:** veranda swing, occasional concerts and lectures

## THE KITCHEN HOUSE
126 Tradd Street
Charleston, South Carolina 29401
**Phone:** 843/577-6362
**Fax:** 843/965-5615
**Website:** www.cityofcharleston. com.kitchen.htm
**E-mail:** loisevans@worldnet.att.net
**Proprietor:** Lois Evans

Dr. Peter Fayssoux, surgeon general in the Continental Army during the Revolutionary War, lived in the

house at 126 Tradd Street. The Kitchen House is a completely renovated eighteenth-century kitchen/dwelling, attached to the Fayssoux house (ca. 1732), but with a separate entrance from the garden. The Kitchen House is centered around its four original fireplaces, and contains a living room and kitchen with dining area on the first floor and two spacious bedrooms and a bathroom on the second. The kitchen is fully equipped with every modern convenience; the refrigerator and pantry stocked with items for a complimentary full breakfast. The house is designed to accommodate up to four people. With its secluded patio overlooking a colonial herb garden and magnolia tree, it offers absolute privacy in the heart of the historic district.

**Open:** year round **Accommodations:** guest house with 2 bedrooms and 1 bath sleeps up to 4 **Meals:** full breakfast included; complimentary refreshments; restaurants nearby **Rates:** $150 to $350 **Payment:** Visa, MC, personal and traveler's checks **Restrictions:** inquire about children; no smoking; no pets **On-site activities:** fish pond, garden, library

PLANTERS INN
112 North Market Street
Charleston, South Carolina
29401
**Phone:** 843/722-2345
**Fax:** 843/577-2125
**Website:**
www.plantersinn.com
**Innkeeper:** Larry Spelts

Planters Inn, an 1844 commercial building at the corner of Market and Meeting streets, is a recipient of the Preservation Society of Charleston's award for renovation. The inn offers spacious guest rooms with traditional high ceilings and oversize baths of marble and hardwood. Furnishings are from Baker's museum-quality Historic Charleston Collection. Each room is distinct from the others in objets d'art, hues, and decor. Television and radio are concealed in an armoire. Many rooms have working fireplaces with adjacent seating areas. Turn-down service and pillow chocolates are standard. Breakfast, served on crystal and china, is brought to each bedroom door on a silver tray. A lobby, sitting room, courtyard, and rooftop deck are public places to relax. Planters Inn is also home to a critically acclaimed restaurant.

**Open:** year round **Accommodations:** 62 guest rooms with private baths; 6 are suites **Meals:** continental-plus breakfast included; complimentary refreshments; restaurant on premises; restaurants nearby **Wheelchair access:** yes **Rates:** $105 to $350; 10% discount to National Trust members and National Trust Visa cardholders **Payment:** AmEx, Visa, MC, DC, Discover, traveler's check **Restrictions:** no pets **On-site activities:** courtyard, carriage tours from inn

## THIRTY-SIX MEETING STREET

36 Meeting Street
Charleston, South Carolina 29401
**Phone:** 843/722-1034
**Fax:** 843/723-0068
**Proprietors:** Vic and Anne Brandt

Legend has it that Thirty-Six Meeting Street was the site of the first Christmas tree in Charleston, beginning with Hessian soldiers quartered here in 1780-1781. Built in 1740, this pre-Revolutionary War single house is distinguished by a two-tiered, columned porch and significant Georgian woodwork. Three elegantly appointed guest suites are furnished with four-poster mahogany rice beds, antiques, oriental rugs, kitchenettes, private baths, central heat and air conditioning, televisions, and telephones. The inn is well suited to families with children. Behind wrought-iron gates, guests can enjoy the home's private walled garden for breakfast or after a day of sightseeing. In the heart of the National Register historic district, less than two blocks from the Battery, the inn is an ideal location from which to explore Charleston's famed historic streets, perhaps on bicycles provided by the inn.

**Open:** year round **Accommodations:** 3 guest suites with private baths **Meals:** continental breakfast included; restaurants nearby **Rates:** $75 to $145 **Payment:** Visa, MC, personal and traveler's checks **Restrictions:** no smoking; no pets **On-site activities:** private walled garden, bicycles

## THOMAS LAMBOLL HOUSE

19 King Street
Charleston, South Carolina 29401
**Phone:** 843/723-3212
or 888/874-0793
**Fax:** 843/724-6352
**Website:**
www.lambollhouse.com/home.htm
**E-mail:** lamboll@aol.com
**Proprietor:** Marie W. Read

Located just off the Battery, this house is known as the Thomas Lamboll House, for its original owner. Built in 1735, the house is a fine example of the Charleston single-house style with raised basement and double-decker porch. Two large bedrooms, elegantly furnished with reproduction and antique furniture, are offered. Each room has a fireplace, cable television, a telephone, central air conditioning, a private bath, and French doors that lead to the third-floor balcony. A continental breakfast is served in the dining room on the first floor.

**Open:** year round **Accommodations:** 2 guest rooms with private baths **Meals:** continental breakfast included; restaurants nearby **Rates:** $100 to $155; 10% discount to National Trust members and National Trust Visa cardholders **Payment:** personal check **Restrictions:** smoking limited; no pets

## TWENTY-SEVEN STATE STREET BED AND BREAKFAST

27 State Street
Charleston, South Carolina 29401
**Phone:** 843/722-4243
**Fax:** 843/722-6030
**Website:** www.charleston-bb.com
**Proprietors:** Paul and Joye Craven

A significant structure in the city's historic district, the house at 27 State Street was built just after 1800 in the Adam, or Federal, style. Its outward appearance has been carefully preserved along with much of the interior, including elegant woodwork. The carriage house, behind wrought-iron gates and beyond the courtyard, contains two guest suites furnished in antiques and reproductions. Each suite has a private entrance and consists of a bedroom, living room, private bath, and kitchenette. Suites are inviting with fresh fruit and flowers, cable television, telephone, and central heat and air. A festive breakfast is provided in each suite, along with a morning newspaper. Twenty-Seven State Street has been the location for several film productions, including the television minseries *Queen* and *Scarlett*. The inn is close to all of Charleston's shopping and dining opportunities.

**Open:** year round **Accommodations:** 2 guest suites with private baths **Meals:** continental-plus breakast included; complimentary refreshments; restaurants nearby **Rates:** $100 to $180 **Payment:** personal and traveler's checks **Restrictions:** no smoking; no pets **On-site activities:** bicycles available

## VICTORIA HOUSE INN
208 King Street
Charleston, South Carolina 29401
**Phone:** 843/720-2944 or 800/933-5464
**Website:** www.charminginns.com
**Proprietor:** Mary Kay Smith

Built in 1889 as the city's second YMCA, this three-story brick building was financed by prominent civic-minded Charlestonians who recognized the need to reestablish the association for young men. One of Charleston's few Victorian-era structures built in the Romanesque Revival style, the building, in the heart of the Market Area, has through the years housed retail shops as well as apartments. In 1991 it was meticulously refurbished to offer distinctive guest rooms and small suites, some with fireplaces and whirlpool baths. Today, the Victoria House is decorated in Victorian furnishings and fabrics. Period wallpapers and paint colors adorn the walls. Guests receive evening turn-down service and a continental-plus breakfast. Victoria House Inn is convenient to shopping, dining, and touring.

**Open:** year round **Accommodations:** 18 guest rooms with private baths; 4 are suites **Meals:** continental-plus breakfast included; complimentary refreshments; restaurants nearby **Wheelchair access:** some guest rooms, bathrooms, public spaces **Rates:** $140 to $245; 10% discount offered to National Trust members and National Trust Visa cardholders **Payment:** Visa, MC, traveler's check **Restrictions:** smoking limited; no pets

## WENTWORTH MANSION
149 Wentworth Street
Charleston, South Carolina 29401
**Phone:** 843/853-1886 or 888/INN-1886
**Fax:** 843/720-5290
**Website:** www.wentworthmansion.com
**Proprietor:** Scott Williams

Designed as an opulent private residence, Wentworth Mansion is a place of hand-carved marble fireplaces, intricate woodwork, Tiffany stained-glass windows, massive crystal chandeliers, frilly wrought iron, and etched brasswork. A pristine example of America's Gilded Age, the 1886 Second Empire manse sits grandly in the heart of Charleston, its iron roof cresting surrounding a cupola that looks out over this historic city. Guests are pampered by sumptuous surroundings in public and guest rooms, all of which are furnished with antiques. The most up-to-date conveniences and comforts have been discretely added: king beds, oversized whirlpool tubs, working gas fireplaces. Amenities include breakfast buffet, afternoon tea, wine tastings, evening cordials, turn-down service, and on-site parking. Private tours of the city can be arranged.

**Open:** year round **Accommodations:** 21 guest rooms with private baths; 7 are suites **Meals:** breakfast buffet included; complimentary afternoon tea; restaurant on premises; restaurants nearby **Rates:** $275 to $675 **Payment:** AmEx, Visa, MC, DC, Discover, personal and traveler's checks **Restrictions:** no smoking; no pets

---

# LATTA

**Nearby attractions:** museums, historic walking tours, art galleries, antiques hunting, golfing, canoeing, kayaking

## ABINGDON MANOR
307 Church Street
Latta, South Carolina 29565
**Phone:** 843/752-5090 or 888/752-5090
**Website:** www.bbonline.com/sc/abingdon/
**Proprietors:** Michael and Patty Griffey

This magnificent Neoclassical mansion with Greek Revival touches was built in 1905 by James H. Manning, the first state senator from Dillon County. With 8,000 square feet of space, the house is the largest in the county. It is accented by more than 2,000 square feet of verandas and porches supported by 40 columns cut from trees on the original plantation. Rooms with 12-foot ceilings, exquisite woodwork, and 11 fireplaces with carved mantels are beautifully restored. The inn provides luxurious accommodations in guest rooms and suites appointed with antique furnishings, private baths, and fireplaces. A full breakfast, early evening refreshments, sherry, and chocolates are among the many amenities included. This premier lodging establishment, listed in the National Register of Historic Places, has been awarded four diamonds by AAA.

**Open:** year round **Accommodations:** 5 guest rooms with private baths; 1 is a suite **Meals:** full breakfast included; complimentary refreshments; restaurants nearby **Rates:** $105 to $140; 10% discount to National Trust members and National Trust Visa cardholders **Payment:** AmEx, Visa, MC, Discover, personal and traveler's checks **Restrictions:** children over 12 welcome; no smoking; no pets **On-site activities:** bicycles, hot tub, exercise equipment

## MT. PLEASANT

**Nearby attractions:** Yorktown Maritime Museum, Boone Hall Plantation, Patriots Point, Charleston, beaches at the Isle of Palms and Sullivans Island

### GUILDS INN
101 Pitt Street
Mt. Pleasant, South Carolina 29464
**Phone:** 843/881-0510 or 800/331-0510
**Fax:** 843/884-5020
**Proprietor:** Lou Edens
**Location:** 5 miles from downtown Charleston

Guilds Inn was built in 1888 as a grocery store. With its white clapboards, green shutters, and neat row of dormers, it is a charming example of Colonial Revival architecture. For 53 years it was the cornerstone of life in the village of Mt. Pleasant. The care with which the venerable building was restored is enhanced by its furnishings. Each guest room is filled with early American reproductions made by Mt. Pleasant native Harry Hitopoulous. Modern conveniences like private telephones, whirlpool baths, and individual climate controls coexist with four-poster canopy beds. A home-baked breakfast is served in the second-floor sun room.

**Open:** year round **Accommodations:** 6 guest rooms with private baths; 1 is a suite **Meals:** continental breakfast included; casual cafe on premises; restaurants nearby **Rates:** $95 to $135; 10% discount to National Trust members and National Trust Visa cardholders **Payment:** AmEx, Visa, MC, personal and traveler's checks **Restrictions:** children over 12 welcome; no smoking; no pets

# SOUTH DAKOTA

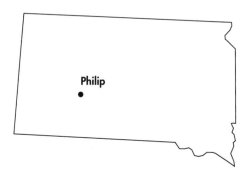

## PHILIP

**Nearby attractions:** Badlands National Park, Bad River, Petrified Gardens, Pine Ridge Indian Reservation, Wounded Knee Memorial, Wall Drugstore, Black Hills, game hunting, fishing

### TRIANGLE RANCH BED AND BREAKFAST
HCR 1 Box 62
Philip, South Dakota 57567
**Phone:** 605/859-2122 or 888/219-1774
**Website:** www.bbonline.com/sd/triangleranch/
**Proprietors:** Lynden and Kenneth Ireland

H. H. Williams, the innkeeper's great-grandfather, lived on this ranch first in a creekbank "dugout," then in a log house before building the Alhambra in 1923. Ordered from Sears, Roebuck & Co., this "Honorbilt" home is a foursquare two-story home adorned with ornate Mission-style parapetting around its three dormers and front porch. The lumber and materials, including crystal chandeliers and bookcases and buffet with leaded-glass doors, arrived marked and stacked in order on two railroad cars at Cottonwood. It took two weeks to haul the materials home by team and wagon. A local German carpenter assembled the house. First-floor interiors are oak in the Arts and Crafts style, complete with window seats and colonnades, plus brick fireplaces. The decor throughout is original 1920s. A hearty mix of Grandma Williams' recipes is served family style in the dining room, sun room, or on the front porch.

**Open:** year round **Accommodations:** 4 guest rooms (2 have private baths) **Meals:** full breakfast included; complimentary refreshments; sack lunches and other meals available **Rates:** $48 to $75 **Payment:** Visa, MC, personal check **Restrictions:** no smoking **On-site activities:** ranch tours, house tours, hiking, fishing, ride your own horse, stargazing

# TENNESSEE

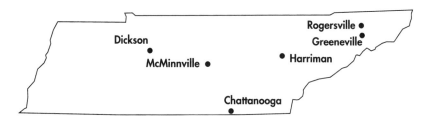

## CHATTANOOGA

**Nearby attractions:** Tennessee Aquarium, Civil War battlefields, the Incline passenger railway, Chattanooga Choo-Choo, Hunter Museum of Art, Children's Discovery Museum, symphony, Tivoli Theater, Rock City, hiking

### ADAMS HILBORNE
801 Vine Street
Chattanooga, Tennessee 37403
**Phone:** 423/265-5000
**Fax:** 423/265-5555
**Website:** innjoy.com
**E-mail:** innjoy@worldnet.att.net
**Proprietors:** Wendy and Dave Adams

Located in the Fort Wood historic district, a neighborhood of architectural diversity, Adams Hilborne is a majestic Richardsonian Romanesque home. Built in 1889 of native mountain stone, the house's castlelike proportions are emphasized by a round-arched entryway, steeply pitched gables, balconies, balustrades,

and a conically roofed round porch. The house, originally designed for former Chattanooga Mayor Edmond G. Watkins, has been renovated by the innkeepers to show off its original hand-carved coffered ceilings, arched doorways, and leaded, beveled, and Tiffany glass windows. It received the National Trust's Great American Home award in 1997. Guest rooms, with 16-foot ceilings and hand-carved moldings, are filled with fine antiques and original art. Many rooms offer fireplaces with original mantels. A continental breakfast is served in the banquet room with its views of historic Lookout Mountain.

**Open:** year round **Accommodations:** 9 guest rooms with private baths; 4 are suites **Meals:** continental breakfast included; restaurant on premises; restaurants nearby **Wheelchair access:** 1 room **Rates:** $125 to $250; 10% discount to National Trust members and National Trust Visa cardholders midweek only **Payment:** AmEx, Visa, MC, personal and traveler's checks **Restrictions:** children over 6 welcome; no smoking; no pets **On-site activities:** gift shop, music

---

## DICKSON

**Nearby attractions:** Natchez Trace, Montgomery Bell State Park, Luther Lake, golfing, antiques hunting

### EAST HILLS BED AND BREAKFAST INN
Highway 70 East
Dickson, Tennessee 37055
**Phone:** 615/441-9428 or 615/446-6922
**Fax:** 615/446-2181
**Website:** www.bbonline.com/tn/easthills/
**Proprietors:** John C. and Anita J. Luther

The innkeeper's father, W. E. Luther, Sr., was the developer of Luther Lake and the East Hills Subdivision in the eastern part of Dickson in the 1940s. He built this traditional, 5,000-square-foot Neoclassical one-story home on four acres in that area. Steeped in southern hospitality and charm, the inn offers five guest rooms with private baths and a separate cottage. Guests are invited to enjoy the spacious living room and library/den with fireplaces and television. The house is furnished with antiques and designer reproductions. The long front porch and enclosed back porch with swing and rocking chairs provide great places for relaxing under stately trees. Guests receive tea and muffins in the evening and a full breakfast.

**Open:** year round **Accommodations:** 5 guest rooms with private baths; 1 separate cottage **Meals:** full breakfast included; complimentary refreshments; restaurants nearby **Rates:** $65 to $95; 10% discount to National Trust members and National Trust Visa cardholders **Payment:** AmEx, Visa, MC, Discover, personal and traveler's checks **Restrictions:** no smoking; no pets **On-site activities:** hiking, walking, bird watching, parlor games, porch rocking

# GREENEVILLE

**Nearby attractions:** historic sites, Smoky Mountain National Park, Cherokee National Forest, hiking, bicycling, golfing, white-water rafting, trout fishing, waterfalls, covered bridges, antiques hunting, Appalachian crafts shops

### BIG SPRING INN, DOUGHTY-RICKER HOME
315 North Main Street
Greeneville, Tennessee 37745
**Phone:** 423/638-2917
**Fax:** 423/638-4230
**Proprietors:** Marshall and Nancy Ricker
**Location:** 70 miles east of Knoxville

Big Spring Inn is a turn-of-the-century classically styled home with hipped roof and dormers, large covered porches, and porte cochere. Two guest parlors have fireplaces and provide diversions with a music collection, library, and games. A swimming pool, porches, and gardens with 100-year-old trees are offered in warm weather. Bedrooms are individually furnished with antiques and special amenities such as fresh flowers, fine soaps, and terrycloth robes. The inn's decor is elegant with its antiques, high quality reproductions, and original chandeliers throughout. A unique feature in the dining room is the early hand-painted wallpaper imported from France. Breakfast includes entrees such as cheese-stuffed French toast with apricot sauce. Located in Greeneville's historic district, the inn has been praised by the *Los Angeles Times* and *Knoxville News Sentinel*.

**Open:** April thorugh October **Accommodations:** 6 guest rooms with private baths; 1 is a suite **Meals:** full breakfast included; complimentary refreshments; dinners and picnics available; restaurants nearby **Rate:** $86; 10% discount to National Trust members and National Trust Visa cardholders **Payment:** AmEx, Visa, MC, personal and traveler's checks **Restrictions:** children over 4 welcome; no smoking; no pets (nearby kennels) **On-site activities:** swimming pool, lawn games, gardens, library, porch sitting

# HARRIMAN

**Nearby attractions:** Cornstalk Heights Historic District, Historic Temperance Building and Heritage Museum, Roane County Museum of History and Art, Fort Southwest Point and Museum, Museum of Appalachia, American Museum of Science and Energy, Walden's Ridge, Obed and Little Emory Rivers, Watts Bar Recreational Area, Great Smoky Mountains National Park, fishing, hiking, antiques hunting

## BUSHROD HALL BED AND BREAKFAST

422 Cumberland Street
Harriman, Tennessee 37748
**Phone:** 423/882-8406 or 888/880-8406
**Website:** www.bbonline.com/tn/bushrod
**Proprietors:** Nancy and Bob Ward

In 1892, during the construction of their homes, two eminent citizens of Harriman—S. K. Paige and Frederick Gates—competed to see who could build the most elaborate structure. Gates won, but his house has been lost to fire. The runner-up stands today as a testimony to the grandeur of that era: a solid red-oak staircase imported from Sweden; woodwork, fireplace mantels, and wainscoting that cost $18,000 at the time it was installed; red and white oak inlaid floors. The many details throughout are splendid and, happily, recently restored in this National Register-listed property. Later used as the Bushrod W. James Hall of Domestic Science for young ladies, the house has also seen service as an apartment house. But, back under private ownership, it now offers three bed-and-breakfast guest rooms and a bountiful breakfast. The house is also available for corporate meetings and private parties.

**Open:** year round **Accommodations:** 3 guest rooms with private baths **Meals:** full breakfast included; complimentary refreshments; restaurants nearby **Rates:** $70 to $115 **Payment:** AmEx, Visa, MC, personal and traveler's checks **Restrictions:** children over 12 welcome; no smoking; no pets **On-site activities:** library, television with VCR, stereoscope, games, gardens

# MCMINNVILLE

**Nearby attractions:** "nursery capital of the world," Cumberland Caverns, Rock Island, Fall Creek Falls, Savage Gulf and Old Stone Fort state parks, Center Hill Lake, Nashville, Chattanooga

### HISTORIC FALCON MANOR

2645 Faulkner Springs Road
McMinnville, Tennessee 37110
**Phone:** 931/668-4444
**Fax:** 931/815-4444
**Website:** FalconManor.com
**E-mail:** FalconManor@FalconManor.com
**Proprietors:** George and Charlien McGlothin

This National Register Victorian mansion was built in 1896 by manufacturer Clay Faulkner (who produced Gorilla jeans, "so strong, even a gorilla couldn't tear them apart"). The 10,000-square-foot brick Queen Anne home is surrounded by gingerbreaded porches filled with rockers and shaded by century-old trees. Inside, 12-foot ceilings, a sweeping staircase, exquisite woodwork, rich colors, and museum-quality antiques create an elegant setting. All guest rooms are lavishly furnished with period antiques, including the double beds. The Honeymoon Suite, across the breezeway in the original kitchen, has a king-size brass bed. The house was used as a country hospital from the 1940s until 1968, after which it sat vacant until 1983. The owner's five-year restoration was first-prize B&B winner of the National Trust's 1997 Great American Home Award.

**Open:** year round **Accommodations:** 5 guest rooms with private baths; 1 is a suite **Meals:** full breakfast included; complimentary refreshments; weekend dining by reservation; restaurants nearby **Wheelchair access:** 3 rooms **Rates:** $85 to $105; 10% discount to National Trust members and National Trust Visa cardholders **Payment:**

Visa, MC, personal and traveler's checks **Restrictions:** children over 11 welcome; no smoking; no pets **On-site activities:** porch rocking, library, complimentary house tours, picnics, creek across the road, weddings, special events, group luncheons

---

## ROGERSVILLE

**Nearby attractions:** Cherokee Lake, museum, walking tours of historic district with the oldest courthouse in Tennessee, swimming, tennis, golfing

### HALE SPRINGS INN
Town Square
Rogersville, Tennessee 37857
**Phone:** 423/272-5171
**Proprietors:** Carl and Janet Netherland-Brown

Built in 1824, this three-story brick hostelry is the oldest continuously operating inn in the state. The Federal-style inn has hosted many famous people through the years, most notably presidents Andrew Jackson, Andrew Johnson, and James K. Polk. Originally called McKinney's Tavern after its founder, the inn became a Union headquarters during the Civil War. It was renamed the Hale Springs Inn in 1884, in honor of the mineral springs 15 miles to the north. Today, the fully restored inn retains its original wainscoting and heart-of-pine floors and is furnished with antiques and reproduction pieces. Eight of the nine guest rooms have working fireplaces.

**Open:** year round **Accommodations:** 9 guest rooms with private baths; 3 are suites **Meals:** continental breakfast included; restaurant on premises; restaurants nearby **Wheelchair access:** dining facilities **Rates:** $45 to $70 **Payment:** AmEx, Visa, MC, traveler's checks **Restrictions:** no pets **On-site activities:** tours of the inn, reading, in-room televisions, garden with gazebo and benches

# TEXAS

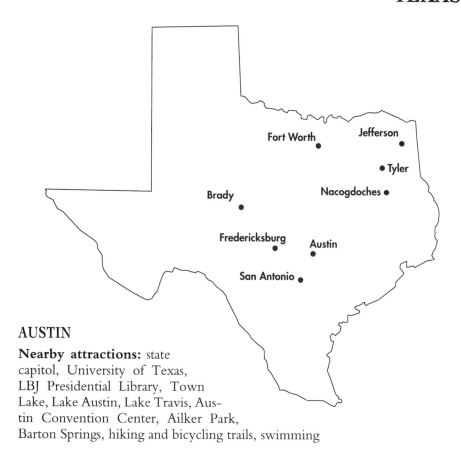

## AUSTIN

**Nearby attractions:** state capitol, University of Texas, LBJ Presidential Library, Town Lake, Lake Austin, Lake Travis, Austin Convention Center, Ailker Park, Barton Springs, hiking and bicycling trails, swimming

## THE DRISKILL
604 Brazos Street
Austin, Texas 78701
**Phone:** 512/474-5911 or 800/678-8946
**Fax:** 512/474-2188
**Website:** driskillhotel.com
**E-mail:** driskhotel.com

Cattle baron Colonel Jesse L. Driskill built his hotel in 1886 to serve as the Frontier Palace of the South in Austin. Constructed in the Richardsonian Romanesque style from local brick and limestone, the hotel is characterized by arched windows, spacious balconies, and exceptional ornamentation. The building's most spectacular architectural features are the floor-to-ceiling arched doorways located at each entrance. Busts of Jesse and his two sons are placed high atop each entrance along with stylized heads of Texas longhorn steers. For more than a century, The Driskill has played host to dignitaries and heads of state (including Lyndon Baines Johnson who celebrated his presidential election here), lobbyists and legislators, as well as socialites, honeymooners, and travelers just passing through. The newly restored guest rooms and suites are luxuriously furnished and feature ceiling fans, safes, and modem-equipped telephones and large work desks. Guest services include valet parking, concierge, business services, and access to a health club. The Driskill is a member of Historic Hotels of America.

**Open:** year round **Accommodations:** 182 guest rooms with private baths; 30 are suites **Meals:** complimentary morning coffee; restaurants on premises; restaurants nearby **Rates:** $155 to $1,500; 10% discount to National Trust members and National Trust Visa cardholders **Payment:** AmEx, Visa, MC, DC, Discover, personal and traveler's checks **Restrictions:** smoking limited; no pets

---

## BRADY

**Nearby attractions:** courthouse square, antiques hunting, Brady Lake, Richards Park, bass fishing, fine dining

**BRADY HOUSE BED AND BREAKFAST**
704 South Bridge
Brady, Texas 76825
**Phone:** 915/597-5265
or 888/272-3901
**E-mail:** bradyhs@centex.net
**Proprietors:** Bobbie and Kelly Hancock

"Miss Nina" Willoughby and "Mr. Willie" White commissioned J. L. Jordan to build this house for them shortly after they were married in 1907. Finished in 1908, the Brady House shows the influence of the Craftsman movement in the use of natural materials, low-pitched gables, and stone porch. The sandstone of the porch and round arch were brought by wagon from Comanche, the brick from Abilene. Interior woodwork of oak accents the dining room with its unusual chandelier. There is a comfortable parlor for reading and visiting. Each of the three spacious gust rooms upstairs has its own private bath and is furnished to create a different period atmosphere. The Brady House sits among pecan and live oak trees on landscaped grounds that cover an acre. A full breakfast is served family style in the dining room.

**Open:** year round **Accommodations:** 3 guest rooms with private baths; 1 is a suite **Meals:** full breakfast included; complimentary refreshments; restaurants nearby **Rates:** $85 to $120; 10% discount to National Trust members and National Trust Visa cardholders **Payment:** AmEx, Visa, MC, Discover, traveler's check **Restrictions:** not suitable for children; no smoking; no pets **On-site activities:** tennis court

---

# FORT WORTH

**Nearby attractions:** Stockyards National Historic District, Tarantula Railroad Station, Billy Bob's Texas, Cowtown Coliseum, Cowtown Rodeo, Livestock Exchange Building and Museum

## MISS MOLLY'S HOTEL

109 1/2 West Exchange Avenue
Fort Worth, Texas 76106
**Phone:** 817/626-1522 or 800/99MOLLY (800/996-6559)
**Fax:** 817/625-2723
**Website:** www.missmollys.com
**Proprietor:** Mark Hancock

Miss Molly's Hotel is on the second floor of this 1910 building, above the Star Cafe, one of the district's oldest and best restaurants. The hotel originated as a legitimate business, but in the 1940s it became a popular bawdy house known as the Gayette Hotel. Operating legally again, Miss Molly's offers eight guest rooms dressed in turn-of-the-century Texas style with iron beds, carved oak furniture, and even a pot-bellied stove in one room. Each room contains memorabilia to honor a different sector of Texas society: cowboys, cattle barons, gunslingers, oilmen, railroad men, and even the establishment's previous madam, Miss Josie. Miss Josie's room features a draped fabric ceiling and a private bath. The remaining rooms share three bathrooms in the hallway—robes are provided for guests' use. Lace curtains and antique quilts are found in all rooms. Breakfast is served in the parlor beneath the stained-glass skylight.

**Open:** year round **Accommodations:** 8 guest rooms (1 has a private bath) **Meals:** continental-plus breakfast included; restaurants nearby **Rates:** $95 to $170; 10% discount to National Trust members and National Trust Visa cardholders **Payment:** AmEx, Visa, MC, DC, Discover, personal and traveler's checks **Restrictions:** children over 12 welcome; no smoking; no pets

# FREDERICKSBURG

**Nearby attractions:** Admiral Nimitz Museum, LBJ State and National Park, Enchanted Rock, wineries and wine tastings, Guadalupe River, Austin, San Antonio, golfing, tennis, swimming, shopping on Main Street

## THE HERB HAUS BED AND BREAKFAST AT FREDERICKSBURG HERB FARM

401 Whitney Street
Fredericksburg, Texas 78624
**Phone:** 830/997-8615 or 800/259-HERB
**Fax:** 830/997-5069
**Website:** www.fredericksburgherbfarm.com
**E-mail:** herbfarm@ktc.com
**Proprietor:** Bill and Sylvia Varney

An organic herb farm internationally known for its natural fragrances, herb condiments, and creative necessities for gardeners, The Fredericksburg Herb Farm sits on 14-plus acres just six blocks off Main Street. During World War II, the pioneer farmhouse was used as a "Victory Garden" cannery operation. Today, amid numerous herb gardens, sits the Herb Haus, a restored 1940s frame cottage, once the home of a prominent midwife. The herb-decorated and scented house has two bedrooms, one with a double bed, the other with a queen-size bed, a bath with footed tub, and a small kitchen. Guests will find an array of natural toiletries supplied by the farm's shop. Breakfast emphasizes a continental herb cuisine: homemade herb breads, sweet herb-n-spice butter, and fresh fruits and juice with edible flowers. Other attractions at the farm include the Tea Room, Quiet Haus (for aromatherapy massages), and Poet's Haus (the farm's gift shop).

**Open:** year round **Accommodations:** 1 guest house with 2 bedrooms and private bath **Meals:** continental-plus breakfast included; complimentary refreshments; restaurant on premises **Rates:** $105 to $125; 10% discount to National Trust members and National Trust Visa cardholders **Payment:** AmEx, Visa, MC, DC, Discover, personal and traveler's checks **Restrictions:** not suitable for children; no smoking; no pets **On-site activities:** day spa by appointment, gardening, roaming 14 acres of gardens, shopping in two stores

## MAGNOLIA HOUSE

101 East Hackberry
Fredericksburg, Texas 78624
**Phone:** 830/997-0306
**Website:** magnoliahouse.com
**E-mail:** magnolia@hctc.net
**Proprietors:** Joyce and Patrick Kennard

This house was built in 1923 by architect Edward Stein for his family. Designer of the Gillespie County Courthouse in Fredericksburg, Stein personally selected each piece of lumber for his own home. The Craftsman-influenced house with clipped front gable and wide low-pitched roofline has been designated a Texas Historic Landmark by the Texas Historical Commission. Inside, the original kitchen has antique glass cabinets, a working cistern in the butler's pantry, and antique built-in iceboxes. Unique antique-decorated guest rooms offer terrycloth robes and Magnolia House soaps. Each room has color television with premium cable channels. Some rooms have fireplaces and private entrances. Bountiful breakfasts are served on antique china in the formal dining or breakfast room. A stone patio with fish pond and waterfall invites guests outdoors. Wicker furniture graces the porches.

**Open:** year round **Accommodations:** 5 guest rooms with private baths; 2 are suites **Wheelchair access:** limited **Meals:** full breakfast included; complimentary refreshments; restaurants nearby **Rates:** $95 to $125; 10% discount to National Trust members and National Trust Visa cardholders, weekdays only **Payment:** AmEx, Visa, MC, Discover, personal and traveler's checks **Restrictions:** children over 12 welcome; no smoking **On-site activities:** patio and porch sitting

## WATKINS HILL
608 East Creek Street
Fredericksburg, Texas 78624
**Phone:** 830/997-6739 or 800/899-1672
**Fax:** 830/997-3755
**Website:** www.watkinshill.com
**Proprietors:** Betty O'Connor and Susan Martin

Watkins Hill comprises seven buildings on two acres, yet is only one block from the shops of Fredericksburg's Main Street. Four of the buildings date to the nineteenth century, including the 1855 Basse-Burrier home, the original stone house on this property, and a transplanted 1835 log house. All have been renovated and custom designed with elegance and comfort in mind. Furnishings throughout range from rare to singular. All the queen-size beds are canopied. Several are massive four-posters (two came over the Appalachians in 1845). Another has posts of saguaro cactus. A full breakfast comes to guest rooms in a wicker basket. A butler's pantry in each guest room provides a variety of refreshments, including a complimentary bottle of wine. One log house contains a library, dining room, parlor, conservatory, and a complete frontier log cabin—incorporated into the larger building—used as a ballroom and meeting hall. In the press, Watkins Hill has received kudos from the *San Antonio Express News*, *Dallas Morning News*, *Southern Living*, and *Country Living* among others.

**Open:** year round **Accommodations:** 7 guest rooms with private baths; 6 are suites **Meals:** full breakfast included; complimentary refreshments; restaurants nearby **Rates:** $82 to $165; 10% discount to National Trust members and National Trust Visa cardholders **Payment:** Visa, MC, personal and traveler's checks **Restrictions:** no smoking; inquire about pets

# JEFFERSON

**Nearby attractions:** museums, riverboat tours, buggy tours of historic district, antebellum house tours, antiques hunting, steam-engine train ride, bayou excursions, Lake Caddo, Lake o' the Pines, golfing, boating, fishing

## PRIDE HOUSE
409 Broadway
Jefferson, Texas 75657
**Phone:** 903/665-2675
or 800/894-3526
**Fax:** 903/665-3901
**Website:**
www.jeffersontexas.com
**E-mail:** jefftx@mind.net
**Proprietor:** Sandra J. Spalding

The Pride House is a two-story Stick Style structure built in 1888 for lumberman George Brown. Painted a rich caramel color with white gingerbread trim and sky-blue accents, Pride House recalls the past with a wraparound porch, original bronze hardware in heavy doors, and stained glass in every window. Rooms have high ceilings and tall windows, and exceptional millwork is evident in the beaded wainscoting and door and window moldings. The house is filled with Victorian furniture. Guest rooms, including those in the guest cottage, contain period decor and wallpaper, armoires, and private baths. (The crimson West Room has an enormous antique claw-foot bathtub that was voted best in the state by *Houston Style* magazine.) The Pride House, which opened to guests in 1980, is said to be Texas's first bed and breakfast.

**Open:** year round **Accommodations:** 10 guest rooms with private baths; 1 is a suite **Meals:** full breakfast included; restaurants nearby **Rates:** $55 to $110; 10% discount to National Trust members and National Trust Visa cardholders **Payment:** Visa, MC, personal and traveler's checks **Restrictions:** no smoking **On-site activities:** reading, porch rocking

# NACOGDOCHES

**Nearby attractions:** tours of historic Nacogdoches, golfing, fishing, hiking, rodeos, horse shows, county fairs, antiques hunting, museums, art galleries, lakes for swimming and water skiing

## LLANO GRANDE PLANTATION BED AND BREAKFAST

Llano Grande Plantation
Press Road, Route 4
Box 9400
Nacogdoches, Texas 75961
**Phone:** 409/569-1249
**Website:** www.llanogrande.com
**E-mail:** llanogr@inu.net
**Proprietors:** Ann and Charles Phillips
**Location:** 5 miles south of Nacogdoches, oldest town in Texas

Llano Grande Plantation contains three separate guest houses, none visible from the other. The Tol Barret House (1840) was the home of the man who drilled the first producing oil well in Texas in 1866. This National Register structure has been restored and furnished with antiques of the period. Its outbuildings include a large detached kitchen, with a second-story bedroom that is now a guest suite. The Sparks House (1851), a restored and antique-filled pioneer structure, is a Texas Historic Landmark offering a two-bedroom suite, complete with wood-burning fireplace and stove. The Gate House is a charming 1938 Texas farmhouse with a parlor fireplace and two sunny bedrooms. It is set among lofty oaks and surrounded by a well house, cattle barns, a corral, and pastures.

**Open:** year round **Accommodations:** 3 2-bedroom houses with private baths **Meals:** full or continental-plus breakfast included (varies with guest house); restaurants nearby **Rates:** $65 to $95; 10% discount offered to National Trust members and National Trust Visa cardholders **Payment:** personal and traveler's checks **Restrictions:** inquire about children; smoking limited; inquire about pets **On-site activities:** 600 acres of forest with hiking trails, fishing in stocked pond, croquet, wildlife watching

# SAN ANTONIO

**Nearby attractions:** King William historic district walking tours, Alamo, Riverwalk, Institute of Texan Cultures, Market Square, Spanish Governor's Palace, Fort Sam Houston, Brackenridge Park and Zoo, Sea World, Fiesta Texas, San Pedro Springs Park, jogging paths, tennis, botanical center, museums

## A YELLOW ROSE BED AND BREAKFAST

229 Madison
San Antonio, Texas 78204
**Phone:** 210/229-9903 or 800/950-9903
**Fax:** 210/229-1691
**Website:** www.bbonline.com/tx/yellowrose
**Proprietors:** Justin (Kit) Walker and Deb Field-Walker

The historic King William district of San Antonio was settled by prosperous German immigrants in the late 1880s. This beautiful home was built in two stages: the first and smaller portion in 1865, and the main house in 1878 by Charles Mueller. This elaborate structure features a 25-foot-high foyer with grand staircase, 14-foot ceilings, leaded-grass transoms, triple-hung, stenciled-glass windows, and 10-foot-tall red pine pocket doors. The foyer, parlor and dining room are appointed with turn-of-the-century antiques and luxurious fabrics. Guest rooms feature canopied, four-poster, or carved Victorian beds. All rooms are equipped with central air conditioning, cable television, alarm clocks, and private baths. After a full breakfast, guests may choose to stroll two short blocks to the city's famous Riverwalk or one block to the trolley.

**Open:** year round **Accommodations:** 5 guest rooms with private baths; 1 larger room can sleep four guests **Meals:** full breakfast included; restaurants nearby **Rates:** $99 to $145; 10% discount to National Trust members and National Trust Visa cardholders midweek only **Payment:** AmEx, Visa, MC, personal check **Restrictions:** children over 12 welcome; no smoking; no pets

## BECKMANN INN AND CARRIAGE HOUSE
222 East Guenther Street
San Antonio, Texas 78204
**Phone:** 210/229-1449
or 800/945-1449
**Fax:** 210/229-1061
**Website:** www.beckmanninn.com
**E-mail:** beckinn@swbell.net
**Proprietors:** Betty Jo and Don Schwartz

This house was built in 1886 by Albert Beckmann for his bride, Marie Dorothea, daughter of the Guenther flour-mill family. Located on the mill grounds, the one-story house gained additions over the years, including a wraparound porch, which resulted in its current rambling floor plan. In the living room, ceilings are 14 feet high, tall windows have beveled glass, and the floor is an intricately designed wood mosaic imported from Paris. Arched pocket doors with opaque glass inserts open to the formal dining room. Guest rooms feature high ceilings with fans, tall, ornately carved Victorian beds, and colorful floral fabrics and wallpapers. Adjacent to the main house is the carriage house with two suites. This building's shuttered windows are adorned with flower-filled boxes. A full breakfast, including dessert, is served daily.

**Open:** year round **Accommodations:** 5 guest rooms with private baths; 2 are suites **Meals:** full breakfast included; restaurants nearby **Wheelchair access:** limited **Rates:** $90 to $140; 10% discount to National Trust members and National Trust Visa cardholders, midweek only based on availability **Payment:** AmEx, Visa, MC, DC, Discover, personal and traveler's checks **Restrictions:** children over 12 welcome; no smoking; no pets **On-site activities:** patio and gardens, wicker-filled sunporch, porch sitting

## BRACKENRIDGE HOUSE, A BED AND BREAKFAST INN
230 Madison
San Antonio, Texas 78204
**Phone:** 210/271-3442 or 800/221-1412
**Website:** www.brackenridgehouse.com
**E-mail:** benniesueb@aol.com
**Proprietors:** Bennie and Sue Blansett

Located in the King William Historic District, the Brackenridge House is a 1901 Greek Revival house, its front gable supported by four Corinthian columns. Inside, the house boasts its original pine floors, double-hung windows, and high ceilings. Guest rooms contain king- and queen-size beds, telephones, private baths, and private entrances. Two suites feature kitchenette/sitting areas; all rooms have mini-refrigerators. Family quilts create a homey ambience. A full breakfast is served on the breezy, shady veranda or in the formal dining room. Porch swings, rocking chairs, and a garden area hot tub offer quiet relations in this quiet neighborhood just six blocks from downtown. The inn also offers a two-bedroom guest house with kitchen, living room, dining room, and bath. The guest house is perfect for extended stays or for guests with young children or small pets.

**Open:** year round **Accommodations:** 5 guest rooms with private baths; 2 are suites; one guest house **Meals:** full breakfast included; complimentary refreshments; restaurants nearby **Rates:** $89 to $175; 10% discount to National Trust members and National Trust Visa cardholders **Payment:** AmEx, Visa MC, Discover, personal and traveler's checks **Restrictions:** children over 12 welcome; no smoking; pets welcome in guest house only **On-site activities:** hot tub, afternoon tea on veranda

## BULLIS HOUSE INN
621 Pierce Street
P.O. Box 8059
San Antonio, Texas 78208
**Phone:** 210/223-9426
**Fax:** 210/299-1479
**Proprietors:** Steven and Alma Cross

General John Lapham Bullis was famous for fighting Indians on the Texas frontier and was instrumental in the capture of the Apache chief Geronimo. Bullis's house, built between 1906 and 1909, is said to be haunted by Geronimo's spirit. The house is a white Neoclassical mansion, notable for the grouped Ionic columns that support the two-story portico. Stairways and paneling are of dark oak and mahogany. Marble fireplaces warm each parlor. The house is also graced with parquet floors and intricately designed ceilings with large plaster medallions framing crystal chandeliers. Several guest rooms have gas- and wood-burning fireplaces and French windows. All are individually decorated with antiques and contemporary furnishings. The Bullis House Inn is located in the Fort Sam Houston Historic District, two miles northeast of downtown.

**Open:** year round **Accommodations:** 7 guest rooms (1 has a private bath) **Meals:** continental-plus breakfast included; catering available with reservations; restaurants nearby **Rates:** $49 to $150; additional adult $10; additional child $6 **Payment:** AmEx, Visa, MC, Discover, traveler's check **Restrictions:** smoking limited; no pets **On-site activities:** badminton; swimming pool; volleyball; table tennis; summer barbecues; cable television with Showtime, movie nights with complimentary popcorn, cookies, coffee, and tea

---

## TYLER

**Nearby attractions:** museums, zoo, antiques hunting, Tyler Municipal Rose Garden, Texas Rose Festival, house tours, golfing, lakes, parks, symphony, theaters, bicycle tours

### CHARNWOOD HILL INN BED AND BREAKFAST

223 East Charnwood
Tyler, Texas 75701
**Phone:** 903/597-3980
**Fax:** 903/592-6473
**Website:** www.tyler.com/charnwood
**E-mail:** chrnwood@ballistic.com
**Proprietor:** Andy Walker

Built in 1855, this residence underwent a series of owners and remodelings until it was purchased by H. L. Hunt in the early 1900s. Hunt remodeled the home extensively, resulting in the Neoclassical style evident today. On the third floor he built an Art Deco suite for his daughters, Margaret and Caroline. This 1500-square-foot suite with skylight, opaque glass walls, two bedrooms, and living room is a luxurious guest room today. The H. C. Miller family, who bought the house in 1938, converted some second-floor space into a wood-paneled and beamed trophy room with built-in gun cabinet and bar. This room is also offered to guests today. Other guest rooms range in style from rustic to sylvan in a room with a willow-canopied bed and garden statuary. Numerous common areas include the great hall, library, gathering hall, balconies, screened swing porch, and gardens. Located in the Azalea historic district, the inn offers off-street parking.

**Open:** year round **Accommodations:** 7 guest rooms with private baths; 1 is a suite **Meals:** full breakfast included; complimentary refreshments; restaurants nearby **Rates:** $95 to $275; 10% discount to National Trust members and National Trust Visa cardholders **Payment:** Visa, MC, Discover, personal and traveler's checks **Restrictions:** children over 13 welcome; no smoking; no pets **On-site activities:** library, television–VCR and video library, walking, gift shop, gardens with fountain

# UTAH

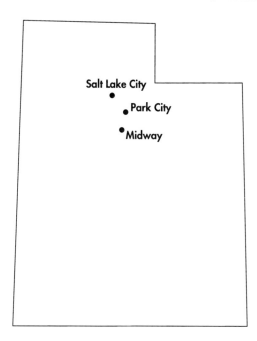

Salt Lake City
• Park City
•Midway

## MIDWAY

**Nearby attractions:**
Wasatch Mountain State Park (golfing, cross-country skiing, hiking, camping), Heber Valley Historic Railroad, eight downhill ski resorts, four golf courses, Deer Creek and Jordanelle Reservoirs (boating, waterskiing, windsurfing, and fishing), historic Park City, Bridal Veil Falls, Timpanogos Caves National Monument, Sundance and Cascade Springs

### THE HOMESTEAD
700 North Homestead Drive
Midway, Utah 84049
**Phone:** 435/654-1102 or 800/327-7220
**Fax:** 435/654-5087
**Website:** www.homestead-ut.com
**E-mail:** HomesUT@aol.com
**General Manager:** Britt Mathwich

More than 100 years ago Simon Schneitter first tried to farm the rocky fields that surround The Homestead. The mountainous mineral springs that frustrated his farming efforts began to draw neighbors for swimming. A smart man, Simon left off agriculture and turned his homestead into a resort. He added a dining room, bath houses, and guest rooms and successfully made the most out of his misfortune. This famous, National Register-listed inn continues to offer the same celebrated service, great food, spectacular scenery, variety of sports, and hot mineral baths that have been its trademarks since 1886. Its various accommoda-

tions include executive cottages and suites, family-style rooms, and the Victorian bed-and-breakfast Virginia House. Decor ranges in style from New England to Southwestern, classic to traditional. The Homestead is located in one of America's most beautiful alpine valleys.

**Open:** year round **Accommodations:** 140 guest rooms with private baths; 27 are suites **Meals:** complimentary refreshments; restaurant on premises; restaurants nearby **Rates:** $109 to $334; 10% discount off regular rack rate to National Trust members and National Trust Visa cardholders **Payment:** AmEx, Visa, MC, CB, DC, Discover, personal and traveler's checks **Restrictions:** smoking limited; no pets **On-site activities:** golfing, horseback riding, sleigh rides, snowmobiling, cross-country skiing, Homestead Crater (tours, swimming, snorkeling, scuba diving, therapeutic mineral bath), mountain bike rentals, indoor and outdoor spas and pools, fitness room, tennis, game room, volleyball, horseshoes, croquet, basketball

## PARK CITY

**Nearby attractions:** museum, historic Main Street, shops, galleries, Town Lift to Park City Ski Area for downhill skiing, cross-country skiing, golfing, tennis, mountain biking, hiking, fishing, hot-air ballooning, horseback riding, concerts, festivals

### OLD MINERS' LODGE – A BED AND BREAKFAST INN
615 Woodside Avenue
P.O. Box 2639
Park City, Utah 84060-2639
**Phone:** 435/645-8068 or 800/648-8068
**Fax:** 435/645-7420
**Website:** www.oldminerslodge.com
**Proprietors:** Hugh Daniels and Susan Wynne

Old Miners' Lodge is located in the National Register historic district of the colorful resort town of Park City. This two-story frame inn was established in 1889 as a boarding house for local miners seeking fortune in the surrounding ore-rich mountains. Named for historic Park City personalities, the lodge's 12 guest rooms are restored and furnished to their period with antique and country pieces, down pillows, and comforters. All guest baths contain terrycloth robes. Guests start the day with a full breakfast in the cozy dining room. A large fireplace in the living room draws guests in the evening. An outdoor hot tub is available year round and extra-large towels are provided in each room. The lodge is equipped to host groups for workshops, seminars, or family gatherings.

**Open:** year round **Accommodations:** 12 guest rooms with private baths; 3 are suites **Meals:** full breakfast included; complimentary refreshments; catering available for groups; restaurants nearby **Rates:** $65 to $275 seasonal **Payment:** AmEx, Visa, MC, Discover, personal and traveler's checks **Restrictions:** no smoking; no pets **On-site activities:** outdoor hot tub

## WASHINGTON SCHOOL INN
543 Park Avenue
Park City, Utah 84060
**Phone:** 435/649-3800 or 800/824-1672
**Fax:** 435/649-3802
**Website:** www.bbju.org
**General Manager:** Nancy Beaufait

The Washington School is the sole remainder of three public schools constructed here in the late nineteenth century, and is one of the few buildings to survive the Great Fire of June 19, 1898. It was built in 1889 of native limestone and contained three large rooms with 16-foot ceilings. Two rooms were added in 1903 and another in 1906. When enrollment dropped off in the 1930s, the building became the property of the Veterans of Foreign Wars, where dances and social events were held. Listed in the National Register of Historic Places, the school's exterior—including its flagpole-topped bell tower and pedimented dormers—has been restored, while inside, 15 charming guest rooms have been fashioned in period decor. Amenities abound, from freshly laundered bathrobes to afternoon appetizers and libations; full breakfasts to full concierge service. The inn is also well suited to small business meetings.

**Open:** year round **Accommodations:** 15 guest rooms with private baths; 3 are suites **Meals:** full breakfast included; complimentary refreshments; restaurants nearby **Rates:** $89 to $379; 10% discount to National Trust members and National Trust Visa cardholders **Payment:** AmEx, Visa, MC, DC, Discover, traveler's check **Restrictions:** children over 10 welcome; no smoking; no pets

## SALT LAKE CITY

**Nearby attractions:** seven ski areas, canyon hiking, bicycling, University of Utah, Temple Square, Family History Library, Symphony Hall, Trolley Square shopping

### SALTAIR BED AND BREAKFAST
164 South 900 East
Salt Lake City, Utah 84102
**Phone:** 801/533-8184 or 800/733-8184
**Fax:** 801/595-0332
**Website:** www.saltlakebandb.com
**E-mail:** saltair@inqual.com
**Proprietors:** Jan Bartlett and Nancy Saxton

The oldest continuously operating bed and breakfast in Utah is this one, Saltair, a 1903 foursquare house embellished by beveled- and stained-glass windows and carved woodwork of oak, an unusual building material in the Salt Lake area. In the 1920s the house became home to the Italian Vice Consul, Fortunato Anselmo, who is notable for several things, among them the national recognition of Columbus Day. Guest rooms at the inn are cozy and comfortable. For extended stays, the inn offers the Alpine Cottages next door. Built around 1870, they combine nineteenth-century charm with all the modern conveniences of such things as cable television and private telephones. Each cottage sleeps four and has a full kitchen, sitting room, and private entrance. Each unit has an original fireplace with unique designs by master craftsmen of the late 1800s. A full breakfast in the family dining room and a comfortable parlor make guests feel at home.

**Open:** year round **Accommodations:** 17 guest rooms (14 have private baths) 12 are suites **Meals:** full breakfast included; restaurants nearby **Rates:** $60 to $159; 10% discount to National Trust members and National Trust Visa cardholders **Payment:** AmEx, Visa, MC, Discover, personal and traveler's checks **Restrictions:** children over 12 welcome; no smoking; no pets **On-site activities:** hot tub

# VERMONT

## ANDOVER

**Nearby attractions:** Okemo Mountain Ski Area, Weston Priory, Green Mountain National Forest, hiking, antiques hunting, Weston Playhouse (seasonal)

## INN AT HIGHVIEW

East Hill Road
R.R. 1, Box 201A
Andover, Vermont 05142
**Phone:** 802/875-2724
**Fax:** 802/875-4021
**Website:**
innathighview.com
**E-mail:** hiview@aol.com
**Proprietor:** Gregory T. Bohan
**Location:** 10 minutes from Weston, Chester, and Ludlow (Okemo Mountain)

A spacious, rambling farmhouse, the Inn at Highview sits high on East Hill, providing panoramic views of the surrounding Green Mountains. Built in 1789, the cozy, yet elegant inn retains much of its original farmhouse appeal, although it has been fully modernized. Guest rooms contain antiques, family heirlooms, and comfortable beds. But the real attention-getters here are the lands around the inn, specifically the trails that were developed for the Swedish Ski Club in the 1950s, and the magnificent gardens and views. After skiing on the inn's own scenic 72 acres and beyond, or cycling through quaint towns and past trout streams and waterfalls, guests return to the inn to relax by the warm fire, cool off in the rock garden pool, or unwind in the sauna.

**Open:** year round **Accommodations:** 8 guest rooms with private baths; 2 are suites **Meals:** full breakfast included; complimentary refreshments; dinner available on weekends; restaurants nearby **Rates:** $95 to $155; 10% discount offered to National Trust members and National Trust Visa cardholders midweek only **Payment:** Visa, MC, personal and traveler's checks **Restrictions:** no smoking; small pets accepted **On-site activities:** cross-country skiing and hiking trails, outdoor swimming pool, relaxing in gazebo

# BRANDON–MIDDLEBURY

**Nearby attractions:** Middlebury College, Shelburne Museum, Fort Ticonderoga, Billings Farm Museum, Drowley Cheese Factory, New England Maple Museum, state parks, Lake Dunmore, swimming, boating, trout fishing, bicycling, hiking, downhill and cross-country skiing, UVM Morgan Horse Farm, antiques hunting, auctions, golfing

**CHURCHILL HOUSE INN**
R.R. 3, Box 3265
Brandon, Vermont 05733
**Phone:** 802/247-3078
**Fax:** 802/247-6851
**Website:**
www.churchillhouseinn.com
**E-mail:**
innkeeper@churchillhouseinn.com
**Proprietor:** Richard Paybell

From the beginning, this century-old farmhouse has offered warm hospitality to weary travelers. Built by the Churchill family in 1871, the house was a stopover for farmers bringing their grain and lumber to the mills. That welcoming spirit remains today, as the Churchill House Inn offers an intimate setting with comfortable rooms that are a blend of original furnishings, antique pieces, and modern bedding. A full breakfast and dinner are included in overnight rates, and guests dine by candlelight around the old oak table. The inn's location at the edge of the Green Mountain National Forest provides numerous recreational opportunities, after which guests often retreat to the inn for a swim in the pool, a session in the sauna, or a drink by the fireplace.

**Open:** year round **Accommodations:** 9 guest rooms with private baths; 1 is a suite **Meals:** full breakfast and dinner included in modified American Plan (MAP) **Rates:** $170 to $220 MAP **Payment:** Visa, MC **Restrictions:** no smoking; no pets **On-site activities:** swimming pool, sauna, hiking, bicycle rentals, cross-country skiing and ski rentals

## LILAC INN

53 Park Street
Brandon, Vermont 05733
**Phone:** 802/247-5463 or 800/221-0720
**Fax:** 802/247-5499
**Website:** www.lilacinn.com
**E-mail:** lilacinn@sover.net
**Proprietors:** Michael and Melanie Shane

In the late nineteenth century, a young Albert Farr left Brandon to seek his fortunes in the Midwest. After establishing himself as a financier and philanthropist, Farr returned to Brandon. In 1909, he built a summer cottage on stately, tree-lined Park Street. With its five-arched facade and grand proportions, the Greek Revival mansion rivaled the finest home in town. After a complete restoration, the inn—with 10,000 square feet of living space—features just nine guest rooms, each uniquely designed and decorated for both aesthetics and practicality, seamlessly blending modern conveniences with period decor. The architectural focal point of the inn is the grand gallery, a vast space where guests may take afternoon tea or perhaps play cards, and the source of the sweeping staircase that rises to the floor above. A favorite setting for weddings, the inn also offers a bridal suite with pewter canopy bed, whirlpool bath, and fireplace. The Lilac Inn has been featured in *Yankee* and *Country Inns* magazines.

**Open:** year round **Accommodations:** 9 guest rooms with private baths **Meals:** full breakfast included; restaurants nearby **Wheelchair access:** limited **Rates:** $130 to $260; 10% discount to National Trust members and National Trust Visa cardholders **Payment:** AmEx, Visa, MC, Discover, personal and traveler's checks **Restrictions:** children over 12 welcome; no smoking; no pets **On-site activities:** putting green, library, tavern, concert series

## CHELSEA

**Nearby attractions:** historic sites and house tours, museums, skiing, boating, hiking, bicycling, golfing, swimming, ice skating, tennis, antiques hunting, auctions

### SHIRE INN
Main Street
Chelsea, Vermont 05038
**Phone:** 802/685-3031
or 800/441-6908
**Fax:** 802/685-3871
**Website:** www.shireinn.com
**E-mail:** trust@shireinn.com
**Proprietors:** Jay and Karen Keller

The elegant Shire Inn, solidly con-
structed of Vermont red brick and granite, has been skillfully restored and
upgraded for modern conveniences. Inside the 1832 Federal-style structure are
a spiral staircase, wide-planked pumpkin pine floors, and 10-foot-high ceilings.
Fireplaces occupy four of the six guest rooms and a spacious, sunny parlor. The
house is furnished with antiques throughout. The inn, listed as part of a National
Register historic district, serves a full breakfast and a gourmet five-course dinner.
Guests are invited to enjoy the parlor, porch, or yard at their leisure. The inn is
located in the heart of what is frequently called "the quintessential New England
village." The *New York Times* describes Chelsea as "one of the prettiest towns in
Vermont."

**Open:** year round **Accommodations:** 6 guest rooms with private baths **Meals:** full
breakfast included (B&B); dinner also included [modified American Plan (MAP)]
**Wheelchair access:** guest rooms, bathrooms, dining facilities **Rates:** $95 (B&B) to $205
(MAP); 10% discount to National Trust members and National Trust Visa cardholders
**Payment:** AmEx, Visa, MC, personal and traveler's checks **Restrictions:** children over
7 welcome; no smoking; no pets **On-site activities:** cross-country skiing, use of inn's
bicycles, hiking, fishing, sledding

# CHESTER
**Nearby attractions:** Vermont Historical Railroad, downhill and cross-country skiing, golfing, swimming, canoeing, picnicking, fishing, hiking, bicycling, tennis, antiques hunting, St. Gaudens National Historic Site, American Precision Museum

## GREENLEAF INN
Depot Street
P.O. Box 188
Chester, Vermont 05143
**Phone:** 802/875-3171
**Fax:** 802/875-6414
**Proprietors:** Jerry and Robin Szawerda

The abundant Italianate and Queen Anne decorations on this house reflect its construction in 1867 and ownership until 1880 by William H. H. Cram, one of Chester's foremost carpenters of that time. The inn is a two-and-a-half-story white clapboard house with gables, porches, bays, dormers, and a cupola. E. J. Davis owned the house during most of the first half of this century, causing it to be called the Cram–Davis House until its transformation in the 1980s to the Greenleaf Inn. Nearly all of the former owners' marks on the house have been carefully preserved, earning the house a National Register listing. Lovely antiques fill the ample guest rooms, which overlook the lawn and brook.

**Open:** year round **Accommodations:** 5 guest rooms with private baths **Meals:** full breakfast included; complimentary refreshments; restaurants nearby **Rates:** $85 to $115; 10% discount to National Trust members **Payment:** Amex, Visa, MC, Discover, personal and traveler's checks **Restrictions:** children over 12 welcome; no smoking **On-site activities:** board games, cards, volleyball, croquet, bicycles, swimming, hiking, golfing

## HENRY FARM INN
Green Mountain Turpike
Chester, Vermont 05143
**Phone:** 802/875-2674 or 800/723-8213
**Fax:** 802/875-6468
**Proprietors:** Stuart and Lee Gaw

Nestled between a sloping meadow and a pond, adjoining 50 acres of forested foothills near a sparkling river, is the Henry Farm and its inn, a mid-eighteenth-century classic New England colonial. With its white clapboards and black roof set off by dark green shutters on its many double-hung windows, the inn retains the ambience of its earlier days, when it served as a stagecoach stop and tavern.

The rooms retain their original wide-planked pine floors, hand-hewn paneling, eight fireplaces, and a beehive oven. Spacious bedrooms with private baths look out on the picturesque landscape. Two cozy sitting rooms and a country dining room welcome guests.

**Open:** year round **Accommodations:** 7 guest rooms with private baths **Meals:** full breakfast included; complimentary refreshments; restaurants nearby **Rates:** $50 to $90; 10% discount offered to National Trust members and National Trust Visa cardholders **Payment:** AmEx, Visa, MC, personal and traveler's checks **Restrictions:** no smoking; no pets **On-site activities:** hiking in the hills, river fishing

## HUGGING BEAR INN AND SHOPPE
Main Street
Chester, Vermont 05143
**Phone:** 802/875-2412 or 800/325-0519
**Website:** www.huggingbear.com
**Proprietors:** Georgette, Diane, and Paul Thomas

Set back from the street on landscaped grounds, the Hadley–Carpenter House— now known as the Hugging Bear Inn—was built in 1850 in the Italianate style. Later came Queen Anne and Colonial Revival additions. The inn's dominant feature is a three-story octagonal tower that rises to a pyramid-peaked roof. Indoors, teddy bears abound as symbols of warmth and family ties, emphasizing the inn's policy of welcoming children of all ages. Guests will find a teddy in each bed, along with sheets and towels decorated with teddy bear motifs. These are accompanied by comfortable, Victorian furnishings. Guests are invited to unwind in the cozy den or on the spacious front porch. The Hugging Bear Inn is located in one of Chester's two National Register historic districts.

**Open:** year round except Thanksgiving and Christmas **Accommodations:** 6 guest rooms with private baths **Meals:** full breakfast included; complimentary refreshments; restaurants nearby **Rates:** $60 to $75 single; $85 to $115 double; 10% discount offered to National Trust members and National Trust Visa cardholders November through June, excluding holidays **Payment:** AmEx, Visa, MC, Discover, personal and traveler's checks **Restrictions:** no smoking; no pets **On-site activities:** Teddy Bear Shoppe (with over 6,000 bears), games, books

## STONE COTTAGE COLLECTIBLES
196 North Street
Chester, Vermont 05143
**Phone:** 802/875-6211
**Proprietors:** Chris and Ann Curran

The Stone Cottage is nestled in the center of Chester's historic stone village. Described in the National Register nomination as "Greek Revivalized Cape Cod executed in stone," it was built in 1840 for Simon Sherwin by the Clark brothers, Scottish stonemasons who worked on the Welland Locks in Canada. The eight houses, church, and schoolhouse that compose the stone structures in this district are built of locally quarried granite, gneiss, and schist in the "snecked ashlar" technique. The home offers guests a parlor, sitting room, library and two guest bedrooms: one queen size with fireplace and one double, both with private baths. The rooms can be combined as a suite for groups. As the name suggests, the Stone Cottage is filled with collectibles and contains a small antiques shop. A pond and flower gardens offer sitting areas for relaxing. A sumptuous full breakfast including homemade breads is provided.

**Open:** year round **Accommodations:** 2 guest rooms with private baths (may be combined with sitting room with sleep sofa as a 6-person suite) **Meals:** full breakfast included; complimentary refreshments; restaurants nearby **Rates:** $65 to $80; 10% discount to National Trust members **Payment:** personal and traveler's checks **Restrictions:** no smoking; no pets **On-site activities:** games, books, television and VCR, collectibles and antiques, gardens, pond

---

# GRAFTON
**Nearby attractions:** historic village, Grafton Historical Society Museum, Grafton Museum of Natural History, antiques hunting, hiking, bicycling, walking trails, downhill and cross-country skiing, tennis, golfing, music festivals

## THE OLD TAVERN AT GRAFTON
Main Street
Grafton, Vermont 05146
**Phone:** 802/843-2231 or 800/843-1801
**Fax:** 802/843-2245
**Website:** www.old-tavern.com
**E-mail:** tavern@sover.net
**Proprietor:** Kevin G. O'Donnell

First opened just 12 years after the American colonies gained independence from

England, the Old Tavern at Grafton was originally a stop along the Boston-to-Montreal stagecoach route. Restored with historical accuracy by the Windham Foundation in 1965, the Old Tavern retains its hand-hewn beams, wide pine flooring, and peace and quiet that were its hallmarks when it hosted such notables as Daniel Webster, Oliver Wendell Holmes, Ulysses S. Grant, Nathaniel Hawthorne, Rudyard Kipling, and Henry David Thoreau. Today's guest rooms—in the main tavern and adjacent cottages—are individually furnished with antiques and comfortable furnishings. A range of outdoor activities is offered year round, from pond swimming to cross-country skiing. A member of Historic Hotels of America, the Old Tavern at Grafton is an integral part of the historic community of Grafton.

**Open:** year round, except month of April **Accommodations:** 65 guest rooms with private baths **Meals:** continental breakfast included; complimentary afternoon tea; restaurant and bar on premises **Wheelchair access:** yes **Rates:** $135 to $295; guest houses sleeping up to 10 are $460 to $510; 10% discount to National Trust members and National Trust Visa cardholders **Payment:** Visa, MC, personal and traveler's checks **Restrictions:** children over 7 welcome (under 7 welcome in some guest houses); no pets **On-site activities:** pond swimming, bicycles, tennis courts, cross-country skiing on groomed trails, shuffleboard, billiards, table tennis, stables for guests' horses

# GREENSBORO

**Nearby attractions:** Green Mountains, White Mountains, Greensboro Historical Society Museum, quaint villages, antiques hunting, golfing, fishing, nature preserve, bicycling

## HIGHLAND LODGE
Caspian Lake Road
R.R. 1, Box 1290
Greensboro, Vermont 05841
**Phone:** 802/533-2647
**Fax:** 802/533-7494
**Website:** www.pbpub.com/vermont.hiland.htm
**E-mail:** HLodge@connriver.net
**Proprietors:** David and Wilhelmina Smith
**Location:** 2 miles north of Greensboro

Highland Lodge was built in 1865 as a Greek Revival farmhouse. Queen Anne–style porches were added in 1910 and 1926, the year it was converted to an inn. The lodge and its cottages are located on 120 acres deep in the Vermont countryside on the shores of Lake Caspian. Each of the eleven cottages has a living room, bath, porch and one, two, or three bedrooms. Guests enjoy imaginative meals served in the dining rooms of the lodge. At the lodge the playroom offers table tennis and other games, the playhouse is base for the supervised play program for youngsters, and the library and living rooms are available for quieter activities. The beach house, with its fireplace and grills, is the center of lake activities. Highland Lodge, in the Smith family since 1954, offers a complete cross-country ski center with 65 kilometers of trails in the Greensboro-Craftsbury snowbelt.

**Open:** late May to mid-October and late December to mid-March **Accommodations:** 11 cottages with private baths **Meals:** full breakfast and dinner included on modified American Plan (MAP) **Wheelchair access:** limited **Rates:** $89.50 to $115 per person MAP **Payment:** Visa, MC, Discover, personal and traveler's checks **Restrictions:** smoking limited **On-site activities:** tennis, lawn games, lake swimming from sandy beaches, rowboats, paddleboats, canoes, sailboats, fishing, cross-country skiing

# HARTLAND

**Nearby attractions:** six golf courses, downhill and cross-country skiing, bicycling, St. Gaudens National Historic Site, Billings Farm and Museum, historic Woodstock, horseback riding, auctions, flea markets

## SUMNER MANSION

Station Road
P.O. Box 346
Hartland, Vermont 05048
**Phone:** 802/436-3386 or 888/529-8796
**Fax:** 802/436-3386
**Website:** www.sumnermansion.com
**Proprietors:** Mary Louise and Ron Thorburn

The Sumner Mansion is one of the few preserved examples of the early work of Asher Benjamin, author of architectural pattern books and designer of the Charles Street Meetinghouse in Boston. The mansion, named for its most prosperous owner, lumberman David Sumner, is one of the best examples of the Federal style in Vermont. The 1807 brick house is adorned by blue wooden window caps and urns perched above the outside pilasters on the Palladian window. Inside, the suspended spiral staircase and ornamental woodwork are beautifully preserved. The first floor features a glass-enclosed dining room and two-story library and music room. Guest rooms with private baths offer four-poster or canopied beds, fireplaces, and air conditioning. A country breakfast and afternoon high tea are served daily. Guests enjoy sports and exercise privileges at the Quechee Club. The entire house and grounds, listed in the National Register of Historic Places, can be rented for private events.

**Open:** year round **Accommodations:** 4 guest rooms with private baths; 1 is a suite **Meals:** full breakfast and high tea included; catered dinners for groups available; restaurants nearby **Wheelchair access:** yes **Rates:** $96 to $135; 10% discount to National Trust members and National Trust Visa cardholders **Payment:** Visa, MC, personal and traveler's checks **Restrictions:** no smoking; no pets **On-site activities:** regulation pool table, croquet, badminton, fitness equipment, country club privileges

# HYDE PARK

**Nearby attractions:** Stowe, downhill and cross-country skiing, hiking, walking, antiques hunting, swimming, golf, tennis, bicycling, opera house, summer theater, Ben and Jerry's, cider mill, Cabot cheese

## FITCH HILL INN

Fitch Hill Road
R.F.D. 1, Box 1879
Hyde Park, Vermont 05655
**Phone:** 802/888-3834 or 800/639-2903
**Fax:** 802/888-7789
**Proprietors:** Richard A. Pugliese and Stanley E. Corklin
**Location:** 9 miles north of Stowe

This Federal style farmhouse was built in 1797 by Darius Fitch, son of a Hyde Park founder and Revolutionary War captain. First a farmhouse, then a school, the house has been used as an inn for more than a decade. The interior is filled with antiques, each guest room exhibiting an individual character. The Quebec Room has a Vermont-made quilt on a hardwood Victorian bed that sits on the original maple wide-board floor. The West is represented in the Wyoming Room with its nineteenth-century bed and quilt. The suite has a country cottage decor. Full breakfasts—with such entrees as raspberry cream cheese–filled French toast—are served on Wedgewood and Lenox china. Sterling silver flatware and Waterford crystal complete the table settings. Guests may relax or read in the sitting room, den, or on one of three porches; outside, guests are welcome to explore the inn's five acres of lawns, fields, and maple and pine groves.

**Open:** year round **Accommodations:** 5 guest rooms with private baths; 1 is a 2-bedroom suite; 1 apartment with kitchen, fireplace, and whirlpool bath **Meals:** full breakfast included; restaurant on premises (dinner available on modified American Plan); restaurants nearby **Rates:** $85 to $175; 10% discount to National Trust members and National Trust Visa cardholders **Payment:** AmEx, Visa, MC, personal and traveler's checks **Restrictions:** children over 10 welcome; no smoking; no pets **On-site activities:** video library, Civil War library, the complete works of Louis L'Amour, barbecue, hiking, walking, hot tub

# MANCHESTER

**Nearby attractions:** Hildene (Robert Todd Lincoln home), Southern Vermont Art Center, summer theater, factory-outlet shops, fishing, canoeing, downhill and cross-country skiing, tennis, golfing, hiking, bicycling

## INN AT MANCHESTER

Historic Route 7A, Box 41
Manchester Village, Vermont 05254
**Phone:** 802/362-1793 or 800/273-1793
**Fax:** 802/362-3218
**Website:** www.innatmanchester.com
**E-mail:** iman@vermontel.com
**Proprietors:** Stan and Harriet Rosenberg

The Inn at Manchester was built in 1880 as a two-story white clapboard home with gray shutters and multiple dormers. Today, the inn has been carefully restored, leaving original architectural details intact. The common rooms and guest rooms are furnished with antiques (most refinished by the owner) and an extensive art collection. The carriage house, recently rehabilitated according to the Secretary of the Interior's Standards for Rehabilitation, also contains antique-furnished guest rooms. Both buildings are listed in the National Register of Historic Places. Good places to unwind include the wraparound front porch, the parlor with its fireplace, the library, and a swimming pool, which hides in a secluded meadow. The congenial innkeepers like to assist their guests with reservations, travel plans, and directions as needed.

**Open:** year round **Accommodations:** 18 guest rooms with private baths; 4 are fireplaced suites **Meals:** full breakfast included; complimentary afternoon tea; restaurants nearby **Rates:** $100 to $168; 10% discount to National Trust members and National Trust Visa cardholders **Payment:** AmEx, Visa, MC, Discover, personal and traveler's checks **Restrictions:** children over 8 welcome; smoking limited; no pets **On-site activities:** swimming pool, ski and golf packages

## WILBURTON INN

River Road
Manchester Village, Vermont 05254
**Phone:** 802/362-2500 or 800/648-4944
**Website:** www.wilburton.com
**E-mail:** wilbuinn@sover.net
**Proprietor:** Georgette Levis

Chicago businessman Albert Gilbert, built this summer estate on a hill overlooking the Battenkill River, but the next owner, James Wilbur, a banker from

Cleveland, gave it its name. The 1902 mansion is an attractive and creative blend of Tudor and the then-modern styling promoted by such architects as Frank Lloyd Wright. The interior exhibits fine craftsmanship from its cherrywood beams and leaded-glass doors to its massive fireplaces and grandly proportioned rooms. Large plate-glass windows afford panoramic vistas of mountain ranges in all directions, while inside the views are equally pleasing with fine antiques, carpets, and a contemporary art collection. Guest rooms are in the mansion and four other buildings on the property. A country breakfast is served. The grounds at Wilburton Inn include sculptures, tennis courts, and a swimming pool. Just two minutes from the village green, the inn is close to all area attractions and is ideal for weddings and corporate retreats.

**Open:** year round **Accommodations:** 35 guest rooms with private baths; 10 are suites **Meals:** full breakfast and afternoon tea included; restaurant on premises; catering for parties; restaurants nearby **Wheelchair access:** yes **Rates:** $125 to $250 **Payment:** AmEx, Visa, MC **Restrictions:** smoking limited; no pets **On-site activities:** beautiful views, 3 tennis courts, swimming pool, sculpture trail

---

# ORWELL

**Nearby attractions:** Sheldon Museum, Shelburne Museum, Vermont Folklife Museum, Fort Ticonderoga, Morgan Horse Farm, horseback riding, golfing, swimming, tennis

### HISTORIC BROOKSIDE FARMS COUNTRY INN
Highway 22A
P.O. Box 36
Orwell, Vermont 05760
**Phone:** 802/948-2727
**Fax:** 802/948-2800
**Website:** www.brooksideinnvt.com
**E-mail:** hbfinnvt@aol.com
**Proprietors:** Joan and Murray Korda

Tall white Ionic columns grace the front of this stately mansion. Known historically as the Wilcox–Cutts House, it was built in 1789 with the proceeds of a sale of two merino rams for $30,000. The original farmhouse was enlarged in 1843 to a design by architect James Lamb, reflecting the Greek Revival style. The building is also significant for having the only coffered ceiling in a private home in the state. A National Register building, the inn has been featured in numerous books about New England architecture. Bedrooms in the restored tenant farmer's house (1810) are furnished in early American style. The main house contains an

enormous library and a major collection of pre-Columbian art. Still a working farm, the 300-acre estate produces maple syrup, feeds farm animals, and grows fresh vegetables and herbs.

**Open:** year round **Accommodations:** 7 guest rooms, 3 with private baths; 1 is a suite **Meals:** full breakfast included; complimentary refreshments; restaurants nearby **Wheelchair access:** 1 guest suite, all common areas **Rates:** $92 to $162; 10% discount to National Trust members and National Trust Visa cardholders **Payment:** personal and traveler's checks **Restrictions:** smoking limited; no pets **On-site activities:** hiking trails, cross-country skiing, canoeing on 26-acre lake, fishing, antiques hunting

## RIPTON

**Nearby attractions:** Middlebury sites, Shelburne Museum, Fort Ticonderoga, hiking the Long Trail and other trails, downhill and cross-country skiing

### CHIPMAN INN
Route 125
P.O. Box 115
Ripton, Vermont 05766
**Phone:** 802/388-2390 or 800/890-2390
**Fax:** 802/388-2390
**Website:** www.bestinns.net/usa/VT/chipman.html
**E-mail:** smudge@together.net
**Proprietors:** Joyce Henderson and Bill Pierce

Built in 1828 by Daniel Chipman, a prominent legislator and founder of Middlebury College, Chipman Inn is situated eight miles from Middlebury in the midst of the Green Mountain National Forest. The inn is small, informal, and very comfortable. Guest rooms are individually furnished with attractive antiques and have private baths. Public rooms include a lounge where guests may relax before a large fireplace. The dining room is lighted by candles, warmed by a fireplace, and decorated with colonial stenciling. Here the innkeepers serve a full breakfast and, with notice, a five-course dinner. The Chipman Inn is located in the picturesque village of Ripton, home of Robert Frost.

**Open:** May 1 through October 31; December 26 through March 31 **Accommodations:** 8 guest rooms with private baths **Meals:** full breakfast included; dinner by reservation **Rates:** $80 to $125 **Payment:** AmEx, Visa, MC, Discover, personal and traveler's checks **Restrictions:** children over 12 welcome; smoking limited; no pets

---

## SHELBURNE

**Nearby attractions:** Shelburne Museum, Vermont Mozart Concert Series, hiking, fishing, biking, sailing, golfing

### INN AT SHELBURNE FARMS
Shelburne Farms
Bay and Harbor Roads
Shelburne, Vermont 05482
**Phone:** 802/985-8686
**Fax:** 802/985-8123
**Proprietors:** Shelburne Farms

Shelburne Farms, originally the agricultural estate of William Seward Webb and Lila Vanderbilt Webb, is a 1,400-acre historic site situated on the eastern shores of Lake Champlain. The Inn at Shelburne Farms, built in 1899, is the Webb's completely restored country manor house, evoking both Queen Anne and Tudor styles. Original furnishings and decor in its 24 bedrooms and spacious common rooms recall the grandeur of the Webb era. Guests may warm themselves before the library fireplace, stroll the formal perennial gardens, or explore the entire farm by walking trails. The grounds were designed at the turn of the century with help from Frederick Law Olmsted. Today, the estate is listed in the National Register of Historic Places. Shelburne Farms is a nonprofit organization that teaches and demonstrates the stewardship of natural and agricultural resources.

**Open:** mid-May to mid-October **Accommodations:** 24 guest rooms (17 have private baths) **Meals:** restaurant on premises serving breakfast, Sunday brunch, afternoon tea, and dinner daily **Rates:** $95 to $350 **Payment:** AmEx, Visa, MC, DC, personal and traveler's checks **Restrictions:** no smoking; no pets **On-site activities:** tennis, walking trails, rowing and canoeing, croquet, lake fishing, swimming, game room, tours of Shelburne Farms, concerts and special events

## STARKSBORO

**Nearby attractions:** Shelburne Museum, shopping and cultural activities in Burlington, Middlebury and Waitsfield, hiking, mountain biking, swimming, boating, golfing

### MILLHOUSE BED AND BREAKFAST

State Prison Hollow Road
P.O. Box 22
Starksboro, Vermont 05487
**Phone:** 802/453-2008 or 800/859-5758
**Proprietors:** Ron and Pat Messer
**Location:** 25 miles south of Burlington, 10 miles north of Bristol, 20 miles north of Middlebury

On a knoll alongside the Great Falls of Lewis Creek is the Millhouse, built in 1831 for the Knight family. It is architecturally elegant for a Vermont country house, with matching detailed moldings inside and out and beautifully arched main entry doors. The attached corn crib makes a unique breezeway. The house changed hands several times and owners in the 1940s restored it as a summer home and antiques shop. After further renovation by the current owners, Millhouse was listed in the National Register of Historic Places and opened as a bed and breakfast welcoming guests from May through October. A variety of accommodations are available, including a studio cottage, all thoughtfully decorated and furnished with period antiques. Mornings begin with classical music and a generous breakfast.

**Open:** May through October **Accommodations:** 4 guest rooms (2 have private baths); 3 can be combined as suites **Meals:** full breakfast included; complimentary refreshments; restaurants nearby **Rates:** $35 to $40 per person; $95 double in studio; 10% discount to National Trust members **Payment:** personal and traveler's checks **Restrictions:** no smoking; pets in studio cottage only **On-site activities:** sitting by the falls of the creek, swinging on breezeway

# STOWE

**Nearby attractions:** Stowe Mountain Resort, Mt. Mansfield, downhill and cross-country skiing, sleigh rides, gondola rides and alpine slide in summer, historic walking tours, covered bridges, Ben and Jerry's Ice Cream Factory, Cold Hollow Cider Mill, ice skating, hiking, bicycling, swimming, golfing, horseback riding, antiques hunting, music festivals, summer theater, concerts in Trapp Family Meadow

## BRASS LANTERN INN

717 Maple Street
Stowe, Vermont 05672
**Phone:** 802/253-2229 or 800/729-2980
**Fax:** 802/253-7425
**Website:** www.brasslanterninn.com
**E-mail:** brasslntrn@aol.com
**Proprietor:** Andy Aldrich

At the edge of this 200-year-old village is the Brass Lantern Inn, a restored 1810 farmhouse and carriage barn. The inn offers nine guest rooms, each with its own identity and decor. Furnished with antiques and handmade quilts, all guest rooms have planked floors and private baths. Most offer spectacular views, and some have wood-burning fireplaces, canopy beds, or whirlpool tubs. A full country breakfast is served up along with views of Mt. Mansfield. A fireplace in the living room is kept burning in winter, and the patio, open in warm weather, is a fine place for viewing a sunset over the mountains. Brass Lantern Inn has earned three diamonds from AAA.

**Open:** year round **Accommodations:** 9 guest rooms with private baths **Meals:** full breakfast included; restaurants nearby **Rates:** $85 to $225 **Payment:** AmEx, Visa, MC, traveler's check **Restrictions:** not suitable for children; no smoking; no pets **On-site activities:** flower garden, putting green, enjoying views from patio

# WARREN

**Nearby attractions:** Sugarbush and Mad River Glen ski areas, Vermont Mozart Festival, sailplanes, tennis, horseback riding, Shelburne Museum

## BEAVER POND FARM INN

Golf Course Road
R.D. Box 306
Warren, Vermont 05674
**Phone:** 802/583-2861
**Fax:** 802/583-2860
**Website:** www.beaverpondfarminn.com
**E-mail:** beaverpond@madriver.com
**Proprietors:** Betty and Bob Hansen

This classically styled farmhouse, built about 1840, has a wing and attached barn built at a later date. The whole has been beautifully restored, leaving Greek Revival and Italianate details intact. Beaver Pond Farm Inn is furnished with antiques; guest rooms have down comforters and candles in the windows. Gourmet breakfasts are served, thanks to Betty Hansen, the chef, who attended the Sorbonne in Paris. Prix fixe dinners are also offered three times weekly in winter. The inn derives its name from several beaver ponds in the rear of the property, which adjoins the Sugarbush Golf Course. Cross-country skiing is just outside the door in winter. Downhill skiing is less than one mile away.

**Open:** December to April; late May to Thanksgiving **Accommodations:** 6 guest rooms (4 have private baths) **Meals:** full breakfast included; complimentary refreshments; dinner available three nights a week in winter; restaurants nearby **Rates:** $92 to $118; 10% discount offered to National Trust members and National Trust Visa cardholders **Payment:** Visa, MC, personal and traveler's checks **Restrictions:** children over 6 welcome; smoking limited; no pets (resident pets) **On-site activities:** Sugarbush Golf Course, cross-country skiing, hiking, biking, trout fishing

# WILMINGTON

**Nearby attractions:** Mount Snow/Haystack skiing, golfing, Lake Whitingham, canoeing, fishing, ice skating, sleigh rides, snowmobile tours, cross-country skiing, bicycling, tennis, horseback riding, antiques hunting

## THE WHITE HOUSE OF WILMINGTON

Route 9
P.O. Box 757
Wilmington, Vermont 05363
**Phone:** 802/464-2135 or 800/541-2135
**Fax:** 802/464-5222
**Website:** www.whitehouseinn.com
**E-mail:** whitehse@sover.net
**Proprietor:** Robert Grinold
**Location:** 1/4 mile east of Wilmington Center

Built in 1915 as a summer home for lumber baron Martin Brown, the White House of Wilmington, with its matching gable-fronted wings and double-decker porches, boasts 14 fireplaces, lustrous woodwork, original French wallpaper, and Victorian-style brass and crystal light fixtures. Guest rooms, each with private bath, are furnished with period pieces befitting a New England country inn. Seven of the rooms are located in the adjacent guest house. Nine rooms have fireplaces, six have balconies or terraces, and four have whirlpool tubs. Three restaurants offer a creative collage of continental dishes. The lower level of the inn contains a spa, complete with indoor swimming pool. The inn is listed in the National Register of Historic Places and has been praised by the *Boston Herald*, *New York Times*, and *Boston Globe*.

**Open:** year round **Accommodations:** 24 guest rooms with private baths; 1 is a suite **Meals:** full breakfast included; restaurant on premises; restaurants nearby **Wheelchair access:** yes **Rates:** $118 to $195 **Payment:** AmEx, Visa, MC, DC, personal and traveler's checks **Restrictions:** smoking limited; no pets **On-site activities:** 33-kilometer groomed cross-country trail network, ski rentals, group and private ski lessons, snowmobile trails and tours, indoor and outdoor swimming pools, spa, whirlpool, sauna, suntan room, hiking

# WOLCOTT VILLAGE

**Nearby attractions:** Cabot Cheese Creamery, Ben and Jerry's Ice Cream Factory, Bread and Puppet Museum, Mount Elmore State Park, Fisher Covered Railroad Bridge, Mount Mansfield, Stowe and Craftsbury villages, fly fishing, canoeing, skiing, bicycling

## GOLDEN MAPLE INN

35 Main Street
Wolcott Village, Vermont 05680-0035
**Phone:** 800/639-5234
**Fax:** 802/888-6614
**Proprietors:** Dick and Jo Wall

The amiable ghost of original owner "Benjamin" Bundy continues to switch off lamps and close doors in this richly elaborated 1865 Greek Revival inn. Architectural details abound, including wide board floors, architrave trim, "bubbled" glass windows, board-and-bead ceilings, and Italianate doors. A superb example of Vermont's connected "big house, little house, back house, barn," the inn offers three spacious guest rooms, each furnished with a variety of antiques, quilts, and comforters. A full breakfast is served in the Victorian dining room on sterling silver, bone china, and crystal, and evening teas and sweets are served in the library and parlor. The inn is situated among century old maples on lawns rolling down to the Lamoille River, famous for fly fishing and quiet canoeing.

**Open:** year round **Accommodations:** 3 guest rooms with private baths; 1 is a suite **Meals:** full breakfast included; complimentary refreshments; dinner available by reservation; restaurants nearby **Rates:** $69 to $89; 10% discount to National Trust members and National Trust Visa cardholders except holidays and peak weekends **Payment:** AmEx, Visa, MC, Discover, personal and traveler's checks **Restrictions:** children over 14 welcome; no smoking; no pets **On-site activities:** fly fishing, canoeing, bicycling, backcountry skiing

# WOODSTOCK

**Nearby attractions:** Billings Farm and Museum, Saint-Gaudens National Historic Site, Calvin Coolidge Homestead, walking tours, Quechee Gorge, Ascutney State Park, covered bridges, swimming, canoeing, golfing, tennis, horseback riding, downhill and cross-country skiing, antiques hunting, art galleries

## JACKSON HOUSE INN

37 Old Route 4W
Woodstock, Vermont 05091
**Phone:** 802/457-2065 or 800/448-1890
**Fax:** 802/457-9290
**Website:** www.jacksonhouse.com
**E-mail:** innkeepers@jacksonhouse.com
**Proprietors:** Juan and Gloria Florin

In 1890, when Wales Johnson, local saw-mill owner, built his classically styled Colonial Revival home, he was able to use the finest woods available. Floors of bird's eye maple and black cherry complement paneling and woodwork of elm, pine, and oak. Furnishings today accentuate this high level of craftsmanship: European antiques, oriental rugs, French-cut crystal, a library of the classics, and a parlor with a welcoming fire. Guest rooms and suites with fireplaces are furnished with period antiques and accented with fine Italian fabrics. The dining room with cathedral ceiling has a granite open-hearth fireplace and magnificent views of the four-acre garden where an arched bridge crosses a brook to lead to the pond. New American cuisine is prepared by Chef Brendan Nolan, previously of the Four Seasons Hotel in Boston. A full breakfast and evening champagne and hors d'oeuvres are complimentary.

**Open:** year round **Accommodations:** 15 guest rooms with private baths; 6 are suites **Meals:** full breakfast included; complimentary refreshments; restaurant on premises **Rates:** $170 to $290; 10% discount to National Trust members and National Trust Visa cardholders **Payment:** AmEx, Visa, MC, personal and traveler's checks **Restrictions:** children over 14 welcome; no smoking; no pets **On-site activities:** swimming pond, four-acre garden, spa with steam room and weight center, aerobic equipment, library, parlor, porches

## KEDRON VALLEY INN

Route 106
South Woodstock, Vermont 05071
**Phone:** 802/457-1473 or 800/836-1193
**Fax:** 802/457-4469
**Website:** www.information.com/vt/kedron
**E-mail:** kedroninn@ad.com
**Proprietors:** Max and Merrily Comins
**Location:** 5 miles south of Woodstock

This 1828 Federal brick building surrounded by graceful porches has had a lively history. Once it hosted cotillions and May balls; later, the house hid runaway slaves during the Civil War. Now it is a New England inn, featured in such publications as *Country Living*, *Country Home*, *Good Housekeeping*, and the *Los Angeles Times*. Guest rooms feature queen-size canopy or antique oak beds, and many have fireplaces or Franklin stoves. Two fascinating collections—one of antique clothing, the other of heirloom quilts—fill the inn. Guests are welcome in the fireplaced living room with hand-crafted oak bar, needlepoint rugs, and a family of antique rockers. In addition to full country breakfasts, the inn's restaurant serves innovative dinners prepared in a style the innkeepers call Nouvelle Vermont, in which the freshest seafoods and local products are used.

**Open:** May to March **Accommodations:** 26 guest rooms with private baths; 3 are suites **Meals:** full breakfast included; restaurant on premises **Wheelchair access:** yes **Rates:** $125 to $230 **Payment:** AmEx, Visa, MC, Discover, personal and traveler's checks **Restrictions:** smoking limited **On-site activities:** swimming lake with beach, ice skating, sledding, croquet, 15 acres of grounds, 50-horse stable for trail rides, sleigh and surrey rides

## LINCOLN INN AT THE COVERED BRIDGE
Route 4 West
Woodstock, Vermont 05091
**Phone:** 802/457-3312
**Fax:** 802/457-5808
**Website:** www.lincolninn.com
**E-mail:** Lilncoln2@aol.com
**Proprietors:** Kurt and Lori Hildbrand

Charles Lincoln, Abraham Lincoln's cousin, once owned this farmhouse. Built in 1870, it sits on six acres of rolling lawn bordered by the Ottauquechee River and a historic covered bridge. (The bridge is the only remaining wooden bridge in America designed by T. Willis Pratt, founder of the Pratt Institute of Design in Brooklyn, New York.) Today at the inn, fireplaces warm the library with its exposed hand-hewn beams, the lounge, and one of the dining rooms. Canopied and brass beds adorn the guest rooms. A full country breakfast is served daily, and rates can also include delicious dinners. Outside, there is a gazebo for relaxing and reading, a swing overlooking the river, an old stone fireplace for cookouts, and a picnic area under a willow tree at the river's edge. The inn is Swiss-Chef owned and operated.

**Open:** year round **Accommodations:** 6 guest rooms with private baths **Meals:** full breakfast included; restaurant on premises; restaurants nearby **Rates:** $99 to $199 **Payment:** Visa, MC, traveler's check **Restrictions:** not suitable for children; no smoking; no pets **On-site activities:** cross-country skiing, fishing, river swimming, hiking, picnicking, bridge- and leaf-watching

# VIRGINIA

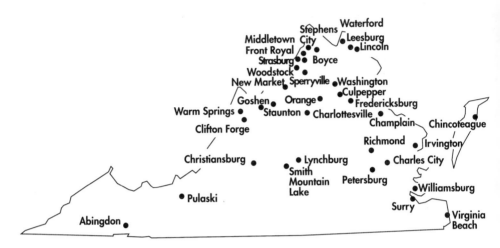

## ABINGDON

**Nearby attractions:** Barter Theater, Virginia Creeper Trail, Mount Rogers National Recreation Area, Appalachian Trail, historic district, antiques hunting, arts and crafts festival in August, hiking, bicycling, boating

### CAMBERLEY'S MARTHA WASHINGTON INN
150 West Main Street
Abingdon, Virginia 24210
**Phone:** 540/628-3161 or 800/555-8000
**Fax:** 540/628-7652
**Website:** www.camberleyhotels.com
**General Manager:** Ron Lamers

Tucked away in Virginia's Southern Highlands is the award-winning Martha Washington Inn, constructed in 1832 as a residence for the large family of Colonel Francis Preston and his wife, Sara. The building has served as a women's college as well as a Civil War hospital. In 1935, "The Martha" opened as one of Virginia's finest hotels. The four historic buildings that compose the inn were painstakingly restored to their original elegance in 1985 at the cost of more than $8 million. Guest rooms and suites are furnished in Victorian antiques and reproductions. Some suites contain fireplaces. The Martha's Dining Room serves continental cuisine and traditional southern dishes. Offering every amenity—including ghost stories—the inn's staff is dedicated to fine service and personal attention. The Martha Washington Inn is a charter member of Historic Hotels of America.

**Open:** year round **Accommodations:** 61 guest rooms with private baths; 10 are suites **Meals:** restaurant and lounge on premises **Wheelchair access:** yes **Rates:** $149 to $300 **Payment:** AmEx, Visa, MC, CB, DC, Discover, personal and traveler's checks **Restrictions:** no pets **On-site activities:** bicycling, hiking, fly fishing, golfing

# BOYCE

**Nearby attractions:** historic sites, antiques hunting, wineries, hiking, bicycling, state arboretum, river activities, horseback riding, foxhunting, fine dining

## RIVER HOUSE
Route 1, Box 135
Boyce, Virginia 22620
**Phone:** 703/837-1476
**Fax:** 703/837-2399
**Website:** www.bbhost.com/Riverhouse.VA
**E-mail:** RVRHOUSE@visuallink.com
**Proprietor:** Cornelia S. Niemann
**Location:** 14 miles east of Winchester; on southwestern corner of U.S. Route 50 and Shenandoah River

Commanding a strategic point on the Shenandoah River, River House sits on property surveyed by a young George Washington. In 1780 the property, known as Ferry Farm, was part of the huge Carter Hall estate. At that time the building was a one-story stone slave quarters. After a major expansion in 1820 that transformed the building into its present three-story configuration, River House was pressed into service as a military hospital during the Civil War. Later, its slave quarters served as tollhouse for the bridge that replaced the old ferry and as a waystation for bridge travelers. Further renovations were made in the early 1940s. Now River House offers five diverse guest rooms, from the original 1780 kitchen with its walk-in fireplace and intriguing theater collection, to the spacious master bedroom with its wide-planked pine flooring and romantic atmosphere. Heirlooms, books, and personal memorabilia fill all corners of the house.

**Open:** year round **Accommodations:** 5 guest rooms with private baths, fireplaces, and air conditioning **Meals:** full breakfast/brunch included; complimentary refreshments; restaurants nearby **Wheelchair access:** limited **Rates:** $99 to $130; $20 surcharge on Saturday-only bookings; 10% discount offered to National Trust members and National Trust Visa cardholders on 2-night bookings **Payment:** Visa, MC, personal and traveler's checks **On-site activities:** 17 acres of woodlands and riverfront for walking and picnicking, reading, relaxing, games, special theatrical weekend packages and house parties

# CHAMPLAIN

**Nearby attractions:** historic Tappahannock, Stratford Hall, Wakefield, Saunders Wharf Steamboat Museum, Rappahannock River, river cruises, boating, fishing, golfing, Ingleside Winery

## LINDEN HOUSE BED AND BREAKFAST

Route 17 South
P.O. Box 23
Champlain, Virginia 22438
**Phone:** 804/443-1170 or 800/622-1202
**Website:** www.bbhost.com/Lindenhousebb
**Proprietors:** Kenneth and Sandra Pounsberry
**Location:** 40 miles south of Fredericksburg

Listed in the National Register of Historic Places and a designated Virginia Landmark, Linden House is the 1750 home of planter Nicholas Faulkner. The stately three-story brick house and adjacent carriage house, joined by a courtyard, offer eight guest rooms, most with queen-size beds (two rooms offer antique high-backed beds). Some guest rooms have fireplaces and sitting areas. The house is furnished with eighteenth-century antiques. A full plantation breakfast is served each morning and guests can help themselves to lemonade, tea, and coffee all day long. The sunroom at the rear of the house overlooks the terraced lawn, where a boxwood-lined path leads to an arbor. The herb garden is surrounded by a white picket fence and a rose-laden trellis. The front of the house looks onto gently rolling pastures populated by grazing cattle and horses.

**Open:** year round **Accommodations:** 6 guest rooms with private baths; 2 are suites **Meals:** full breakfast included; complimentary refreshments; dinners for groups by reservation; restaurants nearby **Wheelchair access:** 1 suite **Rates:** $135 to $150; 10% discount to National Trust members and National Trust Visa cardholders **Payment:** Visa, MC, personal and traveler's checks **Restrictions:** children over 12 welcome; no smoking; no pets **On-site activities:** walking trails, croquet, lawn bowling, gazebo

# CHARLES CITY

**Nearby attractions:** Colonial Williamsburg, James River Plantation tours, Civil War battlefields, Busch Gardens, horse races, antiques hunting, outlet shops, fish hatchery tours, golfing, tennis, bicycling

## EDGEWOOD PLANTATION

4800 John Tyler Highway (historic Route 5)
Charles City, Virginia 23030
**Phone:** 804/829-2962 or 6908
**Fax:** 804/829-2962
**Website:** www.wmbg.com/edgewood
**Proprietors:** Julian and Dot Boulware
**Location:** 28 miles west of Williamsburg, 24 miles east of Richmond in the James River plantation country

Edgewood, a Carpenter Gothic home, was built in 1849 by Spencer Rowland. Once part of nearby Berkely Plantation, it has seen use as a church, post office, and telephone exchange. Completely restored, Edgewood contains 14 large rooms, 10 fireplaces, five chimneys, and a spiral, three-story staircase. Romance is literally etched in this house; in an upstairs bedroom window is scratched the name Lizzie Rowland, who died waiting for her lover to return from the Civil War. Many believe she still waits for him, watching from the upstairs front windows. Guest accommodations are filled with antiques, canopied beds, and old-fashioned country artifacts. Breakfast is served in the country kitchen or by candlelight in the formal dining room. Edgewood, a National Register house, has been featured in *Country Home* and *Southern Living*.

**Open:** year round **Accommodations:** 8 guest rooms (6 with private baths) **Meals:** full breakfast included; complimentary refreshments; restaurants nearby **Rates:** $128 to $188 **Payment:** Visa, MC, personal and traveler's checks **Restrictions:** children over 12 welcome; smoking limited; no pets **On-site activities:** swimming pool, picnic area, creek fishing, walking trails, English gardens

## NORTH BEND PLANTATION BED AND BREAKFAST

12200 Weyanoke Road
Charles City, Virginia 23030
**Phone:** 804/829-5176 or 800/841-1479
**Fax:** 804/829-6828
**Proprietors:** George F. and Ridgely Copland
**Location:** 25 miles west of Williamsburg

This history-steeped house survives as the best preserved expression of the Greek Revival style in the James River plantation country. Federal-style mantels and stair carvings survive from the oldest portion of the house (ca. 1819), as do all of the Greek Revival features from the 1853 remodeling. The house was built for Sarah Harrison, sister of the ninth president of the United States, William Henry Harrison, and was used during the Civil War as the headquarters of Union General Philip Sheridan while his army occupied the area. The house's current owners are members of one of Virginia's oldest families—the innkeeper is a great-great-grandson of Edmund Ruffin, who fired the first shot of the Civil War at Fort Sumter. They have filled North Bend and its spacious guest rooms with family antiques and heirlooms, including collections of rare books and antique dolls. A full country breakfast is served in the formal dining room. North Bend, listed in the National Register, is still an active farm on 850 acres.

**Open:** year round **Accommodations:** 4 guest rooms with private baths; 1 is a suite **Meals:** full breakfast included; complimentary refreshments; nearby restaurants offer complimentary desserts to North Bend guests **Rates:** $115 to $135; 10% discount to National Trust members and National Trust Visa cardholders **Payment:** Visa, MC, personal and traveler's checks **Restrictions:** children over 6 welcome; no smoking; no pets **On-site activities:** swimming pool, croquet, badminton, horseshoes, volleyball, nature trails, tandem bicycle, nature walks, fox hunts in season

# CHARLOTTESVILLE

**Nearby attractions:** Monticello; University of Virginia; Ashlawn; Michie Tavern; National Trust's Montpelier; Blue Ridge Parkway; Skyline Drive; Appomattox; winery tours; antiques hunting; bicycling; golfing; horseback riding; hiking; tennis; James River fishing, canoeing, fishing, rafting, and swimming

## CLIFTON – THE COUNTRY INN
1296 Clifton Inn Drive
Charlottesville, Virginia 22911
**Phone:** 804/971-1800 or 888/971-1800
**Fax:** 804/971-7098
**Website:** www.cliftoninn.com
**Proprietor:** T. Mitchell Willey
**Location:** 5 miles east of Charlottesville

Clifton was originally the property of Thomas Mann Randolph, husband of Thomas Jefferson's daughter Martha and an early governor of Virginia. Perched on a cliff overlooking the Rivanna River, the home was built in 1799. Its appearance is dominated by a full-facade columned portico. The same pine floors, paneled walls, and fireplaces (one in every room) that warmed Randolph family visits still welcome guests. Clifton's guest rooms are large, private, and comfortable, with luxurious baths and air conditioning. All have wood-burning fireplaces and elegant period furnishings combined with tasteful contemporary pieces in a spectacular country setting.

**Open:** year round **Accommodations:** 14 guest rooms with private baths; 5 are suites **Meals:** full breakfast and afternoon tea included; dinners by reservation; restaurants nearby **Rates:** $150 to $315; ask about winter discount **Payment:** AmEx, Visa, MC, DC, personal and traveler's checks **Restrictions:** no smoking; no pets **On-site activities:** tennis, croquet, horseshoes, lake, fishing, swimming pool, spa

## HIGH MEADOWS INN

Route 20 South
High Meadows Lane
Scottsville, Virginia 24590
**Phone:** 804/286-2218 or 800/232-1832
**Fax:** 804/286-2124
**Website:** www.highmeadows.com
**Proprietors:** Peter Sushka and Mary Jae Abbitt
**Location:** 17 miles south of Charlottesville

The only structure of its kind in the state of Virginia, High Meadows Inn is actually two dwellings, built in 1832 and 1882 and connected by a bilevel hall. The early half of the house is built of brick with Federal detailing, while the other half is a Victorian design covered in stucco. Located on a 50-acre estate, the unique home with its 17 rooms, nine fireplaces, and original grained woodwork is listed in the National Register of Historic Places. Five guest rooms are furnished in Victorian style, while two suites reflect the Federal period. The rest are in the late nineteenth-century Queen Anne style. All have original and antique art, sitting and writing areas, and garden or vineyard views, and are furnished with a decanter of port or sherry and working fireplaces. Guests are invited to enjoy the Federal parlor, Victorian music room, grand hall, west terrace, and teahouse, where fresh flowers, fruit, and candy are always on hand.

**Open:** year round **Accommodations:** 12 guest rooms with private baths; 5 are suites **Meals:** full breakfast included; complimentary wine tasting and cheese; four- to six-course candlelight dinners served nightly by reservation **Rates:** $95 to $195; 10% discount offered to National Trust members and National Trust Visa cardholders **Payment:** AmEx, Visa, MC, DC, Discover, personal and traveler's checks **Restrictions:** children over 8 welcome; no smoking; pets allowed with notice **On-site activities:** wine tasting, vineyard tours, horseshoes, croquet, bicycling, badminton, ponds and creeks, picnicking, bird sanctuary, mountain views, nature trails, canoeing, fishing, tubing, skiing, ballooning

## INN AT MONTICELLO

Highway 20 South
1188 Scottsville Road
Charlottesville, Virginia 22902
**Phone:** 804/979-3593
**Fax:** 804/296-1344
**Website:** www.innatmonticello.com
**E-mail:** innatmonticello@mindspring.com
**Proprietors:** Norm and Becky Lindway

Located just two miles from Monticello, Thomas Jefferson's beloved home, and the Michie Tavern, one of Virginia's oldest homesteads, the Inn at Monticello offers a perfect resting spot for visitors to these historic sites. This country manor house, built in 1850, is surrounded by dogwoods, boxwoods, and azaleas. Inside are five guest rooms, each uniquely decorated in period antiques and fine reproductions. Different rooms offer special features, such as a working fireplace, a private porch, or a canopy bed. The breakfast menu is designed to make the most of seasonally available specialties. A crackling fire in the living-room fireplace draws guests in cold weather, while the rocking chair-filled porch awaits on breezy summer days. The inn contains an exhibit about Thomas Jefferson's home life and a gift shop.

**Open:** year round, except Christmas week **Accommodations:** 5 guest rooms with private baths **Meals:** full breakfast included; complimentary refreshments; restaurants nearby **Rates:** $110 to $145; 10% discount to National Trust members and National Trust Visa cardholders, December through March **Payment:** Visa, MC, personal and traveler's checks **Restrictions:** children over 12 welcome; no smoking; no pets **On-site activities:** porch rocking, hammock, croquet, picnicking, bird-watching, fishing on adjacent pond

## INN AT THE CROSSROADS
P.O. Box 6519
Charlottesville, Virginia 22959
**Phone:** 804/979-6542
**Website:** www.crosroadsinn.com

Built as a tavern in 1820 to serve travelers on the Staunton-James River Turnpike, this four-story brick building with timber framing retains many of the features of ordinaries, or inns, of its time, including an English kitchen on the lower level. Once inside, guests are treated to an authentic colonial atmosphere where rooms are furnished with antiques and treasures from days gone by. All guest rooms have private baths, most have king or queen beds, some have fireplaces, and all have breathtaking views. A hearty country breakfast is served in the keeping room on the lower level. The long harvest table on which breakfast is served dates back to the 1800s. Listed in the National Register of Historic Places and a Virginia landmark, the inn is situated on four acres with panoramic views of the Blue Ridge Mountains and is convenient to Monticello and the University of Virginia.

**Open:** year round **Accommodations:** 5 guest rooms and 1 cottage all with private baths **Meals:** full breakfast included; restaurants nearby **Rates:** $85 to $125 **Payment:** Visa, MC, personal and traveler's checks **Restrictions:** children over 8 welcome; no smoking; no pets **On-site activities:** meander among wildflowers, swing under a giant oak tree, sit on the hill and enjoy the countryside

# CHINCOTEAGUE

**Nearby attractions:** Chincoteague Wildlife Refuge, Assateague Seashore, ocean beach, swimming, sailing, fishing, tennis, bicycling, bird-watching, kayaking, canoeing, fine seafood restaurants

### THE GARDEN AND THE SEA INN
4188 Nelson Road
P.O. Box 275
New Church, Virginia 23415
**Phone:** 757/824-0672 or 800/824-0672
**Fax:** 757/824-5605
**Website:** www.gardensea.com
**E-mail:** baker@shore.intercom.net
**Proprietors:** Tom and Sara Baker
**Location:** 15 minutes from Chincoteague Island and Assateague National Seashore

Built in 1802 and known as Bloxom's Tavern, this inn was a hub of hospitality for many years and served as the first voting precinct in New Church. The building was enlarged in 1896 and converted into a Victorian country home with wraparound porch and gingerbread trim. Today, the structure welcomes guests again. Professionally designed bedrooms feature canopied, carved Victorian, and unusual wrought-iron or wicker beds. All guest rooms have spacious private baths, and some feature whirlpool tubs. The inn's dining room, under the direction of the owner/chef, features innovative cuisine prepared using local produce and seafood from the farms and waters of the Eastern Shore. The Garden and the Sea has been praised by the *Washington Post* and the *Los Angeles Times*. The inn is ideally located in an area rich in history, architecture, and natural beauty.

**Open:** late March to December  **Accommodations:** 6 guest rooms with private baths **Meals:** continental-plus breakfast included; complimentary refreshments; restaurant on premises **Rates:** $75 to $175; 10% discount to National Trust members and National Trust Visa cardholders midweek only, excluding holidays and Pony Penning Week **Payment:** AmEx, Visa, MC, Discover, personal and traveler's checks **Restrictions:** inquire about children; no smoking

---

# CHRISTIANSBURG

**Nearby attractions:** Virginia Polytechnic Institute and State University, Radford University, Historic Newbern Museum, New River State Park Bike Trail, Smithfield Plantation, antiques hunting, wineries, Blue Ridge Parkway, caverns, lakes, hiking, Appalachian Trail, boating, fishing, outlet shops

### EVERGREEN, THE BELL-CAPOZZI HOUSE
201 East Main Street
Christiansburg, Virginia 24073
**Phone:** 540/382-7372 or 800/905-7372
**Fax:** 540/382-4376
**Website:** www.bnt.com/evergreen
**E-mail:** evegrninn@aol.com

This 1890 brick mansion was built by Betty Junkin, the sister-in-law of Stonewall Jackson. It shows influences of both the Queen Anne and Colonial Revival styles: varied roof line, bay windows, pillared wraparound porch, pedimented entries and dormers. Guests are invited to relax and enjoy all of Evergreen's public spaces, including parlors and a library with fireplaces, a formal dining room, a wraparound porch with rockers, an in ground pool with gazebo and a wisteria-covered arbor with double swings. The library also features a gallery of the works of local artists. Handsomely styled guest rooms feature king and queen four-poster beds with designer linens, televisions and VCRs, and private baths. A traditional southern breakfast is served. The inn is centrally air conditioned and offers off-street parking and conference facilities for up to 12 people.

**Open:** year round **Accommodations:** 5 guest rooms plus a cottage, all with private baths **Meals:** full breakfast included; complimentary refreshments; restaurants nearby **Rates:** $95 to $125; 10% discount to National Trust members and National Trust Visa cardholders **Payment:** AmEx, Visa, MC, personal and traveler's checks **Restrictions:** not suitable for children; no smoking; no pets **On-site activities:** swimming pool, bocci, fireside or poolside bridge games

## THE OAKS VICTORIAN INN
311 East Main Street
Christiansburg, Virginia 24073
**Phone:** 540/381-1500
**Website:** www.bbhost.com/theoaksinn
**Proprietors:** Margaret and Tom Ray

Three-hundred-year-old oak trees surround this elegant yellow and white Queen Anne home. Built ca. 1890 by Major W. L. Pierce for his family, the house is distinguished by turrets and a wide wraparound porch. Original features, including pine woodwork, ornate mantels, stained-glass windows, and tall windows, have been restored. Guest rooms combine fine antiques and contemporary furnishings with special features such as queen or king canopy beds, fireplaces, and refrigerators. Private bathrooms are stocked with plush towels, terry robes, and toiletries. Guests are invited to use the sun room, study, parlor, and garden, where a gazebo houses a hot tub. Full breakfasts, featuring entrees such as shirred eggs in spinach nests, are served by candlelight in the dining room. The Oaks has been named one of the top 12 inns of 1991 by *Country Inns* magazine. Listed in the National Register, the Oaks holds Mobil three-star and AAA four-diamond ratings.

**Open:** year round **Accommodations:** 7 guest rooms with private baths **Meals:** full breakfast included; complimentary refreshments; restaurants nearby **Rates:** $115 to $155 **Payment:** AmEx, Visa, MC, Discover, personal and traveler's checks **Restrictions:** children over 12 welcome; no smoking; no pets **On-site activities:** hot tub, sauna, library, videotapes

---

## CULPEPER
**Nearby attractions:** Skyline Drive, wineries, walking tours, tennis, hiking, bicycling, golfing, National Trust's Montpelier, Civil War battlefields, museums, antiques hunting

### FOUNTAIN HALL
609 South East Street
Culpeper, Virginia 22701
**Phone:** 703/825-8200 or 800/29-VISIT (800/298-4748)
**Website:** www.fountainhall.com
**Proprietors:** Steven and Kathi Walker

Fountain Hall, nestled in the heart of historic Culpeper County, was built in 1859 in a simple Victorian style. In 1923 it was remodeled to produce the existing

Colonial Revival structure. A brick herringbone walkway leads to the columned front porch with balcony. Inside, the house has been completely renovated and appointed with period antiques and complementary furnishings. Guest rooms are individually decorated and offer various extras, such as balconies or whirlpool tubs. A generous breakfast is served in the morning room. Indoor common rooms include a library of old and new books and two parlors, one with a fireplace. Outside, guests enjoy formal gardens and comfortable lawn furniture. Situated on one of Culpeper's oldest residential streets, Fountain Hall is an easy six-block stroll to the historic downtown.

**Open:** year round **Accommodations:** 6 guest rooms with private baths **Meals:** continental-plus breakfast included; complimentary refreshments; restaurants nearby **Wheelchair access:** yes **Rates:** $85 to $150; 10% discount to National Trust members and National Trust Visa cardholders **Payment:** AmEx, Visa, MC, CB, DC, Discover, personal and traveler's checks **Restrictions:** no smoking; no pets **On-site activities:** lawn games, board games, reading materials, golf packages, tennis, hiking, biking

## FREDERICKSBURG

**Nearby attractions:** Mary Washington College, Rising Sun Tavern, historic plantations and estates (Belmont, Kenmore), Civil War battlefields (Chancellorsville, Fredericksburg, Spotsylvania, Wilderness), James Monroe Museum, Mary Washington House, Stonewall Jackson shrine, Hugh Mercer Apothecary Shop, antiques hunting, National Trust's Montpelier

### LA VISTA PLANTATION

4420 Guinea Station Road
Fredericksburg, Virginia 22408-8850
**Phone:** 540/898-8444 or 800/529-2823 (reservations only)
**Fax:** 540/898-9414
**Website:** www.bbonline.com/va/lavista
**E-mail:** lavistabb@aol.com
**Proprietors:** Michele and Edward Schiesser

Built in 1838 by the Boulware family, this was later the home of Anne Tripp Boulware, first president of the Ladies Memorial Association of Spotsylvania County. LaVista has a past rich in Civil War history, as both armies of the war encamped here. The house reflects the Early Classical Revival style with its two-story front portico. Inside are high ceilings, wide pine floors, and acorn-and-oak leaf moldings. A guest suite, located in the sunny English basement, features a bedroom with fireplace, sitting room, second bedroom, bathroom, and kitchen, all furnished in period antiques. The other guest accommodation is a large room on the main floor furnished with Empire furniture and a king-size mahogany rice-carved four-poster bed. A full breakfast includes fresh farm eggs and homemade jams. The 10-acre grounds are filled with mature trees, shrubs, pastures, woods, gardens, and a stocked pond. The house is listed in the National Register of Historic Places.

**Open:** year round **Accommodations:** 2 guest rooms with private baths; 1 is a 2-bedroom apartment **Meals:** full breakfast included; complimentary refreshments; restaurant nearby **Rates:** $85 single to $105 double **Payment:** Visa, MC, personal and traveler's checks **Restrictions:** no smoking; no pets **On-site activities:** fishing, rowboat, tree swing, bird-watching, country walks, gardens, pick-your-own Christmas tree in December

# FRONT ROYAL

**Nearby attractions:** Skyline Drive, Shenandoah National Park, Luray Caverns, National Trust's Belle Grove Plantation, Civil War reenactments, antiques hunting, horseback riding, wineries, golfing, hiking, canoeing, tennis, fine dining, live theater

## CHESTER HOUSE

43 Chester Street
Front Royal, Virginia 22630
**Phone:** 703/635-3937 or 800/621-0441
**Website:** www.chesterhouse.com
**Proprietors:** Bill and Ann Wilson

This stately Georgian-style Colonial Revival mansion is situated on two acres in Front Royal's historic district. Built in 1905 by international lawyer Charles Samuels, the house exhibits much attention to detail. Local artisans designed the dentil molding, intricate woodwork, and hand-molded decorative ceilings; handsome marble mantels, fountains, and statuary were imported from Europe. Crystal chandeliers, oriental rugs, art, and family antiques blend the old with the new in today's elegant inn. Spacious bedrooms look out on the century-old gardens. In-room amenities include hand-ironed sheets, thick terrycloth robes, personal toiletries, fresh flowers, bedside mints, and homemade cookies. Two rooms have working fireplaces. Refreshments are offered in the fireplaced parlor or on the shaded portico. Shops, restaurants, and historic attractions are a short walk from the inn.

**Open:** year round **Accommodations:** 6 guest rooms (5 have private baths); 1 is a suite; 1 carriage house **Meals:** continental-plus breakfast included; complimentary refreshments; restaurants nearby **Rates:** $65 to $125; carriage house $190 **Payment:** AmEx, Visa, MC, personal and traveler's checks **Restrictions:** children over 12 welcome; smoking limited; no pets **On-site activities:** television lounge, hammock for two, terraced gardens, boxwood mazes

# GOSHEN

**Nearby attractions:** historic Lexington, Goshen Pass, George Washington National Forest, Lime Kiln Theater, Garth Newel Music Center, Warm Springs, Hot Springs, Blue Ridge Parkway, Skyline Drive, Staunton, Virginia Military Institute, Washington and Lee University, Civil War battlefields, George C. Marshall Museum, Virginia Horse Center, golfing, swimming, hiking, skiing, canoeing, fishing, hunting, kayaking

## HUMMINGBIRD INN

Wood Lane
P.O. Box 147
Goshen, Virginia 24439
**Phone:** 540/997-9065 or
800/397-3214
**Fax:** 540/997-0289
**Website:**
www.hummingbirdinn.com
**E-mail:** hmgbird@cfw.com
**Proprietors:** Diana and Jeremy
Robinson
**Location:** 23 miles northwest of Lexington

At the core of the Hummingbird Inn is a 1780 two-room post-and-beam house. The remainder of the inn is the Gothic Revival house that enveloped the older house in 1853. It is adorned with pointed-arch windows, a steeply pitched cross-gabled roof, and decorative cresting along the front porch roof. The house has been operated as an inn for decades, and counts Eleanor Roosevelt among its many guests. One of the guest rooms, named in her honor, looks almost exactly as it did when she slept here in 1935, with its antique bird's-eye maple bedroom set. One guest room, in the 1780 portion of the house, holds a pencil-post canopy bed. All rooms have ceiling fans, natural-fiber linens, down comforters, and Caswell and Massey toiletries. Breakfast, served on antique china, includes the innkeeper's raisin-filled scones from a family recipe.

**Open:** year round **Accommodations:** 5 guest rooms with private baths **Meals:** full breakfast included; complimentary refreshments; Saturday dinner by reservation; restaurants nearby **Wheelchair access:** limited **Rates:** $75 to $125; 10% discount to National Trust members and National Trust Visa cardholders **Payment:** AmEx, Visa, Discover, MC, personal and traveler's checks **Restrictions:** children over 12 welcome; no smoking; no pets **On-site activities:** lawn games, trout stream

---

## IRVINGTON

**Nearby attractions:** Rappahannock River and Chesapeake Bay cruises, fishing, sailing, golfing, antiques and specialty shops

## THE HOPE AND GLORY INN

715 Tavern Road
Irvington, Virginia 22480
**Phone:** 804/438-6053 or 800/497-8228
**Fax:** 804/438-5362
**Proprietor:** William E. Westbrook, Jr.   **Manager:** Joyce Barber

In 1890 a small school opened in Irvington. The clapboard structure with pointed Gothic windows had two front doors: one for boys, one for girls. Today, that school has graduated into what the *Tatler/Cunard Travel Guide* calls one of "The 101 Best Hotels in the World." At the Hope and Glory Inn the two front doors remain, but the lower classrooms are now an expansive, columned lobby with a dramatic stairway, fireplace, and intimate conversational settings. The upstairs bedrooms are elegantly styled. The smallest features a once-hidden passageway to the bath. The largest steps onto a double balcony overlooking the front lawn. All have private baths, beautiful linens, and plenty of soft pillows. Behind the inn are four guest cottages with their own small gardens, each dripping charm and character. At the rear of the property is a small conference center. The grounds are landscaped in the English cottage garden style with winding brick paths and even a moon garden. Hearty breakfasts start leisurely days in this bayside town.

**Open:** year round **Accommodations:** 11 guest rooms with private baths; 4 are cottages **Meals:** full breakfast included; restaurants nearby **Rates:** $95 to $175; 10% discount to National Trust members and National Trust Visa cardholders **Payment:** Visa, MC, personal and traveler's checks **Restrictions:** children welcome in cottages; no smoking; pets accepted in cottages **On-site activities:** bicycles, bocci, croquet, horseshoes, volleyball, wander and sit in gardens

---

# LEESBURG

**Nearby attractions:** historic Leesburg, hunt country, point-to-point and steeplechase races, horseback riding, historic house tours, National Trust's Oatlands, antiques hunting, Civil War battlefields, parks, wineries, Wolftrap Farm Park, golfing

### THE NORRIS HOUSE INN AND STONE HOUSE TEA ROOM
108 Loudoun Street
Leesburg, Virginia 20175-2909
**Phone:** 703/777-1806 or 800/644-1806
**Fax:** 703/771-8051
**Website:** norrishouse.com
**E-mail:** inn@norrishouse.com
**Proprietors:** Pam and Don McMurray

This handsome brick house with green shutters, dentil molding, and roof dormers, was built in 1760 in the heart of Leesburg. It was owned by the Norris family from 1850 until its conversion to an inn in 1983. Built-in cherry bookcases in the library typify the exceptionally fine woodwork found throughout the inn. In addition to the library, guests have full use of the dining room, parlor, sunroom, and veranda overlooking the gardens. Guest rooms are tastefully appointed with antiques and canopy or brass beds. All rooms have comfortable sitting areas and three have working fireplaces. A tearoom, offering weekend service and special event space, is in the adjacent Old Stone House, purported to have been British headquarters in 1754 during the French and Indian War.

**Open:** year round **Accommodations:** 6 guest rooms share 3 baths; private bath available with 15% surcharge **Meals:** full breakfast included; complimentary refreshments; restaurants nearby **Rates:** $85 to $145; 10% discount to National Trust members and National Trust Visa cardholders **Payment:** AmEx, Visa, MC, DC, Discover, personal and traveler's checks **Restrictions:** children over 12 welcome; no smoking; no pets

---

## LINCOLN

**Nearby attractions:** Civil War battlefields, Shenandoah River, Appalachian Trail, wineries, antiques hunting, bicycling, hiking, boating

### SPRINGDALE COUNTRY INN
Lincoln, Virginia 22078
**Phone:** 540/338-1832 or 800/388-1832
**Fax:** 540/338-1839
**Website:** springdalecountryinn.com
**Proprietors:** Nancy and Roger Fones
**Location:** 45 minutes west of Washington, D.C.

Springdale was built in 1832 as a Quaker girls' boarding school. It is a stone-and-frame Federal structure of central passage plan. Front double doors are flanked by Tuscan columns; sidelights and a nine-light transom frame the entrance. A Victorian front porch has turned posts and a hipped roof. Inside, original six-panel doors have reeded trim and bull's-eye corner blocks. Nine fireplaces, with original mantels, are found throughout the building. Guest rooms are meticulously furnished with antiques from the Regency, Federal, and Victorian periods. Lupton's Loft Room on the top floor offers office space and equipment for business travelers. From meetings to weddings, groups can rent a portion or all of the inn.

**Open:** year round **Accommodations:** 9 guest rooms (6 have private baths) **Meals:** full breakfast included; full meal service available for groups; restaurants nearby **Wheelchair access:** yes **Rates:** $95 to $200; 10% discount to National Trust members and National Trust Visa cardholders **Payment:** Visa, MC, Discover, personal and traveler's checks **Restrictions:** no smoking; no pets **On-site activities:** walking paths, croquet

# LYNCHBURG

**Nearby attractions:** Appomattox, Fort Early, Red Hill (home of Patrick Henry), Poplar Forest (home of Thomas Jefferson), City Cemetery, South River Meeting House, historic district walking tours, Blue Ridge Mountains and Parkway, Natural Bridge, Crabtree Falls, Lynchburg Symphony, galleries, colleges and universities, antiques hunting, outlet shops

## LYNCHBURG MANSION INN BED AND BREAKFAST

405 Madison Street
Lynchburg, Virginia 24504
**Phone:** 804/528-5400 or 800/352-1199
**Fax:** 804/847-2545
**Proprietors:** Bob and Mauranna Sherman

The Lynchburg Mansion Inn was built in 1914 for James R. Gilliam, Sr., president of five coal companies, the Lynchburg Shoe Company, and six banks throughout the state. The house, with its 9000 square feet of living space, is located in the Garland Hill Historic District, one of five National Register districts in the city. Neoclassical styling is evident in the huge columns that support the front portico and the paired columns of the porte cochere on side of the building. The front door opens to a 50-foot grand hall with soaring ceilings and cherrywood columns and wainscoting. Lavishly decorated guest rooms contain deluxe linens, padded satin clothing hangers, lace sachets, color cable television, a telephone, and a clock-radio. A full breakfast is served in the formal dining room with fine china, crystal, and silver. The inn has received a three-star rating from Mobil.

**Open:** year round **Accommodations:** 5 guest rooms with private baths; 2 are suites **Meals:** full breakfast included; restaurants nearby **Rates:** $109 to $144; 10% discount offered to National Trust members and National Trust Visa cardholders **Payment:** AmEx, Visa, MC, CB, DC, personal and traveler's checks **Restrictions:** no smoking; no pets **On-site activities:** hot tub, library

# MIDDLETOWN

**Nearby attractions:** Belle Grove Plantation, Cedar Creek Battlefield, Museum of American Presidents, Skyline Drive, Shenandoah National Park, historic Winchester, Stonewall Jackson Museum, Crystal Caverns, Great Strasburg Antique Emporium, fishing, hiking, picnicking, downhill skiing, canoeing on the Shenandoah River

## WAYSIDE INN
7783 Main Street
Middletown, Virginia 22645
**Phone:** 540/869-1797 or 877/869-1797
**Fax:** 540/869-5519
**Website:** waysideofva.com
**E-mail:** info@waysideofva.com
**Proprietor:** William Hammack

Guests have been visiting this quaint country inn—known variously as Wilkinson's Tavern, Larrick's Hotel, and now, the Wayside Inn—since 1797. Steeped in history, the inn witnessed the Battle of Cedar Creek during the Civil War. With the introduction of the automobile, and Wayside's convenient location on the Valley Pike, it became known as "America's First Motor Inn." Guest rooms are decorated with rare antiques, fine art, and a potpourri of memorabilia. Furnishings reflect many periods—early American, Victorian, Empire, French Provincial, and Greek Revival. The Wayside Inn, a member of Historic Hotels of America, is also famous for its restaurant (with seven antique- and pewter-filled dining rooms) serving authentic regional cuisine, including peanut soup, spoon bread, and Virginia ham.

**Open:** year round **Accommodations:** 24 guest rooms with private baths; 2 are suites **Meals:** restaurant on premises **Wheelchair access:** limited **Rates:** $95 to $145; 10% discount offered to National Trust members and National Trust Visa cardholders **Payment:** AmEx, Visa, MC, CB, DC, Discover, traveler's check **Restrictions:** no pets

# NEW MARKET

**Nearby attractions:** Skyline Drive, golfing, skiing, vineyards, caverns, antiques hunting, battlefields

## RED SHUTTER FARMHOUSE BED AND BREAKFAST

17917 Farmhouse Lane
New Market, Virginia 22844
**Phone:** 540/740-4281 or 800/738-8BNB (8262)
**Fax:** 540/740-4661
**Proprietors:** George and Juanita Miller

The oldest part of this farmhouse was built of logs in 1790 by George Rosenberger. Although the outside is covered with clapboard, the interior has exposed logs with stone-and-mortar chinking and exposed-beam ceilings. The dining room is in this old section, with a guest suite on the second floor. In 1870, a large house, with high ceilings and a center entrance hall, was added to the log cabin. Owners in the 1920s added a library and bedrooms. Major Edward M. Brown, who owned the house in the 1930s, entertained extensively in political circles, his guests including Franklin D. Roosevelt, Mrs. Woodrow Wilson, and numerous ambassadors, governors, and other notables. Today's guests enjoy spacious bedrooms, a veranda with rocking chairs, a library, and 20 acres in the beautiful pastoral valley of Smith Creek.

**Open:** year round **Accommodations:** 5 guest rooms (3 have private baths); 1 is a suite **Meals:** full breakfast included; restaurants nearby **Rates:** $60 to $75; 10% discount offered to National Trust members and National Trust Visa cardholders **Payment:** Visa, MC, personal and traveler's checks **Restrictions:** no smoking; no pets **On-site activities:** library, board games, cards, children's toys

## ORANGE

**Nearby attractions:** historic sites, Blue Ridge Mountains, National Trust's Montpelier, antiques hunting, hiking, bicycling, lakes, boating, swimming

### WILLOW GROVE INN

14079 Plantation Way
Orange, Virginia 22960
**Phone:** 540/672-5982
**Fax:** 540/672-3674
**Proprietor:** Angela Molloy

Willow Grove was first a modest frame structure built by Joseph Clark in 1778. In 1820, Clark's son William added the brick portion, built by the same workmen who had recently finished work on Thomas Jefferson's University of Virginia. Today, Willow Grove is an impressive example of Jefferson's Classical Revival style. Guest rooms, named for Virginia-born presidents, showcase a 30-year collection of period furnishings, heirloom linens, hand-hooked rugs, vintage prints, and antique watercolors. Wide pine flooring and original fireplace mantels preserve the traditional character of the rooms. Newly renovated antebellum cottages provide more rooms and suites in the same tradition. The inn, listed in the National Register and designated a Virginia Historic Landmark, has been praised by the *Washington Post, Washingtonian, Washington Times, Town and Country,* and *Country Accents.*

**Open:** year round **Accommodations:** 10 guest rooms with private baths; 5 are suites **Meals:** full breakfast and four-course dinner included; restaurants nearby **Rates:** $225 to $330; 10% discount to National Trust members and National Trust Visa cardholders **Payment:** AmEx, Visa, MC, Discover, personal and traveler's checks **Restrictions:** well-behaved children welcome; smoking limited; no pets **On-site activities:** tree-shaded lawns, gardens, stone barns, picnicking, hammock

# PETERSBURG

**Nearby attractions:** Petersburg historic district, Petersburg National Battlefield, James River plantations, antiques hunting

## MAYFIELD INN

3348 West Washington Street
P.O. Box 2265
Petersburg, Virginia 23804
**Phone:** 804/733-0866 or 804/861-6775
**Website:** www.ims-usa.net/mayfield/
**Proprietors:** Jamie and Dot Caudle **Manager:** Cherry Turner
**Location:** 2 miles west of Petersburg historic district

Listed in the National Register of Historic Places and designated a Virginia landmark, Mayfield Inn is one of the finest mid-eighteenth-century residences in the state. Built in 1750, the house is a one-and-a-half-story brick structure built over a raised basement. Two defense lines were maintained on Mayfield property, giving it an important role in General Robert E. Lee's final attempts to defend Petersburg in 1865. After numerous changes in ownership, and a stint as part of a hospital complex, the 300-ton house was saved from demolition and moved one mile to its present location. The current owners received the Association for the Preservation of Virginia Antiquities award for restoration of this house in 1987. Completely furnished with antiques and period reproductions, the inn offers elegantly decorated rooms with canopied beds, original rugs on pine floors, private baths, and fireplaces. A country breakfast is served in the fully paneled dining room. Four acres of landscaped and natural grounds include an outdoor swimming pool.

**Open:** year round **Accommodations:** 4 guest rooms with private baths; 2 are suites **Meals:** full breakfast included; restaurants nearby **Rates:** $69 to $95; 10% discount to National Trust members and National Trust Visa cardholders **Payment:** Visa, MC, personal and traveler's checks **Restrictions:** smoking limited; no pets **On-site activities:** swimming in a 40-foot-long pool, strolling grounds to enjoy gazebo and herb garden

# RICHMOND

**Nearby attractions:** state capitol, Shockoe Slip, financial district, Sixth Street Marketplace, Richmond Center, the Coliseum, Valentine Museum, White House of the Confederacy, Carpenter Center for the Performing Arts, Virginia Museum of Fine Arts, Edgar Allan Poe house, Virginia Commonwealth University, James River plantations

## EMMANUEL HUTZLER HOUSE

2036 Monument Avenue
Richmond, Virginia 23220
**Phone:** 804/355-4885
**Fax:** 804/355-5053
**Website:** www.bensonhouse.com
**E-mail:** be.our.guest@bensonhouse.com
**Proprietors:** Lyn M. Benson and
John E. Richardson

Designed in the Italian Renaissance style, this 1914 mansion was built by Emmanuel Hutzler, the youngest son of a prosperous dry goods merchant. The dramatic 8,000-square-foot home has been totally restored in recent years. Its mahogany raised paneling and wainscoting, leaded-glass windows, and coffered ceilings with dropped beams create a classical, early Renaissance appearance. A marble fireplace flanked by mahogany bookcases is the centerpiece of the large living room, where guests are invited to relax and converse. Four large guest rooms decorated with coordinating fabrics and wallpaper are appointed with antiques. Queen beds and sitting areas are found in all rooms; two have fireplaces. The largest guest room, which overlooks Monument Avenue, contains a four-poster mahogany bed and an antique sofa and dresser. The adjoining bathroom features a large whirlpool bathtub. Centrally located, the inn is convenient for business and leisure travelers alike.

**Open:** year round (except the week from December 23 through January 1) **Accommodations:** 4 guest rooms with private baths; 2 are suites **Meals:** full breakfast included; restaurants nearby **Rates:** $95 to $155; 10% discount to National Trust members **Payment:** AmEx, Visa, MC, DC, Discover, personal (preferred) and traveler's checks **Restrictions:** children over 12 welcome; no smoking; no pets

## LINDEN ROW INN
100 East Franklin Street
Richmond, Virginia 23219
**Phone:** 804/783-7000 or 800/678-8946
**Fax:** 804/648-7504
**Website:** www.Lindenrowinn.com
**General Manager:** Julia Flowers

Linden Row Inn comprises a block of Greek Revival brick row houses built in 1847. Listed in the National Register of Historic Places, the inn proudly boasts many original features such as plaster cornices, ceiling medallions, marble mantels, and chandeliers. The brick-walled garden behind Linden Row was the childhood playground of Edgar Allan Poe and his inspiration for the enchanted garden in his love poem, "To Helen." The inn's garden quarters offer private entrances. All guest rooms are individually climate-controlled and are appointed with authentic Victorian furnishings. Southern cuisine is featured in the dining room and guests enjoy a complimentary breakfast and wine-and-cheese reception nightly. Complete business-traveler services are available, including fax, modem jacks, photocopier, and free transportation to downtown. For all its services and amenities, Linden Row has received a AAA four-diamond award and is a member of Historic Hotels of America.

**Open:** year round **Accommodations:** 70 guest rooms with private baths; 6 are suites **Meals:** continental-plus breakfast included; complimentary refreshments; restaurant on premises; restaurants nearby **Wheelchair access:** yes **Rates:** $99 to $209; 10% discount to National Trust members and National Trust Visa cardholders **Payment:** AmEx, Visa, MC, DC, Discover **Restrictions:** no pets **On-site activities:** health club privileges

## WEST-BOCOCK HOUSE
1107 Grove Avenue
Richmond, Virginia 23220
**Phone:** 804/358-6174
**E-mail:** brwest@erols.com
**Proprietor:** Mrs. James B. West, Jr.

The West–Bocock House was built in 1871 in the Greek Revival style as a suburban retreat for a wealthy family. In the 1930s and 1940s it belonged to the noted preservationist Elizabeth S. Bocock, who restored the attractive home on fashionable Grove Avenue. This street is now part of the Fan Area Historic District, listed in the National Register of Historic Places. The innkeepers have lived here for more than 20 years, collecting American and English antiques to complement an eclectic art collection. One notable find, now in a guest room, is a bed formerly owned by Lady Astor. One guest room has a sunporch overlooking the back garden, another overlooks the courtyard, and the third has a vista of the nearby cathedral and the city skyline. A plantation breakfast is served in the dining room or on the veranda.

**Open:** year round **Accommodations:** 3 guest rooms with private baths; 1 is a suite **Meals:** full breakfast included; restaurants nearby **Rates:** $75 to $95 **Payment:** personal check **Restrictions:** smoking limited; no pets

## SMITH MOUNTAIN LAKE

**Nearby attractions:** Smith Mountain Lake, Booker T. Washington National Monument, Blue Ridge Parkway, Roanoke, Peaks of Otter, Mill Mountain Zoo, farmers' market, boating, fishing, golfing, swimming, tennis, antiques hunting

### THE MANOR AT TAYLOR'S STORE, A BED AND BREAKFAST COUNTRY INN
Route 1, Box 510
Smith Mountain Lake, Virginia 24184
**Phone:** 540/721-3951 or 800/248-6267
**Website:** www.symweb.com/taylors
**E-mail:** taylors@symweb.com
**Proprietors:** Lee and Mary Lynn Tucker
**Location:** 20 miles southeast of Roanoke

Skelton Taylor, a lieutenant in Virginia's Bedford Militia, established Taylor's Store as a general merchandise trading post at this site in 1799. The Manor at Taylor's Store is a Greek Revival house, built in 1820 as the focus of a prosperous tobacco plantation. The manor, situated on a 120-acre estate next to Smith Mountain Lake, offers six guest rooms, each containing a special feature such as a fireplace, balcony, or porch. Guests also enjoy the formal parlor with its grand piano, a sunroom, a great room, an exercise room, a guest kitchen, and a hot tub. Breakfast features heart-healthy recipes. A separate cottage with a stone fire-

place, three bedrooms, two baths, and a fully equipped kitchen is ideal for families. The estate invites hiking or swimming, canoeing, and fishing in one of six, private, spring-fed ponds.

**Open:** year round **Accommodations:** 6 guest rooms (4 have private baths); 3 are suites; 1 3-bedroom cottage **Meals:** full breakfast included; complimentary refreshments; restaurants nearby **Rates:** $85 to $180; 10% discount to National Trust members and National Trust Visa cardholders **Payment:** Visa, MC, personal and traveler's checks **Restrictions:** children welcome in cottage; no smoking except in cottage; no pets **On-site activities:** swimming, fishing, canoeing, hiking, volleyball, badminton, croquet, billiards, videotapes, hot tub, exercise room

---

## SPERRYVILLE

**Nearby attractions:** Monticello, James Madison's Montpelier, Skyline Drive, Old Rag Mountain, Luray Caverns, Shenandoah National Park, fishing, canoeing, fruit picking, furniture making, golfing, tennis, wineries, dinner at world-famous Inn at Little Washington

### BELLE MEADE BED AND BREAKFAST
353 F.T. Valley Road
Sperryville, Virginia 22740
**Phone:** 540/987-9748
**Website:** www.bnb-n-va.com/bellemeade.htm
**E-mail:** bellemeade@summit.net
**Proprietors:** Susan Hoffman, Michael Biniek, Tobey Wheelock, and Jennifer Simmons
**Location:** 6 1/2 miles south of Sperryville on Route 231

Belle Meade Bed and Breakfast is located on a 137-acre farm in Rappahannock County along the eastern slope of the Blue Ridge Mountains. The newly renovated, spacious Victorian farmhouse is on Route 231, a scenic Virginia byway. Large guest rooms with private baths offer views of the surrounding mountains. One guest accommodation is a cottage. Belle Meade offers a peaceful retreat where guests are invited to soak in the hot tub in view of Old Rag Mountain, explore the fields, small streams, and mountains, and swim in the pool. Guests of all ages are welcome at this family-run establishment.

**Open:** year round **Accommodations:** 5 guest rooms with private baths; 1 is a cottage **Meals:** full breakfast included; dinners and bag lunches available; restaurants nearby **Rates:** $110 to $160; 10% discount to National Trust members and National Trust Visa cardholders for stays longer than 3 days **Payment:** personal and traveler's checks **Restrictions:** no smoking **On-site activities:** hot tub, hiking, swimming, massages available

## STAUNTON

**Nearby attractions:** Woodrow Wilson Birthplace and Museum, Museum of American Frontier Culture, Blue Ridge Parkway, Skyline Drive, Mary Baldwin College, Stuart Hall, Harrisonburg, James Madison University, Lexington, Washington and Lee University, Virginia Horse Center, Virginia Military Institute, Charlottesville, Monticello, University of Virginia, Michie Tavern, Ash Lawn, hiking, skiing

### FREDERICK HOUSE
28 North New Street
P.O. Box 1387
Staunton, Virginia 24401
**Phone:** 540/885-4220 or 800/334-5575
**Fax:** 540/885-5180
**Website:** www.frederickhouse.com
**E-mail:** ejharman@frederickhouse.com
**Proprietors:** Joe and Evy Harman

Frederick House is actually five elegant row houses built between 1810 and 1910, all restored and furnished with American antiques and paintings by Virginia artists. The 1810 Young House, an early Classical Revival structure with a portico, was most likely the work of builders who worked for Thomas Jefferson—the house is similar to a building designed by Jefferson on the campus of the University of Virginia. The building even includes nails from the Jefferson forge. Frederick House guests enjoy oversized beds, ceiling fans, remote cable television, air conditioning, telephone, and private baths. Some rooms have balconies and all have private entrances. A full breakfast is served in Chumley's Tea Room. Frederick House is across from Mary Baldwin College in the heart of Staunton, the oldest city in Virginia west of the Blue Ridge Mountains.

**Open:** year round **Accommodations:** 19 guest rooms with private baths; 6 are suites
**Meals:** full breakfast included; inn-owned McCormick's Restaurant adjacent to property
**Rates:** $75 to 175; 10% discount offered to National Trust members and National Trust Visa cardholders **Payment:** AmEx, Visa, MC, DC, Discover, personal and traveler's checks **Restrictions:** no smoking; no pets

## SAMPSON EAGON INN
238 East Beverley Street
Staunton, Virginia 24401
**Phone:** 540/886-8200 or 800/597-9722
**Website:** www.eagoninn.com
**E-mail:** eagoninn@rica.net
**Proprietors:** Laura and Frank Mattingly

The Sampson Eagon Inn, an 1840 residence, shows an Italianate influence in its low-pitched hipped roof and tall, narrow windows, set in pairs. Several Victorian additions at the rear and sides were made by the house's various owners through the years. The fully restored winner of Historic Staunton Foundation's 1992 preservation award offers five distinctive accommodations, each with period decor. Every air-conditioned guest room has a canopied queen-size bed, a cozy sitting area, cable television with VCR, and a private bath. The innkeepers place chocolates on bedside tables, provide personal baskets of toiletries, and offer a refreshment-stocked refrigerator for guest use. Bone china, cut crystal, and sterling silver are used to serve a full breakfast that may include such specialties as Grand Marnier souffle pancakes or gourmet egg dishes. Sampson Eagon Inn has been lauded by *Gourmet*, the *Baltimore Sun*, and *Country Inns*.

**Open:** year round **Accommodations:** 5 guest rooms with private baths; 2 are suites **Meals:** full breakfast included; complimentary refreshments; restaurants nearby **Rates:** $96 to $120 **Payment:** personal and traveler's checks **Restrictions:** children over 12 welcome; no smoking **On-site activities:** book and video library

## STEPHENS CITY

**Nearby attractions:** Belle Grove Plantation, Shenandoah National Park, Skyline Drive, Glen Burnie House and Gardens, Historic Long Branch, Civil War battlefields, museums, wineries, antiques hunting, canoeing, cross-country skiing, bicycling

## INN AT VAUCLUSE SPRING

140 Vaucluse Spring Lane
Stephens City, Virginia 22655
**Phone:** 540/869-0200 or 800/869-0525
**Fax:** 540/869-9546
**Website:** www.vauclusespring.com
**E-mail:** neil@vauclusespring.com
**Proprietors:** Karen and Mike Caplanis; Neil and Barry Myers

Strother Jones, a captain in the Revolutionary Army, built Vaucluse about 1785. Because of the limestone spring on the property, he named it after the Fontaine de Vaucluse near Avignon, France. Like many Shenandoah Valley homes of its era, Vaucluse is a simple country home. What distinguishes Vaucluse is its large and pleasing scale and architectural features such as seven Greek Revival mantels dating to the 1840s, cherry and walnut doors throughout the first floor (including a pair of 12-foot library doors), and original flooring and woodwork. In 1963, an artist by the name of John Chumley bought Vaucluse and moved to the property an 1850s walnut log home that became the Chumley Homeplace. Guest rooms in both houses are dressed in antiques that emphasize comfort, and have queen-size beds and private baths with whirlpool tubs. All rooms in the Manor House have fireplaces and two in the Chumley Homeplace have private entrances and decks.

**Open:** year round **Accommodations:** 12 guest rooms with private baths; 4 are suites **Meals:** full breakfast included; Saturday dinner available with advance notice; restaurants nearby **Wheelchair access:** limited **Rates:** $135 to $250; 10% discount to National Trust members and National Trust Visa cardholders **Payment:** Visa, MC, personal and traveler's checks **Restrictions:** children over 10 welcome; no smoking; no pets **On-site activities:** swimming pool, walking

## STRASBURG

**Nearby attractions:** Strasburg Museum, Strasburg Emporium for antiques hunting, walking tours, Hupp's Hill Battlefield Park and Study Center, National Trust's Belle Grove, New Market Battlefield Historical Park

### HOTEL STRASBURG
213 South Holliday
Strasburg, Virginia 22657
**Phone:** 540/465-9191 or 800/348-8327
**Fax:** 540/465-4788
**E-mail:** thehotel@shentel.net
**Proprietors:** Gary and Carol Rutherford

The Hotel Strasburg originated as Dr. Mackall R. Bruin's private hospital in 1895. It was converted to a hotel in 1915, accepting overnight and long-term guests. Today, the three-story white clapboard building and two adjacent Victorian houses provide a strong dose of Victoriana in their common areas and guest rooms. Furnishings are an eclectic mix of antiques in Queen Anne, Renaissance Revival, and Eastlake styles. Beds are made of brass, painted iron, or elaborately carved wood. The inn's antiques also are for sale. The dining room, overseen by a framed print of Queen Victoria, displays that era's penchant for indoor plants. Chef-prepared meals may include such items as chicken breast with sauteed Virginia peanuts, apples, and Smithfield ham in apple brandy and cream. Local wines are served. Overnight guests receive a complimentary continental breakfast.

**Open:** year round **Accommodations:** 29 guest rooms with private baths; 9 are suites with whirlpool tubs **Meals:** continental breakfast included; restaurant and pub on premises **Rates:** $74 to $165; 10% discount to National Trust members and National Trust Visa cardholders **Payment:** AmEx, Visa, MC, CB, DC, personal and traveler's checks **Restrictions:** smoking limited; inquire about pets **On-site activities:** antiques shopping, fine dining

# VIRGINIA BEACH

**Nearby attractions:** beach, water sports, state parks for hiking and cycling, Back Bay Wildlife Refuge, Marine Science Museum, Life Saving Museum, Old Coast Guard Museum, Old Cape Henry Lighthouse, golfing, tennis

## ANGIE'S GUEST COTTAGE

302 24th Street
Virginia Beach, Virginia 23451
**Phone:** 757/428-4690
**Proprietor:** Barbara G. Yates

The first aerial photograph of Virginia Beach, taken from a Navy balloon sometime in the 1920s, shows Angie's Guest Cottage. It was built in 1915 in a typical beach-bungalow style and retains that style today with porches and sundecks. In the early days, Angie's housed the families of men who worked at the local Coast Guard station. Today, the Guest Cottage hosts travelers from around the world; it also runs an American Youth Hostel behind the cottage. Rooms are decorated in a casual, beach style with wicker, fresh flowers, and lots of seashells. Some rooms have private entrances, porches, and refrigerators. All guests are welcome to use the community kitchen. Angie's is one block from the beach in the heart of the resort area.

**Open:** April 1 to October 1 **Accommodations:** 6 guest rooms; 1 with private bath **Meals:** continental-plus breakfast included in season (Memorial Day to Labor Day); restaurants nearby **Rates:** $50 single to $84 double (rates drop by a third in off-season) **Payment:** personal and traveler's checks **Restrictions:** no smoking; inquire about pets; 2-night minimum **On-site activities:** barbecue, picnic tables, table tennis, library, sundeck and front porch for relaxing and people watching

## BARCLAY COTTAGE BED AND BREAKFAST

400 16th Street
Virginia Beach, Virginia 23451
**Phone:** 757/422-1956
**Website:** www.inngetaways.com/va/barclay.html
**Proprietors:** Peter and Claire Catanese

Located in the heart of the Virginia Beach recreational area, Barclay Cottage is named for its former owner, Lillian S. Barclay. Used as a schoolhouse for many years, the charming two-story, clapboard house has a pyramidal hipped roof and porches completely surrounding its two floors. While fully modernized, the inn's historical ambience is maintained through antiques and collectibles in every room. A full breakfast is served. Guests enjoy backgammon and other table games

in the living room and complimentary lemonade or iced tea. Just two blocks from the beach, Barclay Cottage provides beach chairs for its guests.

**Open:** April through October **Accommodations:** 5 guest rooms (3 have private baths) **Meals:** full breakfast included; complimentary refreshments; restaurants nearby **Rates:** $78 to $108; 10% discount to National Trust members and National Trust Visa cardholders **Payment:** AmEx, Visa, MC, traveler's check **Restrictions:** children over 12 welcome; no smoking; no pets **On-site activities:** veranda sitting, reading, backgammon, cable television

---

# WARM SPRINGS

**Nearby attractions:** Warm Springs Pools; Garth Newel Chamber Music; scenic drives; hiking trails; swimming in mountain lakes, day trips to historic Lexington and Staunton and to rural Highland and Pocahontas (WV) counties

## ANDERSON COTTAGE BED AND BREAKFAST
Old Germantown Road (Route 692)
Box 176
Warm Springs, Virginia 24484
**Phone:** 540/839-2975
**Proprietor:** Jean Randolph Bruns

The original four rooms of this rambling old house were an eighteenth-century log tavern. The building was joined to a four-room cottage in the early nineteenth century, then gained further additions to reach its current shape in about 1840. There are 12 fireplaces with original mantels, authentic rough-plastered crooked walls, and old wood floors. More than a century of ownership by one family has provided a continuity evident in the furnishings, the library, and the innkeeper's knowledge of the area. Guest rooms range from spacious suites to single rooms, all with electric baseboard heat. Two parlors are available for guests, and spacious porches are ideal for rocking and reading. Behind the main house, an 1820 brick kitchen has been expanded to make a two-bedroom, two-bath cottage with living room and kitchen. A warm stream from the nearby Warm Springs pools flows through the two-acre property.

**Open:** Main House early spring to mid-fall; Kitchen Cottage year round **Accommodations:** 5 guest rooms (4 have private baths); 2 are suites; 1 cottage with kitchen **Meals:** full breakfast included; restaurants nearby **Rates:** $60 to $125 **Payment:** personal and traveler's checks **Restrictions:** Main House not recommended for small children; no smoking; inquire about pets **On-site activities:** reading, rocking, croquet, badminton, volleyball, soccer, cards, board games, unhurried conversation

# WASHINGTON

**Nearby attractions:** Shenandoah National Park, Skyline Drive, Civil War battlefields, antiques hunting, wineries, stables, caverns, museums, waterfall watching, swimming, tennis, canoeing, golfing, climbing, fine dining

## CALEDONIA FARM – 1812 BED AND BREAKFAST
47 Dearing Road
Flint Hill, Virginia 22627
**Phone:** 540/675-3693 or 800/BNB-1812 (262-1812)
**Website:** bnb-n-va.com/cale1812.htm
**Proprietor:** Phil Irwin
**Location:** 4 miles north of Washington, Virginia; 68 miles west of Washington, D.C.

This Federal house and companion summer kitchen have the same two-foot-thick stone walls, 32-foot-long beams, mantels, paneled windows, and wide pine floorboards that were installed when it was built in 1812. The house was constructed of local fieldstone by Captain John Dearing, and the interior woodwork is attributed to Hessian soldiers who stayed in the area and found work as carpenters following the Revolutionary War. The winter kitchen's huge fireplace provides a delightful atmosphere during cold seasons, and three porches and a patio offer views of fields, mountains, and woods. The elegant decor is enhanced by working fireplaces in public rooms as well as in each antique-appointed bedroom. All guest rooms have individual climate controls and enjoy spectacular views of Skyline Drive. Listed in the National Register, Caledonia is a working cattle farm. Caledonia Farm was selected in 1992 by INNovations, a B&B marketing company, as the only bed and breakfast in Virginia, and one of only 23 nationally, to receive "four ovations," designating it as "exceptional" and "significantly exceeding requirements in physical and operational categories." AAA has given Caledonia Farm a three-diamond rating.

**Open:** year round **Accommodations:** 2 guest rooms with semiprivate bath; 2 suites with private baths **Wheelchair access:** limited **Meals:** full breakfast included; complimentary refreshments; superb restaurants nearby (including the world-famous Inn at Little Washington) **Rates:** $80 to $140; 10% discount to National Trust members **Payment:** Visa, MC, Discover, personal and traveler's checks **Restrictions:** children over 12 welcome; no smoking; no pets **On-site activities:** lawn games, bicycles, hayrides, hiking, piano, television and VCR; other on-site extras include balloon flights, carriage rides, limousine service, custom photography, guided battlefield tours

# WATERFORD

**Nearby attractions:** Middleburg, Harpers Ferry, National Trust's Oatlands, Civil War sites, fox hunting

## MILLTOWN FARMS
P.O. Box 34
Waterford, Virginia 20197
**Phone:** 540/882-4470 or 888/747-3942
**Website:** www.vabb.com/milltownfarms
**E-mail:** paul-barbara@erols.com
**Proprietors:** Paul and Barbara Mayville

At the heart of this 300-acre farm is a log home built circa 1765 by Henry Addington. He and his family were Quakers; the land for this farm was deeded to them by Lord Fairfax. The house was enlarged and modernized in 1975 and today offers guests a romantic place to get away from the hectic pace of city life. Located just 2.5 miles north of Waterford and less than an hour from Washington, D.C., the inn is nevertheless secluded and restful. Sporting original chinked log walls and massive stone and brick fireplaces, the house is filled with period antiques, oriental rugs, feather beds, and oil paintings. In an area steeped in Civil War history, Milltown Farm is proud to have hosted Alberta Martin, the subject of the book, *The Last Living Confederate Widow*. Full breakfasts are served up with unlimited pastoral views of horses, cattle, and the Blue Ridge Mountains.

**Open:** year round **Accommodations:** 4 guest rooms (2 have private baths); 2 are suites **Meals:** full breakfast included; restaurants nearby **Rates:** $100 to $125; 10% discount to National Trust members and National Trust Visa cardholders **Payment:** Visa, MC, Discover, personal and traveler's checks **Restrictions:** not suitable for children; no smoking; no pets

# WILLIAMSBURG

**Nearby attractions:** Colonial Williamsburg, James River plantation tours, Civil War battlefields, Busch Gardens, antiques hunting, outlet shops, fish hatchery tours, golfing, tennis, bicycling

## THE CEDARS BED AND BREAKFAST

616 Jamestown Road
Williamsburg, Virginia 23185
**Phone:** 757/229-3591 or 800/296-3591
**Website:** www.ontheline.com/cedars
**Proprietors:** Carol, Jim, and Brona Malecha

The Cedars is the oldest and largest bed and breakfast in Williamsburg. Built by a doctor in the early 1930s, this three-story brick Georgian Revival home was constructed by Colonial Williamsburg restoration craftsmen of 200-year-old brick from a nearby plantation house. Less than a 10-minute walk to the restored area of Williamsburg, and across the street from the College of William and Mary, The Cedars offers candlelight and fresh flowers to enhance the full breakfasts, which are served from a hand-hewn huntboard on the tavern porch. The menu includes such inn specialties as oatmeal pudding with brandied raisins and smoked salmon flan. After breakfast, the porch serves as a meeting place for cards, chess, or other diversions. On cool evenings, the fireplace in the elegant sitting room invites relaxation and conversation. The eight guest rooms and the two-story cottage are graciously appointed, each with a unique style that reflects the romance of the colonial era. Four-poster and canopy beds abound. Each of the two suites in the cottage has a fireplace.

**Open:** year round **Accommodations:** 8 guest rooms with private baths; 1 cottage **Meals:** full breakfast included; restaurants nearby **Rates:** $95 to $165 **Payment:** Visa, MC, personal and traveler's checks **Restrictions:** no smoking; no pets

## GOVERNOR'S TRACE BED AND BREAKFAST

303 Capitol Landing Road
Williamsburg, Virginia 23185
**Phone:** 757/229-7552 or 800/303-7552
**Fax:** 757/220-2767
**E-mail:** Govtrace@widomaker.com
**Proprietors:** Sue and Dick Lake

Governor's Trace derives its name from the fact that it is adjacent to land purchased for the royal governors of Virginia. Built in 1930 during the restoration of Colonial Williamsburg, it is a replica of a Georgian, Flemish-bond brick manor house. Situated on a former peanut plantation, it fronts historic Capitol Landing Road, the route of commerce for goods unloaded from English ships. (Nearby is a recently discovered gallows site where 13 of Blackbeard's pirates were hanged.) Governor's Trace, the closest bed and breakfast to the restored area of Williamsburg, less than one block away, contains three spacious bedrooms with private baths. They are furnished with elegant four-poster beds, family antiques, and collectibles. One room connects to a private screened porch furnished in wicker. Another room sets an eighteenth-century tone with brass candlelighted lanterns, shuttered windows, and a working fireplace.

**Open:** year round **Accommodations:** 3 guest rooms with private baths **Meals:** continental-plus breakfast included; restaurants nearby **Rates:** $105 to $125; 10% discount to National Trust members and National Trust Visa cardholders **Payment:** Visa, MC, personal and traveler's checks **Restrictions:** no smoking; no pets

## PINEY GROVE AT SOUTHALL'S PLANTATION
P.O. Box 1359
Williamsburg, Virginia 23187-1359
**Phone:** 804/829-2480
**Fax:** 804/829-6888
**Website:** www.pineygrove.com
**Proprietors:** Brian, Cindy Rae, Joseph, and Joan Gordineer
**Location:** 20 miles west of Williamsburg, 35 miles east of Richmond in the James River plantation country

Piney Grove (1800), a rare Tidewater log building, and the modest Greek Revival–style Ladysmith House (1857) are situated on property that includes flower gardens, fruit trees, farm animals, and a nature trail. Archeological digs on the grounds have unearthed an ancient Indian site and a deposit of three-million-year-old fossils. The inn includes a unique collection of antiques and artifacts that illustrates the history of the Southall Plantation, Piney Grove, and its residents, who have included planters, tavern keepers, merchants, farmers, and Confederate soldiers. The houses have been restored using original color schemes and furnishings, and all guest rooms contain working fireplaces. Listed in the National Register of Historic Places, the inn contains an impressive library of Virginia history and architecture. The grounds also include Ashland (1835) and the Duck Church (1900).

**Open:** year round **Accommodations:** 5 guest rooms with private baths **Meals:** full breakfast included; complimentary arrival refreshments; bottle of Virginia wine or cider; brandy nightcaps; restaurants nearby offer complimentary desserts to Piney Grove guests **Rates:** $130 to $170; 10% discount to National Trust members and National Trust Visa cardholders for stays of two nights or more **Payment:** personal and traveler's checks **Restrictions:** no smoking; no pets **On-site activities:** nature trails, swimming pool, library, croquet, badminton, bird-watching

# WOODSTOCK

**Nearby attractions:** Civil War sites, National Trust's Belle Grove Plantation, hiking in national forests, canoeing, horseback riding, caverns, museums, shopping, antiques hunting, winery tours, skiing, wineries

## AZALEA HOUSE
551 South Main Street
Woodstock, Virginia 22664
**Phone:** 540/459-3500
**Website:**www.shen.web.works.com.azaleahouse.com
**Proprietors:** Margaret and Price McDonald

Azalea House was built in 1892 as a manse by the United Church of Christ and was used for many years by pastors and their families. The most unique features of the large Victorian house are the almost square bay windows extending from ground to roofline and the adjoining first- and second-floor porches. The house, located near the Massanutten Academy, has unique stenciled ceilings and is decorated with many family antiques. Guests enjoy a full country breakfast. Breathtaking views from the balcony are topped only by the brilliant display of more than 100 azalea bushes blooming in the spring.

**Open:** year round **Accommodations:** 4 guest rooms with private baths; 1 is a suite **Meals:** full breakfast included; complimentary refreshments; restaurants nearby **Rates:** $50 to $70; 10% discount offered to National Trust members except in October and on weekends **Payment:** Visa, MC, personal and traveler's checks **Restrictions:** children over 6 welcome; no smoking; no pets **On-site activities:** bicycling and hiking

## INN AT NARROW PASSAGE
U.S. Route 11 South
P.O. Box 608
Woodstock, Virginia 22664
**Phone:** 540/459-8000
**Fax:** 540/459-8001
**Website:** www.innatnarrowpassage.com
**Proprietors:** Ellen and Ed Markel
**Location:** 2 miles south of Woodstock

This log inn overlooking the Shenandoah River has been welcoming travelers since the early 1740s, when it was a haven against Indians for settlers on the Virginia frontier. Later it was a stagecoach inn on the old Valley Turnpike, and in 1862 Stonewall Jackson made it his headquarters during the Valley Campaign.

Restored to its eighteenth-century character, the inn has its original fireplaces working once again and its pine floors gleaming. The massive limestone fireplace in the living room warms a cozy common area. Furnished in antiques and handmade colonial reproductions, the Inn at Narrow Passage offers comfortable guest rooms, some with wood-burning fireplaces and canopy beds. The back porches and five acres surrounding the inn provide relaxing places to unwind and view the river.

**Open:** year round **Accommodations:** 12 guest rooms with private baths **Meals:** full breakfast included; restaurants nearby **Rates:** $95 to $145; 10% discount offered to National Trust members and National Trust Visa cardholders **Payment:** Visa, MC, personal and traveler's checks  **Restrictions:** smoking limited; no pets **On-site activities:** hiking, canoeing, fishing, bird-watching, horseback riding, historic sites

# WASHINGTON

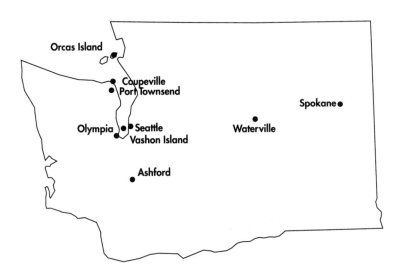

## ASHFORD

**Nearby attractions:** Mount Rainier National Park, Northwest Trek Animal Park, Mount Rainier Scenic Railroad, Pioneer Farm Museum, hiking, skiing, lakes for swimming and boating

**MOUNTAIN MEADOWS INN BED AND BREAKFAST**
28912 SR 706 E
P.O. Box 291
Ashford, Washington 98304
**Phone:** 360/569-2788
**Website:** www.bbchannel.com/bbc/p215352.html
**E-mail:** mtmeadow@mashell.com
**Proprietors:** Harry and Michelle Latimer

The view in 1910 from the front porch of this mill superintendent's house would have taken in the activity at the booming sawmill town of National, near Ashford. Here was the biggest sawmill west of the Mississippi, but the unionization of labor forced the mill and town to close before World War II. Today the house, known as Mountain Meadows Inn, is on 11 acres of serene cedar groves amidst the grandeur of the Northwest landscape. Guests enjoy forested trails, gardens, a wildlife pond, evening campfires, and an impressive Northwest Coast Native American artifact collection. The nature library of more than 1,000 books includes a John Muir archive. Large comfortable guest rooms are highlighted by hearty country breakfasts. There is a two-bedroom suite with kitchen for groups of 3 or 4, or the whole house can be rented.

**Open:** year round **Accommodations:** 6 guest rooms with private baths; 1 is a suite with kitchen **Meals:** full breakfast included; campfire evenings with marshmallow roasts **Rates:** $75 to $165; 10% discount to National Trust members **Payment:** Visa, MC, personal check **Restrictions:** children over 4 welcome; no smoking; no pets **On-site activities:** Native American artifact collection, nature trails, bird watching, nature library, maps and guides to Mount Rainier National Park


## NATIONAL PARK INN
Mt. Rainier National Park
P.O. Box 108
Ashford, Washington 98304
**Phone:** 360/569-2400 or 800/678-8946
**Fax:** 360/569-2770
**Website:** www.guestservices.com/rainier
**General Manager:** Rusty Sproat

James Longmire, an early guide in Mt. Rainier National Park, accidentally stumbled upon a series of soda and iron springs. He laid claim to the 20 acres and, in 1888, built a small cabin that still stands today. Within a few years, he had constructed a small hotel and developed the springs into a health bath. In 1906, the Milwaukee Railroad Company built the National Park Inn to accommodate the tourists arriving by train. This provided stiff competition for the Longmires who, in turn, constructed a new two-story hotel known as the National Park Inn Annex. In 1926, after a fire completely destroyed the original inn built by the railroad company, the Annex became known as the National Park Inn. Remodeled in 1990 and open all year, the Inn offers comfortable guest accommodations and spectacular views of Mt. Rainier. A member of Historic Hotels of America, the inn also is listed in the National Register of Historic Places.

**Open:** year round **Accommodations:** 25 guest rooms (17 with private baths) **Meals:** full breakfast included November through April; restaurant on premises serves breakfast, lunch, and dinner; complimentary refreshments **Wheelchair access:** limited **Rates:** $69 to $128; 10% discount to National Trust members and National Trust Visa cardholders **Payment:** AmEx, Visa, MC **Restrictions:** no pets **On-site activities:** hiking, nature trails, evening campground talks, National Park Service Museum, cross-country ski and snowshoe rentals

## PARADISE INN

Mt. Rainier National Park
P.O. Box 108
Ashford, Washington 98304
**Phone:** 360/569-2400 or 800/678-8946
**Fax:** 360/569-2770
**Website:** www.guestservices.com/rainier
**General Manager:** Rusty Sproat

In the early 1900s, a group of Tacoma businessmen formed a corporation to respond to visitors' requests for lodging in the higher elevations of Mt. Rainier National Park. The resulting Paradise Inn was built in 1917 of Alaskan cedar resurrected from a devastating forest fire. Hand-hewn furniture and two large stone fireplaces in the lobby convey the inn's rustic charm. The original 33 guest rooms, which were offered without private baths, are still available to guests. In the early 1920s, the Annex was added, providing accommodations with private baths. The inn was threatened with demolition in the 1950s, but a public outpouring of protest resulted in a major renovation in 1979. Today, the inn welcomes visitors to the incomparable beauty and scenic grandeur of Mt. Rainier from spring to fall. The Paradise Inn is a member of Historic Hotels of America.

**Open:** mid-May to early October **Accommodations:** 126 guest rooms (93 with private baths) **Meals:** restaurant on premises serves three meals daily and Sunday brunch **Rates:** $73 to $130 **Payment:** AmEx, Visa, MC **Restrictions:** no pets **On-site activities:** hiking, mountain climbing, nature walks, evening programs, gift shop with Native American items

## COUPEVILLE

**Nearby attractions:** Fort Casey State Park, Ebby's Landing National Reserve, historic Port Townsend (via ferry), swimming, skin diving, bird-watching

## FORT CASEY INN

1124 South Engle Road
Whidbey Island
Coupeville, Washington 98239
**Phone:** 360/678-8792
**Proprietors:** Gordon and Victoria Hoenig
**Location:** 1¹/2 hours from Seattle

Fort Casey Inn is a 1909 Colonial Revival structure built as officers' quarters for the then-active defense installation of Fort Casey on Whidbey Island. The restored National Register inn is located next door to Fort Casey State Park, with its bunkers, lighthouse, 10-inch disappearing guns, public beaches, and trails. Built to withstand attacks on Fort Casey, the house has a reinforced basement, which was intended for use as a bomb shelter. All guest accommodations are two-bedroom suites complete with bath, living room, and kitchen. The beautifully appointed Garrison Hall is available for seminars and retreats. Whidbey Island offers countless attractions, from sites of early frontier living to spectacular Deception Pass.

**Open:** year round **Accommodations:** 8 2-bedroom guest suites with private baths **Meals:** continental-plus breakfast included; restaurants nearby **Rates:** $85 to $135 **Payment:** Visa, MC, personal and traveler's checks **Restrictions:** no smoking; no pets **On-site activities:** bicycles

---

# OLYMPIA

**Nearby attractions:** state capitol, downtown shopping and dining, marina, boating, jogging, bicycling, wildlife sanctuaries

### HARBINGER INN BED AND BREAKFAST
1136 East Bay Drive
Olympia, Washington 98506
**Phone:** 360/754-0389
**Fax:** 360/754-7499
**Proprietors:** Marisa and Terrell Williams

The house that is now the Harbinger Inn was constructed in 1910. Its Neoclassical styling was rendered in gray ashlar block with white pillars and broad balconies. All elements have been carefully restored, including interior features such as original wall stenciling and oak pocket doors. The house has two unique features of interest: a mysterious street-to-basement tunnel and a hillside waterfall fed by an artesian well. Bedrooms afford views of the Olympic Mountains, Budd Inlet, or that lovely waterfall. Guests will find a warm, informal atmosphere at the inn and are encouraged to borrow books from the library for night reading, enjoy complimentary late afternoon tea and cookies, or just relax in the sitting room with views across the water to the nearby capitol.

**Open:** year round **Accommodations:** 5 guest rooms with private baths; 2 are suites **Meals:** continental-plus breakfast included; complimentary refreshments; restaurants nearby **Wheelchair access:** limited **Rates:** $60 to $175; 10% discount to National Trust members and National Trust Visa cardholders **Payment:** AmEx, Visa, MC, personal and traveler's checks **Restrictions:** children over 12 welcome; no smoking; no pets **On-site activities:** library, bird watching

## ORCAS ISLAND

**Nearby attractions:** swimming, golfing, windsurfing, fishing, sailing, kayaking, bicycling, shopping, arts and crafts

### TURTLEBACK FARM INN

Crow Valley Road
Route 1, Box 650
Eastsound, Washington 98245
**Phone:** 360/376-4914 or 800/376-4914
**Fax:** 360/376-5329
**Website:** www.turtlebackinn.com
**Proprietors:** Bill and Susan Fletcher

Turtleback Farm Inn is located on Orcas Island, considered to be the loveliest island of the San Juan Archipelago in Puget Sound. A restoration and expansion in 1985 preserved the integrity of the original Folk National-style farmhouse while adding modern amenities. The living room has a Rumford fireplace, comfortable seating, and a corner game table. In 1997, the innkeepers added Orchard House to the property. Nestled among the apple trees, it offers four spacious rooms with individual decks, fireplaces, sitting areas, and full baths. All guest rooms are furnished with a blend of fine antiques and contemporary pieces. A hearty breakfast is served on bone china with silver and linen table settings. Offering outdoor adventure and indoor comfort, Turtleback Farm Inn has been called one of the 12 most romantic spots in the country by the *Los Angeles Times*. The inn is a sanctuary on 80 acres of forest and farmland in the shadow of Turtleback Mountain.

**Open:** year round **Accommodations:** 11 guest rooms with private baths **Meals:** full breakfast included; complimentary refreshments; restaurants nearby **Wheelchair access:** yes **Rates:** $80 to $210 **Payment:** Visa, MC, Discover, personal and traveler's checks **Restrictions:** children over 8 welcome; no smoking; no pets **On-site activities:** bird watching, walking, parlor games

# PORT TOWNSEND

**Nearby attractions:** museums, art galleries, home tours, state parks, marine science center, boating, golfing, tennis, windsurfing, kayaking, hiking, bicycling, swimming, fishing, beachcombing, clam digging, seasonal festivals

## ANN STARRETT MANSION
744 Clay Street
Port Townsend, Washington 98368
**Phone:** 360/385-3205 or 800/321-0644
**Fax:** 360/385-2976
**Website:** www.olympus.net/starrett
**Proprietors:** Edel and Bob Sokol

George Starrett built this elaborate Queen Anne mansion as a wedding present for his wife, Ann, in 1889. The mansion is internationally renowned for its outstanding architecture, frescoed ceilings, and free-hanging three-story spiral staircase. The stairs lead to an eight-sided domed ceiling that is actually a solar calendar with frescoes that depict the Four Seasons and Four Virtues. Small dormer windows are situated so that on the first day of each new season the sun shines on a ruby red glass, causing a red beam to point toward the appropriate seasonal panel. Elsewhere in the house elaborate moldings feature carved lions, doves, and ferns. Guest rooms are furnished with antiques carefully selected to recreate the Victorian era of a century ago. The Ann Starrett Mansion has received praise from many publications, including the *New York Times* and the *London Times*.

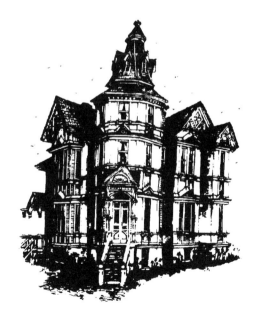

**Open:** year round **Accommodations:** 11 guest rooms with private baths; 6 are suites **Meals:** full breakfast included; restaurants nearby **Rates:** $85 to $225; 10% discount offered to National Trust members and National Trust Visa cardholders midweek November through April **Payment:** AmEx, Visa, MC, Discover, personal and traveler's checks **Restrictions:** children over 12 welcome; no smoking; no pets

## HOLLY HILL HOUSE BED AND BREAKFAST
611 Polk Street
Port Townsend, Washington 98368
**Phone:** 360/385-5619 or 800/435-1454
**Fax:** 360/385-3041
**Website:** www.acies.com/hollyhill/
**E-mail:** hollyhill@olympus.net
**Proprietor:** Lynne Sterling

This charming cross-gabled house with wide front porch was built in 1872 by Colonel R. C. Hill, mayor, state representative, and bank founder. Noted for its well-preserved nineteenth-century wood graining in the formal dining room, the house is also known for its expansive gardens, which feature 185 rose bushes, 17 ancient holly trees, and a 100-year-old Camperdown elm tree. Guest accommodations are bedecked in florals and lace, adding romance to the Victorian furnishings here and throughout the house. Each room offers a view of the gardens, Admiralty Inlet, Mt. Baker, or the Cascade Range. Breakfast is served in the candlelit dining room, with a table set in linens, china, and silver. Afternoon tea and fresh-baked pastries are served in the elegant parlor in front of the Italian fireplace. A cozy library invites browsing among its 2,000 books.

**Open:** year round **Accommodations:** 5 guest rooms with private baths; 1 is a suite **Meals:** full breakfast included; complimentary refreshments; restaurants nearby **Rates:** $78 to $145; 10% discount to National Trust members and National Trust Visa cardholders November through April only **Payment:** Visa, MC, personal and traveler's checks **Restrictions:** children over 12 welcome; no smoking; no pets **On-site activities:** 2,000-book library, extensive gardens, mystery weekends

## QUIMPER INN BED AND BREAKFAST
1306 Franklin Street
Port Townsend, Washington 98368
**Phone:** 360/385-1060 or 800/557-1060
**Website:** www.olympus.net/biz/Quimper/Quimper.html
**E-mail:** Thequimps@olympus.net
**Proprietors:** Sue and Ron Ramage

In 1888, Henry Morgan built a two-story house with hipped roof. A remodeling in 1904 by Harry and Gertrude Barthrop gave the house a third story through the addition of gables and dormers, and a dramatic presence through the further addition of a double front porch. After decades of neglect, the house was restored in the late 1980s and converted to an inn. Workers renewed such features as pocket doors, bay windows, Victorian lighting fixtures, and built-in shelves and cabinets. Guest rooms have been decorated with antiques and individual style. An easy walk takes guests downtown or to uptown districts amid cafes, shops, theaters, and festivities.

**Open:** year round **Accommodations:** 5 guest rooms (3 have private baths); 1 is a suite **Meals:** full breakfast included; restaurants nearby **Rates:** $75 to $140 **Payment:** Visa, MC, personal and traveler's checks **Restrictions:** children over 12 welcome; no smoking; no pets

## SEATTLE

**Nearby attractions:** financial, retail, and historic districts of Seattle; Rose Gardens; Volunteer Park; Seattle Art Museum and Conservatory; University of Washington; Pike Place Market; convention center; parks; bicycling; swimming; kayaking; Chittenden Locks and fish ladder; tennis; zoo; horse-drawn carriages

### CHELSEA STATION ON THE PARK—A BED AND BREAKFAST INN
4915 Linden Avenue North
Seattle, Washington 98103
**Phone:** 206/547-6077 or 800/400-6077
**Website:** www.bandbseattle.com
**E-mail:** jsg@nwlink.com
**Proprietor:** John Griffin **Innkeeper:** Karen Carbonneau

After the Great Fire of 1896 and a second fire in 1899, brick became the building material of choice in Seattle. Chelsea Station, a Federal-style home built in 1929, displays decorative brickwork in an asymmetrical diamond pattern laid vertically on either side of the entrance. Largely decorated in Mission style, the house features antiques throughout. Guest rooms offer king- and queen-size beds with private baths. Second-floor suites reveal peek-a-boo views of the Cascade Mountains. Guests feel refreshed by the warm and casual mood at Chelsea Station. The property was originally part of the 1896 grant that established the Seattle Zoo and is located directly across from the Rose Gardens. The inn, nestled in the Fremont neighborhood, is also convenient to Woodland Park, Greenlake, and downtown.

**Open:** year round **Accommodations:** 9 guest rooms with private baths; 5 are suites **Meals:** full breakfast included; complimentary refreshments; restaurants nearby **Rates:** $95 to $135; 10% discount offered to National Trust members and National Trust Visa cardholders low season only **Payment:** AmEx, Visa, MC, DC, Discover, personal and traveler's checks **Restrictions:** children over 12 welcome; no smoking; no pets

## PIONEER SQUARE HOTEL
77 Yesler Way
Seattle, Washington 98104
**Phone:** 206/340-1234 or 800/800-5514
**Fax:** 206/467-0707
**Website:** www.pioneersquare.com
**E-mail:** info@pioneersquare.com
**General Manager:** Jo Thompson

Pioneer Square is so named for the explorers and founders of this unique city, first established as a mill town. One of the most vibrant in its history was Henry L. Yesler, developer of the first saw mill and much of the early commercial district. One of the ventures of his vast estate, was the design and construction of the Yesler Hotel in Pioneer Square in 1914. Simply detailed, the brick hotel, now called Pioneer Square Hotel, continues to operate today as the only first-class small hotel in the National Register historic district. All 75 guest rooms are equipped with remote-control cable television, direct dial telephones with data ports, full private baths, and individual climate controls. Each room is designed with style and comfort in mind. The hotel is ideally suited for receptions, meetings, and weddings and is convenient to all Pioneer Square attractions.

**Open:** year round **Accommodations:** 75 guest rooms with private baths; 3 are suites **Meals:** continental-plus breakfast included; restaurants nearby **Wheelchair access:** yes **Rates:** $129 to $229; 10% discount to National Trust members and National Trust Visa cardholders **Payment:** AmEx, Visa, MC, CB, DC, Discover, traveler's check **Restrictions:** smoking limited; no pets

## ROBERTA'S BED AND BREAKFAST
1147 Sixteenth Avenue East
Seattle, Washington 98112
**Phone:** 206/329-3326
**Fax:** 206/324-2149
**Website:** www.robertas.com
**Proprietor:** Roberta Barry

Roberta's Bed and Breakfast is located on a tree-lined residential street in Seattle's historic Capitol Hill neighborhood. Volunteer Park, which includes the Seattle Art Museum and Conservatory, is just around the corner. The house, a 1903 classic four-square, shows strong Prairie School influences. Five sunny bedrooms with queen-size beds, are furnished with a variety of antiques and lots of books. Breakfast, beginning with coffee or tea delivered to bedroom doors, is continued in the dining room where hearty, homemade food is served. The living room and wide front porch are good places to relax and meet other visitors or read a

newspaper; the *New York Times* and two local papers are delivered daily. The innkeeper, with a native's knowledge, is glad to recommend activities and restaurants in the Seattle area.

**Open:** year round **Accommodations:** 5 guest rooms with private baths; 1 is a suite **Meals:** full breakfast included; restaurants nearby **Rates:** $100 to $140; 10% discount to National Trust members and National Trust Visa cardholders **Payment:** AmEx, Visa, MC, personal and traveler's checks **Restrictions:** children over 12 welcome; no smoking; no pets

# SPOKANE

**Nearby attractions:** Coeur d'Alene Park, Eastern Washington Historical Society, walking tours, Riverfront Park, golfing, Mt. Spokane, skiing, lakes, fishing

## FOTHERINGHAM HOUSE
2128 West Second Avenue
Spokane, Washington 99204
**Phone:** 509/838-1891
**Fax:** 509/838-1807
**Website:** www.IOR.com/Fotheringham
**E-mail:** Fotheringham.bnb@IOR.com
**Proprietors:** Jackie and Graham Johnson

This late Queen Anne–style house is a primary site in the Browne's Addition National Register historic district. It was built in 1891 by Mayor David B. Fotheringham. Tin ceilings, wood floors, a curved-glass window in the entryway, the first-floor carved and tiled fireplace, intricate ball-and-spindle fretwork separating the entry and living room, and open, carved staircase are all original to the house. Guest rooms are furnished with Victorian-era pieces from England, Ireland, France, and the United States. Each room is decorated differently, from the four-poster bed in the Mayor's Room to the armoire and matching rose-carved bed in the Mansion Room. Evening tea and truffles and morning coffee and juice are set outside guest room doors. Full breakfasts feature a daily changing menu.

**Open:** year round **Accommodations:** 4 guest rooms (1 with private bath) **Meals:** full breakfast included; complimentary refreshments; restaurants nearby **Rates:** $80 to $105; 10% discount to National Trust members and National Trust Visa cardholders **Payment:** AmEx, Visa, MC, Discover, personal and traveler's checks **Restrictions:** children over 12 welcome; no smoking; no pets

# VASHON ISLAND

**Nearby attractions:** beaches, kayaking, golfing, swimming, tennis, art galleries, shopping, massages

## ANGELS OF THE SEA BED AND BREAKFAST

26431 Ninety-Ninth Avenue, S.W.
Vashon Island, Washington 98070
**Phone:** 206/463-6980 or 800/798-9249
**Fax:** 206/463-2205
**Website:** angelsofthesea.com
**E-mail:** AngelsSea@aol.com
**Proprietor:** Marnie Jones

Visitors hop the ferryboat from Seattle or Tacoma and feel their troubles slip away in the wake as they head toward the peaceful sanctuary of Angels of the Sea, a bed and breakfast in a former Lutheran church, tucked into the lush woods and meadows of Vashon Island. The building is quaint with belfry (bell still rings) and Gothic windows. On the first floor there are two guest rooms that share a bath with claw-foot tub and living room; upstairs is a spacious suite with private whirlpool bath and sleeping alcove just right for children. Dressed in angels and mementos of the sea and shore, all accommodations offer television and VCR and coffeemakers. Breakfast is served in the church sanctuary, to the heavenly strains of innkeeper Marnie Jones's private harp concert.

**Open:** year round **Accommodations:** 2 guest rooms share a bath; 1 suite with private bath **Meals:** full breakfast included; complimentary refreshments; restaurants nearby **Wheelchair access:** limited **Rates:** $75 to $125; 10% discount to National Trust members and National Trust Visa cardholders **Payment:** Visa, MC, personal and traveler's checks **Restrictions:** no smoking **On-site activities:** video library, games, books, live harp music, hiking, summer sailing on 18-foot sailboat

# WATERVILLE

**Nearby attractions:** historic downtown Waterville, Douglas County Museum, Badger Mountain, Leavenworth Bavarian Village, Lake Chelan Resort area, golfing, fishing, bicycling, hiking, skiing, swimming

## WATERVILLE HISTORIC HOTEL

102 East Park Street
P.O. Box 692
Waterville, Washington 98858-0692
**Phone:** 509/745-8695
**Fax:** 509/745-8180
**Proprietor:** David Lundgren

Its luster recently restored, this 1903 Tudor hotel with half-timbered gables and dormers, stands sentry over neighboring Pioneer Park. Closed for 20 years, the hotel has been returned to operating status through the hard work of the innkeeper. Original features including claw-foot bathtubs and woodwork in the salon, library, lobby, and front porch are in prime condition. While each guest room is different in character and decor, they all feature original fixtures, antique furnishings, cozy steam heat, a window view, and all the modern comforts and conveniences. This National Register-listed property is surrounded by spectacular views of the Cascade Mountains, rolling wheat fields, and historic Waterville, the most highly elevated incorporated community in the state of Washington at 2,600 feet.

**Open:** year round   **Accommodations:** 12 guest rooms (6 have private baths); 3 are suites **Meals:** complimentary tea and coffee; restaurants nearby **Rates:** $48 to $88; 10% discount to National Trust members and National Trust Visa cardholders **Payment:** Visa, MC, Discover, traveler's check **Restrictions:** children over 8 welcome; no smoking; no pets **On-site activities:** porch sitting, strolling grounds, horseshoes, barbecuing

# WEST VIRGINIA

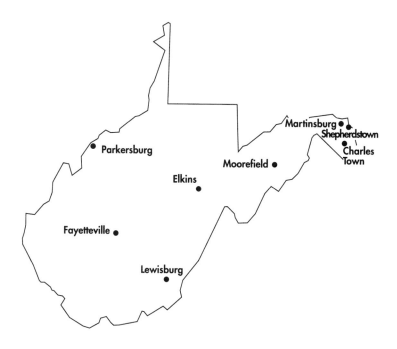

## CHARLES TOWN

**Nearby attractions:** Charles Town Races, Jefferson County Museum, John Brown Gallows site, walking tours, George Washington family homes, Antietam Battlefield, Harpers Ferry National Historic Park, Blue Ridge Outlet Mall, Bunker Hill Antique Mall and Mills, gift shops, antiques hunting, golfing, tennis, hiking, Shenandoah River rafting and canoeing

### GILBERT HOUSE BED AND BREAKFAST
Middleway Historic District
P.O. Box 1104
Charles Town, West Virginia 25414
**Phone:** 304/725-0637
**Proprietor:** Bernard F. Heiler
**Location:** 5 miles west of Charles Town, 11 miles southwest of Harpers Ferry, 60 miles west of Washington, D.C.

Gilbert House is an imposing Georgian colonial structure located in the eighteenth-century village of Middleway, a mill site on the original European settlers' trail into the Shenandoah Valley. Built in 1760, with additions in 1830, and

included in the Historic American Building Survey in 1938, this National Register house has 20-inch-thick gray stone walls and six working fireplaces with original mantels. Some walls bear graffiti from long ago including a child's growth chart begun in 1839 and an 1832 drawing of James K. Polk. Guest rooms are filled with tapestries, antiques, oriental rugs, and oil paintings. Rooms on the second floor have fireplaces, and third-floor guests can enjoy the sound of rain on the metal roof. Sumptuous breakfasts begin with freshly ground coffee from beans regularly brought by the innkeeper from Mexico. The innkeeper also gives tours of a reconstructed eighteenth-century log house in the back yard.

**Open:** year round **Accommodations:** 3 guest rooms with private baths; 1 is a suite **Meals:** full breakfast included; complimentary refreshments; restaurants nearby **Rates:** $80 to $140; 10% discount offered to National Trust members **Payment:** AmEx, Visa, MC, personal and traveler's checks **Restrictions:** inquire about small children; no smoking; no pets **On-site activities:** investigating garden and restored log house; reading; piano; porch with rocking chairs

# ELKINS

**Nearby attractions:** Blackwater Falls State Park, Canaan Valley Resort, Cass Scenic Railroad, Spruce Knob/Seneca Rocks Recreation Area, the historic Swiss Village of Helvetia, Rich Mountain Battlefield, Monongahela National Forest, hiking, bicycling, downhill and cross-country skiing, whitewater rafting, rock climbing, spelunking, bird watching, trout fishing, antiques hunting, specialty shopping, fairs and festivals

## THE WARFIELD HOUSE

318 Buffalo Street
Elkins, West Virginia 26241
**Phone:** 304/636-4555 or 888/636-4555
**Website:** www.bbonline.com
**Proprietors:** Connie and Paul Garnett

Named for its first owners, local bank executive Harry R. Warfield and his wife Susan, this spacious 1901 Queen Anne home is notable for its expansive front hall, parlor, and dining room lavishly enriched with golden oak pocket paneling and wainscoting. A massive terra-cotta fireplace takes center stage in the first-floor library adding to the grand scale of the home. A staircase bathed in rich hues from the two-story stained glass window, rises to four large, comfortable guest rooms on the upper floor. The fifth guest room is tucked over the kitchen with its own private stairwell. The dining room is illuminated by 24 early copper light fixtures shaped like acanthus leaves, which ring the room close to the ceiling. Filled with antiques, the house has been restored and furnished with turn-of-the-century carpets and wallpapers from J. R. Burrows & Co., Sanderson, and other makers of fine home furnishings.

**Open:** year round **Accommodations:** 5 guest rooms (3 have private baths) **Meals:** full breakfast included; complimentary refreshments; restaurants nearby **Rate:** $75; 10% discount to National Trust members and National Trust Visa cardholders **Payment:** personal and traveler's checks **Restrictions:** children over 12 welcome; no smoking; no pets **On-site activities:** bicycles

# FAYETTEVILLE

**Nearby attractions:** New River Gorge National Park, historic district walking tours, museums, white-water rafting

**MORRIS HARVEY HOUSE
BED AND BREAKFAST**
201 West Maple Avenue
Fayetteville, West Virginia
25840
**Phone:** 304/574-1902
**Fax:** 304/574-1040
**Proprietor:** Elizabeth Bush

Morris Harvey was a Civil War veteran, banker, county sheriff, and generous contributor to the failing Barboursville College, now known as Morris Harvey College. In 1902 he commissioned R. H. Dickinson to build this Queen Anne home. It had an elaborate rain-gathering system that used an 800-gallon copper tank to provide indoor plumbing. The Innkeeper has painstakingly rehabilitated the 14-room house, restoring hardwood floors, woodwork, and stained-glass windows with fleur-de-lis patterns like those found on the surrounding wrought-iron fence and in the flower garden. The old copper water tank is visible behind a glass panel on the second floor. The entire house is furnished with period antiques. Each guest room contains a fireplace, private bath with brass-footed tub, and a pendulum clock. Two suites share the tower—one upstairs, one down. Listed in the National Register, Morris Harvey House has been rated by AAA with three diamonds.

**Open:** April to December **Accommodations:** 4 guest rooms with private baths; 2 are suites **Meals:** full breakfast included; restaurants nearby **Rate:** $85; 10% discount to National Trust members and National Trust Visa cardholders **Payment:** Visa, MC, personal and traveler's checks **Restrictions:** inquire about children; no smoking; no pets **On-site activities:** flower garden, Victrola

# LEWISBURG

**Nearby attractions:** historic Lewisburg walking tours, Revolutionary and Civil War sites, Pearl Buck's birthplace, Greenbrier Valley Theater, state parks, lakes, fishing, hunting, cross-country skiing, swimming pools, tennis, golfing, hiking and biking trails, Lost World Caverns

## GENERAL LEWIS INN
301 East Washington Street
Lewisburg, West Virginia 24901
**Phone:** 304/645-2600
**Fax:** 304/645-2601
**Website:** www.generallewisinn.com
**Proprietors:** Mary Noel, Jim Morgan, and Nan Morgan

History permeates every room of the General Lewis Inn. The original 1834 home and its larger 1929 addition contain numerous cupboards filled with early glass, pottery, china, and curios. The front desk was built in 1760. Patrick Henry and Thomas Jefferson registered at this desk when it was in the Sweet Chalybeate Springs Hotel, at one of the many springs in the area visited by Virginia's early aristocrats. The dining room, serving old-fashioned country cooking, is in the first floor of the original 1834 home. Memory Hall, a small museum contained within the inn, pays tribute to the resourcefulness of mountain pioneers in vast collections of tools, guns, household utensils, and musical instruments. Two bedrooms and two suites are in the oldest part of the house and feature original fireplaces and mantels. Every room in the inn is furnished with antiques that highlight the craftsmanship of early settlers.

**Open:** year round **Accommodations:** 25 guest rooms with private baths; 2 are suites **Meals:** restaurant on premises **Rates:** $75 to $112 **Payment:** AmEx, Visa, MC, Discover, personal and traveler's checks **Restrictions:** no smoking **On-site activities:** pioneer memorabilia display, porch rocking, gardens

# MARTINSBURG

**Nearby attractions:** Antietam Battlefield National Park, Harpers Ferry National Park, Berkeley Springs mineral baths, C&O Canal and bicycle trail, Charles Town Thoroughbred Race Track, white-water rafting, auctions, golfing, antiques hunting, outlet shops

## BOYDVILLE, THE INN AT MARTINSBURG
601 South Queen Street
Martinsburg, West Virginia 25401
**Phone:** 304/263-1448
**Proprietor:** La Rue Frye

The 10 acres on which Boydville sits was once part of a large plantation purchased by General Elisha Boyd in the 1790s. Boyd built his stone mansion in 1812, and the house has changed hands only three times since then, leaving original woodwork, wallpaper, window glass, and mantels intact. Foyer wallpaper was handpainted in England in 1812 especially for Boydville. A mural, handpainted in France in the 1830s, graces a bedroom wall. All guest rooms are furnished with functional American and English antiques. Breakfast features native West Virginia products in season. Rocking on the long porch overlooking century-old boxwoods and trees in rockers original to Boydville is a favorite pastime. Guests also enjoy strolling the grounds and the ivy-covered brick-walled courtyard and garden.

**Open:** year round **Accommodations:** 6 guest rooms (4 have private baths) **Meals:** continental-plus breakfast included; complimentary refreshments; restaurants nearby **Rates:** $100 to $125; 10% discount to National Trust members and National Trust Visa cardholders **Payment:** Visa, MC, personal and traveler's checks **Restrictions:** children over 12 welcome; no smoking; no pets **On-site activities:** 10 acres for walking and jogging

# MOOREFIELD

**Nearby attractions:** fishing, horseback riding, golfing, hiking, canoeing, train excursions, wineries

## McMECHEN HOUSE INN BED AND BREAKFAST

109 North Main Street
Moorefield, West Virginia 26836
**Phone:** 304/538-7173 or 800/2WVA-INN (298-2466)
**Fax:** 304/538-7841
**Website:** www.bbonline.com/wv/mcmechen
**Proprietors:** Linda, Bob, and Larry Curtis

S. A. McMechen was a merchant and political activist. He built this three-story Greek Revival brick home in 1853 in what is now the Moorefield historic district. During the Civil War the house served alternately as headquarters to both the Union and Confederate forces as military control of the South Branch Valley changed hands. Listed in the National Register of Historic Places, the inn offers seven graciously appointed guest rooms. The delicate antebellum grace embodied by McMechen House is enhanced by the many antiques found throughout. An antiques and gift shop is also on the premises. A full breakfast and afternoon tea are served. Casual lunches are offered at the inn's Green Shutters Garden Cafe on weekends. The inn is within walking distance of shops and restaurants.

**Open:** year round **Accommodations:** 7 guest rooms (4 have private baths); 1 is a suite **Meals:** full breakfast included; complimentary refreshments; restaurant on premises; restaurants nearby **Rates:** $60 to $98; 10% discount to National Trust members and National Trust Visa cardholders **Payment:** AmEx, Visa, MC, CB, DC, personal and traveler's checks **Restrictions:** smoking limited; no pets **On-site activities:** books, games, antiques shop, live music in outdoor cafe, annual art show and one-man show

# PARKERSBURG

**Nearby attractions:** Blennerhassett Island Historical Park, Middleton Doll Company, Fenton Art Glass, paddle boat rides on Ohio River, museums, Smoot Theater

### THE HISTORIC BLENNERHASSETT CLARION HOTEL
320 Market Street
Parkersburg, West Virginia 26101
**Phone:** 304/422-3131 or 800/262-2536
**Fax:** 304/485-0267
**Website:** wvweb.com/www/blennerhassetthotel
**General Manager:** Larry Demme

On May 6, 1889, a refined Blennerhassett Hotel opened in the rough-and-tumble city of Parkersburg—new laws banned the galloping of horses through town; the hotel's large mirror had to be guarded by steel against errant gunshots—but its collection of 50 finely appointed rooms, the presence of a First National Bank in its lobby, and its popularity with deal-making businessmen made the hotel the centerpiece of the city's move toward sophistication. An imposing brick structure, the four-story hotel shows Richardsonian Romanesque detailing in its paired, arched windows and corner tower. Modernized in 1994, the National Register-listed hotel enjoyed expansion and a detailed renovation in 1986, which incorporated architectural elements and antiques salvaged from historic buildings nationwide: chandeliers, wainscoting, crown molding, mantels, grandfather clocks, desks, and prints. A member of Historic Hotels of America, the Blennerhassett offers tastefully decorated guest rooms and world-class dining.

**Open:** year round **Accommodations:** 104 guest rooms with private baths; 4 are suites **Meals:** full breakfast included; complimentary refreshments; restaurant on premises; full meeting and banquet facilities; restaurants nearby **Rates:** $69 to $129; 10% discount to National Trust members and National Trust Visa cardholders **Payment:** AmEx, Visa, MC, CB, DC, Discover, personal and traveler's checks **Restrictions:** smoking limited **On-site activities:** Friday night seafood buffet and Sunday brunch with live jazz

# SHEPHERDSTOWN

**Nearby attractions:** historic Shepherdstown Museum, C&O Canal and Towpath, Antietam Battlefield, Charles Town Races, Harpers Ferry, Appalachian Trail, Morgan's Grove Park, Thomas Shepherd Grist Mill, Blue Ridge Outlet Center, Berkeley Springs Mineral Baths, golfing, fishing, boating, rafting, hiking, bicycling

## THOMAS SHEPHERD INN
300 West German Street
P.O. Box 1162
Shepherdstown, West Virginia 25443
**Phone:** 304/876-3715
**Fax:** 304/876-3313
**Website:** www.intrepid.net/thomas_shepherd/
**E-mail:** mrg@intrepid.net
**Proprietor:** Margaret Perry

In the heart of historic Shepherdstown, West Virginia's oldest town, the inn, a mid-nineteenth-century Federal structure, originated as the Lutheran Church's parsonage on land once owned by Thomas Shepherd. Later the home and office of a local physician, the house was restored in 1984. Today, it is the Thomas Shepherd Inn with seven spacious guest rooms furnished appropriately for the period. Fresh flowers, thick towels, and scented soaps are stocked in private bathrooms. A living room, two formal dining rooms, a library, and a porch are shared and enjoyed by guests. Specially prepared dinners and picnic lunches are available.

**Open:** year round **Accommodations:** 7 guest rooms with private baths **Meals:** full breakfast included; restaurants nearby **Rates:** $85 to $135; 10% discount to National Trust members and National Trust Visa cardholders; business rates available **Payment:** AmEx, Visa, MC, Discover, personal and traveler's checks **Restrictions:** children over 8 welcome; no smoking; no pets

# WISCONSIN

## CEDARBURG

**Nearby attractions:** Cedarburg historic district, Cedarburg Cultural Center, Cedar Creek Settlement, Kuhefuss House, Covered Bridge Park, Pioneer Village, Cedar Creek Winery, Riveredge Nature Center, art galleries, horseback riding, tennis, bicycling, hiking, cross-country skiing, Lake Michigan fishing and boating, antiques hunting

**STAGECOACH INN**
W61 N520 Washington Avenue
Cedarburg, Wisconsin 53012
**Phone:** 414/375-0208
or 888/375-0208
**Fax:** 414/375-6170
**Website:**
www.stagecoach-inn-wi.com
**Proprietors:** Liz and Brook Brown

When city travelers journeyed by horse and coach up the Lake Michigan shoreline in the 1850s, they rested in Cedarburg at this country inn, known then as the Central House Hotel. It boasted "first class accommodations, choice wines, liquors, and beers. Good stabling and large stock." Restored in 1984 by the innkeepers, the 1853 Greek Revival stone building, now the Stagecoach Inn, continues its tradition of welcoming guests. Nine guest rooms are offered in the stone building and three are in the 1847 frame Weber Haus across the street. Guest rooms are furnished with antique wardrobes and canopy or sleigh beds. Six suites have two-person whirlpool tubs. The Stagecoach Pub and Beerntsen's Chocolate Shop are on the first floor of the main building. The pub features a 100-year-old bar, oak tavern tables, and the original tin ceiling. Stagecoach Inn is located in Cedarburg's historic district, within walking distance of shops, restaurants, parks, and the Cultural Center.

**Open:** year round **Accommodations:** 12 guest rooms with private baths; 6 are suites **Meals:** continental-plus breakfast included; restaurants nearby **Rates:** $70 to $130; 10% discount to National Trust members and National Trust Visa cardholders weekdays, January through April **Payment:** AmEx, Visa, MC, Discover, personal and traveler's checks **Restrictions:** children over 10 welcome; no smoking; no pets **On-site activities:** pub, garden

## WASHINGTON HOUSE INN
W62 N573 Washington Avenue
Cedarburg, Wisconsin 53012
**Phone:** 414/375-3550 or
800/554-4717
**Fax:** 414/375-9422
**Website:**
www.washingtonhouseinn.com
**Proprietor:** Wendy
Porterfield

Washington House was Cedarburg's first inn, built in 1846 on this site. Forty years later the original structure was replaced by the present three-story brick hotel with decorative cornices and parapets. In the 1920s, the building remained but its use changed: the hotel was converted into offices and apartments. But when the building was sold in 1983, restoration began and Washington House was returned to its original use as an inn. Guests find themselves surrounded by a collection of antique Victorian furniture, marble-trimmed fireplaces, and freshly cut flowers. Tasteful guest rooms decorated in country-Victorian style feature antiques, down quilts, whirlpool baths, and fireplaces. Designer fabrics, bed linens, and wallpapers add elegance. Listed in the National Register of Historic Places, the inn has been praised by *Country Home, Innsider, Milwaukee Journal,* and *Milwaukee Magazine.*

**Open:** year round **Accommodations:** 34 guest rooms with private baths **Meals:** continental-plus breakfast included; complimentary wine and cheese; restaurants nearby **Wheelchair access:** yes **Rates:** $69 to $189; 10% discount offered to National Trust members and National Trust Visa cardholders **Payment:** AmEx, Visa, MC, DC, Discover, personal and traveler's checks **Restrictions:** smoking limited; no pets **On-site activities:** sauna, board games, cards, reading

---

## EPHRAIM

**Nearby attractions:** Eagle Harbor, boating, sailing, theater, concerts, music festivals, art galleries, bicycling, historical sites

### HILLSIDE HOTEL OF EPHRAIM
9980 Highway 42
P.O. Box 17
Ephraim, Wisconsin 54211
**Phone:** 920/854-2417 or 800/423-7023
**Fax:** 920/854-4240
**Proprietors:** David and Karen, and David, Gracie Jean, and Iain McNeil

This rambling, white building, constructed over the period 1854 to 1890, was one of the first grand hotels in Ephraim. Today, it is the last of its kind; historic, preserved, renovated, charming. Each guest room has been decorated differently. Victorian wrought-iron beds and mirrored dressers—original to the hotel—mesh comfortably with lace or crisp white cotton curtains; restored Olson quilts are on display and the original hardwood floors have been refinished by hand. In European tradition, the hotel features optional feather beds, and just down the hall are four individual baths, complete with claw-foot tubs with showers, and gleaming brass fixtures. Two cottages on the grounds provide accommodation for up to six people. Nestled between the picturesque steeples of Ephraim and the waters of Eagle Harbor, Hillside is ideally located for sightseeing and leisure activities.

**Open:** year round **Accommodations:** 12 guest rooms share four baths; 2 cottages with private baths **Meals:** full breakfast included; complimentary afternoon tea; restaurants nearby **Rates:** $80 to $119 (rooms); $160 to $180 (cottages); 10% discount to National Trust members and National Trust Visa cardholders **Payment:** Visa, MC, Discover, personal and traveler's checks **Restrictions:** no smoking; no pets **On-site activities:** swimming, jet skiing, fishing

# HUDSON

**Nearby attractions:** Octagon House Museum, St. Croix River activities, St. Croix Meadows Greyhound Racing, golfing, parks, hot air ballooning, Phipps Theater, Mall of America

## PHIPPS INN
1005 Third Street
Hudson, Wisconsin 54016
**Phone:** 715/386-0800
**Fax:** 715/386-0509
**Website:** www.phippsinn.com
**Proprietors:** John and Cyndi Berglund

Called the "Grand Dame" of Queen Anne houses in Hudson, this 1884 architectural treasure was once the home of William Henry Phipps—lumberman, railroad official, bank president, park commissioner, county commissioner, mayor, state senator, philanthropist. From the top of the turret to the five-wood parquet flooring, every inch of the Phipps Inn has been carefully restored and refinished. Six elegantly furnished guest rooms each contain queen-size beds with down comforters and private whirlpool baths with showers. Canopied beds and gas or wood-burning fireplaces are in nearly every room. Antiques and finely crafted furnishings fill the mansion; of note are an 1880s pump organ and a 1920s baby grand Crownstay piano, which has been converted to a player piano. Breakfasts of homemade pastries and entrees are served in the dining room, the porch, or in the privacy of guest rooms.

**Open:** year round **Accommodations:** 6 guest suites with private baths **Meals:** full breakfast included; complimentary refreshments; restaurants nearby **Rates:** $99 to $189 **Payment:** AmEx, Visa, MC, Discover, personal and traveler's checks **Restrictions:** children over 12 welcome; no smoking; no pets

## LA FARGE

**Nearby attractions:** Amish neighbor's furniture-making shop and maple syrup camp (in spring), largest Amish community in Wisconsin, local and state historic sites, three major rivers with related water activities, two state parks, bike trails

### TRILLIUM COUNTRY COTTAGE
Route 2, Box 121
La Farge, Wisconsin 54639
**Phone:** 608/625-4492
**Proprietor:** Rosanne Boyett
**Location:** 7 miles east of Westby, on East Salem Ridge Road

Trillium Country Cottage is a 1929 cedar-shake cottage with a timber-framed porch. It was moved to the innkeeper's farm in 1942 for her grandmother to live in, and today offers travelers a cozy, private refuge tucked into the hills of the Kickapoo Valley. The cottage contains original wood floors, original kitchen fixtures including a wood-burning stove, and a fireplace built with stone from the nearby Kickapoo River. Nearly every item in the cottage is a family heirloom, including the double-wedding-ring quilt, the oak Hoosier kitchen cupboard, and grandma's rocker in the living room. A fresh farm breakfast is brought to the cottage each morning, and guests are free to prepare all other meals in the cottage kitchen. Trillium is surrounded by woods, fields, orchards, and organic gardens.

**Open:** year round **Accommodations:** 1 cottage sleeps 6 in 2 double and 2 twin beds (plus portable crib) **Meals:** full breakfast included; complimentary refreshments; restaurants nearby **Rates:** $60 to $80 double, $25 each additional guest over 12 years old **Payment:** personal and traveler's checks **Restrictions:** no smoking; no pets **On-site activities:** hiking, swimming in pond, bird watching, bicycling, porch swing and hammock, livestock chores and farm and field work in season

---

# LAKE GENEVA

**Nearby attractions:** Geneva Lake Kennel Club dog racing, tennis, boating, swimming, golfing, museums, dining, shopping

## T. C. SMITH HISTORIC INN BED AND BREAKFAST

865 Main Street
Lake Geneva, Wisconsin 53147
**Phone:** 414/248-1097 or 800/423-0233
**Fax:** 414/248-1672
**Website:** wwte.com/tcinn/htm
**Proprietors:** Marks family

Built in 1845 as a private home, the T. C. Smith Inn is a fine example of a pre-Civil War home with the exterior blending elements of Greek Revival and Italianate styling. Listed in the National Register of Historic Places for outstanding architectural, historical, and artistic significance, the inn proudly stands in downtown Lake Geneva surrounded by formal gardens, neoclassical statues, and secluded benches. Guests will discover original nineteenth-century light fixtures, converted from gas to electricity, illuminating the foyer's parquet floor, magnificent hand-tooled black walnut balustrades and staircase, and hand-painted walls with miniature oil paintings and original trompe l'oeil. More history is preserved in the marble fireplaces, intricate woodwork, hand-painted moldings, and immense pocket doors. Most guest rooms offer fireplaces and whirlpool tubs. A fine collection of antiques and paintings, spanning several centuries, add warmth and splendor to the historic inn.

**Open:** year round **Accommodations:** 8 guest rooms with private baths; 2 are suites **Meals:** full breakfast included; complimentary refreshments; restaurants nearby **Rates:** $95 to $350; 10% discount to National Trust members and National Trust Visa cardholders **Payment:** AmEx, Visa, MC, Discover, DC, personal and traveler's checks **On-site activities:** bicycling, bird watching, fish pool, water gardening

# MADISON

**Nearby attractions:** University of Wisconsin and its Arboretum, Lake Mendota swimming and boating, state capitol, bicycling, antiques hunting, cross-country skiing, swimming, sailing, tennis, golfing, shopping

### ARBOR HOUSE, AN ENVIRONMENTAL INN
3402 Monroe Street
Madison, Wisconsin 53711
**Phone and Fax:** 608/238-2981
**Website:** www.arbor-house.com
**Proprietors:** John and Cathie Imes

Arbor House, previously the Plough Inn, has been a Madison landmark since the mid-nineteenth century. Possibly built as early as 1834 as a private home, it was converted to a tavern and inn by 1853. It is a Greek Revival building, having been built in three stages of sandstone and brick. Later the building was covered in stucco. The award-winning inn blends historic features—original wood floors and natural stone fireplaces—with modern amenities that have an environmental emphasis—natural fabrics, energy-saving climate controls, and water-saving bathroom fixtures. Arbor House has five guest rooms with whirlpool baths and fireplaces. In the arbor-adjoined Annex, an environmentally designed building, guest rooms have private balconies. The two buildings are on a large landscaped lot with mature trees and native gardens. Guests can enjoy complimentary canoeing and mountain biking in the University of Wisconsin Arboretum across the street.

**Open:** year round **Accommodations:** 8 guest rooms with private baths; 1 is a suite **Meals:** continental-plus breakfast included on weekdays; full breakfast included on weekends; complimentary refreshments; restaurants nearby **Wheelchair access:** yes  **Rates:** $85 to $195; 10% discount to National Trust members and National Trust Visa cardholders, weekdays only excluding holidays **Payment:** AmEx, Visa, MC, personal and traveler's checks **Restrictions:** no smoking; no pets **On-site activities:** use of Trek mountain bikes

## MANSION HILL INN
424 North Pinckney Street
Madison, Wisconsin 53703
**Phone:** 608/255-3999 or
800/798-9070
**Fax:** 608/255-2217
**Website:**
www.Mansionhillinn.com
**Proprietor:** Janna Wojtal

This elegant Italianate mansion
was built in 1858 for Alexander
A. McDonnell. Lacy wrought-
iron balconies encircle carved
sandstone facades and a
belvedere crowns the roof of
the National Register house. Tall, gracefully arched windows fill rooms with light,
ornate cornices and medallions crown spacious halls, and hand-carved marble and
hardwoods enhance the many fireplaces. A four-story spiral staircase leads to a
rooftop belvedere. Bedrooms are elaborately decorated with silks, lace, damask,
and chintz. All rooms contain fine antiques. Private bathrooms are outfitted in
brightly colored tiles and whirlpool tubs, marble, and skylights. Rooms feature
fireplaces, minibars, and access to a veranda or balcony. A parlor, private wine
cellar, Victorian garden, and entertainment center are offered for guests' use.

**Open:** year round **Accommodations:** 11 guest rooms with private baths; 2 are suites
**Meals:** continental-plus breakfast included; complimentary refreshments; restaurants
nearby **Rates:** $100 to $325 **Payment:** AmEx, Visa, MC, personal and traveler's checks
**Restrictions:** children over 12 welcome; no pets **On-site activities:** gardens, television
and VCR, stereo system, access to health spa and private dining club

# STEVENS POINT

**Nearby attractions:** University of Wisconsin for plays and musical functions, museum, antiques hunting, specialty shopping, golfing, hiking and bicycling on Green Circle scenic trails, square dancing

## DREAMS OF YESTERYEAR BED AND BREAKFAST

1100 Brawley Street
Stevens Point, Wisconsin 54481
**Phone:** 715/341-4525
**Fax:** 715/ 344-3047
**Website:** www.coredcs.com/~dreams
**E-mail:** dreams@coredcs.com
**Proprietors:** Bonnie and Bill Maher

At the Dreams of Yesteryear, guest accommodations are in the restored J. L. Jensen house, an elegant turn-of-the-century Queen Anne home built for a Stevens Point merchant. The house was designed by J. H. Jeffers, who also designed the Wisconsin Exhibition Building at the St. Louis World's Fair of 1904. Three generations of Jensens lived in this house until 1987, when it was purchased by the innkeepers and restored to show off its golden oak woodwork, pocket doors, hardwood floors, leaded-glass windows, and original light fixtures. Guests are invited to curl up with refreshments in front of the original brass-and-iron fireplace or bird watch from the porch. A full breakfast is served in the formal dining room, which contains furniture original to the house. Bedrooms are decorated in Victoriana and antiques. Listed in the National Register of Historic Places, the inn has been featured in *Victorian Homes* magazine.

**Open:** year round **Accommodations:** 6 guest rooms (4 have private baths) **Meals:** full breakfast included; complimentary refreshments; restaurants nearby **Rates:** $55 to $135; 10% discount to National Trust members and National Trust Visa cardholders **Payment:** Visa, MC, Discover, personal and traveler's checks **Restrictions:** children over 12 welcome by prior arrangement; no smoking; no pets **On-site activities:** garden strolls, puzzles, games, reading

## STURGEON BAY

**Nearby attractions:** Door County Museum and Library, Miller Art Center, walking tours of historic district, shipyards, lighthouses, shops, boating, swimming, fishing, golfing, tennis, five state parks for bicycling and hiking, cross-country and downhill skiing

### INN AT CEDAR CROSSING

336 Louisiana Street
Sturgeon Bay, Wisconsin 54235
**Phone:** 920/743-4200
**Fax:** 920/743-4422
**Website:** www.innatcedarcrossing.com
**Proprietor:** Terry Smith-Wulf

Built in 1884 at the corner of what were then called Cedar and Cottage streets, the brick vernacular-style building was originally a street-level drugstore with living quarters above. Over time, the building has been used as a tailor's shop, a soda fountain, doctors' offices, and a clothing store. After a thorough restoration in 1985, the Inn at Cedar Crossing opened as a bed and breakfast. The lobby features a pressed-tin ceiling, fireplace, and curved staircase. The Gathering Room offers another fireplace and a place for comfortable reading or games. Guest rooms are furnished with four-poster, canopy, brass, or cottage beds. Careful use of painting finishes, stenciling, wallpapers, and fabrics complements fine antiques. Down-filled comforters and private baths (some with double whirlpool tubs) add to the comfort of each room. Fireplaces with antique mantels grace many guest rooms. The Inn at Cedar Crossing is listed in the National Register of Historic Places.

**Open:** year round **Accommodations:** 9 guest rooms with private baths **Meals:** continental-plus breakfast included; complimentary refreshments; restaurant on premises serving full breakfast, lunch, and dinner **Wheelchair access:** dining room **Rates:** $95 to $160 **Payment:** Visa, MC, personal and traveler's checks **Restrictions:** supervised children welcome; no smoking; no pets **Onsite activities:** pub on premises, television and telephone in all guest rooms

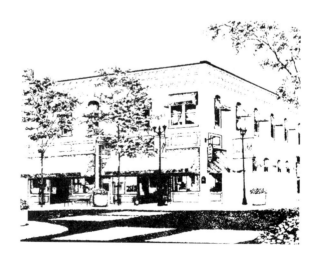

# WYOMING

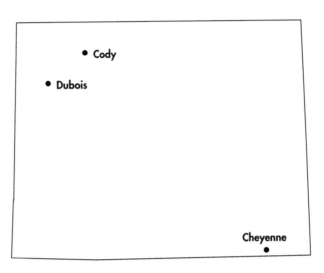

## CHEYENNE

**Nearby attractions:** state capitol, historic governor's mansion, Old West Museum, historical walking tour of downtown, tennis, golfing

### NAGLE WARREN MANSION BED AND BREAKFAST

222 East Seventeenth Street
Cheyenne, Wyoming 82001
**Phone:** 307/637-3333 or 800/811-2610
**Fax:** 307/638-6835
**Website:** colorado_bnb.com/nwmansion
**Proprietors:** Jim and Jacquie Osterfoss

Called "one of Cheyenne's most elegant residences" by the *Smithsonian Guide to Historic America*, the Richardsonian Romanesque three-story, turreted mansion was built in 1888 by Erasmus Nagle and in 1910 became the home of Francis E. Warren, governor and U.S. Senator. The innkeepers have meticulously restored the lavish property, bringing back to original splendor the cherry paneling, cast-bronze fireplaces, stained-glass windows, gas lighting fixtures, and pocket doors. Every room in the house has been decorated in the elegance of the Victorian West. From authentic period wallpaper to antique furniture and nineteenth-century artwork, the era is faithfully recreated. But unlike accommodations of yore, this bed and breakfast offers central air conditioning and a private bath, telephone, and television in each guest room. Business travelers will appreciate the two phone lines and dataport in each room. A conference center can accommodate up to 20 people. A full breakfast and afternoon sherry and tea are served daily. For its superb service and amenities, the inn has received four diamonds from AAA.

**Open:** year round **Accommodations:** 12 guest rooms with private baths; 1 is a suite **Meals:** full breakfast included; complimentary refreshments; restaurants nearby **Rates:** $85 to $145; 10% discount to National Trust members and National Trust Visa cardholders **Payment:** Visa, MC, Discover, personal and traveler's checks **Restrictions:** no smoking **On-site activities:** exercise facility, massage, outdoor hot tub, library, games

---

# CODY

**Nearby attractions:** Yellowstone National Park, Buffalo Bill Historical Center, Old Trail Town, Museum of the Old West Cody Nite Rodeo, horseback riding

## CODY GUEST HOUSES
1401 Rumsey Avenue
Cody, Wyoming 82414
**Phone:** 307/587-6000 or 800/587-6560
**Fax:** 307/587-8048
**Website:** www.wtp.net.cghouses
**Proprietors:** Kathy and Daren Singer

The Cody Guest Houses are a unique collection of historic homes that have been meticulously restored, furnished, and decorated to match the original era of each home. The Victorian House, built in 1906 was the first property acquired by owners Kathy and Daren Singer. Four years were spent on the complete restoration of the Victorian House and the two charming Western Cottages behind it. Since opening business in 1994, the Singers have added five more historic properties, including the Western Lodge, Country Cottage, Grandma's House, and the Mayor's Inn. Houses, cottages and suites are rented privately to one party and range in size from one to four bedrooms. Each offers private bathroom, fireplace, fully equipped kitchen, all modern amenities, beautifully landscaped grounds, convenient in-town locations, and furnishings and decor authentic to the house's period.

**Open:** year round **Accommodations:** 8 guest houses with one to four bedrooms each **Meals:** meals by special request; complimentary refreshments; restaurants nearby **Rates:** $80 to $450; 10% discount to National Trust members and National Trust Visa cardholders **Payment:** Visa, MC, Discover, personal and traveler's checks **Restrictions:** no smoking; no pets **On-site activities:** fresh-water spa, massage therapy, antiques sales, itinerary planning

---

## DUBOIS

**Nearby attractions:** Grand Teton and Yellowstone National Parks

### BROOKS LAKE LODGE
458 Brooks Lake Road
Dubois, Wyoming 82513
**Phone and Fax:** 307/455-2121
**Website:** www.brookslake.com
**Proprietors:** The Carlsbergs and The Rigsbys

Built in 1922 as a way-station for bus travelers on their way to Yellowstone National Park, the Brooks Lake Lodge was constructed by some of the same craftsmen who worked on the Inn at Old Faithful. An impressively rustic creation, the lodge features massive-log walls, plank flooring, log-beamed ceilings, huge stone fireplaces, and a decor that is the ultimate in western sporting lodge motif. The great hall is 30-by-60-feet long and 20 logs high at the eaves. Furnished in wicker, the hall houses a collection of wild game specimens from around the world. The main lodge features six tastefully decorated rooms with hand-crafted lodgepole pine furniture and beds. Each of the restored cabins is distinctive and in character with its name: Trail Boss, Prospector, Hunter, Fisherman, Mountain Man, and Judge's Cabin. Each cabin features a wood stove and separate front room. Perhaps even more impressive than the lodge is the amazing setting. Overlooking Brooks Lake, the lodge is rimmed on the east by the Pinnacle Buttes and on the west by the ridge of the Continental Divide, only two miles away.

**Open:** year round **Accommodations:** 13 guest rooms with private baths; 3 are suites **Meals:** all meals plus high tea included **Rates:** $150 to $225; 10% discount to National Trust members and National Trust Visa cardholders **Payment:** AmEx, Visa, MC, personal and traveler's checks **Restrictions:** smoking limited; no pets **On-site activities:** horseback riding, hiking, canoeing, fishing, snowshoeing, cross-country skiing, snowmobiling, dogsledding